THE VICTORIA HISTORY
OF THE
COUNTIES OF ENGLAND

———

A HISTORY OF
CHESHIRE
VOLUME II

THE VICTORIA HISTORY
OF THE
COUNTIES OF ENGLAND

EDITED BY C. R. ELRINGTON

THE UNIVERSITY OF LONDON
INSTITUTE OF
HISTORICAL RESEARCH

Oxford University Press, Walton Street, Oxford OX2 6DP

OXFORD   LONDON   GLASGOW
NEW YORK   TORONTO   MELBOURNE   WELLINGTON
KUALA LUMPUR   SINGAPORE   JAKARTA   HONG KONG   TOKYO
DELHI   BOMBAY   CALCUTTA   MADRAS   KARACHI
NAIROBI   DAR ES SALAAM   CAPE TOWN

ISBN 0 19 722749 X

Printed in Great Britain
at the University Press, Oxford
by Eric Buckley
Printer to the University

INSCRIBED TO THE

MEMORY OF HER LATE MAJESTY

QUEEN VICTORIA

WHO GRACIOUSLY GAVE THE TITLE TO

AND ACCEPTED THE DEDICATION

OF THIS HISTORY

'THE ORDER OF THE PARLIAMENT OF THE EARLS OF CHESTER'
A late 16th-century representation of Earl Hugh (d. 1101) in his 'parliament' with the spiritual and temporal
'barons' of the earldom

A HISTORY OF THE COUNTY OF CHESTER

EDITED BY B. E. HARRIS

VOLUME II

PUBLISHED FOR

THE INSTITUTE OF HISTORICAL RESEARCH

BY

OXFORD UNIVERSITY PRESS

1979

Distributed by Oxford University Press until 1 January 1982
thereafter by Dawsons of Pall Mall

CONTENTS OF VOLUME TWO

LIST OF ILLUSTRATIONS

For permission to reproduce material in their copyright or in their possession and for the loan of prints and photographs, thanks are offered to the Chester Archaeological Society, Chester City Record Office, the Most Honourable the Marchioness of Cholmondeley, the Right Honourable the Earl Grosvenor, the Grosvenor Museum, Chester, and the John Rylands University Library of Manchester. The drawing of the arms of Cheshire County Council is by H. Ellis Tomlinson.

LIST OF MAPS

The maps were drawn by K. J. Wass, of the Department of Geography, University College, London, from drafts prepared by A. T. Thacker, B. E. Harris, and Judith A. Green. Those of Local Government Divisions, 1937, Local Government Reorganization, 1974, and Parliamentary Constituencies were based on material provided by the Cheshire County Council.

EDITORIAL NOTE

CHESHIRE was one of only eight English counties for which the *Victoria History* published nothing before the First World War and one of only four for which nothing had still been published by the end of the decade following the Second World War. Possibly that neglect reflected the anomalies in the government of the former County Palatine and in the way in which its records were kept. In the nineteen-sixties members of the History Department of the University of Liverpool began to urge that the *Victoria History* should turn its attention to Cheshire, and in 1971 the Leverhulme Trust made a generous grant to the University of London, which owns the *History* and manages it through the Institute of Historical Research, towards the cost of the research, writing, and editorial work that was needed for the compilation of the History of Cheshire. The grant, made for seven years in the first instance and renewed in 1978 for a further period of seven years, was conditional on the securing by the University of London of the remainder of the funds necessary to complete the Cheshire History, and later in 1971 the Cheshire County Council agreed to pay an annual grant to the University sufficient to enlarge, and ultimately to replace, the money received from the Trust to the sum required for the payment of salaries of a County Editor and Assistant Editor and for other necessary expenses and fees.

An Editorial Board on which the County Council, the Trust, and the University of Liverpool are represented supervises the progress and expenditure of the Cheshire History. Dr. B. E. Harris took up his appointment as County Editor in 1972, and was assisted by Dr. Judith Green on a temporary basis and by Dr. S. J. Lander from 1972 to 1975. In 1976 Dr. A. T. Thacker succeeded Dr. Lander as Assistant Editor.

The volume now published is the first to result from the partnership between the Cheshire County Council and the University of London. The University is able to take advantage of its responsibility for publication of the Cheshire History to express its deep and sincere appreciation of the generosity both of the Leverhulme Trust and of the Cheshire County Council, whose share of the total costs of compilation has been increased by the fall in the value of money. It also thanks the University of Liverpool most warmly for its part in inaugurating the project, for making a room available for the editorial staff in the History Department at Liverpool, and for giving other facilities. Cordial thanks are also offered to Chester College, which for the first year provided a room in Chester.

The help of many people in the compilation of this volume is recorded in appropriate footnotes to the articles concerned; they are sincerely thanked, as are also Lady Ashbrooke, Dr. Stephen Baskerville, Sir Walter Bromley-Davenport, Mr. Stephen Lees and the Harvester Press, the Duke of Westminster, and the History of Parliament Trust for allowing access to materials, and to Dr. D. N. Cannadine, Dr. L. Colley, Mr. J. P. Cooper, Dr. A. Crowther, Mr. A. Thomas, and Dr. M. Wanklyn for reading and commenting on parts of the text. Among those having official custody of records that have been consulted it is a pleasure to acknowledge help beyond the normal call of duty from Mr. A. W. Mabbs of the Public Record Office and Mr. T. J. Donovan of the repository at Ashridge, Mr. B. C. Redwood (Cheshire County Archivist), and Miss A. M. Kennett (Chester City Archivist); among the material in Miss Kennett's care is the Earwaker Collection belonging to the Chester Archaeological Society, whose permission to consult documents in the collection is gratefully acknowledged. A particular debt of gratitude is owed to Professor A. R. Myers of the University of Liverpool for his untiring support for the Cheshire History and its editorial staff.

The structure and aims of the *Victoria History* as a whole are outlined in the *General Introduction*, published in 1970.

LIST OF CLASSES OF DOCUMENTS
IN THE PUBLIC RECORD OFFICE
USED IN THIS VOLUME
WITH THEIR CLASS NUMBERS

Chancery
C 231   Crown Office Docket Books

Palatinate of Chester
Chester 2   Enrolments
Chester 3   Inquisitions post mortem
Chester 17   Eyre Rolls
Chester 19   Sheriffs' Tourn Rolls
Chester 20   Calendar Rolls
Chester 24   Gaol Files, Writs, etc.
Chester 25   Indictment Rolls
Chester 26   Mainprise Rolls
Chester 27   Outlawry Rolls
Chester 29   Plea Rolls

Chester 31   Fines and Recoveries
Chester 33   Forest Proceedings
Chester 37   Warrants of Attorney Rolls
Chester 38   Miscellanea

Exchequer, King's Remembrancer
E 178   Special Commissions of Inquiry
E 179   Subsidy Rolls etc.

Exchequer, Office of the Auditors of Land Revenue
L.R. 2   Miscellaneous Books

Special Collections
S.C. 2   Court Rolls
S.C. 6   Ministers' Accounts

SELECT LIST OF ACCUMULATIONS
AND COLLECTIONS IN THE
CHESHIRE RECORD OFFICE
USED IN THIS VOLUME

Private Collections
DAR   Arderne of Alvanley and Harden
DCH   Cholmondeley of Cholmondeley

Quarter Sessions Records
QJB   Sessions Books
QJF   Sessions Files

ACCUMULATION IN THE
CHESTER CITY RECORD OFFICE
USED IN THIS VOLUME

CR 63   Collections and MSS. of J. P. Earwaker

ANALYSIS OF CHESHIRE MATERIAL
IN THE DEPUTY KEEPERS' REPORTS

Frequent reference is made to the lists and calendars of Palatinate of Chester records which appeared as appendices to the *Deputy Keepers' Reports* in the 19th century. The reports are here cited in a way which differs from normal *V.C.H.* usage. The number of the *Report* is given first. The *Reports* are inconsistent in their numbering and pagination of appendices, and the page-number given after *D.K.R.* in footnotes refers to whichever appendix is being quoted. The following key shows the contents of each of the relevant appendices.

25 D.K.R.   App. pp. 23–31: Calendar of Bills and Answers, etc., Hen. VIII, Edw. VI, and Philip and Mary.

App. pp. 32–60: Index to Inquisitions, etc., for Ches. and Flints.

26 D.K.R.   App. pp. 16–31: Calendar of Warrants, Signed Bills, and Privy Seals, Hen. VI to Eliz. I, for Ches. and Flints.

App. pp. 32–5: Calendar of Writs of General Livery, Ouster le Main, etc., for Ches., Eliz. I, Jas. I, and Chas. I.

App. pp. 36–55: Calendar of Deeds, Inquisitions, and Writs of Dower on the Chester Plea Rolls: Hen. III and Edw. I.

27 D.K.R.   App. pp. 94–123: Calendar of Deeds, Inquisitions, and Writs of Dower on the Chester Plea Rolls: Edw. II.

28 D.K.R.   App. pp. 6–19: Calendar of Fines, cos. Chester and Flint: Edw. I.

App. pp. 20–71: Calendar of Deeds, Inquisitions, and Writs of Dower on the Chester Plea Rolls: Edw. III.

29 D.K.R.   App. pp. 49–98: Calendar of Deeds, Inquisitions, and Writs of Dower on the Chester Plea Rolls: Ric. II to Hen. VII.

30 D.K.R.   App. pp. 121–65: Calendar of Deeds, Inquisitions, and Writs of Dower on the Chester Plea Rolls: Hen. VIII.

31 D.K.R.   App. pp. 169–262: List of Officers of the Palatinate of Chester, in cos. Chester and Flint and N. Wales.

36 D.K.R.   App. II: Calendar of Recognizance Rolls of the Palatinate of Chester, to the end of the reign of Hen. IV.

37 D.K.R.   App. II: Calendar of Recognizance Rolls of the Palatinate of Chester, from the beginning the reign of Hen. V to the end of the reign of Hen. VII.

39 D.K.R.   App. pp. 1–306: Calendar of Recognizance Rolls of the Palatinate of Chester, 1 Hen. VIII to 11 Geo. IV.

NOTE ON ABBREVIATIONS

Among the abbreviations and short titles used the following may require elucidation.

Ches. R.O.	Cheshire Record Office
Chester R.O.	Chester City Record Office
D.K.R.	*Deputy Keeper's Report*
J.C.A.S.	*Journal of the Chester Archaeological Society*
Ormerod, *Hist. Ches.*	G. Ormerod, *History of the County Palatine and City of Chester*, 2nd edn. by T. Helsby
R.S.L.C.	Record Society of Lancashire and Cheshire
Sheaf	*The Cheshire Sheaf*: preceded by series number, and followed by volume number within series and page. For the 5th series, beginning in 1976, only the item number is given
T.H.S.L.C.	*Transactions of the Historic Society of Lancashire and Cheshire*

THE EARLDOM OF CHESTER
1070–1301

CHESHIRE was conquered by the Normans in the winter of 1069–70. In 1069 the men of Chester, in alliance with the Welsh, had besieged Shrewsbury. William I led his army across the Pennines from York into Cheshire, and built castles at Chester and at Stafford. At about this time he gave the county of Chester first to the Fleming, Gherbod, and subsequently, after Gherbod's withdrawal to Flanders, to Hugh (I), son of Richard *vicomte* of Avranches.[1] The date of the gift to Hugh is unknown, but Hugh seems to have been in possession of the earldom by 1077.[2]

Evidence for the state of the earldom in the ensuing 170 years is sparse and its interpretation controversial. Few of the *acta* of the first three Norman earls have survived either in original or in later copies, and not all of the survivals relate to Cheshire.[3] They may, as in other counties, be supplemented by private charters,[4] but the records of the Exchequer, Chancery, and *curia regis* contain few references to Cheshire before 1237. Moreover, there is only one chronicle that deals in any detail with events in Cheshire during this period, and this, the annals compiled in St. Werburgh's abbey, Chester, survives only in late manuscripts.[5] Even Domesday Book throws little light on the administration of the county under Earl Hugh (I).[6]

The succession of the earls is indeed known, though precise dates are often hard to ascertain.[7] Hugh (I) died in 1101, and was succeeded by his son Richard, who died in the White Ship in 1120. The earldom then passed to Ranulph (I), nephew of Hugh (I). Ranulph died in 1128 or 1129 and was succeeded by his son Ranulph (II) (d. 1153); this Ranulph was succeeded by his son Hugh (II) (d. 1181), who in turn was succeeded by his son Ranulph (III). Ranulph (d. 1232) left no issue, and was succeeded by his nephew John 'le Scot', the 8th earl of Huntingdon, who died, also without issue, in 1237. Most of the earls were nationally eminent, though their importance derived as much from their possessions and interests outside Cheshire as from their lands and powers within it.[8] Their careers cannot here be traced.[9]

In spite of the paucity of evidence it is possible to reconstruct the administration of Cheshire in the early 13th century, under Ranulph (III). It should not necessarily be assumed, of course, that either Ranulph or his advisers were themselves responsible

[1] Orderic Vitalis, *Eccl. Hist.*, ed. Marjorie Chibnall, ii. 228, 234.

[2] J. Tait, 'An Alleged Chart. of Wm. the Conqueror', *Essays in Hist. presented to R. L. Poole*, ed. H. W. C. Davis, 161. Tait believed that Hugh was made earl after the battle of Cassel (20 Feb. 1071).

[3] A. P. Duggan, 'Chancery of Norman Earls of Chest.', Liverpool Univ. M.A. thesis, 1951, pp. xxi–xxiv, lists only three *acta* of Hugh (I), two of Richard, and four of Ranulph (I). His figures for Ranulph (II), Hugh (II), Ranulph (III), and John are respectively 31, 28, 85, and 13. Further *acta* have come to light since 1951.

[4] See especially G. Barraclough, *Facsimiles of Early Ches. Charts.*

[5] *Annales Cestrienses* (R.S.L.C. xiv), introduction.

[6] A translation of the Domesday survey of Ches. is planned for another volume of the *History*.

[7] *Handbk. Brit. Chronology* (2nd edn.), 420. The dates there given are followed, but the 'surnames' attributed to the earls, with the exceptions of those of Hugh (I) and John, are not used here since they lack contemporary authority. Expressions such as 'Ranulph, the 4th earl' are ambiguous, since such an enumeration depends on whether Gherbod or Hugh (I) be reckoned the first earl.

[8] The importance of lands outside Ches. given to Hugh (I) was noticed by W. J. Corbett: *Camb. Med. Hist.* v. 507. The argument is further developed by G. Barraclough, *Earldom and Co. Palatine of Chest.* (Oxford, 1953, reprinted from *T.H.S.L.C.* ciii), 12–16.

[9] *D.N.B.* contains articles on Hugh (I), Ranulph (I), Ranulph (II), Hugh (II), and Ranulph (III). Sir Peter Leycester's biographies of the earls, with additions by Ormerod and Helsby, are given in Ormerod, *Hist. Ches.* i. 9–44.

for inventing the Cheshire institutions which first appear in records at this time. The county formed one part of the honor of Chester, which included lands in many other English counties.[10] It has been estimated that Ranulph was, at the time of Richard I's death in 1199, the greatest landowner in England after Richard's brother John.[11] There is little evidence about the boundaries of the county in the century and a half following the Domesday survey. To the west the area under Norman control diminished. The cantred of Englefield, the northern part of the modern Flintshire, was lost by the mid 12th century.[12] In September 1146 the Welsh overran Cheshire itself, and were stopped only at Nantwich by Robert of Mold.[13] Henry II's reconquest of Englefield in 1157 was short-lived.[14] Most authorities show the earls of Chester in possession of eastern Flintshire as far as Hawarden and Ewloe castles at the beginning of the 13th century.[15] The boundaries of the county towards England are no easier to define. Clitheroe and Whalley (Lancs.) were described in 1122 as lying in Cheshire.[16] The 'land between Ribble and Mersey', associated with Cheshire in the Domesday survey, was given to Ranulph (II) in Stephen's reign and again to Ranulph (III) by Henry III,[17] but there is no evidence that it was ever administered as a unit with Cheshire. The boundary to the east was the ill-defined area known as the Lyme.[18] Parts of modern Staffordshire may have been in Cheshire in the 12th and early 13th centuries. The farm of the manor of Leek was rendered with the earl's Cheshire farms in 1185 and further references from the late 13th century hint at an earlier association of Leek and its surroundings with Cheshire.[19] Apart from Leek the other demesne manors of whose farms accounts were rendered in 1185 were all within the area of the modern county: Middlewich, Northwich, Frodsham, Weaverham, Over, and Macclesfield.[20]

At the head of the administration stood the earl himself. Since his *acta* are undated it is impossible to discover how much time he spent in Cheshire. Ranulph (III) can only be shown to have been in Chester on four dates during a tenure of the earldom which lasted over forty years.[21] By the 17th century there was a tradition that the earl had his own parliament, consisting of the 'barons' of Cheshire.[22] The lay 'barons' are usually stated to have numbered eight (Halton, Mold, Nantwich, Malpas, Shipbrook, Dunham Massey, Stockport, and Kinderton) but, although the witness lists of comital charters often show that some of the 'barons' were present with the earl, there is no evidence that they constituted a 'parliament'. The engraving of Earl Hugh (I) in his 'parliament' which first appeared in King's *Vale Royal* must be regarded as a flight of fancy: it shows the abbots of Combermere, Norton, and Vale Royal in attendance on the earl, although Combermere and Norton were founded in the 12th century and Vale Royal in the thirteenth.[23] Two of the 'baronies' were associated with hereditary offices, that of Halton with the office of constable of Chester and that of Mold with the office of steward. The former may certainly be traced from the time of Hugh (I).[24]

Below the earl the chief administrative official was the justice, who seems in the time of Ranulph (III) to have held a position rather like that of the justiciar of England

[10] For the hist. of the lands of the honor outside Ches., see W. Farrer, *Honors and Knights' Fees*, ii. 1–293, and *Early Yorks. Charts.* ii. 193–255.

[11] S. Painter, *Reign of King John*, 20.

[12] J. E. Lloyd, *Hist. Wales* (3rd edn.), ii. 469–80.

[13] *Ann. Cestr.* 20.

[14] Lloyd, *Hist. Wales*, ii. 496–500, 519–20.

[15] e.g. W. Rees, *Hist. Atlas Wales* (3rd edn.), pl. 38.

[16] J. Tait, *Medieval Manchester and Beginnings of Lancs.* 155.

[17] Ibid. 170 sqq.; *Cal. Chart. R.* 1226–57, 101–2.

[18] *Liber Luciani de Laude Cestrie* (R.S.L.C. lxiv), 65; Barraclough, *Earldom*, 38; *Cart. St. Werburgh's Abbey, Chest.* i (Chetham Soc. N.S. lxxix), 105.

[19] *Ches. in Pipe R.* (R.S.L.C. xcii), 13; *Cal. Chest. Co. Court R.* (Chetham Soc. N.S. lxxxiv), 116, 237; cf. J. W. Alexander, 'New Evidence on Palatinate of Chest.', *E.H.R.* lxxxv. 726–8.

[20] *Ches. in Pipe R.* 13.

[21] *Ann. Cestr.* 50, 56–8; Barraclough, *Earldom*, 31; Barraclough, *Early Ches. Charts.* 47.

[22] W. Stubbs, *Const. Hist. Eng.* (5th edn.), i. 392 and n.

[23] The picture is reproduced in Ormerod, *Hist. Ches.* i, facing p. 358. For the painting on which it was probably based see frontispiece.

[24] *Domesday Survey of Ches.* (Chetham Soc. N.S. lxxv), 48–9; Ormerod, *Hist. Ches.* i. 52.

under the king. In the absence of the earl he presided over the county court.[25] In witness lists of Ranulph's *acta* he usually occurs after the constable among the lay witnesses,[26] although sometimes his name takes precedence over that of the abbot of Chester.[27] In the time of Ranulph (II) there is a reference to Adam, the earl's justice,[28] and a Ralph who may have been another occurs twice,[29] but the importance of the office seems to begin in the time of Ranulph (III), when a continuous succession of known justices begins. The first was Ranulph de Mainwaring, who was succeeded, probably in 1202 or 1203, by Philip of Orby.[30] Philip's tenure of the office lasted until 1229.[31] He was a frequent witness of charters of Ranulph (III). From 1229 the office was regarded as sufficiently important for changes to be recorded in the annals of St. Werburgh's abbey.[32] After Cheshire was taken into the king's hands in 1237 the justice became responsible for accounting for it at the Exchequer, thus assuming one of the characteristics of an English sheriff. There is, however, no evidence that those who farmed the earls' lands earlier, during the minorities of Hugh (II) and Ranulph (III), were justices of Chester.

Other officials included the chamberlain, the chief clerk, and the sheriff. Several chamberlains are known by name, but the nature of their office before 1237 remains obscure. The chief clerk occupied a position like that of a royal chancellor: both Peter the clerk, who witnessed at least 48 of the charters of Ranulph (III) and was rewarded for his services by grants of land and privilege, and his successor Simon, who replaced him *c.* 1226, were referred to on occasion as chancellors, though the term seems to have lacked official recognition.[33] The sheriff of Cheshire occupied a subordinate position with far less power and prestige than his counterparts elsewhere in England.[34] Below him was a staff which included, for maintaining law and order, some itinerant serjeants of the peace with power to billet themselves locally. Their number was limited to twelve and their power to requisition provender was defined in the 'Magna Carta' of Cheshire issued by Ranulph (III).[35]

Among the institutions of the county at this time there is evidence of the existence of an exchequer which may have been modelled on that of the king.[36] There is, however, little reliable evidence of its operation.[37] The earl may have had his own court apart from and superior to the county court.[38] The few references to the earl's 'pleas of the sword' do not enable us to understand their precise nature: they were apparently the counterpart in Cheshire of pleas of the Crown in England. The earliest known mention of them occurs in a charter of Ranulph (III) to Peter the clerk, dated *c.* 1208–13, when they are reserved to the earl, as they are also in the 'Magna Carta' of Cheshire.[39] The county court seems to have been a kind of *curia regis* in miniature with the addition of a minor jurisdiction. It dealt, for example, with actions of novel disseisin and mort d'ancestor.[40] Ranulph (III) is said to have facilitated procedure by providing the court with a register of original writs.[41] No plea rolls have survived

[25] 3 *Sheaf*, xx, pp. 1, 4, 11, 17.
[26] e.g. *Reg. Antiquissimum*, vi (Linc. Rec. Soc. xli), 83-4; *Coucher Bk. Whalley Abbey*, i (Chetham Soc. [1st ser.], x), 10-11, 12-13; *Cart. St. Werburgh's Abbey, Chest.* ii (Chetham Soc. N.S. lxxxii), 338.
[27] e.g. *Dieulacres Cart.* (Staffs. Hist. Collections, N.S. ix), 315; *J.C.A.S.* N.S. i. 24-5.
[28] *Cart. Chest. Abbey*, i. 234.
[29] F. M. Stenton, *First Cent. Eng. Feudalism*, 271; *Danelaw Charts.*, ed. F. M. Stenton, 362-3.
[30] 3 *Sheaf*, xx, p. 6; xxxv, p. 40.
[31] *Ann. Cestr.* 54-6.
[32] Ibid. 56 sqq. The justices are listed in *Cart. Chest. Abbey*, i, pp. iv-vi.
[33] Barraclough, *Early Ches. Charts.* 20.

[34] For his duties later in the 13th and in the 14th cents. see *Cal. Chest. Co. Ct. R.*, pp. xxvi-xxvii.
[35] *Cart. Chest. Abbey*, i. 105-6. On the hist. of serjeants in Ches., see R. Stewart-Brown, *Serjeants of Peace in Medieval Eng. and Wales*, cap. I.
[36] *Close R.* 1234-7, 539.
[37] Barraclough, *Earldom*, 18 n. 5.
[38] Ibid. 31.
[39] G. Barraclough, 'Some Charts. of Earls of Chest.', *Medieval Miscellany for Doris M. Stenton* (Pipe R. Soc. N.S. xxxvi), 41; *Cart. Chest. Abbey*, i. 102-3; cf. Barraclough, *Earldom*, 17 and n. 9.
[40] *Close R.* 1234-7, 538; 3 *Sheaf*, xx, p. 9.
[41] *Abbrev. Plac.* (Rec. Com.), 268-9.

from his time, but there are examples of final concords made in the county court, 'in the earl's court', and 'before earl Ranulph and Llywelyn prince of Wales'.[42] Sometimes final concords, and charters produced and read in the county court, were enrolled on what became known as the Cheshire Domesday Roll. The original of this is now lost, and its nature and contents were long misunderstood.[43] It was a means by which the details of transactions could be preserved. Its authenticity was later unsuccessfully challenged by Roger of Sandbach on the ground that Ranulph (III) had arbitrarily decided what should be enrolled.[44] The roll continued to be used until the end of the 13th century, and in 1324 or 1325 it was delivered by the deputy of one justice of Chester to the deputy of another.[45] Payments for enrolment are recorded on the early plea rolls.[46]

The 'Magna Carta' which Ranulph (III) issued in favour of his Cheshire 'barons' in 1215 or 1216 shows the development of some characteristic Cheshire institutions.[47] The 'barons' were exempted from military service beyond the Lyme except with their consent, and at the earl's expense. They were allowed to hear in their own courts all pleas except 'pleas of the sword'. The charter accepted the local customs known as 'avowries' and 'thwertnic', about the origins of which little is known. By means of avowry strangers were allowed to settle on the lands of the earl and of his 'barons' and enjoy their protection in return for an annual payment. Surviving references to the institution from the 12th century are few.[48] 'Thwertnic', better known in the form 'thwert-ut-nay', allowed a 'baron's' man to clear himself, if impleaded without witnesses in the county court, by an absolute denial. The later plea rolls demonstrate its use.[49] The charter also laid down maximum amercements of two shillings for a doomsman and one shilling for a suitor at hundred and county courts.[50]

Little can be said of the financial organization of Cheshire before 1237. The county only appears on the Pipe Rolls during the minorities of Hugh (II) and Ranulph (III), when it was in the hands of royal keepers.[51] The accounts rendered in those years present puzzling features. They are absent for the period of Hugh's minority between 1156 and Easter 1158, and for the period between 1174 and January 1177, when the earldom was apparently in the king's hands following Hugh's participation in the rebellion of 1173–4. The accounts from 1158 to 1162 are headed *terra comitis Cestrie*. They make no attempt to distinguish between income derived from Cheshire and that from the earl's estates outside it. The lands were farmed for £294 except during the financial year 1161–2, when the farm was increased to £304. Between 1181 and 1187 the arrangements made for the custody of the lands of Ranulph (III) during his minority were more complex. Separate accounts for the possessions outside Cheshire were rendered until Michaelmas 1184, the sums being described in the first year as 'issues' and subsequently as a farm, though they varied from year to year. At Michaelmas 1184 the keeper's debt outstanding from the previous fiscal year was described as arising *de veteri firma comitatus Cestrie*. The accounts for Cheshire itself show some confusion. For the first three years they are headed 'Cheshire', and afterwards 'honor of Chester'. The change appears to coincide with a change of keeper at Easter 1185. In one account only, that of Michaelmas 1185, the farms of the earl's demesne manors

[42] *Cart. Chest. Abbey*, i. 200–2; Barraclough, *Early Ches. Charts.* 47; Barraclough, *Earldom*, 32; *Dieulacres Cart.* 328.
[43] Ormerod, *Hist. Ches.* i, p. xxxv and n.; R. Stewart-Brown, 'Domesday Roll of Ches.', *E.H.R.* xxxvii. 481–500; 3 *Sheaf*, xx, *passim*.
[44] *E.H.R.* xxxvii. 497; *Cal. Pat.* 1247–58, 431.
[45] 3 *Sheaf*, xx, p. 66.
[46] *Cal. Chest. Co. Ct. R.* pp. xv, 137, 138, 140.

[47] Text in *Cart. Chest. Abbey*, i. 102–7.
[48] R. Stewart-Brown, 'Avowries of Ches.', *E.H.R.* xxix. 41–55; Pipe R. Soc. N.S. xxxvi. 35–7.
[49] *Cal. Chest. Co. Ct. R.*, *passim*; R. Stewart-Brown, *E.H.R.* xl.
[50] For the later working of the co. ct. see pp. 15 sqq.
[51] The Pipe R. entries are transcribed, with notes, by R. Stewart-Brown, in *Ches. in Pipe R.* 1–25. This is the source of what follows.

are separately listed. Macclesfield was also accounted for separately in 1183 and 1184. In the account for 1181–2 it is said that Earl Hugh (II) had placed some of the Cheshire manors at farm, but otherwise it is impossible to tell whether the royal keepers were using an administrative machinery inherited from the late earl, or whether they were attempting to introduce a new organization. After 1237, when Cheshire once again appears on the Pipe Rolls, a similar difficulty is encountered.[52] The 12th-century accounts throw little light on the administration of the county.

The foregoing review of Cheshire administration under the later Norman earls, although necessarily incomplete, provides a background against which the extraordinary status of Cheshire among English counties may more clearly be seen. As early as 1450 it was claimed that Cheshire 'hath been a county palatine, as well before the conquest of England, as continually since, distinct and separate from the crown of England'; it was supposed that Hugh (I) had been given the earldom by the Conqueror 'to hold as freely to him and to his heirs by the sword, as the king should hold all England by the crown'.[53] The assumption remained unquestioned by writers of both national and local history until the fourth decade of the 20th century: Cheshire could be described as an *imperium in imperio*.[54] The use of the term 'palatinate' to describe Cheshire before 1237 appears to lack contemporary authority: the term itself is not indeed sanctioned by official usage until the 1290s.[55] In 1293 a royal serjeant asserted that Earl Ranulph (III) had not been an earl palatine.[56] Attempts have been made to show that evidence is also lacking for the quasi-regal powers traditionally claimed for the Norman earls.[57] Nevertheless, there appears to be abundant evidence that Cheshire stood apart, in the minds of contemporaries, from England. Although the importance of the county's absence from the Pipe Rolls has been minimized,[58] that absence reflects a considerable degree of independence. Thus there was no royal demesne in Cheshire. The chief administrative official, the justice of Chester, was neither appointed by the king nor responsible to him. The king derived no benefit from scutages or tallages levied in the county. Royal justices did not visit it; fines and amercements levied there did not reach the king. To this negative evidence may be added the absence of Cheshire from the inquests of military service taken in 1166 and 1212.

These arguments, derived mainly from the absence of evidence, receive substantial positive confirmation by the end of the 12th century. In 1200 the king's court respited an action so that inquiry could be made into the earl's liberties in Chester: the result of the inquiry has not survived.[59] To the monk Lucian the earl of Chester is a *princeps*. Lucian describes the independence of the earls, achieved through their own excellence and the indulgence of kings.[60] The term *princeps*, implying territorial sovereignty, was also used of Earl Ranulph (III) in 1254, twenty-two years after his death.[61] Matthew Paris, who said of Earl John (d. 1237) that as *comes palacii* he had power to coerce an errant king,[62] praised the attitude of Ranulph (III) in refusing, in 1229, to allow clergy in his lands to pay tenths to the pope.[63] The distinction between Cheshire and England, made already by Lucian and repeated in the 'Magna Carta' of Cheshire in 1215 or 1216, continued to be recognized into the 13th century.[64] The repetition in substance of

[52] See p. 7.
[53] Ormerod, *Hist. Ches.* i. 126–7.
[54] e.g. Stubbs, *Const. Hist.* i. 294, 392; *Ches. in Pipe R.* p. xiv.
[55] Barraclough, *Earldom*, 20; Margaret Tout, 'Comitatus Pallacii', *E.H.R.* xxxv. 418–19; cf. S. Painter, *Studies in Hist. of Eng. Feudal Barony*; G. T. Lapsley, *Co. Palatine of Durham*, 28.
[56] *Plac. de Quo Warr.* (Rec. Com.), 714, quoted by J. W. Alexander, *E.H.R.* lxxxv. 727.

[57] *E.H.R.* lxxxv. 723–6; Barraclough, *Earldom*, 10–11, 17.
[58] *E.H.R.* lxxxv. 724; cf. J. Boussard, *Gouvernement d'Henri II Plantagenêt*, 198.
[59] *Cur. Reg. R.* i. 392.
[60] *Liber Luciani*, 65.
[61] *E.H.R.* xxxvii. 497.
[62] *Chron. Maj.* (Rolls Ser.), iii. 337–8.
[63] Ibid. 189.
[64] *Liber Luciani*, 65; *Cart. Chest. Abbey*, i. 105; *Ann. Cestr.* 72; *Cal. Pat.* 1247–58, 369.

four articles of the English Magna Carta in the Cheshire document implies that the former was not regarded as valid within the county.[65] There seem, in fact, to have been few exceptions to the general proposition that, where substantial evidence is available, Cheshire was largely autonomous. The Cheshire lands of the bishops of Coventry and Lichfield may indeed have been outside the earls' control; these were of little significance, consisting, at the time of the Domesday survey, of the manors of Wybunbury, Farndon, Tarvin, Guilden Sutton, and probably Burton in Wirral, and of some land in Chester itself.[66] During the minority of Earl Ranulph (III) Henry II could arrange for the transfer of lands, and made provision for the abbey of St. Werburgh; but after attaining his majority Ranulph was able to procure the removal of the king's nominee as abbot.[67] The tradition, current by the end of the 14th century, that Cheshire had rejoiced in a royal prerogative (*regali gaudebat prerogativa*),[68] is easy to understand. By 1237 Cheshire had, through a process obscured by lack of evidence, attained a position analogous to that of Durham: the comparison cannot be pursued in depth, however, since evidence of the powers and administration of both palatinates only becomes abundant later in the 13th century.[69]

The death without issue of Earl Ranulph (III) in October 1232 resulted in the partition of his lands outside Cheshire. His nephew, John 'le Scot', already earl of Huntingdon, succeeded him as earl. When John died, also without issue, in 1237, the lands belonging to the earldom outside Cheshire were again partitioned. Cheshire itself was administered by royal servants.[70] Stephen of Seagrave, Henry of Audley, and Hugh Despenser were sent to take over the administration of the county on 6 June, and sixteen days later detailed instructions were addressed to them.[71] Seagrave was formally appointed justice of Chester.[72] By 10 July, however, custody of the county had been given to John de Lacy, constable of Chester and earl of Lincoln.[73] Associated with him were a new justice, Richard de Draycott, and a new chamberlain, Richard de Gatesden.[74] John de Lacy had married Ranulph's niece, and was, as constable of Chester, the leading Cheshire 'baron', but no attempt was made to re-create the earldom in his favour. In 1240 he died, and after what appear to have been interim arrangements[75] a new administrative practice was devised whereby the justice was made directly responsible for the county to the Crown, rather than to a *custos*. In 1243 Cheshire was assigned as part of Queen Eleanor's dower,[76] and four years later its annexation by the Crown was declared permanent.[77] In February 1254 it formed part of the large grant made by Henry III to his son Edward, who was not, however, styled earl of Chester.[78]

Under the Crown Chester was used as a point of muster and departure for royal operations against North Wales. Henry III first visited it in the late summer of 1241,[79] and used it as his base for the conquest of eastern North Wales from David ap Llywelyn.[80] Chester was used similarly in 1245, 1257, 1277, 1282, 1287, and 1294.[81] Lands conquered from the Welsh were at first placed under the control of the justice

[65] *Cart. Chest. Abbey*, i. 105. Cf. J. C. Holt, *Magna Carta*, 270 and n. 5.

[66] *Domesday Surv. Ches.* 27.

[67] *Ann. Cestr.* 30, 34, 44.

[68] R. Higden, *Polychronicon* (Rolls Ser.), viii. 210.

[69] Cf. Lapsley, *Durham*, cap. II.

[70] The partitions, and the litigation arising from them, are described by R. Stewart-Brown, 'End of Norman Earldom of Chest.', *E.H.R.* xxxv. 26–54.

[71] *Cal. Pat. 1232–47*, 185; *Close R. 1234–7*, 538–9.

[72] *Cal. Pat. 1232–47*, 188. The appointment is ignored by *Ann. Cestr.*, but Seagrave was addressed as justice in letters of 1 and 3 July: *Cal. Lib. 1226–40*, 278.

[73] *Cal. Pat. 1232–47*, 189.

[74] *Ann. Cestr.* 60; 3 *Sheaf*, xix, p. 16; *Ches. in Pipe R.* 36.

[75] *Ches. in Pipe R.* 54–5, 62; *Cal. Lib. 1226–40*, 451, 460.

[76] *Cal. Pat. 1232–47*, 394.

[77] Ibid. 501.

[78] *Cal. Pat. 1247–58*, 272; cf. *Handbk. Brit. Chronology*, 420. The county was briefly in the hands of Simon de Montfort: *Handbk. Brit. Chronology*, 421; *Ann. Cestr.*, 89; *Cal. Pat. 1258–66*, 397.

[79] *Ann. Cestr.* 62.

[80] Lloyd, *Hist. Wales*, ii. 697–8.

[81] Ibid. 703–5, 721–2; J. E. Morris, *Welsh Wars of Edw. I*, 127–30, 158–60, 209, 254.

of Chester. In 1241 an allowance of 100 marks made to the justice was stated to be for keeping the county and the castles of Chester, Beeston, and Dyserth.[82] Dyserth (Flints.) and Deganwy (Caern.) castles were included in the Queen's dower in 1247.[83] In 1249 the justice's bailiwick was extended to cover the Four Cantreds (Rhos, Rhufoniog, Dyffryn Clwyd, and Englefield).[84] These lands were, however, lost to Llywelyn ap Gruffudd by 1256, a position confirmed by the treaty of Montgomery in 1267.[85] The Welsh war of 1277 enabled Edward I to recover Englefield and Rhos, together with the castles of Flint and Rhuddlan (Flints.).[86] The two cantreds, but not Rhuddlan castle, were included in the bailiwick of Reynold de Grey in 1281.[87] Part of Rhos was granted to the earl of Lincoln late in 1283[88] and in the following year, by the statute of Rhuddlan, the new county of Flint was created, with a sheriff subordinate to the Chester justice and chamberlain.[89]

In some ways the annexation of Cheshire brought the county more closely into line with 'normal' English counties. Except during the period 1254-72, when it was in the hands of the Lord Edward, Cheshire appears regularly in Exchequer and Chancery records from 1237 to 1301. Administrative orders were directed to the justices in the same terms as those addressed to the sheriffs of other counties; general writs were addressed 'to the sheriffs of England and the justice of Chester'.[90] Edward I's commissions of inquiry issued in October 1274 included Cheshire, and the replacement of many of the English sheriffs in the same month was paralleled by the appointment of Guncelin de Badlesmere as justice of Chester in place of Reynold de Grey.[91] Under Edward Cheshire was made to contribute to the fifteenths exacted throughout the kingdom in 1275, 1281, and 1292.[92] From 1237 first the *custos* and subsequently the justice accounted at the Exchequer, and Cheshire thus appeared once more on the Pipe Rolls. The county was not, however, treated by the Exchequer as a normal one. At first the practice was for detailed accounts of the farms of the demesne lands (the city of Chester, Frodsham, two-thirds of Shotwick, Gayton, Rushton, Weaverham, Over and Darnhall, Northwich, Middlewich, and Macclesfield) and of amounts arising from pleas of the county court and forests to be rendered.[93] It has been suggested that the amounts concerned, which show considerable increases over those brought in between 1181 and 1187, reflect the extent to which Earl Ranulph (III) had exploited the county's resources.[94] It is, however, equally likely that the organization of the county's revenues had been undertaken or at least begun by Stephen of Seagrave in 1237.[95] In January 1249 the justice, John de Grey, entered into a new arrangement by which he was to hold the county, together with the Four Cantreds, at farm for 500 marks a year.[96] Confusion was soon apparent, since Grey wrongly believed that he was no longer to be responsible for paying the fixed alms.[97] The placing of the county at farm angered the men of Cheshire.[98] The arrangement was renewed after a year,[99] but only until the quindene of Easter 1250, after which Grey once more accounted as keeper.[1] In the following July Alan la Zouche was appointed justice, with

---

[82] *Cal. Lib.* 1240-5, 128.
[83] *Cal. Pat.* 1232-47, 501.
[84] Ibid. 1247-58, 35.
[85] Lloyd, *Hist. Wales*, ii. 739-41.
[86] T. F. Tout, 'Flints.: its Hist. and Recs.', *Flints. Hist. Soc.* i. 13-14; *Cal. Chanc. R. Var.* 160; *Cal. Pat.* 1272-81, 256.
[87] *Cal. Pat.* 1272-81, 464.
[88] Ibid. 1281-92, 82.
[89] *Flints. Hist. Soc.* i. 16-21.
[90] e.g. *Cal. Pat.* 1272-81, 104, 342-3; *Cal. Close,* 1272-9, 516; *Cal. Fine R.* 1272-1307, 317-18.
[91] *Cal. Pat.* 1272-81, 59; *Cal. Fine R.* 1272-1307, 30-5.

[92] P. H. W. Booth, 'Financial Admin. of Lordship and Co. Chest.', Liverpool Univ. M.A. thesis, 1974, 166.
[93] The form of the accounts is discussed by Mabel H. Mills, *Ches. in Pipe R.* 30-3.
[94] J. W. Alexander, 'A Pinchpenny Patron: Ranulf III of Chest.', *Cîteaux*, i. 23.
[95] *Ches. in Pipe R.* 30-1; cf. *Close R.* 1251-3, 455-6.
[96] *Cal. Pat.* 1247-58, 35.
[97] *Close R.* 1247-51, 221.
[98] See p. 8.
[99] *Cal. Pat.* 1247-58, 70.
[1] *Ches. in Pipe R.* 93.

control over the Four Cantreds as well as over Cheshire, in return for an annual payment of 1,000 marks.[2] There is no evidence about the financial arrangements made under the Lord Edward before 1270, when Reynold de Grey became justice:[3] his farm, of Cheshire only, was 800 marks.[4] Guncelin de Badlesmere, who succeeded Grey in October 1274, accounted once more as keeper; from December 1277, however, the revenues of the county were applied to the building of the abbey of Vale Royal.[5] In 1281 Grey was reappointed, farming Cheshire and the cantreds of Englefield and Rhos for 1,000 marks a year for eight years,[6] but the Welsh war necessitated a temporary suspension of the arrangement,[7] and alienation by Edward I of some of the Welsh lands in Grey's custody led to remissions of part of the farm in 1283, 1284, and 1285; when Grey's appointment was renewed for a further eight years in 1290, the farm was set at 727 marks 8s.[8] In 1299 Richard de Massey replaced Grey, and although it was apparently intended at first that he should be responsible, as approver, for all the issues of Cheshire and Flintshire, it was eventually arranged that he should hold the counties at farm for 1,000 marks a year.[9]

A paradoxical result of the annexation of Cheshire by the Crown was renewed emphasis on the county's individuality. It has indeed been argued with force that this period witnessed the creation of what might be called the 'palatinate tradition'.[10] When Stephen of Seagrave was sent to Cheshire in 1237, he was admonished to do justice according to the custom of the region.[11] In 1249 the 'barons' and community of Cheshire sent to Henry III a list of complaints about infringements of local customs. On three of them the king ordered that the customs existing in the time of Earl Ranulph should be observed. At the same time the royal prerogative was emphasized: complaints that the king had infringed Cheshire custom in placing the county at farm and in appointing an escheator were dismissed.[12] Moreover, the concessions made were suspended four months later;[13] when, however, the county was placed at farm, emphasis was laid on the maintenance of local law and custom.[14] In 1251 further concessions were made in favour of local custom, repeating those granted and subsequently revoked in 1249.[15] The justice at that time, Alan la Zouche, provoked both complaints and resistance by high-handed actions towards the men of the county and of North Wales.[16] In 1255 the authority of the Cheshire Domesday Roll was upheld.[17] In 1258 the Lord Edward issued letters patent confirming the customs of Earl Ranulph's time.[18] In the following year a further unsuccessful attempt was made to challenge the appointment of an escheator for the county.[19] The charter of liberties issued by Ranulph (III) was confirmed in 1265 and 1300.[20] In 1273 Reynold de Grey, like Alan la Zouche twenty years earlier, was alleged to have contravened local custom.[21] By 1301 Cheshire's status within the kingdom was still in many respects exceptional. The term 'county palatine' was apparently first used, in an official record, to describe it in 1297.[22]

[2] *Cal. Pat.* 1247–58, 70.
[3] *Ann. Cestr.* 100.
[4] *Ches. in Pipe R.* 108.
[5] Ibid. 111–45; *Cal. Pat.* 1272–81, 247; *Cal. Close,* 1272–9, 460.
[6] *Cal. Pat.* 1272–81, 476.
[7] *Cal. Close,* 1279–88, 216–17.
[8] *Cal. Pat.* 1281–92, 82, 133, 172, 369.
[9] *Ches. in Pipe R.* 183–4; *Cal. Fine R.* 1272–1307, 428–9.
[10] Barraclough, *Earldom,* 22.
[11] *Close R.* 1234–7, 538.

[12] Ibid. 1247–51, 185–6.
[13] Ibid. 342–3.
[14] *Cal. Pat.* 1247–58, 35, 60, 70.
[15] *Close R.* 1247–51, 442.
[16] Ibid. 541, 551; 1251–3, 179; 1253–4, 310; *Cal. Pat.* 1247–58, 106, 171.
[17] See p. 4.
[18] *Cal. Pat.* 1292–1301, 519.
[19] *Cal. Chest. Co. Ct. R.* 2.
[20] *Cal. Pat.* 1292–1301, 499–501.
[21] Ibid. 1272–81, 6.
[22] *E.H.R.* xxxv, 419.

THE PALATINATE 1301–1547

Cheshire, the Earldom of Chester, and the Crown[1]

IN February 1301 Edward 'of Carnarvon', son of Edward I, was created prince of Wales and earl of Chester.[2] In the following April the prince's Cheshire tenants did homage and swore fealty to him, and appointments were made to the chief administrative offices of the county, those of justice and chamberlain of Chester.[3] During the 14th and 15th centuries it became the normal practice for the king's heir to receive the titles, although no rule was established about a suitable age for the creation. Edward 'of Carnarvon' was nearly seventeen when he was made prince and earl; his own son appears to have received the titles when only eleven days old. Between 1301 and 1547 only two kings' heirs never received the titles. Henry, son of Henry V, was less than nine months old when he succeeded to the throne in 1422.[4] Edward, son of Henry VIII, although he was nine when he succeeded his father as king, had never been created prince of Wales or earl of Chester.[5] If there was no earl, the administration of the county was conducted in the king's name: that happened for rather more than half the period. The creation of a new earl did not necessarily result in an immediate assumption by him of administrative power. Between 1454 and 1456, for example, and again between 1471 and 1473, sessions of the county court were held in the king's name rather than in the earl's.[6] In 1506 letters patent confirming and extending the franchise of the city of Chester were issued from the Chester Exchequer in the king's name, though his son was earl of Chester.[7]

After 1301 it was rare for kings or earls of Chester to visit the county. Occasionally such visits had administrative significance: thus the Black Prince's visit of 1353 was expressly undertaken in order to deal with disorder in Cheshire.[8] That of Prince Arthur in 1499 was connected with the institution of *quo warranto* proceedings in the county.[9] No such importance appears to attach to the visits of Edward II to Chester in 1309[10] or of Henry VII in 1495.[11] Writers have occasionally been misled into inferring the presence of king or earl at Chester from the formula *teste me ipso apud Cestriam* which appears at the end of some of the charters granted to the city.[12] The phrase, which appeared in all 15th-century letters patent issued by the Chester Exchequer and in all original writs, merely referred to the location of the palatinate seal.

Since earls of Chester were usually infants at the time of their creation, the

[1] The help of Miss Dorothy J. Clayton of Liverpool University in reading this section, in making valuable suggestions for its improvement, and in making available the results of her researches into 15th-cent. admin. hist. of Ches. is gratefully acknowledged.

[2] For dates of creation of earls of Chest., see *Complete Peerage*, s.v. Chester.

[3] *Ches. Chamberlains' Accounts* (R.S.L.C. lix), 13–14; *Cal. Pat.* 1343–5, 227–8.

[4] *Handbk. Brit. Chronology*, 37.

[5] Ibid. 39.

[6] See headings of Chester 29/159–61 and Chester 29/175–6.

[7] Chester R.O., CH/32.

[8] *Blk. Prince's Reg.* iii. 111. For administrative significance of the visit see P. H. W. Booth, 'Taxation and Public Order: Ches. in 1353', *Northern Hist.* xii. 16–31.

[9] R. Stewart-Brown, 'Ches. Writs of *Quo Warranto* in 1499', *E.H.R.* xlix. 676–84.

[10] *Cal. Fine R.* 1307–19, 43–4; *Cal. Pat.* 1307–13, 163; *Cal. Close*, 1307–13, 161; *Chrons. of Reigns of Edw. I and Edw. II* (Rolls Ser.), ii. 161.

[11] Gladys Temperley, *Henry VII*, 415.

[12] e.g. R. H. Morris, *Chest. in Plantagenet and Tudor Reigns*, 54, 61, 64, followed by J. T. Driver, *Ches. in Later Middle Ages*, 38.

administration of their estates was entrusted to councillors appointed by the king. Such a council might be authorized expressly to appoint ministers within Cheshire.[13] In the later 15th century the council in the marches of Wales played a prominent part in Cheshire administration.[14] Representatives of the king's or earl's council were considered to be almost permanently associated with sittings of the Chester Exchequer: those who made recognizances to keep the peace before the chamberlain of Chester in the 15th century were bound to appear within Chester castle before the king's council there.[15] In 1436 representatives of the community of the county were ordered to appear *coram consilio nostro apud Cestriam in scaccario ibidem* to negotiate over the grant of a subsidy to the king: the deputy justice of Chester, the chamberlain, and two others including a baron of the national Exchequer met them on the king's behalf.[16]

Under the successors of Edward 'of Carnarvon' as earls of Chester, whether they happened to be the kings themselves or their heirs, the institutions of the palatinate which have been observed in their early stages of growth were encouraged to develop more fully. The existence of those institutions, and of the distinctive records which they produced, has sometimes led to an exaggerated view of the county's independence. Although it was possible for an official record to refer to 'England and Wales and the county of Chester' as late as 1399,[17] the county was, in general, subject to English statute law. Moreover, the appointment of officials in the palatinate often reflected national political developments. Thus Sir Robert Holland's appointments as justice of Chester in 1307, 1311, and 1318–19 reflect the influence of his patron, Thomas of Lancaster.[18] The overthrow of Roger Mortimer in 1330 was accompanied by the replacement of his supporter, Sir Oliver Ingham, as justice by Sir William Clinton.[19] From the late 14th century onwards, the justices of Chester were almost always figures of national political importance who could have had very little to do with the day-to-day judicial routine of the palatinate. In Richard II's reign appointments of sheriffs and escheators in Cheshire often coincided with those of the same officials throughout the kingdom.[20] The dynastic changes of 1399 and 1461 were accompanied by sweeping changes among the administrative personnel of the county.[21]

Whenever the earldom changed hands, purges of the administrative officials of Cheshire might be expected. It is, however, impossible to trace a consistent policy governing such changes. In 1301 the justice, the chamberlain, and the sheriff were all replaced,[22] but no such dramatic developments followed the creation of the Black Prince as earl in 1333. What appear to have been significant changes in 1376, following the resumption of the county by Edward III, become on closer examination mostly confirmations of existing appointments, and only the chamberlain was possibly replaced.[23] In 1377 a new sheriff and, apparently, an associate justice, were appointed, but the existing justice, chamberlain, and escheator were confirmed in their offices.[24] Similarly, the appointments of chamberlain, escheator, and sheriff in 1502, shortly after the death of Prince Arthur, were in fact confirmations.[25]

---

[13] *Cal. Pat.* 1330–4, 419.

[14] See p. 34.

[15] e.g. Chester 2/115 rot. 3. Such recognizances must be distinguished from mainprises for appearance at the county court: see p. 21.

[16] Chester 2/107 rot. 6. For a commission by the prince of Wales's council in 1474 to treat with the community of Ches. over a subsidy, see Chester 2/146 rot. 1.

[17] *Cal. Pat.* 1399–1401, 175.

[18] For Holland's career see J. R. Maddicott, 'Thos. of Lanc. and Sir Rob. Holland', *E.H.R.* lxxxv. 449–72.

[19] *Cal. Pat.* 1330–4, 13.

[20] *Cal. Fine R.* 1383–91, 112–13, 274, 305–7, 341–2;

1391–9, 6–8, 166–8, 194–5.

[21] *36 D.K.R.* 99–100; *37 D.K.R.* 138–9.

[22] *Ches. in Pipe R.* 195, 214–15.

[23] *Cal. Fine R.* 1369–77, 355, 357. The writs are dated 6 June, two days before the Black Prince's death. No evidence has been found for the identity of the chamberlain immediately before this: the last to be recorded was Robert Paris who accounted in 1373–4 (*21 D.K.R.* 32).

[24] *Cal. Pat.* 1377–81, 72; *Cal. Fine R.* 1377–83, 36, 38.

[25] *37 D.K.R.* 144. There is no evidence in the appointments as calendared that they were mere confirmations: the fact can only be checked by reference to the last recorded holders of the offices.

In 1397 Cheshire, together with Flintshire and the confiscated lands of the earl of Arundel, was made into a principality by Richard II. The internal administration of the county appears to have been but little affected by the creation, which did not survive Richard's deposition.[26]

The appointment of officials in Cheshire was, throughout the period, unfettered by such restrictions as controlled similar appointments elsewhere in the kingdom. As a result many of the leading offices became, in the late 14th and 15th centuries, hereditary, or sinecures, or both. As early as 1318 Edward II claimed that he was unable to accede to Parliament's request that he dismiss the justice of Chester, since the appointment belonged to his son as earl rather than to himself.[27] Nevertheless kings could, and did, influence the appointment of Cheshire officials even when their heirs were in control of the earldom. In 1355 Edward III directed the appointment by his son of Thomas Warwick as constable of Chester castle, and in the following year the chamberlain was ordered to pay Warwick's wages from the date of his appointment rather than from the time of his arrival to take up the post, since that too was the king's will.[28] In 1457 Richard Tunstall was appointed chamberlain of Chester for life by Henry VI. The appointment, however, required ratification in the name of the three-year-old prince of Wales, and on ratification the tenure was converted from life to pleasure.[29]

Administration of Justice

At the beginning of the period the justice of Chester had wide administrative powers. In 1308 he was said to be *tenens locum domini regis*.[30] In April 1301 Sir William Trussell was given custody of Cheshire and Flintshire, and of the manors of Macclesfield and of Overton (Flints.), with the castles of Chester, Rhuddlan (Flints.), and Flint. He was to appoint constables to the castles, and was to receive £100 a year as his fee.[31] His predecessor had been empowered to lease out demesne lands and offices,[32] and that power seems to have continued to be exercised by the justices. Trussell's predecessor had held his office at farm, and it was often farmed in the early 14th century. Sir William Ormesby succeeded Trussell before May 1307;[33] the terms of Ormesby's appointment are unknown, but his successor, Sir Robert Holland, appointed in August 1307,[34] seems to have farmed the office, since Sir Pain Tiptoft who replaced him on the same terms in 1309 was accounting for a farm of 1,000 marks in 1311. The farm was then increased to £1,000. Shortly afterwards Holland was reappointed, with his farm set at the lower figure, but it too was increased within a month of his appointment.[35] Wardships, reliefs, escheats, marriages, and the like were reserved to the king.[36] When Edward, son of Edward II, was given Cheshire in 1312, Holland was replaced by Sir Hugh Audley the elder.[37] The chamberlain's account surviving for 1312–13 implies that Audley did not farm the office, but no mention was made of his fee. From Easter to Michaelmas 1315, however, he was granted £50 for the expenses of his household.[38]

There is no evidence whether the succeeding justices, Sir John Sapey (1318), Sir Robert Holland (1319–22), and Sir Oliver Ingham (1322–5) were farmers or not, but Sir Richard Damory (1325–8) was paid a proportion of his fee of £100 for the period from December 1326 until the following Michaelmas.[39] In February 1328 Ingham

[26] R. R. Davies, 'Ric. II and Princip. of Chest.', *Reign of Ric. II: Essays in honour of May McKisack*, ed. F. R. H. du Boulay and Caroline M. Barron, 256–79.
[27] T. F. Tout, *Place of Reign of Edw. II in Eng. Hist.* 116.
[28] *Blk. Prince's Reg.* iii. 205, 227.
[29] 37 *D.K.R.* 726.
[30] Booth, 'Financ. Admin.', 61.
[31] *Ches. in Pipe R.* 214–15.
[32] Ibid. 194–5; *Ches. Chamb. Accts.* 2.

[33] Tout, *Place of Reign of Edw. II*, 337–8.
[34] 31 *D.K.R.* 209.
[35] *Cal. Fine R.* 1307–19, 50, 121, 122, 124.
[36] *Cal. Pat.* 1307–13, 427.
[37] *Cal. Chart. R.* 1301–26, 202.
[38] *Ches. Chamb. Accts.* 78, 86 (the latter account wrongly dated by the editor).
[39] Ibid. 103.

was appointed once more, at first in return for the usual annual fee but from November as farmer, for life, at 1,000 marks yearly.[40] As a supporter of Mortimer, Ingham lost his office in 1330, and his successors Sir William Clinton (1330–5) and Sir Hugh Frene (1335–6) were paid the yearly fee of £100.[41] Nevertheless at Michaelmas 1336 Sir Henry Ferrers received the county at farm, and continued so to hold it until his death in 1343, as did his successor and relative Sir Thomas Ferrers.[42] The latter surrendered his office in July 1346, although his agreement with the Black Prince's council had three more years to run, and was re-granted it with £100 a year. The appointment was intended to last until Easter 1349, when it was apparently renewed, since Ferrers remained justice until his death in 1353.[43] The reason for the change in his terms of service is unknown, but it may have been financial: in 1347 he was said to be trying to recover debts due to him from the time when he had been farmer.[44]

From the mid 14th century the justice's position as the supreme head of county administration declined, and he became almost exclusively concerned with judicial administration. Thus in 1377 Sir Thomas Felton and John de la Pole were made 'justices of Chester for holding pleas', an appointment far removed in tone from that of Trussell in 1301.[45] At the same time the office became increasingly a sinecure to be performed by deputies. It has been argued that Sir Thomas Ferrers was the last of the medieval justices to exercise his office in person.[46] Deputies in the office occur, indeed, as early as 1307.[47] In 1325 the appointment of a new justice was accompanied by the transfer of the 'bag called Domesday' to his deputy by his predecessor's.[48] In the 1320s writs were addressed to 'the justice or his deputy', a form of address which became common in the 1340s and 1350s.[49] Conversely, there is evidence of the personal involvement of some of the justices of the early 14th century in the office. In 1310 Tiptoft refused to obey a royal command to remove a man appealed of felony and held in Macclesfield gaol to Nottingham. He defended his action in the county court by claiming that it would be *contra statum domini regis, comitis Cestrie* to do so.[50] Ingham's appointment in 1322 was avowedly made for military reasons, and implies that he was expected to take action within the county.[51] At the first county court held by Damory in 1325 it appears that he asked for information about the status of the doomsmen and suitors there.[52]

The first deputy justice about whom much evidence has survived was John Delves, who held a like position in North Wales, and who in 1354–5 was receiving £40 as his fee out of the £100 a year allotted to his superior.[53] Although Delves was always addressed as deputy, it is clear that the Black Prince's council treated him as effectively justice. In 1354 he was ordered to prolong the county court session for as long as should be necessary. Five years later the chamberlain was notified that Delves could not be present at the next county court.[54] His superior, Bartholomew Burghersh the younger, was empowered on his appointment in 1353 to act himself or by deputy.[55] Burghersh and his successor Sir Thomas Felton, appointed in 1370, spent much of their periods

[40] *Cal. Pat.* 1327–30, 242; *Ches. Chamb. Accts.* 108; *Cal. Fine R.* 1327–37, 113–14.

[41] *Cal. Pat.* 1330–4, 13; *Ches. Chamb. Accts.* 110, 113. Ingham's first appointment in 1322 had expressly been 'political', resulting from Scottish invasion and siege of Tickhill (Yorks. W. R.): *Cal. Pat.* 1321–4, 72.

[42] *Ches. Chamb. Accts.* 111; Booth, 'Financ. Admin.' 53. The appointment of Hugh Berwick in place of Sir Henry in Feb. 1341 (*Cal. Fine R.* 1337–47, 214) does not seem to have taken effect.

[43] *Blk. Prince's Reg.* i. 47; Booth, 'Financ. Admin.' 174.

[44] *Blk. Prince's Reg.* i. 108.

[45] *Cal. Pat.* 1377–81, 72.

[46] Booth, 'Financ. Admin.', 53–4.

[47] *Arley Charts.* ed. W. Beamont, 35.

[48] 3 *Sheaf*, xx, p. 66.

[49] *Ledger Bk. Vale Royal Abbey* (R.S.L.C. lxviii), 55; *Blk. Prince's Reg.* vols. i and ii, *passim*.

[50] *E.H.R.* xxxv. 419.

[51] *Cal. Pat.* 1321–4, 72.

[52] Chester 29/37 rot. 10.

[53] *Blk. Prince's Reg.* iii. 128, 149; *Ches. Chamb. Accts.* 228.

[54] *Blk. Prince's Reg.* iii. 168, 370.

[55] Ibid. iii. 128.

of office abroad in the Black Prince's service.[56] Under Richard II a succession of noblemen held the post of justice of Chester: the king's half-brother, John Holland, appointed in 1381; Edmund, duke of York, in 1385; Robert de Vere, duke of Ireland, in 1387; Thomas, duke of Gloucester, in 1388; Thomas, earl marshal and earl of Nottingham, in 1394; and William le Scrope, earl of Wiltshire, in 1398.[57] Most of them appointed deputies.[58] One such deputy, Thomas Molineux, who was killed at Radcot Bridge in 1387, was described by a chronicler as justice.[59] No change of policy resulted from the change of dynasty in 1399. Henry IV's first justice of Chester was Henry Percy; other noblemen to hold the office were Gilbert, Lord Talbot, appointed in 1403, Thomas, duke of Exeter, in 1420, Humphrey, duke of Gloucester, in 1427, William de la Pole, earl of Suffolk, in 1440, John, earl of Shrewsbury, in 1459, and Thomas, Lord Stanley, in 1462.[60] Thomas, created earl of Derby in 1485, remained in the office until his death in 1504. His son George, Lord Strange, was appointed jointly with him, in survivorship, in 1486, but died in 1497.[61]

Records of the county court, such as judicial writs, final concords, and the headings of plea rolls, assume the presence of the justice at the court's sessions. It has been shown that that type of evidence is not conclusive elsewhere in the kingdom as early as the 13th century.[62] Two examples from the time when Humphrey, duke of Gloucester, was justice of Chester will illustrate its unreliability for Cheshire. Gloucester is shown on the plea rolls as presiding over sessions of the county court on 25 April 1430 and on 22 May 1431.[63] On the first occasion he is said to have been at Canterbury. Five days before the second he was at Abingdon (Berks.), and it is unlikely that he could have travelled thence to Chester in time for the county court.[64] In any event it is doubtful whether Gloucester's position at the centre of English affairs would have allowed him to spend time on routine judicial matters in a remote part of the realm. Nevertheless, even the most 'political' of justices could arouse passions among the inhabitants of the county. In 1393 a rising in Cheshire was said to have been caused by fears that the justice was plotting to withdraw the county's franchises.[65]

The earl of Derby's death in 1504 was followed by an apparent change in the policy of appointments to the office of justice of Chester. Derby's successors were men with legal experience. The first was the elder Sir Thomas Englefield, who had been made a deputy justice in 1486 and had regularly appeared in that capacity since 1498.[66] From 1513 his son Thomas was associated with him.[67] The younger Thomas succeeded to the office on his father's death, and he and his successors Sir William Sulyard (1538–40), Sir Nicholas Hare (1540–5), and Robert Townshend (appointed in 1545) were lawyers.[68] Nevertheless the practice of exercising the office by deputy continued to the end of the period. Among Thomas Cromwell's notes made in October 1533 of 'acts necessary to be made at this Parliament' appears, 'that the justice of Chester shall not occupy by deputy'.[69] The intention was not carried out. In 1537 Bishop Lee of Coventry and Lichfield wrote to Cromwell to notify him of Englefield's death. The latter's activities with Lee in the Welsh marches could have left little time for him to exercise the office of justice of Chester.[70] On the following day John Packington wrote

[56] D.N.B. For Felton's appointment see *36 D.K.R.* 179.
[57] *Cal. Pat.* 1377–81, 624; 1385–9, 24, 450; 1391–6, 404; 1396–9, 284; *36 D.K.R.* 494. Gloucester and Wiltshire were also made justices of N. Wales.
[58] *36 D.K.R.* 95, 347, 426, 494; *Cal. Pat.* 1385–9, 288.
[59] *Bull. Jn. Rylands Libr.* xiv. 168.
[60] *Cal. Pat.* 1399–1401, 37; 1436–41, 376; *31 D.K.R.* 196; *36 D.K.R.* 102; *37 D.K.R.* 133, 138, 139.
[61] *37 D.K.R.* 143.
[62] *R. of Justices in Eyre for Lincs. . . . and Worcs.* (Selden

Soc. liii), p. xliv.
[63] Chester 29/134 rot. 24; Chester 29/135 rot. 18.
[64] K. H. Vickers, *Humph. D. Glouc.* 220, 223.
[65] T. F. Tout, *Chapters in Med. Admin. Hist.* iii. 482–3.
[66] *31 D.K.R.* 195; *37 D.K.R.* 20, 157.
[67] *39 D.K.R.* 55.
[68] For biogs. see E. Foss, *Judges of Eng.* For appointments see *L. & P. Hen. VIII*, xiii (1), p. 62; xv, p. 509; xx (2), p. 422.
[69] Ibid. vi, p. 550.   [70] Ibid. xii (2), p. 274.

to Cromwell to offer 100 marks for the office, which he obviously regarded as a source of income rather than as a position requiring his personal attendance, since he mentioned it as a means of overcoming his financial burdens. [71] Both Hare and Townshend appointed deputies soon after their own appointments. [72] The system had reached extravagant limits by the end of the period, for in 1480, 1481, and 1537 the deputy justices had themselves had others appointed to act for them. [73]

From 1388 there is evidence of special commissions of justices to afforce the county court. Such commissions were sometimes emergency measures taken during a vacancy in the office of justice. The first, in January, 1388, was headed by the duke of Ireland, who had in fact fled after the battle of Radcot Bridge and had been replaced as justice two days before the commission was issued. [74] Between March and August 1388 there were five more such commissions; they may have been intended to provide men to preside over the county court until the appointment of a new justice had taken effect. The duke of Gloucester was appointed on 8 June, but his deputy was not appointed until 31 July. [75] The *pro hac vice* commissions are dated between March and August. [76] The next date from January 1393 and March and April 1394. [77] The earl of Nottingham was made justice in March 1394, and his period of office is marked by further such commissions in September 1394, March, April, and August 1395, May 1396, and February, July, and October 1397. [78] Their numbers then decreased until 1413–14 and again until 1427–31. [79] Those of January, February, and April 1427 appear to be emergency measures between the death of the justice, Thomas duke of Exeter, in December 1426, and the appointment of his successor, Humphrey duke of Gloucester, in the following May. [80] Under Gloucester such commissions were issued in June and December 1429, in June, August, and September 1430, and in January and March 1431. [81] During those years they were dated on the day when the county court session began, and were enrolled at the head of the plea roll which recorded its proceedings. The session was then said to be held before all the justices named, including the justice himself. [82] It is impossible to establish a link between the appointments and the known absence of the justice. On the two dates mentioned above on which it is unlikely that Gloucester can have been present, the county court was not afforced. [83] His absence from one session when it was afforced might be deduced from the fact that the clerk writing the heading of a rotulet of the plea roll omitted to write the duke's name first and had to insert it. [84]

After 1431 the *pro hac vice* commissions become rare. That of May 1461, which included the earl of Warwick, fell between the accession of Edward IV and the appointment of John Needham as justice in the following July. [85] The commission of August 1504, which included Thomas Englefield, followed the death of the justice, the earl of Derby, by less than a month, and preceded Englefield's permanent appointment as justice. [86]

Those appointed to the *pro hac vice* commissions were usually either men of local standing, such as the abbots of Combermere and St. Werburgh's, Chester, and John Bruen of Tarvin, or men of legal training such as Hugh Holes, who was appointed a King's Bench justice in 1389, and Henry Birtles, serjeant at law. Some at least of

[71] *L. & P. Hen. VIII*, xii (2), p. 275.
[72] *31 D.K.R.* 205, 255.
[73] Ibid. 174, 199.
[74] *36 D.K.R.* 95; *Cal. Pat.* 1385–91, 381, records appointment of Wm. Hornby, but no evidence that it took effect has been found.
[75] *Cal. Pat.* 1385–9, 450; *36 D.K.R.* 95.
[76] *31 D.K.R.* 190; *36 D.K.R.* 95.
[77] *36 D.K.R.* 97.
[78] *Cal. Pat.* 1391–6, 404; *31 D.K.R.* 226; *36 D.K.R.* 97–8.
[79] *36 D.K.R.* 100–2; *37 D.K.R.* 49, 132, 133.
[80] *37 D.K.R.* 133.
[81] Ibid. 55, 98, 134.
[82] e.g. Chester 29/134 rott. 33, 35; Chester 29/135 rott. 1, 7, 11.
[83] See p. 13.
[84] Chester 29/135 rot. 2.
[85] *37 D.K.R.* 138–9.
[86] Ibid. 144.

the deputy justices were also men of law. Before his appointment John de la Pole had acted as the earl of Chester's advocate in *quo warranto* pleas.[87] James del Holt rose from the position of serjeant at law to that of justice of Chester.[88] Hugh Holes, Roger Horton, and John Needham may indeed have found the service of the law in Cheshire a useful stepping-stone to a wider legal career.[89]

The Cheshire county court was distinguished from other similar courts in the kingdom more by reason of its rules of procedure than because of the law which it administered. The law of Cheshire was, in general, that of the kingdom as a whole.[90] The court itself had competence over all civil and criminal actions.[91] It could also review decisions of other courts, such as the Pentice Court of Chester, through the issue of a writ of error.[92] It met eight or nine times a year, at intervals which could be as short as two or three weeks.[93] The most regular date of meeting in the mid 15th century was the Tuesday after the close of Easter: sessions began on that day in every year between 1442 and 1485 except 1461 and 1471. In the same period sessions opened more often than not on the Tuesday after Trinity and the second or third Tuesday in January.[94] In 1339 sessions were said to last from 'prime on Tuesday to sunset on Wednesday', but soon afterwards it was held that they could be extended until adjourned, and in 1354 the deputy justice was ordered to hold the court for as long as should be necessary.[95] Judicial writs were usually dated on the Wednesday of a county court session, but occasionally on a Thursday.[96]

In Cheshire the county court was nominally held not before the sheriff as in England, but before the justice of Chester, although in practice, as has been shown, either his deputy or a group of *pro hac vice* justices must often have presided. Final concords were said to be made before the justice and a group of persons whose names replaced those of the justices of the bench in a normal English concord. Of 78 final concords which have been examined for the period from 20 Henry VI to 22 Edward IV (both years inclusive), all but 12 were said to be made before the justice (two joint justices between 22 and 28 Henry VI) and 5 others, of whom 3 were always knights.[97]

Among the others present at county court sessions were doomsmen and suitors. In the normal English county court there seems to have been a progressive tendency to regard the doomsmen and suitors as a single body, but that was not so in Cheshire.[98] In 1325 a newly appointed justice sought information on the role of the two groups. He was told that both held their lands in return for the obligation to serve. They helped the justice to render judgements. First the doomsmen gave their opinion, which the suitors either accepted or rejected. In case of disagreement a majority decision was taken, though it is not clear how it was reached. Any party dissatisfied with a judgement could procure a writ of error from the king. When the writ reached the county it might be debated during three sessions, and the judgement could be reversed. If, however, it stood, and was later found to be false, the doomsmen and suitors were liable to an amercement of £100.[99] Such an amercement occurs in 1342.[1] At that time 31 doomsmen

[87] e.g. *Ledger Bk. Vale Royal Abbey*, 134. He was acting as deputy justice in 1364: *Blk. Prince's Reg.* iii. 466.
[88] 36 *D.K.R.* 242.
[89] Foss, *Judges of Eng.* iv. 204–5, 332, 446–7.
[90] *Cal. Chest. Co. Ct. R.* p. xix.
[91] Ibid. p. xvii.
[92] Chester R.O., SFW/5/1–13.
[93] e.g. sess. were held on 4 and 25 Apr. and 13 and 27 June 1430: Chester 29/134 rott. 20, 24, 28, 33.
[94] Ex inf. Miss Clayton from analysis of Chester 29/147–87.
[95] Margaret Sharp, 'Contributions to Hist. of Earldom

and Co. Chest. 1237–1399' (Manchester Univ. Ph.D. thesis, 1925), i. 175, 178; *Blk. Prince's Reg.* iii. 168.
[96] Ex inf. Miss Clayton from analysis of Chester 24/36–58.
[97] Chester 31/31–5. Of the remainder, 7 were levied before the justice and 6 others, 2 before the justice and 7 others, 2 before the justice and 8 others, and 1 before the justice and 4 others.
[98] Cf. T. F. T. Plucknett, *Concise Hist. Common Law* (4th edn.), 89–90.
[99] Chester 29/37 rot. 10.
[1] Sharp, 'Contributions', i. 178.

were mentioned. A 17th-century copy of a list of doomsmen and suitors dating from 36 Edward III (1362–3) names a total of 52 doomsmen and 69 suitors from the six hundreds which were represented at the county court; Macclesfield hundred, which had its own courts, sent no doomsmen or suitors to the county court.[2] Each doomsman or suitor was regarded as representing a particular vill; the same man or woman could represent a group of vills, and those liable to service could appoint others to act in their place. In 1418 Peter Dutton was given custody of two-thirds of the lands of Hugh Venables of Kinderton during the minority of Hugh's heir. In 1423 Dutton was allowed to perform by attorney the duty of the younger Venables as doomsman for Kinderton, Witton, and Sproston.[3] In the 1530s doomsmen from 46 vills were each fined 6s. 8d. 'because they did not come to render judgement on felons convicted of felony, as they used to do'; it has been argued that the fines represented an attempt to revive a practice which had been extinct for some time.[4] In 1390 ten doomsmen were each fined 2s. for non-attendance at the county court.[5] Judgement on convicted felons was said to be given by the doomsmen in 1464.[6]

At each county court session a grand jury[7] was impanelled, whose task was to consider bills of indictment. Not all those impanelled were sworn to the jury. Between 1442 and 1460 the numbers of jurymen on panels varied between 11 and 25, though most panels contained between 18 and 21 names. The number actually sworn varied between 9 and 17, with most juries consisting of 12 to 14 men. Jury service was extremely burdensome to some individuals. Seventeen men were each impanelled on 20 or more occasions between 1442 and 1461. Thus Hamon del Lee appeared on 48 jury panels in that period, and he was sworn to the jury on all but 6 occasions. Thomas Kyncy, on the other hand, was impanelled 20 times but only sworn on 11. The figures represent a minimal estimate of jury service performed by those named, since only 107 jury lists have survived from the 161 county court sessions held during those 20 years, and in 31 cases only the names of those actually sworn are known. What appears to be a list of those liable to jury service in all seven hundreds of Cheshire for 1445 lists 493 names.[8] It is obvious that, as was to happen in the late 16th and 17th centuries, jury service fell most heavily on a small group of men rather than evenly throughout the group.

Civil actions in the Chester county court seem to have resembled those of the central courts of the kingdom in most particulars. They were begun by original writs in the name of the earl or king, attested at Chester.[9] There were, however, some divergences from common English practice. In the 14th century the limit of legal memory, in actions of novel disseisin, was placed at the accession of John *de Scotia* as earl of Chester (1232); in those of mort d'ancestor it was set at the time when Earl Ranulph III took the Cross (1215).[10] Furthermore, there were no law terms in Cheshire; business was adjourned to the next county court session.[11] There is no evidence how far ahead the court's sessions were planned. Judicial writs returnable at the following session always give its exact date, while long-term mainprises use a more general date. Thus of five mainprises recorded at the county court session of 3 October 1441, two were to extend until the court after Christmas next, one to the county court after

[2] Chester R.O., CR63/2/26, ff. 108–9.
[3] Ibid., CR63/2/24, p. 36.
[4] 3 *Sheaf*, x, p. 46.
[5] Chester 38/15 rot. 3.
[6] Chester 29/168 rot. 17d.
[7] The following paragraph is based on inf. supplied by Miss Clayton from analysis of Chester 24/36–43 and Chester 25/14.

[8] Chester R.O., CR63/1/7, unfoliated: a 19th-cent. transcript of a 16th-cent. copy of the original list. Cf. J. P. Earwaker, *East Ches.* i, pp. xxv–xxvi and 16.
[9] See examples among the sess. files (Chester 24).
[10] Sharp, 'Contributions', i. 88–9.
[11] e.g. successive postponements of an action of debt, Chester 29/165 rot. 2d.

Midsummer next, and the remaining two to the county court after Michaelmas a year thence; the courts actually met on 9 January, 24 July, and 2 October.[12]

The court entertained all criminal actions. Criminal process was usually begun by a grand jury indictment, though indictments made before the justice in his eyre, and before the sheriff in his tourn, as well as those sent up from the Macclesfield courts and the forest courts were also taken up by the county court, and the names of those indicted at the inferior courts were inserted on the calendar roll.[13] In the mid 15th century the heading *placita corone* on the county court plea roll normally introduces the record of the various stages in criminal process: an indicted person whose appearance had not been secured by writs of *venire facias* (in criminal trespass), *capias, alias,* or *pluries* was exacted at four consecutive county court sessions. If he still failed to appear, he was mainprised by the crier of the court to yet another session and finally outlawed.[14]

Those indicted for trespass usually preferred to submit to the court's mercy and to pay a fine rather than undergo the uncertainties of jury trial. Five men indicted for trespass on 10 January 1464, having been exacted four times in the county court, placed themselves in the court's mercy on 5 March 1465.[15] In cases of felony, however, the accused, if brought to court at all, would be tried at gaol delivery. A routine task of the court was the delivery of Chester castle gaol. One or more gaol delivery juries were usually impanelled and sworn at those county court sessions whose records have been examined for the mid 15th century; there is no apparent connexion between the jurors and the localities where the crimes were committed, since one gaol delivery jury could try a group of people accused of crimes committed at different times and places and, indeed, indicted at different courts.[16] Although technically delivered from the gaol in Chester castle, many of the accused had in fact been released on mainprise. If they were subsequently acquitted, they had to pay a fine *pro sueta prisone*.[17]

The record keeping of the county court was of a high standard. Sessional files have survived from the mid 14th century.[18] Those for the period 1442–85 have been assigned to their sessions and examined in detail. They contain original and judicial writs in civil actions; judicial writ in criminal cases; grand jury panels and the bills of indictment that were found; gaol delivery juries with notes on their verdicts; writs of summons for juries in civil actions, with jury panels attached and, where possible, notes of the verdicts; indictments sent up from other courts; notes of final concords attached to the writs of *precipe* which originated the actions; notes of mainprises, attorneys, and pledges of fines.[19] It is likely that many of the more formal records of the court were compiled between its sessions from the notes which appear on the files.[20] Of those formal records the most important are the plea rolls which record the various stages in civil and criminal actions, gaol deliveries, and amercements imposed. The names of the grand jurors who were sworn, and the details of the bills of indictment

[12] Chester 26/16 rott. 5–5d compared with Chester 29/147–8.

[13] e.g. Chester 20/3.

[14] e.g. process against Wm. son of Lawr. Starky late of Northwich between Jan. 1464 and Jan. 1465: Chester 25/15 rot. 5 (indictment); Chester 24/46, sess. Tues. in 5th wk. of Lent, Tues. after close of East., Tues. after Trinity, 4 Edw. IV (*capias, alias,* and *pluries*); Chester 29/168 rott. 14, 16d, 20d, 25d, 29, 33 (enrolments of process on plea roll); Chester 27/1 rot. 4 (outlawry roll).

[15] Chester 25/15 rot. 5; Chester 29/168 rot. 33; Chester 29/169 rot. 3d.

[16] Ex inf. Miss Clayton from analysis of Chester 24/35–58 and Chester 25/14–15.

[17] e.g. Chester 24/58, sess. Tues. after Trinity, 1 Edw. V. Cf. R. Stewart-Brown, 'Suete de Prisone', *E.H.R.* xxiv. 506–10, and for earlier use of the term *sueta prisone,* R. B. Pugh, *Imprisonment in Medieval Eng.* 168.

[18] Chester 24: see *P.R.O. Lists & Indexes No. XL,* 13.

[19] Chester 24/35–58. A paper slip has been attached to each file giving its session date, and a detailed list of the contents of those pieces has been given to the P.R.O. with a brief analysis of their contents.

[20] The following description is based on an analysis of Chester 20/3, Chester 25/14–15, Chester 26/16–19, Chester 27/1–2, Chester 29/147–87, Chester 31/31–5, and Chester 37/6 made by Miss Clayton.

which they found true, were enrolled formally on the indictment roll. From that roll a calendar roll was compiled, giving merely the names of those indicted and the type of indictment, felony or trespass being the most common. The purpose of the calendar roll was presumably to enable the clerks to compose writs of *capias*, etc., and records of process enrolled on the plea rolls, without the need to read through the detailed indictments on the indictment roll. The names of those eventually outlawed were enrolled on an outlawry roll. Where parties in an action chose to be represented by attorneys, the names of the latter were enrolled on the warrants of attorney roll.

The term 'eyre' in the legal history of Cheshire had two distinct meanings. In 1353 the Black Prince proclaimed a general eyre in the county; the community of the county complained that such an eyre would contravene their liberties, and in return for a proffer of 5,000 marks it was respited for thirty years and a commission of trailbaston substituted.[21] In 1499 a general eyre was again proclaimed, this time as a vehicle for the investigation of franchises.[22] The term more usually refers to a visitation conducted by the justice of Chester, in theory once a year, of all the hundreds of Cheshire except Macclesfield.[23] During the course of the eyre juries were impanelled in the places visited by the justice, and their indictments were subsequently transferred to the county court for action.[24] The justice also heard civil pleas, initiated by bill rather than by writ. Actions could be adjourned from one place to another on the justice's circuit, and from the eyre to the county court.[25] A sheriff's tourn is also recorded for the first time in 1377.[26] By Edward IV's reign it displayed, in criminal cases, similar characteristics to the justice's eyre: in each of the six hundreds (Macclesfield again being excluded) a jury was impanelled, and indictments for felony and trespass were recorded.[27] The indictments were, like those made before the justice in his eyre, transferred to the county court.[28]

The Exchequer of Chester

The chamberlain of Chester emerged in the 14th century from comparative obscurity to become the leading administrative official of the palatinate. Throughout the period he appears as a financial officer, accounting to the king or earl for the issues of Cheshire and Flintshire, except during those periods when the justice of Chester farmed his office.[29] The accounts were normally audited in Chester.[30] During the early 14th century, however, the chamberlain was expected to travel outside his bailiwick at need. In 1320 Richard Bury spent nine days in London at the Exchequer at the close of his predecessor's account.[31] Some six years later a former chamberlain claimed expenses which he had incurred in travelling to make liveries of money from Chester to London, Kenilworth (Warws.) (twice), and Woodstock (Oxon.). He had spent in all fifty days in those journeys.[32] By the mid 14th century the chamberlain was making six or seven liveries a year to the Black Prince's receiver-general at Westminster, though not, by that time, in person. Much attention was paid, under the Black Prince, to the chamberlain's account. In 1347 a clerk was appointed, at a fee of £10 yearly (half as much as the chamberlain's) as controller of all pleas, receipts, and issues belonging to

[21] *Northern Hist.* xii. 16–31.
[22] *E.H.R.* xlix. 678–82.
[23] Sharp, 'Contributions', i. 192–4; *Cal. Chest. Co. Ct. R.*, p. xxix.
[24] Chester 24/38 contains a bdle. of indictments before the justice in his eyre from 20 to 32 Hen. VI.
[25] e.g. Chester 17/8 rott. 20, 23, 28.
[26] Sharp, 'Contributions', i. 204. An earlier date has been suggested by Mr. P. H. W. Booth from analysis of

Chester 19/1.
[27] Chester 19/6.
[28] Cf. Chester 19/6 rot. 6 and Chester 29/48, sess. Tues. after Trin. 8 Edw. IV.
[29] See pp. 11–12.
[30] What follows relies much on Booth, 'Financ. Admin. *passim*.
[31] *Ches. Chamb. Accts.* 94.
[32] Ibid. 97–9.

the offices of justice and chamberlain. Four months after the appointment it became obvious that the new system was not working satisfactorily: the chamberlain was told to let the controller attend both his petty receipts and his liveries, and to provide locks and keys for the treasury door in Chester castle, and a locked chest for keeping current records. The chamberlain, the justice, his deputy, or their clerk, and the controller were each to hold keys. All fines were to be taken openly in the Exchequer or some other suitable place, in the presence of the justice or his deputy and either the chamberlain or the controller. The detailed arrangements may have represented part of a general search for improved financial efficiency after the change in the status of the justice from a farmer to a paid official in 1346 and the appointment of a new chamberlain, John Brunham the younger.[33] The controllership seems to have been abandoned by 1350, but was revived in a modified form towards the end of the period.[34] The Black Prince's council nevertheless continued to look for better means of accounting, and by the early 1350s the form of the chamberlains' account itself was radically changed.[35] The survival from 1349-50 onwards of the accounts of subordinate ministers may reflect another aspect of the reforms.[36]

The survival of the accounts, and the attention paid to the financial aspects of the chamberlain's office under the Black Prince, together provide a one-sided view of that office. Within the palatinate the chamberlain occupied a position akin to that of the chancellor in the kingdom: he had custody of the Chester seal and was responsible for making out and sealing writs and charters. From 1348 he was authorized to take 16s. 4d. for every charter sealed with the prince's seal, and by 1354 a further 'great fee' had been imposed with respect to certain charters.[37] The fees were waived when grants were made in return for services to the Black Prince in Gascony, but the recipients had still to pay the clerks' fees.[38] If the chamberlain was absent from Chester, difficulties could arise with regard to the seal. In 1394 John Woodhouse was dismissed as chamberlain, and set off for London on the king's business. Before his departure he enclosed the Chester seal in a bag and delivered it to his clerk to keep until the arrival of Robert Paris, his successor. Over a month later, on 9 June, Paris had not arrived in Chester, and the seal was needed for the county court session. It was decided by the deputy justice, the sheriff, the escheator, and three serjeants at law that the bag should be opened and the seal used, and the decision was solemnly enrolled on the 'recognizance roll'.[39]

While the chamberlain resembled the English chancellor in some ways, in others he was akin to an English sheriff. There is an obvious parallel between the accounts of the chamberlain of Chester and those of a sheriff for a normal county. In the 13th century such accounts had been rendered by the justice rather than by the chamberlain, and letters addressed by the royal chancery to all the sheriffs of England were addressed to the justice of Chester. By the early 15th century the chamberlain had become the recipient of such letters.[40]

The chamberlains of Chester during the 14th century were usually clerks. William Melton, who held the office for four years and a half from April 1301, rose to be archbishop of York.[41] Richard Bury, who was chamberlain in the early 1320s, became

[33] *Blk. Prince's Reg.* i. 20, 65, 100-1. Brunham held office until his death in 1370.

[34] The controller is not mentioned in chamberlain's accounts after 1348-9. For the later appointments see *37 D.K.R.* 422; *39 D.K.R.* 56; *L. & P. Hen. VIII*, x, p. 527.

[35] The changes are described in detail in Booth, 'Financ. Admin.', 17-29.

[36] *Ches. Chamb. Accts.* 132 sqq.

[37] *Blk. Prince's Reg.* i. 161; *Ches. Chamb. Accts.* 210, 227. Dr. Sharp argued that this led to the practice of enrolling writs and charters on the 'recognizance rolls', thus changing their character: 'Contributions', i. 109.

[38] *Blk. Prince's Reg.* iii. 244.

[39] *36 D.K.R.* 97.

[40] *Cal. Pat. 1405-8*, 361-2.

[41] *D.N.B.*

bishop of Durham.[42] Thomas Blaston, chamberlain in 1328, was rector of Solihull (Warws.), and eventually became a baron of the Exchequer at Westminster.[43] John Ashby (who occurs as chamberlain in 1329), John Painel (appointed in 1330), John Brunham the younger (chamberlain 1346–70), and John Woodhouse (chamberlain 1376–94) all held livings in the Church.[44] The importance of the office at the end of the 14th century was such that the appointment of Robert Paris in 1394 was made conditional on his personal occupancy of it.[45] It was the first of the Cheshire posts to be filled by Henry IV: the appointment of John Trevor, bishop of St. Asaph, as chamberlain was made when Henry was in Chester in August 1399, before he had assumed the kingship.[46] In the 15th century the office followed the trend set earlier by that of the justice. In 1412 William Troutbeck was made chamberlain during pleasure.[47] Twenty-five years later his appointment was renewed for life, and the reversion of the office was granted during good behaviour to his son John.[48] In 1439 William resigned, and John was appointed for life, with power to appoint a deputy, which he exercised within fourteen days of appointment.[49] His successor, Richard Tunstall, appointed in 1457, also immediately appointed deputies.[50] In 1461 Sir William Stanley was made chamberlain for life.[51] Robert Frost, almoner to the prince of Wales, was appointed in succession to Stanley in 1495, but held office for less than two months; his successors were Sir Reynold Bray (1495–1500) and Sir Richard Pole (1500–6).[52] From 1504 Randal Brereton appears regularly as Pole's deputy, and in 1506 he was made chamberlain.[53] The appointment, said to be during pleasure in 1509, was altered to a life appointment two years later.[54] In June 1530 Randal was succeeded by his son William Brereton, who held office together with several others in Cheshire until 1536, when he shared in Anne Boleyn's fall.[55] An agreement survives by which Randal Lloyd undertook to exercise the office of chamberlain as William's deputy.[56] His successor as chamberlain was Sir Rice Maunsell, whose naval and military career made it inevitable that his office would be exercised by deputy.[57] The deputy was another William Brereton, whose term of office was distinguished by a feud with Sir Peter Dutton. By the late 1530s even the deputy chamberlainship could be exercised *in absentia*, for Brereton was sent to Ireland.[58]

The chamberlain was poorly paid in comparison with the justice . His fee of £20 a year in 1301 had not been increased by 1500 except as a personal favour to John Brunham, who was awarded an extra ten marks a year in 1351.[59] The fee was said to be inadequate. William Melton's arrears of £80 were pardoned because of his expenses in his four years and a half as chamberlain.[60] John Painel petitioned the king for pardon of part of his arrears, in 1330, claiming that his expenses in office had exceeded his fee.[61] It may consequently seem surprising that the office was considered so desirable in the 15th and 16th centuries. The reason may well have been the patronage which the chamberlain could exercise within Cheshire. Many of the

[42] N. Denholm-Young, 'Ric. de Bury', *Trans. R.H.S.* 4th ser. xx. 135–69.
[43] Foss, *Judges of Eng.* iii. 397–8.
[44] Chester 2/18 rot. 1; *36 D.K.R.* 67, 410, 538.
[45] *Cal. Fine R. 1391–9*, 115.
[46] *Cal. Pat. 1396–9*, 591. His com. included N. Wales.
[47] *36 D.K.R.* 104.
[48] *Cal. Pat. 1436–41*, 77.
[49] Ibid. 275; *37 D.K.R.* 136.
[50] *37 D.K.R.* 138.
[51] Ibid. He was brother of Thos., Lord Stanley, who shortly afterwards became justice.
[52] *26 D.K.R.* 27; *37 D.K.R.* 73, 144, 299.
[53] *21 D.K.R.* 30; *37 D.K.R.* 42, 48, 501, 816.
[54] *39 D.K.R.* 28, 55.

[55] *Letters and Accts. of Wm. Brereton of Malpas* (R.S.L.C. cxvi), 104. A list of his Ches. offices is printed in *L. & P. Hen. VIII*, x, pp. 365–6. For his career see E. W. Ives, 'Court and Co. Palatine in Reign of Hen. VIII: career of Wm. Brereton of Malpas', *T.H.S.L.C.* cxxiii. 1–38.
[56] *L. & P. Hen. VIII*, x, p. 217.
[57] Ibid. x, p. 527. On Maunsell's career see C. A. Maunsell and E. P. Statham, *Hist. Fam. of Maunsell*, i. 283–348.
[58] *L. & P. Hen. VIII*, xiv (2), pp. 114–15; cf. *Handbk. Brit. Chronology*, 157.
[59] *Ches. in Pipe R.* 207; *26 D.K.R.* 27; *Blk. Prince's Reg.* iii. 11.
[60] *Ches. Chamb. Accts.* 45–6.
[61] *Rot. Parl.* ii. 31.

lesser offices there seem to have been in the chamberlain's gift. William Brereton was said to have been able to appoint coroners.[62] His namesake as deputy chamberlain claimed the power to refuse to admit an under-sheriff in 1538, and a letter of Bishop Lee later the same year implies that both the office of sheriff and that of deputy chamberlain were in the chamberlain's gift.[63] The chamberlainship may also have acted as a magnet to attract other offices and sources of profit. Between 1417 and 1439 William Troutbeck received custody of William Beeston's lands during his minority, two annuities of £10, a joint appointment as steward of Hawarden and Moldsdale (Flints.), confirmation of a further annuity of £10, custody of Thomas Holes's lands during the minority of his heiress (who married William's son John), the park-keepership of Shotwick, and the sheriffdom of Cheshire for his son.[64] Sir Reynold Bray acquired a wardship and marriage soon after his appointment.[65] Sir Randal Brereton was able to procure advancement for his family during his tenure of the deputy chamberlainship and of the chamberlainship.[66]

In spite of assertions made in the late 16th century and later that the chamberlain of Chester had in early times exercised a jurisdiction akin to that of the English chancellor, evidence of his jurisdiction in equity does not survive before the 16th century. In 1310 the community of the county stated that an action of debt brought in the Chester Exchequer belonged properly to the county court or the eyre.[67] In 1351 the chamberlain was directed to hold at the Chester Exchequer all pleas belonging there, as far as possible according to the usages of the English Exchequer.[68]

Sessions of the Exchequer often, in the 15th century, coincided with those of the county court.[69] Just as individuals were put under mainprise at the county court to keep the peace, or to appear at a subsequent session, so at the Exchequer they might be bound by recognizances. Although the effect of the two forms was similar, the wording of county court mainprises and Exchequer recognizances differed widely. The mainprise carried a penalty for failure to carry out its terms. The recognizance acknowledged that the person bound by it owed a debt to the king or earl, but that the debt would be cancelled if the condition of the recognizance (to keep the peace, or to appear later) should be fulfilled. Both types of bond specified an appearance on the day of a future county court session, but while the mainprise provided for the delivery of the person bound by the justice at the county court, the recognizance provided for his delivery by the council of the earl or king. A recognizance could, though rarely, be converted on its expiry into a mainprise;[70] normally mainprises and recognizances were renewed in the form in which they had originally been made. Some of the renewals were repeated over a long period: thus William, son of Thomas Dod, first made a recognizance to keep the peace towards Hugh Dod of Harthill in January 1444, and the recognizance was renewed in April and July, in January and December 1445, in July and October 1446, and at intervals until July 1454.[71] Many of the county court mainprises were associated with civil or criminal actions which were pending in that court. The Exchequer recognizances, on the other hand, can rarely be related to such actions.

Recognizances to keep the peace occupy much space on the 15th-century enrolments of the Chester Exchequer. The class of records formerly known as 'recognizance rolls'

[62] *L. & P. Hen. VIII*, x, pp. 365–6.
[63] Ibid. xiii (1), pp. 6, 194.
[64] *37 D.K.R.* 717–18.
[65] Ibid. 73.
[66] *T.H.S.L.C.* cxxiii. 3–5.
[67] Booth, 'Financ. Admin.' 58.
[68] *Blk. Prince's Reg.* iii. 9.

[69] The following paragraph is based on info. supplied by Miss Clayton from analysis of recognizances on Chester 2/115–57.
[70] e.g. Chester 2/115 rot. 1, renewed on Chester 26/16 rot. 5d.
[71] *37 D.K.R.* 205–6.

but more correctly as 'enrolments' survives from 1307.[72] Their main purpose seems at first to have been to record recognizances of debt made before the chamberlain or the justice. The plea rolls of the county court were also sometimes used for that purpose.[73] From their beginning the Exchequer rolls were also regarded as an alternative to the so-called 'Domesday Roll' for the enrolment of charters and other evidences; the first example of the usage occurs at the head of the second membrane of the first surviving roll.[74] One of the early rolls is entirely taken up with evidences relating to the land transactions of a Chester merchant, William Doncaster.[75] The changes in the chamberlain's office later in the 14th century coincide with changes in the form of the rolls, which became the equivalent for the palatinate of the Chancery enrolments at national level.[76] The development is illustrated by a change in the headings of the rolls, from 'recognizances' in the early 14th century to 'recognizances . . . together with charters, pardons, and licences' by the middle of the century, and 'recognizances . . . together with enrolments of charters, writings, and other muniments' in the 15th.[77] By that time charters, letters patent, and writs, particularly those concerned with the administration of the escheator's office, accompanied the recognizances and enrolled deeds which formed the earlier contents of the rolls.[78]

The accounts of the chamberlains of Chester begin in the fiscal year 1300–1, and extend in an almost unbroken series from the mid 14th century to the end of the period. From the mid 14th century they are supported by the accounts of other ministers such as the escheator, the sheriff of the county, the sheriffs of the city of Chester, the foresters, and the bailiffs of demesne manors.[79] The accounts were regularly audited, usually at Chester.[80] Like the Exchequer enrolments they embodied details of Flintshire administration as well as that of Cheshire, since the chamberlain, like the justice of Chester, was responsible for both counties.[81]

The Cheshire lands held at one time or another in demesne included the city of Chester, Macclesfield, Middlewich, Northwich, Shotwick, Frodsham, and Drakelow. The city of Chester was held at farm by the citizens throughout the period. Other demesne lands were often leased to individuals or groups in return for a fixed annual farm. Thus at the beginning of the period the manors of Macclesfield and of Overton (Flints.) were leased for £220, Northwich for £76, and Middlewich for £92.[82] Since the leases were annual, it was possible for the farms to be increased: that of Macclesfield with Overton was raised to £232 in 1302–3 and £240 in 1303–4.[83] Conversely, it might prove impossible to find a lessee if the farm demanded was thought to be excessive. The farm of Middlewich declined from £90 in 1302–3 to £84 in 1320; by 1325–6 the chamberlain of Chester was complaining of the default of its farmer, and in 1327–8 both Middlewich and Northwich were 'in the king's hand for lack of farmers'.[84] On occasions the demesne lands were the subject of outright grants, free of account. After Edward I's death Macclesfield passed to Queen Isabel.[85] In 1386

[72] Chester 2, listed in *P.R.O. Lists & Indexes No. XL,* 1–3. The contents of the rs. are listed alphabetically in apps. to *36, 37,* and *39 D.K.R.*; the lists are misleadingly entitled a 'calendar' but omit headings, marginal notes, cancellations of recognizances, and *posteas.* See B. E. Harris, 'The Chest. Recognizance Rolls', *Medieval Ches. Seminar Papers,* Liverpool University, 1974–5, pp. 1–5.

[73] e.g. Chester 29/37 rot. 1d.

[74] *36 D.K.R.* 35.

[75] Chester 2/8.

[76] Sharp, 'Contributions', i. 109.

[77] e.g. Chester 2/1 rot. 1; Chester 2/35 rot. 1; Chester 2/118 rot. 1.

[78] Miss Clayton has reconstructed the rs. for the period 1441–2 to 1484–5 from *37 D.K.R.* and has checked the results against the original rolls (Chester 2/115–57).

[79] The accts. have been taken out of the Chester group and placed in Special Collections: Ministers' and Receivers' Accts. (S.C. 6); they are listed in *P.R.O. Lists & Indexes Nos. V* and *XXXIV.* Selective translations of those from 1301 to 1360 are in *Ches. Chamb. Accts.,* where some of the dates given are inaccurate. The chamberlain's acct. for 1300–1 is printed in *Ches. in Pipe R.* 193 sqq.

[80] Booth, 'Financ. Admin.', *passim.*

[81] Flints. info. is disregarded here.

[82] *Ches. Chamb. Accts.* 2.

[83] Ibid. 16, 38.

[84] Ibid. 38, 90, 95, 104.

[85] *Cal. Chart. R.* 1301–26, 202.

Frodsham was granted to Radegund Becket free of all charge.[86] If the demesne was retained in the hand of the king or earl, it could be placed under the supervision of a bailiff who would account for all rents and other issues arising from it. The bailiffs of Frodsham and Shotwick accounted for 'rents and other issues' in 1315–16.[87] Alternatively, the bailiff could be made responsible for the actual cultivation of the land. Under the Black Prince's council experiments in demesne cultivation were carried out. In 1355 the demesnes of Frodsham were to be cultivated by the bailiff, while those of Drakelow were to be leased out to tenants.[88] At the same time a cattle herd and stud were built up at Macclesfield which by 1376 are calculated to have yielded over £800.[89] The manor of Drakelow was a new creation of the mid 14th century, resulting from a systematic survey of lands in Rudheath and Overmarsh in 1346–7.[90] Experiments in direct farming of Drakelow and of the other available demesne lands were, however, soon abandoned in favour of leases, either because the latter were found to yield greater or more certain sums, or because of the administrative convenience of leasing. In the 15th century such leases were very common. For example, between August and October 1474 ten-year leases were granted of the demesnes in Drakelow and Rudheath, various customs in Middlewich, the pasture and moor of Overmarsh, and the manor and lordship of Frodsham.[91]

It is difficult to estimate the value of the Cheshire lands to the king or earl.[92] Records of liveries of money give some idea of the resources available from the county. In 1302 the chamberlain sent £1,000 to London; in 1325–6 liveries totalled £1,470, and in 1359–60, £2,600.[93] Those sums included income from Flintshire. They also included income from proffers and amercements, from fees of the seal, from forest administration, and the like.

The annual income was supplemented by a succession of taxes granted by the county community. As a county palatine Cheshire claimed immunity from national taxation, since it was not represented in Parliament. The claim was accepted in 1380, 1441, and 1450.[94] The first recorded exaction of a subsidy from Cheshire was in 1346, when the community of the county granted the Black Prince £1,000. Nothing had been paid towards this by April 1347, but in the following fiscal year money began to flow in.[95] A document of 26 Edward III (1352–3) seems to indicate that the sums demanded from each hundred in the county had by that time become fixed by tradition: it was said that at each mize of £100 Bucklow hundred should pay £14 and Northwich £13.[96] The mize was the name traditionally given to the later Cheshire taxes. In 1353 a grant of 5,000 marks was made in return for the abandonment of a projected general eyre in Cheshire. The assessment of individual burdens was left to the justice or his lieutenant and the chamberlain. Men were to be charged in proportion to their wealth, and no one with less than 20s. in land, rent, or chattels was to contribute. The duke of Lancaster was pardoned his contribution. Complaints of unjust assessment soon began to be made. The tax was described variously as a 'common fine', a 'composition', and a 'mize'.[97] A further large communal fine was imposed later in the 1350s on the forest communities of Wirral and Mere and Mondrem.[98] Taxes of 2,500 marks and 3,000 marks were granted to the Black Prince in 1368 and 1373.[99] In 1398 a grant of 3,000 marks was made to Richard II, apparently in return for his confirmation of the

---

[86] *36 D.K.R.* 192.
[87] *Ches. Chamb. Accts.* 83.
[88] *Blk. Prince's Reg.* iii. 210.
[89] Booth, 'Financ. Admin.', 107–13.
[90] *Blk. Prince's Reg.* i. 37; cf. *Ches. Chamb. Accts.* 193–9.
[91] *37 D.K.R.* 106, 173, 176, 298.
[92] Cf. *Ches. Chamb. Accts.* pp. xiv–xvii.
[93] Ibid. 12, 97–9, 274.

[94] *Cal. Close, 1377–81*, 472; *Sel. Cases in Exchequer Chamber* (Selden Soc. li), p. 83; Ormerod, *Hist. Ches.* i. 126–7.
[95] *Blk. Prince's Reg.* i. 67; *Ches. Chamb. Accts.* 122.
[96] *28 D.K.R.* 54.
[97] *Blk. Prince's Reg.* iii. 115, 146, 153, 165, 172.
[98] *Ches. Chamb. Accts.* 247.
[99] Booth, 'Financ. Admin.', 184.

county's charters of liberties.[1] Another was made to the prince of Wales in 1403 in return for pardons to those of the county who took part in Henry Percy's rebellion.[2] Yet another was made to Henry V in 1416.[3] Henry VI's imminent departure for France in 1430 produced a grant of 1,000 marks.[4] In 1436 inquisitions as to freeholders, set on foot in connexion with the subsidy granted by Parliament in 1435, were authorized for the counties palatine of Chester, Lancaster, and Durham as well as for the remainder of England;[5] although the parliamentary subsidy did not extend to Cheshire, the county community granted 1,000 marks to the king.[6] A further confirmation of charters and grant of pardons was made in return for a grant of 3,000 marks in 1441.[7] In 1463 the justice and chamberlain were ordered to consult with the county 'touching the subsidy customarily granted to the king on his coming into his inheritance': the result was a grant of 3,000 marks, and a confirmation of charters soon followed.[8] The next such grant was made in 1474.[9] The accession of Henry VII was followed by a grant in 1486, but the community of the county sought that, since it was rumoured that the queen was pregnant, this mize should stand instead of that which would otherwise be granted should the child prove to be male.[10] A commission for the levy of an aid was issued in 1491, but does not seem to have resulted in a grant.[11] Its purpose was a proposed expedition to France. War against Scotland produced a grant of 1,000 marks in 1497.[12] Three years later it was belatedly realized that no mize had been granted to Arthur, prince of Wales, on his creation.[13] A mize was then granted, and another followed in 1517.[14]

Payment of the mize was made in fixed half-yearly instalments from the seven hundreds of Cheshire. A mize of 3,000 marks was normally payable in six instalments, and collectors for each hundred were appointed annually.[15] Within the hundreds the assessment of each township had become fixed by 1406, the date of the first surviving 'mize book' or list of assessments.[16] In the mize book and its successors the hundreds appear in a regular order, which is also preserved in the enrolments of the collectors' appointments.[17] Within each hundred the townships also appear in a fixed order: the order in Eddisbury hundred is not arbitrary but seems to follow a number of routes around the hundred, perhaps reflecting the routes taken by the original assessors of the first mize.[18] Each township is given an assessment, and a note is made of the proportion payable by the lord, thus: *de Tervyn* (Tarvin) *dominus pro dimidia . . . xxvj s. viij d.* In the mize book of 1406 the collectors' names or initials are written against the townships for which they were responsible, in some of the hundreds.[19] The sums mentioned in 1352–3 as payable by Bucklow and Northwich hundreds are proportionately exactly the same as those which appear in the later mize books. That fact implies that the assessments were fixed by the mid 14th century. It is not known, however, how individual burdens were assessed in each township.

---

[1] *Cal. Chart. R.* 1341–1417, 313–15; *36 D.K.R.* 95–6.
[2] *36 D.K.R.* 43, 103, 411–12.
[3] *37 D.K.R.* 75.
[4] Ibid. 670.
[5] *Cal. Fine R.* 1430–7, 262.
[6] *37 D.K.R.* 671.
[7] *Cal. Pat.* 1436–41, 560–1; 1441–6, 32, 50.
[8] *37 D.K.R.* 95, 140, 693; *Cal. Chart. R.* 1427–1516, 202.
[9] *37 D.K.R.* 141, 694.
[10] Ibid. 201.
[11] *26 D.K.R.* 21.
[12] *37 D.K.R.* 694.
[13] *26 D.K.R.* 25.
[14] *39 D.K.R.* 55.
[15] For 15th-cent. examples see *37 D.K.R.* s.v. Broxton,

Bucklow, Eddisbury, Macclesfield, Northwich, Wich-Malbank, and Wirral.
[16] John Rylands Libr. Tatton MSS. 345: reference supplied by Mr. P. H. W. Booth. A so-called 'assessment of Broxton temp. Edw. III' (Chester 38/25/2) is a mize book of 1444.
[17] Eddisbury, Broxton, Wirral, Northwich, Bucklow, Nantwich, Macclesfield.
[18] e.g. Tarvin, Little Barrow, Great Barrow, Bridge Trafford, Thornton, Ince, Elton, Hapsford, Dunham, Helsby, Alvanley, Manley, Mouldsworth, Ashton, Horton and Little Mouldsworth, Kelsall: John Rylands Libr. Tatton MSS. 345. The order is lost in the alphabetical rearrangement of the 1442 mize book in Ormerod, *Hist. Ches.* i. 398; ii. 895–7; iii. 883–4.
[19] John Rylands Libr. Tatton MSS. 345.

As has been shown above, the consent of the county community was held to be essential before a mize could be exacted. The process of summoning a meeting of the community and the negotiations which followed are described in detail in a document of 1436.[20] The community was described in 1474 as 'all the lords, abbots, priors, knights, esquires, freeholders, and commons having livelihood or dwelling within the said shire'.[21] The occasion of its meeting then (2 August 1474) was also a county court session day.[22] There can be little doubt that such assemblies were the reality behind the later tradition of a 'Cheshire Parliament'.[23] By the mid 15th century the grant of the normal mize of 3,000 marks was associated with the first entry of a king or earl into his inheritance. [24]

The Escheators

At the beginning of the period the escheator appears as an official accounting for lands temporarily in the king's or earls custody.[25] His fee in 1312–13 was 6d. a day, although by 1328 it was only 2d.[26] The escheators of that time were clerks, whose accounts were rendered separately from those of the chamberlains.[27] In the early 1350s the Black Prince's council reorganized the office. From Michaelmas 1350 the daily fee was increased by 10 marks yearly, as a special favour to Hugh Hopwas.[28] Hugh's successor in 1352 was given the additional duty of holding courts and views of frankpledge at the demesne manors, for which he was allowed 40s. a year above his daily fee. He was to answer for the issues of his office at the Chester Exchequer rather than at the prince's Exchequer at Westminster.[29] In 1353 his duties were extended to include Flintshire.[30] Two years later he was empowered, on the advice of the justice and chamberlain, to sell all wardships and marriages within his bailiwick which were worth 10 marks a year or less, without the need to consult the prince's council. By 1359 the three officers were authorized to sell all wardships and marriages by mutual agreement, and to arrange profitable leases of escheated lands.[31] Meanwhile the escheator's fee was increased to 10 marks a year and, from Michaelmas 1356, to £10, because of his increased expenses. In spite of the fact that a separate escheator for Flintshire was appointed from 1357, the fee of the Cheshire escheator remained £10 a year until the end of the period.[32] The office was often combined with others. From October 1359 until December 1361 Thomas Young was both escheator and sheriff of Cheshire.[33] John Scolehall was appointed escheator, steward of foreign courts, and attorney of the Black Prince in Cheshire in 1365; in 1367 he became sheriff, and he held both offices until 1370.[34] William Brereton, who became chamberlain c. 1530, had been escheator since April 1527.[35] The escheatorship was also often combined with the office of attorney-general in Cheshire, but there were exceptions. Matthew del Mere was appointed attorney-general in 1399 when Richard Manley was made escheator, but himself became escheator in 1403.[36] John Bruen of Tarvin, who became escheator at the end of 1428,

[20] Chester 2/107 rot. 6, inadequately calendared in *37 D.K.R.* 671. For commentary see 5 *Sheaf*, no. 1.
[21] Chester 2/146 rot. 1.
[22] Chester 29/178 rot. 16.
[23] Cf. G. T. Lapsley, *Co. Palat. of Durham*, 116–30.
[24] *Ad primum adventum sive introitum suum in hereditatem suam* (1463); the same with *comitatus* [*sic*] *Cestr' et Flynt* added (1474): Chester 2/135 rot. 2d; Chester 2/146 rot. 1.
[25] e.g. *Ches. Chamb. Accts.* 3.
[26] Ibid. 79; 3 *Sheaf*, xxiv, p. 66.
[27] *Cal. Fine R. 1307–19*, 8; *Ches. Chamb. Accts.* 122; *Blk. Prince's Reg.* i. 6; 3 *Sheaf*, xxiv, pp. 58–69.
[28] *Blk. Prince's Reg.* iii. 44.
[29] Ibid. 78.

[30] Ibid. 136.
[31] Ibid. 193, 368.
[32] Ibid. 268, 288; *36 D.K.R.* 93; *L. & P. Hen. VIII*, x, pp. 365–6.
[33] *Blk. Prince's Reg.* iii. 369, 428.
[34] Ibid. 476; *36 D.K.R.* 423. Scolehall seems to have remained escheator until 1385 (ibid. 94), since appointment of John Helegh (ibid. 228) recorded in 1379 does not appear to have taken effect (Ches. R.O., DCH/B/664). Lawr. Dutton appears as sheriff from Oct. 1370 (ibid., DCH/C/25; *21 D.K.R.* 34).
[35] *39 D.K.R.* 56.
[36] *36 D.K.R.* 100, 102, 340.

had been attorney-general for more than seven years.[37] Thomas Wolton, who held the two offices for nearly 38 years from August 1467, was in 1495 replaced by Roger Mainwaring as escheator and by Edmund Bulkeley as attorney-general.[38]

During Richard II's reign appointments to the escheatorship show a curious vacillation. Adam Kingsley had served in the post from 1361 to 1365.[39] On John Scolehall's death in 1385 he was appointed again.[40] In March 1387 he was replaced by John Ewloe, only to be reappointed in the following July. He then kept the office for nearly three years until his replacement by John Leche of Chester in June 1390; Leche's appointment, and those of Thomas Masterson of Nantwich in February 1391 and of Kingsley once more in the following August, were among many new appointments of escheators and sheriffs in England. After only three months, however, Masterson replaced Kingsley, only to be displaced in his turn by Kingsley in February 1392. On that occasion Kingsley's appointment was annulled within about six weeks, and Masterson regained the office. He remained escheator until November 1395 when, again as one of many appointments to escheatorships in England, Kingsley was reappointed. In October 1397 Kingsley was replaced by Hugh Leigh, but the latter's appointment lasted only a little over a month. In December Kingsley was appointed yet again, and he held the office until November 1399.

In the 15th century, like other major offices in Cheshire, the escheatorship became hereditary. John Leigh of Ridge, who had been appointed during pleasure in 1434, was reappointed for life in 1439, and less than three years later he and his son Ralph were granted the office in survivorship.[41] Another grant of the office in survivorship was made in 1509.[42] Deputy escheators are recorded in 1460 and 1529.[43]

In 1389 the county community stated that livery of the inheritance of the heirs of tenants holding in chief in Cheshire ought to be sued out only at the Exchequer of Chester.[44] Writs involving the escheator, such as *diem clausit extremum*, were issued from the Chester Exchequer and returned there.[45] Occasionally commissions to others than the escheator to take such inquisitions have survived.[46] The processes following the death of a tenant in chief were apparently conducted with reasonable speed and efficiency. Thomas Beeston died on 20 October 1476; his heir was granted livery on 10 November following, two days after the inquisition post mortem had been held.[47] Sir William Booth died on 6 April 1477. A writ of *diem clausit extremum* was issued on 17 April, the inquisition was taken on the 26th, and livery followed on the 29th.[48] Receipts from the escheator's office were small. In 1334–5 the escheator's wages were said to exceed the receipts.[49] The accounts of 1349–50 and 1350–1 show gross receipts respectively of £54 and of less than £21.[50]

The Sheriffs

It has been shown above that the status of the sheriff of Cheshire before 1301 was markedly inferior to that of his counterparts elsewhere in England. Until 1349 it is impossible to establish the succession of sheriffs beyond doubt; some appointments have survived, but several sheriffs can only be traced through their appearance as

[37] *37 D.K.R.* 97, 98.
[38] Ibid. 140, 143.
[39] *Blk. Prince's Reg.* iii. 428, 476.
[40] For what follows see *Cal. Fine R.* 1383–91, 176, 306, 342; 1391–9, 8, 18, 168; *36 D.K.R.* 94, 96, 98, 100, 272.
[41] *37 D.K.R.* 135, 136, 451.
[42] *39 D.K.R.* 54.
[43] *37 D.K.R.* 292; *L. & P. Hen. VIII*, iv, p. 3179.

[44] *36 D.K.R.* 187.
[45] Ex inf. Miss Clayton, based on analysis of Chester 3/41–50 and Chester 2/115–57.
[46] e.g. *L. & P. Hen. VIII*, iii (2), p. 593.
[47] *37 D.K.R.* 38; Chester 3/48/16 Edw. IV, no. 1.
[48] *37 D.K.R.* 59–60; Chester 3/49/17 Edw. IV, no. 1.
[49] *Ches. Chamb. Accts.* 112.
[50] Ibid. 156, 205.

witnesses to private deeds.[51] Nevertheless it is clear that most sheriffs appointed before 1349 farmed the office, rendering amounts varying from 200 marks in 1301 to more than £240 in 1327.[52] From September 1347 to June 1348 the office was temporarily in the hands of an 'approver' who had to answer for all its issues. That arrangement became permanent from 1349–50, and the sheriff received an annual fee 'by agreement made by the justice and chamberlain'. The fee was the same as the chamberlain's. Net receipts for that year amounted to nearly £248, and by 1359–60 to more than £335.[53]

In the 15th century the office of sheriff followed the same course as the justiceship and the chamberlainship. Sir Robert Booth, who was appointed in 1439 during good behaviour, received a life appointment in 1441, altered in 1443 to a joint appointment with his son in survivorship.[54] Sir William Stanley, appointed in 1465,[55] resigned the office in favour of his son William in 1488.[56] From 1495 to 1524 John Warburton was sheriff, and on his death the office passed to Thomas, his son.[57] The more frequent occurrence of deputy sheriffs in the records while the Stanleys and Warburtons were sheriffs, implies that the office was being exercised by deputy at the end of the 15th century and early in the sixteenth.[58]

After only five months in office Thomas Warburton was replaced by George Holford.[59] The appointment of sheriffs subsequently became, with occasional exceptions, annual, with Cheshire participating in the system in operation for the rest of the country. A 'sheriff roll' was presented to the king, with the names of three candidates for the sheriffdom of each county, one of whom was 'pricked' by the king. The Cheshire entries on the rolls of 1525 and 1526 are illegible, but the names of those chosen then and in years for which no sheriff rolls survive can be discovered from the Chester enrolments.[60] The appointment of sheriffs remained, as before, by letters patent of the Chester Exchequer issued on receipt of a royal warrant.[61]

The only name which deserves special mention among those chosen between 1524 and 1547 is that of Sir Peter Dutton, who was first made sheriff in 1534.[62] In the following year his name was inserted by the king in preference to those submitted to him. He was reappointed in 1536 and 1542.[63] His first period of office was marked by a succession of events which throw some light on the sheriff's powers. While both sheriff and under-sheriff were in London the under-sheriff's clerk fraudulently levied fines from people in the county.[64] In 1536 Dutton arrested the abbot of Norton and three canons, and was said to wish to execute them without trial.[65] He and the deputy chamberlain, William Brereton, soon became involved in disputes about the abbot and canons, about another prisoner, and about the stewardship of Halton.[66] Although Dutton was replaced by Sir Henry Delves in 1537, he remained influential and tried to impose his own nominee on Delves as under-sheriff.[67] Bishop Lee believed that the quarrel between Dutton and Brereton was undermining order within the county.[68]

[51] *P.R.O. Lists & Indexes No. IX*, 17a, is based mainly on recorded appointments of the early 14th cent. and on the few surviving chamberlains' accts. of the period.
[52] *Ches. in Pipe R.* 195; *Ches. Chamb. Accts.* 90; *Cal. Fine R.* 1327–37, 88.
[53] *Ches. Chamb. Accts.* 119–20, 132–8, 264.
[54] *37 D.K.R.* 58; the calendar entry of the appt. of Rob. and his son in survivorship, ibid. 59, is inaccurate: Chester 2/116 rot. 1d.
[55] *37 D.K.R.* 680.
[56] Ibid. 143; *21 D.K.R.* 37.
[57] *37 D.K.R.* 143; *39 D.K.R.* 55.
[58] e.g. *37 D.K.R.* 48, 587, 645, 748.
[59] *39 D.K.R.* 55.

[60] *L. & P. Hen. VIII*, iv, pp. 798, 1182.
[61] For an example of such a warrant see *Ches. Quart. Sess. Recs.* (R.S.L.C. xciv), 35, interpreted as unusual by Joan Beck, *Tudor Ches.* 5.
[62] *L. & P. Hen. VIII*, vii, p. 558.
[63] Ibid. ix, p. 309; xi, p. 491; xvii, p. 640.
[64] Ibid. ix, p. 380; x, pp. 95–6.
[65] Ibid. xi, p. 413.
[66] Ibid. xi, p. 487; xii (1), pp. 61, 585; xii (2), pp. 19–21, 221–2, 428–9.
[67] Ibid. xii (2), pp. 393, 406; xiii (1), p. 6. Brereton was no happier about Delves's own choice of deputy.
[68] Ibid. xiii (1), p. 194.

Thomas Cromwell eventually intervened to bring 'a loving end' between the ex-sheriff and the deputy chamberlain, but the latter was still afraid in 1539 that Dutton, given the opportunity, would use his influence to obtain a sheriff 'to his mind', and asked Cromwell to try to see that 'an indifferent sheriff' was chosen for the ensuing year.[69]

The duties of the sheriff enabled him to exercise much local influence. By 1350 he was acting as an intermediary for the payment of some of the lesser rents and farms which at the beginning of the 14th century had been rendered direct to the chamberlain. Thus in 1349–50 the sheriff accounted for the rent of the fee of the serjeanty of the countess of Warwick, the chamber rent, the farm of the avowries, and the farm of the passage of Lawton. He collected the fines and amercements arising from sessions of the county court and the justice's eyre. Together with the chamberlain he leased the beadleries of the hundreds. He collected as much of the income from the hundred courts as had not been granted to the beadles, and the fines of suitors and doomsmen for avoiding their obligation to attend county and hundred courts. Those who were liable to be put on assizes and juries could avoid the duty by paying the sheriff a sum known as freemen's silver. When money was adjudged to a party to an action in the county court, the sheriff's aid could be purchased in its collection. He claimed a fee of oxen for his aid in recovering tenements.[70] During his tourn he carried out inquiries into blocked roads.[71] Certain townships in all the hundreds except Nantwich and Macclesfield were liable to the annual shrieval impost called 'sheriff's tooth'.[72] The sheriff was evidently much in demand as a witness to transactions in land. As in other counties he was responsible for the execution of original and judicial writs in connexion with the business of the county court, and for co-operating with the escheator in impanelling juries for inquisitions post mortem.

Further duties resembling those of sheriffs elsewhere in England were occasionally given to the sheriff of Cheshire. In 1368 he was ordered to inquire into infringements of the statutes of labourers,[73] and in 1394, 1395, and 1423 commissioned to arrest disturbers of the peace.[74] He was ordered to make proclamations.[75] In 1436 he was ordered to keep the peace at the impending visitation of Vale Royal abbey.[76] In 1450 he was charged with carrying into effect the first Act of Resumption.[77] In 1481 he was ordered to arrest all ships which might attempt to discharge their cargoes elsewhere than at the port of Chester.[78] Seven years later his duty of supervising the election of a hundred coroner is mentioned.[79]

Complaints about sheriffs are sometimes recorded. In 1332 the 'charterers' of Cheshire gained release from the payment of various burdensome customs to the sheriff.[80] Twenty years later a complaint was made that the sheriff was levying a fee of oxen when he was not entitled to do so, since such a fee could be exacted only from a disseisor after an action of novel disseisin.[81] In 1353 complaint was made that the sheriff was refusing to help in recovering sums adjudged, until granted 2d. in the shilling. The Black Prince's council ruled that payments for his aid must be voluntary, but a similar complaint to that of 1353 was made two years later.[82] In view of the marriage bonds uniting leading members of the gentry, it is not surprising that jury panels had to be quashed because the sheriff was a kinsman of one of the parties in

[69] L. & P. Hen. VIII, xiv (2), pp. 114–15.
[70] The foregoing description is based on Ches. Chamb. Accts. 133–7, 173, 174.
[71] e.g. Ches. R.O., DCH/A/131, DCH/C/334.
[72] Ches. Chamb. Accts. 133, 171; for liability of individual townships see Chester R.O., CR63/2/26, pp. 1–5.
[73] 36 D.K.R. 423.
[74] Ibid. 97–8; 37 D.K.R. 227.
[75] 36 D.K.R. 98.

[76] 37 D.K.R. 735.
[77] Ibid. 137.
[78] Ibid. 222.
[79] Ibid. 254.
[80] Cal. Close, 1330–3, 509–10.
[81] Blk. Prince's Reg. iii. 63.
[82] Ibid. 101, 198: both complaints were made against Thos. Danyers, first of the regular succession of approver-sheriffs.

an action, or likely to be partial. In 1459 a jury panel summoned in an action of debt between the prince of Wales and five leading Cheshire gentlemen was quashed because of the sheriff's affinity to one of the defendants; a new writ of summons was sent to the coroner of Northwich hundred, but the panel which he returned was also quashed because of his partiality towards the defendants, and the coroner of Nantwich hundred was ordered to impanel yet another.[83]

Other County and Hundred Officers

Throughout the period the collection of avowry rents[84] was leased. In the 14th century the leases varied between one and three years, and the farms between 26s. 8d. and £48 a year.[85] On two occasions the leases were for life.[86] By the early 1540s the avowries had become no more than a form of debt evasion, and they were abolished in 1543.[87]

Vendors of the goods and chattels of felons, fugitives, and intestates occur between 1344 and 1498, with annual fees of 60s. or 40s.[88] The appointment of a bailiff-errant to levy amercements was first made as an experiment after the Chester trailbaston session of 1353.[89] There was a suggestion that such an officer ought to be appointed generally 'to levy the prince's money in default of the other ministers' in 1355, but no appointment seems to have been made until 1362.[90] The office was granted for life, to be exercised in person or by deputy, in 1437, and in survivorship in 1444.[91] It was still in existence in 1540 when the holder was censured by the mayor of Chester for allegedly infringing the city's liberties.[92]

The serjeants of the peace in Cheshire continue to be mentioned at the beginning of the period.[93] In 1301–2, for example, Sir Richard Sutton and his wife, hereditary serjeants of the peace for the county, claimed 2s. for the heads of two robbers beheaded by their deputies.[94] In 1327 it was said that the serjeants had leased their offices to others, and that their efficiency had declined in consequence.[95] In 1357 and 1363 serjeants were appointed for Bucklow hundred but their office, with its wages of 2d. a day, was abolished in 1365.[96] The relationship between the serjeants and the hundred officials who emerge during the 14th century is obscure. The hundred courts are said to have met fortnightly, under the hundred bailiffs.[97] The offices of bailiff and beadle of the hundreds may have originated separately, but during the period they coalesced.[98] In 1349–50 the beadleries of the six Cheshire hundreds outside Macclesfield were leased out by the chamberlain and sheriff on a yearly basis at sums varying between 73s. 4d. (for Eddisbury) and £7 19s. 2d. (for Broxton). In return the beadles took puture, or a composition for it, from those lands which bore the obligation to provide it, fines from the 'charterers' whose lands were worth less than 40s. yearly, in order to avoid the obligation to make summonses, one-third of the goods of felons, a fine for respiting attachments, and half the perquisites and amercements of the hundred

---

[83] Chester 24/43, sess. Tues. after Conception of B.V.M., Tues. before St. Matthias, 38 Hen. VI.

[84] For a description of avowries see p. 4.

[85] *Ches. Chamb. Accts.* 2, 112, 120, 171, 208; *36 D.K.R.* 52, 64, 114, 187, 196, 243, 280, 285, 327, 460; *37 D.K.R.* 4, 48, 141.

[86] *Cal. Pat.* 1381–5, 362; 1385–9, 370.

[87] See p. 35.

[88] *36 D.K.R.* 105, 108, 522; *37 D.K.R.* 92; *Ches. Chamb. Accts.* 235.

[89] *Blk. Prince's Reg.* iii. 123.

[90] Ibid. 210; *36 D.K.R.* 380.

[91] *Cal. Pat.* 1436–41, 127; *37 D.K.R.* 697.

[92] *L. & P. Hen. VIII*, xvi, p. 15.

[93] Most of the evidence quoted by Stewart-Brown, *Serjeants of Peace*, 3–10, is early.

[94] *Ches. Chamb. Accts.* 6.

[95] *Cal. Close*, 1327–30, 226.

[96] *Blk. Prince's Reg.* iii. 253, 483.

[97] Sharp, 'Contributions', i. 194.

[98] Stewart-Brown, *Serjeants of Peace*, 15–19.

courts.[99] In 1331 the beadles were accused of extortion.[1] Nevertheless they sometimes found difficulty in enforcing their claims to puture and in collecting debts due to them.[2] No consistency of policy has been found with regard to the leasing of the hundreds during the period. The length of such leases varied widely, and appointments to the beadleries were made for one or more lives, during good behaviour, and during pleasure.[3]

Coroners, either one or two, were appointed for each hundred. In 1427 there were two each in Nantwich and Northwich hundreds, probably two in Broxton, and one in each of the other four hundreds.[4] In the 14th and 15th centuries, like their counter-

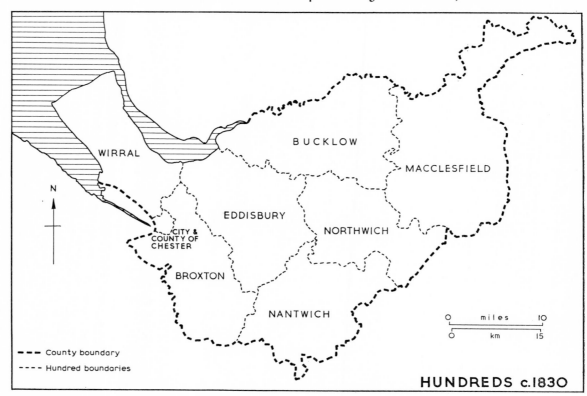

parts in the rest of England, they carried out inquests into sudden deaths, and the inquests were presented at the county court.[5] As elsewhere in England a man who wished to turn approver when charged with felony could ask for a coroner, before whom he would make his allegations.[6] If a jury impanelled by the sheriff was said to favour a party to an action, a new *venire facias* was issued to the coroner of the hundred where the cause of the action arose, and if his panel in turn was said to be partial, to the coroner of the next hundred, and so on.

Franchises

Franchises in the county were twice investigated, first under the Black Prince in the 1340s and again by Prince Arthur's council in the eyre of 1499.[7] Most of the

[99] *Ches. Chamb. Accts.* 136.
[1] Stewart-Brown, *Serjeants of Peace*, 9; *Sel. Cases in Ct. of King's Bench under Edw. II* (Selden Soc. lxxvi), pp. 66–9.
[2] *Blk. Prince's Reg.* iii. 80, 86, 118; *37 D.K.R.* 135, 194, 252, 379, 518.
[3] *36 D.K.R.* 2, 3, 200; *37 D.K.R.* 95, 97, 245, 254, 291, 573; *39 D.K.R.* 108, 301.
[4] *37 D.K.R.* 153.

[5] Some examples are given in 3 *Sheaf*, xviii, pp. 45–6, 58, 84, 102–3; xx, pp. 33, 43.
[6] e.g. Chester 24/44, sess. Tues after St. Bartholomew, 1 Edw. IV.
[7] On what follows see *E.H.R.* xlix. 676–84, and 3 *Sheaf*, xxx–xxxi, where the claims made in 1499 are listed. The topographical hist. of the franchises is reserved for treatment elsewhere.

liberties claimed were of types common throughout England, including view of frank-pledge, infangthief, freedom from suit of shire or hundred court, and the right to markets, fairs, tolls, and fisheries and boats on the Dee. Some were of more distinctive origin, such as the claims to jurisdiction over minstrels and harlots, to the master serjeanty of Macclesfield hundred, and to the privileges of the Cheshire 'baronies', though the latter had by the end of the 15th century become little more than ordinary judicial and economic immunities under a grandiose name.[8] The city of Chester attained considerable independence from the county. In 1300 it gained jurisdiction over pleas of the Crown within its limits, and the right to elect its own coroners. In 1354 the mayor became *ex officio* escheator, and was granted admiralty powers over the Dee. In 1506 the city was granted the status of a county.[9] Stockport, Macclesfield, and Congleton had by the end of the 15th century obtained mayors and borough courts, and North-wich, Middlewich, Nantwich, and Frodsham enjoyed some of the characteristics of borough status.[10]

Macclesfield hundred enjoyed some judicial immunity. It was excluded from the jurisdiction of the county court, but instead was visited annually by the justice or by *pro hac vice* commissioners, who held sessions known as 'the three hundreds of the eyre of Macclesfield'.[11] In 1444 and 1447 Macclesfield gaol was delivered by the justice of Chester; normally indictments from Macclesfield were sent to the county court, and the accused dealt with in Chester gaol delivery sessions.[12] The doomsmen of the Macclesfield hundred court were liable to amercement for false judgement, like those of the county court.[13] The *poker* of Macclesfield claimed return of writs and in 1347 the sheriff of Cheshire claimed that he could not enter the liberty without the *posse comitatus* for fear of his life.[14] In the same year the Black Prince gained control of Macclesfield hundred by exchange with Queen Isabel, but although an inquiry was set on foot in 1353 to determine its status, the hundred was not fully integrated with the county for judicial purposes, although it was included in commissions of array, arrest, and tax collection in the 15th century.[15] Other hundreds are occasionally mentioned. The 'hundred of Halton' included the Cheshire lands of the constable of Chester, which early in the 14th century came into the possession of Thomas of Lancaster as part of the Lacy inheritance, and descended to the dukes of Lancaster and thus, from 1399, to the Crown.[16] Its court, like the county court, was attended by suitors and doomsmen.[17] A 'hundred of Malpas' occurs in 1354, but probably repre-sented no more than a vestigial title of the court of the 'baron' there.[18] Similarly, the 'hundred of Caldy' entitled its holder to no more than minor jurisdiction over a small group of manors in Wirral, appurtenant to the manor of Gayton.[19]

The Distinctiveness of Cheshire and its Assimilation to England

During the period Cheshire was characterized by its reputation for disorder, and by its use as a recruiting area. Adam of Usk likened the county to a 'nest of wicked-ness'.[20] In 1318 there occur references to acts of terrorism on the part of men of the

[8] Ormerod, *Hist. Ches.* i. 36, 526, 703-5; ii. 601; iii. 189, 426; J. P. Earwaker, *East. Ches.* i. 345; ii. 3-4; Stewart-Brown, *Serjeants of Peace*, 10-11; T. P. Highet, *Early Hist. of Davenports of Davenport* (Chetham Soc. 3rd. ser. ix), *passim*.
[9] Morris, *Chest.* 490-1, 496, 524 sqq.
[10] For a summary of hist. of Ches. boros., see J. T. Driver, *Ches. in Later Middle Ages*, cap. ii.
[11] For lists of 15th-cent. commissioners see *37 D.K.R.* 482-5.

[12] Chester 17/8 rott. 22, 26.
[13] *Blk. Prince's Reg.* iii. 64.
[14] Sharp, 'Contributions', i. 199, 344.
[15] *Blk. Prince's Reg.* i. 147; iii. 92.
[16] Ormerod, *Hist. Ches.* i. 699-705.
[17] Ches. R.O., DCH/E/93.
[18] *Blk. Prince's Reg.* iii. 149.
[19] 36 *D.K.R.* 342; 3 *Sheaf*, ii, p. 95; xviii, p. 105.
[20] *Chron. Ade de Usk*, ed. E. M. Thompson, 175-6.

county against those of the city of Chester.[21] Wounding, beating, and ill-treatment were said to be rife in the county even after the Black Prince's visit in 1353. His proclamation against riding armed had to be repeated in 1362.[22] From the mid 14th century to its end there were complaints of incursions by men from Cheshire into neighbouring counties, whence, having performed various criminal acts, they retired immune from prosecution into Cheshire.[23] It is difficult to gauge the effectiveness of the various attempts made to punish disorder in the county, or to compare violence there with that which prevailed elsewhere in England.[24] Commissions to arrest malefactors, disturbers of the peace, and those who spread false rumours occur in Cheshire from the late 14th century.[25] In 1400 the new prince of Wales appointed keepers of the peace in each hundred, chosen from among the leading Cheshire families, but the experiment does not appear to have been successful, and Cheshire remained without justices of the peace for more than a century.[26]

Complaints of disorder continued until the end of the period. In 1534 and 1536 Cheshire was rumoured to be on the verge of rebellion.[27] In 1538 Bishop Lee alleged that 'more murders and manslaughters are done this year in Cheshire than in all Wales these two years', and that juries were refusing to co-operate with him. Nevertheless he could claim a year later that order had been restored within the county.[28] It is often assumed that the many recognizances made by individuals to keep the peace towards each other in Cheshire in the 15th century arose from real violence between them.[29] The involvement, either as the subjects of such recognizances or as the mainpernors, of many of the leading Cheshire gentlemen, and the large proportion of the Chester enrolments which the recognizances occupy, may give a disproportionate importance to them. In the four quarter sessions between October 1660 and July 1661 the justices of the peace in Cheshire took 189 recognizances to keep the peace and 159 recognizances for good behaviour.[30] The 15th and early 16th centuries, when 'the county was disturbed by riots, feuds, and the abuse of livery and maintenance' with 'the gentry . . . all too often the main source of unrest', witnessed the rise to prosperity of many Cheshire families, who were able to build large houses for themselves and to enrich churches.[31] The paradox illustrates the need for further work on the Cheshire records, and their comparison with what has survived for other counties.

The use of Cheshire as a recruiting area, especially for archers, is well known. In 1301 the justice of Chester was among those ordered to choose 'Welsh footmen' from the county and its surroundings for service in Scotland.[32] Such service contravened the freedom which Cheshire men had traditionally claimed from military service outside the county, but in spite of a promise made in 1322 that such a levy would not be treated as a precedent, commissions of array continued to be issued.[33] Under the Black Prince they occur in 1346, 1355, 1356, 1359, 1362, and 1363.[34] Richard II sought 1,000 archers from Cheshire in 1386 and 2,300 in 1397–8.[35] In 1400 a force of 500 Cheshire archers went to the Scottish war, and further commissions of array were

[21] Cal. Pat. 1317–21, 200; Cal. Close, 1318–23, 12.

[22] Blk. Prince's Reg. iii. 129, 383–4.

[23] Ibid. 265, 267, 383–4; Rot. Parl. ii. 352–3; iii. 42, 62, 81, 139, 201, 280, 308, 440.

[24] J. Bellamy, Crime and Public Order in Eng. in Later Middle Ages, makes no special mention of Ches. Cf. Eng. Hist. Docs. iv, pp. 969, 1221–36.

[25] Cal. Pat. 1391–6, 433; 36 D.K.R. 497, 532; 37 D.K.R. 96, 109, 121, 184, 185, 231–2, 497, 644, 645, 667.

[26] 36 D.K.R. 100–1.

[27] L. & P. Hen. VIII, vii, p. 520; xi, pp. 441, 476.

[28] Ibid. xiii (1), pp. 384–5, 523; xiv (1), p. 565.

[29] e.g. by Driver, Ches. in Later Middle Ages, 17.

[30] Ches. R.O., QJB 3/1, ff. 1–32.

[31] Cf. Barraclough, Earldom, 24, 26, with Driver, Ches. in Later Middle Ages, caps. iii and iv. For activities of a Ches. gentry family in 15th and early 16th cents. see J. T. Driver, 'Mainwarings of Over Peover', J.C.A.S. [2nd ser.], lvii. 27–40.

[32] Cal. Pat. 1292–1301, 598.

[33] Ibid. 1321–4, 177.

[34] Blk. Prince's Reg. i. 7; iii. 199–200, 205, 224, 331, 350, 449, 454.

[35] Cal. Pat. 1385–9, 217; 36 D.K.R. 98; on the Ches. archers, see J. L. Gillespie, 'Ric. II's Ches. Archers', T.H.S.L.C. cxxv. 1–39.

FIRST FOLIO OF A CHESHIRE MIZE BOOK FOR 1405 [see p. 24]

Sir John Done (d. 1629), Master Forester of Delamere and Mondrem

The Delamere Forest Horn, said to be of the 12th century

issued throughout the 15th and early 16th centuries.[36] A thousand Cheshire men are said to have served at Flodden.[37] Nevertheless by that time Cheshire was no longer the leading source of soldiers. In 1386 its contingent, forming 20 per cent of the total demanded from the whole country, was more than twice the size of those of the next most heavily burdened counties, Yorkshire and Lancashire, which were each to supply 400 archers.[38] In 1524, however, Devon's archers outnumbered the 3,606 which Cheshire could supply, and in numbers of billmen Cheshire came only eighth among the counties.[39]

In spite of the distinctiveness of Cheshire's palatine institutions the county was never, during the 14th, 15th, or early 16th centuries free from outside interference. Statute law was generally enforced there, except where it infringed the prerogative of king or earl to appoint palatine officials. The statutes of labourers were enforced in the county.[40] A statute of 1400 which prohibited Welshmen from purchasing lands in towns on the Welsh marches was expressly extended to Chester, and was enforced in 1427.[41] That of 1429 against livery and maintenance was again expressly extended to include the palatinates of Chester and Lancaster.[42] In 1434 the chamberlain and his deputy were ordered to swear the inhabitants of the county to the fulfilment of an Act against maintenance of peacebreakers.[43] The Act of 1477 forbidding the currency of Irish money was to be proclaimed in Cheshire by the sheriff.[44] A complaint by the mayor of Chester that the statute of 1532 restricting the sale of tanned leather appeared to violate the liberties of the county palatine was ignored.[45]

The judicial immunity of Cheshire was in some respects more apparent than real. In 1323 the right of the bishop of Coventry and Lichfield to cite the archdeacon of Chester before him was upheld by the king in spite of the justice's protests.[46] More than a century later the chamberlain of Chester, on his own authority, issued a writ of prohibition against the bishop, who had cited the rector of Northenden to appear before him: the bishop appealed to the privy council, and the prohibition was withdrawn as contrary to the king's coronation oath. The chamberlain, John Troutbeck, was reproved.[47] Although there was no regular process available in the 14th century to a person who had suffered injury outside Cheshire by a native of the county, it was possible for the injured party to seek a remedy by petitioning the king or earl.[48] In 1352 three men who had been outlawed in Yorkshire and had fled to Cheshire were to be arrested, detained, and removed to York.[49] In 1399 the immunity of Cheshire men from prosecution was much curtailed by statute.[50]

Sessions of the Chester county court could be either afforced or supplemented by special commissions of the king or earl. In 1304 a commission of oyer and terminer in favour of William Inge, Sir William Trussell (the justice of Chester), Richard Massey (Trussell's predecessor), William Bliburgh, and Thomas Cambridge, had as its terms of reference alienations of the earl's lands, unauthorized encroachments, and the unjust levy of imposts.[51] In March 1309 two commissions of oyer and terminer related to specific events, the murder of a prior of Combermere and damages allegedly committed by the justice and his bailiffs against the abbot of Vale Royal.[52] A commission of April 1318 was concerned with extortion by bailiffs, farmers, and other

---

[36] 37 *D.K.R.* 7, 95, 96, 117, 139, 140, 682, 703; 39 *D.K.R.* 280; *L. & P. Hen. VIII*, v, p. 632.
[37] *L. & P. Hen. VIII*, i (2), p. 1005.
[38] *Cal. Pat.* 1385–9, 217.
[39] *L. & P. Hen. VIII*, iv, p. 426.
[40] H. J. Hewitt, *Ches. under the Three Edwards*, 96.
[41] 2 Hen. IV, c. 12; 37 *D.K.R.* 380.
[42] 8 Hen. VI, c. 4.
[43] 37 *D.K.R.* 135.
[44] Ibid. 141.
[45] *L. & P. Hen. VIII*, vi, pp. 275, 658.
[46] *Cal. Close*, 1323–7, 45. The decision overrode or ignored the earl of Chester's authority.
[47] Earwaker, *East Ches.* i. 289–90.
[48] *Rot. Parl.* i. 107; *Blk. Prince's Reg.* iii. 265, 267.
[49] *Blk. Prince's Reg.* iii. 58.
[50] 1 Hen. IV, c. 18.
[51] *Cal. Pat.* 1301–7, 238.
[52] Ibid. 1307–13, 128–9.

ministers in Cheshire and Flintshire. The commissioners were empowered to remove incapable ministers.[53] In 1333, 1346, and 1347, men were sent from the king or earl to observe sessions of the county court.[54] Between 1341 and 1342 Hugh Berwick and others were in Chester as justices of oyer and terminer for 'all trespasses and felonies perpetrated in Cheshire and Flintshire'.[55]

Under Edward IV, and particularly under the first two Tudors, measures were taken which resulted in the assimilation of Cheshire in several ways to normal English counties. At first Cheshire was brought into association with the council in the marches of Wales. Among the commissioners of the prince of Wales appointed in 1474 to oversee the prince's demesnes in Cheshire and Flintshire, and to negotiate with the inhabitants for a mize, John Alcock, bishop of Rochester, Thomas Vaughan, the prince's chamberlain, John Needham, and Richard Hawt were members of the prince's council.[56] In 1500 and 1501 the members of Prince Arthur's council included Sir Richard Pole, Sir Thomas Englefield, Peter Newton, William Greville, and Robert Frost. Pole was made chamberlain of Chester in January 1500; the warrant for his appointment was, significantly, dated at Bewdley. Englefield was acting as deputy justice of Chester. Peter Newton, secretary to the council, had been made park-keeper of Shotwick in 1494, steward of Frodsham in 1495, and lessee of Shotwick manor in 1497. William Greville had been the prince's advocate in the recent Chester *quo warranto* proceedings. Robert Frost, the prince's almoner, had briefly held the chamberlainship of Chester.[57]

Early in Henry VIII's reign Cheshire and Flintshire were included in commissions of justices of oyer and terminer and of the peace for Wales and the marches, Shropshire, Herefordshire, Gloucestershire, and Worcestershire.[58] The association of Cheshire with the marches was not, however, invariable. In 1517 the county was included with Nottinghamshire and Derbyshire, Staffordshire, Shropshire, and Lancashire in an inquiry into concealed inclosures.[59] Four years later an inquiry into concealed lands had within its purview Derbyshire, Leicestershire, Shropshire, and Staffordshire as well as Cheshire.[60] In 1522 Cheshire was included in the earl of Shrewsbury's commission of array with Shropshire, Staffordshire, Derbyshire, Nottinghamshire, Yorkshire, and Northumberland, and in the following year the earl of Surrey's commission included the same counties, with Cumberland, Westmorland, and Lancashire.[61]

From the 1520s the appointment of sheriffs in Cheshire coincided with similar appointments elsewhere; it was carried out in the same way, although the sheriff's commissions were issued from the Chester Exchequer. In 1536 the Act introducing justices of the peace into the counties of 'shired' Wales included Cheshire and Flintshire. Amercements and fines arising from the justices' sessions there were to be estreated into the Chester Exchequer.[62] The first surviving peace commissions for Cheshire were issued in July 1539, February and May 1540, and June 1543; no records of the justices' sessions have, however, survived from the period.[63]

A further Act of 1536 regulated the issue of original and judicial writs in counties palatine. They were henceforth to run in the name of the king alone. In this Act the position of Sir Thomas Englefield as justice of Chester was expressly preserved.[64]

[53] *Cal. Pat.* 1317–21, 134.
[54] Ibid. 1330–4, 432; *Blk. Prince's Reg.* i. 17, 22, 113.
[55] *Ches. Chamb. Accts.* 114–16.
[56] Caroline A. J. Skeel, *Council in Marches of Wales*, 20, 24–5.
[57] P. Williams, *Council in Marches of Wales under Eliz. I*, 10; *26 D.K.R.* 27; *37 D.K.R.* 562; *E.H.R.* xlix. 682.
[58] *L. & P. Hen. VIII*, i (1), pp. 195, 605–6; i (2), p. 933; ii (1), p. 193; ii (2), pp. 1282, 1387; iii (2), p. 915.
[59] Ibid. ii (2), p. 1054.
[60] Ibid. iii (2), p. 594.
[61] Ibid. iii (2), pp. 1027, 1211.
[62] 27 Hen. VIII, c. 5. For commentary on this and subsequent Acts see Stewart-Brown, *Serjeants of Peace*, 106–8; Barraclough, *Earldom*, 27.
[63] *L. & P. Hen. VIII*, xiv (1), pp. 584–5; xv, pp. 108, 348; xx (1), p. 316.
[64] 27 Hen. VIII, c. 24.

The sessions of the Cheshire justices of the peace were said in 1540 to impose an additional heavy burden on those freeholders who also owed suit at the county court. It was then enacted that the county court should be held only twice each year, with one session after Michaelmas and the other after Easter. Such sessions were to be extended for as long as should be necessary.[65] The Act resulted in two anomalies. It restricted the justice's freedom to decide the dates of the county court sessions in accordance with expediency. It also inadvertently led to the abolition of the sheriff's *retro-comitatus* at which minor pleas were held and outlawries were proclaimed.[66] As a result an Act of 1541 set up a sheriff's court for Cheshire, to be held once a month for determining civil pleas where the sums involved were less than 40s. and for the proclamation of outlawry. Procedure in Cheshire was thus brought into line with that in similar courts in other counties. The same Act restricted the number of Cheshire coroners to two.[67] The county's avowries, which had by that time become a mere means of debt evasion, were abolished by the Act which gave the county representation in Parliament.[68] In 1543 the standing of the justice of Chester was changed. He was now to hold sessions twice a year in Denbighshire and Montgomeryshire as well as in Cheshire and Flintshire. Original writs for Cheshire and Flintshire were to be issued from the Exchequer of Chester, as were writs *de coronatore eligendo* for the two counties. A new seal in the keeping of the justice, however, was to be used for sealing judicial writs for all four of the counties over which he had jurisdiction.[69]

In 1450 the leading inhabitants of Cheshire petitioned against the attempt to enforce a Parliamentary subsidy in the county. Cheshire, it was claimed, had been a county palatine since before the Norman Conquest, with its own parliaments, 'chancery exchequer', and justice.[70] It has been asserted that Cheshire suffered only disadvantages from its exceptional status;[71] those who subscribed to the petition, however, evidently wished to remain as they were. Nevertheless in the preamble to the Act of 1543 which gave parliamentary representation to the county and to the city of Chester, another petition was recited in which the disadvantages of non-representation in Parliament were set out.[72] The reason for the Cheshire men's change of mind was almost certainly the fact that, particularly since the late 1520s, Cheshire had lost much of that administrative distinctiveness which it had still enjoyed in 1450. A final blow to the county's traditional independence of status must have been the imposition of parliamentary subsidies there; Cheshire paid the subsidy of 1540.[73]

[65] 32 Hen. VIII, c. 43.
[66] For the *retro-comitatus* see *Cal. Chest. Co. Ct. R.* p. xxiii.
[67] 33 Hen. VIII, c. 13. For first appointment of coroners, see *39 D.K.R.* 56.
[68] *E.H.R.* xxix. 41–55.

[69] 34 & 35 Hen. VIII, c. 26.
[70] The petition, with the king's acceptance of it, is printed in Ormerod, *Hist. Ches.* i. 126–7.
[71] Barraclough, *Earldom*, 23–5.
[72] 34 & 35 Hen. VIII, c. 13.
[73] E 179/85/10.

PALATINE INSTITUTIONS AND COUNTY GOVERNMENT
1547–1660

The Survival of the Palatine Institutions

BETWEEN the death of Henry VIII and the Restoration Cheshire's administration resembled in most respects that of any other English county. Power was largely in the hands of a local élite, and was exercised through such offices as the magistracy and the deputy-lieutenancy. Nevertheless the distinctive institutions of the county, which had survived the reforms of the 1530s and 1540s, continued to function effectively throughout the period, except during the short-term disruption caused by the Civil War.

Only during two brief periods between 1547 and 1660 were there earls of Chester. Henry, son of King James I, was created earl of Chester in June 1610, and died two and a half years later; his younger brother Charles received the earldom late in 1616 and held it until he succeeded to the throne early in 1625.[1] Neither earl exercised, either personally or through a council, any real power in the county. The grant of the earldom to Prince Henry, indeed, was followed by the transfer of responsibility for paying the fees of the justices of Chester from the local receiver to the national Exchequer.[2] The limited extent to which the earls were thought to be in control of Cheshire is neatly illustrated by the administration of inquisitions post mortem under them. In the time of Prince Henry inquisitions were always said to be held before the king's escheator, by virtue of the king's writ or commission.[3] Under Prince Charles they were so described until June 1617; after that they were sometimes held in the prince's name, though not consistently.[4]

Even before the county had obtained representation in Parliament it had been made subject to parliamentary taxation. Nevertheless the traditional mize continued to be exacted whenever the county changed hands, as it had in the Middle Ages. In January 1560, for example, a body representing the community of the county appeared before the deputy chamberlain in the Chester Exchequer and conceded a mize in return for the confirmation of their liberties.[5] Grants of the mize, or the appointments of collectors, are recorded for the accessions of Edward VI and James I, and also in 1612.[6] An anonymous writer early in the 17th century believed that the preservation of palatine rights depended on the ancient association of the grant of the mize with the concession of those rights, and with the assent of a representative body of the inhabitants.[7] A generation earlier the opinion had received support from the judges.[8]

In practical terms the most prized possessions of the palatinate were its courts and

---

[1] *Handbk. Brit. Chron.* 421.
[2] *Cal. S.P. Dom.* 1611–18, 45.
[3] *Ches. Inquisitions Post Mortem, 1603–60,* R.S.L.C. lxxxiv. 109, 153, 160, 189; lxxxvi. 152, 161; xci. 1, 82, 155, 164.
[4] Three inqs. of 1624 illustrate the confusion: ibid. lxxxiv. 154, 159; xci. 72.

[5] Chester 2/211.
[6] *List of Exchequer (K.R.) Lay Subsidy R.* (List & Index Soc. xliv), 115; Ches. R.O., DAR/I/17.
[7] *Rights and Jurisdiction of Co. Palatine of Chest.* (Chetham Soc. [1st ser.] xxxvii), 26.
[8] Ibid. 32–4.

its legal immunities. The courts of Great Sessions and Exchequer set Cheshire apart from other English counties in the minds of contemporary lawyers.[9] The courts claimed exclusive jurisdiction except in treason, error, foreign plea, and foreign voucher, and when in the Interregnum it seemed that much of their business had been lost to Westminster, the sheriff, justices of the peace, and grand and second juries at the Great Sessions addressed a petition to Parliament seeking its restoration.[10]

The court of Great Sessions had taken over the functions of the medieval county court in Cheshire. Whereas in the Middle Ages its judges had been responsible only for Cheshire and Flintshire, they afterwards had charge of a circuit which also included Denbighshire and Montgomeryshire. Furthermore, they occupied leading places in the Council in the Marches of Wales, and continued to do so even after Cheshire had been excluded from the Council's jurisdiction.[11] Like other judges of assize the justices of Chester were usually chosen from lawyers who had no previous connexion with the county. At first they were assisted by deputies, but in 1576 provision was made for an associate justice.[12] The first associate, Henry Towneshend, had already acted as a deputy justice in Chester; he held his post for over forty years.[13]

Statutes of Henry VIII's reign had enacted that there should be two six-day sessions a year in each of the counties comprising the circuits.[14] In Chester the spring sessions were usually held in April, and the autumn sessions in September or October.[15] Under Sir John Throckmorton, justice of Chester from 1558 to 1580, they were held less regularly: the first sessions were held in February in five years, and autumn sessions varied in date from August to December.[16] Political and personal difficulties seem to have made Throckmorton an unsuccessful justice.[17] Under his successors the pattern of sessions in April and September or October was consistently maintained. Departures from it were usually the result of the death of a justice and delay in the appointment of his successor, as in 1589, 1600, 1616, and 1625.[18] The postponement of a spring session until July in 1608 may have resulted from Justice Lewkenor's absence in London, where he was upholding the claim of the Council in the Marches of Wales to jurisdiction over Gloucestershire, Herefordshire, Shropshire, and Worcestershire.[19] Work on the Chester circuit, indeed, was seen as a complement of work on the Council rather than vice versa. In his *Liber Famelicus* Justice James Whitelocke devoted far more attention to matters concerning the Council than to those concerning the circuit, noting, for example, the length of the Council's sessions, the number of causes heard, and disputes over precedence there in which he was involved. When he was offered promotion to the King's Bench in 1624 he accepted, being then 'very weary of the life I led at the Council'.[20]

The Civil War interrupted the court's operations. The only occasion on which it sat between 1643 and 1647 was in February 1644, while Chester was in royalist hands. A grand jury, later said to have been 'packed', indicted Sir William Brereton and other Parliamentarians for their rebellious activities between July 1643 and January 1644.[21] In the following September Parliament ensured that the performance would not be repeated. The operation of the palatine seal, then in the hands of the royalist chamberlain of Chester, was suspended, and the king's writ was to run in Cheshire; inhabitants

---

[9] Coke, *Fourth Institute*, cap. xxxvii.
[10] Chester R.O., CR63/2/692, ff. 70–1.
[11] Skeel, *Counc. in Marches*, 287, n. 3.
[12] 18 Eliz. I, c. 8.
[13] W. R. Williams, *Hist. of Great Sessions in Wales, 1542–1830*, 56–7.
[14] 32 Hen. VIII, c. 43; 33 Hen. VIII, c. 13; 34 & 35 Hen. VIII, c. 26.
[15] P.R.O. *Lists and Indexes No. IV*, 87–8.
[16] Ibid. 87.

[17] A. L. Browne, 'Sir John Throckmorton of Feckenham, Chief Justice of Chest.', *J.C.A.S.* N.S. xxxi (i), 55–71.
[18] *Lists and Indexes No. IV*, 87–8; Williams, *Gt. Sess.* 33–5.
[19] Skeel, *Counc. in Marches*, 138.
[20] *Liber Famelicus of James Whitelocke* (Camden Soc. [1st ser.] lxx), 80–97.
[21] *Civil War Tracts of Ches.* (Chetham Soc. N.S. lxv), 146–62.

of the county were to sue and to be answerable at Westminster.[22] Once order had been re-established the court was able to resume its functions, and it sat from April 1648. The first justices appointed by Parliament were local men, John Bradshaw of Marple and Peter Warburton. Bradshaw is said to have been particularly zealous in his control of the Cheshire justices of the peace.[23]

Like the other courts of Great Sessions in the Welsh circuits that of Chester combined the jurisdiction of an ordinary assize court with that of the superior courts at Westminster.[24] In 1548 it was empowered to have fines with proclamation levied before it.[25] Fourteen years later both it and the Chester Exchequer were acknowledged to be courts of record within the meaning of the Statute of Enrolments.[26]

The Exchequer of Chester was a more distinctive palatine institution than the court of Great Sessions.[27] The office of chamberlain might be held by an absentee nobleman, but his subordinate officials were permanently based in Chester castle. As in the Middle Ages the Exchequer combined the functions of a court and a secretariat. By the beginning of Elizabeth I's reign, however, it had lost most of its earlier financial importance. Before 1547 the Court of Augmentations had taken over responsibility for the financial administration of Crown lands in the county. From November 1559, when customs accounts were removed from its purview, the Exchequer's financial responsibility lay merely in its liability to account for profits and fees of the seal and for its receipts as a court of justice.[28]

Following the death of Sir Rice Maunsell in 1559 Edward, earl of Derby (d. 1572), was made chamberlain of Chester for life.[29] In 1565, however, he was replaced by the earl of Leicester, who held the office for 23 years and was in turn succeeded by Henry, earl of Derby (d. 1593).[30] Derby's death was followed by a vacancy lasting 5 months, at the end of which the Attorney-General, Thomas Egerton, was appointed. He remained chamberlain after his elevation to the office of Lord Keeper in May 1596, but in August 1603, soon after he became Lord Chancellor, he was made to give it up.[31] His successor, William, earl of Derby (d. 1642), apparently made some hereditary claim to the office; he was appointed for life, and in 1626 his son James, Lord Strange, was associated with him in it.[32] James took the royalist side in the Civil War, and in 1647 was removed from the chamberlainship, being replaced by the speakers of the two Houses of Parliament. William Lenthall occurs as chamberlain in 1650 and just before the Restoration, although the appointment of Humphrey Mackworth is recorded in 1654.[33]

The chamberlains visited Chester infrequently. The office of vice-chamberlain therefore became more prominent during the period, especially in the first two decades of Elizabeth I's reign when it was held by William Glasiour.[34] Under his leadership the Exchequer gained important jurisdictional victories, against the Council in the Marches of Wales and the corporation of the city of Chester. In the late 1560s, Thomas Radford, who had been imprisoned by Glasiour for refusing to give sureties for keeping the peace, successfully appealed to the Council in the Marches of Wales for his release. Glasiour objected to the Council's action so strenuously that in 1568 a commission of judges under Sir James Dyer was appointed to inquire into the jurisdiction and liberties of the

[22] *Acts & Ords. of Interr.*, ed. Firth and Rait, i. 503–5.
[23] Williams, *Gt. Sess.* 36–7, 57; J. S. Morrill, *Ches. 1630–60*, 231–2, 243.
[24] 34 & 35 Hen. VIII, c. 26.
[25] 2 & 3 Edw. VI, c. 28: on significance of the concession see *Abstracts of Surr. Feet of Fines, 1509–58* (Surr. Rec. Soc. xix), xxv–xxvii.
[26] 5 Eliz. I, c. 26.
[27] For what follows see W. J. Jones, 'Exchequer of Chest. in Last Years of Eliz. I', *Tudor Men and Institu-*

tions, ed. A. J. Slavin, 123–70.
[28] *Chest. Customs Accts.* (R.S.L.C. cxi), 6–7.
[29] *Cal. Pat.* 1558–60, 104.
[30] Williams, *Gt. Sess.* 73.
[31] *39 D.K.R.* 61; *Handbk. Brit. Chron.* 87; *Cal. S.P. Dom.* 1603–10, 27.
[32] *Cal. S.P. Dom.* 1603–10, 27, 50.
[33] Williams, *Gt. Sess.* 73–4; *39 D.K.R.* 64.
[34] *39 D.K.R.* 60, 133.

county palatine and into the chamberlain's office. Its report vindicated the exclusive jurisdiction of the palatine courts, except in cases of error, foreign plea, and foreign voucher, and affirmed that by the Laws in Wales Act 1542, Cheshire and Chester were excluded from the purview of the Council in the Marches of Wales.[35]

Glasiour's disputes with the corporation of Chester, of which he had himself been mayor in 1551–2, lasted for some fifteen years. Soon after his appointment as vice-chamberlain a defendant in a suit before the Exchequer complained about its jurisdiction to the mayor of Chester, claiming that since the city was a county of itself, distinct from the county palatine, he as a citizen should not be compelled to answer in the Chester Exchequer. The mayor committed the plaintiff in the action to prison, and he and his sheriffs ignored Glasiour's attempts to bring the plaintiff back into the Exchequer by a writ of *corpus cum causa*. Glasiour complained to his superior, the earl of Derby, who came to Chester and summoned the mayor and sheriffs before him. No agreement could be reached, and the dispute was taken before the national Exchequer, where it was held that the city was a parcel of the county palatine and liable to answer the Chester Exchequer's writs.[36] Shortly afterwards the city obtained a new confirmation of its liberties from the queen, and within a decade the mayor was claiming that a clause in the confirmation excluded the city from the Exchequer's jurisdiction.[37] Once again Glasiour's writs were ignored. In March 1573 a commission under Sir Francis Walsingham was appointed to hear the dispute: it found that the clause in question had been fraudulently obtained, and ordered the letters patent containing it to be returned. A new confirmation of the city's liberties was to be obtained, and detailed disputes between the city and the Chester Exchequer were to be settled by compromise.[38]

Glasiour's relations with his subordinates were as inharmonious as those with the city of Chester and the Council in the Marches of Wales. The office of baron or clerk of the Exchequer was held jointly by William Tatton and John Yerworth, with Alexander Cotes as their deputy.[39] The three were involved in disputes with Glasiour in the 1570s and 1580s. Cotes was accused of embezzlement and suspended from office, though the charge was later found to be false.[40] Both sides appealed to the earl of Leicester as chamberlain, and Leicester attempted to impose more rigid control over Glasiour. New instructions issued for the running of the Exchequer in 1574 were designed to ensure the attendance at its sessions of qualified assistants; nevertheless the orders were ignored, and further ones had to be issued in 1578 and 1584. By the latter the vice-chamberlain's freedom of action was severely curtailed: he could do little except in the presence of an assistant learned in the law.[41]

Seen against the success of Glasiour in freeing the Exchequer from the jurisdiction of the Council in the Marches of Wales, the result of the disputes within the Exchequer was ironical. Leicester asked George Bromley, justice of Chester, to sit in the Exchequer whenever possible; Henry Towneshend, the associate justice, was also among the recognized assistants by 1584: both were prominent in the Council in the Marches of Wales. The new instructions of 1584 limited the dates of the Exchequer's sessions, which were to open on the same day as the Great Sessions. Furthermore, the Exchequer was increasingly staffed by common lawyers. Among the assistants was Peter Warburton, who became vice-chamberlain in 1593 and who late in 1600 became a justice of the Common Pleas.[42] An anonymous writer at the beginning of James I's reign accepted the need for the justices of Great Sessions to be associated with the vice-chamberlain

[35] *Rights & Jurisd.* 32–4.
[36] Ibid. 16–24.
[37] Morris, *Chest.* 546.
[38] *Acts of P.C.* 1571–5, 210, 223–8.

[39] *39 D.K.R.* 58, 60.
[40] Ibid. 60, 258; Jones, 'Exch. of Chest.' 130–2.
[41] Jones, 'Exch. of Chest.' 129–32.
[42] Ibid. 130–2; *39 D.K.R.* 287.

in an advisory capacity, but believed that the vice-chamberlain himself 'must be no common lawyer'.[43] Nevertheless the new vice-chamberlain appointed in January 1604 was Henry Towneshend, already second justice of Chester, who held both offices until his death in 1621.[44]

As vice-chamberlain Towneshend, like Glasiour, found his powers threatened. It was rumoured in 1604 that the city of Chester was once again about to try to exclude itself from the Exchequer's jurisdiction.[45] In 1605 Towneshend was complaining about encroachments on his authority by the Westminster courts, and three years later his superior, the earl of Derby, made a similar complaint.[46] Meanwhile disputes among the Exchequer officials continued unabated.[47] When Towneshend died in 1621 he was said to be 84 years old; if this was correct, he had already been in his late sixties when appointed vice-chamberlain.[48] After his death the experiment of combining the offices of vice-chamberlain and second justice was discontinued.[49]

At the beginning of James I's reign the officials of the Exchequer were said to number twenty-four. They included the chamberlain, the baron or clerk, the controller, the attorney-general, four serjeants, an examiner, a bailiff-errant, a messenger, a crier, and nine attorneys, besides the mason, carpenter, and surveyor.[50] To the list should be added the vice-chamberlain, his assistant, and the deputy baron.[51]

As a court of equity the Exchequer was held to have exercised its authority from the time of the creation of the earldom of Chester.[52] No records of its judicial activities earlier than 1500 have, however, survived.[53] Its procedure was similar to that of the court of Chancery, although its standards both of procedure and of record keeping are said to have been much lower.[54] It exercised powers of review over local courts, transferring actions, for example, from the Pentice Court of Chester to the Portmote Court, and issuing prohibitions of tithe suits in the ecclesiastical courts. Most of the causes heard before it were minor local disputes involving debt in some form, and it could offer the inhabitants of Cheshire more moderate fees and quicker hearings than they would obtain in Chancery. A suit in 1593 is said to have cost the plaintiff less than £5. Peter Warburton heard twelve causes in one day. When Henry Towneshend wrote to Cecil in the early years of the 17th century he recited the number of actions which he had heard in the Exchequer: they amounted to 80 shortly before October 1605, more than 65 in the week before Christmas, 65 again in April 1606, and 60 early in 1608.[55]

The Exchequer continued its medieval function as the palatine chancery, executing commissions and other documents under the Chester seal. Its activities in this respect are, as in the earlier period, shown in the 'recognizance rolls', and the roll of 36 and 37 Elizabeth I (1594–5) may be taken as a convenient illustrative example.[56] It contains appointments of the county sheriff, and of a serjeant at law. Commissions issued during the year dealt with such matters as arrest, the sequestration of land in pursuance of an Exchequer decree, binding an offender to keep the peace, and inquiries into the removal of building materials from Chester castle, the responsibility for bridge repairs in Cheshire, and 'libels and rhymes' disseminated in Nantwich. Other writs enrolled included one of *ouster le main* and three of general livery, an exemption from service

[43] *Rights & Jurisd.* 25–6; cf. Jones, 'Exch. of Chest.' 167.
[44] *39 D.K.R.* 62–3.
[45] Hist. MSS. Com. 9, *Salisbury*, xvi, p. 432.
[46] Ibid. xvii, p. 466; xx, pp. 17–18.
[47] Jones, 'Exch. of Chest.' 134–5, 164; Hist. MSS. Com. 9, *Salisbury*, xviii, p. 115.
[48] *Liber Famelicus of James Whitelocke*, 90–1.
[49] Williams, *Gt. Sess.* 75.
[50] *Rights & Jurisd.* 28.

[51] *39 D.K.R.* 62.
[52] *Rights & Jurisd.* 15, 33; Coke, *Fourth Institute*, cap. xxxvii.
[53] *P.R.O. Lists & Indexes No. XL*, 5, 7.
[54] For what follows see Jones, 'Exch. of Chest.' 135–68.
[55] Hist. MSS. Com. 9, *Salisbury*, xvi, p. 466; xviii, p. 115; xx, pp. 70–1.
[56] Chester 2/260, calendared in *39 D.K.R.* 18, 26, 35, 38, 54, 61, 76, 115, 147, 176, 192, 193, 201, 215, 219, 228, 250, 258, 301.

on assizes, and an order for the levy of a county rate for bridge repairs. One charter, two indentures of sale, an inquisition post mortem, and proceedings and orders of the Exchequer were enrolled at the instance of interested parties.

The Personnel of Local Administration

Like those of other counties the commissions of the peace in Cheshire always included a proportion of 'dignitaries', chief among whom were the greater officers of state.[57] Others who normally took little or no part in the routine work of justices of peace included, in Cheshire, the judges of the Great Sessions and some members of the Council in the Marches of Wales. The Council continued to be represented on the Cheshire commissions after Cheshire was excluded from its jurisdiction, and two of its members, William Glasiour the vice-chamberlain of Chester and Sir Hugh Cholmondeley (d. 1597), were prominent among the active justices of the peace.[58] Among churchmen, the bishops of Chester were normally on the commission, and occasionally attended quarter sessions, while in the 17th century lesser ecclesiastics were sometimes appointed. They included George Byrom, rector of Thornton, Thomas Dod, rector of Malpas and Astbury and archdeacon of Richmond, Thomas Mallory, rector of Davenham and Mobberley, Richard Murray, rector of Stockport, William Nicholls, rector of Cheadle, George Snell, rector of Wallasey and archdeacon of Chester, and William Forster, rector of Barrow and (in 1634) bishop of Sodor and Man, besides two chancellors of the diocese of Chester, David Yale and Edmund Mainwaring.[59] Nevertheless the core of the active bench during the period was provided by members of the local gentry.

Some 220 Cheshire laymen served as justices of the peace in Cheshire between 1539 and 1642.[60] Detailed changes in the commissions of the peace in the period cannot here be traced, but certain general conclusions about their composition may be drawn. The size of commissions, exclusive of dignitaries, tended to increase during the 16th century in spite of government proposals to reduce it. In 1539 there were only fourteen local gentlemen on the commission. The number rose to 23 in 1547, up to thirty during the 1570s, 38 by 1587, and over forty by the 1590s.[61] Its size remained roughly the same under James I, but fell to an average of just over thirty under Charles I.[62] The commission of September 1626, numbering 83 altogether, was exceptional, and the additional justices are said to have been appointed merely in order to facilitate the collection of the Free Gift authorized two months earlier. By October the commission had been reduced to its normal size, with a total of 47 justices on it.[63]

Many justices, once appointed to the commission, served on it for the remainder of their active lives. Of the 220 laymen who served between 1539 and 1642, fourteen were only appointed temporarily in September 1626 and dismissed within a month. Some twenty others were still serving when the Civil War began. Of the remainder, it is virtually certain that 98 were on the commission at the time of their death. The removal of justices of the peace thus appears to be exceptional. Occasionally it was the result of age or infirmity. Ralph Arderne (d. 1609), who was removed from the commission in 1601, was aged over seventy three years before, when he had surrendered his estates

[57] For what follows see Patricia J. Marriott (née Turner), 'Commission of Peace in Ches. 1536–1603' (Manchester Univ., M.A. thesis, 1974), and G. P. Higgins, 'Co. Govt. and Society in Ches. c. 1590–1640' (Liverpool Univ., M.A. thesis, 1973). The help of Mrs. Marriott and of Mr. Higgins, and their permission to make use of their research, are gratefully acknowledged.

[58] Marriott, 'Com. of Peace', 84; Williams, Counc. in Marches under Eliz., 344–5, 348–9.
[59] Higgins, 'Co. Govt. & Soc.' 66, 71–2, 254–60.
[60] See lists of justices in Marriott, 'Com. of Peace', 138–43, and Higgins, 'Co. Govt. & Soc.' 254–60.
[61] Marriott, 'Com. of Peace', 41, 90, 108.
[62] Higgins, 'Co. Govt. & Soc.' 68. [63] Ibid. 69–70.

to his son.[64] Richard Birkenhead, recorder of Chester, surrendered that office through old age in 1601; he had been off the commission of the peace since 1593 or 1595.[65] Both William Moreton in 1616 and Peter Warburton of Arley in 1623 were removed at their own request.[66] Outlawry was the cause of the removal of two justices in 1616, but one was reinstated within a month.[67] Elizabethan governments sponsored various inquiries into the religious persuasions of the justices and of other leading gentlemen, but there is little evidence that 'purges' resulted. In 1564, for example, nine justices were listed as unfavourable to the religious settlement. Five (John Bruen, John Dutton, Urian Brereton, William Davenport, and Robert Tatton) were removed from the commission in 1564, and one (Peter Legh of Lyme) in 1565, but Dutton and Legh were soon restored to it, and the other three were not disturbed at all.[68] Further reports dated *c.* 1580 and *c.* 1583 apparently produced even fewer changes; the nearest event to a major 'purge' occurred in 1595, when nine justices were removed, but five of them had only recently been appointed and the remainder are said to have been too poor to sustain the burden of office.[69]

It has been said that the membership of the Cheshire commissions in the late 16th and early 17th centuries reveals a 'tendency to élitism', 'the increasingly hereditary nature of the office', and its restriction to 'a narrow section of society'.[70] Such claims can be supported by some of the available evidence, but they represent on over-simplification. No members of the peerage were regularly resident in Cheshire during the period, but men of the rank of knight or baronet could generally expect to be included in the commission. All but one of the knights enumerated in a list of Cheshire freeholders in 1578 were justices.[71] The 13 families which, it is claimed, constituted a county élite at the time, with annual incomes sufficient to enable them to lend large sums to the Crown and to head the muster rolls, altogether furnished 43 of the 220 lay justices, with the Savages of Rock Savage and the Calveleys of Lea each providing five justices, and the Fittons of Gawsworth, the Venables of Kinderton, the Breretons of Brereton, and the Booths of Dunham Massey each providing four.[72] Nevertheless other families were equally prominent. The Delves of Doddington, the Dones of Utkinton, and the Masseys of Puddington each provided 5 justices between 1539 and 1642. There are several instances of sons succeeding their fathers on the bench. Sir John Done, one of the first Cheshire justices to be appointed, died in 1561. His son Ralph was appointed in 1565; on his death his son John immediately succeeded him on the bench, and John's own son and grandson followed equally quickly. Similar successions may be traced for the Masseys of Puddington and the Savages of Rock Savage.[73] Nevertheless the tendency should not be exaggerated. The son of Thomas Aston (d. 1552) was not appointed to the commission, although his son Sir Thomas (d. 1613) was. Sir Thomas's son John (d. 1615) was excluded, but John's son Thomas, who attained his majority *c.* 1621, was appointed in 1637.[74] William, Lord Brereton, and his son John were both justices in the 1620s. John predeceased William, but although John's son William, who attained his majority in 1633, inherited the title, he was not appointed to the commission of the peace.[75] When Sir Edward Fitton of Gawsworth died in 1606 his son was not appointed, even though three generations of Fittons had been on the commission.[76]

[64] Earwaker, *East Ches.* i. 469.
[65] Ormerod, *Hist. Ches.* i. 221.
[66] C 231/4, ff. 14, 149.
[67] Ibid. ff. 14, 16v.
[68] Marriott, 'Com. of Peace', 83.
[69] Ibid. 93, 99, 104.
[70] Ibid. 67; Higgins, 'Co. Govt. & Soc.' 66, 67.
[71] *List of Freeholders in Ches. 1578* (R.S.L.C. xliii), 3–23.
[72] B. Coward, 'Lieutenancy of Lancs. and Ches. in 16th

and Early 17th Cents.', *T.H.S.L.C.* cxix. 43.
[73] Marriott, 'Com. of Peace', 139, 141, 142; Higgins, 'Co. Govt. & Soc.', 256, 258, 259.
[74] Marriott, 'Com. of Peace', 138; Higgins, 'Co. Govt. & Soc.', 254; *Pedigrees made at Visitation of Ches. 1613* R.S.L.C. lviii), 12–13.
[75] Higgins, 'Co. Govt. & Soc.' 254; R.S.L.C. lxxxiv. 75.
[76] Marriott, 'Com. of Peace', 140.

There were few professional lawyers among the active justices of the peace in Cheshire, although like gentlemen's sons elsewhere many of the justices had attended one of the Inns of Court.[77] The Birkenhead family, however, combined landed status and hereditary succession on the bench with professional expertise. John Birkenhead (d. 1550) and his illegitimate son Richard (d. after 1601) were recorders of Chester; Henry (d. 1613) and his son, also called Henry (d. 1646), were prothonotaries of the court of Great Sessions, and thus linked the court with the bench.[78]

Service on the commission of the peace formed only one, though a very important, aspect of the civic responsibilities demanded of local gentlemen during the period. The county sheriffs, though not always members of the bench at the time of their appointment, came from the same social rank as most of the justices. Some men were asked to bear the burden of that office more than once: Thomas Brooke of Norton (d. 1623) and George Booth of Dunham Massey (d. 1652) were each made sheriff of Cheshire twice, and Sir John Savage, who sat as a justice of the peace from 1550 until his death in 1597, acted as sheriff of Cheshire seven times.[79] Although most of the sheriffs' work was undertaken by deputies, the office imposed certain burdens and responsibilities up to and beyond the Restoration. A particularly irksome duty imposed on the sheriffs in the 1630s was the collection of Ship Money. The difficulties involved, when the sheriff was placed in a position of maximum discomfort between the Privy Council and the high and petty constables of the county, are amply demonstrated by the letters of Sir Thomas Cholmondeley of Vale Royal, who was sheriff from 1637 to 1638.[80] Gentlemen of substance were also made responsible for the collection of parliamentary subsidies. The assessment of the subsidy for Bucklow hundred in 1593 was in the hands of Sir Hugh Cholmondeley, Peter Warburton, and Thomas Brooke, all of whom were justices of the peace at the time.[81] In June 1631 commissions concerning distraint of knighthood were made out in favour of the earl of Derby and his son (joint chamberlains of Chester) and thirteen Cheshire gentlemen, all of whom except Edward Warren of Poynton were serving as justices of the peace.[82]

Administrative as well as financial duties were imposed on the county gentry, in addition to their work as justices of the peace. In 1595 the chamberlain, vice-chamberlain, and two justices of Chester appointed a commission to inquire into the responsibility for bridge repair in Cheshire. Fourteen local gentlemen were named, and the list was headed by Sir Rowland Stanley, a long-serving justice of the peace. Two of the commissioners, Sir Randal Brereton and Thomas Wilbraham, had been among those asked a month earlier to investigate the removal of building materials from Chester castle. Another member of that commission had been Sir Hugh Cholmondeley; he and Thomas Wilbraham were among those deputed earlier in the year to inquire into the spread of 'libels and rhymes' in Nantwich.[83] The practice of appointing commissioners to assist the escheator and feodary in taking inquisitions post mortem imposed yet another duty on the same class. Sir Henry Bunbury (d. 1634) served as a commissioner on seven occasions between 1614 and 1621.[84] Sir Richard Wilbraham of Woodhey (d. 1643) attended fifteen inquisitions as a commissioner between 1613 and 1636.[85]

Public service of the kinds enumerated above might well occupy most of the active lifetime of a Cheshire gentleman. Some 29 of the 220 justices held the office for over

[77] Higgins, 'Co. Govt. & Soc.' 78.
[78] Marriott, 'Com. of Peace', 138; Higgins, 'Co. Govt. & Soc.' 254; *39 D.K.R.* 19–20.
[79] *P.R.O. Lists & Indexes No. IX,* 17b–18.
[80] Higgins, 'Co. Govt. & Soc.' 166–95; Elaine Marcotte, 'Ship-Money in Ches. 1637', *Bull. Jn. Rylands Libr.* lviii. 137–72.
[81] 3 *Sheaf,* xxviii, p. 8.
[82] *Obligatory Knighthood temp. Chas. I* (R.S.L.C. xii), 199.
[83] Chester 2/260 rott. 2, 3d.
[84] R.S.L.C. lxxxiv. 1, 13, 20, 37, 38, 54; lxxxvi. 101.
[85] Ibid. lxxxiv. 1, 42, 78, 88, 134; lxxxvi. 65, 116; xci. 38, 52, 69, 80, 147, 173–4, 175, 178.

thirty years, and Sir George Booth (d. 1652) served for over sixty. Attendance at quarter sessions varied between individuals. For example, 28 justices are recorded as attending between April 1577 and January 1580.[86] Sir Hugh Cholmondeley attended 9 of the 12 sessions, and Sir Randal Brereton attended 8, but the 10 justices who each attended 4 or 5 sessions out of the 12 were more typical. On average 7 or 8 justices sat at each session. When special commissions were appointed, it was generally assumed that not all those named would participate. The commission appointed to investigate the removal of building materials from Chester castle in 1595 contains 9 names, but the quorum was set at two.[87] In 1607 a committee of 11 justices was nominated to view the causeway between Warrington Bridge and Wilderspool; its quorum was 8, and that number duly attended and reported.[88]

Freeholders of lesser rank, who could not normally aspire to a position on the county bench, were nevertheless expected to participate in administration. The office of escheator, normally held for life in Cheshire, was in the 16th century usually given to men of knightly rank, but in the 17th century both escheators and feodaries were labelled esquire or gentleman.[89] Those freeholders who were styled gentlemen also normally filled the office of head constable, which carried a heavy financial responsibility in addition to the obligation to attend quarter sessions and Great Sessions.[90] At any one time there were fourteen head constables in Cheshire, two from each of the seven hundreds of the county. The most interesting of the administrative obligations of the lesser gentry of the county, however, was their duty to perform jury service at Great Sessions, quarter sessions, and inquisitions.

Throughout the period there is evidence that grand jury service was a burden which was unequally distributed among the Cheshire freeholders. In the 11 quarter sessions grand jury panels which survive for the sessions between April 1577 and January 1580 325 men were impanelled.[91] The jury usually numbered 15, but the panels from whom the jurors were chosen varied in size between 24 and 38. Those summoned included men who were styled esquires and gentlemen; the esquires, however, were less frequently sworn to service. John Domvile, for example, was impanelled on 7 out of the 11 occasions, and Thomas Vernon on 5, but neither was placed on a jury. Conversely, James Browne of Hulse, styled gentleman, was impanelled and sworn on 8 occasions, and Peter Filkyn of Tattenhall and Robert Buckley of Bickerton each on seven. An investigation of grand jurymen at Great Sessions and quarter sessions from 1629 to 1659 reveals similar tendencies.[92] In that period 609 men were sworn to jury service; 117 served on more than 10 occasions, and 28 of the latter were sworn on more than twenty. Philip Antrobus, William Tomlinson, John Middlehurst, and Humphrey Page, who had each served on juries before 1629, each acted on more than 40 occasions in the following 30 years. In the selection of jurymen a balance was maintained between experienced men and newcomers to the service, but there were also widely varying degrees of experience which cannot easily be explained. If juries at inquisitions post mortem are also taken into account, the pattern is emphasized.[93] Humphrey Page, for example, served on more than 100 inquisition juries after 1603, or more than one in three of all those that were held under James I and Charles I. In 1619 17 inquisitions

[86] What follows is based on Ches. R.O., QJB 1/2 ff. 24, 28v; QJF 7/1 no. 32; 7/2 no. 31; 7/3 no. 38; 7/4 no. 43; 8/1 no. 42; 8/4 no. 41; 9/1 no. 34; 9/2 no. 32; 9/3 no. 33; 9/4 no. 74.

[87] Chester 2/260 rot. 2.

[88] Ches. Q.S. Rec. 61.

[89] 39 D.K.R. 57, 59, 60; Cal. S.P. Dom. 1603–10, 209; R.S.L.C. xci, p. ix; J. Hall, 'Feodary's Returns for Ches. in . . . 1576', J.C.A.S. N.S. xvii. 19–54.

[90] J. S. Morrill, Ches. Grand Jury, 1625–59, 59–60.

[91] For what follows see Ches. R.O., QJF 7/1 nos. 19, 20; 7/2 no. 21; 7/3 no. 11; 7/4 nos. 34, 35; 8/1 nos. 24, 25; 8/3 nos. 11, 13; 8/4 nos. 27, 28, 29; 9/1 no. 28; 9/2 nos. 18, 19; 9/3 no. 16; 9/4 nos. 36, 38.

[92] Morrill, Ches. Grand Jury, 18–19.

[93] For what follows see R.S.L.C. lxxxiv, lxxxvi, and xci, passim.

post mortem were held. John Birtles, Edmund Mouldsworth, and Humphrey Page each served on 9 of them. The liability to serve on such juries as well as on grand juries at Great Sessions and quarter sessions could impose a heavy burden. There were two Great Sessions and four quarter sessions a year; the number of inquisitions averaged seven a year, although in the years from 1619 to 1624 it rose steeply, the number for each year being respectively 17, 21, 13, 11, 16, and eleven. Further service might be demanded at the private sessions held from time to time by justices of the peace, where jurors were again impanelled and sworn. At Bunbury in March 1568, for example, a panel of 34 was drawn up, of whom 17 were sworn as jurors.[94]

Jurors were sometimes fined for non-attendance. At the quarter sessions held in May 1559, for example, 3 esquires were each fined 3s. 4d., and 10 gentlemen 2s. 6d.[95] In 1585 the fines for default were set at 13s. 4d. for esquires and 6s. 8d. for gentlemen.[96] Fines imposed at the sessions of April, July, and October 1594 amounted to a total of £10 6s. 8d., including 3 at the higher rate and 25 at the lower.[97] In March 1608 7 men were each fined £1 for non-attendance at a private session, and ten years later 4 were fined similarly for non-attendance at quarter sessions, but in the 17th century such fines are rarely recorded, a fact which may well reflect the severity of the penalty.[98] It is impossible to reach a firm conclusion on the extent to which jury service was resented, although the frequency with which some men served could be taken to indicate their enthusiasm. Humphrey Page certainly felt that he was on familiar enough terms with the clerk of the peace to be able to ask him to suspend process until after he should have been able to speak to the clerk in person.[99]

The effect of the Civil War in Cheshire was to raise to the bench men who could previously not aspire to it, since many members of families traditionally active as justices were excluded by virtue of their political sympathies. It has been estimated that only 9 of the 30 justices who served between 1645 and 1659 were of families represented on the pre-war bench.[1] Four of the 30 had served as head constables.[2] Like the earlier justices they were frequently concerned in other tasks. Among 19 local justices named in the commission of the peace in the autumn of 1650, for example, 17 were among the commissioners for the parliamentary assessment of April 1649, and 15 among those named in the similar commission of June 1657.[3] Service on the many local committees appointed during and after the Civil War may indeed have taken up more time than that performed by the same men as justices of the peace.[4]

Quarter Sessions and County Administration

Between 1559, when continuous records begin, and 1660, the general sessions of the peace for Cheshire were with a single exception[5] held in five towns: Chester, Knutsford, Middlewich, Nantwich, and Northwich.[6] The table shows the location of each session. It is obvious that the justices made various attempts to establish acceptable patterns of rotation between the five towns, either in order to deal fairly with business from the different parts of the county in turn, or to reduce their own need to travel. Thus the

[94] Ches. R.O., Private Sess. File 10–44 Eliz. I no. 9.
[95] Ibid., Estreats File 2–44 Eliz. I no. iv.
[96] Ibid., QJB 1/2 f. 137.
[97] Ibid., Estreats File 1576–1600 no. 47.
[98] Ibid., QJB 2/4 f. 110v; 2/5 f. 9v; Morrill, *Ches. Grand Jury*, 16.
[99] Ches. R.O., QJF 55/1 no. 67.
[1] Morrill, *Ches. 1630–60*, 224.
[2] Ibid. 224–5.

[3] Chester R.O., P/Cowper [1956], vol. ii, facing f. 1; *Acts & Ords. of Interr.* ii. 31, 1063–4.
[4] Morrill, *Ches. 1630–60*, 225.
[5] A session held at Congleton in July 1561.
[6] The following paragraph and table are based on tables in 3 *Sheaf*, lviii, p. 30, and Higgins, 'Co. Govt. & Soc.', 262–3, corrected and supplemented by Ches. R.O. Quarter Sessions Order Bks. and Files.

LOCATION OF QUARTER SESSIONS 1559–1660

Meeting-places:

C	Chester	M	Middlewich
Co	Congleton	N	Nantwich
K	Knutsford	No	Northwich

Year	Ep.	East.	Mids.	Mich.	Year	Ep.	East.	Mids.	Mich.
1559	—	—	—	M	1610	C	K	N	M
1560	No	C	M	N	1611	C	K	N	K
1561	No	C	Co	N	1612	C	M	N	K
1562	No	C	M	N	1613	C	M	N	K
1563	No	C	M	N	1614	C	K	No	N
1564	No	C	M	N	1615	C	K	N	M
1565	No	C	M	N	1616	C	K	N	M
1566	No	C	M	N	1617	C	K	N	M
1567	No	C	M	N	1618	C	K	N	M
1568	No	C	M	N	1619	C	K	N	M
1569	No	C	M	N	1620	C	K	N	M
1570	No	C	M	N	1621	C	K	N	M
1571	No	C	M	N	1622	C	K	N	M
1572	No	C	M	N	1623	C	K	N	M
1573	No	C	M	N	1624	C	K	N	M
1574	No	C	M	N	1625	C	K	N	M
1575	K	C	M	N	1626	C	K	N	M
1576	No	C	M	N	1627	C	K	N	M
1577	K	C	M	N	1628	No	K	N	M
1578	K	C	M	C	1629	C	K	N	No
1579	K	C	C	C	1630	C	K	N	M
1580	No	C	C	C	1631	C	K	N	M
1581	K	C	C	C	1632	C	No	N	M
1582	K	C	C	C	1633	C	K	N	No
1583	K	C	C	C	1634	C	K	N	M
1584	K	C	C	C	1635	C	K	N	No
1585	K	C	C	C	1636	C	K	N	M
1586	K	C	C	C	1637	C	K	N	No
1587	K	N	C	N	1638	C	K	N	M
1588	No	N	C	C	1639	C	K	N	No
1589	K	C	C	N	1640	C	K	N	M
1590	C	N	K	N	1641	C	No	N	K
1591	No	C	N	No	1642	C	No	N	K
1592	C	N	C	No	1643	C	—	—	—
1593	C	N	C	N	1644	—	—	—	—
1594	No	N	C	N	1645	—	—	—	K
1595	C	N	C	N	1646	—	No	N	M
1596	C	N	C	N	1647	C	K	—	—
1597	C	No	C	N	1648	K	No	N	K
1598	K	N	C	N	1649	M	No	N	K
1599	C	N	C	N	1650	C	M	N	No
1600	No	N	C	N	1651	K	M	N	No
1601	C	No	N	N	1652	K	M	N	K[a]
1602	C	C	N	M	1653	—	K	N	K
1603	C	C	N	M	1654	C	M	N	K
1604	N	C	No	C	1655	No	M	N	K
1605	K	M	N	N	1656	C	M	N	K
1606	M	K	N	C	1657	C	M	N	K
1607	N	K	C	M	1658	C	M	N	K
1608	C	No	N	K	1659	C	M	N	K
1609	C	M	N	K	1660	—	—	—	K

[a] Adjourned to Northwich.

routine established in 1560 was only broken three times before the end of 1578, while from 1601 until the end of the period there were few exceptions to the rule that the Epiphany sessions should be held at Chester and the Midsummer sessions at Nantwich. Surviving records give no indication of the factors which lay behind the justices' decisions about the location of sessions, except when the Privy Council intervened in 1578. In May of that year the justices were ordered, except in times of sickness, to hold sessions only at Chester or Nantwich. The instruction was not carried out, since the earl of Leicester, as chamberlain of Chester, issued a further order that three sessions a year should be held at Chester, while the fourth should be at Knutsford or Northwich: the result may be seen in the location of sessions between Michaelmas 1578 and Epiphany 1587.[7]

Quarter sessions in Cheshire are usually said in the records to have lasted for one day only. On two occasions in the 1570s they were adjourned, and three of the sessions between July 1615 and July 1616 were said to have lasted for two days.[8] They were usually described as general sessions of the peace, although in July 1607, January 1614, and January 1616 the words 'and of gaol delivery' were later inserted into the headings in the Order Books.[9] No unusual features have, however, been noticed in the business recorded at those sessions.

A broken line of clerks of the peace is traceable from the establishment of the court and of deputy clerks from 1614.[10] An important part of the clerks' work was making and keeping the records, of which from the beginning of Elizabeth I's reign there is an unusual abundance in comparison with what exists for other counties at that time. From the first the records form continuous series, of which the most important are the sessions books and files. It was decided at an early date to preserve the formal records of each session in two distinct series of books. One contained brief entries of those indictments which resulted in the imposition of a fine: the name of the person indicted, the nature of the offence, pledges for the fine, and subsequent action taken were all noted, although the amount of the fine is not normally given. By the end of the 16th century the indictments at each session were supplemented by notes of the grand jury's presentments.[11] The second series of books originally contained notes of recognizances dealt with at each session. Administrative orders made by the court, which are occasionally mentioned briefly in the earliest indictment books, were by the 1590s being more fully and formally entered in the recognizance books; the latter also, from January 1627, give regular lists of head constables.[12]

From the early 1570s the sessions books are supplemented by sessions files.[13] Like those of other counties, the files, which until their restoration in the 1930s were kept in their original state as sessions rolls, contain documents of miscellaneous character, including writs of summons, jury panels, bills of indictment endorsed by the grand jury, examinations, recognizances taken before justices out of sessions, petitions, and letters to or from the bench. During the period the number of documents filed increased. The files for the year 1572–3 contain an average of 39 documents a session,[14] or 156 in all. Those for 1602–3 contain 336 documents, and those for 1622–3 589.[15] The effect of the outbreak of civil war is shown in a decline in the number of documents filed: there are 99 in the file for Easter 1642 and 132 in that for the Midsummer session, but

[7] *Acts of P.C.* 1577–8, 236; 3 *Sheaf*, lviii, p. 28.

[8] Ches. R.O., QJB. 2/3 ff. 43v, 103v; 2/4 ff. 164v, 176; 1/4 f. 133.

[9] Ibid., QJB 1/3 f. 239; 1/4 ff. 87, 123.

[10] The following account corrects *Ches. Q. S. Recs.* 23, 31–3. For clerks of the peace during the period see

E. Stephens (ed.), *Clerks of Counties 1360–1960*, supplemented by Ches. R.O. List of Clerks of the Peace.

[11] Ches. R.O., QJB 2/1–7.

[12] Ibid., QJB 1/1–6.

[13] Ibid., class QJF.

[14] Ibid., QJF 2/1–4.

[15] Ibid., QJF 31/1–4, 51/1–4.

the Michaelmas file contains only 37 documents and that of the following Epiphany session 52.[16] By the early 1650s business had once again increased, and the average of 150 documents filed at each session of the year 1652–3 represents a return to the level of activity of the early 1620s.[17] The file for July 1653 contains 333 documents.[18] Material to be filed was originally rolled up, with the outer wrapper containing notes of recognizances. The material on the wrapper for April 1619, for example, duplicates the entries in the recognizance and order book for that session.[19] Later the outer membrane became a mere wrapper, containing only the heading giving the date and place of the session, often ending with the word *coram*, indicating that it was written before the session opened and before the names of justices attending could be recorded.

Among other records surviving from the period may be mentioned private sessions files, which exist for the reigns of Elizabeth I and James I; indictment rolls, which cover the period from 1568 to 1578 and are fair copies of the bills found by the grand juries; and rolls of estreats, which survive from the whole of Elizabeth's reign.[20] In spite of the quantity of material available, however, there are some surprising deficiencies in the records. Few details are available of the justices' work in fixing wages. Indictments for felony and subsequent proceedings are also imperfectly recorded.

Judged from the headings to files and order books, a source not wholly reliable,[21] justices' attendance at quarter sessions varied widely. The sessions of the years 1577–80 were typical, in that attendance, averaging between 7 and 8 justices, varied in individual instances from 3 to twelve.[22] In the early 17th century sessions at Chester and at Nantwich tended to command the highest attendances.[23] It was rare for more than 15 justices to attend a session: such attendances are only recorded on 21 occasions between 1590 and 1640, or about a tenth of the total sessions. Unusually high attendances of more than 20 justices were recorded at Chester at Midsummer 1598, Easter 1603, and Midsummer 1607, and at Nantwich at Michaelmas 1605. Average attendance figures taken decade by decade show attendances of just under 9 justices during the 1590s, nearly 11 in the first decade of the 17th century, nearly 10 in the second, and over 10 in the 1620s, but from 1631 the average for the decade fell to less than eight. Since the order book for the 1650s has not survived, nothing can be said of the attendance of justices during that decade.

Attendance at quarter sessions was, of course, only one of the many duties imposed on justices of the peace. Stress has rightly been laid on their work out of sessions, as shown, for example, by the number of documents which they signed and which were subsequently filed.[24] Nevertheless it is obvious that if only small numbers of justices attended sessions it might be difficult to achieve consistency, especially in administrative projects which might require action over several months or even years. Thus in June 1631, after the receipt of the Book of Orders, it was decided that the house of correction at Northwich was too small and out of the way, and that two new ones should be built. Ten months later the bench decided that Northwich was, after all, the town nearest the centre of Cheshire, and that the old house of correction there should be retained. This might seem like mere vacillation, but an examination of the headings for each session shows that only Sir William Brereton was present at both: none of the other six justices at Nantwich in June 1631 joined him at the Easter session

---

[16] Ches. R.O., QJF 71/1–4.
[17] Ibid., QJF 80/1–3.
[18] Ibid., QJF 81/2.
[19] Ibid., QJB 1/5 ff. 1–6v; QJF 41/1, no. 87.
[20] Ibid., Private Sess. Files 1568–1602, 1605–19; Indictment Rolls, 1568–70, 1571–4, 1574–8; Estreats Files, 2–44 Eliz. I, 1560–75, 1576–1600. In 1976 none of

these recs. had Ches. R.O. call-numbers.
[21] e.g. Ches. R.O., Estreats File 1576–1600 ff. 47–47v, compared with QJB 1/3 ff. 4, 11.
[22] See above, n. 91.
[23] Higgins, 'Co. Govt. & Soc.', 262–3.
[24] Morrill, *Ches. 1630–60*, 16 and n. 2, 184.

'HUGH LUPUS'S HALL AND THE EXCHEQUER IN CHESTER CASTLE'
as rebuilt in the late 1570s

THE NEW COUNTY HALL, CHESTER, *c.* 1835
with a court in session

HUGH LUPUS GROSVENOR, 1ST DUKE OF WESTMINSTER (d. 1899)
M.P. for the City of Chester 1847–69, and Lord Lieutenant of Cheshire 1883–99

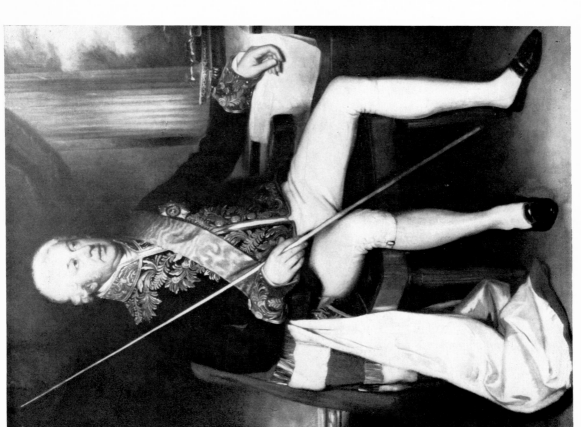

GEORGE JAMES CHOLMONDELEY, 1ST MARQUESS OF CHOLMONDELEY (d. 1827)
Lord Lieutenant of Cheshire 1770–83, and Chamberlain of Chester 1770–1827

of 1632 which was, unusually, held at Northwich. On that occasion Brereton was joined by only three justices.[25]

Little can be said of the justices' dealings at quarter sessions with the more serious criminal matters which came within their competence. No calendars of prisoners in Chester castle delivered at quarter sessions have survived for the 16th century. The first such record that has been found dates from the years 1603 and 1604, and consists of two calendars of prisoners written at the end of the book of recognizances and orders.[26] Later recognizance and order books also include *nomina prisonarum* with notes of action taken, but such entries are unusual. It appears, however, that Chester castle was delivered of prisoners by the justices if they held their Epiphany sessions there.[27] Whipping, branding, or the pillory were the usual punishments imposed.[28] In 1604 a woman was sentenced to be hanged for burglary after a pregnancy inquest.[29]

Cases recorded in the indictment books and supporting documents seem to be those for which a monetary punishment was imposed. Offences mentioned between October 1594 and January 1595, for example, included trespass, forcible entry, assault, cutting down oak trees and other wood, rescuing a mare which had been levied in distraint, profaning the Sabbath, enclosing a highway, diverting a water-course, erecting a cottage without licence, conducting an alehouse without licence, unlicensed trading as a badger or drover, and non-payment of money due for the relief of poor prisoners. Fines imposed varied from 6d. to £1.[30]

A long period could elapse between the indictment of an offender and his trial, and between the trial and the assessment of a suitable fine. The earliest estreat roll which has survived is headed 'Fines for the first year of Elizabeth I taxed in the second'.[31] Lists of those offenders to be fined were drawn up in rolls which each covered a year's sessions, and submitted to the justices for the assessment of the fines at the following session. The amounts of the fines were then entered on the rolls, and a second copy was made, presumably in addition to the copy which had to be sent to the national Exchequer. The estreats for the four sessions from July 1568 to April 1569 inclusive, for example, were signed by four justices who were present at the session of July 1569.[32] By comparison of the estreats with the indictment books and bills it can be seen that delays were accepted as inevitable. Many of those indicted were absent from the court at the time of their indictment, and had to be pursued by mesne process, the various stages in the execution of which might occupy altogether five sessions.[33] If appearance was not thus secured outlawry in the county court, which could take another five months, would follow. The result of such delays is shown in the roll of estreats for the year from April 1594 to January 1595. The roll was signed by six justices who were present at the session held in May 1595, which must have been the date when the fines were assessed. Those listed as liable to fines in April 1594, however, had been indicted at the session of May 1593; those listed at the October 1594 session had been indicted in May, July, and October of the previous year; and those listed at the session of January 1595 had been indicted at the sessions of October 1593 and the four sessions of 1594.[34]

The increase in the administrative powers and duties of the justices of the peace under the Tudors and early Stuarts is widely known.[35] The administrative activities

[25] Ches. R.O., QJB 1/5 ff. 283v, 286v–287, 303, 306v–307.
[26] Ibid., QJB 1/3 ff. 279v–280v.
[27] e.g. ibid., QJB 1/4 ff. 127, 153, 178.
[28] e.g. ibid., QJB 1/3 ff. 279v–280v; 1/5 ff. 87–8.
[29] Ibid., QJB 1/3 ff. 279v–280.
[30] Ibid., Estreats File 1576–1600 ff. 47–47v.

[31] Ibid., Estreats File 2–44 Eliz. I f. 1.
[32] Ibid., Estreats File 1560–75 ff. 12–14.
[33] Ibid., QJB 2/4 f. 98v, for an example of 1607–8.
[34] Ibid., Estreats File 1576–1600 ff. 47–47v; QJB 1/3 f. 19; 2/4 ff. 6–13v.
[35] For summaries see Esther Moir, *Justice of the Peace*, caps. 2 and 3; G. R. Elton, *The Tudor Constitution*, 454–5.

of the justices in Cheshire mirrored in most ways those of their contemporaries else-where.[36] Their clearest expression is to be found in the orders which the justices made in quarter sessions; such orders were fully and formally enrolled from the 1590s.[37] Earlier administrative orders were recorded informally in recognizance or indictment books.[38] Informal notes of orders continued to be made even after the 1590s, in the form of summaries written on the face of petitions submitted to the bench and filed among the sessions documents; the practice was in 1604 recorded in the order book, and in the 1650s, when no order book has survived, it is the only means of identifying action taken by the justices.[39]

As in other counties the action taken by the justices was founded partly on statute law but also on orders made by the Privy Council and by the judges at the court of Great Sessions. Orders from the Privy Council were preserved on the sessions files.[40] No copy of the Book of Orders of 1631 has been found among the Cheshire records, but it was mentioned in June of that year in connexion with orders about the house of correction and the appointment of provost-marshals.[41] The court of Great Sessions often issued administrative directions to the justices. In 1606, for example, the judges ordered the justices to repair the road between Warrington bridge and Wilderspool; in 1616 they issued a general order that individual hundreds should be responsible for the repair of decayed bridges; in 1638 they required the suppression of superfluous alehouses in Bunbury; and in 1652 they referred petitions about bridges in disrepair to the justices.[42] The chamberlain and his deputy could join the judges in issuing adminis-trative directions.[43]

Much of the justices' work in quarter sessions was concerned with the problems of individuals. Decisions had to be taken on such matters as the issue of licences to brew and sell ale, to act as badgers, maltsters, or drovers, and to erect cottages; the maintenance of bastard children; and the claims of maimed soldiers for pensions. Such action was sometimes taken after recommendations from local justices. In 1572 three justices from Wirral hundred submitted to quarter sessions the names of persons whom they considered fit to conduct alehouses; in 1629 Sir Richard Grosvenor recommended a maimed soldier to the consideration of the bench for a pension.[44] Most often, however, action followed the submission of a petition to the justices. Petitions reached the bench in such numbers that in 1622, because some of them appeared to be 'of no moment nor fitting to be heard in the sessions', it was decided that before being heard they must be accepted as worthy by (presumably local) justices.[45] Large numbers of petitions con-tinued to be submitted, and others were referred to the justices by the judges of Great Sessions and by the lord lieutenant.[46]

Where the problems of the county, as distinct from those of an individual or a small group, were to be dealt with, the justices were often less certain in their actions. The Privy Council's orders were not always quickly carried out. In 1605 the Council complained about the justices' negligence in organizing relief for victims of plague in Chester.[47] Five years later the justices were said to have disregarded orders for the suppression of superfluous alehouses.[48]

---

[36] More detailed surveys of individual admin. activities will be found in Marriott, 'Com. of Peace', 115–22; Higgins, 'Co. Govt. & Soc.', cap. 3; Morrill, *Ches. 1630–60*, *passim*. Selections drawn from the sess. files, illustra-tive of admin. work of Ches. justices of the period, are in *Ches. Q.S. Rec.* 36–169.

[37] Ches. R.O., QJB 1/3 *passim*.

[38] e.g. ibid., QJB 1/1 ff. 17, 45v; 2/3 ff. 148v, 157.

[39] Ibid., QJB 1/3 f. 165; *Ches. Q.S. Rec.* 141–68.

[40] e.g. *Ches. Q.S. Rec.* 46–7, 53–4, 65, 66–7.

[41] Ches. R.O., QJB 1/5 ff. 286–286v.

[42] *Ches. Q.S. Rec.* 57, 93–5, 160; Ches. R.O., QJB 1/4 f. 144.

[43] *Ches. Q.S. Rec.* 79.

[44] Ibid. 37–9, 82–3.

[45] Ches. R.O., QJB 1/5 f. 72.

[46] e.g. *Ches. Q.S. Rec.* 67–8, 84–5, 131.

[47] Ibid. 53–4.

[48] Ches. R.O., QJF 38/4 no. 3.

If action affecting the whole county needed to be taken, a preliminary survey might be needed; such surveys were taken from time to time during the period, using the hundred as a basis. For example, between the end of November 1609 and the middle of January 1610 small groups of justices met in each hundred to draw up lists of those who were presented for selling ale without licence. Presentments were made by each township: thus in Eddisbury hundred 99 illegal alehouses were presented from a total of 31 townships. In several of the townships the person making the presentment included himself among those breaking the law, as did Ralph Bryne of Tarvin and Richard Trafford of Bridge Trafford.[49] A more ambitious project was the survey of bridges throughout Cheshire made between 1618 and 1621.[50]

The justices' difficulty in framing and following a consistent policy is shown by their attempts to provide an adequate house of correction. The first record of an order for the erection of a county house of correction is in a note in the indictment book for 1593.[51] Further orders in 1611 provided for the conversion of a tithe barn in Altrincham, and rules for its supervision were drawn up.[52] Nevertheless within three years a new decision was taken: 600 marks was to be raised for building two new houses of correction, one for Bucklow, Macclesfield, and Northwich hundreds and the other for the remaining four.[53] The text of the order refers to a previous one, apparently unrecorded, for the building of a single house; but after three months yet another order for a single house of correction, to be built at Northwich, was entered.[54] By January 1615 the house had been built, at a cost of 300 marks, and a governor had been appointed.[55] It ran into difficulties within five years: the governor's sureties defaulted, and the owner of the land on which the house was built was complaining about the non-payment of rent due to him.[56] Early in 1623 the house was said to be in decay, and the implements and tools there to have been lost.[57] There had meanwhile been several changes of master, and yet another followed in 1624 after petitions had been addressed to the justices complaining of the master's misbehaviour.[58] The Book of Orders of 1631 caused the bench to reconsider the provision of the house of correction: Northwich, they decided, was too remote from some parts of Cheshire, and it would be preferable to have two houses, one at or near Chester castle, and the other at Knutsford. The governors should have £25 each a year instead of the £10 allowed to the master at Northwich.[59] At the following session a third house was proposed at Tarvin.[60] Nevertheless after six months the justices decided that Northwich was as convenient a site as any, and that the house there should continue, with the master's payment raised from £10 to £25 a year.[61] For the next five years nothing is heard of the house of correction, but in 1637 the master, who was then said to have allowed prisoners to escape and to have been negligent in imposing punishments, was dismissed.[62] Between 1638 and 1641 a new house of correction was built at Middlewich.[63] During the Civil War it was occupied by squatters.[64]

Such problems as those of the house of correction could arise from several factors. Changes in the commission of the peace, and the varying diligence of individual justices in attending quarter sessions, could lead to vacillations in administrative policy. Further difficulties were caused by the division of administration between county,

[49] Ibid., QJF 38/4 nos. 101–11.
[50] Chester R.O., CR63/2/692 ff. 38–47.
[51] Ches. R.O., QJB 2/3 f. 148v.
[52] Ibid., QJB 1/4 ff. 43v, 47v–48, 49v–50v.
[53] Ibid., f. 97.
[54] Ibid., f. 104v.
[55] Ibid., f. 108.
[56] Ches. R.O., QJB 1/5 ff. 42v, 70v; QJF 51/1 no. 118.
[57] Ibid. QJB 1/5 ff. 86v–87v.
[58] Ibid., ff. 121v, 127–127v.
[59] Ibid., ff. 286–286v.
[60] Ibid., f. 294.
[61] Ibid., ff. 306v–307.
[62] Ibid., f. 461.
[63] Ibid., ff. 488–488v; QJB 1/6 ff. 14v, 22v, 53.
[64] Morrill, *Ches. 1630–60*, 93.

hundred, parish, and township, by the heavy reliance placed on unpaid local officials, and by the difficulty of raising money both for ordinary and for extraordinary expenditure.

No attempt was made in the commissions of the peace to provide a sufficient number of justices for each hundred. In 1559, for example, of the 31 justices who were resident in the county, 8 were from Broxton, 6 each from Bucklow and Macclesfield, 4 from Wirral, 3 from Eddisbury, and only 2 each from Nantwich and Northwich.[65] In 1605 the distribution was different but no more even: 10 of the 47 justices named were from Bucklow, 8 each from Nantwich and Macclesfield, 7 from Eddisbury, 5 each from Broxton and Wirral, and 4 from Northwich.[66] Whether or not individual justices were of the quorum might be another problem. In 1572 three Wirral justices discovered that they had exceeded their powers by taking recognizances from alehouse-keepers, since none of them was of the quorum, and in the same year Ralph Done wrote to ask Sir Hugh Cholmondeley to join himself and Richard Hurleston in granting a writ of restitution 'since there is none of the quorum near but you'.[67] The only instance of a justice's residence being taken into account at the time of his appointment seems to be that of Edward Warren in 1634.[68]

The justices fulfilled their obligation to supplement general sessions of the peace with regular hundred meetings. The justices who wrote to quarter sessions from Wirral in 1572 mentioned their frequent practice of calling 'the country' before them 'for reformation of disorders and abuses'.[69] Monthly meetings in the hundreds are mentioned in 1603 and 1630, and the Book of Orders in requiring justices to hold such meetings was thus formalizing a practice already well-established in Cheshire.[70] In 1659 one of the head constables of Macclesfield hundred declared that he had nothing to present to the grand jury at quarter sessions 'in regard that the honourable justices of the peace within the said hundred do keep their usual month's meetings, before whom offenders are presented and punished, so that I have no more but that I am your humble servant'.[71]

Each of the seven Cheshire hundreds was in two divisions, with a head constable in charge of each. The head constables were drawn from the same ranks of the gentry as those which provided the grand juries. Methods of election and length of service varied between hundreds, although the head constables were under the general supervision of quarter sessions: changes were usually recorded in the order books, and from 1627 head constables were regularly listed there.[72] Early in 1642 it was decided that they should remain in office for only one year, but the disruption caused by the Civil War frustrated the decision.[73] The justices tried to ensure that head constables carried out their duties adequately: in 1641, for example, they ordered the constables to ride through their divisions at least once a week to seek out rogues and vagabonds.[74] Non-attendance at quarter sessions could lead to the imposition of a fine on the defaulting constable, as in 1594 when four of them were fined.[75] Complaints arose most frequently over the failure of the constables to levy or to pay in sums of money with which they were charged. In January 1605 two meetings were arranged at which present and former head constables were to present their accounts of receipts for the previous three years, but six months later seven of them had still failed to render accounts, and they were threatened with imprisonment.[76] In 1609 the clerk of the peace, who was an attorney at

[65] Marriott, 'Com. of Peace', 108.
[66] Ches. R.O., QJB 1/3 f. 279.
[67] Ches. Q.S. Rec. 37–8; Ches. R.O., QJF 2/1 no. 3.
[68] Morrill, Ches. 1630–60, 6.
[69] Ches. Q.S. Rec. 37.
[70] Ibid. 51; Ches. R.O., QJB 2/5 f. 148v.
[71] Ches. R.O., QJF 87/1 no. 10.

[72] Morrill, Ches. Grand Jury, 59–60; Ches. R.O., QJB 1/5 ff. 174–174v.
[73] Ches. R.O., QJB 1/6 ff. 62v, 78.
[74] Ibid., f. 46.
[75] Ches. R.O., Estreats File 1576–1600, f. 47.
[76] Ibid., QJB 1/3 ff. 191, 202v–203.

the Chester Exchequer, was ordered to begin a suit there against those head constables who were in arrears.[77] The building of the new house of correction at Middlewich was said in 1640 and 1641 to be hampered by the failure of the head constables to gather the money allotted to it, and defaulters were again threatened with imprisonment.[78] In 1649 the head constables of Broxton, Macclesfield, Nantwich, and Wirral hundreds were alleged to have paid little or nothing towards a rate imposed six months earlier for bridge repairs: each was to be fined.[79] In 1650 the bench tried to solve the problem by insisting that no head constable should be discharged from office until his accounts should have been rendered, any election of a successor notwithstanding.[80] The head constables in turn complained that their failures were not the result of their own negligence. In 1649 one of those for Macclesfield hundred complained that the church-wardens would not pay their allotted sums for the relief of maimed soldiers, and the justices fined every churchwarden and ordered petty constables to collect the arrears due.[81]

The size and nature of the Cheshire parishes imposed further difficulties in local administration. Parishes in Cheshire could consist of thirty or more townships, dispersed over a wide area.[82] Between 1599 and 1601 quarter sessions were called on to discuss the question of those townships in the county which had to pay money for poor relief to parishes in Chester.[83] By 1640 it had become usual in large parishes for each township to maintain its own poor, but doubts as to the legality of the practice were expressed.[84] A further problem might then arise over the definition of a township. In 1639 Edward Warren asked the bench whether it might be possible for the three hamlets which together constituted Poynton township in Prestbury parish to be charged separately for poor relief. The request was referred to the justices for Macclesfield hundred, but the outcome is unknown.[85]

Although Cheshire was after 1540 subject to Parliamentary taxation, and although subsidies there were assessed on the same basis as those elsewhere, the ancient mize assessments on each township, which had been fixed at least as early as the 14th century, became the normal basis of assessment for county rates. In 1567 the payment of a year's mize was ordered for the repair of all county bridges.[86] The mize was used as the assessment rate for the money provided for plague relief, payments made from 1619 to the captain-trainer of the Cheshire trained bands, and the construction of a new house of correction.[87] Such expenditure, however, was extraordinary. Ordinary annual expenditure in Cheshire included sums raised for the relief of maimed soldiers and of prisoners in the King's Bench and Marshalsea prisons and in Chester castle, and a composition for 25 oxen a year. In the early 1620s the amounts levied for maimed soldiers (£38 15s. 8d.) and for the King's Bench, Marshalsea, and the master of the house of correction (£15 12s.) were levied by head constables as a mize of 2s. 9d. in the pound, and paid to the two elected county treasurers in quarterly instalments.[88] Money raised for the relief of prisoners in Chester castle formed the basis of a separate mize rate of 1s. 9d. in the pound, which brought in over £25 a year. The rates were consolidated before July 1632, when they were all raised by a quarter.[89] Although the mize itself was based on assessment by townships, the new lists drawn up were arranged by parishes, which

---

[77] Ibid., f. 271.
[78] Ches. R.O., QJB 1/6 ff. 23, 30v–31.
[79] Ibid., f. 210.
[80] Ibid., ff. 253v–254.
[81] Ibid., ff. 209–209v.
[82] See table in Dorothy Sylvester, 'Parish and Township in Ches. and NE. Wales', *J.C.A.S.* [N.S.], liv. 29.
[83] Ches. R.O., QJB 1/3 ff. 72, 84, 94.

[84] *Ches. Q.S. Rec.* 98–9.
[85] Ibid. 97–8.
[86] Ches. R.O., QJB 1/1 f. 97.
[87] Ibid., QJB 1/5 ff. 17, 488–488v; *Ches. Q.S. Rec.* 52, 54, 56.
[88] Chester R.O., CR63/2/692 ff. 145–6.
[89] Ibid., f. 148.

were listed according to the head constables' divisions. A further increase of a quarter in the rates was authorized in April 1642.[90] During the Civil War payment of maimed soldiers' pensions lapsed. In 1648 the justices in response to a parliamentary ordinance ordered the election of treasurers for each hundred and a levy of three times the former amount; the order was, however, quickly rescinded.[91] The election of county treasurers is first recorded in 1593, when 'the two ancient justices of peace as they are placed in Her Majesty's commission' were chosen to act as treasurers for the money raised for the relief of maimed soldiers.[92] From 1620 they were given the additional responsibility of collecting and distributing money raised for 'charitable uses'.[93]

By the early 1650s the eccentricities of the mize were causing concern. It had been used not only as the basis of assessment of county rates, but also as that of Ship Money during the 1630s and weekly and monthly parliamentary assessments after the Civil War.[94] In July 1651 the rector of Burton in Wirral complained that his parish, with only two townships, was assessed for prisoners and maimed soldiers at three times the rate of Neston, which had eight. The inhabitants of Baddiley showed that their assessment for prisoners and maimed soldiers, compared with those of Audlem and Marbury parishes, bore no relation to the 'old rents'.[95] Nevertheless the mize was to remain the basis of assessment for local taxation for more than another century, and much time was taken up in devising tables to enable its incidence to be calculated: an example has been preserved from the early 1650s, compiled by one William Hankinson and prefaced by some verses entitled *A Remonstrance of the Mize*.[96]

The Lieutenancy

For most of the period the lieutenancy of both Lancashire and Cheshire was held by the earls of Derby.[97] Earl Edward (d. 1572) was made lieutenant of Lancashire in 1551, and two years later his commission was renewed for Lancashire, Cheshire, Flintshire, and Denbighshire. In 1557 and 1559 the earl again acted as lieutenant in Lancashire and Cheshire. He received another commission from 1569 to 1570, and his son and successor Henry (d. 1593) was commissioned from 1585. Disputes within the Stanley family are said to have lain behind the failure of William, earl of Derby (d. 1642), to obtain the lieutenancy until 1607: from 1593 to that year it was in commission, under the control of the sheriff and a number of local gentlemen.[98] In 1607 Earl William was created lieutenant, and his son James, Lord Strange, was associated with him in the office from 1626.[99]

The Stanleys were a Lancashire rather than a Cheshire family, and their absence from Cheshire enhanced the role of their deputies. The latter were drawn from the leading ranks of Cheshire society, and were otherwise prominent as members of the commission of the peace. Sir John Savage and Sir Hugh Cholmondeley, for example, occur as deputy-lieutenants in 1569 and as commissioners of musters ten years later. Sir George Booth occurs as a deputy-lieutenant from 1619, and Robert Cholmondeley, Sir Thomas Savage, and Richard Wilbraham occur from 1625.[1]

In 1578 there were 356 knights, esquires, gentlemen, and freeholders in Cheshire charged with providing horses and armour; at about the same time there were just

[90] Ches. R.O., QJB 1/6 ff. 70v–72.
[91] Ibid., ff. 168v–169, 183v, 195v.
[92] Ches. R.O., QJF 23/2 no. 64v; for names of justices elected from 1593 to 1624 see QJB 1/5 ff. 115v–116.
[93] Ibid., QJB 1/5 f. 37v.
[94] Morrill, *Ches. 1630–60*, 28, 97 et seqq.
[95] Ches. R.O., QJF 79/2 nos. 129, 141.
[96] Ches. R.O., DAR/I/17.
[97] For much of what follows see *T.H.S.L.C.* cxix. 39–64.
[98] Higgins, 'Co. Govt. & Soc.' 121–2.
[99] *Cal. S.P. Dom.* 1625–6, 438, 461.
[1] *T.H.S.L.C.* cxix. 44–5.

over two thousand able-bodied but unarmed men able to serve in the county.[2] As in the Middle Ages, Cheshire was a recruiting ground for soldiers, and about a thousand are said to have been impressed, mostly for service in Ireland, between 1585 and 1602.[3] In 1595, of a total of 4,000 able-bodied men in Cheshire aged between 16 and 60, 1,100 were arrayed in bands. The nucleus of this force consisted of 600 trained foot-soldiers arranged in 6 bands corresponding to 6 of the 7 hundreds of Cheshire. Eddisbury hundred had no band of its own, but supplied men to its neighbours. The remainder were untrained men. There were also 500 pioneers, and the county's quota of horsemen was said to be 89, although there was a deficiency of eighteen.[4] In 1628 there were again said to be 1,100 armed soldiers in the county; the number of pioneers had fallen to 113, and there were 68 horsemen.[5] The cost of training men, and of recruitment for overseas service, was said to amount to over £2,400 in the decade from 1586 to 1596.[6]

Musters in Cheshire were notoriously inadequate until the 1620s.[7] A temporary improvement in the quality and training of soldiers followed the accession of Charles I; the professional soldiers sent by the Privy Council in 1626 to train the bands were afterwards retained by the deputy-lieutenants at their own charge, and companies of foot were maintained at full strength, with the aged and impotent removed.[8] The number of horsemen was, however, never brought up to the standard required, and the improvements of the late 1620s were not maintained during the next decade.[9]

[2] *List of Freeholders in Ches. in 1578*, 3–24; *Cal. S.P. Dom. 1547–80*, 469.

[3] Higgins, 'Co. Govt. & Soc.' 130.

[4] Ches. R.O., DDX 358/1 ff. 1, 11v.

[5] Chester R.O., CR63/2/6 f. 42.

[6] Ches. R.O., DDX 358/1 f. 40.

[7] *Cal. S.P. Dom. 1581–90*, 14; *1619–23*, 33. Cf. L. Boynton, *The Elizabethan Militia*, 24–5.

[8] Higgins, 'Co. Govt. & Soc.' 153; Morrill, *Ches. 1630–60*, 26.

[9] Higgins, 'Co. Govt. & Soc.', cap. 4.

THE PALATINATE 1660–1830

The Court of Great Sessions, p. 56. The Exchequer of Chester, p. 57. The Abolition of the Palatine Institutions, p. 59.

The Court of Great Sessions

CONTEMPORARIES regarded the Chester court of Great Sessions as the equivalent of the assizes in other counties. The term 'assizes' was used to describe the court both by lawyers and by laymen.[1] With regard to pleas of the Crown it certainly resembled the Crown side of an ordinary assize court, a fact which probably explains the loose use of the term.[2] In civil actions its competence, in causes arising within Cheshire, paralleled that of the courts at Westminster, whose practice it took as its model unless varied by special rule of the Chester court.[3] In the late 17th century it was claimed that certain real actions were subject to much longer delays at Chester than at Westminster, partly because the court of Great Sessions sat only twice each year, and then briefly, and also because defendants who lived outside the county could force the preliminary stages of such actions into interminable delays.[4] Nevertheless it remained, until its abolition, popular for perfecting conveyances through fines and recoveries. In 1767, for example, 61 fines were levied and 34 recoveries suffered at the two Chester sessions.[5] It has been claimed that in the 1680s the civil work was as 'considerable' as the criminal, and a bitter complaint was made in the House of Commons about Judge Jeffreys, who had only held one session in 1680 and had then left a number of actions untried, to the great inconvenience of the parties.[6]

The chief justice determined when each session should be held.[7] Normally spring sessions were held in March or April and autumn sessions in September or October.[8] They were held at Chester, except in 1716, when it was decided, apparently because of the many Jacobite prisoners in Chester castle, to hold them at Nantwich.[9] Sessions were attended by elaborate ceremonial, involving the county sheriff in much expense.[10] In 1745 an association was formed to provide financial relief to sheriffs, particularly in assize weeks: its first rule was that the sheriff was not then to entertain or treat jurors or others. Subscribers were if possible to dine and sup with the sheriff at their own expense 'to prevent any sheriff being neglected or wanting company at the assizes'. During the scheme's currency, from 1745 to 1778, more than two hundred subscribed to it. The entrance fee was £10 and the annual subscription two guineas.[11] The opening of sessions of the court was preceded by a service in Chester cathedral; sermons preached on those occasions were sometimes published.[12] The session itself was an excuse for a social gathering of the leading Cheshire gentry. In March 1748 Sir Richard Brooke, foreman of the grand jury, declared that 'there is no bill of any sort brought before this jury, nor any business of any kind whatever, save eat, drink, smoke, and be

---

[1] J. Faulkner, jun., *Practice of Ct. of Session for Co. Chest.*, 2, 3, etc.; J. Hall, *Hist. Nantwich*, 205, 213–16.

[2] Proceedings of the Crown side of the court are noted in the Crown books, Chester 21/5, 21/7, and 21/8. The gap between 10 Anne and 31 Geo. II is partly filled by a Crown book now in Chester R.O., CR63/2/13.

[3] Faulkner, *Practice*, 1.

[4] G. Booth, *Nature and Practice of Real Actions* (2nd edn., 1811), 159, 160–3.

[5] Listed in 3 *Sheaf*, xii, pp. 74–90.

[6] G. W. Keeton, *Lord Chancellor Jeffreys and the Stuart Cause*, 156, 159.

[7] Faulkner, *Practice*, 69.

[8] *P.R.O. Lists & Indexes No. IV*, 88–91.

[9] Hall, *Hist. Nantwich*, 215.

[10] Ibid. 214–15.

[11] 1 *Sheaf*, i, pp. 218–19. The order of procession for the assizes of Aug. 1831 is described ibid. ii, p. 68.

[12] e.g. in 1784: ibid. i, pp. 160–1.

jolly'. In the autumn session of 1751 the grand jurors spent £25 on food and drink at the Ship tavern, and in April 1753 'an exceeding good dinner' was had at the Yacht.[13] In such respects the Chester sessions resembled the assizes of other counties in England.

The office of chief justice of Chester was apparently desirable both in its own right and as a rung on the ladder of judicial promotion. Sir Job Charlton is said to have been extremely reluctant to give it up in Judge Jeffreys's favour in 1680.[14] In 1702 the chief justice refused to send in his patent for renewal, lest the renewal be refused, and towards the end of the 18th century John Morton successfully resisted suggestions that he should resign.[15] The posts of chief justice and of puisne or 'other' justice could be given as political rewards, as in 1680 when Jeffreys was appointed and in 1689 when Sir John Trenchard and Littleton Powys became respectively chief and 'other' justice; both had been prominent opponents of James II.[16] The chief justiceship was described after its abolition as 'a prize for ratting' and 'a trap . . . baited with Cheshire cheese', and, more recently, as 'a sure stepping-stone for promotion to the English Bench'.[17] Of the 29 men who held it between 1660 and 1829, 9 died in office, but of the remainder 7 became masters of the Rolls, 6 chief justices of the Common Pleas, 3 chief justices of the King's Bench, and 2 chief barons of the Exchequer; Jeffreys and J. S. Copley (later Lord Lyndhurst) became Lord Chancellors.[18] The average length of each chief justice's term of office was just under 6 years. Of the 'other' justices, 2 were promoted to the chief justiceship, as was the last holder of the office, in effect, since he acted alone after the death of the last chief justice in 1829; 9 died in office. None of the others reached high judicial office, although 2 became barons of the Exchequer and a third was made a justice first of the King's Bench and later of the Common Pleas.[19] Twenty men served as 'other' justices between 1660 and 1830.

After the Restoration the court of Great Sessions continued to supervise some branches of county administration. Presentments were made to it, as to the quarter sessions, concerning the failure of townships to repair their highways. In April 1714 two individuals and the inhabitants of nine townships were so presented.[20] In 1686 the court imposed a fine of £500 on the county for its failure to repair part of the Chester–Nantwich road.[21] County buildings also came within its purview. In 1766 the grand jury drew attention to the inconvenience of the prothonotary's room in Chester castle, where the county records were kept.[22] In 1784 it presented the gaol at Chester castle as out of repair and insufficient.[23] A table of fees to be taken by clerks of the justices of the peace, settled at quarter sessions in 1809, was submitted to the Court of Great Sessions for its approval.[24] The judges also apparently had the power to confirm royal charters: the charter of 1568, which affirmed the exemption of the citizens of Nantwich from service on juries which concerned matters not arising within the town's limits, was confirmed several times by the judges.[25]

The Exchequer of Chester

In the late 17th and earlier 18th century the Exchequer's position as a local court of equity seemed strong. In a manual of its practice, compiled c. 1740, an anonymous

[13] Ibid. ii, p. 4.
[14] Keeton, *Jeffreys*, 149–52.
[15] W. R. Williams, *Gt. Sess.* 25–6.
[16] Keeton, *Jeffreys*, 148; Williams, *Gt. Sess.* 43–4, 62–3.
[17] Williams, *Gt. Sess.* 29.
[18] Ibid. 38–55.
[19] Ibid. 56–69.

[20] Chester R.O., CR63/2/13 ff. 2v–3.
[21] Ches. R.O., QJB 3/4 ff. 53, 54v–55v.
[22] Ibid., QJF 194/4 no. 39.
[23] Ibid., QA/Gaol & Co. Hall at Chest. 1 p. 1.
[24] Ibid., table of clerks' fees, 1809.
[25] Hall, *Hist. Nantwich*, 79, 206, 216.

author wrote of 'the great regard and extraordinary care which courts of equity have in their decrees: here is no hasty determination made with a haughty arbitrary air, but done with the greatest deliberation after the fullest information, and conscience is the judge'.[26] Nevertheless, as the author admitted, there were difficulties. Much of the court's business concerned the settlement of small debt claims through the process of common bill and confession. As an alternative to an action of debt at common law, a plaintiff would allege that the bond or note embodying the debt had been lost, and thus the action was brought within the purview of a court of equity. The process was both quick and effective, but the author of the manual claimed that it was 'illegal and of dangerous consequence, as it introduces a method of determining property in an arbitrary manner and without the interposition of a jury'; normally such actions were settled by the mere order of the baron or of his deputy. Apparently the vice-chamberlain had wished to abolish the practice, but was prevented from doing so by the fact that then 'the business of the court would be so small that probably no attorney of reputation would attend, and so the court become contemptible'.[27] In fact the court quickly lost favour at the end of the 18th century. Its records, abundant until the early part of George III's reign, become meagre thereafter.[28] In 1816 it was described as 'completely superannuated'; the deputy baron confessed his ignorance of its procedure, and of the two clerks then in attendance, one was said to be too sick to deal with important business, the other 'almost childish'.[29] In 1822 John Faulkner published a manual of its practice, based largely on that written some eighty years earlier, 'which, if the business of that court should be revived, may, it is hoped, be useful'.[30]

Whereas the chief and 'other' justice of Chester normally attended the court of Great Sessions in person, the offices in the Exchequer were usually performed by deputy. The chamberlainship was, after the Restoration, entirely honorific, being held by the earls of Derby from 1660 to 1736 (except from 1672 to 1677), by the third and fourth earls of Cholmondeley (1736–1827), and by the earl of Stamford and Warrington from 1827 until its abolition.[31] Sessions were usually held twice a year by the vice-chamberlain.[32] At other times business was managed by the clerk or baron of the Exchequer, who could himself act by deputy.[33]

The baron of the Exchequer, or his deputy, was also responsible for the other aspect of the Exchequer's functions, as the office from which writs and letters patent of the palatinate were issued. Original writs initiating actions in the court of session were obtained from it.[34] The diplomatic of the issue of letters patent concerning palatinate offices in the period has not been thoroughly examined, but it appears that those relating to officers of the court of Great Sessions were issued by the Chancery of England, while Exchequer officials and the sheriffs of Cheshire received their patents from the Chester Exchequer.[35] The Exchequer enrolments, especially after the beginning of the 18th century, contain little other than records of appointments, together with a few enrolments of deeds and pleas, and records of the admission of attorneys at the Exchequer.[36] There are fourteen rolls for the reign of Charles II, but only four thereafter.[37]

[26] Ches. R.O., DDX/15 p. 174.
[27] Ibid. pp. 151–2. For commentary on the process see Jones, 'Exchequer of Chest. in last years of Eliz. I', 145–6.
[28] P.R.O. Lists & Indexes No. XL, 5–11.
[29] 3 Sheaf, lvii, p. 42.
[30] Faulkner, Practice, pp. vi, 75–118.
[31] Williams, Gt. Sess. 73–4.
[32] Ibid. 75–7; Ches. R.O., DDX/15 p. 149.
[33] Ches. R.O., DDX/15 pp. 149–50.

[34] Faulkner, Practice, 55, 57, 62, 76; judicial writs were made out by the prothonotary: ibid. 5–6, 25, 30.
[35] For examples, see Ches, R.O., DDX/24/18 (appointment of John Lloyd as prothonotary and clerk of the Crown, 1822), DAR/C/83 (appointment of John Arden as sheriff, 1790).
[36] e.g. 39 D.K.R. 35, 99, 117, 257, 261, 282.
[37] P.R.O. Lists & Indexes No. XL, 3.

The Abolition of the Palatine Institutions

Both the Court of Session and the Chester Exchequer were abolished by an Act of 1830 which took effect that October.[38] Reform of the Welsh courts of Great Sessions, with which the Chester court was associated, had been discussed for some thirty years.[39] The proposal to abolish the Chester courts was opposed both by the county and by the city of Chester, and petitions were drawn up against it.[40] The county justices of the peace authorized a printed statement which pointed out the convenience with which suits could be initiated and brought to trial at Chester. It was claimed that 'the principles and practice of the palatinate courts have not been understood by the parties recommending their abolition, but have been confounded with the judicature of Wales, from which they are and always have been totally distinct'. The point was pertinent with regard to the Chester Exchequer, but more dubious with regard to the court of Great Sessions, whose judges had since 1542 been responsible for the administration of justice in Flintshire, Denbighshire, and Montgomeryshire as well as in Cheshire. A contrast was drawn between the proposed abolition of the Chester courts and the retention of similar institutions in Lancaster and Durham. It is, however, difficult to see how the court of Great Sessions could have been retained after the abolition of the Great Sessions of Wales. The Exchequer might have presented a special case for retention; its advantages were argued in an open letter from the vice-chamberlain, R. G. C. Fane, to the attorney-general. Fane pointed out that the recent Common Law Commission had been incompetent to report on such courts of equity as the Exchequer, and proposed reforms which, he claimed, would 'render it more extensively useful'. Nevertheless, he had to admit that 'of late years the business of the court of Exchequer has been very trifling', and it might have been argued that, having held the vice-chamberlainship for some six years, Fane had hitherto done little to bring about the improvements which he now advocated.

Shortly after the abolition of the courts Joseph Hemingway described the Act as 'obnoxious' and 'an ungracious proceeding'; he believed that it would harm both the legal profession in Chester and the inhabitants of the county.[41] The description was exaggerated, reflecting hurt local pride rather than a realistic view of the situation. Chester remained an assize town, being part of a circuit which until 1876 included all Wales.[42] Although Hemingway had alleged that 'serious delays and expenses will be imposed in the collection of debts', there remained in the county some ten courts where small debts could be recovered, including the sheriff's county court at Chester and various hundred and town courts.[43] They in turn were replaced by the new county courts set up after 1846. In 1882 the county was served by county courts at Chester, Altrincham, Birkenhead, Congleton, Crewe, Hyde, Macclesfield, Nantwich, Northwich, Runcorn, Sandbach, and Stockport, and it was then said that they had largely replaced the many manorial courts which had still functioned early in the 19th century.[44]

A bizarre and unforseen result of the abolition of the Court of Session concerned the execution of condemned criminals.[45] Until 1830 felons condemned at the court were handed over to the sheriffs of the city of Chester rather than to the county sheriff for execution. Executions took place originally at Boughton in the eastern suburbs of the

[38] 11 Geo. IV & 1 Wm. IV, c. 70. For the background see Williams, *Gt. Sess.* 26–7; Holdsworth, *Hist. Eng. Law,* i. 131.

[39] Williams, *Gt. Sess.* 26–7.

[40] What follows is based on the contents of an unlisted box of documents labelled 'abolition of palatine jurisdiction' at Ches. R.O.

[41] J. Hemingway, *Hist. Chest.* ii. 181 n.

[42] *Guide to Contents of P.R.O.* i. 127.

[43] Holdsworth, *Hist. Eng. Law,* i. 680.

[44] Ormerod, *Hist. Ches.* i, p. xx and n. In 1962 there were county courts at all those places except Nantwich and Sandbach: *Law List* (1962), 37–8.

[45] This paragraph is based on R. Stewart-Brown, 'Execution of Criminals in Ches.', *J.C.A.S.* N.S. xxii 91–116.

city, and afterwards at the city gaol.[46] In 1834 the city sheriffs claimed that the abolition of the palatine jurisdiction had relieved them of their obligation to execute county criminals. The county sheriff in turn denied responsibility, and for more than three months the execution of two condemned felons was delayed while a solution was sought. With nothing decided, the felons were eventually removed from Chester castle by *habeas corpus* and hanged in London. In 1835 statutory provision was made for execution, as before, by the city sheriffs, but in 1867 the responsibility was transferred to the sheriff of Cheshire.

Concern had been expressed about the deterioration of the records of the palatine courts before 1830. By the Public Record Office Act, 1838, the records were placed under the charge of the Master of the Rolls.[47] Faithful Thomas, a solicitor whose father had been gaoler in Chester castle,[48] was paid to make abstracts of some classes of the records during the first quarter of the 19th century.[49] In 1840 W. H. Black, Assistant Keeper of the Public Records, listed the common-law records in detail, relying on Thomas's descriptions of the Exchequer records.[50] In 1854 all the palatinate records were removed from Chester castle to the Public Record Office, where they were arranged and repaired.[51]

[46] Accounts of some of the executions are given in H. Hughes, *Chronicle of Chest.*, cap. 10.
[47] 1 & 2 Vic. c. 94, s. 1.
[48] Ches. R.O., subject file 'Faithful Thomas'.
[49] Ormerod, *Hist. Ches.* i. 61 n.; Ches. R.O., unlisted material on palatinate records. Thomas's abstracts are

Ches. R.O., Acc. 1320.
[50] *1 D.K.R.* App. pp. 79–85, 108–11.
[51] *P.R.O. Lists & Indexes No. XL*, p. iii. The rec. are described briefly, and references to published lists and calendars given, in *Guide to Contents of P.R.O.* i. 172–6.

COUNTY GOVERNMENT
1660–1888

Lieutenants and Justices of the Peace

FOR most of the period from the Restoration to 1689 the earls of Derby were lieutenants both of Cheshire and of Lancashire.[1] In the early 1660s William, Lord Brereton, was associated with the 8th earl in the lieutenancy but the experiment appears to have led to friction and confusion.[2] Some local feeling was expressed against both men, ostensibly because of their absence from the county.[3] For most of the 18th century the offices of lord lieutenant and *custos rotulorum* were held by the earls of Cholmondeley; from 1783 to 1845 they were held by the earls of Stamford and Warrington. In 1845 Richard, 2nd marquess of Westminster, was appointed; he held the office until his death in 1867, when he was succeeded in it by Lord Egerton of Tatton (d. 1883). From 1883 to 1900 the lieutenancy and office of *custos* were again under Grosvenor control, in the person of the 1st duke of Westminster. It had been said in the late 18th century that the then Lord Grosvenor had felt himself slighted at being passed over for the lieutenancy.[4]

No study has been made of the Cheshire commissions of the peace for the period. Changes in the commission belong, of course, rather to the study of political than to that of administrative history, particularly in the 18th century when 'the prospect of the issue of a new commission of the peace was the signal for plots to begin'.[5] Commissions were much larger than in the 17th century; thus that of October 1758 contained 87 new names in addition to those who had served earlier.[6] From the point of view of administrative history it is of more concern to know how many of the justices were actively concerned in county administration. Many of those whose names were included in the commission failed to take the oaths qualifying them to act. In 1853 only 176 of the 556 justices in the commission were qualified.[7] Patterns of attendance by the justices at quarter sessions indicate an aspect of their involvement in the work of the office. In 1755, for example, only 15 of the justices were recorded as having attended general sessions of the peace. Only one, Roger Comberbach, attended all four sessions. He was a professional lawyer, his father being prothonotary of the court of Great Sessions.[8] Two justices attended 3 sessions each, 4 attended 2, and the remaining 8 attended only once.[9] Ten years later of the 14 justices attending general sessions, none attended more

[1] Lord lieutenants to 1882 are listed in Ormerod, *Hist. Ches.* i. 79. From the late 18th century the office of *custos rotulorum* was generally held by the lord lieutenant. For a list of holders see Ches. R.O., subject file 'Quarter Sessions Officeholders'.

[2] *Cal. S.P. Dom.* 1661–2, 483, 509, 596. The entries there make it clear that Lord Brereton was Derby's associate rather than his deputy: cf. Ormerod, *Hist. Ches.* i. 79.   [3] *Cal. S.P. Dom.* 1661–2, 596.

[4] 3 *Sheaf*, xiii, p. 34. The successors of the 1st duke of Westminster as lord lieutenants were the 1st Earl Egerton of Tatton (d. 1909), who resigned in 1905, the 2nd duke

of Westminster (d. 1953), who resigned in 1920, Sir W. Bromley-Davenport (d. 1949), and the 3rd Viscount Leverhulme: Ches. R.O., subject file: 'Quarter Sessions Officeholders.'

[5] Moir, *Justice of Peace*, 80.

[6] 2 *Sheaf*, i, pp. 99–100.

[7] J. M. Lee, *Social Leaders and Public Persons*, 16.

[8] Williams, *Gt. Sess.* 71, 83.

[9] Ches. R.O., QJB 3/11 sess. 14 Jan., 15 Apr., 15 July, 7 Oct. 1755. The pattern of attendance at general quarter sessions at ten-yearly intervals from 1665 to 1795 is shown in Table I.

than two.[10] Low attendance at quarter sessions caused concern in 1846, when it was decided that lists of justices should be drawn up, excluding those who had not qualified, those over sixty-five, clergymen having clerical duties, and practising medical men; 6 justices should then receive, in alphabetical rotation, summonses in person to appear at quarter sessions.[11]

Attendance at quarter sessions was, of course, only a part of the justices' work, much of which was done at monthly meetings, the later petty sessions, or in the justices' own homes. From the beginning of the 19th century there is evidence of work by various committees of quarter sessions, including visitors of the county gaols at Chester castle and Knutsford, and of the county lunatic asylum at Upton by Chester. Between December 1826 and December 1827, for example, 15 meetings of the committee of visitors of

TABLE I: *Attendances of Justices at General Quarter Sessions 1665–1795*

Year[a]	Number attending sessions				No. of sessions attended by individuals				Total attending
	Ep.	East.	Mids.	Mich.	1	2	3	4	
1665	8	9	17	8	10	3	6	2	21
1675	13	9	17	10	6	5	7	3	21
1685	6	11	8	9	6	4	4	2	16
1695	5	6	7	3	4	3	1	2	10
1705	4[b]	8[b]	24	9	12	12	3	0	27
1715	10	13	12	12	7	6	4	4	21
1725	2	7	10	7	9	4	3	0	16
1735	12	9	11	12	12	5	2	4	23
1745	8	8	6	9	4	4	5	1	14
1755	4	6	7	9	8	4	2	1	15
1765	8	7	6	4	3	11	0	0	14
1775	8	7	13	12	9	10	1	2	22
1785	9	10	11	7	6	12	1	1	20
1795	8	9	10	10	8	13	1	0	22

[a] i.e. modern calendar year beginning in Jan.   [b] Lists incomplete.

Knutsford house of correction were held. The number of justices present averaged 5; Trafford Trafford and Sir J. T. Stanley each attended 10, however, and E. V. Townshend attended nine.[12]

In 1848 156 acting justices were listed by their divisions.[13] Eight of them had served for over forty years each. The senior justice was Trafford Trafford of Oughtrington Hall, who had qualified in January 1797.[14] He was chairman of quarter sessions, and although he had asked to be replaced in 1846, no substitute had then been found. Two years later he again tried to resign, and an arrangement was made by which he was persuaded to continue to preside over the hearing of appeals and over administrative business, but not over the trial of criminals. He was only finally able to retire in February 1858, after more than sixty years' service on the bench; he died just over a year later.[15] Of the other justices active in 1848 fifty had been appointed since the beginning of 1841, and seventy during the 1830s.

Traditionally the justices of the peace had been drawn from the landed gentry, although in the 18th century clergymen were more often placed on the commission. In 1758 thirteen of the 87 new justices were clerks, and 22 of the 156 acting justices in 1848 were given the title 'Reverend'.[16] During the 19th century industrialists were sometimes appointed. Those placed on the commission during the 1870s and 1880s

[10] Ches. R.O., QJB 3/12 sess. 15 Jan., 23 Apr., 16 July, 8 Oct. 1765.
[11] Ibid., QJB 6/1 sess. 6 Apr. 1846.
[12] 4 *Sheaf*, i, pp. 8–50.
[13] *Ches. Quarter Sessions Standing Orders* (1848), pp. xv–xx.

[14] Ibid., p. xvi.
[15] Ches. R.O., QJB 6/1 sess. 19 Oct. 1846; 6/2 sess. 26 Aug. 1848, 22 Feb. 1858, 27 June 1859.
[16] 2 *Sheaf*, i, pp. 99–100; *Ches. Q.S. Stand. Ord.* (1848), pp. xv–xx.

included W. E. Garforth, a mining engineer, William Laird, a shipbuilder, Sir Joseph Leigh, a cotton manufacturer, and Thomas Ward, owner of salt works.[17]

Quarter Sessions

The five sessions towns used before the Restoration (Chester, Knutsford, Middlewich, Nantwich, and Northwich) continued to be used after 1660.[18] Until 1679 the January sessions were held at Chester, those of April alternately at Middlewich and Northwich, those of July at Nantwich, and those of October at Knutsford. From 1679 the locations of the first two sessions were reversed. Middlewich ceased to be used after January 1723, but otherwise this pattern (Northwich, Chester, Nantwich, Knutsford) remained in use until 1745. From then until 1759 the positions of Nantwich and Northwich in the cycle were reversed, breaking a traidtion of some century and a half during which summer sessions had always been held at Nantwich. The sessions house there had collapsed in 1737, and while it was being rebuilt the Nantwich sessions were held in the house of correction.[19] The earl of Cholmondeley agreed to build a new sessions house and market hall, but that building in turn appeared dangerous by the end of the 1750s, and as a result Nantwich ceased to be used as a quarter sessions town after January 1760.[20] Meanwhile a new sessions house had been built at Northwich in 1731,[21] but it too was abandoned after July 1759, and from 1760 general quarter sessions were held only at Chester, in January and April, and Knutsford, in July and October. The sessions house at Knutsford was repaired in the 1770s.[22] In the early 19th century a new sessions house was built there, with a house of correction attached.[23]

In the 17th century the amount of business was usually small enough to allow it to be completed within the general quarter sessions. Between 1660 and 1700 there are only a handful of references to adjourned sessions.[24] Adjournments remained infrequent until the 1730s, but appear much more often thereafter. It is not always clear what the business of the adjourned sessions was: no business, for example, is recorded in the order book for the sessions of 27 May, 24 June, and 12 August 1775.[25] A routine cause of adjournment arose whenever the April sitting happened to coincide with the spring assizes in Chester.[26] Sometimes adjourned sessions were held to meet a particular emergency, as in 1749, when six adjourned sessions took place in January, February, and March, to take precautions against the spread of cattle plague.[27] By the mid 19th century the details of regular adjournments, and the type of business to be transacted at both general and adjourned sessions, had become established in the court's standing orders.[28]

Petty Sessions and the Cheshire Hundreds

The genesis of petty sessions lay in the monthly meetings which, in Cheshire, had been held in each hundred since at least the late 16th century. In the 18th century they were still known as monthly meetings.[29] In 1838 justices of the peace were listed

---

[17] *Ches. Leaders, Social and Political* (1896), 18, 61, 64, 67.

[18] What follows is based on an analysis of Ches. R.O., QJB 3/1–15 and 6/1–2.

[19] Hall, *Hist. Nantwich*, 220; Ches. R.O., QJB 3/9 sess. 12 July 1737, 11 July 1738, 10 July 1739, 15 July 1740.

[20] Ches. R.O., QJB 3/10 sess. 13 July 1742; Hall, *Hist. Nantwich*, 220.

[21] Ches. R.O., QJB 3/8 sess. 12 Jan. 1731.

[22] Ibid., QJB 3/14 sess. 4 Oct. 1774, 11 July 1775.

[23] Ormerod, *Hist. Ches.* i. 493.

[24] Ches. R.O., QJB 3/4 ff. 65, 79, 136v, 176v, 187; 3/5 sess. 15 Oct. 1695.

[25] Ibid., QJB 3/14.

[26] The first example found is of 1714: Ches. R.O., QJB 3/6 f. 113.

[27] Ibid., QJB 3/10.

[28] e.g. *Ches. Q.S. Stand. Ord.* (1838), pp. 1–7.

[29] See, for example, 1 *Sheaf*, iii, p. 218; Ches. R.O., DCH/A/465/26e.

according to the hundreds in which they lived; ten years later they were listed by petty sessional divisions.[30] In Broxton, Eddisbury, Nantwich, Northwich, and Wirral, the boundaries of hundred and petty sessional division coincided until 1839, when three townships in Nantwich hundred were annexed to Northwich.[31] In the same year Bucklow hundred was split into the two divisions of Daresbury and Bucklow (East).[32] Before 1820 Macclesfield hundred was in two petty sessional divisions, Prestbury and Stockport,[33] but a third, known as the Hyde division, was subsequently created, the appointment of a new high constable being authorized for it in 1848.[34] In 1867 the new Runcorn division was created, based on nine townships taken out of the Daresbury division of Bucklow.[35] In 1870 following the recommendations of a committee a new division known as Chester Castle was formed, consisting of 25 townships taken from Broxton, six from Eddisbury, and 18 from Wirral; another, Leftwich, was formed from 28 townships taken from Daresbury, Bucklow (East), Eddisbury, and Northwich.[36] In 1874 nineteen townships were removed from Bucklow (East) to form Altrincham division.[37] There were then fourteen petty sessional divisions within the county, none of which corresponded exactly with the original hundred boundaries.

From the beginning of quarter sessions records in Cheshire there is evidence of the appointment of two high constables for each hundred in the county. In the two centuries after 1660 they continued to perform important functions. They were responsible for the policing of their divisions by constables of individual townships.[38] They collected rates, and had to ensure that township officials acted properly in that respect. Thus in 1783 the high constable of one division of Broxton hundred issued printed orders to the constables of the townships in his division. In August they were to notify alehouse keepers that their licences were due for renewal, and persons aggrieved by window-tax assessments that they could appeal; they were to make their payments towards the 'county stock', and to return lists of the freeholders in their townships. In the following month they were given notice of the next month's hundred meeting and special session for the highways, and ordered to list persons qualified to serve as overseers of the highways, and to notify the collectors of land tax, house duty, and window tax, and of the duty on inhabited houses, that their Michaelmas instalments were due.[39] A book of tables showing the amounts due from each Cheshire township according to the traditional valuations, published in 1726, was appropriately entitled *The Head-Constable's Assistant*.[40] High constables were responsible for drawing up lists of freeholders qualified to serve on juries.[41] From the 1820s, however, they began to lose their powers. The appointment of special high constables relieved them of much of their duties with regard to crime prevention and the prosecution of offenders. Their responsibility for collecting county rates was transferred to the boards of guardians. By 1861 they were still obliged to attend quarter sessions, but only at Michaelmas of each year, and must appear before the grand jury if they had any nuisances to present of their own knowledge.[42] Although a new high constable's division had been created as recently as 1848, the office was of little significance by the 1860s. It was abolished early in 1870.[43]

The hundred itself retained vestigial functions up to the end of the period. Its liability for providing damages in the case of property destroyed during riots is well

[30] *Ches. Q.S. Stand. Ord.* (1838), pp. 12–17; (1848), pp. xv–xx.
[31] Ches. R.O., QJB 6/1 sess. 14 Oct. 1839.
[32] Ibid., sess. 1 July 1839.
[33] Ches. R.O., QJB 4/1 pp. 466–7.
[34] Ibid., QJB 6/2 sess. 16 Oct. 1848.
[35] Ibid., QJB 6/3 sess. 30 Dec. 1867.
[36] Ibid., sess. 11 Apr. 1870, 3 Apr., 26 June 1871.
[37] Ibid., sess. 5 Jan. 1874.

[38] e.g. Ches. R.O., QJB 3/6 f. 204v: orders of 1717 concerning watch and ward in the townships.
[39] Ibid., DCH/A/465/26d, 26e.
[40] By J. Jolley (London, 1726).
[41] Ches. R.O., QJB 3/3 sess. 10 Jan. 1682.
[42] *Ches. Q.S. Stand. Ord.* (1861), p. 46.
[43] Ches. R.O., QJB 6/2 sess. 16 Oct. 1848; 6/3 sess. 3 Jan. 1870.

known: examples for Cheshire have been found in 1841, 1853, and 1863.[44] In 1848 twenty-five bridges in the county were listed as hundred bridges, the obligation to repair which lay on the hundred rather than on the county.[45] In 1849 Bucklow, Macclesfield, and Northwich hundreds were fined for failure to repair bridges.[46] A rate for the repair of hundred bridges was levied in Bucklow and Macclesfield hundreds in 1887.[47]

County Finance

Such sums as had been levied for county purposes by the justices of the peace in the period before the Restoration had been raised from each township according to the traditional assessment known as the mize. The mize was also payable by the county whenever the earldom of Chester changed hands, in return for a confirmation of the palatine privileges. Anciently set at £2,000 payable over three years, the mize itself would have been of little significance to royal finance after 1660. Nevertheless Charles II's government tried to secure payment of it late in 1665; the proceeds were to be used for the repair of Chester castle.[48] A year later nothing had been done to collect it by the earl of Derby, who, as chamberlain of Chester, was responsible for the issue of warrants directing its collection.[49] The traditional mize was again levied on the creation of Frederick, George II's son, as prince of Wales and earl of Chester in 1729. The prince remitted it to the county, for the purpose of building quarter sessions houses, but by 1733 the treasurer appointed to supervise the work was dead, and it was not known what had become of the money.[50]

In the mid 17th century the mize assessments were used as the basis of Cheshire's contribution to national taxation. In the parliamentary assessments from December 1649 Cheshire's total contribution was 1·22 per cent of the national total, and of that, Chester city paid one tenth. Thus when an assessment of £70,000 a month was levied, Chester paid £85 11s. 2d. and the county £770. The £770 was apportioned between hundreds according to the mize assessments. That is proved by a calculation based on one quarter of a month's assessment (£192 10s.) in which the hundreds are set out in the same order as in warrants for collection of the mize (Eddisbury, Broxton, Wirral, Northwich, Bucklow, Nantwich, Macclesfield) and where each hundred's payment is 58·3 per cent of the hundred's nominal mize assessment.[51] The royal aid granted in 1665 used the same basis of assessment.[52] Taxation of land during the later years of Charles II's reign, however, used new bases.[53]

The mize remained in use for assessment of county rates from 1660 until late in 1821. Early in the period each item of expenditure required a separate warrant. The quarter sessions order books record the amount required, and analyse it by hundreds according to the mize assessment.[54] The sums appear at first as marginal notes, but by the early 18th century they are neatly tabulated. Thus at the end of the orders of the session of July 1703, nine items are listed, with each demand analysed by hundreds. In all, demands set out in this way in 1703 amounted to £640 1s., raised for 23 different purposes.[55] In addition to the extraordinary items, which varied from session to session,

44 Ibid., QJB 6/1 sess. 18 Oct. 1841; 6/2 sess. 27 June 1853; 6/3 sess. 29 June 1863.
45 *Ches. Q.S. Stand. Ord.* (1848), p. xiv.
46 Ches. R.O., QJB 6/2 sess. 9 Apr. 1849.
47 Ibid., QJB 6/4 sess. 4 Apr. 1887.
48 1 *Sheaf*, i, p. 159.
49 Ibid., pp. 163–4.
50 Ches. R.O., QJB 3/8 sess. 9 Jan. 1733.

51 Chester R.O., CR63/2/692 f. 69; Ches. R.O., DAR/I/2.
52 *Eng. Hist. Documents*, viii, p. 318; Chester R.O., CR63/2/692 f. 69.
53 Examples given in Ches. R.O., DAR/I/2.
54 For a published example of 1671 see *Ches. Q.S. Rec.* 182 (where the hundreds are listed in an unusual order).
55 Ches. R.O., QJB 3/5 sess. 12 Jan., 13 Apr., 13 July, 5 Oct. 1703.

payments were also demanded towards what became known as the county stock. In 1680 a levy of £100 a year was authorized, to support the houses of correction and prisoners in Chester castle and the King's Bench and Marshalsea prisons. Pensions for maimed soldiers, which had hitherto occurred as a regular item, were temporarily in abeyance.[56] In 1700 quarterly payments for the county stock were raised from £25 to £37 10s., and they were raised again in 1701 (to £50) and 1703 (to £75).[57] Thus in the latter year the total demand, for county stock and extraordinary expenditure, was more than £800.

Amounts for individual items of expenditure were assessed and collected until 1739, and individual treasurers were appointed to supervise payments in connexion with each. The result was that a township constable might have to levy, as in 1703, some twenty or more different rates, some of which might be very small. The publication of mize tables in 1726 must have eased the problems of both high and petty constables.[58] Using them, the amount due from any township, when a given rate was imposed in the hundred in which it lay, could be ascertained to within one thousandth of a penny. The inherent inefficiency of the separate rating system was recognized by statute in 1739, when quarter sessions were authorized to levy a single rate for all county purposes.[59] The power was first used in Cheshire in October 1739, when £250 was demanded.[60] By late 1741 quarterly payments were fixed at £500.[61] In 1742 Macclesfield borough successfully claimed exemption from rates levied for the repair of county bridges, unless they lay within its boundaries. That made it impossible to retain the system of making a block demand for the county stock, and at the first three sessions of 1742 the demand was once more divided into two parts, one for the 'county stock commonly called the quarterly pay' and the other for bridge repair.[62] The arrangement was, apparently, considered unsatisfactory, and in 1743 it was arranged that Macclesfield, together with Congleton which had also claimed exemption from bridge repair rates, should in future simply pay half the amount at which they were assessed for general county stock rates.[63]

From October 1742 the demands for quarterly pay disappear from the quarter sessions order books, and the loss of the county treasurers' accounts makes it impossible to know what demands were being made on the county. From time to time the treasurers' accounts were audited by quarter sessions, but little can be deduced from the entries concerning the audits in the order books. In July 1764 the 'quarterly pay' was £400.[64] At the end of the 18th century the rateable value of Cheshire was said to be exactly £1,000; the values given for each hundred except Macclesfield and Northwich show that the estimate was based on the mize, since for the five hundreds they represent the mize assessment multiplied by 3·048.[65]

At the level of the individual township, the amount demanded for county rates had to be apportioned among the ratepayers, and it is obvious that the comparative values of their land were taken into consideration. In 1748 the sum of 14s. was apportioned among thirty-eight occupiers in Grappenhall, the payment demanded varying from ½d. to 2s. 1d.; in Latchford 26 occupiers had to pay sums between ¼d. and 1s. 6¾d.[66] In 1784 the constables of Cholmondeley township made a succession of assessments based on land values, and paid the instalments of the 'quarterly pay' together with other expenditure from the money so raised.[67] Such local levies were sometimes based on

[56] Ches. R.O., QJB 3/3 sess. 15 July 1680.
[57] Ibid., QJB 3/5 sess. 16 July 1700, 6 May 1701, 13 Apr. 1703.
[58] Jolley, Head-Constable's Assistant.
[59] 12 Geo. II, c. 29.
[60] Ches. R.O., QJB 3/9 sess. 2 Oct. 1739.
[61] Ibid., sess. 14 July 1741; QJB 3/10 sess. 6 Oct. 1741.
[62] Ibid., sess. 12 Jan., 27 Apr., 13 July 1742.
[63] Ibid., sess. 11 Jan. 1743.
[64] Chester 38/33 (unnumbered rate assessments).
[65] Aikins, General Account of Ches. (1795), quoted in 3 Sheaf, xxviii, p. 67.
[66] 3 Sheaf, xiii, pp. 47–8.
[67] Ches. R.O., DCH/A/465/26i.

a 'pound rate', sometimes on traditional rental values, the 'old rents'. In 1701 quarter sessions ordered that, since it appeared that the assessment for poor relief in Clive, made according to the 'old rents', was unfair, a new one should be made 'by way of the pound rate'.[68] Between 1714 and 1716 a succession of appeals and counter-appeals reached quarter sessions from the inhabitants of Church Minshull over the same issue. The court first decided in favour of assessment based on the 'old rents', but later changed its mind.[69] It was said in 1686 that the 'old rents' in Bunbury parish, amounting to about £273, represented about one twenty-fourth of the real annual value of lands there.[70] The inhabitants of a township could appeal to quarter sessions for leave to make a new assessment. That was done by the inhabitants of Christleton in 1694: a new survey was made and returned into quarter sessions, which referred it to the next monthly meeting for Broxton hundred and afterwards confirmed it.[71]

In 1815 quarter sessions were empowered to replace such stereotyped assessments as the mize by new equitable bases of rateable value.[72] No advantage was taken of the statute in Cheshire until late in 1820, by which time the 'quarterly pay' had risen to £5,000.[73] In October quarter sessions ordered a return of land values to be made to the local justices in their petty sessional divisions; they in turn were to report at the next quarter sessions.[74] The returns were found to be inadequate, and, because they still appeared unsatisfactory in August 1821, three local surveyors were asked to check them. Their recommendations were accepted in September.[75] A rate of 1½d. in the pound was then levied, the expected product of which was about £5,363.[76] Under the new assessments the proportion of county rates paid by each division of the seven hundreds of Cheshire changed considerably, as is shown in Table II. Under the old system the two divisions of Wirral hundred appear to have been greatly over-burdened, while Bucklow and Macclesfield hundreds paid much less than their fair share towards county expenses. Similar changes in distribution of the demand occurred within the parishes. Table III shows how this worked in the eleven townships forming the ancient parish of Tarvin. Adjustments in the assessments could be made fairly easily. From time to time full-scale reassessments of rateable values throughout the county were ordered.[77] Collection remained the responsibility of the head constables within each division of the hundreds until 1844, when it was transferred to the poor-law unions.[78]

A further source of income from the mid-18th century was found in the profits of the Weaver Navigation. In 1720 an Act for making the river Weaver navigable between Winsford and Frodsham bridges had provided that, once the trustees' debts were paid off, surplus income might be devoted to bridges and highways in Cheshire.[79] The trustees' accounts were audited by the clerk of the peace each year from 1761, but no income was received from the source until 1777–8.[80] Between then and 1894, when the county council lost its revenues from the Weaver, the navigation contributed on average more than £9,000 a year to county funds.[81] Such projects as the rebuilding of Chester castle in the late 18th century and the construction of the county lunatic asylum at Upton early in the 19th were partly financed from that source.[82]

From the late 18th century capital expenditure was also financed by loans. An Act for the rebuilding of Chester castle empowered the commissioners to raise money on

[68] Ibid., QJB 3/5 sess. 15 July 1701.
[69] Ibid., QJB 3/6 ff. 125, 132, 149, 160v, 164–164v, 170v.
[70] Ibid., QJB 3/4 ff. 54v–55v.
[71] Ibid., ff. 217, 221v, 225.
[72] 55 Geo. III, c. 51.
[73] Ches. R.O., QJB 4/1 p. 465.
[74] Ibid., pp. 466–7.
[75] Ibid., pp. 618, 631–4, 675, 679–82.
[76] Ibid., pp. 747–57.

[77] e.g. Ches. R.O., QJB 6/2 sess. 30 June 1851, 27 June 1859; 6/3 sess. 7 Apr. 1873; 6/4 sess. 15 Oct. 1883.
[78] Ibid., QJB 6/1 sess. 1 July, 14 Oct. 1844.
[79] 7 Geo. I, c. 10.
[80] Ches. R.O., QJB 3/12 sess. 14 July 1761; 3/14 sess. 7 Oct. 1777.
[81] Lee, Soc. Leaders, 68.
[82] Hemingway, Hist. Chest. ii. 177, 226. The account bks. of the trustees are in Ches. R.O.

mortgage of the county rates.[83] Other such loans included £5,000 for alterations to Knutsford house of correction in 1853, and £16,500 for alterations to Upton lunatic asylum in 1853 and 1855.[84] In 1866 the county had to borrow £270,000 to pay compensation for cattle slaughtered during the cattle plague of 1865–6. The debt could not be paid off until 1897.[85]

Until 1843 the county treasurers' accounts were audited by *ad hoc* committees of justices of the peace. From that year, however, a finance committee of quarter sessions was regularly appointed. It consisted of five justices appointed by the Michaelmas quarter session and one from each petty sessional division.[86] From the early 1850s it met at the Crewe Arms Hotel at Crewe.[87] The treasurers' accounts were passed at the Michaelmas quarter sessions. Since rates were assessed quarterly, there tended to be wide variations in the balances each year, and in the amounts of the rates demanded. For example, a rate of ¼d. in the £ was levied by each of the seven quarter sessions before October 1850, when there was a balance in the treasurer's hands of nearly

TABLE II: *Mize and Rateable Value by Hundreds*

Hundred and Division	Percentage of total mize assessment	Percentage of total rate assessment (*1821*)
Broxton W.	7·08	5·34
Broxton E.	7·83	5·16
Bucklow E.	7·08	10·29
Bucklow W.	7·02	8·59
Eddisbury W.	6·89	6·7
Eddisbury E.	3·89	4·8
Macclesfield Stockport	6·97	13·06
Macclesfield Prestbury	9·85	12·28
Nantwich Audlem	9·09	6·17
Nantwich Nantwich	7·68	6·16
Northwich Middlewich	6·17	5·59
Northwich Congleton	6·95	7·76
Wirral W.	6·12	3·44
Wirral E.	7·36	4·65

Sources: for mize, Jolley, *Head-Constable's Assistant*; for rate Ches. R.O., QJB 4/1, p. 756.

£4,700. Apparently the justices felt that the balance was healthy enough for them to need no levy during the following year. The result was a deficit of £205 by October 1851, which had increased a year later to more than £3,800 in spite of two levies of ¼d.[88] The hand-to-mouth flavour of county financial administration in the mid-19th century is illustrated by the levies made between June 1869 and October 1871, which varied between ⅜d. and 4d.[89] From 1852 an additional levy was made for police purposes, at first for the county as a whole but soon for every police district. After 1857 there were two different police rates levied, one for general police expenditure and the other varying between districts.[90]

County Officials

Eleven clerks of the peace have been noted in Cheshire during the period from 1660 to 1888.[91] The longest-serving was John Stephens, who was appointed by the *custos*

---

[83] 28 Geo. III, c. 82.
[84] Ches. R.O., QJB 6/2 sess. 15 Aug., 28 Nov. 1853, 26 Mar. 1855.
[85] *Ches. C.C. Triennial Report* (1898), 16.
[86] Ches. R.O., QJB 6/1 sess. 16 Oct. 1843.
[87] Lee, *Soc. Leaders*, 15.

[88] Ches. R.O., QJB 6/2 sess. 3 Jan. 1849–18 Oct. 1852.
[89] The sums levied were ½d., 2d., 1¾d., ¾d., 4d., ⅜d., ¾d., ¾d., 3½d., and ¾d.: Ches. R.O., QJB 6/3 sess. 28 June 1869–16 Oct. 1871.
[90] Ches. R.O., QJB 6/2 sess. 18 Oct. 1852–16 Feb. 1857.
[91] Ches. R.O., List of Clerks of the Peace.

rotulorum, the earl of Cholmondeley, in October 1781 and held office until 1818.[92] Clerks, when they took office, appointed deputies, who sometimes succeeded them in the office: thus William Adams, who became clerk of the peace in 1714, appointed Thomas Tagg as his deputy, and Tagg succeeded to the clerkship in 1716.[93] Charles Potts took the oath as deputy clerk of the peace to George Johnson in 1846, and was made clerk some time between January and April 1860. He remained clerk of the peace until 1890.[94] The Potts family also served in the county treasurership during the period.

In the reigns of Charles II and James II the pre-Civil War practice of appointing two treasurers annually was continued.[95] They appointed deputies, who were allowed to receive 10s. a quarter.[96] In 1697, Thomas Bailey, who was said to have been deputy treasurer for many years, died, and John Hussey was made treasurer 'for the Quarterly Pay'. He presented his first accounts to quarter sessions in 1701, when a balance of more than £23 was recorded as due to him.[97] Two years later the deficit was more than

TABLE III: *Mize and Rateable Value in a Sample Parish*

Township	Percentage of total mize for ancient parish	Percentage of rate assessed in 1821
Ashton	14·75	12·45
Bruen Stapleford	4·92	8·11
Burton	2·95	3·19
Clotton-Hoofield	12·29	10·76
Duddon	4·49	5·04
Foulk Stapleford	12·42	8·98
Hockenhull	4·43	4·04
Horton cum Peel	3·93	3·15
Kelsall	11·31	14·02
Mouldsworth	8·85	6·09
Tarvin	19·67	24·17

Note: although the ancient parish was not used as a unit of assessment or collection either for the mize or for the county rate, the table indicates changes in the relative amounts levied between 11 townships.

Sources: for mize, Jolley, *Head-Constable's Assistant*, 301, 335; for rate, Ches. R.O., QJB 4/1 pp. 747, 750.

£62; Hussey was then allowed a salary of £10 a year.[98] He remained county treasurer until 1726, when he was said to be old and infirm; he then retired in favour of his son.[99] The new appointment lasted less than two years, John Hussey the younger being replaced by Thomas Lunt of Macclesfield in January 1728.[1] Lunt died in 1734, and was succeeded by Charles Potts of Ollerton.[2] The appointment began the long association of the Potts family with Cheshire administration; after thirty-four years' service Potts was succeeded by his son (also named Charles) in 1768.[3] Henry Potts was appointed in 1815.[4] Charles William Potts, who succeeded to the treasurership on Henry's death in 1845, was also deputy clerk of the peace, but resigned the office of treasurer in 1860 when he became clerk of the peace.[5] In 1867 the salary of Charles Townshend, then treasurer, was increased.[6] Four years later a county auditor was appointed for the first time.[7]

The office of county bridgemaster and surveyor apparently originated in *ad hoc* surveys

[92] Ibid.; Ches. R.O., QJB 3/15 pp. 389–90.
[93] Ibid., QJB 3/6 f. 110; List of Clerks of the Peace.
[94] Ibid.; Ches. R.O., QJB 6/1 sess. 5 Jan. 1846; 6/2 sess. 18 Jan., 20 Apr. 1860.
[95] e.g. Ches. R.O., QJB 3/3 sess. 12 Apr. 1681, 25 Apr. 1682, 28 Apr. 1685, 13 July 1686.
[96] Ibid., QJB 3/1 f. 170.
[97] Ibid., QJB 3/5 sess. 12 Jan. 1697; QJF 129/2 no. 2.
[98] Ibid., QJB 3/5 sess. 13 July 1703.

[99] Ibid., QJB 3/7 sess. 12 July 1726.
[1] Ibid., QJB 3/8 sess. 9 Jan. 1728.
[2] Ibid., sess. 23 Apr. 1734.
[3] Ibid., QJB 3/13 sess. 19 Apr. 1768.
[4] Ibid., QJB 6/1 sess. 28 June 1841.
[5] Ibid., sess. 13 Oct. 1845, 5 Jan. 1846; QJB 6/2 sess. 14 Feb. 1860.
[6] Ches. R.O., QJB 6/3 sess. 30 Dec. 1867.
[7] Ibid., sess. 26 June 1871.

of county bridges commissioned in the late 17th and the 18th centuries.[8] In 1776 the question of appointing a permanent official was considered, but nothing was immediately done.[9] Such an appointment occurs early in the 19th century, however; the county bridgemaster's duties are expounded in standing orders of quarter sessions in 1838.[10] In 1876 Stanhope Bull was appointed; his duties included the management of county police stations and magistrates' offices, and in 1881 his salary was increased in recognition of new duties under the Highways and Locomotives (Amendment) Act of 1878.[11]

At the beginning of the period there were two coroners working within Cheshire. In 1752 a statute enacted that coroners' fees should be paid from county rates, and within the next two years quarter sessions authorized payments to the two county coroners and to those of Halton Fee and Macclesfield borough.[12] In 1840 a new coroner's district, to be known as 'Stockport', was formed from the Stockport and Hyde divisions of Macclesfield hundred; the other two districts were to be known as 'Knutsford' and 'Chester'. The first included the remainder of Macclesfield hundred, Northwich hundred, and parts of Bucklow, Eddisbury, and Nantwich. The second embraced the remainder of the county.[13] In 1848 a newly appointed coroner of Halton Fee claimed an allowance in respect of an inquest held at Barnton. It was disallowed by quarter sessions, because Barnton was believed to lie within the Knutsford coroner's district of Cheshire. The Halton coroner, however, claimed that many more townships lay in his area than the eleven which had been enumerated at the time of the rearrangement in 1840. The question was delegated to a committee, which was empowered to look for 'the original grant of the manor of Halton Fee' among the records of the duchy of Lancaster. As a result seventeen townships were removed from the Knutsford district, and five from the Chester district, and placed within the Halton coroner's authority. His claim had been supported by the chancellor of the duchy of Lancaster. The Chester and Knutsford coroners unsuccessfully claimed compensation.[14]

Highways, Bridges, and County Buildings

For much of the period the duty of quarter sessions towards highways was supervisory. Townships were authorized to levy rates for highway repair.[15] Those townships which neglected to carry out their statutory obligations to repair highways were fined, and quarter sessions directed the fines to be used for carrying out the appropriate repairs. In October 1718 twelve fines were imposed.[16] From 1762 quarter sessions issued orders for highways to be made wider.[17] Only when a highway was extra-parochial did the justices undertake the cost of repairs from county funds. From the early 18th century highways in Delamere forest were signposted and repaired at county expense.[18]

The Highways Act, 1862,[19] empowered justices in quarter sessions to divide counties into highway districts, and a committee was immediately constituted in Cheshire to recommend how it should be done. In 1863 twelve highway boards were established, based on the hundreds and petty sessional divisions.[20] That done, quarter sessions

[8] e.g. Ches. R.O., QJB 3/5 sess. 10 July 1705; 3/12 sess. 1 May 1759.

[9] Ibid., QJB 3/14 sess. 9 Jan. 1776.

[10] *Ches. Q.S. Stand. Ord.* (1838), p. 30.

[11] Ches. R.O., QJB 6/3 sess. 23 May, 16 Oct. 1876; 6/4 sess. 4 Apr. 1881.

[12] 25 Geo. II, c. 29; Ches. R.O., QJB 3/11 sess. 3 Oct. 1752, 2 Oct. 1753, 15 Jan. 1754.

[13] Ches. R.O., QJB 6/1 sess. 19 Oct. 1840.

[14] Ibid., QJB 6/2 sess. 9 Apr., 2 July 1849.

[15] e.g. ibid., QJB 3/4 ff. 201–201v.

[16] Ibid., QJB 3/6 ff. 234–234v.

[17] e.g. 7 orders in Oct. 1762 and 6 in Jan. 1763: ibid., QJB 3/12 sess. 5 Oct. 1762, 11 Jan. 1763.

[18] Ibid., QJB 3/6 ff. 110, 125, 145v.

[19] 25 & 26 Vic. c. 61.

[20] Ches. R.O., QJB 6/3 sess. 13 Oct. 1862, 4 Mar. 1863. The board districts were Broxton (East), Broxton (West), Bucklow (East), Bucklow (Daresbury), Eddisbury (East), Eddisbury (West), Macclesfield (Prestbury), Macclesfield (Stockport and Hyde), Nantwich (Audlem), Nantwich (Nantwich), Northwich, and Wirral.

resumed a supervisory role, authorizing, for example, a highway board to borrow money in 1876.[21] Following the Highways and Locomotives (Amendment) Act, 1878,[22] quarter sessions established a highways committee, with two justices representing each of the highway board districts. Regulations were made for traffic on county highways.[23] The definition of 'main road' in Cheshire was said to be wide, including any road leading to a railway station.[24]

A list of county bridges and causeways printed in 1848 names 176 structures as subject to repair at county expense.[25] In addition there were 25 hundred bridges.[26] Not all the bridges listed were the sole responsibility of Cheshire; where they crossed the county boundaries, liability to repair them was shared between two counties,[27] and Stone Bridge in Wirral hundred lay between Cheshire and Chester city. A list made c. 1741 had named 127 county bridges.[28] Major repairs to them could only be undertaken after the grand jury at quarter sessions had presented them as out of repair.[29] Such indictments were to be drawn up by the county surveyor, who was to report annually on the state of all county bridges.[30]

At the beginning of the period the county's responsibility for buildings other than bridges and causeways extended only to parts of Chester castle and to the house of correction at Middlewich. Responsibility for repairs to Chester castle seems at first to have been accepted by the Crown, which appointed its governors. In 1663 John Shaw, master mason and surveyor of the county, petitioned for reimbursement of money which he claimed to have spent in repairs to the castle.[31] Such claims had to be submitted to the judges of the court of Great Sessions before they could be sent to the government.[32] Nevertheless, quarter sessions at the same time acknowledged its responsibility for contributing towards the repair of the shire hall, or common hall of pleas, in the castle.[33] By the 1690s this duty had extended to include repair of the gaol there, which had been expressly excluded from county liability in 1681.[34] By 1709 the county was also contributing towards repair of the Exchequer court and the prothonotary's office.[35] A slater for the shire hall was employed on a permanent contract in 1723.[36] A list of county bridges and causeways written c. 1741 included all structures for which the county was liable, mentioning the shire hall, gaol, Exchequer, and prothonotary's office.[37]

Prisoners in Chester castle were not the responsibility of the county sheriff but came under the care of the constable of the castle, who in turn appointed a deputy to act as gaoler.[38] In 1772 quarter sessions complained that the constable had appointed a woman gaoler, who was thought to be unsuitable.[39] Howard likened the felons' quarters in the gaol to what he had heard of the Black Hole of Calcutta; Thomas Pennant thought Howard's description an under-statement.[40] In 1784 the grand jury at the court of Great Sessions presented the gaol as out of repair and insufficient.[41] In the

[21] Ches. R.O., QJB 6/3 sess. 20 Oct. 1876.
[22] 41 & 42 Vict. c. 77.
[23] Ches. R.O., QJB 6/3 sess. 30 June 1879; 6/4 sess. 27 June 1881.   [24] Lee, *Soc. Leaders*, 25.
[25] *Ches. Q.S. Stand. Ord.* (1848), pp. vii–xiii.
[26] Ibid. p. xiv.
[27] e.g. Brinksway bridge (between Ches. and Lancs.), Broadbottom bridge (between Ches. and Derb.), Farndon bridge (between Ches. and Denb.), Saltersford bridge (between Ches. and Yorks.).
[28] Ches. R.O., QJB 3/9.
[29] *Ches. Q.S. Stand. Ord.* (1838), pp. 28–30.
[30] Ibid. (1861), p. 36.
[31] *Cal. Treas. Bks.* 1660–7, 479, 536.
[32] Ches. R.O., QJB 3/3 sess. 12 Apr. 1681.
[33] Ibid., QJB 3/1 ff. 186v–187; 3/3 sess. 11 July 1682,

9 Jan., 24 Apr. 1683, etc.
[34] Ibid., sess. 12 Apr. 1681; QJB 3/4 f. 193.
[35] Ches. R.O., QJB 3/6 ff. 3v, 15.
[36] Ibid., QJB 3/7 sess. 3 Aug. 1723.
[37] Ibid., QJB 3/9.
[38] J. Howard, *State of the Prisons* (1780 edn.), 400.
[39] Ches. R.O., QJB 3/13 sess. 14 Jan. 1772.
[40] Howard, *State of Prisons*, 400–3; Hemingway, *Hist. Chest.* ii. 177.
[41] What follows is based on Ches. R.O., QA/Gaol & Co. Hall at Chest./1–3. For a description of the new bldg., based on Harrison's, see Hemingway, *Hist. Chest.* ii. 177–84. Harrison's plan is printed in Lyson's, *Mag. Brit.* ii (2), between pp. 570 and 571. Detailed treatment of the architecture of Chester castle and other county bldgs. is reserved for treatment elsewhere in the *History*.

following year a competition was held for designing new buildings on the castle site, to serve as a shire hall and Exchequer as well as a county gaol. An Act was obtained for taking down and rebuilding the gaol and other parts of the castle, and a commission consisting of the acting justices for the county, was established to supervise the work.

The county's one house of correction, for the imprisonment of minor criminals and vagabonds, was set up in the early 17th century at Middlewich. In 1677 money was raised for building another at Nantwich. The inhabitants of the town promised that the building, which was also to be used as a local workhouse, would not be a further charge on the county.[42] The master's salary was, however, paid by the county treasurer.[43] In 1718 the building was said to be superfluous, but no action was taken.[44] Five years later it was used for housing impressed soldiers;[45] in the late 1730s, following the collapse of the sessions house at Nantwich, it was used to accommodate quarter sessions. By 1767 it had been sold and converted into alms-houses, though the sale of the land on which it stood took long to complete.[46] Meanwhile a building known as the Old Quay House at Neston had been converted into a house of correction; it remained in use at the end of the 18th century.[47] Another is recorded in the late 18th century at Stockport,[48] but that at Middlewich remained the principal house of correction in Cheshire and was named in 1780 as the place where prisoners sentenced to hard labour were to be sent, as an alternative to transportation.[49]

During the 18th century sessions houses are recorded at Knutsford,[50] Nantwich,[51] and Northwich.[52] In the second decade of the 19th century it was decided to build a new sessions house and house of correction at Knutsford. The building was said to be nearing completion by 1819.[53] The house of correction was accommodating more than 225 prisoners by 1826–7.[54] In 1839 a new wing containing ninety cells and new workrooms was authorized, at a cost of £8,000.[55] In 1877 both Chester castle gaol and Knutsford house of correction were taken over as government prisons.[56]

In 1829, under the provisions of the Act of 1828,[57] a county lunatic asylum was built at Upton by Chester, for the maintenance of pauper lunatics.[58] Major extensions to it were authorized in 1848 and 1859.[59] In 1867 it was decided to purchase a site for a second asylum at Macclesfield, where accommodation was to be provided for 400 inmates.[60]

Police

Although some of the larger towns in Cheshire had made their own arrangements to provide full-time paid police forces within their limits, no general force for the county was instituted until 1857.[61] An Act of 1829 gave the justices in quarter sessions the power to appoint special high constables for any hundred or division of a hundred. Assistant petty constables could be appointed for individual townships or groups of

[42] Ches. R.O., QJB 3/3 sess. 10 July 1677; Hall, *Hist. Nantwich*, 209.
[43] Ches. R.O., QJB 3/3 sess. 15 July 1680.
[44] Ibid., QJB 3/6 f. 209v.
[45] Ibid., QJB 3/7 sess. 16 July 1723.
[46] Ibid., QJB 3/10 sess. 20 Apr. 1747; 3/14 sess. 8 Oct. 1771, 10 Jan. 1775.
[47] Ibid., QJB 3/11 sess. 10 July 1750; 3/17, p. 478.
[48] Ibid., QJB 3/17, p. 535.
[49] Ibid., QJB 3/15, pp. 196–8.
[50] e.g. Ibid., QJB 3/8 sess. 7 Oct. 1729.
[51] First mentioned in Ches. R.O., QJB 3/7 sess. 14 July 1724.

[52] Built in 1731; ibid., QJB 3/8 sess. 12 Jan. 1731.
[53] Ormerod, *Hist. Ches.* i. 493. A full description is given in *Bagshaw's Dir. Ches.* (1850), 551–2.
[54] *4 Sheaf*, i, pp. 6–20.
[55] Ches. R.O., QJB 6/1 sess. 30 Dec. 1839.
[56] Ibid., QJB 6/3 sess. 8 Apr. 1878, 7 Apr. 1879.
[57] County Lunatic Asylums Act: 9 Geo. IV, c. 40.
[58] For a description see Hemingway, *Hist. Chest.* ii. 226–9.
[59] Ches. R.O., QJB 6/2 sess. 3 Jan. 1848, 4 Apr. 1859.
[60] Ibid., QJB 6/3 sess. 8 Apr., 1 July 1867.
[61] R. W. James, *To the Best of our Skill and Knowledge*, 108 sqq.

townships on the recommendation of three local justices.[62] In 1839, 1840, and 1841, quarter sessions refused to adopt the Counties Police Act of 1839.[63] By 1838 special high constables had been appointed only for the hundred of Bucklow and for the Prestbury and Stockport divisions of Macclesfield hundred.[64] Ten years later there were nine, one for each of the three divisions of Macclesfield hundred and one for each of the other six hundreds.[65] The appointment and payment of assistant petty constables depended on *ad hoc* arrangements between the justices and the overseers of individual townships, as did the provision of local lock-ups. Thus in 1842 quarter sessions agreed to contribute towards the provision of a lock-up in Tarvin, in aid of a similar amount to be raised by the inhabitants of the parish.[66]

Quarter sessions tried to secure uniformity of standards among the constabulary. In 1840 it was ordered that instructions provided for constables in Bucklow hundred be printed and circulated among the forces in other parts of the county.[67] In 1848 lock-ups were placed under the control of the special high constable of each division.[68] From 1852 the salaries of assistant petty constables were levied from hundreds rather than from individual townships, and such constables were henceforth appointed to divisions of hundreds rather than to *ad hoc* groups of townships.[69] Police rates were levied in varying amounts from each division. In April 1853, for example, they varied from $\frac{1}{4}d$. in the £ in Northwich hundred to 2*d*. in the £ in Wirral, while in October, of the 9 divisions, 3 were rated at $\frac{1}{4}d$., 3 at $\frac{3}{8}d$., and 3 at $\frac{1}{2}d$. in the £.[70] A police superannuation fund was established in 1852.[71]

The Police Act, 1856,[72] compelled the county, which then had a force of about eighty assistant petty constables in the nine divisions, to create a county police force. A police committee of quarter sessions was set up in January 1857.[73] A chief constable was appointed.[74] Police districts under the new Act were, with the exception of Macclesfield hundred, which was divided into three, based on the hundreds, but in 1868 a tenth division was created, to include the Daresbury and Runcorn petty sessional divisions of Bucklow hundred.[75] In 1861 the force consisted of 9 superintendents, 4 inspectors, 27 sergeants, and 160 constables at divisional level, with a central reserve force of one superintendent, one inspector, one sergeant, and 8 constables.[76] In the early years of the new system there was a high turnover of constables: 112 of those appointed in the first year were discharged within three years.[77]

Militia

In the two decades after the Restoration the number of deputy lieutenants in Cheshire varied between 14 and sixteen.[78] In a list made *c.* 1715 20 deputy lieutenants were named, of whom four acted for Chester as well as for the county.[79] In 1733 54 men were recommended to the king for appointment, and all but 5 appear to have received commissions.[80] The deputy lieutenants, under the authority of the lord lieutenant, were sometimes involved in the local side-effects of national political crises. In 1683

[62] 10 Geo. IV, c. 97 (Local and Personal).
[63] Ches. R.O., QJB 6/1 sess. 25 Mar. 1839, 23 Mar. 1840, 4 Jan. 1841.
[64] *Ches. Q.S. Stand. Ord.* (1838), p. xvii.
[65] Ibid. (1848), p. xxi.
[66] Ches. R.O., QJB 6/1 sess. 28 Mar. 1842.
[67] Ibid., sess. 19 Oct. 1840.
[68] Ches. R.O., QJB 6/2 sess. 10 Apr. 1848.
[69] Ibid., sess. 14 Apr., 28 June, 16 Aug. 1852.
[70] Ibid., sess. 11 Apr., 17 Oct. 1853.
[71] Ibid., sess. 18 Oct. 1852.
[72] 19 & 26 Vic. c. 69.

[73] Ches. R.O., QJB 6/2 sess. 5 Jan. 1857.
[74] Ibid. sess. 13 Oct. 1856.
[75] Ches. R.O., QJB 6/3 sess. 29 June 1868.
[76] *Ches. Q.S. Stand. Ord.* (1861), pp. 47–51.
[77] James, *To the Best of our Skill and Knowledge*, 34. James's book contains a detailed account of the Ches. police force from 1857 to 1957.
[78] For appointments of 1665, 1673, and 1676 see Chester R.O., CR63/2/8–11.
[79] Ches. R.O., DCH/X/9/B.
[80] Ibid., DCH/1692, p. 1.

they ordered the confiscation of the arms of men suspected of supporting the duke of Monmouth.[81] The landing of William of Orange in November 1688 came at a delicate time for the Cheshire militia. James II, having some time earlier removed the 9th earl of Derby from the office of lord lieutenant, had agreed to reinstate him. Derby, while awaiting the arrival of his commission and of the king's approval of the deputies whom he had nominated, was secretly negotiating with Lord Delamere, a supporter of William of Orange. Two days after William's landing Derby met his proposed deputy lieutenants at Northwich, but his own commission as lord lieutenant had still not arrived and another week elapsed before he was able to appoint his deputies. Soon afterwards Delamere complained of Derby's delays in raising the Cheshire militia against attacks by Roman Catholics; in the following spring Delamere replaced Derby as lord lieutenant and Derby's deputies and militia officers lost their positions.[82] In 1696 the militia was again used to search for and seize the arms of those suspected of disaffection.[83]

In 1684 a muster of Cheshire militia was held at Knutsford. The force then numbered 1,085 foot-soldiers and 105 horsemen.[84] Thirteen years later the county's force included two troops of horse and a regiment of foot, and latter divided into seven companies each representing one of the hundreds. The number of foot-soldiers for Wirral hundred is not recorded, but the numbers for the other six hundreds totalled 821.[85] Eddisbury, which provided 101 soldiers in 1697, was said to be responsible for providing 95 in a list compiled c. 1715. Of the total, 72 were sent from 53 townships in the hundred, and the remainder were found by freeholders.[86]

The militia appears to have become disorganized by 1745. In November, when there were fears that the Jacobite army would attack Chester, the lord lieutenant informed the duke of Newcastle that the Cheshire militia rolls were lost, and that there were no arms.[87] It also appeared that there was no provision for paying militiamen.[88] In 1757 the English militia was reorganized by statute, with Cheshire's quota of soldiers set at 560.[89] In 1769 the Royal Regiment of Cheshire Militia consisted of 28 commissioned officers and 607 non-commissioned officers and privates.[90] Five years later the strength was said to be respectively 30 and 612.[91] In 1802 Cheshire's quota of soldiers for the regular militia was reassessed at 885; in addition the county had since 1796 been liable to provide 1,460 men for the supplementary militia.[92]

The Regulation of the Forces Act, 1871,[93] transferred command of the militia in England from the lords lieutenant to the Crown. As a result the two militia barracks in Cheshire, at Chester castle and at Macclesfield, ceased to be county institutions. In 1874 quarter sessions allowed the Chester barracks to be sold to the War Department, and in 1881 they agreed that the War Department should lease the Macclesfield barracks.[94]

[81] Hist. MSS. Com. 13, *10th Rep. IV, Kilmorey*, pp. 363–4. For those accused of disaffection in 1683 see also Ormerod, *Hist. Ches.* i, p. lxvii.
[82] Hist. MSS. Com. 35, *14th Rep. IV, Kenyon*, pp. 198–202, 205–7, 212–13.
[83] Ches. R.O., DCH/X/9/B.
[84] Hist. MSS. Com. 13, *10th Rep. IV, Kilmorey*, p. 364.
[85] Ches. R.O., DCH/X/9/B.
[86] Ibid.
[87] Ches. R.O., DCH/X/9/A no. 9.

[88] R. C. Jarvis, 'Lieutenancy and Militia in Lancs. and Ches. in 1745', *T.L.C.A.S.* lxii. 111–32.
[89] 30 Geo. II, c. 25, s. 16. The total included Chester city.
[90] Ches. R.O., QJB 3/13 sess. 9 Jan. 1770.
[91] Ibid., DCH/X/9/B.
[92] 37 Geo. III, c. 3, s. 3; 42 Geo. III, c. 90, s. 19.
[93] 34 & 35 Vict. c. 86.
[94] Ches. R.O., QJB 6/3 sess. 5 Jan. 1874; 6/4 sess. 17 Oct. 1881.

NEW LOCAL AUTHORITIES

Poor-Law Unions, p. 75. Urban and Rural Districts, p. 77.

Poor-Law Unions

BEFORE 1834 poor-relief in Cheshire was usually undertaken by individual townships in isolation. The parishes in Chester, however, combined in the mid 18th century to provide a workhouse.[1] In 1777 it was said to afford accommodation for 250 inmates. Of the other 30 workhouses in Cheshire in that year, some, such as Macclesfield and Stockport, were fairly large. Macclesfield workhouse could house 160 paupers, and Stockport 60. Others were very small; the workhouse at Rode had only 6 places, and that at Faddiley only four. The total accommodations available in the Cheshire workhouses in 1777 was 1,181 places.[2] By the early 19th century 61 of the 491 places in Cheshire which made returns to Parliament were supporting some of their poor in workhouses. Occasionally townships contributed to the upkeep of establishments outside their boundaries; 18 townships were said to subscribe to a workhouse at Grappenhall. The proportion of paupers who received indoor relief was very small, amounting to only 273 out of nearly 26,000 persons relieved in 1802–3.[3]

During the late 18th and early 19th centuries expenditure on poor-relief in Cheshire, like that elsewhere, rose steeply. In 1775–6 it totalled almost £30,000; by the mid 1780s it averaged more than £39,000 a year; by 1802–3 it had reached nearly £70,000, and by 1833–4 nearly £93,000. The increase was not disproportionate. In 1775–6 and 1783–5 Cheshire was ranked twenty-third of 44 English counties in total expenditure on poor-relief, and in 1802–3 and 1833–4 twenty-fifth out of 42. Because of the increase of population in Cheshire in the early 19th century expenditure per head of population fell, from 7s. 3¼d. in 1802–3 to 5s. 6d. in 1833–4; in the latter year only 3 counties in England had a lower *per capita* expenditure.[4]

As a result of the Poor Law Amendment Act, 1834,[5] poor-law unions were established throughout the county, with the exception of Chester where the 'incorporation' remained distinct. When the assistant poor-law commissioner Digby Neave reported in July 1836 only one union, Wirral, had been formed.[6] The organization of the remaining unions that comprised places in Cheshire took another year and a half to complete. The last, Hayfield (Derb.), was established in December 1837.[7] In forming the unions the commissioners ignored existing county and hundred boundaries. Altrincham, Macclesfield, Nantwich, Northwich, Runcorn, and Wirral unions lay wholly within Cheshire. Great Boughton, Congleton, and Stockport included places in counties outside Cheshire.[8] Similarly, places in Cheshire were included in the unions of

---

[1] 2 Geo. III, c. 45. For poor-relief in Chest. before the Act see R. V. H. Burne, 'Treatment of Poor in 18th Cent. in Chest.', *J.C.A.S.* [N.S.] lii. 33–48; for an outline hist. of the admin. of the 'incorporation' see Chester R.O., intro. to list of class TRU (Chest. poor-law union rec.).

[2] *Abstracts of Returns made by Overseers of the Poor, 1777*, pp. 14–20.

[3] *Abstracts of Answers and Returns relative to Expense and Maintenance of the Poor in Eng. 1804*, H.C. 175, pp. 48, 60 (1804), xiii.

[4] Ibid. pp. 60, 714–15; *7th Ann. Rep. Poor Law Com.*

1841 [327], table facing p. 17, H.C. (1841), xi.

[5] 4 & 5 Wm. IV, c. 76.

[6] *2nd Ann. Rep. Poor Law Com. 1836*, p. 405, H.C. 595–I (1836), xxix (I).

[7] *Return of Names of Unions governed by Boards of Guardians under the Poor Law Amendment Act*, pp. 1–3, H.C. 425–II (1840), xxxix.

[8] Great Boughton union included Hawarden and Higher Kinnerton (Flints.); Congleton union included Biddulph (Staffs.); Stockport union included Heaton Norris and Reddish (Lancs.).

Ashton-under-Lyne (Lancs.), Hayfield (Derb.), Market Drayton (Salop.), and Wrexham (Denb.).[9]

During the 19th century several alterations were made to the union boundaries. In 1845 Grappenhall, Latchford, and Thelwall were transferred from Runcorn union to that of Warrington (Lancs.). In 1853 12 townships were detached from Great Boughton union and added to the one newly established at Hawarden (Flints.). At the same time 12 of the Cheshire townships in Wrexham union, together with 2 from Great Boughton and 8 from Nantwich, were placed in Whitchurch (Salop.) union. In 1861 9 townships were taken from Wirral union to form a new one named Birkenhead.[10] The Chester

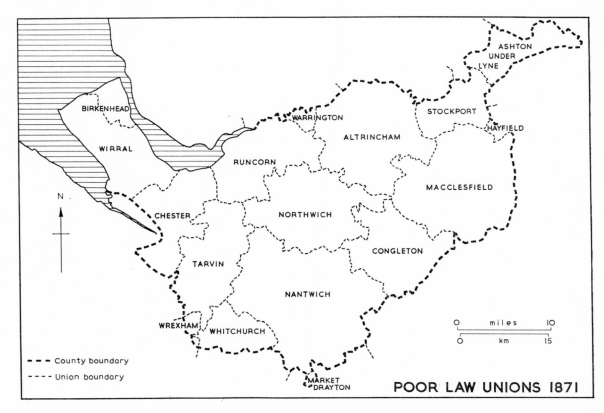

POOR LAW UNIONS 1871

- – - – County boundary
- - - - Union boundary

'incorporation' became a poor-law union in 1869,[11] and was enlarged in 1871 by the addition of 13 townships from Hawarden union and 30 from Great Boughton, which was renamed Tarvin.[12] In 1895 Altrincham union was renamed Bucklow.[13] The Local Government Boundary Commission, 1888, recommended several more changes in the boundaries of the Cheshire unions, including the creation of two new ones named Dukinfield and Malpas; other changes would have made county and union boundaries coincide.[14]

In the late 1830s the new unions slowly faced the task of building workhouses. By 1840 the only new workhouses to be completed were those for Northwich and Wirral unions. Altrincham's was being built; Congleton and Nantwich had converted and improved existing workhouse buildings. Macclesfield and Stockport were renting buildings; Great Boughton had contracted with the Chester 'incorporation' for the admission of its poor into Chester workhouse. Runcorn union was altogether without

[9] *Return of Names of Unions*, pp. 1–3.
[10] *Return of Area and Population of Poor-Law Unions*, pp. 23, 87, 193, 201, H.C. 485 (1862), xlix, pt. ii.
[11] *22nd Ann. Rep. Poor Law Crs. 1869–70*, [c. 123], p. 365, H.C. (1870), xxxv.

[12] Ches. R.O., QJB 4/47 pp. 34, 40, 250, 254.
[13] Ches. R.O., intro. to list of Bucklow union rec. (class LGB).
[14] *Rep. Local Govt. Boundary Crs. 1888*, H.C. 360, pp. 65, 67–8, 79, 181–2, 187, 313, 327–8, 513–14 (1888), li.

workhouse accommodation.[15] Ten years later Runcorn union still had no workhouse, but Congleton, Macclesfield, and Stockport had built new workhouses;[16] Great Boughton built one in 1857.[17]

Because expenditure on poor-relief had already been fairly low in Cheshire, and because the poor-law unions were not formed until 1836–7 and not supplied with adequate workhouses until later, the Act of 1834 resulted in much smaller savings in Cheshire than in many other counties. By 1839–40 expenditure was 18 per cent lower than in 1833–4, while the average decrease in England was 28 per cent.[18] Expenditure per head of population remained low in comparison with other counties. In 1890–1 and 1911 only 4 English 'union counties' spent less per head than Cheshire on poor-relief.[19] Nevertheless unions in the county were said in the early 1890s to be too ready to give outdoor relief. In 1891 a conference of the Cheshire unions supported a suggestion for by-laws for the more uniform administration of out-relief. Most unions accepted the model by-laws.[20] Between 1890–1 and 1900–1 the percentage of expenditure on out-relief in Cheshire fell from 63·3 to 54·6, while the average for England and Wales rose from 55·2 to 61.[21] In 1910 the 11 workhouses belonging to the unions in Cheshire were said to offer accommodation for some 5,000 paupers;[22] the total number in residence in 1921 was 2,440.[23]

Urban and Rural Districts

At the beginning of the 19th century Chester, Congleton, Macclesfield, and Stockport were the only municipal boroughs in Cheshire. Since the early 16th century Chester had been a county of itself.[24] During the 19th century Cheshire's population grew rapidly, especially in the eastern and western extremities of the county towards Manchester and the Mersey estuary. The desire of newly urbanized areas for more effective local government resulted in the creation of new local authorities. In the early decades of the century such authorities were usually created by individual Improvement Acts which set up boards of commissioners to undertake specified duties. Birkenhead, Runcorn, and Stalybridge were governed by such boards. The Public Health Act, 1848,[25] resulted in the creation of local boards of health at Nantwich in 1850, at Altrincham in 1851, at Wallasey in 1853, and at Dukinfield in 1857.[26] The Local Government Act, 1858,[27] simplified the procedure for establishing local boards of health. Higher Bebington, Monks Coppenhall, and Tranmere had established such boards by 1860, but between 1862 and 1867 17 more local board districts were formed.[28]

It has been claimed that the promotion of local board districts after 1862 was a direct consequence of the Highways Act of that year[29] which exempted such districts from the

[15] Returns of Workhouses and Bldgs. erected under the Poor Law Amendment Act, pp. 6–9, 100–1, H.C. 425–I (1840), xxxix; Bagshaw's Dir. Ches. (1850), 459.

[16] Bagshaw's Dir. Ches. (1850), 215, 276–7, 499, 575.

[17] Kelly's Dir. Ches. (1857), 47.

[18] 7th Ann. Rep. Poor Law Com. 1841, table facing p. 17.

[19] 21st Ann. Rep. Loc. Govt. Bd. 1891–2 [C. 6745], p. lxix, H.C. (1892), xxxviii; 42nd Ann. Rep. Loc. Govt. Bd. 1912–13 [Cd. 6980], p. xxvi, H.C. (1913), xxxi.

[20] 21st Ann. Rep. Loc. Govt. Bd. 1891–2, pp. 164–5.

[21] Ibid. pp. lxvi–lxvii; 31st Ann. Rep. Loc. Govt. Bd. 1901–2 [Cd. 1231], pp. lxxv–lxxvi, H.C. (1902), xxxv.

[22] Kelly's Dir. Ches. (1910), 77, 78, 223, 277, 399, 430, 472, 496, 522, 572, 632. Figures for Northwich and Wirral workhouses are not given there, but those for the other 9 total 4,595.

[23] Census, 1921, Co. Chest. 48.

[24] Detailed info. about urban areas mentioned in the following paragraphs is reserved for treatment elsewhere in the History.

[25] 11 & 12 Vic. c. 63.

[26] Return of Places where Public Health Act, 1848, or Local Govt. Act, 1858, is adopted, H.C. 80, pp. 2, 8, 14, 21 (1867), lix.

[27] 21 & 22 Vic. c. 98.

[28] Bollington, Bowdon, Bredbury, Buglawton, Chorley, Hollingworth, Hoole, Hyde, Lower Bebington, Lymm, Mossley (in Lancs., Yorks., and Ches.), Northwich, Oxton, Sandbach, Tarporley, Witton cum Twambrooks, and Yeardsley cum Whaley: Return of Places where 1848 and 1858 Acts adopted, pp. 4–24.

[29] 25 & 26 Vic. c. 61.

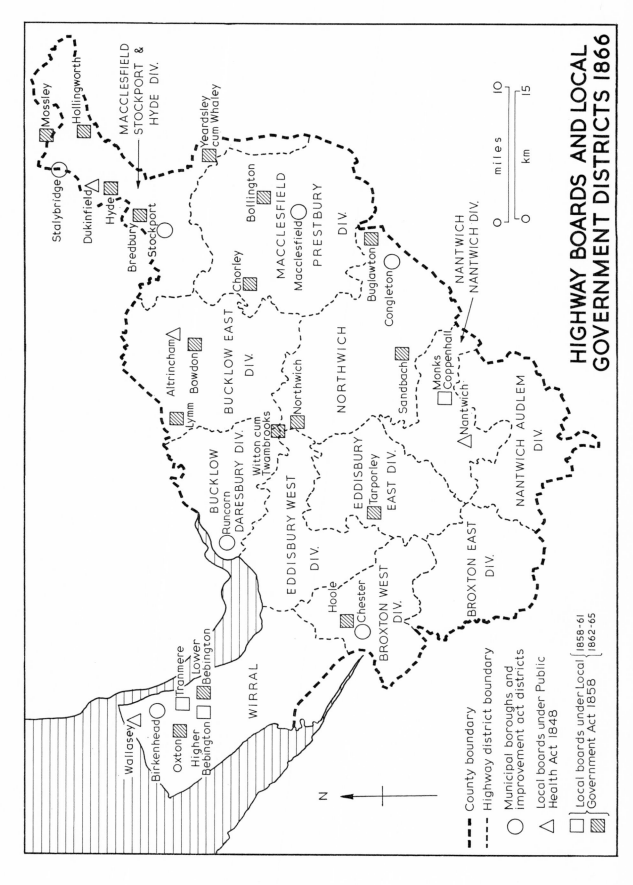

HIGHWAY BOARDS AND LOCAL
GOVERNMENT DISTRICTS 1866

control of the new highway boards.[30] Twelve highway boards were established under the Act in Cheshire in 1863. They were based on the petty sessional divisions of the county, which in turn were based on the ancient hundreds.[31] Other new authorities created before 1894 included school boards[32] and burial boards; 8 of the latter were enumerated in 1865, and 16 in 1877.[33]

As a result of the Public Health Act, 1872,[34] areas controlled by borough corporations by improvement commissioners, and by local boards of health were constituted urban sanitary districts, while the parts of poor-law unions which lay outside such districts were constituted rural sanitary districts. It remained possible for areas to adopt the Local Government Act, 1858; by 1894 10 more places in Cheshire had become local board districts. By then Birkenhead, Crewe, Hyde, and Stalybridge had become municipal boroughs, while under the Local Government Act, 1888,[35] Birkenhead, Chester, and Stockport became county boroughs.[36]

The rationalization of the local government structure in England and Wales which had begun in 1872 was carried further by the Local Government Act, 1894.[37] The new rural districts set up by that Act, unlike the rural sanitary districts which they replaced, did not extend beyond the administrative county. The Cheshire parishes formerly in Whitchurch (Salop.) rural sanitary district became the Malpas rural district; the three Cheshire parishes in Ashton-under-Lyne (Lancs.) rural sanitary district became Tintwistle rural district; Disley parish was co-terminous with the rural district of the same name. Grappenhall, Latchford, and Thelwall, formerly in Warrington rural sanitary district, were placed in Runcorn rural district and thus returned to a unit from which they had been separated in 1845.

Urban growth and the consequential development of urban government continued after 1894. Alsager, Ashton on Mersey, Compstall, Ellesmere Port, Handforth, and Knutsford became urban districts before the First World War; Dukinfield and Wallasey became municipal boroughs, Wallasey becoming a county borough in 1913.[38] Altrincham, Bebington, and Sale became municipal boroughs in the 1930s, as did Ellesmere Port in 1955.[39]

In 1933 Wirral rural district was abolished. Parts of it were transferred to neighbouring county boroughs and urban districts; the remainder was reconstituted Wirral urban district.[40] Three years later more sweeping changes affected the local government divisions of Cheshire. Buglawton, Compstall, Handforth, Hollingworth, Mottram in Longdendale, and Tarporley urban districts and Malpas rural district were dissolved. A new urban district, Longdendale, was created. Most of the parishes in the former Malpas rural district were transferred to that of Tarvin, but three were placed in Nantwich rural district. Ten parishes were wholly or partly transferred from Tarvin to Chester rural district. Seventy parishes were abolished, and their places taken by new parishes or by neighbouring urban authorities.[41] In 1954 Hoole urban district was absorbed into Chester.[42] By 1974, when local government was reorganized, the ancient

---

[30] V. D. Lipman, *Local Govt. Areas 1834–1945*, 57.
[31] *Returns of Places in Cos. of Eng. and Wales which have adopted the Highways Act*, H.C. 147, pp. 3–4 (1864), I.
[32] A description of the Ches. school boards is reserved for treatment elsewhere in the *History*.
[33] *Shaw's Union Officers' and Local Bds. of Health Manual for 1865*, 186–93; *Local Govt. Dir., Almanac, and Guide, 1877*, 455–69.
[34] 35 & 36 Vic. c. 79.
[35] 51 & 52 Vic. c. 41.
[36] The new local board districts were Bromborough,

Cheadle and Gatley, Marple, Middlewich, Mottram in Longdendale, Neston and Parkgate, Sale, West Kirby and Hoylake, Wilmslow, and Winsford: *Return relating to Areas and Population, etc., of Cos. in Eng. and Wales*, H.C. 437, p. 6 (1893–4), lxxvii.
[37] 56 & 57 Vic. c. 73.
[38] *Ches. Co. Council Yr. Bk.* (1913–14), 195–9; Lee, *Soc. Leaders*, 50.
[39] Lee, *Soc. Leaders*, 116.
[40] *Co. Chest. Review Order, 1933*.
[41] *Co. Chest. Review Order, 1936*.
[42] *Chest. (Extension) Order, 1954*.

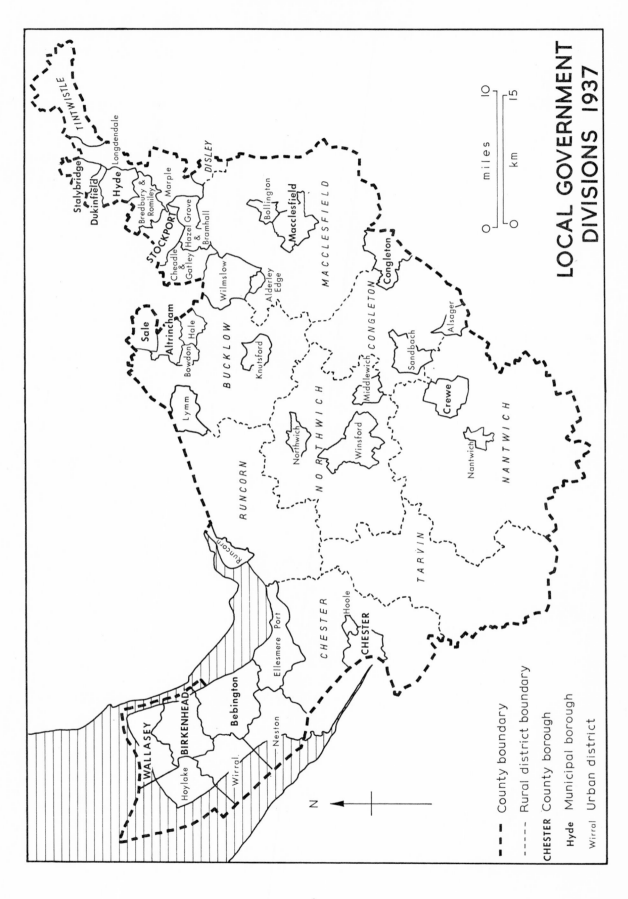

LOCAL GOVERNMENT DIVISIONS 1937

County boundary
Rural district boundary
CHESTER County borough
Hyde Municipal borough
Wirral Urban district

county of Chester contained, in whole or in part, 4 county boroughs,[43] 10 municipal boroughs,[44] 22 urban districts,[45] and 10 rural districts.[46]

[43] Birkenhead, Chester, Stockport, Wallasey.

[44] Altrincham, Bebington, Congleton, Crewe, Dukinfield, Ellesmere Port, Hyde, Macclesfield, Sale, Stalybridge.

[45] Alderley Edge, Alsager, Bollington, Bowdon, Bredbury and Romiley, Cheadle and Gatley, Hale, Hazel Grove and Bramhall, Hoylake, Knutsford, Longdendale, Lymm, Marple, Middlewich, Nantwich, Neston, Northwich, Runcorn, Sandbach, Wilmslow, Winsford, Wirral.

[46] Bucklow, Chester, Congleton, Disley, Macclesfield, Nantwich, Northwich, Runcorn, Tarvin, Tintwistle.

THE COUNTY COUNCIL
1889–1974

Composition of the County Council, p. 82. County Buildings, p. 83. Committees, p. 84. Clerks to the County Council, p. 85. County Finance, p. 86. Education, p. 87. Health and Social Services, p. 90. Planning, p. 91. Public Protection Services, p. 92. Roads and Bridges, p. 93. Agriculture and Small-holdings, p. 93. County Records, p. 94. Boundary Changes and Local Government Reorganization, p. 94. County Seals and Arms, p. 96.

Composition of the County Council

THROUGHOUT 1887 and 1888 the justices of the peace in quarter sessions had to deal with local government reorganization. Early in 1888 they memorialized the Royal Commission on Local Government Boundaries against the removal of any large areas from Cheshire, and they pointed out the disadvantages of the existing poor-law union structure which overlapped county boundaries at many points.[1] Later in the year they undertook the division of the county into electoral districts for the election of the new county council. Under the Local Government Act, 1888, Birkenhead, Chester, and Stockport became county boroughs.[2] The remainder of the county was divided into 57 electoral districts. Of the municipal boroughs Macclesfield was divided into four county electoral divisions, and Crewe, Hyde, and Stalybridge into three each; Congleton constituted a single division.[3]

The number of county councillors was increased to 58 in 1891, when a new district was created in Crewe, and to 59 in 1893 with the creation of one for New Brighton.[4] In 1907 Wallasey's representation on the council was enlarged from three to five members, but all five disappeared after 1913, when Wallasey became a county borough.[5] The number of aldermen remained nineteen except between 1907 and 1913. In 1936 Cheshire underwent various boundary changes,[6] and the electoral divisions were re-constituted. Councillors increased from 56 to 69, and aldermen from 19 to 23. The new structure was not altered until 1955, when the Hoole division was incorporated in the city of Chester.[7] In 1958 the number of divisions was increased by six, in order to provide new seats for the suburban areas in the east and west of the county which had grown up since 1945.[8] The 74 seats were increased to 82 before the elections of 1970.[9] From 1958 to 1970 there were 24 aldermen; their number was increased by three from 1970.

In the first election, held in 1889, 35 of the 57 seats for county councillors were contested.[10] Thereafter the number of contested seats never rose above 14 before the First World War, and only exceeded that number twice before 1939.[11] In the first election held after the Second World War 51 of the 69 seats were contested, but three years later the number of contests fell to 35, and in all the elections from 1952 to 1961 inclusive, less than half the seats were fought. In 1964, 1967, and 1970 the number of

[1] Ches. R.O., QJB 6/4 sess. 2 Jan. 1888. For poor-law unions see pp. 75–6.
[2] 51 & 52 Vic. c. 41.
[3] For commentary see Lee, *Soc. Leaders*, 55–6.
[4] Ibid. 56 and n.
[5] Ibid.
[6] See p. 95.
[7] Lee, *Soc. Leaders*, 161.

[8] Ibid. 161–2.
[9] J. M. Lee and B. Wood, Barbara W. Solomon and P. Walters, *Scope of Local Initiative: a Study of Cheshire Co. Council, 1961–74*, 200.
[10] The following paragraph is based on Lee, *Soc. Leaders*, 232, and on Lee, Wood, Solomon, and Walters, *Scope of Local Initiative*, 200.
[11] 22 seats were contested in 1931, and 26 in 1937.

contests was respectively 43, 42, and 43. Between 1889 and 1946, it has been claimed, 'unopposed returns were almost the normal procedure', with unofficial agreements between party leaders limiting the number of contests.[12] Even when contests took place, sitting councillors were likely to be re-elected. Between 1892 and 1958 the number of retiring councillors unseated at contests exceeded four on only three occasions: in 1946 (9 defeats), 1949 (6 defeats), and 1952 (5 defeats). From 1961 to 1970 the number of defeats of sitting councillors (10, 13, 6, and 8) was larger, though still small in relation to the number standing for re-election.

In political composition the council remained under Conservative control throughout its history.[13] The party obtained most seats on the council, if both triennial elections and the subsequent elections of aldermen are aggregated, after every election except those of 1904 and 1928. In 1904 Liberals obtained 37 seats, equalling the number held by the Conservatives. In 1928 the 32 seats held by Liberals exceeded by one the number held by the Conservatives. Following the eight elections held before the First World War Conservatives gained overall majorities on the county council. They were only able to do so twice between the wars, in 1919 and 1937, but from 1946 to 1970 they always gained overall majorities. Liberals never won less than one-third of the seats between 1889 and 1931, but thereafter their share fell rapidly, and after 1949 they could never secure more than 9 seats. The Labour Party gained one seat on the council in 1904, but lost it three years later. Until 1934, when they gained 5 seats, they had never had more than two. After the Second World War their position on the council improved, with their total representation varying between 6 in 1949 and 24 in 1964. Except in 1949, they never had fewer than 13 seats on any post-war council. Independent representation never exceeded single figures before the First World War, but from 1922 to 1970 averaged fifteen.

Between 1889 and 1963 only eight men served as permanent chairmen of the county council.[14] All were Conservatives, except Sir William Hodgson, a Liberal, who served from 1922 to 1935. The vice-chairmanship was held by Liberals except under Hodgson's chairmanship, until 1952, after which both chairman and vice-chairman were Conservatives.

Thirty-four of the acting justices of the peace in Cheshire stood as candidates in the county council elections of 1889. All but 6 were elected, and another 4 were brought into the council as aldermen. Nevertheless there was a significant change in the social character of Cheshire administrators as a result of the Local Government Act of 1888, and the replacement of the great landowners as 'social leaders' by business and professional men, which had already been indicated in the later 19th-century commissions of the peace, was emphasized.[15]

County Buildings

Meetings of the full council were held at Chester castle, inconvenient though that was for councillors from eastern Cheshire. Committee meetings, however, were often held at the Crewe Arms Hotel at Crewe until 1957.[16] Chester castle could not house many of the council's administrative officers, and most departments were therefore located in other places in Chester or elsewhere in the county. In 1902, for example, the only officers whose addresses are given as Chester castle are the surveyor, the auditor,

[12] Lee, *Soc. Leaders*, 59.
[13] For detailed analysis of party allegiances see Lee, *Soc. Leaders*, 233, continued by Lee, Wood, Solomon, and Walters, *Scope of Local Initiative*, 200.
[14] Lee, *Soc. Leaders*, 179.
[15] Ibid. 57-8.
[16] Ibid. 15.

and the chief inspector of weights and measures. The clerk to the county council, the treasurer, and the architect had premises elsewhere in Chester. The county analyst worked from Manchester, the medical officer of health from Birkenhead, and the secretary for technical education from Crewe.[17] Early in the 1930s the marquess of Crewe offered Crewe Hall for conversion into a headquarters building for the county council. The offer was declined, partly because the county officials opposed it, and also because the house had long been unoccupied, and repairs would have been expensive.[18] In 1934 it was decided to build a county hall in Chester, on land adjoining the castle. Work was begun shortly before the Second World War, but suspended during and immediately after it, and as a result the new building was not opened until 1957.[19] All departments of the council were then housed there except those of the surveyor and the chief fire officer, which were at Backford Hall. Nevertheless the large increase in staff employed by the council made the new county hall and the old offices in the castle inadequate, and accommodation had to be sought elsewhere. In 1965 more than a hundred officers were moved to a building in Pepper Street, Chester, and two years later some two hundred went to Commerce House in the city.[20] At the time of re-organization in 1974 the offices of the chief executive, the secretary, treasurer, architect, director of education, and land agent were at the county hall; the planning and social services departments were at Commerce House; the fire officer's department at Walmoor House, Chester; the headquarters of the libraries and museums department at Hoole; and the trading standards and highways and transportation departments at Backford Hall.[21] Accommodation of smaller departments and offices was found in other scattered places. Thus in 1974 a group of rooms over a motor-car showroom in Northgate Street, Chester, housed the county emergency planning department, the Chester district road safety office, and the *Victoria History of Cheshire*; all three were transferred in 1976 to a house in Nicholas Street which they shared with the sites and surveys office of the county architect's department.[22]

Such accommodation problems reflected an increase in the staff employed by the county council, which in turn resulted from the increased scope of its activities. In 1925, shortly after the council had adopted the Local Government and Other Officers Superannuation Act, 1922, there were fewer than 300 officers employed in pensionable posts.[23] In 1953 the number of whole-time administrative staff employed was 1,284; ten years later it had reached 1,835, and over the next decade it doubled to 3,656.[24] The growth had already been sufficiently apparent in the late 1940s to force the architect of the new county hall to redesign it with an additional floor.[25]

Committees

At the beginning of its existence the county council appointed five standing committees, apart from the standing joint committee which controlled the police force. Two of them, for general purposes and for the administration of the Contagious Diseases of Animals Acts, were committees of the whole council; the other three were for finance, main roads, and lunatic asylums. By 1920 the number of committees had increased to

[17] Addresses in *Kelly's Dir. Ches.* (1902), 9.
[18] Lee, *Soc. Leaders*, 143.
[19] Ibid. 123, 143.
[20] Lee, Wood, Solomon, and Walters, *Scope of Local Initiative*, 141.
[21] Information supplied with map, *New Cheshire*, 1974.

[22] Ex inf. Dr. B. E. Harris.
[23] *Ches. C. C. Triennial Rep.* (1925), 2.
[24] *Ches. Finance* (1953), 21–2; (1963), 27; (1973), 19.
[25] W. Dobson Chapman, *County Palatine: A Plan for Ches.*, frontispiece.

nineteen.[26] Twenty committees are enumerated in a list of 1938.[27] In 1965 and 1966 a sub-committee considered the simplification of county administration. The parliamentary and general purposes committees were amalgamated; so were the diseases of animals, land drainage, and smallholdings committees. The weights and measures and local taxation committees became sub-committees. The number of sub-committees was reduced from 53 to 28. The limit of expenditure which chief officers could sanction on their own authority was raised from £100 to £1,000. As a result of the changes the number of committee and sub-committee meetings was reduced from 398 in 1965 to 148 in 1967. The number of places on committees was reduced from 476 in 1964 to 302 by 1970. The burden of councillors' attendance at committees was thus much eased. In 1964 one-third of council members were serving on more than six committees, whereas in 1970 none served on more than five.[28]

Clerks to the County Council

When the county council was formed, C. W. Potts, who was already clerk of the peace, became its first clerk. On his death in 1890 his son Reginald succeeded to both offices and retained them until his own death in 1931.[29] Both men used as their offices the premises where they practised as solicitors, Northgate House, Chester. They recruited their own staff.[30] The next clerk to hold office, Geoffrey Scrimgeour, had been deputy to Reginald Potts for some five years. He was the first man to hold the appointment of clerk as a full-time post, and served for thirty years.[31] Under him the clerk's department emerged from the rather passive role which it had played under the Potts family. Scrimgeour was closely involved in negotiations on Cheshire's boundaries in the 1930s, and put forward proposals for remodelling them after the Second World War.[32] Soon after taking office he promoted the Cheshire Publicity and Industrial Development Council,[33] and during the Second World War he recommended the council to commission a planning consultant, W. Dobson Chapman, to prepare a county plan.[34] As clerk of the peace Scrimgeour was responsible for organizing the arrangement and repair of quarter sessions records.

Scrimgeour was succeeded in 1952 by Hugh Carswell, under whose supervision the move to the new county hall and the abandonment of Crewe as a centre for committee meetings took place in 1957.[35] His deputy in the post was Mr. A. C. Hetherington, who succeeded him as clerk in 1959. Among Hetherington's achievements were the beginning of a system of regular meetings of the chief officers of the county in the county hall, and the establishment of an organization and methods unit.[36] In 1964 he was replaced by Mr. J. K. Boynton, who was still in office at the time of reorganization in 1974.[37] Boynton was responsible for the simplification of the committee structure described above. He expanded the work of the clerk's department partly by instituting a succession of new offices within it, such as those of training officer, information officer, print manager, transport co-ordinator, and purchasing officer, and partly by making it the centre of co-ordination of the various departments of the council, through

[26] Lee, Soc. Leaders, 137.

[27] County agricultural; children's road safety; general purposes; weights and measures; staffing and salaries; roads and bridges; public assistance; polling districts; parliamentary; milk and dairies; mental deficiency acts; maternity and child welfare; local taxation and road fund licences, etc.; local government acts; finance; education; difficulties at elections; public health and housing; local pensions; air raid precautions: Jubilee of Co. Councils: Ches. 80–1.

[28] Lee, Wood, Solomon, and Walters, Scope of Local Initiative, 87–96, 110.

[29] Lee, Soc. Leaders, 67, 125.

[30] Ibid. 125.

[31] Ibid.

[32] Ibid. 121.

[33] Ibid. 86.

[34] Ibid. 119.

[35] Ibid., 123–4.

[36] Ibid. 124, 133.

[37] For an evaluation of Boynton's work, see Lee, Wood, Solomon, and Walters, Scope of Local Initiative, passim.

steering committees and working parties. In 1966 he introduced a new device for county council stationery and publicity, consisting of three concentric C's. An estimate of the growth of the work of the clerk's department under Carswell, Hetherington, and Boynton can be gained from the fact that whereas in 1953 it employed 52 full-time staff, the numbers had increased to 83 by 1963 and to 250 ten years later.[38]

County Finance

The county council took pride in the fact that its rates were low. In 1922 it was claimed that, out of 42 administrative counties in England, only two had total rates lower than Cheshire's.[39] Between 1889 and 1907 the rate levied for general county purposes never exceeded 6½d. in the £; that figure was, in fact, the rate levied in the first year of the council's existence, and resulted from the omission of quarter sessions to levy any rate at all in the last quarter of its existence as an administrative body. From the mid-1890s rates were only kept low at the cost of a substantial increase in the county's debt. Between 1892 and 1895 the debt stood at less than £35,000 a year. Between 1904 and 1907, however, it averaged nearly £280,000 a year, and by 1922 it stood at nearly £1,250,000. Meanwhile the rate levied for general purposes steadily increased. In 1919–20 it exceeded 1s. in the £ for the first time, and from 1924–5 to 1929–30 it remained between 1s. 3½d. and 1s. 5d. After the county council took over the administration of the poor law in 1929, the rate rose to 4s. 1d. in the £; during the 1930s and early 1940s it varied between 3s. 7d. (in 1931–2) and 4s. 4¾d. The general county rate was only one of those which the council levied. Police rates between 1889 and 1907 varied between 1d. and 2½d. During the First World War they ranged between 3⅛d. and 3¾d., while in the 1920s they did not fall below 5½d. From 1931 to 1946 they varied between 6½d. and 11¾d., the higher figure being that for 1942–3. Higher education rates were 1d. in 1903–4, 2d.–2½d. until after the First World War, 4½d.–5d. in the 1920s, 6d.–7d. between 1930 and 1939, and from 8d. to 8½d. during the Second World War. In 1903–4, the first year after the 1902 Education Act came into operation, the rate for elementary education was 3d. In the next year it doubled, and from 1912 to 1918 it varied between 10d. and 1s. 0½d. Between 1919 and 1930 it varied from 1s. 6½d. to 2s.; in the 1930s and until the end of the Second World War it remained between 2s. and 2s. 3d. In 1942–3 the total rate demanded for county purposes amounted to nearly 7s. 9d., including, besides the rates enumerated above, smaller sums for libraries, from 1929, maternity and child welfare, from 1937, and the administration of the Shops Acts and Food and Drugs Acts, from 1939. Ten years later the rate had almost doubled.[40] By 1962–3 the county rate precept had reached 15s. 7d. out of a total rate which, for the whole of the administrative county, averaged 22s. 7d. in the £; in April 1963, however, a reassessment of rateable values took place throughout the country, which in Cheshire resulted in the product of a penny rate rising from c. £52,000 to c. £150,000. The county rate precept of 6s. in the £ for the year 1963–4 represented a substantial increase over the previous year's, though the chairman of the council could still claim that only five administrative counties had lower rates.[41] In 1973–4 the rate levied for county purposes was 26·18p in the £. The product of a 1p rate was now some £1,400,000, and therefore the real cost to ratepayers had risen by some 339 per cent over the previous decade.[42]

[38] Ches. Finance (1953), 21; (1963), 27; (1973), 18.
[39] For following figs. see Ches. C.C. Triennial Reps. (1892, 1907, 1919, 1922, 1925, 1928, 1931, 1934, 1937, 1943).
[40] Ches. Finance (1953), 5.
[41] Ibid. (1963), 29; Ches. C.C. Triennial Rep. (1964), 53.
[42] Ches. Finance (1973), 31.

Those figures reflect the vast growth in all forms of expenditure by county authorities in the post-war period. Capital expenditure by the county council rose from a total of £1,329,000 in 1952–3 to £4,497,000 in 1962–3 and to more than £17,000,000 ten years later. During the same twenty-year period the county's outstanding debt rose from £5,431,000 in 1953 to £13,241,000 in 1963 and £48,189,000 in 1973.[43] The rise occurred in spite of a change of policy after 1950, by which capital expenditure was financed from revenue rather than from loans. During the following decade buildings completed included, besides the new county hall, 75 schools, 2 colleges of further education, 24 homes for children or for the elderly, 8 clinics, 5 ambulance stations, and 4 fire stations.[44]

Education

Following the Technical Instruction Act, 1889, the county council for the first time became involved in education, by providing grants for technical instruction in schools and institutions of higher education.[45] The cost was not at first met from local rates, but from the so-called 'whisky money' raised under the Local Taxation (Customs and Excise) Act.[46] The amounts granted in Cheshire rose from just over £10,000 in 1891–2 to nearly £18,000 in 1900–1.[47] By the latter year grants were also being made to nine boys' grammar schools in the county, and to two girls' high schools.[48] During the 1890s the county council acquired the Worleston Dairy Institute.[49] Saltersford Hall was leased, as a site for an agricultural training college and farm, and was opened, with accommodation for 60 students, in September 1895.[50]

Under the Education Act, 1902,[51] the council took control in the following year of 28 board schools and more than three hundred voluntary elementary schools.[52] An education committee of the council, consisting at first of 54 members, was established. Sub committees dealt with higher education, agricultural education, and finance, while for purposes of elementary education 23 area sub-committees were set up. Within a short time after the Act came into operation, however, the six non-county boroughs in Cheshire, Congleton, Crewe, Dukinfield, Hyde, Macclesfield, and Stalybridge, took over control of their own elementary schools. Another sub-committee area dealt with Wallasey urban district, and that in turn disappeared after 1913, when Wallasey, as a county borough, assumed control of all educational provision inside its boundaries. There thus remained 16 sub-committee areas, which had been reorganized into 17 by 1938; the sub-committees consisted of county councillors, representatives of all county districts within their areas, and co-opted members.[53]

The council had the duty to maintain existing elementary schools which had been placed under its control, and to build new ones where necessary. By February 1910 20 new elementary schools had been completed, 4 were in course of erection, and another 13 had been planned. Thirty-two more voluntary schools had been transferred to county control. On the other hand 21 schools had been closed.[54] A further 17 new elementary schools had been opened by 1913.[55] The First World War put an end to

43 Ibid. 10, 14.
44 Lee, *Soc. Leaders*, 147.
45 52 & 53 Vic. c. 76.
46 H. C. Barnard, *Short Hist. Eng. Educ.* 209–10.
47 *Ches. C.C. Triennial Rep.* (1895), 9; (1901), 23–4.
48 Ibid. (1901), 24–5.
49 E. Driver, *Ches.: its Cheese-Makers*, 64–8.
50 *Ches. C.C. Triennial Rep.* (1895), 10; (1898), 13; for a description see *Kelley's Dir. Ches.* (1902), 342.

51 2 Edw. VII, c. 42.
52 *Ches. C.C. Triennial Rep.* (1904), 29–32, describes the process. Treatment of the hist. of elementary and secondary educ. before 1902 is reserved for another volume.
53 *Ches. C.C. Educ. Cttee. Official Manual, 1915–16*, 76; *Jubilee of Co. Councils: Ches.* 71–3.
54 *Ches. C.C. Triennial Rep.* (1910), 12–13.
55 Ibid. (1913), 7.

school building. In 1922 the chairman of the county council could only report the transfer to it of one voluntary school and the closure of two small schools. The gloom of this announcement was emphasized by the news that the adoption of national scales for teachers' salaries had meant a large increase in the elementary education rate.[56] Teachers' salaries, which had cost the county £171,000 in 1912–13, amounted to more than £450,000 by 1923–4.[57]

In the period between the World Wars the construction of new schools continued, but very slowly. Thus between 1931 and 1934 7 new elementary schools were opened, while 5 old ones were closed.[58] In the same period 5 schools were reorganized as senior elementary schools, taking pupils over eleven, in accordance with the recommendations of the Hadow Report.

Under the Education Act, 1944,[59] the non-county boroughs which had maintained their own primary schools lost control of them to the county council. All the old administrative sub-committees, except those of Tarvin and Knutsford, were replaced by divisional executives.[60] In 1955 Cheshire maintained 464 primary schools, of which a hundred were all-age schools. The latter were mostly situated in rural areas, 13 being in the Mid-Cheshire division, 25 in Nantwich, 10 each in Ellesmere Port and Chester Rural, and 17 in Tarvin.[61] The county council pursued an energetic policy of replacing the all-age schools, so that by 1965 there were only 6, while the total number of primary schools under county control remained practically the same as in 1955.[62] Much new primary school building took place. By 1970 the number of primary schools under county council control had reached 531, and the all-age schools had disappeared.[63] Thirty more primary schools were provided by 1973.[64] The expansion reflected the rise in the number of children of school age after the Second World War. In 1955 there were 82,300 children on the rolls of the county primary schools. Eighteen years later there were 128,000, an increase of more than 50 per cent.[65] The numbers of primary schools given above include those which were still partly under voluntary control. In 1958 107 of the 463 primary schools in Cheshire were listed as 'voluntary aided', 142 as 'voluntary controlled', and one as 'voluntary special agreement'; the status of 16 had not yet been determined. Three years later the number of aided schools had fallen slightly, to 101, and the number of controlled schools had risen to 148.[66] The difference between the two classes lay in the fact that in 'controlled' schools the authority was responsible for the entire cost of maintenance, while external repairs and structural alterations to 'aided' schools had to be financed in part by the voluntary bodies responsible for them.[67] The number of primary school teachers in Cheshire increased from 2,338 in 1953 to 4,809 twenty years later; in the same period the average number of pupils on the schools' rolls per teacher fell from 33 to fewer than 27.[68]

Before the First World War the county council provided only 9 secondary schools: in Altrincham (2), Crewe, Hyde, Macclesfield, Nantwich and Acton, Runcorn, Sale, and West Kirby. The total number of pupils on their books in January 1915 was 1,720. It also joined with Chester city council in providing a secondary school, and supported 5 other schools with grants.[69] The 1902 Education Act had only permitted councils to levy a rate of 2d. in the £ for higher education. The number of children in Cheshire

[56] *Ches. C.C. Triennial Rep..* (1922), 3–4.
[57] Ibid. (1919), 18; (1925), 4.
[58] Ibid. (1934), 15–16.
[59] 7 & 8 Geo. VI, c. 31.
[60] *Educ. in Ches.* (1945–55), 120–6.
[61] Ibid.
[62] Ibid. (1955–60), 104; (1960–5), 159.
[63] Ibid. (1965–70), 159.

[64] *Ches. Finance* (1973), 20.
[65] *Educ. in Ches.* (1945–55), 120; *Ches. Finance* (1973), 20.
[66] *Ches. C.C. Triennial Rep.* (1958), 23; (1961), 28.
[67] Barnard, *Short Hist. Eng. Educ.* 348–9.
[68] *Ches. Finance* (1953), 16; (1973), 20.
[69] *Ches. C.C. Educ. Cttee. Official Manual, 1915–16,* 94–6.

receiving secondary education reached 4,517 by 1922 and nearly doubled between then and 1934. In the latter year 8,500 Cheshire pupils were receiving education in 13 schools owned by the county council, 6 non-county grammar schools in Cheshire, 8 schools in Chester and Stockport, and 15 schools outside the geographical county.[70]

The 1944 Education Act abolished the category of elementary school and provided that all pupils must receive a secondary education. The secondary system chosen in Cheshire was that based on secondary modern and grammar schools. In the first ten years after the Act came into operation, the county provided 62 secondary modern and 18 grammar schools. The number of pupils in each type was respectively 20,063 and 10,420 in 1955.[71] Ten years later the numbers of secondary modern and grammar schools had increased respectively to 81 and 28, and two-fifths of the 55,000 pupils in secondary schools were receiving grammar-school instruction.[72] Meanwhile the number of direct-grant and independent schools receiving county pupils had fallen to ten. Between 1965 and 1970 one comprehensive school was built, in the Hyde and Longdendale division. It had 771 pupils in 1970.[73]

The years after the Second World War witnessed growth in the demand for further education. In 1953 the 45 technical schools and evening institutes supported by the county council were providing courses for 7,648 pupils. The number of students enrolled exceeded 34,500 ten years later and 48,000 by 1973.[74] In 1956 the council provided full-time further education establishments at Eastham, Crewe, Northwich, Sale, Hyde, Macclesfield, and Runcorn, and supported 43 evening institutes.[75] The agricultural college at Saltersford was found inadequate after the First World War, and Reaseheath Hall near Nantwich was bought by the council, converted into an agricultural college, and opened in 1921.[76] In 1967 it was providing three courses: general agriculture, dairy technology, and rural domestic economy.[77]

In September 1908 temporary premises were opened for the training of teachers, at Crewe.[78] By 1913 Crewe training college, which had been opened in the previous year, had 119 students.[79] A second college was opened for the emergency training of teachers at Alsager in 1947, and permanently established two years later.[80] By 1953 the two colleges were between them providing 420 places, but with the increasing demand for trained teachers in the two decades after the end of the Second World War, rapid expansion was allowed, and the numbers of students had risen to 2,120, of whom 1,330 were at Alsager, by 1967, and to 2,400 by 1973.[81]

When it was inaugurated in 1922, the county library service was under the authority of the director of education. At first it operated from a central headquarters in Chester through local centres run by volunteers.[82] The number of branches rose from some 250 in the 1920s to 392 in 1953 and 619 ten years later.[83] In 1965, following the Public Libraries and Museums Act, 1964,[84] the library service was separated from the education department, and a director of libraries and museums was appointed.[85] In 1973 the number of library service points was 1,233, and the total stock of books was more than 1,400,000.[86]

[70] Ches. C.C. Triennial Rep. (1922), 5; (1934), 17.
[71] Educ. in Ches. (1945–55), 120.
[72] Ibid. (1960–5), 159.
[73] Ibid. (1965–70), 159.
[74] Ches. Finance (1953), 16; (1963), 20; (1973), 20.
[75] Ches. C.C. Co. Services Guide (1956), 16–20.
[76] Jubilee of Co. Councils: Ches. 74–5, for a description of 1938.
[77] Ches. C.C. Triennial Rep. (1967), 34.
[78] Ibid. (1910), 19.
[79] Ibid. (1913), 13.
[80] Educ. in Ches. (1945–55), 80.
[81] Ches. C.C. Triennial Rep. (1967), 33; Ches. Finance (1973), 20.
[82] Ches. C.C. Triennial Rep. (1928), 4–5.
[83] Ches. Finance (1953), 17; (1963), 21.
[84] 1964, c. 75.
[85] Ches. C.C. Triennial Rep. (1967), 66.
[86] Ches. Finance (1973), 22.

Health and Social Services

A county medical officer of health was first appointed in 1893, but until 1895 his appointment was part-time.[87] The county council was empowered to provide isolation hospitals, and in 1896 the medical officer recommended the division of the county into 9 districts for that purpose.[88] By 1910 hospital boards had been established in the Bucklow, Congleton, Nantwich, Northwich, and Wirral areas.[89] Their function was to ensure that adequate accommodation was provided in existing hospitals, rather than to provide new ones. In 1916, however, the county joined with the county boroughs of Birkenhead, Chester, Stockport, Wallasey, and Stoke-on-Trent (Staffs.) to provide a joint sanatorium committee, which purchased a site for a sanatorium at Burntwood (Staffs.). The sanatorium was opened in 1923, and accommodated 240 patients by 1928.[90] A colony for the treatment and rehabilitation of tuberculosis patients was opened at Wrenbury Hall in 1922.[91] The county council joined the county boroughs of Birkenhead, Chester, and Wallasey in creating a joint board for the mentally defective in 1928, which developed in institution at Cranage Hall.[92] In 1935 the county's first general hospital was opened, at Clatterbridge. It contained about 300 beds.[93] West Park hospital at Macclesfield was taken over by the county in 1940, and in the following year the Mary Dendy homes for the mentally defective at Alderley Edge passed into its control.[94] By 1936 the two mental hospitals which the county had taken over from quarter sessions in 1889, at Upton by Chester and at Macclesfield, accommodated respectively 1,753 and 1,344 patients.[95] After the Second World War most of the county institutions, apart from Wrenbury Hall, passed into National Health Service control.

The county provided school medical inspection of pupils, and clinics for the welfare of expectant mothers and children of school and pre-school age.[96] In 1935 there were 7 district medical officers of health employed full-time by the county, while another 30 doctors combined work for the county with private practice.[97] In 1972 129 child health clinics were controlled by the county, which employed 180 health visitors and school nurses, 189 home nurses, and 143 midwives; Cheshire was divided into 11 areas each with a divisional medical officer in control.[98] The county ambulance service owned 75 vehicles in 1953 and 123 twenty years later.[99]

As a result of the Local Government Act, 1929,[1] the county council took over responsibility for public assistance from the 8 poor-law unions which were wholly in Cheshire and the 6 of which parts lay in the county.[2] In the early 1930s there was a steep rise in the number of unemployed requiring relief; the average weekly number rose from 806 in 1931 to 1,322 in 1932, 2,205 in 1933, and 2,679 in 1934. The number of persons relieved in the former poor-law institutions averaged 2,442 between 1931 and 1933 but declined to 2,110 in the next triennial period and to 1,484 between 1937 and 1939.[3] After the Second World War the public assistance department of the county council was replaced, under the National Assistance Act, 1948,[4] by a welfare department; a children's department had already been set up in 1946.[5] The children's and welfare departments were amalgamated with parts of the health and education depart-

[87] *Ches. C.C. Triennial Rep.* (1895), 5; (1898), 5–6.
[88] Ibid. (1898), 6.
[89] *Kelly's Dir. Ches.* (1910), 76, 276, 399, 471, 495.
[90] *Ches. C.C. Triennial Rep.* (1919), 35–6; (1925), 10; (1928), 24.
[91] *Kelly's Dir. Ches.* (1939), 479.
[92] Ibid. 123; *Ches. C.C. Triennial Rep.* (1934), 10.
[93] *Ches. C.C. Triennial Rep.* (1937), 30; *Jubilee of Co. Councils: Ches.*, 79.
[94] *Ches. C.C. Triennial Rep.* (1943), 13.
[95] *Jubilee of Co. Councils: Ches.* 83.

[96] For a description of the services shortly before the Second World War see ibid. 76–7, 79, 80.
[97] Lee, *Soc. Leaders*, 127.
[98] *Ches. C.C. Health Services* (1972), pp. iii, 63, 65.
[99] *Ches. Finance* (1953), 18; (1973), 22.
[1] 19 & 20 Geo. V, c. 17.
[2] *Ches. C.C. Triennial Rep.* (1931), 22.
[3] Ibid. (1934), 25–6; (1937), 29, 31; (1940), 15.
[4] 11 & 12 Geo. VI, c. 29.
[5] *Ches. C.C. Triennial Rep.* (1949), 10, 44.

ments to form a new social services department in 1971.[6] The children's department had been responsible for providing homes and hostels: in 1955 it controlled 2 reception and short-stay homes, 8 long-stay homes and nurseries, 2 family group homes, and 2 hostels for working boys and girls.[7] The welfare department had, on its creation, taken over three old people's homes from the public assistance committee. In 1949 its first objective was said to be the creation of 21 such homes.[8] By 1967 the number of homes provided had reached 41, and accommodation was provided for 1,314 old people.[9] In 1973 the social services department owned 24 homes and hostels for children providing 358 places, and 61 homes for aged and infirm persons providing 1,766.[10]

Planning

In the 1930s and for some time afterwards planning was thought of as an extension of the county's responsibility for roads and bridges.[11] The county was then divided into 10 planning areas, each with a committee composed of representatives of the county council and of other authorities. For example, the Mid-Cheshire (Area No. 2) Joint Planning Committee as constituted in 1937 contained 9 representatives of the county council and two of Chester R.D.C., three of Nantwich R.D.C., and four of Tarvin R.D.C. Its main task was to consider proposals for housing and other development, rather than to make schemes for the future.[12]

During the Second World War a post-war reconstruction committee was set up, as a result of a conference of all local authorities in Cheshire summoned in 1943.[13] A planning consultant, W. Dobson Chapman, was commissioned to prepare a county plan, which was printed for private circulation in 1946 and published three years later.[14] In 1948 the county was divided, under the Town and County Planning Act, 1947,[15] into 7 planning areas, and a planning officer was appointed for the whole county. By March 1949 an average of 477 planning applications was being considered each month.[16] The county planning officer prepared a development plan for the whole county, which was submitted to the Ministry of Housing and Local Government in two stages. The first, dealing with Hoole urban district and parts of Chester rural district, was approved by the Minister in 1952, but was soon rendered ineffective by the transfer of most of the area to Chester city. The second part, covering the remainder of the county apart from the area within the Peak Park, was also submitted in 1952 but not finally approved until 1958.[17] The plan provided for an increase in Cheshire's population of about 190,000, of which some three-fifths would be accommodated in Ellesmere Port, Bebington, Crewe, and district, Stockton Heath, Macclesfield and district, Sale, Altrincham, Hale and Bowdon, Wilmslow and Alderley Edge, Bredbury and Romiley, Cheadle, Gatley, Hazel Grove, and Bramhall; about 85,000 new dwellings would be needed.[18] While the plan was under consideration, two other proposals were made: one was for a new town with a population of c. 60,000 at Congleton, the other for new towns for Manchester 'overspill' based on Lymm and Mobberley. Both were rejected.[19]

[6] Lee, Wood, Solomon, and Walters, *Scope of Local Initiative*, 9.

[7] *Ches. C.C. Triennial Rep.* (1955), 8–9.

[8] Ibid. (1949), 44.

[9] Ibid. (1967), 108.

[10] *Ches. Finance* (1973), 27.

[11] *Jubilee of Co. Councils: Ches.* 92, where 'planning' appears under the heading 'roads and bridges'.

[12] *Mid-Ches. Jt. Planning Cttee. Annual Report* (1938).

[13] Lee, *Soc. Leaders*, 119–20.

[14] W. Dobson Chapman, *County Palatine: a Plan for Ches.*

[15] 10 & 11 Geo. VI, c. 51.

[16] *Ches. C.C. Triennial Rep.* (1949), 39–40.

[17] Ibid. (1955), 42; (1961), 77; *Ches. C.C. Development Plan, Pt. 2, Written Statement, 1959*, p. 1. and note facing.

[18] Ibid. 2–3.

[19] *Ches. C.C. Triennial Rep.* (1952), 41; (1958), 62.

By the mid 1960s, in spite of objections from the county council, Runcorn had been selected as a site for a new town of 60,000 inhabitants.[20] Meanwhile the county had become involved in difficult and protracted negotiations with Manchester over the accommodation of the city's 'overspill' population, following Manchester's request in 1962 for 22 sites in Cheshire.[21]

Meanwhile planning applications from developers were reaching an annual total of more than ten thousand.[22] In 1968 it was decided to centralize planning by replacing the 6 area planning offices then existing by 2, one of which would be based in county hall at Chester.[23] In 1973 the county planning department, which had employed 80 staff twenty years earlier, numbered 225; in the year 1972–3, 12,688 planning applications were considered, of which 11,873 were made by private developers.[24] The work of the department then included advice on conservation areas under the Civic Amenities Act, 1967.[25] A series of booklets was produced, each dealing with one conservation area, describing the areas and offering advice to residents on the terms of legislation on conservation.

Public Protection Services

In 1889 the police in Cheshire came under the control of a standing joint committee consisting of one justice of the peace and one county councillor from each of the 14 petty sessional divisions, and the chairman and vice-chairman of both the county council and quarter sessions.[26] In 1902 the county police force consisted of the chief constable and his deputy, 11 superintendents, 13 inspectors, 79 sergeants, and 334 constables, organized in eleven divisions. Eight years later the number of divisions had increased by two, and the force included 404 constables.[27] During the 1920s and 1930s the size of the force increased by about 50 per cent.[28] Under the Police Act, 1946,[29] the former independent police forces of Congleton, Hyde, Macclesfield, and Stalybridge were brought under county control, and that of Chester city followed in 1949.[30] In 1963 the total police strength in the county was 1,191; it was within 2 per cent of its authorized strength. Seven per cent of the annual cost was borne by Chester city.[31] Within the next ten years the police forces of Birkenhead, Stockport, and Wallasey were brought under the control of the county police authority, bringing its strength up to 2,825 by 1973. The county then bore roughly seven-tenths of the cost, the remainder being met by the county boroughs.[32] A new headquarters building was constructed in Chester between 1964 and 1967.[33]

In 1936 an air-raid precautions scheme was designed for Cheshire, and a year later the county council was officially made responsible for air-raid precautions. By the end of July 1938 8,000 persons had enrolled as air-raid wardens, and anti-gas courses had been held for between three and four thousand civilians.[34] Between August 1940 and November 1941 there were 80 incidents involving the service. The majority of them occurred in Wirral.[35] A civil defence committee was established in 1949 and Cheshire was divided into 9 civil defence groups. More than 2,000 persons enrolled for training before 1952.[36] The enrolment doubled within the next three years, but in the 1960s

---

[20] *Ches. C.C. Triennial Rep.* (1964), 79–80.
[21] The negotiations are fully described by Lee, Wood, Solomon, and Walters, *Scope of Local Initiative*, 28 sqq.
[22] *Ches. C.C. Triennial Rep.* (1964), 80.
[23] Lee, Wood, Solomon, and Walters, *Scope of Local Initiative*, 45.
[24] *Ches. Finance* (1953), 22; (1973), 19, 23.
[25] 1967, c. 69.   [26] Lee, *Soc. Leaders*, 66.
[27] *Kelly's Dir. Ches.* (1902), 13; (1910), 15.

[28] *Jubilee of Co. Councils: Ches.* 96.
[29] 9 & 10 Geo. VI, c. 46.
[30] James, *To the Best of our Skill & Knowledge*, 108.
[31] *Ches. Finance* (1963), 24.
[32] Ibid. (1973), 24.
[33] Pevsner and Hubbard, *Buildings of England: Ches.* 158.
[34] *Jubilee of Co. Councils: Ches.* 85.
[35] *Ches. C.C. Triennial Rep.* (1946), 13.
[36] Ibid. (1952), 19–23.

central government policy led to a reduction of the force, and at the end of 1966 the numbers stood at 1,627 on the active list and 955 in reserve.[37] The Cheshire division of the Civil Defence Corps was then under the authority of a county control at Chester and 5 county sub-controls.

Cheshire became a fire authority under the Fire Services Act, 1947.[38] The county was divided into 5 districts, based respectively on Hyde, Wilmslow, Crewe, Chester, and Ellesmere Port; 28 fire stations were under county control by March 1949, of which 11 were manned by part-time personnel.[39] In 1963 the Cheshire fire brigade had a whole-time establishment of 840 out of a total authorized strength of 916. The gap between authorized and actual strengths had widened ten years later, when the figures were respectively 997 and 773.[40]

Inspectors of weights and measures had been appointed in the 19th century, but their duties had after 1857 been discharged by local police superintendents in their divisions. In 1889 the county council appointed a weights and measures committee and the county was divided into 4 inspection districts.[41] The county analyst appointed by quarter sessions in 1876 was retained by the council until his death in 1913.[42] The duties of the weights and measures department included the checking of weights and measures, the analysis of samples of food and drugs, and the registration of premises for the sale of poisons. Its staff numbered 21 in 1953.[43] By 1973 its functions had been assumed by the trading standards department and its staff had doubled.[44]

Roads and Bridges

In the mid 1890s the county council was responsible for some 570 miles of main roads, of which 450 miles lay in rural and 120 in urban districts.[45] In addition there were more than 300 county and hundred bridges to be maintained, and some 50 approach roads to railway bridges.[46] The Local Government Act, 1929, brought all highways in rural areas and all classified roads in municipal boroughs and urban districts under county council management. In terms of mileage that meant an increase from 630 to nearly 2,300.[47] Ninety-seven miles of roads in Cheshire were designated trunk roads under the Trunk Roads Act, 1936.[48] Among the projects completed between the wars were a new road from Shotwick to Frodsham, and the first stages of the Northwich by-pass on the road from Chester to Altrincham and Manchester.[49] The first lengths of motorway in Cheshire were opened in 1961 and 1963, and covered a total of 25 miles from Barthomley to the Lancashire boundary north of Lymm.[50] In 1961 a new bridge was completed across the Manchester Ship Canal and the Mersey at Runcorn.[51] In 1973 the county council was responsible for maintaining 51 miles of motorway and 201 of trunk roads; the total mileage of roads under its control was nearly 2,500.[52]

Agriculture and Smallholdings

The executive committee set up by the county council in accordance with the Diseases of Animals Act, 1894,[53] was replaced by an agricultural committee under the Ministry

[37] Ibid. (1955), 10; (1967), 14–15.
[38] 10 & 11 Geo. VI, c. 41.
[39] Ches. C.C. Triennial Rep. (1949), 21–2.
[40] Ches. Finance (1963), 21; (1973), 21.
[41] Ches. C.C. Triennial Rep. (1892), 6.
[42] Lee, Soc. Leaders, 69–70.
[43] Ches. Finance (1953), 22.
[44] Ibid. (1963), 27; (1973), 19.
[45] Ches. C.C. Triennial Rep. (1895), 3–5.
[46] Ibid. (1919), 30.

[47] Ibid. (1931), 10.
[48] Ibid. (1937), 10; 1 Edw. VIII & 1 Geo. VI, c. 5.
[49] Jubilee of Co. Councils: Ches. 92.
[50] Ches. C.C. Triennial Rep. (1964), 87.
[51] Ibid.
[52] Ches. Finance (1973), 25. Detailed treatment of road communication in Ches. is reserved for another volume of the History.
[53] 57 & 58 Vic. c. 57.

of Agriculture and Fisheries Act, 1919.[54] By 1938 the committee had six sub-committees working under it, dealing respectively with cultivation, diseases of animals, land drainage, light horse breeding, livestock, and smallholdings and allotments.[55] In 1912 the executive committee supervised 24 veterinary inspectors under the Act of 1894 and its successors.[56]

As a result of the Smallholdings Act, 1907,[57] a land agent's office was set up by the county council in the following year, and estates were bought for conversion into small-holdings. By 1910, 1,341 acres of land had been purchased, with the largest area (853 a.) the Ledsham estate. It was divided into 24 smallholdings of areas varying between 14 and 50 acres, and 5 market garden plots each of 7 acres. Each smallholding was provided with a three-bedroomed dwelling house, and farm buildings. Average rents charged were 46s. a year for each acre of the smallholdings and 83s. 6d. an acre for the market garden plots. Another estate purchased from the Ecclesiastical Commissioners at Tarvin contained one large smallholding and 30 much smaller plots of between 1 and 4 acres each.[58] By the end of the First World War the total land acquired amounted to 4,740 acres, but that amount was doubled over the next three years.[59] In 1925 the county owned 365 holdings, and there were almost as many applicants, most of them ex-servicemen, on its waiting list.[60] Thereafter the total acreage owned by the county did not expand greatly; it was 12,672 acres in 1937 and 13,109 in 1946.[61] In 1973 there were 350 holdings, and a register of 164 approved applicants waiting.[62]

County Records

Although the records of the palatinate of Chester had been removed from Chester castle to the Public Record Office in 1854, those of quarter sessions and its associated offices remained in Chester. A record office was established there in 1934 and in 1949 a full-time archivist was appointed.[63] Two years later the records of the Chester diocesan probate registry were deposited at the county record office.[64] The staff of the office, which came under the control of the clerk's department, numbered six in 1964.[65] In 1940 the county council financed the publication of lists and selections of the quarter sessions records up to 1760 by the Record Society of Lancashire and Cheshire.[66] In 1972 work began on the *Victoria History of Cheshire*, locally financed partly by the county council and partly by a grant from the Leverhulme Trust.

Boundary Changes and Reorganization

After 1888 the ancient county of Chester suffered several changes of boundary.[67] The Local Government Act, 1888, made Birkenhead and Stockport along with Chester into county boroughs independent of county administration, and Wallasey gained the same status in 1913. Cheshire lost territory both to the county boroughs and to the neighbouring counties. The parish of Tittenley, which had been almost surrounded by Shropshire, was transferred to that county in 1895.[68] In 1901 1,728 acres of land with a population of more than 13,000 was transferred to Stockport. Between 1927 and 1936

[54] 9 & 10 Geo. V, c. 91.
[55] *Jubilee of Co. Councils: Ches.* 81.
[56] *Ches. C.C. Yr. Bk.* (1912–13), 169–76.
[57] 7 Edw. VII, c. 54.
[58] *Ches. C.C. Triennial Rep.* (1910), 37–40.
[59] Ibid. (1919), 33; (1922), 17.
[60] Ibid. (1925), 18–19.
[61] Ibid. (1937), 32; (1946), 6.
[62] *Ches. Finance* (1973), 26.

[63] *Ches. C.C. Triennial Rep.* (1937), 45, 46; (1940), 27; (1952), 17.
[64] Ibid. (1955), 15.
[65] Ibid. (1964), 26.
[66] *Ches. Q.S. Rec.*
[67] For details of changes see under individual places in table of population, below.
[68] 58 & 59 Vic. c. 86 (Local).

Cheshire lost territory to Derbyshire and Lancashire, and to Birkenhead, Chester, Manchester, Stockport, Wallasey, and Warrington county boroughs, only partly offset by the gain of Ludworth and Mellor parishes from Derbyshire in 1936. The net loss sustained by Cheshire between 1901 and 1954 was more than 28,000 acres.[69] Some of the losses were resisted by the county council, especially those of Baguley, Northenden, and Northen Etchells to Manchester in 1931 and of the area between the Manchester Ship Canal and the Mersey to Lancashire in 1932.[70]

Until the late 1960s Cheshire county council believed that reorganization of local government could be carried out without any large-scale revision of the established

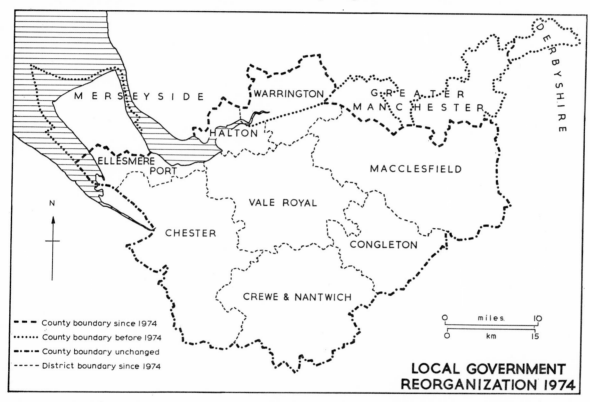

LOCAL GOVERNMENT REORGANIZATION 1974

- – – County boundary since 1974
- ······· County boundary before 1974
- –·–·– County boundary unchanged
- – – – District boundary since 1974

county boundaries. In 1962, in reply to the questionnaire sent out by the Local Government Commission which had been set up under the Local Government Act, 1958,[71] the council said, 'The size of the administrative county is perfectly satisfactory. . . . The shape is generally satisfactory. . . . Communications across it are extremely good, and are becoming even better, and neither the shape nor the size is any hindrance to the provision of effective and convenient local government.'[72] In 1966 the county council proposed changes which would have revived the administrative unity destroyed in 1506; Birkenhead, Chester, Stockport, and Wallasey would lose their autonomy and become second-tier authorities under the county council.[73] The Redcliffe-Maud Report of 1969 recommended instead the dismemberment of Cheshire; the ancient county was to be apportioned between the Merseyside and South East Lancashire/North East Cheshire (SELNEC) metropolitan areas and the Stoke and North Staffordshire unitary area.[74] The county council objected strongly, and in 1971 its

[69] *Reply of Ches. C.C. to Questionnaire of Loc. Govt. Com. 1962*, 6.

[70] Lee, *Soc. Leaders*, 111–15.

[71] 6 & 7 Eliz. II, c. 55.

[72] *Reply of C.C. to Questionnaire*, 7.

[73] *Ches. C.C., Submissions to Royal Com. on Loc. Govt.*

in *Eng. 1966*, 7–8.

[74] *Rep. Royal Com. on Loc. Govt. in Eng. 1969*, [Cmnd. 4040], pp. 212–14, 219–22, 236–7, H.C. (1968–9), xxxviii; Lee, Wood, Solomon, and Walters, *Scope of Local Initiative*, 61 (map).

objections were largely accepted by the government. Cheshire was to lose territory to Greater Manchester and to Merseyside, but was to receive land north of the Mersey in compensation. The county council accepted the new proposals once it became clear that Ellesmere Port and Neston were to be included in Cheshire rather than in Merseyside, and that Alderley Edge was not to be lost to Manchester. By amendments to the original proposal Wilmslow and Poynton were also retained in Cheshire.[75]

Under the Local Government Act, 1972,[76] all Wirral north-west of Neston urban district and of Ellesmere Port municipal borough was transferred to Merseyside. The parts of Cheshire beyond the parishes of Lymm, Agden, Bollington, Rostherne, Ashley, Mobberley, Wilmslow, Mottram St. Andrew, Prestbury, Adlington, Poynton with Worth, Lyme Handley, and Disley were lost to Greater Manchester. Tintwistle was transferred to Derbyshire. Cheshire gained from Lancashire the county borough of Warrington, the municipal borough of Widnes, Golborne urban district, and 10 civil parishes. Eight new districts were created in Cheshire in succession to the old county borough of Chester, the municipal boroughs, and the urban and rural districts; they were named Chester, Congleton, Crewe and Nantwich, Ellesmere Port, Halton, Macclesfield, Vale Royal, and Warrington.[77]

The first election to the new county council was held in April 1973. Of the 67 seats, 61 were contested; nevertheless the composition and functions of the new council seem not to have excited the electorate, since only 41 per cent voted, compared with 36 per cent at the previous election of the old council held in 1970. Twenty-seven retiring councillors and 3 former aldermen were elected to the new council. In political composition the new body differed from the old; the Conservatives, with 31 seats, were closely followed by Labour with 29; the Liberals won 1 seat, and Independents six. A former Conservative county alderman, Mr. C. L. S. Cornwall-Legh, was elected chairman of the new council; the vice-chairman, Dr. J. K. Walley, was an Independent.[78]

County Seals and Arms

Before the 14th century it is difficult to distinguish between the personal seals of individual earls of Chester and an 'institutional' seal of the county palatine. From the late 1340s references occur to a seal of the Chester Exchequer, fees for the use of which were established.[79] The seal remained in the custody of the chamberlain of Chester, but it was personal to the earl or king and was therefore changed on most occasions when the earldom changed hands. After 1536, however, it could be altered only after a change of ruler.

Before Richard II made Cheshire a principality in 1397 his seal for the county palatine was 1·6 in. in diameter and one-sided.[80] A surviving impression of that of the principality of Chester is much larger, and has both obverse and reverse.[81] Under Richard's successors large double-sided seals continued to be used.[82] As an example of the palatinate seals used in the 15th century a good impression of that of Richard III, attached to letters patent issued by the Chester Exchequer in 1484, may be taken.[83] The seal is round, 3·25 in. in diameter. The obverse shows the king seated on a galloping

[75] The discussion is described by Lee, Wood, Solomon, and Walters, *Scope of Local Initiative*, 66.

[76] 1972, c. 70.

[77] See map.

[78] Lee, Wood, Solomon, and Walters, *Scope of Local Initiative*, 188–90, 200.

[79] *Ches. Chamb. Accts.* 137.

[80] Examples in Chester R.O., CH/20–1.

[81] J. Hall, 'Royal Grants to City of Chest.', *J.C.A.S.*

N.S. xviii. 46 and plate facing.

[82] Ibid. 50, 51, 56; *Cat. of Seals in B.M.*, ed. W. de G. Birch, ii. 48–51.

[83] Chester R.O., CH/30, described in *J.C.A.S.* N.S. xviii. 51–2 and illustrated in R. H. Morris, *Chest.* 517 (line drawing), and Margaret J. Groombridge, *Guide to Charters, Plate, and Insignia of City of Chest.* 22 (photograph).

horse, holding in his right hand a drawn sword, and on his left arm a shield of arms. The reverse shows the arms of England and France quarterly impaling the earldom of Chester (three garbs) beneath a coronet; supporters a lion and a boar. Legend, obverse and reverse, black letter: SIGILLUM RICARDI DEI GRACIA REGIS ANGLIE ET FRANCIE ET DOMINI HIBERNIE COMITATUS SUI PALATINI CESTRIE. The obverse and reverse have minor variations in abbreviation.

From Elizabeth I's reign palatinate seals included references to the county palatine of Chester and Flintshire. From 1603 they were dated.[84] Charles II's seal, for example, is round, 3·6 in. in diameter. The obverse again shows the king seated on a galloping horse, holding in his right had a drawn sword. Above the horse's tail is a small representation of the arms of the county palatine. The reverse shows the arms of the county palatine (three garbs) surmounted by a coronet; supporters two wyverns holding feathers. Legend, roman, obverse: SIGILLUM CAROLI II DEI GRATIA MAGNÆ BRITANNIÆ FRANCIÆ ET HIBERNIÆ REGIS FIDEI DEFENSORIS; reverse, COMITATUS PALATINI SUI CESTRIÆ ET FLINT ANNO 1660.[85] A seal bearing the date 1706 is said to have been that in use when the palatine courts were abolished.[86]

The seal in use by Cheshire county council from 1889 to 1938 was round, 2·5 in. in diameter, and showed a shield bearing three garbs with feathers as supporters, surmounted by a coronet. Legend, black letter: CHESHIRE COUNTY COUNCIL ANNO MDCCCLXXXIX. After the grant of arms to the county council in 1938, a new seal was used, round, 2·25 in. in diameter, showing the arms with supporters, ground, and motto; legend, roman: THE COUNTY COUNCIL OF THE COUNTY PALATINE OF CHESTER.[87] After local government reorganization a new seal was brought into use early in 1976: round, 2·25 in. in diameter, showing arms with supporters, ground, and motto: legend, roman, CHESHIRE COUNTY COUNCIL.[88]

[84] P.R.O. Lists & Indexes No. XL, p. iv; Cat. of Seals in B.M., ii. 51–2.
[85] Chester R.O., CR63/2/687. Another impression is illustrated in E. Cust, 'Investigation into the Right of Co. Palatine of Chest. to bear a Coat of Arms', T.H.S.L.C. ii. 9–18.
[86] H. Taylor, Co. Palatine of Chest.: its Place in Hist., 14.

For an example of 1821 see Ches. R.O., DTW/Acc. 2406 Box 7.
[87] Examples in Ches. R.O., CCL/F/87.
[88] The help of Mr. G. Gordon in describing the hist. and use of the most recent co. council seal is gratefully acknowledged.

CHESHIRE COUNTY COUNCIL. Arms: azure a sword erect between three garbs or. Crest: upon a mural crown gules a lion statant guardant or between two ostrich feathers argent, mantled azure doubled or. Supporters: on either side a lion or supporting between the forelegs an ostrich feather argent. Motto: Jure et dignitate gladii. Badge: in front of an oval wreath of oak leaves a sword erect, the blade surmounted of a garb, all or.   [Arms granted 1938, badge 1958]

PARLIAMENTARY
REPRESENTATION 1543-1974

T HE statute of 1543[1] granting parliamentary representation to the county palatine and city of Chester completed the revolution in government which assimilated Cheshire to the other English counties. The preamble of the statute rehearsed a petition from the freeholders of Cheshire, asking the King for the right to share in the making of those laws by which they were bound. The petition implicitly acknowledged that most of the distinctive institutions of the palatinate had already been altered, and that it had lost the benefits of remaining outside the parliamentary system and above all, since 1540, its immunity from paying parliamentary subsidies.

There is no evidence of objections to the granting of members of parliament to the county and city. Two double-member constituencies were created, allowing the palatinate four members, a number unchanged until 1832.[2] In that year the number of seats within Cheshire was increased to ten by creating two double-member county seats and three double-seat boroughs, Chester, Macclesfield, and Stockport. Birkenhead was granted a single seat in 1859. Two more county seats added in 1867 brought the total representation to thirteen, which was increased to fourteen in 1918 and to fifteen in 1945.

The Act of 1543 had laid down a procedure which differed from that operating elsewhere. The Lord Chancellor sent election writs to the chamberlain of Chester, head of the palatine jurisdiction, who in turn passed them to the mayor and the sheriff. That deference to the continued status of the palatinate probably had little actual effect, although it did give the chamberlain some control over the timing of the elections, which could be crucial. The chancellor of the Duchy of Lancaster, who enjoyed similar powers in Lancashire elections, certainly gained considerable influence in elections there.

The Act made no specific provision for the franchise, beyond requiring that the form of the elections should be the same as that 'in the county palatine of Lancaster or any other county and city in England'. That was taken to mean that in the county the franchise belonged to all forty shilling freeholders, and that in Chester the parliamentary franchise should be the same as that laid down for the election of borough governors in the charter of 1506.[3]

The term 'forty shilling freeholder' was not strictly construed in the 16th and 17th centuries. No registers of electors were compiled,[4] and in most counties custom rather than legal title determined the electorate. Indeed it has recently been shown that in most counties little attention was paid to the freehold requirement, and even less to the value qualification, so that 'in many areas most people with any land at all could make a plausible claim to vote if they wished'.[5] Cheshire, with no developed local tradition, with no succession of contested elections until the end of the 17th century which would

---

[1] 34 & 35 Hen. VIII, c. 13.
[2] Except for two elections (1654, 1656) during the Protectorate, at each of which the county returned 4 members and the city one.
[3] J. Hemingway, *Hist. Chest.* ii, *passim*.

[4] The so-called 'freeholders' books', compiled as jury lists, contained only some of those entitled to vote: J. S. Morrill, *Ches. Grand Jury 1625-59*, 13-15.
[5] D. Hirst, *Representative of the People?* 42.

have helped to develop one, and with an agricultural economy which led to the continued existence of a large number of tenant farmers holding land on long leases and at nominal rents,[6] was particularly affected by that point. It may help to explain why the county had one of the largest electorates in the early 18th century. It has been estimated that 4,800 actually voted in 1681.[7] An electorate of 5,500 has been suggested for the reign of Anne,[8] and one of 5,000 voters in the period 1715–54.[9] Both estimates give Cheshire the sixth largest county electorate in the country. In fact, it was almost certainly more numerous. In 1727 the poll book shows that over 5,800 actually cast votes.[10] In 1734 two of the candidates of 1727 stood. Unless the proportion of plumpers, who only used one of their two votes, was drastically lower, and the Excise crisis had so polarized opinion as to make that unlikely, the number of those voting would have been rather higher, possibly around 7,000–7,200,[11] giving Cheshire the third largest electorate in Britain.

The size of the county electorate raised problems common to all county seats. The problems of the borough franchise were at once more particular and more long-lasting. Most commentators have assumed that Chester was a freeman borough,[12] but it has been argued that its electorate in the early 17th century consisted of all adult males.[13] A case can be made out for each view, but the balance of evidence supports the latter. Only a minority of 16th- and 17th-century parliamentary elections for the city were contested. Possibly, indeed, there were no formal contests until 1621, the matter having already been decided informally within the corporation before the mayor opened the writ. In that sense Chester was developing a governing body franchise. Nevertheless when in 1621 a discontented oligarch appealed to the citizens at large, the corporation made no attempt to disclaim a wider franchise. The charter of 1506 had granted Chester a very open electoral system. The mayor, aldermen, and councillors were to be elected annually, and the recorder periodically, by 'the citizens and commonalty'. Much of that open government was altered during the 16th century; aldermen and councillors were co-opted by the corporation and, once chosen, served for life. The commonalty, however, still played a limited role in the annual election of the mayor.[14] It is reasonable to assume that the parliamentary electors would be the same as those who retained that vestigial part in borough government. It remains uncertain whether the phrase 'citizens and commonalty' was held to mean all male inhabitants or all freemen of the city. Nevertheless it was consistently used in relation to local elections. The avoidance of the precise term 'freemen' is suggestive. Moreover, several mayors sold the freedom of the city to large numbers of men to raise money during Elizabeth I's reign. All criticisms of the practice concentrated on its adverse economic consequences; no mayor was accused of interfering with the electoral system.[15]

The evidence from the 1621 election is more positive. The corporation, in its petition to the Commons against the result, claimed that the victor had canvassed amongst the poor of the city and particularly amongst 'those of the suburbs, the basest sort, as labourers and hired workmen and even beggars, and not with these only but also with

[6] M. D. G. Wanklyn, 'Structure of Parties in Ches. & Salop. during the Civil War' (Manchester Univ. Ph.D. thesis, 1974).

[7] Hist. Parl. Trust, constit. rep. Ches. 1660–90.

[8] W. A. Speck, *Tory and Whig*, 126.

[9] *Hist. Parl., Commons*, 1715–54, i. 202. The editors divided the total number of votes cast by two, on the assumption that each elector cast both votes.

[10] 32·7 per cent plumped for one candidate, Sir Robt. Salisbury Cotton, accounting for 86 per cent of his support. The poll book is Ches. R.O., P/4/17/2.

[11] Extrapolation from the above analysis of the 1727 poll book to the result as given in *Hist. Parl., Commons*, 1715–

54, i. 202.

[12] Hemingway, *Hist. Chest.* ii. 378–80; R. H. Morris, *Chest. in Plantagenet and Tudor Reigns, passim*; A. M. Johnson, 'Some Aspects of Political, Const., Social, and Econ. Hist. of City of Chest. 1550–1662' (Oxford Univ. D.Phil. thesis, 1974), cap. 2; Hist. Parl. Trust, constit. rep. Chest. 1509–58, 1558–1603.

[13] Hirst, *Repr. of People?* 99, 255 n.; J. K. Gruenfelder, 'Chest. Election of 1621', *T.H.S.L.C.* cxx. 35–44, does not discuss the nature of the electorate but consistently talks of the voters as the 'commonalty'.

[14] Hemingway, *Hist. Chest.* ii. 382–6.

[15] Morris, *Chest.* 74.

divers apprentices and foreigners, such as were not capable of voices'.[16] Although the corporation might be thought to be objecting to non-freeman voters, significantly they did not use the term. It seems more reasonable to suppose that they objected to the extension of the franchise to those not living within the boundaries of the city as established by the charter, and to apprentices who were too young to vote. The 1628 election again affords evidence which on balance supports belief in a franchise wider than that of the freemen. More than 900 voters took part.[17] A recent careful estimate of the population of Chester concludes that there were 4,500 inhabitants about 1640.[18] Assuming a ratio of adult males to the population as a whole of between 1:4 and 1:6,[19] at most there would be only 1,100 adult males in Chester in 1628. Not only did 900 men vote in 1628: it has been suggested that 800–1,000 regularly voted in mayoral elections in that period.[20] Even if in Chester, as in York, more than 75 per cent of the adult male population were freemen, Chester during the period up to 1640 apparently had an inhabitant franchise. If there was genuine indecision and doubt about the question, it would result in practice in a very open franchise indeed.[21]

After the Restoration, however, Chester had a clearly established freeman franchise. The crucial contest may have been a by-election in 1673. An outside observer wrote to the Secretary of State: 'The mayor was a great stickler for the recorder and made many freemen to vote for him after the writ was opened and the election going on, near 30 as I am informed. Now the recorder having 17 more freemen's votes than the colonel [Colonel Robert Werden] makes him bustle and make the under-sheriff certify for him; but if the freemen the mayor made during the election were withdrawn, as they ought to be, the colonel would have the major vote of freemen, but it has always been practicable here for all inhabitants that pay duties to king and church to vote.'[22] The final clause suggests that the nature of the electorate may have been in dispute. The Commons Journal does not record details of Werden's subsequent petition, but the House, on the recommendation of the Committee of Privileges, set aside the election of the recorder and declared Werden elected.[23]

By 1690 no one disputed that the electorate should consist of freemen. Sir Thomas Grosvenor and Richard Leving were elected with 498 and 494 votes against 484 and 457 for the sitting members, Roger Whitley and George Mainwaring. The defeated candidates, basing their petition to the Commons firmly on the ground that 'the right of election lies in the freemen of Chester', asked for the result to be set aside because the mayor had created 125 freemen after the opening of the writ, some from ineligible categories such as almsmen, minors, and apprentices. The mayor replied that none under sixteen had been enfranchised and that all freemen 'young or old, rich or poor' were entitled to vote. He and several other witnesses carefully specified, that that had been the custom since the Restoration. The failure to use such phrases as 'time out of mind', 'time immemorial', may well signify an awareness of recent changes in local electoral practice. In the event the election of Grosvenor and Leving was upheld by 186 votes to 185 in the Commons.[24] Forty years later a new problem arose. Lawsuits undertaken in the 1730s by a dissident group to force the corporation to allow open elections of aldermen and councilmen made great play with the charter's entrusting elections to 'the citizens at large', but the dissidents were not arguing for adult manhood suffrage. Their principal aim was not to extend the franchise, but to restrict it by

[16] Chest. Libr., MS. 94.3, f. 33v.
[17] J. S. Morrill, Ches. 1630–60, 31–2.
[18] Johnson, 'Chest. 1550–1662', 8.
[19] Hirst, Repr. of People? 253 n., citing the Cambridge Group for the Study of Population and Social Structure.
[20] Johnson, 'Chest. 1550–1662', cap. 2.
[21] Hirst, Repr. of People? 95.
[22] Cal. S.P. Dom. 1672–3, 559.
[23] C.J. ix. 342, 346.
[24] Ibid. x. 357, 491–2.

depriving of their votes the non-resident freemen, almost one-third of the electorate, whom they believed to be generally dependent upon their landlords, and especially upon the Grosvenors, whom they feared to be turning Chester into a proprietary borough.[25] That appeal to the courts failed, but thirteen years later, in 1747, the dissidents once again contested a parliamentary election for the city. They were heavily defeated, but challenged the result before the Commons' Committee of Privileges, which ruled that 'the right of election of citizens to serve in Parliament for the city of Chester is in . . . such of the freemen . . . not receiving alms, or [who] shall have been commorant within the said city or liberties thereof, for the space of one whole year next before the election'.[26] At last a clear-cut ruling had been made. For the last 75 years of the unreformed Parliament, and for some time thereafter, candidates had the relatively uncomplicated task of bribing and cajoling a clearly defined electorate.

THE COUNTY SEATS 1543–1660

The listing of Members of Parliament drawn up from official sources after the 1867 reform bill is incomplete for Cheshire.[27] Two local antiquarians have suggested names for all the blanks in the Blue Book,[28] but some of their suggestions have proved unsatisfactory.[29]

Two facts immediately appear from the list of members for the years 1543–1642. The first is the absence of parliamentary dynasties in Cheshire. Of 37 different men elected to the 26 parliaments during those years, 25 sat once, 6 twice and 5 thrice.[30] The 37 men came from 28 families, and only one family, the Cholmondeleys of Cholmondeley, furnished more than two members.[31] Secondly, 30 of those 37 sprang from county families which had lived in Cheshire since at least the 13th century.[32] That confirms the well-established view that 16th- and 17th-century Cheshire had a remarkably homogeneous and stable ruling class, which, together with the distinctiveness of its local institutions, made the county insular and conservative.[33] The very high incidence of intermarriage within that group, the fairly narrow range of families appointed to the commissions of the peace,[34] and the fact that 34 of the 37 M.P.s were Cheshire J.P.s at the time of their election all support that view.[35] Finally the absence of any great

[25] F. O'Gorman, 'Gen. Election of 1784 in Chest.', *J.C.A.S.* lvii. 41–50.

[26] *C.J.* xxv. 505; *Hist. Parl., Commons, 1715-54*, 203–4.

[27] *Return of Members of Parl. 1213-1702*, H.C. 69 (1878), lxii(1) gives no returns for 1545, 1547, 1584, 1597, 1614, 1654, 1656, 1659.

[28] 'Parl. Repr. of Ches.' ed. W. D. Pink and A. B. Beavan, *Local Gleanings*, i. 371–81, 405–11 (for 1543–1660). A brief biog. of each member is given.

[29] For the period 1543–1603 the Hist. Parl. Trust unpubl. files differ from Pink and Beavan as follows: 1545 Sir Lawr. Smith and Sir Hugh Calveley; 1547 Sir Wm. Brereton of Brereton and Sir Hugh Cholmondeley; 1572 Sir Hugh (not Thos.) Calveley; 1597 Thos. Egerton of Dodleston and Sir Wm. Brereton of Brereton. Pink and Beavan are also probably mistaken about the M.P.s in 1604 and 1614. For 1604 they give, as the original colleague to Sir Thos. Holcroft, Sir Bart. Ascock, for whom there is no other evidence, instead of Sir Roger Aston, named, without source, by Ormerod, *Hist. Ches.* i. 76, and accepted by Pink in Jn. Rylands Libr., Eng. MS. 296, written later. In 1614 Pink and Beavan suggest Sir Wm. Brereton of Brereton and Randle Crewe, the Speaker, later placed at Saltash: Jn. Rylands Libr., Eng. MS. 299. T. L. Moir, *Addled Parl. of 1614*, 32, 191, gives Sir Roger

Wilbraham as the second member. Brereton may also be a mistake for Hugh Beeston of Beeston, who certainly sat in 1614, for an unknown constituency, possibly Ches.

[30] Sir Wm. Brereton of Brereton (1577, 1614, 1621); Sir Wm. Brereton of Handforth (1628, 1640 spring and autumn); Sir Ric. Grosvenor of Eaton (1621, 1626, 1628); Sir Thos. Holcroft of Vale Royal (1593, 1601, 1604); Ric. Wilbraham of Woodhey (1554 spring and autumn, 1555).

[31] Sir Hugh Cholmondeley (1547), his son Hugh (1584), and great-grandson Rob. (1625).

[32] The others were two members of the Booth family of Dunham Massey, which had settled in the county in the early 15th century; the Holcrofts, Sir Ric. Cotton, Sir Lawr. Smith, and Sir Ant. St. John.

[33] e.g. G. P. Higgins, 'Co. Govt. and Society in Ches., *c.* 1590–1640' (Liverpool Univ. M.A. thesis 1974), caps. 1 and 2; Morrill, *Ches. 1630–60*, 1–6.

[34] Patricia Marriott, 'Commission of the Peace in Ches. 1536–1603' (Manchester Univ. M.A. thesis, 1974), conclusion, shows that only 69 families had served as J.P.s for Ches. before 1603. The total for the period up to 1640 was 90–95.

[35] Based on the appendices in the theses by Marriott and Higgins.

peerage family resident in the county must have helped to develop in local affairs a natural oligarchy, self-sufficient and capable of common action against external threats to its autonomy. The Stanley earls of Derby, although lords lieutenant for most of that period, took little active interest in Cheshire affairs.[36] In any case they generally distanced themselves from the court, and their influence and interest in the government of the realm was spasmodic. Their holding the office of chamberlain of Chester for half the period impeded an alternative form of government intervention through manipulating the timing of elections. Although two other chamberlains, the earl of Leicester (1563–88) and Lord Keeper Egerton (1593–1603), were much closer to the centre of power, there is no evidence that they used their position to influence Cheshire elections, although they did intervene in Chester city's politics.

There is no doubt that, by Elizabeth I's reign at the latest, a distinct leading group of families had arisen in Cheshire, which generally acted together. Only in the 1620s is there evidence of a division of the gentry into competing groups. Elizabethan Cheshire was dominated by a united élite of 13 families, ten of whom were amongst the 28 families providing M.P.s. Five others of the 28 were cadet lines of those leading families.[37]

More dynamic forces should not be ignored. The continuity represented by the survival and prosperity of ancient Cheshire lines such as the Breretons, the Delveses, the Grosvenors, the Fittons, the Leghs, the Masseys, and the Savages,[38] did not preclude the entry into the élite of new families, mostly from outside Cheshire. There were three such rising families in the 16th century. The Smiths of Hough were successful Chester goldsmiths and benefactors, who bought lands in Wirral and remained prominent in the city as well as establishing themselves in county society. Sir Lawrence Smith was the only man before the 19th century to sit for both county and city.[39] The Holcrofts and the Cottons, whose founders had been prominent household officials under Henry VIII, were the two major purchasers of monastic lands in Cheshire. Both families settled on their newly acquired estates and soon sent members to Parliament.[40] As their arrival suggests, Cheshire was not immune from external influences. Its gentry did not sit sullenly at home, holding all central authority and the court's ethos and values at arm's length. Sixteenth-century Cheshire may have received relatively few newcomers, but it sent to court very many of its native gentry, including numerous younger sons. Those who succeeded there did so by making their own contacts and finding their own patrons. Thus, while there were many links between county and court, Cheshire politics never became an arena of conflict between groups representing the interests of court factions. Exactly half of all those who sat for Cheshire between 1543 and 1603 held, or had held, court office, but most were minor figures for whom such office was still secondary. Only for two men did the centre of gravity of their lives lie outside Cheshire. Sir Richard Cotton, the son of a Shropshire gentleman, had risen to be comptroller of the king's household and privy councillor just before Edward VI's death. However, when elected knight of the shire in Mary's third Parliament, he was out of office. The more important courtier was Thomas Egerton (later Lord Ellesmere), illegitimate son of Sir Richard Egerton of Ridley, from a cadet branch of an old county family. When he represented Cheshire (1584, 1586) he was solicitor-general

---

[36] Higgins, 'Co. Govt. and Soc.', caps. 1 and 2.
[37] B. Coward, 'Lieutenancy of Lancs. and Ches. in 16th and 17th Cents.', *T.H.S.L.C.* cxix. 41.
[38] H. J. Hewitt, *Ches. under the Three Edwards*, 20, 110–11.
[39] For Ches. in 1554 and 1555, and for Chest. in 1558

and 1559. His grandson, Sir Thos., was elected M.P. for the city in 1640.
[40] Sir Thos. Holcroft, who bought the Vale Royal estates, sat in the first 2 Parls. of Mary's reign, and Sir Ric. Cotton, purchaser of the Combermere Abbey lands, in 1554.

and a rising man.[41] A forceful lawyer and legal reformer, he carefully distanced himself from the factions at court and was one of the few who retained the confidence of both the Cecils and the earl of Essex. He made no attempt to influence local politics in Cheshire and indeed as time went by came to Cheshire less, settling instead on the estates he acquired in Northamptonshire.

As has been demonstrated elsewhere, no attempt was made by the Crown after the fall of Sir William Brereton of Malpas in 1536 to control the county through royal nominees.[42] By Elizabeth I's reign a handful of local families controlled local government, two of whom stand out: the Cholmondeleys and the Savages. Both restricted their interests to the county. Cheshire politics remained turbulent. Several of those who represented the county in Tudor parliaments were involved in violent clashes with their neighbours. Sir Hugh Calveley (M.P. 1545) was several times summoned before the Star Chamber for riot and trespass, and was probably pilloried in 1556 for one such offence.[43] Sir John Done of Utkinton (M.P. 1558) was involved in violent clashes with the master forester of Delamere; in 1552 the Privy Council wrote to the Cheshire justices to prevent him from disinheriting his brother and heir apparent.[44] Sir Edward Fitton (J.P. 1553) sued Ralph Done, Hugh Cholmondeley, and Sir John Savage (M.P.s 1584, 1586, 1589) for their ignoring his rights as *custos rotulorum*. Fitton claimed that, when he summoned quarter sessions to meet at Knutsford, the others persuaded most of their fellow justices to attend a session elsewhere while he and a few supporters had waited in vain at Knutsford.[45] Although Tudor Cheshire clearly remained a turbulent county, the trouble apparently arose from rugged individualism and isolated disputes. The élite gradually forming was willing to arbitrate and to impose order on the county, and, at least until the 1620s, was broadly united. There is no evidence at all of the grouping of county families into two or three major factions as in Elizabethan Norfolk.[46] Parliamentary elections in Cheshire were a matter for consensus, for debate and resolution within the élite, rather than an arena of conflict in which each group appealed beyond itself to the freeholders in a series of trials of strength. The élite managed the elections in their own interests, without pressure from outside the county, but intent on using contacts with the centre to strengthen the hands of the elected members in serving the needs of the county as articulated by the leading group of gentry.[47]

1543–58

Given in 1545 their first opportunity to send men to Parliament, the freeholders chose men whose main interest were rooted in the county, but who yet had wider experience of the world outside. Sir Lawrence Smith, son of a Chester goldsmith by the daughter of Sir Andrew Brereton of Brereton, had himself settled in county society and married the widow of Sir William Brereton of Malpas. He had fought under the

---

[41] Based on Hist. Parl. Trust, biog. Egerton was attorney-general (1592–4), master of the Rolls (1594–1603), Lord Keeper (1596–1603), Lord Chancellor (1603–17), and was successively created Lord Ellesmere (1603), and Viscount Brackley (1616). Cotton and Egerton were also two of only four men in this period who sat both for Cheshire and for other constituencies. Egerton represented Reading in 1589, Cotton Hampshire in 1553. The others were Sir Thos. Holcroft (Lancs. and Arundel) and Sir Ric. Wilbraham (Tavistock).

[42] E. W. Ives, 'Court and Co. Palatine in Reign of Hen. VIII', *T.H.S.L.C.* cxxiii, 1–38; 'Patronage at the Court of

Hen. VIII: Ralph Egerton of Ridley', *Bull. Jn. Rylands Libr.* cii. 346–74.

[43] *Lancs. and Ches. Cases in Ct. of Star Chamber* (R.S.L.C. lxxi), 46, 95, 113, 122; *Acts of P.C. 1554–6*, 264; Hist. Parl. Trust, biogs.

[44] *Acts of P.C. 1552–4*, 20.

[45] Sta. Cha. 5 F24/8, F30/2; Sta. Cha. 7 21/32. These references were provided by Mr. A. Thomas.

[46] Cf. A. Hassell Smith, *Co. and Court: Govt. and Soc. in Eliz. Norf.*

[47] This paragraph is based on discussions with Mr. A. Thomas of Birmingham Univ.

earl of Hertford in Scotland, being one of the fourteen Cheshire men knighted during that campaign. So too had Sir Hugh Calveley whose brief service in the duke of Richmond's household had given him further contacts with the Court. But by 1545 neither occupied any office of profit and both were primarily local figures. Both had been included in the first Cheshire commission of the peace in 1543.[48]

The Members elected in 1547 and 1552 were of similar types. All were knighted during their service in Scotland, all were in the original commission of the peace and all had been on the fringes of the Court: Sir Hugh Cholmondeley as a friend of Hertford's counsellor, Sir John Thynne; Sir Thomas Venables as a former gentleman of Prince Edward's chamber; Sir William Brereton as a close companion of Hertford during the Scottish campaign. The most interesting was Sir Thomas Holcroft. A Lancashire gentleman by birth, he rose rapidly in the royal household and the Duchy of Lancaster administration, and as an acknowledged expert on Scottish affairs, was active in secret negotiations and organizing a spy network. His interests, however, were closely tied to those of Somerset, and his power collapsed in 1549 with the Protector's fall. He was imprisoned for several months, but served as M.P. for Cheshire in 1552, after his disgrace. What such choices prove, therefore, is not that Cheshire seats were at the disposal of the Seymours in the early years, nor that men were selected who could exploit current contacts, but rather that those early M.P.s were men with more experience of the ways of government than others of the county gentry. All were men whose preoccupations and commitments at the time of their election were those of the country gentleman. Thus Holcroft was involved in rationalizing the estates of Vale Royal abbey which he had purchased in 1545.[49]

The Marian elections present a similar picture. Six of the eight men who served in Mary's parliaments were former household officials whose Crown service appeared to have ended by 1553. Two of them had actually served in the household of the then Princess Mary;[50] a third, a former agent of Thomas Cromwell, had retired to his estates in 1540.[51] Sir Thomas Holcroft served again, before unexpectedly resuming his public career as an active diplomat. He may have used his new office of Knight Marshall to forewarn protestants against whom the Council was contemplating action and secretly aided their escape.[52] Several of the other M.P.s were also probably religious moderates;[53] the general impression is of the county choosing local men (all eight were J.P.s) with experience of national affairs, but no complicity in the current régime. An exception was the return of Richard Wilbraham to three successive parliaments in 1554 and 1555. A younger son of an old Cheshire family, he had already spent thirty years at court, many of them in the household of Princess Mary. Throughout her reign he was master of the Jewel House, and staunchly supported the queen's policy in parliament.[54] Whether the county yielded to royal pressure to elect him, or spontaneously chose him as an insurance policy, while consistently sending as his colleagues men with no current involvement with the government, is unclear.

1559–1603

As before, Cheshire's representation was fairly evenly divided. Different men were chosen for each of Elizabeth's first five parliaments. They were mostly leading county

[48] *L. & P. Hen. VIII*, vi, xii, xix, xx, *passim*; Ormerod, *Hist. Ches.* ii. 252; *Acts of P.C.* 1552–4, 20; Hist. Parl. Trust, biog.
[49] Hist. Parl. Trust, biog.
[50] Sir Ric. Cotton, Sir John Done.
[51] Ric. Hough.
[52] Hist. Parl. Trust, biog.
[53] e.g. Ric. Hough, Sir Lawr. Smith.
[54] He sat for Tavistock in Oct. 1553; cf. Hist. Parl. Trust, biog.

gentlemen and justices of the peace, 'the county families taking it in turns to sit'.[55] Thereafter the pattern is a little more complex, with Thomas Egerton, Sir John Savage, and Sir Thomas Holcroft each elected twice. Of those chosen during the reign as a whole only Egerton stood high at court although six others held minor office or had other links with the court. Sir George Beeston was in charge of the shore defences at Gravesend in 1576 and of 'four great ships' at Chatham during the Armada campaign. Perhaps that, together with his strong protestantism, led to his election in 1589. He was the only M.P., apart from Egerton, who did not spend most of his time in Cheshire. Thomas Egerton of Ridley (1597), recently appointed clerk of the Chester Exchequer, where he acted by deputy, served with the earl of Essex in the Azores, and in Ireland where he was later killed. Hugh Cholmondeley (1584) was vice-president of the Council in the Marches of Wales. Some more prominent office-holders like Edward Fitton (lord president of Connaught 1569-72, vice-treasurer of Ireland 1572-9, *custos rotulorum* of Cheshire in the 1570s, and a former M.P. in 1553) were bypassed. As before, the county wanted more than anything else to choose men whose primary interest and experience were in its own affairs.[56] Experience of the world at large was valuable, but not essential. Nine of the 16 members who served in Elizabethan parliaments never owned houses or held office outside the county. Four members were connected with the Stanleys, but only two at all closely. William Massey (1563) was a steward for their Wirral estates. Piers Legh of Lyme (1601) a former page in the Stanley household, accompanied the 4th earl on his embassy to France in 1585.[57]

The evidence about the religious leanings of Cheshire M.P.s is ambiguous. The four members chosen in 1558 and 1571 were said by Bishop Downham in 1564 to be 'favourable' at that time to the religious settlement. By contrast the two chosen in 1562, William Massey of Puddington and Sir Thomas Venables, were said to be 'not favourable'. One of the 1572 members had been 'favourable' in 1564 and was again in 1580 listed as well affected to the church. His companion in 1572, William Booth, apparently a radical, was the patron of a minister noted for his opposition to vestments. Later, in 1589, the two members were Sir John Savage, earlier listed as 'cold' and later convicted as a recusant, and Sir Hugh Beeston, a strong protestant. Probably, therefore, religious affiliation was not an important consideration in the choice of M.P.s.[58]

Few Cheshire M.P.s were active at Westminster. The only member known to have spoken regularly, Sir Thomas Egerton, did so as a law officer of the Crown.[59] Thomas Holcroft spoke three times during debates in 1601, and Thomas Egerton of Dodleston sat on the monopolies committee in 1597.[60] Similarly, no evidence survives that Cheshire M.P.s sought or obtained bills relating to the county. On the other hand, the election of Sir Thomas Egerton, who had launched his career from the Chester Exchequer, may have been connected with the county leaders' attempt to preserve the autonomy of the palatine jurisdiction from the encroachment of the courts in Westminster Hall and from the provincial jurisdiction of the Council in the Marches. Such men well-placed at court could help to strengthen the rights and foster the independence of local communities. There was no conception of 'court and country' in Tudor Cheshire.[61]

[55] Hist. Parl. Trust, constit. rep.
[56] Hist. Parl. Trust, biog.
[57] W. Beamont, *Hist. House of Lyme*, 109-30; Evelyn, Lady Newton, *The Leghs of Lyme*, passim; J. Croston, *Historic Sites of Lancs. and Ches.* 354-9.
[58] 3 *Sheaf*, v, p. 113; vii, p. 99; K. R. Wark, *Elizabethan Recusancy in Ches.* (Chetham Soc. [3rd ser.] xix), app.;

Hist. Parl. Trust, biogs.
[59] J. E. Neale, *Eliz. I and her Parls.* ii. *passim*.
[60] Hist. Parl. Trust, biog.
[61] Cf. G. R. Elton, 'Tudor Govt.: the Points of Contact (i) Parl.', *Trans. R.H.S.* 5th ser., xxiv. 183-200; Smith, *County and Court*, esp. pp. 307-33.

The first two Stuart elections followed the pattern discussed above, two local gentlemen who held minor court office sitting alongside two prominent squires. The five elections of the 1620s, however, suggest that changes were taking place within the county. First, all the members chosen were 'mere gentlemen' and open hostility was expressed towards those with court connexions. The candidates had to be uncontaminated by contact with the corruption of Whitehall. Secondly, there is evidence of divisions within the county, as two distinct factions arose, neither representing a court interest. Their origins are obscure but were essentially concerned with local precedence. As a consequence, the decade witnessed what were probably the county's first contested elections.

In 1624 Sir Richard Grosvenor, then sheriff, addressed the freeholders of Cheshire. In presenting to them the nominees of a group of leading gentlemen who sat by him on the platform, he discussed at length the role of M.P.s, emphasizing their particular commitment to the interests of the county. In that respect his speech was thoroughly conventional. He then, however, attacked the men who surrounded the king in a remarkably forthright and bitter manner.[62] In particular, he assailed the *de facto* toleration afforded to Catholics, the consequent 'dependence upon foreign princes, dangerous to any state', and the multitude of patents and monopolies.[63] Grosvenor's own activities as an M.P. in 1621 and 1629 offer equally striking proof of those same attitudes. In 1621 he made two major speeches on the fate of the Rhenish Palatinate, manifesting extreme hostility to Spain, distrust of the king's policy of negotiation, and reluctance to grant supply before war was declared. He also spoke against the monopolists and gave an example of the ill consequences for Cheshire of Sir Giles Mompesson's patent to license alehouses.[64] In February 1629 he brought in the report of the committee on Popery which not only called for severer laws against recusants and their stringent enforcement, but also demanded sanctions against the Arminian clergy. Once again he showed marked hostility to the current government. He now attacked it directly, claiming that 'our good endeavours have vanished into smoke', as they had done in the last years of James's reign, because beneath sweet words and assurances from the king, 'the secret directions and command of some eminent ministers of state' hindered the enforcement of the recusancy laws.[65] The report as a whole has been described as 'fastidious and accurate'. Grosvenor, however, is said to have been 'easily taken advantage of by those more wily than himself, in commercial matters more concerned as to winning advantage for his own locality than as to carrying out a national policy of mercantilism'.[66]

The published papers of the 1621 Parliament also suggest the constituency business with which local members were concerned. The knights and burgesses of Cheshire headed a committee to investigate complaints against the Chester Exchequer. A private act allowed a Cheshire gentleman to break the entail on his lands. Grosvenor's fellow knight, Sir William Brereton, moved a clause to include Cheshire in a bill enabling royal tenants to obtain licences of alienation more easily, and a similar amendment to include the palatine courts in a bill to regulate court fees.[67]

[62] Grosvenor as lessee of the Crown's lead mines in Flints. and Denb. was not entirely outside court circles, but never seems to have visited the Court or sought office.
[63] Eaton Hall, Grosvenor MSS., papers of Sir Ric. G., item 25.
[64] *Commons Debates in 1621*, ed. W. Notestein, F. H.

Relf, and H. Simpson, ii. 454; iii. 347; v. 216, 405, 519.
[65] *Commons Debates of 1629*, ed. W. Notestein and F. H. Relf, 65–9.
[66] Ibid. pp. lxiii–lxv; cf. ibid. 172–244 for Grosvenor's journal of the 1628–9 parliament.
[67] *Commons Debates in 1621*, ii. 385; iii. 149; iv. 404; vi. 22.

In his speech of 1624 Sir Richard Grosvenor nominated William Brereton of Ashley and William Booth of Dunham Massey, who were duly elected without a contest. Grosvenor said that the nomination represented 'the opinion and resolution of those worthy gentlemen who sit about me, upon whose careful judgement and experience' the well-being of the county depended.[68] That is the earliest overt reference to caucus politics in the county. Probably the leading families met before every election and argued out amongst themselves which of them should serve, thus avoiding the costs and uncertainties of a poll. That may explain why the representation was shared by so many families. The precondition of such politics was that the county leaders were willing to act together. Increasingly, from the accession of Charles I onwards, that ceased to be the case.[69] In the mid 1620s three families, the Cholmondeleys, the Needhams, and the Breretons of Brereton, acquired Irish peerages, and fought for local supremacy with other families, their equals in wealth and lineage, who had purchased baronetcies. The latter group were led by Sir George Booth and Sir Richard Wilbraham. Throughout England the baronets and the Irish peers were disputing precedency and Charles I's compromise, granting the peers technical precedency, but removing them from acting on the commissions of the peace, was not successful.[70] The rivalry in Cheshire continued, each group attempting to demonstrate its superiority over the other in the parliamentary elections. In 1626, for example, Sir Richard Grosvenor, himself a baronet, was quickly accepted for the first place, but no agreement could be reached about the other seat. Two members of the 'baronet' group drew lots, Peter Daniell, Grosvenor's son-in-law, beating Sir William Brereton of Handforth, Sir George Booth's son-in-law, but the winner was challenged by John Minshull, brother-in-law of Lord Cholmondeley. Only after two days of polling did Minshull withdraw. Nothing seems to have been at stake except local prestige and precedence.[71] Similarly in 1628 large crowds gathered at Chester expecting a contest but the 'barons' backed down at the last minute, to the discomfort of local butchers who had laid in large quantities of meat, hoping to repeat the large profits they had made in 1626.[72]

1640–59

The mutual suspicions of the two groups of Cheshire squires did not diminish during Charles I's personal rule. Yet the centralizing tendencies and dubious legality of many royal policies in the 1630s did not give an ideological edge to those local disputes. Both groups were determined to use the parliamentary elections of 1640 to renew their struggle for control, but they did so by outbidding one another in opposition to the Crown. There was agreement about what needed to be done, and each group maintained that it was best equipped to present the county's grievances.[73] The initiative lay with the 'baronets' who controlled local government, but the Irish peers and their supporters, having been excluded from or relatively inactive in local government, put forward two strong candidates, Sir Thomas Aston, a former ship-money sheriff now campaigning vigorously and knowledgeably against royal fiscal practices, and Sir William Brereton of Handforth, the most active of all the J.P.s, known to be strongly

[68] Eaton Hall, Grosvenor MSS., papers of Sir Ric. G., item 25; Hirst, *Repr. of People?* 217, noting that it was contested, is a misprint.

[69] For the general background, see Morrill, *Ches. 1630–60*, caps. 1 and 2.

[70] For a discussion of this question, see Wanklyn, 'Structure of Parties', *passim*, which disagrees with the views of Morrill, *Ches. 1630–60*, caps. 1–2, that the origins of the party conflict lay in the 1620s.

[71] Chester R.O., CR 63/2/89, fam. notes of Thos. Stanley of Alderley, 1590–1601, 1621–8, unfol.; cf. Morrill, *Ches. 1630–60*, 30.

[72] B.L. Harl. MS. 2125, f. 59.

[73] Morrill, *Ches. 1630–60*, 32–5.

anti-Laudian and popular amongst the 'religious', a man estranged from his father-in-law, Sir George Booth, and his friends.[74] The fact that Aston was later to be a royalist and Brereton a parliamentary commander in Cheshire further suggests that there was no ideological gulf between the factions in 1640. Furthermore, it was specifically reported that the contest had arisen from the bitter distaste felt by the lords at 'the neglect given them' by the baronets, and that all men 'were raised in their own profit' rather than for the public good.[75] In the event, after a 'temperate' declaration by the lord lieutenant for Aston and Brereton, the baronets withdrew.[76]

In the election to the Long Parliament later in the year, the baronets stood down, and the choice lay between Aston, now running with Peter Venables, Lord Cholmondeley's brother-in-law, and Brereton, campaigning independently.[77] Probably the Cholmondeley–Kilmorey faction abandoned Brereton both because he had served their purpose and because his religious radicalism had become far clearer during the spring and summer.[78] After 'much contention' Brereton was elected to the first and Venables to the second seat.[79] Sir William's sensational triumph in the face of the whole county establishment exemplifies the case recently argued that the gentry sought to avert polls, not simply because of the expense, but also because the volatility of the electorate made the outcome unpredictable.[80]

The autumn election saw a further innovation. It was decided that the new members be assisted in presenting the grievances of the county by compiling reports detailing the damaging effects of royal policy. The idea, ironically, was propounded by Sir Thomas Aston, but was taken up at quarter sessions and led to the appointment of committees in every hundred to receive complaints.[81]

In 1642 Peter Venables, like his sponsors, became a royalist. Brereton established himself as Cheshire's principal military and civilian leader for the parliament, using his position in the Commons to engross power and influence in the north midlands.[82] When, after the defeat of the king, the Lower House decided to fill vacancies created by the expulsion of royalist members, Brereton sought to have his own friends and colleagues elected to seats in several counties. Ironically he was less successful in Cheshire than elsewhere. The moderate opposition to his hard-line government of the county, led by Sir George Booth and others of the pre-war 'baronets' party, possessed an overwhelming electoral advantage in 1646 when anti-militarism and demands for a return to pre-war 'normality' were voiced on every hand. Sir George Booth the younger was returned unopposed.[83] He was expelled from the Commons, however, at Pride's Purge in December 1648, so that for the next four years Brereton was once again the county's sole member.[84]

In the 1650s the old county élite, split by political and religious differences in the 1640s, was gradually reunited by a dislike for increased centralization, hatred of army rule, and continuing religious anarchy.[85] One sign of the return to older patterns was the resumption of traditional methods of electoral management. In 1654, 1656, and 1659 the leading gentry met together to agree a slate of candidates.[86] Such agreement was the more necessary because the Instrument of Government had increased the number

[74] See R. N. Dore, 'Early Life of Sir Wm. Brereton', *T.L.C.A.S.* lxiii. 1–26.
[75] *Cal. S.P. Dom.* 1639–40, 564.
[76] Ibid., 580.
[77] Morrill, *Ches. 1630–60*, 35.
[78] B.L. Harl. MS. 2125, f. 133.
[79] Morrill, *Ches. 1630–60*, 34–7.
[80] Hirst, *Repr. of People? passim.*
[81] Morrill, *Ches. 1630–60*, 38–9; Ches. R.O., QJB 1/6 f. 7; QJF 69/3 nos. 11–14.

[82] Morrill, *Ches. 1630–60*, caps. 3–4.
[83] Ibid. 174–9; D. Underdown, 'Recruiter Elections 1645–7', *E.H.R.* lxxxii. 252–6. Brereton was accused of delaying the issue of the writ so that he could set up his own candidate, John Bradshaw: B.L. Add. MS. 11332, ff. 70, 119–20.
[84] D. Underdown, *Pride's Purge*, 366–90.
[85] Morrill, *Ches. 1630–60*, caps. 6–8.
[86] Ches. R.O., DDX 384/1, Diary of Sir Thos. Mainwaring, unfol.

of county seats to four. In 1654 their slate, consisting of the leading civilians willing to serve under the Protectorate, was returned unopposed.[87] In 1656 the gentry were opposed by Major-General Bridge and the leading army and militia commanders, who produced a separate slate.[88] After negotiations between the two groups, Bridge withdrew his list in exchange for an undertaking by the gentry that they would withdraw their support from John Bradshaw, the minor Cheshire gentleman and lawyer who had presided at the trial of Charles I and over the Rump Parliament's Council of State, and, although chief justice of Chester, was now a bitter opponent of the Protectorate. Bradshaw chose to run independently,[89] as did Sir William Brereton, who had taken up residence in Surrey and withdrawn from Cheshire affairs.[90] On the day of the election the sheriff refused to allow a poll to be taken, and insisted that on a show of hands the gentry's nominees were elected.[91] Sheriff Egerton may have been prompted by his obstinate preference for those candidates,[92] but could have had another reason. The Instrument of Government by replacing the forty-shilling freehold qualification with one which enfranchised only those householders with a personal estate of £200,[93] reduced the size of the electorate substantially.[94] That, together with the exclusion of all former royalists, would have made the task of conducting an accurate poll impossible. Indeed, one account of the election, which spoke of Bradshaw's support as coming from 'the generality of freeholders and some gentlemen', suggests that the old county radical was attracting the support of a disenfranchised group which it would have been difficult or impolitic for the sheriff to have excluded from a poll.[95]

By the 1659 election the old franchise and distribution of seats had been restored. Once again a meeting of gentry nominated two men to serve.[96] One of them, Peter Brooke, was quickly accepted for the first place, but the other, Richard Legh of Lyme, the son of a royalist, had to fight John Bradshaw for the second seat. Legh was supported by almost all the new county establishment; Bradshaw, in contrast, by a curious coalition of all the Cheshire republicans and by a cabal of disillusioned former royalists.[97] Bradshaw, possibly defeated in 1656 by the efforts of one sheriff, was certainly victorious in 1659 through the guile of another, John Leigh of Booths, an old Cheshire radical. Finding the result of the poll at Chester too close for comfort, Leigh adjourned the county court to Congleton, Bradshaw's Cheshire base.[98] Bradshaw had defended the Quakers' right to vote without taking an oath, and had denounced the caucus's nominations as a denial of the freeholders' 'birthright'.[99] That made him repugnant to the rapidly evolving monarchist interest by 1659. Certainly it was the most violent contest ever held in the county, with both freeholders and gentry on both sides coming to blows, and bitter recriminations continuing for months afterwards. The poll was eventually concluded and, despite a vigorous campaign at Westminster by his opponents to have the result overturned, Bradshaw took his seat.[1] It had needed

[87] The four were Sir Geo. Booth, Hen. Brooke of Norton, John Crewe of Utkinton, and John Bradshaw.
[88] P. J. Pinckney, 'Ches. Election of 1656', *Bull. Jn. Rylands Libr.* xlix. 387–426; Morrill, *Ches. 1630–60*, 287–93.
[89] The letter-book of Bradshaw's brother Henry contains letters setting out his view of the contest: Bodl. MS. Top. Ches. e. 3.
[90] For Brereton's position, see Pinckney, 'Ches. Election', 417; Chester R.O., CR 63/2/702 (Brereton letter-book), pp. 39–42 (paginated from the rear).
[91] Bodl. MS. Top. Ches. e. 3, ff. 20–1; Chester 24/131, unfol., grand jury presentment.
[92] Morrill, *Ches. 1630–60*, 290–2.
[93] S. R. Gardiner, *Const. Docs. of Puritan Revolution*, 407–11.

[94] Hirst, *Repr. of People?* 3; J. Cannon, *Parl. Reform 1640–1832*, 17–19.
[95] Bodl. MS. Top. Ches. e. 3, ff. 20–1.
[96] They included most of the pre-war élite, also all the leaders of the abortive Booth rising in Aug. 1659 and all the men most active as J.P.s in the early 1660s: Morrill, *Ches. 1630–60*, 293–9.
[97] Ibid. It contained no known supporters of Booth and only two future J.P.s.
[98] Ibid., and the sources there given. Also P. de M. Grey-Egerton, 'Papers relating to Elections . . . for Ches.', *J.C.A.S.* [1st ser.] i. pt. 2, pp. 102–3.
[99] A dangerous word in view of its use by the Levellers.
[1] Jn. Rylands Libr., Legh of Lyme MSS., unfol. letters of Ric. Legh; Bodl. MS. Top. Ches. e. 3, f. 22.

a polarization of opinion far more extreme than that of 1640 to produce the first completed poll of the county's electoral history. A new era in its political history was dawning.

THE CITY OF CHESTER 1543–1660

CHESTER was one of the very few boroughs in the country, probably no more than six or seven, which held out throughout the period against attempts by outsiders to promote candidates at parliamentary elections, and consistently chose as its members freemen of long standing. There were probably only three contested elections in the whole period (1621, 1628, 1659), and for the first hundred years the recorder was almost invariably returned as a member.[2] Only 2 of the 32 members were neither aldermen, nor lawyers in the employment of the corporation.[3] As with the county representatives most men sat once only. Between 1547 and 1659, 24 men other than the recorders represented the city, 17 of them once, 5 twice and 2 thrice.[4]

According to Henry VII's charter of 1506 the assembly and the chief officers were to be elected annually by the inhabitants. Gradually, however, over the 50 years from 1514, the corporation was made close, and popular rights of election, despite considerable opposition, virtually extinguished, the whole of the assembly[5] being recruited by co-option. Only the election of mayors was left to the citizens at large, and they were limited to a choice between two nominees of the assembly.

While the government of the city was moving towards oligarchy, Chester's company of Merchant Adventurers was gaining a stronger grip on its economy. In particular the late 16th century saw bitter disputes about two of the most prosperous of all its trades, the export of calfskins and the import of sweet wines. The activities of the Merchant Adventurers led to considerable tensions between them and the craft guilds, particularly the fifth of all the freemen working in the leather crafts, whose business was affected by the calfskin patent. After 1590 there was intense conflict even within the Adventurers after a small group gained exclusive grants for themselves.[6] At times, inevitably, disputes about local government and about economic problems overlapped, since the oligarchy seeking to close the corporation consisted largely of Merchant Adventurers and men from a few other guilds. Although such quarrels may have affected the choice of M.P.s, the evidence is elusive.

The nearest possibility of a connexion is in the elections of 1547–55. The recorders occupied one seat throughout. The other was held alternately by William Aldersey (1547, spring 1553, and 1554) and by Thomas Massey (1552, autumn 1553). The elections coincided with major developments in the struggles for political and economic control within the city. Between 1552 and 1554 the Exchequer of Chester gave a final and decisive ruling that the choice of new common councillors lay with 'the mayor, aldermen, and the residue of the common council'. At precisely the same time the

---

[2] When in 1597 and 1601 the recorder, Ric. Birkenhead, was too weak and old to serve, the city sent instead men whom it paid to act as special legal counsel.

[3] What follows is based on the corrected lists in the files of the Hist. Parl. Trust (1509–1603). No record survives of any return for 1545. The Blue Book is accurate except for having no names for 1547, 1614, 1621, 1654, 1656, or 1659, which are provided by articles in 1 *Sheaf*, ii and iii, *passim*. Hemingway, *Hist. Chest.* ii. 381–2, gives the wrong names for 1555, when recorder Thos. Gerard and alderman Wm. Aldersey were chosen, and for 1559, when Gerard and Sir Lawr. Smith served. The M.P.s in 1547 are tentatively identified by the Hist. Parl. Trust as

Ric. Sneyd and Wm. Aldersey.

[4] Wm. Aldersey (1547, 1554, 1555), Peter Warburton (1586, 1589, 1597).

[5] The arrangements were complex. Two sheriffs were chosen annually from the 40 common councillors, and vacancies among the 24 aldermen filled from ex-sheriffs. The mayor was elected from amongst the aldermen. The assembly met as a single body of 80–5 members, each with an equal voice, but effective power lay with the mayor and ex-mayors.

[6] Morris, *Chest.*, *passim*; Hemingway, *Hist. Chest.* ii. *passim*; Johnson, 'Chest. 1550–1662', caps. 2, 6, 7.

Merchant Adventurers were agitating for a strengthening of their power to control both overseas trade and retailing within the city. In 1553, during Mary's second parliament, Aldersey obtained a new charter for the company direct from the Lord Chancellor. If the assembly was 'very keen to prevent guilds from applying direct to the government for a charter',[7] Aldersey's action would be bitterly resented. Massey, the younger son of a Cheshire gentleman, was asked by the assembly during the following parliament to raise in the Commons questions about the grant to Aldersey. The latter had already been in dispute with the assembly over his expenses as member in 1547, and long remained at odds with the city during the 1560s, ultimately provoking the grave crisis over the interpretation of the charter in 1572. The alternation of Aldersey and Massey as M.P.s suggests a struggle for power which found expression in the parliamentary elections. But whether the struggle for the nomination was fought out entirely within the assembly or by appeal to the citizenry there is no evidence.[8]

The city had an uneasy relationship with the palatine Exchequer court, since the city's charter gave its courts an exclusive jurisdiction which the Exchequer challenged. Yet Chester had an interest in protecting the Exchequer's autonomy against the courts at Westminster, and the palatinate courts themselves brought business to the city and provided posts for the sons of its leaders. Thus John Yerworth, clerk of the Pentice in the 1550s,[9] on becoming a baron of the Chester Exchequer in 1563, was promptly elected M.P. for the city.[10] Shortly afterwards a jurisdictional dispute between the Exchequer and the city's Portmote court was settled behind the scenes, by a compromise, under which the Exchequer no longer used writs of *certiorari* to convoke cases from the Portmote and which was apparently the work of the chamberlain, the earl of Leicester. Leicester's deputy, William Glasiour, mayor 1551–2, sat for Chester in the parliaments of 1571 and 1572 and obtained a new charter for the city in 1574, which maintained the rights of the Exchequer. Glasiour was still an alderman, and although he had initially championed the Exchequer, his election presumably reflected a new spirit of compromise. Significantly, when in 1572 a minority within the assembly tried to reopen the question of the popular electoral rights re-stated in the new charter, Leicester refused to consider their petition.[11] The connexion of the city with the Exchequer did not end with the resolution of that crisis. At the parliamentary election of 1584, the earls of Leicester and Derby both wrote to the city, supporting the candidature of Peter Warburton, the court's paid legal adviser. The assembly refused and elected instead Thomas Bavand, a former mayor and leading merchant. In 1586, however, after being irregularly elected an alderman in 1585 and buying city property, Warburton was elected. In 1593 he became vice-chamberlain of Chester and was re-elected as M.P.[12]

All the M.P.s were already freemen, and most of them already aldermen, but some had important interests outside the city. John Bingley, a former merchant, had, before his election (1614), transferred his business interests to London. John Savage (1624, 1625), himself an alderman and son of a man who was three times mayor, was primarily a country gentleman and J.P.[13] The Savages were just one of ten gentle families owning extensive property in the city and regularly represented in the city assembly, who perhaps helped to mediate in the jurisdictional and fiscal disputes which frequently simmered between city and county. But the election of Savage, together with those of

[7] Johnson, 'Chest. 1550–1662', 46.

[8] *C.J.* i. 2–15; *Cal. Pat.* 1553–4, 326; 1554–5, 38; Chest. R.O., M/L/5/265; Hist. Parl. Trust, biogs. of Aldersey and Massey, and constit. rep. for Chest.

[9] Equivalent to clerk of the peace.

[10] Hist. Parl. Trust, biog.

[11] Johnson, 'Chest. 1550–1662', caps. 2 and 4; Hemingway, *Hist. Chest.* ii. 384–5; Morris, *Chest.* 93–5; Hist. Parl. Trust, biogs. of Yerworth and Glasiour.

[12] Also an official of the Duchy of Lancaster, and after his last term as M.P. Justice of the Common Pleas 1600–21: Hist. Parl. Trust, biog.   [13] 1 *Sheaf*, ii. *passim.*

Sir Lawrence Smith in 1558 and 1559 and of his grandson in 1640, represents another variation from the simple characterization of Chester's parliamentary history given above. Even some of the recorders had interests distinct from those of the city. Thus William Gerard (1555–75) was also a member of the Council in the Marches from 1560, and Vice-Justice of the Great Sessions of Cheshire from 1561, and resigned as recorder to become Lord Chancellor of Ireland.[14] Moreover, fewer than half of the M.P.s who served for the city were natives.[15]

Yet the decision whom to elect was normally made within the city. On every known occasion when outsiders attempted to influence the choice of candidates, the city asserted its independence: the earl of Leicester was resisted in 1584,[16] as was the prince of Wales's council in 1621 and again in 1624,[17] and the county gentry were routed when they put forward two candidates in 1628.[18]

In 1621, 1628, and the spring of 1640, the city elections were contested, and so provide a clearer picture. The 1621 contest arose from two distinct events. The first was a conflict within the city between a majority of the assembly and Edward Whitby, recorder 1612–38, and his family. Over the previous twenty years, they had brazenly engrossed offices (Edward's father, mayor in 1612, and elder brother Thomas, sheriff the same year, serving as clerks of the Pentice, 1602–17) and had been at odds with successive mayors. A counter-attack in 1617 led to Thomas Whitby's dismissal and an unsuccessful attempt was made to remove Edward as recorder in 1619, when also the assembly overruled the citizens' choice for mayor, perhaps a Whitby partisan, after a bitter contest. There was a major riot in 1620. When the next parliament was summoned, several outsiders tried to put pressure on the assembly. The prince of Wales's council nominated two candidates, neither connected with the city, Sir Thomas Edmondes, a privy councillor and comptroller of the king's household, and Sir Henry Cary. Lord Savage proposed his brother and also supported John Bingley, a former city M.P. The assembly's problems were eased by the election of Cary for Hertfordshire, but the mayor and aldermen surprisingly endorsed the candidature not only of the recorder, but also of Edmondes. That breach of the charter, Edmondes not being a freeman, and of custom gave Whitby his chance for revenge. He dissociated himself from the official choice and canvassed for his own candidate, John Ratcliffe, a former mayor and long-standing ally of his family. After the mayor, Thomas Gamull, had nominated Whitby and Edmondes, Whitby denounced Edmondes as ineligible, and nominated Ratcliffe. The latter nomination was loudly acclaimed by the citizenry, and the assembly were forced to give way. Nonetheless, they appealed to the House of Commons, alleging that Whitby had canvassed unenfranchised groups and had addressed himself to the 'mere inhabitants . . . of the basest sort', labourers, hired workmen, and even beggars, besides apprentices and foreigners. The assembly was clearly trying to implicate Whitby generally with rabble-rousing, but no attempt was made expressly to assert a freeman franchise. In general the election reveals confusion about the franchise, considerable hostility to 'foreign' intervention, but above all that 'Chester politics were primarily concerned with local issues which divided its ruling élite.'[19] The conflict between the Whitbys and the assembly may simply have been a general struggle for authority in local affairs, but two other factors should be borne in mind. The mayor during the election was Thomas Gamull. His family, involved in the struggle

---

[14] Hist. Parl. Trust, biog. See also Ric. Sneyd, recorder 1550–4, and Sir Rob. Brerewood, recorder 1639–46.
[15] Hist. Parl. Trust, biogs.
[16] Morris, *Chest.* 191.
[17] Gruenfelder, 'Election of 1621', 35–44; Hirst, *Repr. of People?* 94–5, 198–9.
[18] B.L. Harl. MS. 2125, f. 59.
[19] Gruenfelder, 'Election of 1621', 35–44; Hirst, *Repr. of People?* 94–5, 198–9; Johnson, 'Chest. 1550–1662', cap. 2; Chest. Libr. MS. 94.3, f. 33.

with the Whitbys since 1602, was also a leading one in the group of merchants clinging to a monopoly in vital city trades. Whitby may well have opposed their monopolistic practices. Secondly, a suppressed part of the assembly's account of the election speaks of Ratcliffe as 'the chief countenancer of the sect of puritans'. The leading opponent of Gamull's patents, William Edwards, was also a puritan. It is commonly asserted that puritanism in Chester was weak, yet several of the city's M.P.s had strong puritan sympathies: Richard Bavand, William Brock, Gilbert and William Gerrard, and John Ratcliffe.[20]

Between 1621 and 1627 the disputes in the city lay dormant, and in the elections of 1624, 1625, and 1626 the nominees of the assembly were returned unopposed. In 1627 Whitby returned to the offensive by demanding a Privy Council inquiry into the activities of Robert Brerewood, the new clerk of the Pentice. After much cross-petitioning and several arbitration hearings before commissioners appointed by the Council, Brerewood was forced to resign. In the ensuing parliamentary election, Whitby and Ratcliffe were challenged by two of Brerewood's allies, Sir Randal Mainwaring and Sir Thomas Smith, Cheshire squires who were also aldermen of the city. Despite allegations of undue pressure by the gentry on their tenants, including threats to dispossess those who failed to vote for the knights, Whitby and Ratcliffe secured two-thirds of the votes and retained the initiative.[21]

By the first election of 1640 Whitby was dead, Thomas Gamull, who had defended Brerewood in 1627, and his fellow patentees controlled the assembly, and Brerewood himself was recorder. In December 1639 the inner circle at Chester met and chose the recorder and Sir Thomas Smith as their nominees. In January 1640 the mayor told Smith about unsuccessful attempts by the vice-chamberlain, a son of the bishop of Chester, and the local gentry to gain the nomination for themselves. In March Smith was informed that everything seemed under control, but, in view of 'the inconstant disposition of the people of this city', was advised to ensure that his tenants turned out on election day. Then, at the last minute, a report that the recorder might raise in Parliament the question of the Dee mills, one of the monopolistic concerns of the inner circle of merchants, apparently made Gamull decide to stand for election himself. Sir Richard Grosvenor and others mediated, gaining satisfactory assurances from Brerewood, and Gamull withdrew. The election itself, held at the end of March, saw a minor revolt by opponents of the oligarchy, which came to nothing.[22]

At the autumn election Smith was returned with Gamull, and the recorder was dropped, perhaps without a struggle, and simply because the assembly's controlling group had come to think him insufficiently committed to their interests. There is little likelihood of wider political disagreements. Gamull, Smith, and Brerewood were all royalist *ultras* from the outset of the Civil War. Furthermore, letters sent from Westminster by Gamull during 1641 and 1642 suggest that the assembly was obsessed with preserving the city's rights. Gamull continued to defend his group's patents from attacks within the House and advised the mayor on the fiscal burdens that would follow from the settlement with the Scots and the movement of troops to Ireland via Chester. He also answered questions about the status of apprentices who volunteered to join the army going over to Ireland. Not until the summer of 1642 did his letters reveal a deepening concern with the breakdown of relations between king and Parliament. Hitherto Gamull had seen his role as an M.P. as to uphold the particular

---

[20] For the first four see Hist. Parl. Trust, biogs.; for Ratcliffe, see Hirst, *Repr. of People?* 198; R. C. Richardson, *Puritanism in North-West Eng.* 133.

[21] Hirst, *Repr. of People?* 198; Johnson, 'Chest. 1550–1662', cap. 2; B.L. Harl. MS. 2125, f. 59.

[22] *Cal. S.P. Dom.* 1639–40, 168, 341, 538, 564, 590.

interests of Chester, while the struggle for power, which he assumed would be resolved, went on.[23]

Both Smith and Gamull actively supported Charles I and in 1644 both were disqualified from taking their seats in the Commons. Chester remained a royalist stronghold until January 1646. Subsequently by-elections were held to replace the expelled members. Sir William Brereton had groomed John Bradshaw, a local lawyer working for the Committee for Compounding, as his nominee for Chester,[24] but in the event the city chose William Edwards, the leader of the anti-Gamull group in the 1630s, and one of the few aldermen who had fought against the king, and John Ratcliffe, the new recorder and son of the M.P. of 1621 and 1628. Their correspondence once again suggests that their principal concern was to shield the city from the evils of the war, above all from subordination to the county committee of Cheshire.[25]

The Instrument of Government reduced Chester's representation from two to one. As a consequence, the recorders' claim to sit for the city was apparently suspended. In 1654 the man chosen was Charles Walley, in 1656 Edward Bradshaw. Walley, a prewar alderman, had served throughout the royalist occupation, during which he was mayor for three successive years. He was a noted defender of the rights of the assembly against the governors imposed by the king and the commissioners of array, and above all, a violent opponent of the excise. In 1646 he led the group prepared to surrender the city to Sir William Brereton. His role had been sufficiently ambiguous for him to be reinstated in 1648 as an alderman.[26] Similarly Edward Bradshaw, a common councillor and sheriff before the war, had remained in the city, but not attended the assembly, during the siege, and had been elevated to the aldermanic bench in 1646. In 1655 he led an attempt to get the Lord Protector to confirm the city's charter. Both Walley and Bradshaw survived a purge in 1659 and showed themselves willing to work with the restored Rump Parliament. The assembly as a whole at that time has been described as 'temperamentally neutralist and inclined to wait upon events', more committed to maintaining the city's independence than to invoking central government authority to achieve religious or political change. Walley and Bradshaw were good representatives of that attitude. Yet the cause they maintained would not long survive the Restoration.[27]

THE COUNTY SEATS 1660–1832

The Civil Wars and Interregnum left a confusing impᵣ   t on the politics and society of Cheshire. For seventy-five years or more, the political élite was deeply divided, and the electoral history of the period is dominated by conflicts over the great 'national' issues of the day, the terms 'Whig' and 'Tory' expressing a profound ideological division amongst the gentry. From 1678 to 1701 the Whig party was in the ascendant in the county, only ceding the seats to the Tories in a bitterly contested election in 1685, and for much of the time it was too powerful even to be challenged. From 1702 to 1734 the parties were more evenly matched. Cheshire was probably the most regularly polled of all counties in these years, at eight out of ten elections. Between 1701 and 1715 it was one of five counties which 'came close to changing their representation in accordance with the prevailing swing', and was the only county far from London to do

[23] Ches. R.O., DCC/14 (Cowper MSS.), ff. 61–74; B.L. Harl. MS. 2081, f. 93.

[24] B.L. Add. MS. 11333, f. 83.

[25] Hist. MSS. Com. 7, *8th Rep. I, Chester Corp.* pp. 384–6; A. M. Johnson, 'Politics in Chest. 1640–62', in *Crisis and Order in Eng. Towns,* ed. P. Clark and P. Slack, 214–18; Chester R.O., M/L/2, nos. 304, 305, 308, 312, 313, 315, 319, 320.

[26] Morrill, *Ches. 1630–60,* 189; Johnson, 'Politics in Chest.' 213.

[27] Johnson, 'Politics in Chest.', *passim.* The above is also based on the evidence of the Assembly Files in Chester R.O.

so.[28] Yet paradoxically the rage of party was declining in intensity after 1701, and from 1734 something resembling a consensus was once again restored so that there were no more contests in the century before the Great Reform Bill. Instead the county was content to return men who prided themselves on their independence.

Although the eras before and after 1734 must be distinguished on one level, there were also very important continuities throughout the period as a whole. Only 26 men drawn from 13 families represented Cheshire between 1660 and 1832. Eight of the 13 families had provided county members of parliament before 1640; 10 of them were descended from men who had served on the commission of the peace under the Tudors.[29] The closed nature of Cheshire landed society and the importance of ancient lineage were thus as important in the 18th century as in the 16th. The government of the county was, however, controlled by a much smaller group of families. It was rare before 1640 for one man to represent the county in successive parliaments; no one served more than thrice. Thirteen of the 26 members in the years 1660–1832 served in three or more parliaments, some in far more. Robert Cotton served in 8 parliaments between 1679 and 1701,[30] and Davies Davenport in all 8 between 1806 and 1832.[31] Charles Cholmondeley served in 7 between 1710 and 1756,[32] and Sir John Mainwaring (1689–1702) and John Crewe of Crewe (1768–1802) sat in 6. Furthermore, that control by a handful of great landed families had sufficient momentum to carry it far beyond the Great Reform Bill, and only ceased to be the major feature of Cheshire politics after 1885.

1660–88

The most striking point about the thirty years after the Restoration was the bitter conflict which developed within the governing élite of Cheshire.[33] It culminated at the assizes in September 1682 when a Tory grand jury accused 32 leading Whig gentlemen of sedition. The origins of the split may, however, go back almost to the Restoration itself. A hint of the divisions to come might even be seen in the contrast between the elections of 1660 and 1661. The representatives of the county in the Convention Parliament, both parliamentarians in the 1640s, were Sir George Booth, an opponent of the Commonwealth and Protectorate and a 'Presbyterian' politician in 1659–60, and Sir Thomas Mainwaring, an active J.P. who had upheld the *de facto* governments of the 1650s. In 1661, they were replaced by William Brereton of Brereton and Peter Venables, two staunch loyalists who had fought for the king and been sequestered as delinquents. When Charles II reconstructed the commission of the peace, all four men were prominent in it. The active Cheshire bench in the 1660s carefully balanced former royalists with former 'Presbyterians' and Cromwellian conservatives, but probably that had a divisive rather than a healing effect. In Cheshire at least the enforcement of the ecclesiastical settlement seemingly created tension: one knot of active justices, led by Venables, Sir Peter Leycester, and Lord Cholmondeley, sought a rigorous enforcement of the Act of Uniformity and the Conventicle Acts, but others, headed by the

---

[28] Speck, *Tory & Whig*, 77.
[29] Sir Fulk Lucy (by-election, 1664), a younger son from a Warwickshire family, had married the heiress of the Davenports of Davenport; Sir Roger Mostyn (1702) was a North Wales landowner with property and kin in Cheshire; the Crewes of Crewe, an ancient Cheshire family, rose in the 17th century through office and marriage.
[30] Defeated in 1685.

[31] First elected at a by-election just before the dissolution of 1806.
[32] Defeated in 1722.
[33] There is no good study of Restoration Cheshire. For some general remarks see C. T. Gatty, *Mary Davies and the Manor of Ebury*, i. *passim*; for a lucid account of county politics in the 1680s, see G. W. Keeton, *Lord Chancellor Jeffreys and the Stuart Cause*, cap. 7.

Booths and the Mainwarings, wished to ease the full rigours of the Acts, particularly for the clergy.[34] On the whole the leading Cheshire factions do not seem to have formed close ties with the court through office and patronage, although several men, including indeed the Booths, received pensions or cash as rewards for their loyalty during the troubles, so that there was no Court and Country polarization. In addition, inextricably entangled with the differences over matters of security and religion, there developed a private feud between Sir Peter Leycester and Sir Thomas Mainwaring, which originated in a slight to his ancestors found by the latter in Leycester's genealogical writings. The paper warfare which followed became a *cause célèbre* among literary circles throughout the country, but locally the effects of an increasingly acrimonious debate probably heightened the mutual antipathy of the groups of gentry already divided over larger issues of county government.[35]

At the by-election caused by the death of Peter Venables in 1670 however the divisions were not yet fully established. Two candidates came forward, Sir Philip Egerton of Oulton and Thomas Cholmondeley of Vale Royal. Both were already hard-line Anglicans, and both were later to be Tories.[36] But 'they not agreeing which should stand, went to poll, which continued till Wednesday, when Sir Philip desisted . . .'.[37] If a 'Presbyterian' or tolerationist faction did exist at the time, it either felt disinclined, or was unable, to present a candidate. Even in 1678, at the election to the first Exclusion Parliament, the divisions were not fierce enough to produce an open trial of strength. The leading gentlemen met in conclave and came to an arrangement whereby the representation should be shared by two men of widely differing views:[38] Philip Egerton was to vote against the Exclusion Bill, while Henry Booth, son of Sir George, now Lord Delamere, was already a committed supporter of Shaftesbury and was soon to make his mark as a radical Exclusionist.[39] Indeed, in a speech on the Exclusion Bill, he came nearer than almost anyone else to rejecting a hereditary monarchy.[40]

Nothing is known about the elections to the second Exclusion Parliament except that the anti-Exclusionist Egerton was replaced by an active Whig, Robert Cotton.[41] In 1681 the county community was totally split and the first full-scale contest between Tory and Whig took place. Sir Robert Leycester and Sir Philip Egerton took Booth and Cotton to a poll. Initially both sides were confident of success, Lord Cholmondeley, for one, being informed by his bailiff that the Tories could expect victory. Cholmondeley's disdain for Booth and Cotton and his alarm at their principles were powerfully expressed in his letters, and the contest greatly exacerbated the divisions within the county. Cotton and Booth had already prudently closeted themselves with the sheriff to work out an election strategy, but Cotton also canvassed Cholmondeley's tenants to deflect them from following their lord's direction, 'a thing so treacherous & base that [Cholmondeley] did not think he had so little of a Gentleman in him'.[42] Henry Booth claimed that the Whig victory was overwhelming, by 4 to 1, and that most of

[34] A. Martindale, *Autobiography* (Chetham Soc. [1st ser.], iv.), *passim*; H. Newcome, *Autobiography* (Chetham Soc. [1st ser.] xxvi), *passim*; W. Urwick, *Hist. Sketches of Nonconf. in Ches.*, *passim*; D. Lacey, *Dissent and Parl. Politics in Engl.*, app.

[35] *Tracts written in the Controversy respecting the Legitimacy of Amicia* (Chetham Soc. [1st ser.] lxxviii–lxxx), *passim*.

[36] For both, see Hist. Parl. Trust, biogs. For Egerton, see also *J.C.A.S.* i. pt. 2, 94–106; for Cholmondeley, see also Evelyn Lady Newton, *Leghs of Lyme* and *Lyme Letters*, *passim*.

[37] *Cal. S.P. Dom.* 1670, 30.

[38] Ches. R.O., DDX/384/2, unfol.

[39] Between 1675 and 1678 Delamere consistently op-

posed the Court. He formally protested against the Non-Resisting Test, and voted for dissolution in 1675 and 1677, and for the impeachment of Danby. All his domestic chaplains after 1660 were nonconformists: Hist. Parl. Trust, biog.; Lacey, *Dissent & Parl. Politics*, biog. appendix; *D.N.B.*

[40] *Works of Hen. Booth, earl of Warrington* (1694), unpag. He had called for a bill to exclude all placemen and pensioners from the Commons.

[41] Cotton sat on the Exclusion Bill committee in the Oxford Parliament of 1681, and vigorously supported Monmouth: Hist. Parl. Trust, biog.; cf. H. Horwitz, *Parl., Policy, and Politics in Reign of Wm. III*, 344.

[42] Ches. R.O., DCH/K/3/3 and 4, unfol.; ibid., DDX/384/2, unpag.

the Tory voters were papists.[43] Cholmondeley however dismissed it as 'the giddy zeals of a fanatical bruits'.[44] Booth himself published a fighting election address which clearly demonstrated that one group of Whigs at least were still using the language and conceptual framework of those who had advocated a mixed monarchy in and after 1641.[45]

Although they had lost the election, the Cheshire Tories were determined to counterattack. The Whig address presented to the Commons calling for Exclusion was met with another, ingeniously asking both for the further investigation of the Popish Plot and for the execution of the 'wholesome laws' enacted against Dissenters, who, the Tories stressed, had perpetrated 'the barbarous murder of the best of kings'. They also called for a 'cheerful' grant of supply, which the Whigs were known to want to withhold until the Exclusion Bill had been passed. The Tory petition was signed by 38 men of standing, including several leading J.P.s, and, significantly, eight clergymen. In the petition, as in most of their declarations and private letters in the 1680s, the Cheshire Tories were Anglican loyalists first, and defenders of the Crown second. But it was all to no avail. The Whig leadership in the Commons avoided formal acceptance of the address on a technicality.[46]

The Cheshire Whigs, headed by the Booths and by Charles Gerard, newly created earl of Macclesfield,[47] had been ruthless in their pursuit of their political objectives. They were to reap the whirlwind they had sown. The occasion was to be the visit to Cheshire of the duke of Monmouth. Attempting to maintain a momentum of popular support which might yet carry him to the throne, the duke made a progress through the north midland counties in September 1682, and was attended and royally entertained by most of the Cheshire Whigs, while large crowds lined the roads and shouted his praises 'in such volley as wanted nothing but a *Vive le Roi* to complete a Rebellion'.[48]

The Whigs had gone too far and given the Government the opportunity to act without alienating moderate support. The commission of the peace was purged, and the Booths and Mainwarings displaced for the first time for generations.[49] At the same time a grand jury at the assizes, with the leading Tory Sir Thomas Grosvenor as foreman, presented 32 leading Whig gentlemen for promoting sedition. The presentment linked the Whigs' address of 1681 which 'tended to alter the succession of the Crown, with other dangerous and seditious purports', with their use of 'an instigated rabble, in a broad mixture of various secretaries' to welcome Monmouth, 'a prime confederate in the late treasonable conspiracy', and their 'connivance and indulgence' of dissenters of all kinds, 'the ready road to rebellion, popery and arbitrary power'.[50] Sir George Jeffreys, chief justice of Chester 1680–3, did not pursue the presentment to the uttermost; but the 32 were made to give recognizances and to plead before him. The presentment was also published to secure a greater effect. The earl of Macclesfield indignantly, but unsuccessfully, brought an action of *scandalum magnatum* against the grand jury. At the same time, the deputy lieutenants were ordered to search the houses of all the leading Whigs for arms.[51] Yet the Tories did not sweep all before them. Sir Thomas Grosvenor's forcing the city of Chester to surrender its charter in order that the king

[43] *Cal. S.P. Dom.* 1680–1, 198, Booth to Ld. Conway, 5 March 1681: Booth and Cotton, c. 1,200 votes; Sir Rob. Leycester 340, Egerton 280.

[44] Ches. R.O., DCH/K/3/4, unfol.

[45] *Works of Hen. Booth, passim*; J. R. Jones, *The First Whigs*, 173.

[46] E. Lipson, 'Elections to Exclusion Parl.', *E.H.R.* xxviii. 68, 85; D. George, 'Elections and Electioneering, 1679–81', *E.H.R.* xlv. 574 n., 576 n.; Jones, *First Whigs*, 172–3; *J.C.A.S.* [1st ser.] i. pt. 2, 105–6.

[47] Gerard, a senior royalist commander in the civil war, was in exile 1646–60. His Whiggery may have stemmed

from frustration at royal failure to reward his sacrifices, and from anger at the court intrigues which hindered his efforts to secure full possession of the disputed Fitton inheritance: *D.N.B.*; Keeton, *Jeffreys*, 148–85.

[48] Quoted without source in Gatty, *Mary Davies*, ii. 7–8.

[49] Henry Booth was also *custos*. He recorded his reactions in 'A Speech on the Occasion of some Justices being put out of Commission': *Works*, unpag.

[50] Quoted without source in Gatty, *Mary Davies*, ii. 9–11.

[51] Ibid. 11–15; Keeton, *Jeffreys*, 148–85; Newton, *Leghs of Lyme*, 198–203; *Cal. S.P. Dom.* 1682–3, *passim*.

might remodel it, and the jurisdictional heavy-handedness of Jeffreys in setting aside local courts and attempting, unsuccessfully, to take control of the judicial inquiry into the riots that followed Monmouth's visit, both alarmed local sentiment, and gave the Whigs some leeway.[52] When James II came to the throne and issued writs for a new parliament, political society in Cheshire was more completely split and more evenly balanced than ever before. The election was bound to be bitter. The Tories put up the two men who had previously served in their interest, Thomas Cholmondeley of Vale Royal and Philip Egerton of Oulton, both of whom had been involved in harrying the Whigs and searching their houses for arms. Since Henry Booth had now succeeded to his father's title, his place as Whig candidate alongside Sir Robert Cotton was taken by John Mainwaring, son of Sir Thomas. Both candidates had been among the 32 presented by the grand jury. The Tories seemed well organized. A year before Charles's death they had met and drawn up a resolution 'to assist each other and stand the charge of a Poll against all opposers'. An impressive list of gentry in every hundred either committed the support of themselves and their tenants, or were listed as 'hopeful'. When the election came, however, much of their support was wavering. One man noted on the agreement: 'this hopeful list was taken a year ago; but it is suspected many of them will fail'. How far national issues were raised is not known, but the election itself, spread over six days, proved bitter and violent. A Tory account described extensive rioting by dissenting mobs who broke windows and cried 'down with the parsons', 'down with the bishops'. One leading gentleman was knocked down in the street. The militia was called out but kept discreetly out of sight and 'without influencing any awe upon the election'.[53] The Whig, Thomas Mainwaring, in contrast, emphasized discriminatory practices by the sheriff, who closed the poll early after many Whig voters had gone home for the weekend expecting to vote on the following Monday. Mainwaring agreed that there were scuffles and some window-breakings, and that the militia was kept out of sight, but did not say to which faction the rioters belonged.[54] Whichever account was correct, the outcome was clear, a Tory majority of 300 in a poll of about 4,000.[55]

It was to be the last Tory victory until 1702. The six intervening elections were all won by the Whigs, mostly without a contest. Mainwaring and Cotton, who sat continuously from 1689 to 1702, had revenge for their defeat in 1685. The triumphant Tories of 1685 were divided and ruined by the policies of James II. They had defended his right to the Crown only to find themselves betrayed by his actions as king. In 1688 they split asunder; many, refusing to acknowledge the Revolution, became Jacobite in sympathy, or at least non-jurors, distancing themselves from local office and influence. Initially only a minority were willing to accept the Revolution *de facto* and to take William's early offer to work with a bipartisan bench of magistrates. The Whigs seized the county machinery and its electoral patronage. The Cheshire Whigs led by Delamere, created earl of Warrington in 1689, and Macclesfield had been early conspirators against James in 1688, and led the most vigorous and open wing of the Northern Rising which accompanied William's landings. They remained confident and united, and could expect to be honoured by the new régime.

What made the plight of the Tories in 1688 worse was their indecision. Alienated by James's actions,[56] but impaled on the principle of passive obedience, they remained

[52] Keeton, *Jeffreys*, 162–8.
[53] Ches. R.O., DCH/K/3/6, unfol. letter of 3 March 1685; *J.C.A.S.* [1st ser.] i. pt. 2, 106–9.
[54] Ches. R.O., DDX/384/2, unfol.; R. George, 'Elections and Electioneering in 1685', *Trans. R.H.S.* 4th ser. xix. 178.

[55] Cholmondeley: 2,099; Egerton: 1,966; Mainwaring: 1,682; Cotton: 1,552.
[56] Their clerical supporters almost all refused to read out the second Declaration of Indulgence in 1688, despite heavy episcopal pressure.

fatally inactive. The earl of Derby, for example, was privy to the invasion plan long before November, but could not bring himself either to denounce or to support it. During the Northern Rising he simply dithered. Thus the Tories neither retained the respect of the new government nor could plausibly claim to have remained unsullied by events.[57] They had compromised themselves. In the ensuing elections they had nothing to offer. In 1690 the best they could do was to attack the Whigs for voting for changes in the land tax assessments detrimental to the county's interests.[58] Meanwhile their leaders were subjected to vigorous searches for arms by the new Whig deputy lieutenants, a harassment which continued for some years.[59]

1689–1734

Most gentlemen and many freeholders in Cheshire were deeply committed to one or other of the Whig or Tory ideologies during these years. The cleavages on matters of principle, indeed, were more clear-cut in Cheshire than elsewhere: in terms of electoral practice however the situation was more confused.

The Cheshire Whigs were a party rooted in a constitutional tradition and with clearly defined political goals; the Cheshire Tories were a party of the Church. The letters and writings of the two sides bear this out clearly. Men like the earls of Warrington and Macclesfield, Sir Thomas Mainwaring, and Sir Willoughby Aston were aggressively Whiggish in matters of the constitution, and defensive or evasive over religion,[60] while the Leghs of Lyme, the Grosvenors, the Shakerleys, the Warburtons, and the Cholmondeleys of Vale Royal were obsessed with the danger to the Church of England, and amazingly inarticulate when writing on politics.[61]

The leading Cheshire Whigs were radical in their views. Booth and Cotton had developed theories of mixed and contractual monarchy during the Exclusion crisis. Yet even then the Tories had not answered their published arguments. In the counter-address to Parliament in 1681, in the assize presentment of 1682, and in the election of 1685 the Cheshire Tories had emphasized the hazards of a divided church and the growth of dissenting congregations as the crucial issues. The correspondence of the Leghs of Lyme in the 1670s, too, rarely mentioned the political issues of the day, but demonstrated vigilant concern and alarm over the Crown's ecclesiastical policies. Sir Richard Legh wrote of 'devil presbyterians' and spoke of the hands of dissenting ministers 'stinking with the guilt of the blood' of King Charles I.[62]

The events of 1688–9 certainly shattered the unity of both parties. The Tories in particular were so hopelessly divided that not until the 1720s did they work together in local government or at parliamentary elections. Three groups can be distinguished. The marriage of Sir Charles Bunbury to the sister of Sir Thomas Hanmer brought one group into the orbit of the Hanoverian-Tory leader, the earl of Nottingham. A second group, headed by Sir George Warburton, liked neither the Stuarts nor the Revolution. Sir George himself refused all oaths of allegiance until after the death of James II, and noisily opposed the cost and bureaucracy of war during his time in parliament (1702–5, 1710–15), but never toyed with Jacobitism. A third group, headed by the Grosvenors and the Leghs of Lyme, held a far more ambivalent position, distancing themselves from

---

[57] D. H. Hosford, *Nottingham, Nobles, and the North*, 37–8, 61, 86–9, 93, 105.
[58] H. Horwitz, 'General Election of 1690', *Jnl. Brit. Stud.* xi. 85–6.
[59] Hist. MSS. Com. 71, *Finch*, ii, pp. 210–11.
[60] e.g. *Works of Hen. Booth, Speeches of Earl of Warring-* ton, *passim*.
[61] See the family collections of the Cholmondeleys of Cholmondeley (Ches. R.O., DCH, particularly boxes K, L, and X), and of the Grosvenors (Eaton Hall, papers of the 3rd and 4th Bts.).
[62] Newton, *Leghs of Lyme*, 246 sqq.; *Lyme Letters*, 77.

local government yet deploring the activities of those in the commission of the peace. They drank toasts to the 'king over the water' but dissociated themselves from all plots to bring him back.[63] The Whigs however were also divided, with a small group led by Lord Cholmondeley and the Cottons, which looked to the Court, becoming increasingly isolated from the mainstream of Cheshire Whiggery, led by the Booths. The Cholmondeleys and their allies stood for the defence of the new régime against the threat of popery and arbitrary rule posed by James and Louis XIV, even if that meant unpleasant increases in the powers of the executive and the scale of taxation. The Booths came to believe that the Revolution had been betrayed by the Junto and that the people were being delivered into a new bondage.[64] Those internal divisions help to explain why, in most of the eight contested elections between 1701 and 1734,[65] renegade groups of Whigs and Tories could be found canvassing and voting for candidates of the opposing ideology.

Nonetheless party principle remained a primary feature of the county's political life throughout the period.[66] The social relationships and daily correspondence of the gentry were saturated with a conventional wisdom drawn from party traditions. There was no talk of neutrality, only of traitors, converts, or allies across the frontiers of the two-party system. The Whigs saw Tories as either incipient rebels or, at best, as men who had merely acquiesced in the Revolution.[67] The Tories wrote of all Whigs as pseudo-Republicans and crypto-Presbyterians.[68] In part the longevity of party alignments is to be explained by the depths of the antagonisms of the earlier period. When Sir Robert Cotton voted against the Junto in 1695 he retained the support of Whigs like Sir John Crewe who said that they had suffered with him in 1683 and would not part company with him now.[69] In part the Tories, though in disarray in the 1690s, remained bound together, unlike the Whigs, because of the implacable hostility of the earl of Warrington. In addresses to the grand juries in the 1690s, he propounded the doctrine of contractual kingship, gloried in the actual resistance which had overthrown James II, and accused the Cheshire Tories of Jacobite associations and of religious hypocrisy.[70] His Tract *The Interest of Whig and Tory* (1694) was directed against the Junto, but his 'Country' ideals were combined with other statements precluding a coalition with 'Country' Toryism like those forming elsewhere.[71]

The Tories were divided in their attitudes to the Revolution, and later by their views on the Hanoverian succession, but retained a genuine commitment to the Church of England.[72] In the 1690s they invariably called themselves the 'Church Party'; their greatest electoral victory, in 1710, was unashamedly gained on a 'church in danger' platform; in 1715 many Tories refused to support a compromise whereby the parties were to share the representation because any Tory who joined 'with a person of known disaffection to the Church and clergy, had likewise deserted his old principles'.[73] Above all the clergy were united. Cheshire was one of only four counties where the clergy

[63] S. W. Baskerville, 'Management of the Tory Interest in Lancs. and Ches., 1715–54', (Oxford Univ. D.Phil. thesis, 1976), *passim*, and the papers of the Grosvenors (Eaton Hall, papers of 3rd and 4th Bts.); Jn. Rylands Libr., Legh of Lyme MSS., and Warburton of Arley MSS.; Tabley House, Leycester–Warren MSS. (lists and access at Ches. R.O.).

[64] Lord Cholmondeley was a Tory in the 1680s, but a noisy convert to Whig ideology in 1696, following the Assassination plot. See Ches. R.O., DCH/K/8; DCH/L/ *passim*; DCH/X/8/10.

[65] The elections of 1708 and 1713 were not contested.

[66] Baskerville, 'Tory Interest', *passim*. The following narrative, though drawing heavily on Dr. Baskerville's work, and on transcripts of documents which he made

freely available, differs considerably in emphasis from his interpretation.

[67] *Works of Hen. Booth, passim*; Ches. R.O., DCH/K/ *passim*; Chester R.O., CR 63/2/691 (Utkinton MSS.); CR 72 (Cotton of Combermere MSS.).

[68] Eaton Hall, Grosvenor MSS., 3rd and 4th Bts.; Tabley House, Leycester–Warren MSS.; Jn. Rylands Libr., Legh of Lyme MSS., Warburton of Arley MSS., Mainwaring of Baddiley MSS.

[69] Chester R.O., CR 63/2/691, f. 184.

[70] *Speeches of Earl of Warrington, passim*.

[71] *Works of Hen. Booth, passim*.

[72] Baskerville, 'Tory Interest', 296–309.

[73] Eaton Hall, Grosvenor MSS., 4th Bt., unfol., J. Fowler to Sir Ric. G., 16 April 1715.

were overwhelmingly Tory in 1710,[74] and a similar solidarity has been demonstrated for the elections of 1715, 1722, and 1727, when the Tory squires were far from united.[75] The intrusion of dissenting justices in the 1690s, the activities of the Whig Bishop Peploe, whom many saw as heretical, and the fact that there were few popish recusant gentry amongst the Cheshire Tories, all contributed to that strong clerical Toryism.[76] Furthermore the exceptionally large proportion of electors who were dissenters, perhaps as high as a quarter,[77] mostly regular Whig voters, would sharpen the Tories' self-image as the party of the Church.

However great the differences within each party, then, the vocabulary and assumptions of Cheshire politics were grounded upon a Whig–Tory dichotomy. Yet it must be emphasized that the only contested election in the period 1689–1734 in which the two parties clashed clearly and straightforwardly was that of 1705. In each of the other seven contests there were organized Whig groups supporting Tory candidates and organized Tory groups supporting Whigs. Three major reasons for this can be suggested.

First, there was a struggle amongst the Whig magnates for control of county government and in particular there was the Janus-like role of the earl of Cholmondeley, whose public pronouncements were those of an orthodox Whig and whose voting record at Westminster was impeccably partisan,[78] but who just as consistently supported Tory candidates in Cheshire elections.[79] The Whig interest was tied, by prescription and 'County preference', to the moral and political leadership of the Booths, and to gain a dominant position in county politics the Cholmondeleys found it expedient to offer their services to the demoralized Cheshire Tories. Their aid was insufficient to unseat the Whig members in 1701, but was probably decisive in 1702 and 1710. The 1705 result, the only Cheshire contest in Anne's reign to go against the national trend,[80] followed Cholmondeley's withdrawal of support from the Tories, after a stern warning from Godolphin that the earl's position at Court would become unsafe if he persisted.[81]

Secondly, Court and Country issues temporarily cut across deeper alignments. As the 1690s progressed both the Whig members, Sir John Mainwaring and Sir Thomas Cotton, drifted into dependency upon the Junto ministers and began to accumulate offices and pensions. Sir Thomas Cotton, for example, pursued a 'Country' Whig line against executive encroachments in the early 1690s, but became more complaisant after his appointment as lord lieutenant of Denbighshire. Sir John Mainwaring accepted a place in William III's Household and then supported the Junto against 'Country' Whig and Tory attacks, even voting to maintain a standing army. He also supported Sir Thomas Grosvenor's election at Chester in 1695 since the Junto found him preferable to Sir William Williams, the *ultra* 'Country' Whig.[82] The campaign to unseat those two in 1701 and 1702 was unashamedly a 'Country' one and made many Whigs swallow their principles for a day and support two 'Country' Tories.[83]

Thirdly, and most decisively, issues of essentially local significance could transcend party allegiance. The most important, concerning the river Weaver navigation, divided

[74] Speck, *Tory and Whig*, 24.
[75] Baskerville, 'Tory Interest', 300 and app. A ii.
[76] Ibid., *passim*.
[77] W. Urwick, *Hist. Sketches of Nonconf. in Ches.*, p. lxi, discusses a list of the constituent churches of the Ches. Association of Presbyterian and Congregational churches, drawn up in 1718, which names 894 dissenting electors. To them must be added perhaps 300 Quakers and Baptists.
[78] G. Holmes, *Brit. Politics in Age of Anne*, 226–8, 292.
[79] Baskerville, 'Tory Interest', *passim*; Ches. R.O.,

DCH/K/3/8, 10, 16, 18, 26; DCH/L/34, 42, 50.
[80] Thus the Whigs held the seats in 1690–1702, 1705–10 and the Tories in 1702–5 and 1710–15.
[81] Both M.P.s had voted to tack the Occasional Conformity clause to the money bill, something the government would not forgive.
[82] Hist. Parl. Trust, biogs.
[83] *J.C.A.S.* [1st ser.] i. pt. 2, 103–4; Ches. R.O., DCH/L/50. Cholmondeley insisted that the Tory candidates swear allegiance to William.

the county from 1699, and most notably in the election of 1715. The issue was complex. On the one hand, if the Weaver was made navigable as far upstream as Northwich the nascent rock-salt industry would become economically viable, to the benefit of many leading gentry and prospective employees. The consequences for the owners of the brine wells, and for the 3,000 Cheshire families whose livelihoods depended upon the carriage of coal to the salt-pans and of the refined salt to Liverpool, would, however, be dire.[84] In 1715, despite the intensity of party conflict throughout England, the Weaver Navigation Bill dominated the Cheshire election.[85] Groups of Tory and Whig magnates who favoured the navigation met at Northwich and agreed on a 'compromise' whereby each party should put forward one man committed to the Bill.[86] Their candidates were the hard-line Whig, Langham Booth, and the anti-Hanoverian Tory Sir George Warburton. The anti-navigationists put up one candidate, the Hanoverian Tory Charles Cholmondeley. The poll-book[87] reveals the extent to which individuals were compelled to make personal choices between conflicting interests. Most of the Whigs, including many hard-liners, supported the two 'compromise' candidates, but a minority, led by the earl of Cholmondeley, supported the anti-navigationist Tory. The Tories were more deeply divided. The quasi-Jacobites and the real backwoodsmen, such as the Grosvenors and the Leghs, would have nothing to do with the 'compromise' and put party principle above economic self-interest. The Hanoverian Tories were divided according to their views on the navigation.[88] One group, led by the earl of Barrymore and Sir Peter Shakerley, although opposed to the navigation, supported the 'compromise' because they believed the alternative to be that the Whigs would put up two candidates and win both seats.[89] The group who adhered most faithfully to their principles, however, were the clergy, who rejected the 'compromise' by 49–12. In contrast 11 of the 26 J.P.s identifiable as Tories voted for both Warburton and Booth.[90] At the close of the poll therefore the county was confronted by the ironical spectacle of a radical Whig and a 'reactionary' Tory in harness, supported by the 'Country' Whigs and a cross-section of the Tories, defeating a moderate Tory backed by the backwoods squires and the Courtier Whig earl of Cholmondeley. In such circumstances the Whig–Tory dichotomy can be seen as a necessary, but hardly as a sufficient, dimension in the electoral history of the period.

In 1722 the Weaver Navigation was still a major issue,[91] and the original line-up of candidates suggests that it was expected to dominate the election: Booth and Warburton were confronted by Charles Cholmondeley again, this time running with John Offley Crewe, former Whig member for Newcastle-under-Lyme (1703–5) and for Cheshire (1705–10). It has been suggested that Crewe had become a Tory since 1715, but no evidence of his conversion has been presented.[92] He is more likely to have been chosen to balance the ticket as an 'independent' Whig opposed to the navigation. The fact that the Whig earl of Cholmondeley agreed with the Grosvenors to support their

[84] E. Hughes, *Studies in Admin. and Finance*, 226–36, 253–64; T. S. Willan, *Navigation of the River Weaver* (Chetham. Soc. 3rd ser. iii), 1–21; S. Lambert, *Bills and Acts*, 153–67; additional information from B.L. Add. MS. 36914 (Aston of Aston MSS.); Jn. Rylands Libr., Legh of Lyme MSS. and Warburton of Arley MSS.; Ches. R.O., DCH/K (Cholmondeley MSS.), all unfol.

[85] The following draws much material from Baskerville, 'Tory Interest', 36–8, 47–54, 60–4, 114–18, but differs radically in its interpretation.

[86] Ibid. 47–54; Eaton Hall, Grosvenor MSS., papers of 4th Bt., unfol. letters; Jn. Rylands Libr., Legh of Lyme MSS., unfol. letters; Ches. R.O., DCH/X/5, unsorted correspondence.

[87] Ches. R.O., QDV/1/1–7.

[88] Their attitudes can be discovered from the following: Baskerville, 'Tory Interest', 47–54, 114–18; Hughes, *Studies in Admin.*, 226–35, 264; Willan, *Weaver*, 1–21; Ches. R.O., DCH/X/5; Jn. Rylands Libr., Legh of Lyme MSS., T. Patten to Peter Legh, 3 March 1711.

[89] Baskerville, 'Tory Interest', 48–54.

[90] Calculated from ibid., app. A and B.

[91] For the continuing debate see the works listed in n. 84 above; also numerous letters in Jn. Rylands Libr., Legh of Lyme MSS., and B.L. Add. MS. 36914.

[92] *Hist. Parl., Commons*, 1715–54, i. 593–4; Baskerville, 'Tory Interest', 126–8, 166.

campaign in Chester in exchange for their support for Crewe suggests that many Tories were unhappy with the latter's candidature.[93] Subsequently Warburton withdrew from the contest, leaving Booth to fend for himself 'in great straits', suggesting that many Tory navigationists would find it difficult to support a single Whig candidate.[94] The navigation again divided the parties. A limited study of the poll books for gentry voting shows more than a quarter of the Tory J.P.s, most of them known supporters of the navigation, plumping for Booth.[95]

Those two elections were to prove a watershed. Men of the two parties had overcome ancient prejudices and were working more closely together than had seemed possible; the generation revered as the leaders of Whiggery in the 1680s had died out; a twenty-year stranglehold on local patronage by the Cholmondeleys had given them the control of local government so long denied them by the moral leadership of the old guard. By 1727 a restructuring of politics is evident. At first sight, the election in that year appears to be a Whig–Tory confrontation, with the Cholmondeleys and the Booths working together for the first time since 1688 for the election of Sir Robert Cotton, a client of Walpole, against the combination of Charles Cholmondeley and John Offley Crewe. It is more convincing, however, to see the election as the first of a new pattern in which Court and 'Country' divisions prevailed. Crewe was not a real Tory, but rather an Independent set on opposing any further extension of executive power. Equally, Booth's support for Cotton may have had less to do with the latter's Whiggery than the former's hopes, after attaching himself some years earlier to the interest of the prince of Wales, now George II, of advancement at court.[96]

The pattern is clearer in 1734.[97] Cotton had topped the poll in 1727,[98] but at the next election he found his support for Walpole's excise bill a serious electoral liability.[99] He was opposed once more by the veteran Charles Cholmondeley and by John Crewe, son of the man defeated in 1722 and 1727. Party rhetoric was reserved for public meetings. The correspondence suggests that the issues cut across the old alignments.[1] Many gentry from secure Tory backgrounds supported Cotton, the government candidate, for the sake of security and peace. Yet even more Whigs, outraged by the excise bill, voted for the Cholmondeley–Crewe interest, most notably the Booths, once again in self-imposed exile from the court. Cruder pressures were also at work, with Cotton's connexions with the government being exploited to barter jobs in the excise office or as inspectors of pedlars, and even ecclesiastical preferments in exchange for votes.[2] Cotton was even successfully advised to secure the interests of the Adlington tenants by pandering to Sir Thomas Legh's dislike of his own son and to Lady Legh's craving for 'some wonderful curiosity . . . to add to her heap of wonders. A rusty nail or a Pebble may do the business, if you can but tack a suitable pedigree from the Temple of Jerusalem or St. Stephen the Martyr.'[3] It was all in vain. Cholmondeley topped the poll, just ahead of Crewe, while Cotton trailed the latter by 700 votes.[4] During the campaign Cotton had attempted to make an alliance with Crewe, appealing to the latter's Whig prejudices against the 'Jacobite' menace, and formal consultations had

93 Eaton Hall, Grosvenor MSS., papers of 4th Bt., L. Cholmondeley to Sir Ric. G., 12 Dec. 1721. Grosvenor, who opposed the navigation, would hardly have needed inducements to back Crewe if the latter had been a Tory.
94 Cited in Baskerville, 'Tory Interest', 128.
95 Calculated from ibid., app. A. and B.
96 Ibid., cap. 4.
97 Ibid. 182, where Dr Baskerville argues that a coalition of Country Whig and Tory elements grew up in most parts of the north-west in the 1730s.
98 *Hist. Parl., Commons*, 1715–54, 202; Ches. R.O.,

P/4/19/2 (Lower Peover parish rec.), poll book.
99 P. Langford, *Excise Crisis, passim*, esp. 121–3, for reactions in the north midland counties.
1 See particularly the 40 letters relating to the campaign in Chester R.O., CR 72/6, bdle. marked 'from box 37'.
2 Ibid., e.g. G. Coope to C[otton], 17 Feb. 1734; P. Davenport to C., 20 Feb. 1734; J. Mainwaring to C., 2 Mar. 1734.
3 Ibid. P. Davenport to C., 4 Mar. 1734.
4 *Hist. Parl., Commons*, 1715–54, 202: Cholmondeley: 3,817; Crewe: 3,710; Cotton: 3,005.

taken place, but in the event Crewe's 'Country' ties to Cholmondeley had proved the stronger bond.[5]

That was to prove the last contested election for almost a hundred years. The fusion of 'Country Tory' and 'Country Whig' interests between 1722 and 1734 prepared the way for a century of 'independent' back-bench members. The strength of that alliance and the near-bankruptcy of the earls of Cholmondeley, the one family capable of challenging their hegemony, inhibited further strife.[6] The country squires reverted to the selection of candidates by agreement. There was one other reason. The detailed correspondence kept by Sir Robert Cotton during the 1734 campaign, far from confirming the idea of a 'tamed and eroded' electorate in the early 18th century, suggests a high degree of volatility and independence amongst the freeholders. Some landlords, like Sir Thomas Aston, could still haughtily 'forbid [his tenants] to promise their votes till they heard further from him',[7] and often the procurement of a letter of recommendation was seen as a guarantee of success. Cotton's agents also expressed conventional views about what was needed to keep voters in order: 'Free ale is the *primum mobile* of the vulgar' wrote one,[8] while another expressed regret that so many landowners now expected the candidates to treat their tenants, and neglected to do so themselves.[9] Much more frequent, however, is the evidence of elation or dejection at the principled resistance of tenants to their landlords' pressure. Thus Cotton clearly expected many dissenters to defy Tory landlords.[10] In many townships freeholders met independently to discuss the issues, and in some the support of two or three prominent freeholders was expected to bring the rest into line, whatever the landlord decreed.[11] The canvass returns from the north Cheshire townships around Lyme and from Wirral suggest a movement of support during the campaign not accounted for by changes in gentry opinion.[12]

The 1734 election was unusually tense, following the excise crisis. The Cotton letters speak of riots at Nantwich, Macclesfield, Congleton, Stockport, and Knutsford between opposing crowds shouting the names of the candidates and traditional party slogans, such as 'no Jacobites', 'down with the Presbyterian justices'.[13] At Macclesfield several people were injured in clashes, and the anti-Court candidates sued Cotton's agent Peter Davenport, mainly as propaganda; the writ was later dropped and redress given by the arbitration of gentlemen from the two sides. In Nantwich, Crewe's supporters staged an impromptu football match outside the inn where three Whig J.P.s were holding their monthly meeting, but it subsequently got out of hand and a riot developed.[14]

There is no evidence of similar demonstrations at most other elections, although Tory–Anglican mobs were reported to have rampaged during the 'Church in Danger' elections of 1705 and 1710.[15] But the strength of freeholders' feeling and the unpredictability of the electorate may have been more usual features. In 1705 the poll books show that voters in more than half the Cheshire townships voted solidly for one party or the other, but in 1710 one-fifth of Lord Bulkeley's tenants supported neither of his

[5] Chester R.O., CR 72/6, P. Davenport to C., 4 Mar. 1734; C. Legh to C., 27 Mar. 1734; T. Eyre to C., 27 Mar. 1734. G. Mainwaring to C., 25 Feb. 1734, speaks of an alliance between 'the tories and Mr Crewe', implying that Crewe was not one himself.

[6] Baskerville, 'Tory Interest', 279 sqq.

[7] Chester R.O., CR 72/6, P. Wenson to C., 18 Feb. 1734.

[8] Ibid. W. Maisterson to C., 14 Jan. 1734.

[9] Ibid. P. Davenport to C., 25 Feb. 1734.

[10] Ibid. e.g., M. Finney to C., 23 Oct. 1733; J. Mainwaring to C., 6 Mar. 1734; H. Cotton to his bro., 11 Mar.

1734; G. Duchenfield to C., 16 Mar. 1734.

[11] Ibid. G. Legh to C., 11 Feb. 1734; J. Mainwaring to C., 15 Feb., 16 Mar. 1734.

[12] Ibid. W. Maisterson to C., 14 Jan., 25 Feb. 1734; R. Leicester to C., 18 Feb. 1734; G. Legh to C., 27 Feb. 1734; H. Cotton to C., 4 Mar. 1734; P. Davenport to C., 4 Mar. 1734, etc.

[13] Ibid. P. Davenport to C., 16 Feb., 25 Feb., 4 Mar. 1734.

[14] Ibid. W. Maisterson to C., 14 Jan. 1734.

[15] G. Holmes, *Trial of Dr. Sacheverell*, 235, 243.

candidates.[16] A copy of the 1727 poll book which lists the votes township by township shows a similar pattern.[17] In more than half of 100 larger townships, two-thirds of the electors voted in the same way. In those where an ancient manor was still owned by a single family, the proportion would appear to be even higher. Yet in not one of those townships did every single elector vote in the same way. Some came very close to it. In the Cholmondeley of Cholmondeley manor of Bickley, 31 men plumped for Cotton, and 1 for Cotton and Crewe; in the Stanley manors of Alderley, Nether Alderley, and Over Alderley, 10 out of 11, 19 out of 20, and 18 out of 22 respectively plumped for Cotton, but in each case, one or two voted for the other candidates. At Adlington 60 out of 62 voters followed their landlord and voted for Cotton. One conjoined Cotton and Cholmondeley, and one voted for Cholmondeley and Crewe. Yet, as in 1705, it should be emphasized that while in more than half of the townships most electors voted together, in nearly half of them there was a major division of opinion. Although no poll book for 1734 has been found, Cotton's defeat may be plausibly ascribed to a revolt of the freeholders. Yet it is clear that such freedom as they possessed could be realized only if there was a prior division amongst the gentry.

1734-1830

In the 96 years covered by this section, five families divided the county representation between them.[18] Of the ten members who served in that period four sat on until their deaths, and all the others sat for between 12 and 34 years. Throughout the decades after 1734, therefore, Cheshire politics was kept firmly in the grip of the county élite, and no 'out-of-doors' political movements disturbed their hold. In the early 1780s the duke of Portland reported to Lord Rockingham that a county Association, for parliamentary reform, was planned, but he was not confident of its coming to fruition since the Cheshire Whigs had 'forgot the substance though they are very attentive to the shadows of their principles'.[19] John Crewe introduced a bill to disqualify revenue officers from sitting in the Commons in 1782, but by 1784 the embryonic Cheshire Association had disbanded.[20]

Three times in the period the county came close to a poll. In 1796 Sir Robert Cotton announced very late in the day his decision to retire from parliament, and both Lord Grey, son of the earl of Stamford,[21] and Thomas Cholmondeley of Vale Royal began to canvass for his seat. Grey eventually withdrew. The decisive factor may well have been the support Cholmondeley received from the Grosvenors, occasioned less by common Pittite sympathies than by the Grosvenors' fear that Cholmondeley had an eye on one of the Chester seats, both of which they intended to take for themselves.[22] In 1812 Cholmondeley himself was challenged by a group distinctly Whiggish in outlook, headed by the earl of Stamford, Lord Crewe, and Sir John Stanley of Alderley. They proposed Stanley in his place, but their campaign concentrated not on Cholmondeley's support for the Tory administration but on his marked inattentiveness to his parliamentary duties and infrequent attendance at the House. The outcome bears all the signs of a compromise. Both men stepped down to be replaced by Wilbraham Egerton of Tatton, son of a former Pittite M.P., who proved a general but not invariable supporter of the Liverpool administration. The Whigs could rely on his fellow member,

[16] Speck, *Tory & Whig*, 26, 45.
[17] Two copies exist of the poll book, Ches. R.O., Egerton of Oulton MSS., unlisted, and Ches. R.O., P/4/19/2.
[18] i.e. 3 Egertons of Oulton, 3 Cholmondeleys of Vale Royal, 2 Crewes of Crewe, Sir Robt. Salisbury Cotton, and Davies Davenport of Capesthorne.
[19] Quoted in E. Black, *The Association*, 47.
[20] Cannon, *Parl. Reform*, 77, 82 n.
[21] The Greys had inherited the Dunham Massey estates through marriage to the heiress of the Booths.
[22] Hist. MSS. Com. 35, *14th Rep. IV, Kenyon*, pp. 543-4.

Davies Davenport, a genuine independent who more often than not went into the lobbies with them.[23] When the two men presented themselves for re-election in 1818, it was reported that there would be no opposition, 'a mutual understanding subsisting between the leading landed interests of the county'.[24]

In 1820, as in 1796, the unexpected announcement by one member, Davies Davenport, that ill-health compelled him to retire, precipitated a conflict. There was little time for the gentry to agree on a single name, and two separate candidates came forward, George Legh of High Legh, and Richard Legh of Lyme. George Legh presented himself as a man 'unshackled by any party or connexion whatever'.[25] Plans were already well-advanced for a poll; for example, Lords Cholmondeley and Egerton of Oulton had agreed to unite their tenantry for an orderly progress into Chester on polling day.[26] Davenport was, however, persuaded to stand again. George Legh immediately withdrew, but the Lyme party took more persuading. Richard Legh's friends claimed that the requisition addressed by the gentry to Davenport had been obtained in an underhand fashion and that 'the reasons which he gave for retiring from Parliament, and which still unfortunately exist, are such as ought to excuse him from so laborious a duty'.[27] In the end, after mediation by Sir John Stanley and other friends, Richard too agreed to stand down, provided Davenport issued a declaration in praise of his conduct and forbearance.[28] The unity of the Cheshire élite was thus preserved, only finally to be shattered by the Great Reform Bill.

Not one of the ten men who served for Cheshire in the years 1734–1830 can be said to have been first and foremost a party man. Most of them followed their consciences above all things, and on occasion broke ranks with the party they generally supported. Thus Samuel Egerton was listed as a 'Tory' by Bute in 1762 and by Newcastle in 1765, but as a 'Whig' by Rockingham in 1765 and again in 1766. He voted with the opposition on the land tax in 1767 and the Middlesex election in 1769.[29] John Crewe opposed the American War throughout, supported the Fox–North coalition, opposed Pitt in the 1790s, and, while he supported parliamentary reform measures in the 1780s, was opposed to the abolition of slavery and the amelioration of the position of apprentices in the cotton industry.[30] Most Cheshire members spoke very little in the Commons; Samuel Egerton made only one recorded speech in 36 years in the House, on a navigation bill in 1771; John Crewe spoke only in support of economical reform and against a tax on maidservants; Thomas Cholmondeley (M.P. 1796–1812) only spoke once, to denounce Fox's proposal to repeal the anti-sedition laws (1797); after Wilbraham Egerton had sat in the House for seven years, his cousin said of him that he was 'quite unused to public speaking'; and Sir Robert Salisbury Cotton made no speech during his sixteen years in the House.[31] Nevertheless, for the most part, they attended regularly and cast their votes with care. Several of them were well-read with strong views on important matters: Crewe was a friend of Thomas Coke and reputedly one of the finest improving landlords in the county;[32] Davies Davenport was an expert on the cotton industry and a pamphleteer for the free trade movement;[33] Wilbraham Egerton knew much of the salt industry.[34]

They were not like the resolute 'Country' members of the period 1660–1734. Increasingly they would take each government on its merits, supporting any which appeared

[23] Hist. Parl. Trust, constit. rep. 1790–1820.
[24] Ibid., constit. rep. and biogs.
[25] Printed handbill in Jn. Rylands Libr., Bromley–Davenport MSS., correspondence, 5 iii, unfol.
[26] See letters in Ches. R.O., DCH/X/5/22.
[27] Jn. Rylands Libr., Bromley–Davenport MSS., correspondence 5 iii, unfol.
[28] Ibid.
[29] Hist. Parl., Commons, 1754–90, ii. 385.
[30] Ibid. ii. 276.
[31] Ibid. ii. 260–1.
[32] Ibid. ii. 276; Hist. Parl. Trust, biog.
[33] Hist. Parl. Trust, biog.
[34] Ibid.

to be successfully defending or advancing the national interest abroad, and maintaining social stability and economic advance at home, although they differed amongst themselves over the means. What was essential to them was their freedom to dissent: to protest whenever any government challenged the system of local government which they themselves dominated, or when it proposed unnecessary increases in taxation. No government was unacceptable on principle, but any which was expensive or which sought fresh powers for itself would face an almost instinctive opposition from the Cheshire M.P.s, as from the independents generally.[35] Those M.P.s had thus modified the nature of their independence by the early 19th century. Although their attitudes to government were outmoded in an industrializing society, they were acceptable to sufficient voters to keep the Cheshire gentry dominant at county elections for fifty years more after the Reform Bill.

THE CITY OF CHESTER 1660–1832

1660–98

The exigencies of civil war temporarily destroyed much of the jurisdictional independence of the city, subjecting it to the authority of the county. In 1660, however, the whole system of committees established by the parliamentarians was abandoned. By 1662 the city was fully restored to its ancient rights. Yet, from the elections of 1661 onwards, it was clear that fundamental changes were taking place in its electoral history. Chester had thrown off the county's jurisdiction, but other influences were at work to undermine the insularity of its politics and institutions. It was not until the early 18th century that the new pattern was fully established. The recorder was chosen at seven of the eight general elections between 1660 and 1690,[36] and never thereafter; eight of the men who sat between 1660 and 1698 were already aldermen when first elected. The interests of few of them, however, lay primarily within the city, even though they could be expected to support the corporations' interests at Westminster. Only two men, one in each Convention parliament, were city merchants;[37] two more were country gentlemen with town houses in Chester,[38] two more gentlemen-courtiers.[39] From the election of 1698 onwards the seats passed entirely into the hands of the gentry. In the 31 parliaments between 1698 and 1832 a total of 20 men served for the city. Eleven of them were members of the Grosvenor family; 7 sprang from leading Cheshire county families, and the other 2 were lawyers who had married county heiresses and performed professional services for the Grosvenors. It is important not to oversimplify, however. The drift away from the merchant oligarchy was well-established before the Grosvenors made, after 1715, their bid for a control only consummated after a succession of bitter disputes between 1732 and 1734, and maintained, not without struggles thenceforward.

Chester was a declining port. The silting of the Dee reduced its capacity to handle long-distance trade and cargo, which increasingly moved to Liverpool. Heavily dependent on leather trades, it was seriously affected by changes in the demand for leather goods and by government regulations which increasingly hindered the import of cheap

[35] N. Baker, 'Changing Attitudes towards Govt. in 18th-cent. Eng.' in *Statesmen, Scholars, and Merchants*, ed. A. Whiteman and J. S. Bromley, 202–19.

[36] Recorder William Williams was defeated at a by-election in 1673 held to replace recorder John Ratcliffe; in 1685 recorder Leving was not elected, perhaps because his appointment was in dispute: Hist. Parl. Trust, files.

[37] Wm. Ince (1660), Geo. Mainwaring (1688).

[38] Sir Thos. Smith (1660), son of the M.P. of 1640; Sir Thos. Grosvenor (1678, 1679, 1685, 1690, 1695, 1698).

[39] Robert Werden (by-election 1673, 1685); Roger Whitley (1681, 1688, 1695).

Irish calfskins.[40] The city could resolve neither problem by its own efforts. Any scheme to make the Dee navigable, for example, would affect the interests of the gentry of Wirral who were farming the mudflats created by the silt, or through whose land any new cut would have to pass. Since the passing of a local Act to improve the navigation depended upon agreement among the interested parties,[41] the city could not act alone. The city's independence had rested upon that of its strong oligarchy. If the oligarchy was penetrated and controlled by an outside interest, that interest would in turn become self-perpetuating. Once the Grosvenors had won control in the early 18th century their grip could be loosened only by a democratization of local government, restoring effective control to the resident freemen. The political struggle in Chester in the period 1690–1734 thus involved fresh attempts to revive the direct election of members of the assembly.[42]

The city could not escape from the political divisions within the nation as a whole over the succession to the throne, the nature of the constitution, and the integrity of the Church of England. The exclusion crisis and the Revolution both divided the county and city élites, and the rights of dissenters and the cry of 'Church in Danger' very clearly divided the commonalty. Organized Whig and Tory groups were struggling for control of Chester throughout the 1690s, and the regular return between 1700 and 1715 of two Tory M.P.s connected to leaders of one of the Tory factions at Westminster ensured that city politics would be involved in the regional struggle for power. Peter Shakerley, city M.P. from 1698 to 1715, was active as Tory whip for a wider area. In 1708 he organized the Tory lobby for several north midland counties.[43] So the money and influence of outside interests were drawn into party politics within the city.[44] When party conflict abated in the 1730s and 1740s the Grosvenors were ideally placed to consolidate a position created in the time of struggle. Between 1734 and 1832 they were to combine constructive independence in national politics with an expressed concern for local interests, and maintain an absolute stranglehold on the city's institutions. Questions of the franchise, of trade, and of party interest were to remain completely inseparable; Chester was always an uncomfortable pocket borough for the house of Eaton.

The elections of 1660 returned men in the traditional mould: the recorder on both occasions, an alderman who had sat in the assembly while Chester was a royalist garrison, but who had retained his office throughout the Interregnum and conformed to all régimes, hoping thereby to restrict the damage to the city's independence,[45] and the son of the city's M.P. of 1640–6. The death of ex-recorder Ratcliffe in 1672 inaugurated a period of deep political division which was to result in the emergence first of Tory and later of Grosvenor family hegemony. Yet the outcome was long in doubt. The interaction of municipal, commercial, and national problems which characterized the years 1673–98 can best be studied in the biographies of four men who dominated the parliamentary representation of Chester in those years: Robert Werden (1673, 1685), William Williams (1675, 1678, 1679, 1681), Roger Whitley (1681, 1689, 1695), and Sir Thomas Grosvenor (1678, 1679, 1685, 1690, 1695, 1698).[46]

[40] T. S. Willan, 'Chest. and the Navigation of the Dee', *J.C.A.S.* 2nd ser. xxxii. 64–7; R. C. Gwilliam, 'Chest. Tanners and Parl.', *J.C.A.S.* [2nd ser.], xliv. 41–9; H. Hankinson, 'Ches. River Navigation with Special Reference to the River Dee', *J.C.A.S.* [2nd ser.] lv. 63–88; Hist. MSS. Com., *8th Rep.*, pp. 388–96.

[41] Lambert, *Bills and Acts*, 155.

[42] H. T. Dutton, 'Stuart Kings and Chest. Corporation', *J.C.A.S.* 2nd ser. xxviii. 195–8, 207–8; Hemingway, *Hist. Chest.* ii. 263–5, 392–8.

[43] For the general context, see Speck, *Tory & Whig*; Holmes, *Brit. Politics*. For party issues in Chest., see also

Baskerville, 'Tory Interest', *passim*. For Shakerley, see Holmes, *Brit. Politics*, 301, and for details of his role as a regional 'whip', Chirk Castle, Clwyd, Myddleton MSS., Box E, nos. 994, i and ii.

[44] For an illuminating comparison and contrast, see M. Mullett, 'Politics of Liverpool, 1660–88', *T.H.S.L.C.* cxxiv. 31–56.

[45] Wm. Ince. See Hist. Parl. Trust, biog.

[46] The only other men to serve during these years were recorder Richard Leving (1690), and George Mainwaring, a leading dissenter and alderman (1689 convention).

Werden's election in 1673 was a major upset, since he comfortably defeated the recorder, William Williams.[47] Furthermore Werden was 'an incomparable courtier, a cavalier and most faithful servant of the royal family'.[48] He was personally backed by the duke of York, in whose household he served,[49] and through whose patronage he had gained an army commission. Yet he had roots in the city. His father had been an attorney there,[50] he had been brought up there, and had been one of the most persistent and incompetent local conspirators during the Interregnum.[51] In 1664 he had become a baron of the Chester Exchequer. Given Williams's subsequent behaviour the by-election was probably a Court–Country struggle in which Werden defended the politics of the Cabal, particularly the Declaration of Indulgence, while Williams,[52] whose father, a well-connected Anglican clergyman from Wales, had been deprived during the 1650s, opposed them. Werden's election in 1685 reflected the Tory triumph after the collapse of the Exclusion movement nationally and in Chester.

Williams, recorder from 1667 to 1684, did not have to wait long for the parliamentary seat denied him in 1673, being returned unopposed in a by-election in 1675 on the death of Sir Thomas Smith. He rose rapidly in opposition circles and became a leading proponent of Exclusion. In 1680–1 he was made Speaker of the House of Commons as Shaftesbury's candidate.[53] His continued unopposed election as the city's M.P. suggests a strong anti-government bias in Chester by the late 1670s. In 1684 the city charter was surrendered to the Crown and Williams was expelled from the assembly and the recordership. Soon, however, he became one of the most notable Whig collaborators of James II, being appointed solicitor-general in 1687, and leading for the Crown in the prosecution of the Seven Bishops.[54] In the Convention Parliament[55] he quickly rediscovered his Whiggish principles and argued that the throne had been vacated by James's flight. He became an archetypal 'Country' Whig in the 1690s.

The careers of the other two leading figures became so intertwined that it will be best to begin by briefly outlining their backgrounds. Although he did not know it, 1677 was to prove the decisive year in Sir Thomas Grosvenor's life. The twenty-year-old baronet, heir to ancient and substantial Cheshire estates and a manor house close to the city, was made an alderman of Chester, a courtesy extended to many country gentlemen before him, and married Mary Davies, daughter of a London merchant who eventually became heiress to the then undeveloped Mayfair, Belgravia, and Pimlico. The combination was to be fatal for the city's independence. Roger Whitley was a former royalist exile, who had helped to plan the 1659 uprisings to restore Charles II, and subsequently served in several second-ranking government offices, notably as deputy postmaster-general, 1672–9, and represented the Flint boroughs in Parliament from 1660 to 1680. An alderman of Chester at the Restoration, he had attempted unsuccessfully to become mayor in 1669. He owned a country seat at Bromborough in Wirral, and was a confidant of the earl of Macclesfield.[56]

By 1690, Grosvenor represented the Tory interest in Chester, and Whitley the Whig interest, but those positions were only taken up as they and the city reacted to the national political crisis. In 1678 Grosvenor sought and was offered the second seat after

[47] Cal. S.P. Dom. 1672–3, 587. The voting in Werden's favour was 601 to 551.
[48] R. North, Autobiog. 374.
[49] As groom of the bedchamber.
[50] The elder Werden had written to Sir Thos. Smith before the 1640 elections. See pp. 108, 113.
[51] D. E. Underdown, Royalist Conspiracy in Eng. 46, 148–9, 251, 288–9, 318; Morrill, Ches. 1630–60, 254–5, 280.
[52] A persecuting J.P. described him in 1667 as 'a true

son of the Church': Cal. S.P. Dom. 1667, 25.
[53] In 1677 he was leading counsel for Shaftesbury when he applied for habeas corpus, after his imprisonment by the House of Lords.
[54] Hist. Parl. Trust, biog. He was fined £1,000 for his offences as Speaker between 1679 and 1681, and hoped to obtain remission of that fine by assisting James II.
[55] As M.P. for Beaumaris.
[56] Gatty, Mary Davies, passim; L. A. Dasent, Grosvenor Square, 16–21.

Williams. His qualification was an anti-court attitude[57] and an ability to mediate with neighbouring landowners over a scheme to make the Dee navigable. Probably the further decline of trade, and the measures prohibiting the import of Irish cattle had hardened the city's governors against the court. At any rate, Grosvenor was re-elected in 1680. In 1681, however, he was replaced by Whitley, who, as M.P. for Flint boroughs, had developed a reputation as a good lobbyist and indefatigable private bill man. The crucial reason for the change, however, may have been the course of the Exclusion crisis. Grosvenor had abstained from voting on the Exclusion Bill and was moving towards the court. In particular, he was and remained opposed to the duke of Monmouth.[58] Williams and Whitley were both supporters of the duke, as was the assembly, since it sent up an address to the Oxford Parliament on his behalf.[59]

The years 1682–4 witnessed the Tory reaction throughout England. Monmouth's progress through the north-west gave the Crown a pretext for a purge of leading Whigs in Cheshire and elsewhere. When Chester's charter, like so many, was challenged, Grosvenor, now firmly in the Tory camp, led the campaign for its voluntary surrender and the negotiations for a new charter drawn up in 1685, which excluded all the leading Whigs, including Whitley and Williams by name, but left the actual composition of the new assembly obscure, apart from naming Grosvenor as mayor. Since the parliamentary elections were held before the new assembly was chosen, moderates dared not oppose the man with all the patronage in his hands: Grosvenor and Werden were returned unopposed.[60]

In 1688 the Tories' position temporarily collapsed. James's policies had destroyed their credibility and self-confidence, and his precipitous fall left the Whigs briefly with the initiative. By invoking the old charter Whitley and alderman George Mainwaring, a leading dissenter, were returned.[61] The future of the city now lay in the balance, but after a bitter eight-year struggle (1690–8) the Tories regained control. On the one side stood a Whig group determined to proclaim the achievements of the Revolution, to put into effect the rights accorded to dissenters, to protect the city from further outside domination, and to restore the 'open' government laid down in the 1506 charter, including the free election of members of the assembly and city officers. On the other side stood the Tories, upholders of the Anglican supremacy, the purely *de facto* nature of William III's rule,[62] and the customary closed membership of the assembly.

The reasons for the Tory success in 1698, when both the local and parliamentary elections went decisively in their favour, have never been studied. The result may simply have been a reaction against the policies of the Whig Junto in power at Whitehall, but factors more deeply rooted in local conditions can be suggested. The local Whigs in committing themselves to freedom of worship for dissenters may well have alienated many of the commonalty. Both earlier and later there is evidence of religious rioting in the city. Secondly the Whigs, greatly dependent on Roger Whitley, were left disorganized by his death in 1697. Moreover, Grosvenor could present himself as the man able to alleviate the economic ills of the city, for which the Whig leaders failed to find remedies, while the heavy taxation imposed to finance the war effort may well have contributed to the city's continuing decline. Whitley's career had been largely

[57] Shaftesbury called him 'worthy': Hist. Parl. Trust, biog.

[58] In 1685 he raised a regiment to help suppress Monmouth's rebellion: SP 44/70 no. 75. See Hist. Parl. Trust, biog.

[59] Jones, *First Whigs*, 169.

[60] *J.C.A.S.* 2nd ser. xxviii. 201–3; Hemingway, *Hist. Chest.* ii. 388; Hist. Parl. Trust, biog.

[61] Grosvenor withdrew, on being ruled ineligible as sheriff of Cheshire, and the Whigs won by default: Bodl. MS. Eng. Hist. c. 711, diary of Roger Whitley, unfol., 11 Jan. 1689.

[62] e.g. in 1696 Grosvenor refused to take the oath of Association pledging loyalty to William III as 'rightful and lawful' king: Hemingway, *Hist. Chest.* ii. 388.

spent as a tax-farmer.[63] As a gentleman of the Privy Chamber, 1689–97, he was associated with the government, while Grosvenor represented both Tory principles and a Country programme.[64] It was probably the connexion between economic and political issues which caused the ending of the four-year experiment in a directly-elected assembly. The old oligarchic principle, once restored in 1698, became inviolable.[65] During those disputes, however, the long-standing confusion over the parliamentary franchise was partially resolved.[66]

1698–1734

The Tories' triumph of 1698 could well have proved illusory; self-perpetuating oligarchy was immune from external pressure, but could easily have been wrecked either by the potential contradictions within Tory thought, or by divisions within the assembly on how to solve Chester's pressing economic problems. Paradoxically, the long-term Grosvenor interest may have been best served by Sir Thomas's death in 1700, and the emergence as the city's M.P.s of Sir Peter Shakerley, M.P. for Wigan (Lancs.) 1690–8, and for Chester 1698–1715, and Sir Henry Bunbury (1700–27). Their length of service alone was a source of stability, but their avoidance of party rancour and assiduous attention to the particular needs of their constituency were more important.

Grosvenor's politics were probably confused, his Jacobitism latent but a matter of public comment. Shakerley and Bunbury, by contrast, were amongst the minority of Cheshire Tories who fully accepted the fact of the Revolution, and from 1702 onwards declared themselves for the Hanoverians. Bunbury, as Sir Thomas Hanmer's brother-in-law, was drawn with his fellow M.P. into the connexion of the Tory earl of Nottingham. Shakerley was an advocate of the Cheshire 'compromise'.[67] Such men avoided dividing the city on party lines, and held the middle ground between 1711 and 1714 as the Tory party in Parliament split asunder. They could present the city to the Grosvenors with a united assembly in 1715.

They also showed constant and energetic attention to the city's economic interests at Westminster. Letters from Shakerley to the assembly reveal not only his activity in promoting several local bills, but his concern to watch out for anything in proposed legislation that might prejudice the city's welfare. Thus he wrote about the Dee navigation, about improvement schemes elsewhere for which other ports were seeking bills, about the effects of the customs duty clauses in the Act of Union and the trade treaty with France (1713), and about the cost to the city of a general Act 'for providing nightly watches'.[68] The Chester tanners were also in constant touch with the M.P.s between 1711 and 1717 about the consequences of new legislation concerning duties on leather, and the export of oak bark to Ireland which was resulting in the rise there of a tanning industry detrimental to Chester's interests.[69] It was not just talk: one of the first acts of the newly chosen oligarchy in 1698 was to make an agreement with a London merchant, Francis Gell, who was to make the Dee navigable for vessels up to 100 tons. By 1700 Shakerley, Grosvenor, and Bunbury were actively promoting a local Act embodying the arrangements agreed with Gell, and trying to placate the opposition of

[63] As registrar of customs, excise farmer for North Wales, and hearth tax receiver.

[64] He opposed the king's land grants to his Dutch favourites: Hist. Parl. Trust, biog.

[65] Hemingway, *Hist. Chest.* ii. 392–4. The reasons for the Tory victory require fuller investigation.

[66] See p. 100.

[67] See p. 122; also Eaton Hall, Grosvenor MSS., papers of 4th Bt., unfol., Shakerley to Sir Ric. G., 2 Dec. 1714.

[68] Hist. MSS. Comm., *8th Rep.*, pp. 392–6.

[69] Chester R.O., Guild Records, T/4 nos. 4–74; *J.C.A.S.* 2nd ser. xliv. 41–9.

Wirral and Flintshire landowners. For some years the improvements seem to have been successful and a new wharf was built.[70] In the 1710s, the M.P.s worked hard for the tanners, negotiating with the Treasury concessions which hindered the export of oak bark, and successfully delaying adverse changes in the excises on leather.[71]

That care for the city's interests ensured that its seats were not contested after 1701 until the new head of the Grosvenor family, Sir Richard, decided to seek one in 1715.[72] Apparently he had agreed not to stand in 1710 provided that he could take one seat at the next election. He had, however, made no move in 1713, possibly being undecided on the question of the succession. By 1715 George I was on the throne, and however much Grosvenor may have regretted his accession he did not mean to become involved in armed uprisings. When he demanded of Bunbury and Shakerley that one of them make way for him, they maintained that, by not acting in 1713, he had forfeited his claims under the 1710 agreement, and both refused to give way. A fight between three Tories was forced upon the city. Some leading citizens refused to help Grosvenor, claiming that they would not spurn members who had 'behaved themselves like gentlemen' and discharged their responsibilities so conscientiously. Neither of the sitting members could match the wealth of the Grosvenors,[73] who reportedly 'spent near £1,000 among the mob.' One friend suggested that he purchase the freedom for 150 poor journeymen, which would be more efficient than 'the charges of treating saucy innkeepers and other pragmatics'. Grosvenor topped the poll and Shakerley lost his seat.[74] The Whigs were too weak to take advantage of those divisions, and when in 1722 a city alderman, Thomas Brereton, a former employee of the Grosvenors, capitalizing on his profits from the South Sea Bubble and seeking to ingratiate himself with the new Whig ministry,[75] challenged the Grosvenors both for the mayoralty and the burgess-ship, he was ignominiously defeated by two to one.[76] Significantly, however, Brereton did not try to reopen party quarrels. His broadsheet denied that he was urging a party cause, and claimed that the question was 'whether this city . . . ought to idolise one neighbouring family'.[77]

The opposition movement subsided and the Grosvenor control tightened. In 1727 the elderly Bunbury was swept aside by Sir Richard Grosvenor and his younger son.[78] For the first time the family had outright control. Nevertheless between 1732 and 1734 Sir Richard had to fight a succession of battles on all fronts. The struggle began because the Dee was once more silting up. Grosvenor, mindful of the problems the Weaver navigation had encountered in the 1720s,[79] was concerned to work in co-operation with the neighbouring gentry, but allowed himself to be out-manoeuvred. An entirely new scheme for cutting a new channel from Chester to the sea, supported by Bereton and his allies in the city, was backed by a group of London financiers and engineers associated with the Walpole administration. The Grosvenors were trapped, unable to support a scheme which cut across the interests of many landed families, and was promoted by their enemies, yet aware that it was an emotive issue in the city. Sir Richard's prevarication, compounded of feigned public support and private lobbying

[70] *J.C.A.S.* 2nd ser. xxxii. 65–6.

[71] Ibid. [2nd ser.] xliv. 41–9.

[72] There were no contested elections during Anne's reign, but seven between 1715 and 1747, including two by-elections, the very reverse of the pattern in other areas. Between 1747 and 1832 there were only 3 further contests (1784, 1812, 1819).

[73] Sir Richard warned Shakerley of 'the consequences of dividing an interest that hath been established at the expense of my family.'

[74] Baskerville, 'Tory Interest', 38–41, 63–4; Eaton

Hall, Grosvenor MSS., papers of 4th Bt., unfol. letters, 1714–15; Jn. Rylands Libr., Warburton of Arley MSS., unfol., Shakerley to Leycester, Feb. 1715.

[75] He was later the Whig electoral manager in the north-west, and himself M.P. for Liverpool.

[76] Baskerville, 'Tory Interest', 120–4, 131; *Hist. Parl., Commons,* 1715–54, i. 203–4.

[77] Eaton Hall, Grosvenor MSS., papers of 4th Bt., unfol.

[78] Baskerville, 'Tory Interest', 166.

[79] See pp. 121–3.

against the bill, was uncovered.[80] The opposition at Chester, although genuinely concerned that the scheme should succeed, also wanted to use the issue to destroy the Grosvenor interest. They thus reopened the old question of the direct election of aldermen and councillors and took it before the courts. Aware that the Grosvenors intended to use the mayor's unlimited power to create freemen to manipulate the electorate, the opposition attempted to wrest the mayoralty from Grosvenor control,[81] and also began a campaign, later to be carried on in the House of Commons, to restrict voting rights to freemen resident in the city. Their campaign failed in 1733, but succeeded in 1747. Unable on their own to match Grosvenor wealth the Whig minority, despite their talk of the city's liberties having been destroyed by outside interests, turned for money to the Whig landlords of Cheshire. In return they offered the Cholmondeleys a burgess seat at the next election, and told the mayor that, if Col. James Cholmondeley were made a freeman and thus qualified as a candidate, the mayor's clerical son would be offered a rich country living. Grosvenor's agents heard what was happening in time, and offered the son a fatter one.

Grosvenor cash secured the mayoralty, but the opposition retained the initiative, since the Navigation Bill was still before Parliament. At that precise moment both the Grosvenor M.P.s died. The city was faced with two by-elections. Once again large sums of money were spent,[82] but the question of the Dee remained paramount. Swallowing their pride, the Grosvenors asked Sir Charles Bunbury to stand. Son of the man whom the Grosvenors had pushed aside in 1727 after twenty-five years' devoted service to the borough, Sir Charles could succeed, where the Grosvenors had failed, in distinguishing between the need for a new navigation scheme and opposition to the particular one put forward. He did so, and pledged himself to work for a separate one.[83] Moreover, the position of Brereton, Manley, and the anti-Grosvenor group was probably weakened by the association of their scheme with the Walpole ministry, then, early in 1733, at the nadir of its unpopularity over Walpole's Excise Bill.[84] In the event the Grosvenors' triumph was complete: they won the mayoral election of 1732, the by-elections of 1733, and the general election of 1734, and fought off the legal actions over the charter. The controversial navigation scheme was passed, however, and its very passage paradoxically destroyed the opposition's principal weapon. The Grosvenor interest had surmounted its severest test.[85]

1734–1832

In the 112 years from 1547 to 1659 Chester was represented by 32 burgesses. Excluding the eight recorders who held one seat almost *ex officio*, all but two sat for the borough only once or twice. Two men sat thrice, but the parliaments they sat in were all short ones, even by Tudor standards. By contrast, in the 114 years from 1715 to 1829, only 15 men represented Chester, 10 of them Grosvenors. Only 2 of those 15 sat in only one

---

[80] Baskerville, 'Tory Interest', 183–7; *J.C.A.S.* 2nd ser. xxxii. 65–6.
[81] Sir Richard spent £6,500 on the mayoral election of 1732 alone.
[82] *Gent. Mag.* iii. 87, spoke of the purchase of votes at £20–£30 each.
[83] The objections to the Whig scheme were (a) that the engineer in charge was unreliable and had been responsible for a similar scheme at Rye that had failed, (b) that the main beneficiaries would not be the city (since the proposed channel would be too shallow) but those who owned mudflats which would be reclaimed for agriculture, (c) that the scheme would be partially financed by duties on

cheese which would damage local interests, (d) that the existing channel would result in the silting up of the Mersey mouth and the decline of Liverpool.
[84] Langford, *Excise Crisis*, 121–3.
[85] Hemingway, *Hist. Chest.* ii. 397–400; Baskerville, 'Tory Interest', 182–99, 207–9; H. Taylor, 'An unpublished Diary of Revd. Peter Walkden', *J.C.A.S.* [1st ser.] iii. 151–61; Hist. MSS. Com., *15th Rep. VII*, pp. 313–14; *Gent. Mag.* iii. 87; *C.J.* xxii. 53–4, 335; Chester R.O., P/Cowper [1956], i. pp. 270–4; Eaton Hall, Grosvenor MSS., papers of 4th, 5th, and 6th Bts.; estate papers, boxes 42/1 and 58/2.

parliament and they died early. Grosvenors held the first seat from 1715 to 1874, and for 42 of the 114 years between 1715 and 1829 occupied both seats. Two junior members of the family, Thomas, brother of the first earl, and his younger son Thomas, held one seat continuously from 1755 to 1826. Of the five non-members of the family, the one closest to them politically and the one who owed most to their patronage and generosity, Richard Wilbraham Bootle, was a member for 30 years.[86]

The success of the Grosvenors has been ascribed to 'a complex intermixture of traditional attitudes and material interests', above all to their control over the corporation, their influence with the guilds, their generosity to the poor, their extravagance at election times, and an efficient political machine.[87] The Grosvenors saw to it that the oligarchy was careful in its recruitment of new members. As one of the richest families in England they were generous to the city, expending perhaps £4,000 a year between elections, with seemingly limitless funds when faced by a contest. They leased from the Crown many dwellings, which they let cheaply on short leases, but whose rents they could raise if the tenants proved ungrateful. They were always willing to buy the freedom for poor men, particularly at election time. What counted above all was their vigilance and a political reputation for independence which made opposition almost impossible. In every contested election between 1732 and 1820[88] the opposition were at pains to proclaim that they shared the political principles of the Grosvenors.[89]

Before the House of Commons ruled in 1747 that non-resident freemen could not vote, the Grosvenors kept several lists of 'country freemen' for Chester who lived in Lancashire, Shropshire, Denbighshire, Flintshire, and Cheshire, and were regimented into Chester on election days.[90] A list of 1732 was marked to show the dependability of each such freeman. It was also noted which freeman families had sons soon to come of age.[91] A late 18th-century letter to Earl Grosvenor, recommending additional forms of patronage, shows meticulous attention to detail. The author suggested that a register of the numerous half-pay officers and others recently arrived in the town should be compiled, since they carried great weight with the tradesmen; that it was more profitable to concentrate attention on the 'little attorneys, who advance small sums', and on the common brewers, to whom most alehouse-keepers were indebted, than on the mass of tradesmen; and that it was wise to ensure the support of the leaders, who were named, of the Methodists and Congregationalists in the city.[92] If the Grosvenors carefully managed the city's electorate, they also campaigned assiduously for its causes, just like their predecessors Bunbury and Shakerley. In 1743 the mayor and assembly wrote pompously to Sir Robert Grosvenor 'to express a grateful sense of that noble spirit of liberty and patriotism so gloriously exerted by our grand representative'; and beseeched him 'to postpone granting any supplies, till the secret committee of inquiry be renewed, the number of placemen in the . . . Commons sufficiently limited, and frequent and free elections restored to us'. In 1758–9 they likewise instructed the two Grosvenors serving in Parliament to argue for government intervention to regulate the grain trade. The family papers are full of such letters.[93] It would be naïve to see such instructions as totally unsolicited. Several, like the petition asking Grosvenor to secure the freedom of William Pitt in 1757, were organized by caucuses of M.P.s at Westminster and distributed in many constituencies. At times, leading members of the Grosvenor family, hoping to gain a peerage or else the lord lieutenancy of Cheshire, offered their services

[86] Based on Hist. Parl. Trust, biogs., published and unpubl.

[87] *J.C.A.S.* [2nd ser.] lvii. 41–50.

[88] i.e. 1747, 1784, 1812, 1819.

[89] e.g. Chester R.O., printed poll book and papers of 1784 election; Ches. R.O., DEO/21, election papers of

John Egerton, 1806 and 1812.

[90] Eaton Hall, Grosvenor MSS., papers of 4th Bt., unfol.

[91] Ibid., papers of 6th Bt.

[92] Chester R.O., CR 74/328/IX. Only page 11 survives.

[93] Eaton Hall, Grosvenor MSS., papers of 5th Bt., folder B; papers of 1st earl, box 2, unfol.

to the administration. In 1758 a Grosvenor even seconded the loyal address. For most of the period, however, they represented the new type of Independent. While Philip Henry Warburton (M.P. 1742–54) voted against the government in every recorded division and represented the old 'Country' Independent tradition, the Grosvenors can be found judging many issues on their merits, the hallmarks of the new Independent.

Politicians of every group saw them as unpredictable. There were still traces of Jacobitism in Sir Richard, the 4th baronet (d. 1732), but thereafter the heads of the family were loyal to the Hanoverians. They were not all averse to office: Robert Grosvenor (later the 2nd earl) served as a Lord of the Admiralty 1789–91, and as commissioner for Indian affairs and privy councillor, 1793–1808, but even he followed his own principles and was unconcerned by the loss of office. He was one of the few Pittites who supported Addington. He later called himself a Whig, but he voted for Peel's paternalistic reforms. His speeches have been described as frequent, verbose, and pompous.[94] More typical was Thomas Grosvenor, younger brother of the 1st earl, M.P. for Chester 1755–95. He supported the government's peace proposals in 1763, but opposed their handling both of the Wilkes affair and of the general warrants controversy. Having stood by Lord North over the prosecution of the war in America, he became alarmed by the prolonged political crisis following North's fall, and he led the St. Albans Tavern group which argued for a Fox–Pitt coalition in 1783.[95]

The views of the Grosvenors at a national level accorded perfectly with what is known of popular political attitudes in Chester at that time. Chester took no part in the Wyvillite association; there were anti-Fox and pro-Pitt demonstrations in 1783–4, and a loyal address to the Crown was sent up at the time of Dunning's motion. All the candidates in the 1784 election carefully associated themselves with those views. In the early 1790s a branch of Reeves's High Tory Association was founded in Chester to prevent any incipient agitation for radical reform. In the contested elections of 1812 and 1819 the opposition were careful to declare that their principles and those of Eaton Hall were identical on everything except the rights and liberties of the citizens or electors.[96] The earliest Chester newspaper, the *Courant*, was firmly attached to the Grosvenors' interests and although a second paper, the *Chester Chronicle*, having survived an early attempt by the family to suppress it, supported their opponents, it did not differ from the *Courant* in its treatment of national events.[97] When a radical paper, the *Chester Guardian*, was launched in 1817 it failed for lack of support.[98]

After 1734 there was no serious challenge to the Grosvenor interest for fifty years. A contest in 1747 arose largely through Sir Robert Grosvenor's indifference to the fate of his colleague since 1742, Philip Henry Warburton, with whom he had quarrelled. Grosvenor refused to issue a declaration associating himself with Warburton, and did not try to make his tenants vote for him. Grosvenor was possibly troubled by Warburton's Jacobite connexions,[99] but was reluctant to upset Warburton's powerful Welsh friends and patrons by openly opposing him. In the event the third candidate, Mainwaring, came a poor third.[1] Unfortunately for Grosvenor, although Mainwaring failed to get the result set aside by the House of Commons, he did get a ruling that the right of election lay only with all freemen resident for twelve months or more and not in

[94] Hist. Parl. Trust, biog.
[95] Ibid., *Hist. Parl., commons*, 1715–54, i. 558–9.
[96] H. Hughes, *Chronicle of Chest.* 48–65, 79–87; Black, *The Association*, 263.
[97] D. Nuttall, 'Hist. of Printing in Chest.', *J.C.A.S.* liv. 37–96; Hughes, *Chronicle, passim*.
[98] Hemingway, *Hist. Chest.* ii. 264.

[99] One correspondent stated that if Grosvenor chose another colleague the Whigs would not contest the seat.
[1] Baskerville, 'Tory Interest', 280–1; Eaton Hall, Grosvenor MSS., papers of 6th Bt., folders B, C, H; estate papers, box 43/1; Hist. MSS. Com. 38, *14th Rep.* IX, p. 311.

receipt of alms. Given the Grosvenor's control of the non-resident freemen, the ruling could increase their problems in the event of a serious challenge.[2]

In 1767 Henry Aston, a local squire, announced that he would seek election in order to render the citizens 'truly free men'. After a month's canvassing, and before the expensive part of the election began, he acknowledged defeat and withdrew. In 1771 the opposition tried, largely in vain, to use the issue of the projected Middlewich canal to accuse the corporation of negligence in safeguarding the city's trade, and contested a shrievalty election. That opposition consisted entirely of city merchants, tradesmen and professional men excluded from the assembly and anxious from both principle and self-interest to open up the oligarchy.[3]

Their next opportunity came in 1784.[4] The part played by the sitting members, Thomas Grosvenor and Wilbraham Bootle, in the abortive scheme to create a Fox–Pitt coalition, perhaps gave the opposition an issue they could use for their purposes, for Fox's reputation in the city had certainly been destroyed by his union with North the year before. Fortunately for the city members Fox refused the overtures of their group and made sharp comments about Grosvenor, which the latter gratefully republished at home, restoring his reputation. The candidate brought in by the opposition, John Crewe, a Cheshire gentleman of moderate fortune, was thus forced on the defensive. He asserted that neither the political principles nor the personal qualities of the sitting members were in question, and that the only issue was whether the 'nomination of both the Members for this city should remain in one family, however respectable'. The attack was concentrated on Bootle, described as more the 'representative of Eaton House than of the city of Chester'. The Grosvenors were attacked in only one pamphlet, which accused them of abandoning their earlier concern for the borough's interests and of offering less and less hospitality to the citizenry as time went by.[5]

The opposition spent as much money on creating freemen as did the Grosvenors, but could only find £10,000 for 'entertainment'. In contrast the Grosvenors spent £15,000 on drink alone. A surviving account book[6] shows that they set up 90 alehouses as 'treating' centres. Agents were appointed who scrutinized the publicans' accounts closely, in many cases disallowing extravagant claims. In the end about three-quarters of the claims were met. A further £1,600 was paid for ribbons and cockades.[7] It was not in vain. For nine days Bootle and Crewe polled neck and neck, with Grosvenor well ahead. But the Crewe support dried up, while the Grosvenors had plenty in reserve. They piled up votes for two more days before Crewe abandoned the quest. More cash and better organization were the principal reasons for the Grosvenor success. There is also no doubt that there was indecision in Crewe's camp. They decided too late, on the ninth day of the poll, to run a second candidate to secure the second votes of Crewe's supporters; they did not seek extraordinary support from any particular class, polling a steady quarter of all main occupational groups. Above all they could not answer the Grosvenor challenge that whatever Crewe's private virtues, his principles were unknown: 'why then should we quit a certainty for an uncertainty?'[8]

For the next six years the opposition tried by a succession of actions in the courts to open elections to the corporation. By 1790 they were financially exhausted and demoralized, unable to enforce a ruling of the House of Lords in their favour, which the

---

[2] *C.J.* xxv. 425, 492, 497–8, 504–5.
[3] Eaton Hall, Grosvenor MSS., papers of 1st earl, unfol.
[4] The following is based on *J.C.A.S.* [2nd ser.] lvii. 41–50, unless otherwise noted.
[5] Chester R.O., printed poll book and papers of 1784 election.
[6] Eaton Hall, Grosvenor MSS., papers of 1st earl.
[7] Ibid.
[8] *J.C.A.S.* [2nd ser.] lvii. 46–50; Hughes, *Chronicle*, 48–65; Chester R.O., printed poll book and papers of 1784 election.

assembly simply ignored.[9] They contemplated contesting the parliamentary election, but desisted.[10]

In 1807 the opposition suddenly, and to their own surprise, gained a victory. The M.P.s since 1802 had been two nephews of the earl, General Thomas Grosvenor, a consistent Pittite, and Richard Erle Drax Grosvenor. Richard had deeply offended the earl by opposing Catholic emancipation, and after a heated debate at Eaton Hall early in 1807, was dismissed as 'refractory'. The Earl set up an old army colleague, Col. Thomas Hanmer, as his second candidate but did not give advance notice to the assembly, many of whom were already discontented by the family's use of London workmen to alter the fabric of Eaton Hall. Furthermore Hanmer was not a freeman. When Sir John Egerton of Oulton, well known in the city and a man of means, offered to stand, the assembly voted to support him against Hanmer. Grosvenor's agents told him that there was no way the family's interests could be preserved. Egerton was returned unopposed to the second seat.[11]

Egerton promised his constituents 'the best exertions of an honest and independent mind' and his voting record in the next six years bore him out.[12] In 1812, however, he faced a tremendous onslaught from the Grosvenors. His declining an offer to serve as their stated candidate cost him dear. He could not match them in cash, but fought a brilliant propaganda campaign, exploiting Catholic emancipation, which he opposed, and General Grosvenor's support for Addington. Once again he concentrated on local issues and on the weaknesses of the second Grosvenor candidate, Sir Richard Brooke, whom his pamphlets attacked mercilessly, dubbing him Sir Pertinax McSycophant and casting doubts on his ability to understand the principles of the constitution. They savagely satirized a repetitive and condescending speech by General Grosvenor, made more absurd by his habitual stammer. The Grosvenors' counter-propaganda was lack-lustre, uncertain of its targets, inelegant in its expression. They vainly republished the results of all previous contests with a gloss intended to implant a sense of hopelessness in the freemen. Their campaign slogan, 'Grosvenor, Brooke, and Independence', was ridiculed by Egerton, whose own cry 'England Expects Every Man to Do His Duty' was unanswerable. In the poll Grosvenor always led, but by the end Egerton was increasing his lead over Brooke and narrowing the gap between himself and Grosvenor.[13]

The Grosvenor monopoly had been broken. In 1819 and 1820 they fought back, spending vast sums in blatant bribery in order to unseat Egerton, whose popularity had been damaged by his support for the suspension of *habeas corpus*. Egerton complained to the House of Commons and a select committee was appointed to sift evidence of corrupt practices. In addition to allegations of traditional forms of pressure and corruption, the opposition claimed that the Grosvenors had hired hundreds of voters as musicians, 'a system of getting votes under a pretence'. Their petition failed, and the Egertons abandoned their interest in Chester politics.[14] Indeed, Sir John's grandson later confessed that those contests had compelled the family to sell property and timber to its permanent loss.[15]

The Grosvenors won the election and survived the investigation, but could not

[9] Hemingway, *Hist. Chest.* ii. 402–5.
[10] D. Ginter, *Whig Organization and the Election of 1790*, 241–4.
[11] Hist. Parl. Trust, biogs.; Ches. R.O., DEO/21, letters and papers relating to 1807 election.
[12] Hist. Parl. Trust, biog.
[13] Hemingway, *Hist. Chest.* ii. 410–14; Eaton Hall, Grosvenor MSS., papers of 2nd marquess, unfol. letters;

Ches. R.O., DEO/21, *passim*; J. Hemingway, *Hist. of Contested Election in Chest., 1812* (copy in Chester R.O.).
[14] Hemingway, *Hist. Chest.* ii. 414–19; *Rep. of Proc. before Cttee. of House of Commons appointed to decide Merits of Late Controverted Election for City of Chest.* (copy in Ches. R.O. DEO/21).
[15] Sir Phil. Egerton, *Egertons of Oulton* (priv. print. 1869. Copy in Camb. Univ. Libr.), 34–5.

recover their old domination. The shrievalty elections were now fought almost every year, and the opposition contested both seats in the parliamentary election of 1826. Although neither of their candidates appeared before polling day, the result was very close. The cost and the bother were becoming too great even for the Grosvenors, who could, in any case, place their friends and relatives in several rotten boroughs elsewhere. In 1829 Robert Grosvenor publicly announced that henceforward the family would only put forward one candidate. The era of the proprietary borough was coming to an end.[16]

ELECTORAL GEOGRAPHY 1832–1974

THE most obvious effect of the Great Reform Bill upon Cheshire was the increase in the number of its representatives. The county had its representation increased from four to ten. In the following decades that figure was further increased, reaching 18 in 1948. In other ways, however, the most important developments in the electoral geography of Cheshire occurred not in 1832, but in 1885. A study of the size of the various electorates, the incidence of contested elections, and the length of service of the county's members suggests that, in the county constituencies at least, the old political system survived for half a century after 1832. In all these respects 1885 was to prove a decisive turning-point.

Neither the 1832 not the 1867 Reform Bills seriously attempted to relate the number of seats in any particular county to the number of its inhabitants or the putative size of the electorate. Both were based on general political considerations of 'balance' between the old agricultural and new industrial interests, and aimed at a pragmatic redistribution of seats towards the rural and industrial areas away from decayed corporate boroughs. Only in 1885 was an attempt made to create seats with roughly similar electorates and thus to allot to each county or region an appropriate number of seats.[17] Nonetheless, as Table I, below, suggests, economic developments within Cheshire, played some part in the allocation of seats at every stage.

Between 1801 and 1881 the population of Cheshire rose rapidly; thereafter growth was slower.[18] The rapid growth in the 19th century largely resulted from major developments in communications, above all the spread of the railways and the development of the Manchester Ship Canal. Crewe became an important railway engineering centre.[19] The Mersey Navigation and Manchester Ship Canal brought major soap, chemical, and oil-refining industries to the north Cheshire plain, and the salt industry was extended in the same region. The spread of suburban railways promoted the building of middle-class dormitory towns at Altrincham, Bowdon, Hale, Alderley Edge, and elsewhere on the verges of the Manchester conurbation,[20] and similar developments in Wirral as the middle classes moved out from Liverpool. The latter had a slower tempo, however, because of the need to cross the Mersey by ferry until the opening of a railway tunnel under the river at the end of the 19th century.[21]

The above suggests limits to the value of treating Cheshire as a compact political area after the late 19th century. Nor was it really part of a single regional economy. It has been argued that it was part of a 'Lancastrian' region, which consisted of five

[16] J. Hemingway, *Electioneering Interests, 1807*, 12.
[17] C. Seymour, *Electoral Reform in Eng. and Wales, passim*; J. R. Hanham, *Elections and Party Management, passim*.
[18] See table of population below.
[19] J. M. Lee, *Social Leaders, and Public Persons*, 22–5;

W. H. Chaloner, *Social and Econ. Development of Crewe*, 135–72.
[20] Travel from those towns was also assisted by a fast packet boat on the Bridgewater canal.
[21] Lee, *Soc. Leaders*, 14–43.

contrasted sub-areas: the distinct Manchester and Liverpool conurbations, the small eastern towns (Stockport, Macclesfield, Hyde, etc.) which were part of the south Lancashire textile belt, the heavy industrial area which straddled the Mersey, and the southern agricultural area, largely part of a rural hinterland merging with Shropshire.[22]

Successive redistributions took account of those changes, but only, until 1885, in so far as they were compatible with the aims of the reforming politicians. In 1832 most newly created seats went to the counties, a minority to the larger industrial towns. Cheshire was only one of the 26 English counties which was divided to make two double-member constituencies. The geographical division was neatly achieved, the north westerly hundreds of Bucklow and Macclesfield forming the northern division, the other five hundreds the southern.[23] Although that divided the population unevenly, when the registration process was completed the number of electors in the two divisions was almost exactly the same.[24] Little attempt to maintain the integrity of the ancient hundreds was made in the later redistributions, although the names of the divisions continued, and continue, to suggest otherwise.

By 1832 two Cheshire towns had a strong case for separate representation: Stockport, a thriving cotton-spinning and hat-making centre with 41,000 inhabitants, and Macclesfield, a centre of the silk industry, with 25,000. In both there had been strong popular agitation for economic and parliamentary reform during the previous decade.[25] They were amongst 22 boroughs given double representation in 1832. In 1857 two boroughs, St. Albans and Sudbury, were disfranchised for corrupt practices, and one of the redistributed seats was allotted to Birkenhead, a town rapidly developing both as a suburb of Liverpool and as a shipbuilding centre. Its population by 1861 had reached 51,000.[26] The redistribution in 1867 was much more modest than that of 1832. The borough representation of Cheshire was unchanged, but the county was one of eleven to be divided again to create a third double-member constituency.[27] The reforms were piecemeal. No attempt was made to create constituencies of approximately equal numbers of electors or inhabitants, and even after 1867 Cheshire was under-represented in comparison with other counties. In the 1850s, for example, the national ratio of members to inhabitants in each county seat was 1:70,000, the Cheshire ratio 1:125,000. Similarly the electorate, at slightly over 4,000 per seat, was well above the national average of 3,400. The 1867 reform did not redress the balance.[28]

The 1885 Redistribution Bill represented a conscious effort to move towards a more equal system. The number of county seats was to be proportionate to the number of inhabitants, not to that of registered voters. The average size was to be 52,000, and most counties fell within 10, and virtually all within 20, per cent of that figure. Cheshire, with eight single-member constituencies, had an average of 54,383 inhabitants per seat.[29] Each county, in addition, was to be awarded a number of borough seats which, altogether, would give a similar M.P.: inhabitant ratio, although it was acknowledged that particular borough seats would have to be much larger or smaller than the norm. In applying that principle the commissioners decided neither to continue Macclesfield's borough status nor to grant it to Crewe, but to make both those towns the centre of county constituencies, balancing the urban votes with those from the rural hinterland. In the case of Macclesfield that was also in part a penalty for the corrupt practices revealed there after the 1880 election. In the case of Crewe it was a misfortune for the

[22] H. Pelling, *Social Geog. of British Elections, 1885–1910*, 239–87.
[23] *Dod's Electoral Facts*, ed. H. J. Hanham, 60–1.
[24] Ibid.; *McCalmont's Parl. Poll Books . . . 1832–1918*, ed. J. R. Vincent and M. Stenton, 55–6.
[25] C. Stella Davies, *Hist. Macclesfield*, 288–92; Seymour, *Electoral Reform*, 68.
[26] Seymour, *Electoral Reform*, 97.
[27] Ibid. 337.
[28] McCalmont, 55–7; *Dod's Electoral Facts*, 60–1; Seymour, *Electoral Reform*, 292 n.
[29] Seymour, *Electoral Reform*, 320–46, and app.

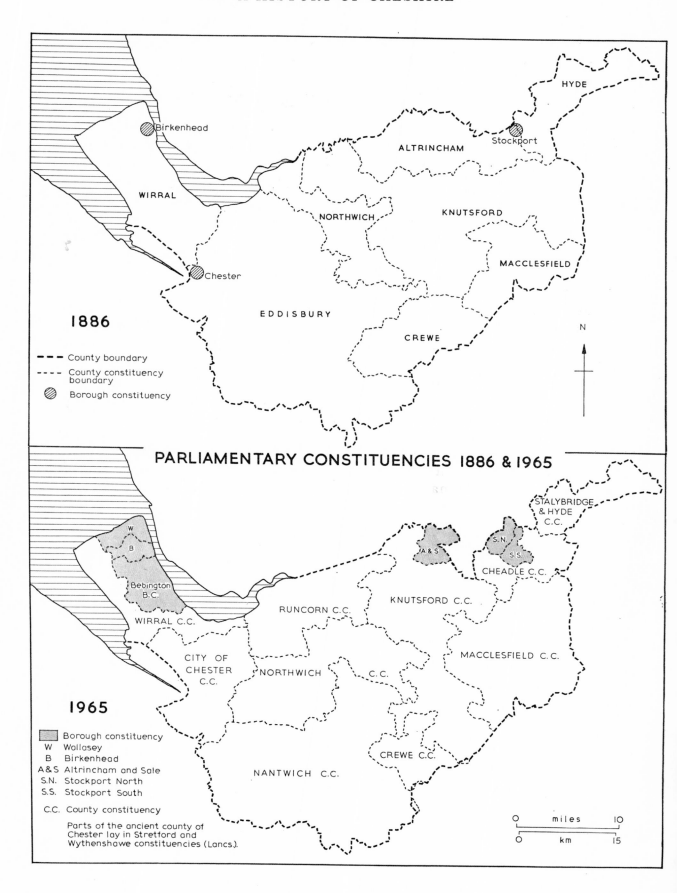

1886

- – – County boundary
- – – – County constituency boundary
- ⊘ Borough constituency

HYDE
ALTRINCHAM
Stockport
Birkenhead
WIRRAL
NORTHWICH
KNUTSFORD
Chester
MACCLESFIELD
EDDISBURY
CREWE

N

PARLIAMENTARY CONSTITUENCIES 1886 & 1965

STALYBRIDGE & HYDE C.C.
W
B
A&S
S.N.
S.S.
CHEADLE C.C.
Bebington B.C.
WIRRAL C.C.
RUNCORN C.C.
KNUTSFORD C.C.
CITY OF CHESTER C.C.
NORTHWICH C.C.
MACCLESFIELD C.C.
NANTWICH C.C.
CREWE C.C.

1965

- ▨ Borough constituency
- W   Wallasey
- B   Birkenhead
- A & S Altrincham and Sale
- S.N. Stockport North
- S.S. Stockport South
- C.C. County constituency

Parts of the ancient county of Chester lay in Stretford and Wythenshawe constituencies (Lancs.).

miles 0 — 10
km 0 — 15

directors of the L.N.W.R. Co., who had successfully campaigned for corporate status for the town in 1877, and had hoped to turn it into a pocket borough of the company. In the first election for the new Crewe division their candidate, himself a director, was easily defeated by a local landowner who carried the solid support of the rural voters.[30]

One principle behind the 1885 bill was to create constituencies of equal size. Another motive was to create safe seats for each party. In 1832 and 1867 the constituency boundaries were taken from the ancient hundreds. In 1885 the boundaries were so draw as to separate the industrial from the purely rural and 'commuter' areas. In consequence seven of the eight county constituencies became relatively 'safe' seats: three industrial ones for the Liberals (Crewe, Northwich, and Macclesfield), two rural (Eddisbury, Knutsford) and two suburban (Altrincham, Wirral) for the Conservatives. The remaining 'mixed' constituency of Hyde remainedo pen.[31] The commissioners left Cheshire with four borough seats: Chester, reduced to a single member, Birkenhead, which retained its single member, and Stockport, which remained a double constituency. That Birkenhead, with 95,000 inhabitants returned one M.P., and Stockport with 70,000 inhabitants two, is evidence that prescription still carried some weight.[32]

The 20th-century changes more precisely reflected the attempts of the Boundary Commission to create 'equal' constituencies which kept pace with population changes without unduly violating local government boundaries.[33] In 1918 Birkenhead was divided into two constituencies, and a new borough seat was awarded to the commuter town of Wallasey. Stockport remained a double-member constituency, one of the very few left undivided. The one unwonted development was the creation of a new 'county' seat, Stalybridge and Hyde, which straddled the Lancashire–Cheshire border, and which brought together two cotton towns and some rural villages from the two counties.[34] The other major change was that Chester, with fewer than 50,000 inhabitants, lost its separate representation. The division now included the city's rural hinterland and was listed as a county seat. In all, the 1918 reforms increased the county's representation from twelve to fourteen. In the limited reshuffling of seats introduced by the Speaker's conference in 1944 two old seats, Altrincham and Knutsford, were divided into three new ones: the residential and light industrial towns of Altrincham and Sale, with the intervening area, becoming one seat, the south and west of Altrincham and the old Knutsford seat being made into two, Knutsford and Bucklow. In 1948, however, the Boundary Commission redesigned almost every seat, creating three more constituencies for the county in the process. Between 1948 and 1974 there were 18 M.P.s returned from the ancient county.[35]

It was argued above that the electorate of Cheshire in 1734 was about 7,000. On a national scale the number of enfranchised freeholders rose by 6 per cent in the period 1754–1831.[36] Hypothetically, since there was no contest in Cheshire from 1734 to 1831, the Cheshire electorate in 1831 would have been about 7,500. As a consequence of the 1832 Act the number of registered electors for the county constituencies of Cheshire rose to 10,300,[37] a probable increase of 35 per cent. Clearly elaborate efforts were made by the leading families and by nascent political organizations in the county to ensure

[30] Chaloner, *Crewe*, 152–60.
[31] Crewe constituency was formed from the county borough of Crewe, the unincorporated towns of Nantwich and Sandbach and intervening countryside; Northwich constituency from the salt towns of the Weaver valley and adjacent countryside; Macclesfield from the towns of Macclesfield and Congleton, and their rural hinterland: Lee, *Soc. Leaders*, 37–8; Pelling, *Soc. Geog.* 239–87.
[32] *McCalmont*, 55–7.

[33] D. E. Butler, *Electoral System in Britain since 1918* (2nd edn. 1968), 1–14.
[34] Stalybridge had returned a single member as a Lancs. borough since 1867.
[35] Butler, *Electoral System*, 102–22; F. W. S. Craig, *Brit. Parl. Election Results, 1918–49, passim*, and *Boundaries of Parl. Constits. 1885–1972, passim*.
[36] Cannon, *Parl. Reform*, 290.
[37] *Dod's Electoral Facts*, 60–1.

the registration of their supporters and dependants,[38] but probably in Cheshire, as elsewhere, the feebleness of the registration procedures and the one-shilling registration fee led to incomplete and inaccurate recording of electors.[39] Many gentlemen and substantial non-resident freemen later told Earl Grosvenor that their agents had failed to register them.[40] As late as 1847, when registration was better supervised, in just half the districts of the South Cheshire constituency 36 of those registered had died before the listings were drawn up, 40 had already sold up and moved, 53 had left their tenant farms, and 114 were listed under an out-of-date address. That represents a 10 per cent margin of error amongst those included, without taking account of those entitled to vote who had not registered.[41] By the 1860s the number of county electors had risen to 12,800, an increase of 24 per cent, considerably less than the rise in the size of the population, which was about 60 per cent.[42] The ratio of electors to population was also very low compared with other counties. The county ratio in 1850 for all counties was 1:20·7; in South Cheshire it was 1:25·8, in North Cheshire 1:33·3.[43]

The effect of the franchise reform in 1867 was far more marked than that of 1832. By the early 1870s there were over 20,800 registered voters in the three county constituencies, an increase of 60 per cent. The elector:inhabitant ratio for Cheshire was now very close to that in other counties (at 1:15), which suggests that the previous low ratio was due to the large number of tiny smallholdings in the county.[44] Much greater, however, was the effect of the 1885 franchise act extending the vote to all male householders. It increased the number of electors in the eight county seats to almost 100,000, which had risen to 120,000 by the early 1900s, although the individual constituencies still had quite a wide range of electorates from the 9,000 in Macclesfield division to the 22,000 in Wirral.[45]

The growth of the electorate in the boroughs can best be gauged by reference to Table II. The effect of the £10 household franchise introduced in 1832, although very different in the different towns, was in line with the pattern elsewhere in the country. The ratio of voters to inhabitants in all cathedral cities averaged 1:12, and that in the industrial towns averaged 1:29. The 1867 Bill, which enfranchised all ratepayers, brought the figures for all towns closer together and made a far higher proportion of the inhabitants entitled to vote. But only after the 1885 Act had made the franchise comparable in town and countryside did the number of inhabitants in all the seats come close together,[46] and only then did the borough and county divisions of Cheshire come to resemble one another in respect of the numbers of electors and the relationship between the number of electors and the number of inhabitants. There were other important respects in which the two types of constituency differed from one another between 1832 and 1885, but became indistinguishable in the years after 1885.

As Table III shows, there were far fewer contested elections for the county seats than for borough ones in the years 1832–85. Between 1832 and 1867 there were only six contests in the county seats: the northern division was polled in 1832 and 1841, and saw a contested by-election in 1848, while the southern division was polled in 1832, 1837, and 1841. The new Mid Cheshire division was the only one polled in 1868 and there was no contest in any of the divisions in 1874. In 1880, however, there were

[38] There are many references to such activity in the Grosvenor MSS., papers of 2nd marquess, unfol., bdles. of letters 1831–2.

[39] Seymour, *Electoral Reform*, 184.

[40] Eaton Hall, Grosvenor MSS., papers of 2nd marquess, letters 1831–2, unfol., e.g. from Thos. Brooke, vicar of Wistaston, Loyd Hesketh of Thurstaston. J. H. Leche remarked 'I think many have not registered in this part of the county and I daresay it is the same everywhere'.

[41] Seymour, *Electoral Reform*, 131.

[42] *McCalmont*, 55–7.

[43] Ibid.

[44] Seymour, *Electoral Reform*, 292 n.

[45] F. W. S. Craig, *Brit. Parl. Election Results, 1885–1918*, 230–8.

[46] *McCalmont, passim*; Seymour, *Electoral Reform*, 342–50, 489–518.

contests in all three. Meanwhile the new boroughs were contested on almost every occasion, the only exception being Macclesfield in 1859. Chester lay somewhere in between: the seats were uncontested in 1835, 1841, 1847, and 1852, but fought in 1832, 1837, 1857, and consistently thereafter.[47]

In 1832 all five Cheshire divisions were polled, but in the next seven general elections (1835–59) most of the seats were uncontested. Then came a change: in 1865 4 out of 6, in 1868 and 1874 5 out of 7, and in 1880 and 1885 all the divisions were fought. The transition to regular contests was not, therefore, a simple development from the reforms of 1885, but was probably connected with the development of better party organizations in the wake of the reforms of 1867.[48]

In the period 1885–1918 5 constituencies were polled at all 8 general elections;[49] 3 were polled 7 times;[50] and 2 more 6 times.[51] Knutsford was polled only 4 times, and, not surprisingly, was the last of the seats dominated by a single family: the park of the Egertons' county seat runs to the very edge of the town of Knutsford. The Egerton influence was still dominant even in the 1890s. The M.P. from 1886 to 1906 was a member of that great county family, the Hon. Alan de Tatton Egerton. It took the Liberal landslide to dislodge him. He and his father had then occupied county seats in parliament uninterruptedly since 1832.[52] After the First World War uncontested seats were very rare. Four seats were not polled in 1918, Eddisbury, Knutsford, Stockport, and Wirral, one in 1922, Eddisbury, and one in 1931, Altrincham.[53]

One final contrast between the periods 1832–85 and 1885–1974 lies in the average length of service of individual M.P.s. There had been a considerable contrast between the periods 1547–1660, 1660–1734, and 1734–1832 in that respect. Whereas in the earliest period very few men served more than once or twice, the 18th century had seen the emergence of long-serving members both for the county and the city.

The period between the 1832 and 1885 Acts saw little change in the pattern of tenure for the county seats from that which had prevailed in the previous century. Once elected to serve, the members stayed on until death or entry to the House of Lords removed them. One or two county M.P.s were defeated at the polls in that period: George Wilbraham and Edward Stanley, two radical Whig gentlemen, both first elected in 1832, were both defeated in 1841. Only one of the 17 county members sat in fewer than 3 Parliaments, and 9 of them sat in 6 or more. By contrast, the borough representatives had much shorter parliamentary careers. Indeed, their average length of service, if the two Brocklehursts, who between them occupied Macclesfield seats for 65 years, are excluded, would be less than half that of the county members. Of the 31 borough representatives in the period 21 sat in only one or two Parliaments. Yet the main cause was not the higher incidence of contested elections in the boroughs. Only 7 incumbent members were defeated at the polls in the period.[54] Many more died or retired while in office. The difference is connected with the social background of the M.P.s. The county M.P.s, being gentlemen and noblemen, were mainly young, when first elected, while the borough representatives were frequently self-made businessmen, manufacturers, and lawyers, entering politics in middle age. The average age of the borough members on first entering the House of Commons was 19 years higher than that of the county members.

After 1885 there was little difference in the parliamentary 'longevity' of M.P.s for

47 McCalmont, passim.
48 Ibid.
49 Altrincham, Crewe, Hyde, Northwich, Stockport.
50 Birkenhead, Chester, Eddisbury.
51 Macclesfield, Wirral.
52 Hanham, Elections & Party Management, 405.

53 Craig, Election Results, 1918–45, passim.
54 T. Marsland (Stockport 1841); T. Grimsditch (Macclesfield 1847); A. J. Williams (Macclesfield 1851); E. Salisbury (Chest. 1859); E. W. Watkins (Stockport 1859); W. Tipping (Stockport 1874); H. C. Raikes (Chest. 1880).

the two types of constituency. Most strikingly, over 40 per cent of those who ceased to represent a Cheshire constituency between 1885 and 1945 were defeated at the polls. In that period the trend towards short periods of service in the Commons was more marked. Almost half of all the members sat in only one Parliament, and 82 out of 97 sat in three or fewer.[55] Yet the turnover was not so great as that suggests. Between 1832 and 1949 there were 27 general elections. In only 7 of them were a majority of those returned for Cheshire constituencies newcomers: in 1832 6 out of 10; in 1885 9 out of 12; in 1906 10 out of 12; in 1918 9 out of 14; in 1922 and 1924 8 out of 14; in 1945 11 out of 14.[56]

Most striking was the disappearance of the old county families after 1885. In 1880 5 of the 6 county members came from landed families who had served on Elizabeth I's commissions of the peace. In 1885 only Alan Egerton survived to perpetuate that tradition. At the same election a man not born and resident in Cheshire was elected to serve for a county constituency, the first of a new breed. Beside these changes the landslides of 1906 and 1945 are of a different and lesser order of significance. In the electoral geography of Cheshire 1885 was the great turning point.

CHESHIRE POLITICS 1832–1974

Political Biography

The years since 1832 have witnessed a gradual collapse of aristocratic control of Cheshire politics. Initially the old élite, who for so long had based their economic and social power upon their landed wealth, retained their dominance by diversifying their interests into industrial and commercial concerns. By the late 19th century, however, they were being forced to surrender political control to a new group of men whose interests were less expressly local, whose election was less a reflection of status long since acquired, and whose success owed more to membership of national political organizations than to local connexions.[57] Thus, to take a straightforward illustration, the proportion of all members of parliament born in the county declines from 95 per cent between 1734 and 1832 to 70 per cent between 1832 and 1885, 30 per cent between 1885 and 1918, 25 per cent between 1918 and 1945, and 20 per cent from 1945 onwards.[58]

Tables V and VI analyse the place of birth and the principal occupations of Cheshire members of parliament. There is an obvious contrast in the years 1832–85 between the figures for the county seats and those for the boroughs. The most striking feature is the domination of the county seats by the old county families. In the 1870s Cheshire landowning was still dominated by a small group of great families to a greater extent than almost any other county. Almost three-fifths of its total acreage belonged to 88 families with 1,000 acres or more each, and 27 per cent to 7 families with over 6,000 acres each. Many of the landowners lived outside Cheshire: 29 of the 88 maintained no house in the county, and at least 20 of the remaining 59 lived principally in London.

---

[55] The full figures are: 45 men sat in 1 parl.; 25 in 2; 12 in 3; 5 in 4; 3 in 5; 5 in 6; 2 in 7.
[56] The above is based on information from *McCalmont*; *Who's Who* (every fifth year from 1898); *Who's Who of Brit. M.P.s*, ed. M. Stenton, i. 1832–85, and (in proof) ii. 1885–1918; *Dod's Parl. Companion* (for every year following a general election from 1867 on); *D.N.B.*

[57] Lee, *Soc. Leaders*, 22–3, 29–38.
[58] The biog. information here, and later in this section, is derived principally from *Who's Who of Brit. M.P.s*; *Dod's Parl. Companion* (for year following every general election since 1867); *Who's Who* for every 5th year since 1898, also 1910, 1924, 1931, 1950, 1965; *D.N.B.*

Political control resided with a minority within the landowning group,[59] who divided the representation of the county seats amongst themselves. Only one 'outsider' penetrated that charmed circle, W. Cunliffe Brookes, a Manchester banker, who sat for East Cheshire from 1869 to 1885.[60] The other 15 came from ten county families, who owned an average of 6,700 acres in Cheshire.[61] Their average income from land alone was over £19,000. The poorest of the group, the Leghs of High Legh, owned 2,800 acres in Cheshire, 3,400 acres altogether, and had a landed income of £7,050 a year. Three of them, the Grosvenors, the Egertons of Tatton, and the Leghs of Lyme, each had rentals of more than £30,000 a year.[62]

Those ten families had two other distinguishing characteristics. First, they were not, when they furnished M.P.s, headed by peers. Lord Grosvenor, elected in 1830, had retired after 1835. The county's other peerage families, the Cholmondeleys, Stamfords, de Tableys, Crewes, Combermeres, Delameres, and Vernons, did not put up sons for county seats.[63] Secondly, 9 of the 10 were lineally descended from families of the same name and abode who had served as J.P.s in the 16th century: the tenth, the Tollemaches of Dorfold, descended from the heiress of one of the most ancient of all Cheshire families, the Wilbrahams. The county members represented the oldest and wealthiest families in the shire.

The borough seats differed both from those of the county, and among themselves. Only Stockport shook itself clear of the control of its leading economic and social élite, and developed a genuinely popular political base. At Chester the Grosvenors continued to nominate one member from 1832 to 1874, when Norman Grosvenor, brother of the first duke of Westminster, retired. The election of 1874 was the first for over 150 years not contested by the family. But their influence was not yet extinct. In 1880 the duke sponsored his nephew, Beilby Lawley, son of Lord Wenlock by Lady Elizabeth Grosvenor. Only 6 of the 11 men who sat for Chester between 1832 and 1885 were born in the city or adjoining county: three Grosvenors, W. O. Stanley of Alderley (1850–7), and two men born at the Deanery, H. C. Raikes (1868–80) and P. S. Humberstone (1859–65). Four others had close connexions with the city: Lawley as Grosvenor's nephew; Sir John Jervis (1832–50), a barrister who had practised in Chester for some years before his election, W. H. Gladstone (1865–8), son of the Liberal Prime Minister whose country house at Hawarden lay close to the city; and Enoch Salisbury (1857–9), a Flintshire barrister who also owned Chester gas works. The only 'outsider' was J. G. Dodson, son of a Sussex landowner, a barrister who had risen as M.P. for East Sussex (1857–74) to be chairman of the Committee of the Whole House and Financial Secretary to the Treasury. Although the Grosvenors made little attempt to break their 1829 pledge not to claim the second seat for the city, the men chosen were in the traditional mould, 6 landowners and 5 lawyers.

Local men were also dominant at Macclesfield where two Brocklehursts, father and son, held one seat continuously from 1832 to 1886. The Brocklehursts were the largest employers in the town, and probably among the largest and oldest silk-weaving manufacturers in the country. Between 1832 and 1847 they shared the representation with two other local men: the banker John Ryle, son of a leading figure in the silk and cotton trades of the town, and Thomas Grimsditch, a prominent local solicitor. In 1847 Brocklehurst's colleague was the London Chartist leader A. J. Williams, himself a silk mercer. More surprisingly, the member from 1852 to 1868 was E. C. Egerton, fourth

[59] Lee, *Soc. Leaders*, 17–19.
[60] *Who's Who of Brit. M.P.s*, i. s.v. Brookes.
[61] Their average landholding, including land in all counties, was over 9,000 a.
[62] J. Bateman, *Great Landowners of Great Britain, passim*.
[63] Cf. R. J. Olney, *Lincs. Politics, 1832–85*, 233.

son of Lord Egerton of Tatton, recently a barrister on the northern circuit, who stood as a Protectionist at a time when both parties were moving towards free trade, but when the silk industry was being hard hit by competition. Finally from 1868 to 1885 the M.P. was David Chadwick, whose father was a Macclesfield man, but who was himself born and brought up in Manchester, where he had become an accountant and subsequently treasurer to Salford corporation.[64]

Between 1859, when it received its single member, and 1885, only two men sat for Birkenhead. John Laird, a Glaswegian who had moved his father's shipbuilding business to Merseyside and had made a fortune by pioneering the manufacture of iron ships, retired from business in 1861 to sit as Birkenhead's first M.P.[65] The *Birkenhead Advertizer*, not a paper sympathetic to him, admitted in 1865 that his election owed nothing to party principle, but was 'dictated by faith in good works and . . . a lively sense of favours yet to come'.[66] On Laird's death in 1874 his place was taken by David MacIver, chairman of the managing owners of Cunard shipping, a long-serving Liverpool councillor and second-generation Liverpudlian.[67]

Stockport differed from the other boroughs. There too men already established as the economic and social leaders of the town sought to establish control. In particular Thomas Marsland (1832–41) and Henry Marsland (1835–47), two unrelated local cotton manufacturers tried hard to monopolize the representation. Although they differed in politics, Henry preferred, in 1835 and 1837, to ally with Thomas rather than let a 'foreigner' who shared his own Radical ideas gain a seat. But the strength first of the anti-Corn Law League and then of the Chartists was too great for the local manufacturers, and 1847 saw the election of two Manchester textile printers, Richard Cobden and James Heald, the first occasion when a Cheshire constituency returned two 'outsiders'. Between 1832 and 1885 Stockport returned three 'local' members, four 'Lancastrians', and four others, including two London-born Radical barristers. Stockport politics were far more concerned with 'national' issues than were those of the other boroughs. At least 8 of its 11 M.P.s during that period were, however, concerned with the cotton trade.

The period from 1885 to 1918 witnessed some striking changes, yet there remained a difference between county and borough members. Although only 12 of the 28 county members had been born in Cheshire, and although only 6 were county landowners, most of the remainder were prominent local figures, men who had established themselves as 'social leaders' rather than as 'public persons'.[68] The old aristocracy retained a near-monopoly up to 1885 and then surrendered it very quickly to their partners, the managerial and entrepreneurial *arrivistes*. A very similar change took place with the first election to the county council in 1889. The manufacturers, bankers, and lawyers, who had become active members of the magistracy alongside the old landowning families, dominated the first elected council. The shift in the parliamentary sphere was achieved without rancour or dispute. In 1880 the old aristocracy triumphed for the last time.[69] In 1885 and 1886 men from three of the old county families were returned: H. J. Tollemache was to sit for Eddisbury,[70] and Alan Egerton for Knutsford, both from 1885 to 1906,[71] and Sir William Bromley-Davenport for the new county division of Macclesfield from 1886 to 1906. A fourth landowner, E. T. J. Cotton-Jodrell, who

[64] Davies, *Macclesfield*, 288–98, and *passim*; M. Crozier, *An Old Ches. Silk Family*, *passim*.

[65] *D.N.B.*

[66] *Birkenhead Advertizer*, 18 Mar. 1865.

[67] *Who's Who of Brit. M.P.s*, ii. unpubl., biog.

[68] Lee, *Soc. Leaders*, 5: 'the essential difference between a social leader and a public person is that the former can surrender public office and still retain his social standing, while the latter acquires social status by taking up public life.'

[69] Ibid. 32–8, 56–61.

[70] Previously M.P. for West Ches. 1880–5.

[71] Previously M.P. for Mid-Ches. 1880–5.

sat for Wirral from 1885 to 1900, did not belong to the county establishment. His father had been bishop of Calcutta, he had been born and educated in the Midlands, and his 4,800 acres had come to him through his mother, the daughter of a wealthy clergyman. The other four county seats fell to the new élite.[72] In Altrincham the victorious candidate in 1885 was the barrister John Brookes, who in 1886 resigned the seat in favour of his uncle Cunliffe Brookes. At Crewe, the winner in 1885 was G. W. Latham, of a lesser Cheshire gentry line, himself a barrister interested in the land question and founder of the Farmer's Alliance. At Hyde J. W. Sidebotham, a local millowner, was returned from 1885 to 1900. At Northwich the M.P. from 1885 to 1918 was Sir John Brunner, chairman of Brunner and Mond's rapidly growing alkali works, soon to be largest in the world. Brunner, the son of a Swiss schoolteacher who had emigrated to England in the 1830s and worked in Everton, was the perfect example of the new élite. His political career was based on the successful management of a local industry strengthened by active service on numerous public bodies and extensive philanthropy.[73] No Cheshire landowner came forward thereafter to contest a seat until Sir Walter Bromley-Davenport won Knutsford in 1945.[74] More typical were Cunliffe Brookes (Altrincham 1886-92), W. S. B. Maclaren, the worsted cloth manufacturer (Crewe 1886-91), Joseph Hoult, a Liverpool shipping magnate (Wirral 1900-6), Sir Andrew Sykes, chairman of the Bleachers' Association (Knutsford 1910-22), and W. H. Lever, later Viscount Leverhulme, founder of Lever Brothers (Wirral 1906-10), like Brunner, a major local benefactor and philanthropist. Between them the landowners, manufacturers, and bankers dominated the county representation in those years. There were in addition six barristers all practising on the northern circuit, and mostly connected with the county establishment. A. Lyulph Stanley (Eddisbury 1906-10) was the fourth son of Lord Stanley of Alderley; Henry Barnston (Eddisbury 1910-29) came from a minor but ancient Cheshire landowning family, as did G. W. Latham (Crewe 1885-6). Although only 12 of the 28 county M.P.s were born in Cheshire, 9 more were born in Lancashire, mostly in Manchester or on Merseyside. All of them had business interests in Cheshire, as did three of those born far from Cheshire.

In general, then, the years 1885-1918 saw the county seats occupied by members of a new élite, who were still very much local men. In the boroughs it was already very different. None of the M.P.s for Chester in this period were born in the north-west. B. W. Foster (1885-6) was an Irish physician who had practised in the county; R. A. Yerburgh (1886-1906, 1910-18), a Lincolnshire man, had practised as a barrister on the northern circuit, as had Alfred Mond (1906-1910), the son of Ludwig Mond, co-founder with Brunner of I.C.I. Birkenhead, too, abandoned men of local birth, selecting in turn a retired general,[75] the son and heir of an earl,[76] the proprietor of a national newspaper,[77] and, as the county's first Labour M.P. in 1906, a former carpenter who was a leading figure in the Co-operative movement.[78] Two of Stockport's nine M.P.s during the period were born there, but one of them (B. Melville) had left as a boy, and when elected in 1895, had lived in Surrey for 20 years. Only Sir Joseph Leigh (1892-3, 1900-6) was born and still worked in Stockport, where he owned a cotton factory.

[72] The 'new men' defeated the old aristocracy not at the polls, but in the committee rooms. None of them faced a squire in the elections.

[73] Lee, *Soc. Leaders*, 33-4. His philanthropy included giving a public library to Northwich and guildhalls to Runcorn and Winsford, his public service included founding a Salt Compensation Board to help the victims of subsidence, and the vice presidency of Ches. Football Assoc.

[74] R. A. Ward, younger son of the earl of Dudley, sat for Crewe, 1895-1900, though he had neither land nor close family ties with Ches.

[75] Sir Edw. Hamley.

[76] Arnold, Vct. Bury, son of the 7th earl of Albermarle, who had married the daughter and heir of Ld. Egerton of Tatton.

[77] Elliot Lees, owner of the *People* and master of the South Dorset Hunt.

[78] H. H. Vivian, also chairman of the Co-operative Tenants' Housing Association.

Others owned mills in Lancashire, but few had any close contacts with Stockport before their adoption as candidates.

During the succeeding period, 1918–45, however, the characteristics of the M.P.s for county and borough constituencies were very similar, and divergencies can be explained by the Labour party's control of the boroughs. In general there was a decline in the number of members with Cheshire connexions. Only a sixth were born in the county, and the proportion born outside 'Lancastria' rose from a third to a half. Very few of them worked in Cheshire: there were three barristers from the north-western circuit, three Merseyside shipping-line directors, and a director of I.C.I. The members were not county leaders. There were no great landowners amongst them, nor any great entrepreneurs or county benefactors like Brunner and Leverhulme. Indeed no fewer than five of the eight Cheshire-born M.P.s were born and educated at Birkenhead, the sons of middle-class parents. Of the 49 M.P.s for the 14 Cheshire seats in those years, all but a few could be counted as the new 'public persons': men who had established themselves comfortably in business, the professions, or, on the Labour side, in the trade union bureaucracy, and who looked to parliamentary service to acquire recognition. Most of the Cheshire county members in the period 1832–1918 warranted entries in county directories and in the nascent *Who's Who* before they served in Parliament. That was not true of most of those who served after 1918. There were men who were 'social leaders', but significantly none of them had any prior connexion with the county.[79] It is notable that several of the more prominent Cheshire members were men seeking refuge after losing seats elsewhere in the country. That had not happened in the previous periods, but between 1918 and 1945 8 former M.P.s found themselves new seats in Cheshire.

The process was completed after 1945. The election of that year saw a clean sweep of all the sitting members except for Sir Arnold Grisley (1935–55). Three of the new members had local connexions: Sir Walter Bromley-Davenport at Knutsford (1945–70), Dennis Vosper (Runcorn 1945–64), a former Conservative Party agent at Knutsford, and Selwyn Lloyd (Wirral 1945–74), a district councillor at Hoylake before the war. The other candidates of both major parties were chosen from the lists provided by Central Office and Transport House. During the next 25 years 7 Cheshire men were elected from the 18 constituencies. Rather more were men who had moved into the county and like Vosper and Selwyn Lloyd, had worked their way up through serving for their party in local government. They included most of the teachers and lecturers, who formed a new occupational grouping amongst the M.P.s. The period since 1918 had already seen the election of fewer of the manufacturers and entrepreneurs who had dominated the representation in the decades before the Great War. Since 1945 only one such man has represented a Cheshire seat. The background of the M.P.s in the 1950s and 1960s was professional: engineers, accountants, barristers, working directors, teachers. Until 1974 only one woman, Eveline Hill (1950–64) had represented a constituency within the ancient boundaries of Cheshire. In that year, however, two others were elected.[80]

There were other notable differences in the backgrounds of representatives of the parties after 1885. Table VII shows strikingly the extent to which the Conservatives rather than the Liberals looked outside the north-west for their candidates. Half of all Cheshire Liberal M.P.s were born in the county, and several others had set up in

[79] Lord Colum Crichton Stuart, 3rd son of the marquess of Bath, a diplomat; Sir Edward Grigg, former Governor of Kenya; J. S. Allan, diplomat; J. T. C. Moore-Brabazon, the aeronautics pioneer.

[80] Tables VII, VIII, and IX are based on the material cited in n. 58 above.

business there as manufacturers or barristers. The Conservatives recruited more than half their members from men not previously connected with Cheshire by birth or economic ties. The Liberals, moreover, preponderated among the manufacturers, representing the new élite. For the later periods after 1918, the numbers are not large enough for any conclusions to be drawn, except for noting the trend common throughout the country towards Tory strength among the new managers and industrial bureaucrats, and the rise of the Labour intellectuals, after the Second World War, at the expense of working trade unionists, which appears from Table IX, giving the educational background of the M.P.s of each party since 1885.

Of the minority of the county members between 1832 and 1885 educated at public schools and Oxford or Cambridge University,[81] most had gone to Eton and Christ Church. After 1885 a majority of all members had gone to public schools, or had been tutored privately at home, but less than half had been to university. Several future Conservatives went straight into the army, usually for a short period. In the second period, from 1918 to 1945, more than three-quarters of the Tory M.P.s went to a public school, while barely a quarter of the non-Tory M.P.s did so: the proportion of graduates was one half among Conservatives and a fifth for the other parties combined. In the period since 1945 the proportion of Conservatives who had had a public school and university education remained unchanged, but there was a new kind of Labour member. While only one of the 13 Liberal or Labour M.P.s was at public school, 10 had been at university: 5 of the Labour members were teachers and lecturers; a sixth, Edmund Dell, was a former Oxford don who had become an executive with I.C.I.; one was a nonconformist minister, G. Lang, two were barristers, S. Schofield Allen and Sir Frank Soskice, and two others, M. Orbach, a former engineer,[82] and P. H. Collick, were trade union officials. Two Labour members newly elected in 1974 were respectively director of a public film corporation, and an official of the National Union of Teachers.

The Rise of Party Politics

By the late 19th century and throughout the 20th all the Members of Parliament were primarily 'party' men. Although they might differ from the party leaderships in particular matters, they stood as candidates of national parties, acknowledged themselves generally bound by party whips, and had their elections managed by party organizations attached to national political bodies. Before 1885 the nascent electoral organization in most constituencies was essentially local and autonomous, and only sprang to life at election time. Although most M.P.s had principles which allowed contemporaries clearly to identify them as Tories, Whigs, or Radicals, most of them attempted to disown such labels, and proclaimed themselves 'independents' in the 18th-century tradition.

At the 1832 elections most candidates defined themselves predominantly with reference to the Reform Bill. In 1835 the candidates were at pains to stress, above all things, that they were 'independents'. Thus John Jervis, standing for Chester, claimed that he had assiduously applied himself to all his public duties, paying devoted attention to the electors' interests, and sought neither place not preferment.[83] George Wilbraham, in South Cheshire, said that although his record 'may not have met the views of the violent of either side, it has been in the truest sense, independent'.[84] At Macclesfield

---

[81] The totals are uncertain, and the sources incomplete, for the period before 1885.
[82] Formerly M.P. for Willesden, 1945–50.

[83] *Chest. Chron.* 2 Jan. 1835.
[84] Ibid.

Thomas Grimsditch claimed that it mattered not to him which party of the aristocracy was in power; he would support any ministry which aimed to promote prosperity of trade and manufacturing, 'on principles of pure independence'.[85] At Stockport Major Thomas Marsland boasted that he had not systematically supported or opposed the Government.[86]

Such claims were reiterated at succeeding elections at least until the end of the 1850s, and as much in the new boroughs as in the county seats. Thus in 1852 James Heald told the 'independent' electors of Stockport that he was 'a true independent tied to no party'.[87] In 1857 William Gibb promised to give 'independent' support to Palmerston, but not 'to follow implicitly the dictates of any minister'.[88]

The notion of 'independence' compounded several meanings. It referred to the freedom of the candidate from dependency upon others. Just as, in the 18th century, candidates sponsored by the Grosvenors were said to be 'dependents' of the house of Eaton, so candidates at Stockport often stressed their freedom from the corporate interest of the Manchester chamber of commerce. Secondly it meant freedom to act in accordance with conscience, rather than being bound by pledges given to the electorate. Several candidates emphasized their role as representatives rather than delegates, and refused to be drawn on the burning questions of the moment, even though, by taking sides, they might gain the second votes of electors committed for or against particular reforms. Thus William Tatton Egerton, contesting North Cheshire in 1832, said that 'he would do everything upon experience and not upon theory'.[89] Only one candidate ever abandoned that notion of the M.P.'s freedom of action. The veteran Cheshire Whig, Edward Davies Davenport, fighting Stockport in 1832, declared that once elected he would stand down if ever asked to do so by the electors.[90] The word 'independent' also implied an intention to refuse any place in the government or at court which would bind a member to support the party in power.

Only two men representing Cheshire constituencies occupied ministerial or court office in the years 1832-67, Robert Grosvenor (Chester 1832-47), comptroller of William IV's household, and E. J. Stanley (North Cheshire 1832-47), Secretary to the Treasury 1835-41 and a founding member of the Reform Club.[91] Between 1868 and 1885 two M.P.s for Chester held office: H. C. Raikes (1868-80), deputy speaker 1874-80, and J. G. Dodson (1874-85), Chancellor of the Duchy of Lancaster 1882-4. There is little evidence that any other Cheshire members were place-seekers. The image of independence was easier to maintain because much parliamentary time was occupied with local and private Acts[92] which were non-party issues, dividing men on a regional basis or members for urban seats from those from rural areas. At other times, as over farming issues such as the problems of the graziers after 1846, members might follow personal interests or those of their tenant farmers against those of their party.[93]

Not all candidates stressed their independence. In 1835 John Ryle at Macclesfield made a qualified commitment to the Tory cause when he said that he 'approved of the declared intention and policy of the new ministry and would support them so long as they adhered to their programme',[94] and in the North Cheshire election in the same year John Tollemache asked all 'independent men' to support his campaign as 'a constitutional Whig'.[95] But the only uncompromising declaration of party allegiance came, surprisingly, from a Grosvenor. Robert Grosvenor, again in 1835, wrote that he

85 *Macclesfield Courant and Herald*, 10 Jan. 1835.
86 *Stockport Advertizer*, 2 Jan. 1835.
87 Ibid. 2 Apr. 1852.
88 Ibid. 27 Mar. 1857.
89 *Chest. Chron.* 21 Dec. 1832.
90 *Chest. Courant*, 18 Dec. 1832.

91 N. Gash, *Politics in Age of Peel*, 405, 407-9, 420.
92 T. J. Nossiter, *Influence, Opinion, and Political Idiom in Reformed Eng.* 3.
93 Hanham, *Party Management*, 387-96.
94 *Macclesfield Courant*, 3 Jan. 1835.
95 *Chest. Courant*, 23 Dec. 1834.

had never hesitated to avow himself a party man, because he believed that it was by party alone that important results could be obtained.[96]

Independence, however, remained a respectable credential, and was claimed by most up to the 1860s; and the Grosvenors, Robert notwithstanding, most proudly proclaimed it. Thus in 1832, when Earl Grosvenor had everything to gain by allying with a candidate of equally impeccable Whig views, he insisted that he was an independent. Sir John Stanley, canvassed for his support, revealingly replied that Grosvenor 'will not allow me to call you a decided Whig, but I know you are not a Tory, and that you would be sorry to see a party opposed to all correction of abuses triumph'.[97] Grosvenor declared at his nomination that his principles forbade him to be bound by ministry or electorate and required him to judge every issue on its merits. From long before 1832 until beyond 1867 the Grosvenors were temperamentally Whigs, and they gave general support to reforming governments from the 1830s down to the 1860s. The arrival of Gladstone, through his marriage, at Hawarden Castle brought the two families into close ties of neighbourliness, cousinage and political sympathy. In 1866-7, however, Hugh Grosvenor helped both to defeat Gladstone's reform bill and to secure Disraeli's, believing that any new reform bill must be achieved as a bi-partisan or non-party measure. He even attempted to found a non-party 'independent' newspaper.[98]

By 1885 far less was heard of 'independence'. Its credibility had been eroded from the 1850s, as the electorate increasingly demanded clear commitments from candidates, but was finally destroyed by the rise of party organization. After 1850, particularly with the emergence of two or more newspapers in each of the parliamentary boroughs, candidates could not evade direct questions and pledges, particularly about religious questions and foreign policy. Even candidates for county seats, when they were contested, were more specific about their political attitudes than before. By the late 19th century, M.P.s were also subject to more lobbying from pressure groups amongst their constituents. William Bromley-Davenport (Macclesfield 1886-1906) was bombarded with advice and requests from his constituents, which ranged from a demand that he support a bill permitting local authorities to build crematoria, or another bill restricting vivisection, to a request from the Homing Pigeon Fanciers Society that he should vote for a private bill to 'stop the evil of poachers and pot-hunters' shooting their birds. Dozens of such letters and petitions survive amongst his papers.[99]

So long as the members financed their own campaigns, and were nominated by local caucuses and not national bodies, they could claim a freedom to proceed solely according to conscience. Thus the growth of national party organizations in the period between 1867 and 1885 was a decisive turning point in determining the role of the M.P.[1] Earlier national party agencies, before 1867 most importantly the national political clubs of the 1830s and 1840s, and the agents of the party whips' offices, had been essentially advisory or co-ordinating services, offering propaganda, and information on how to register electors, and helping to promote or defend petitions about election infringements. Cheshire men were involved in both; E. J. Stanley was a founding member of the Reform Club which brought together the old Whigs and the Radicals, and James Coppock, a Stockport solicitor, became 'the indispensible Whig party factotum', a crucial liaison man between the Whips and the constituencies. Nevertheless

[96] Ibid. 6 Jan. 1835.
[97] Eaton Hall, Grosvenor MSS., polit. papers of 2nd Marquess, unfol.
[98] G. Huxley, *Victorian Duke*, 75-86.
[99] Jn. Rylands Libr., Bromley-Davenport MSS., correspondence 5/x, *passim*.
[1] e.g. Hanham, *Party Management*, *passim*.

such bodies played, as yet, little part in choosing candidates, financing campaigns, or providing directives on policy which local parties must heed.[2]

More significant in that transitional period were the local parties which replaced the old informal caucuses of gentry. A formal caucus had certainly existed at Chester in the early 19th century, and promoted the triumph of Sir John Egerton. But it was almost exclusively concerned with breaking Grosvenor control over the corporation and the parliamentary representation. The Cheshire Whig Club, founded in 1821, was a more advanced body. It aimed to find policies sufficiently drastic to avert the contempt of ultra-reformers without alienating moderate opinion. That plan involved claiming the restitution of the constitutional rights established between 1689 and 1701, embodied notably in the place bills and triennial parliaments, which had since been lost.[3] Despite attacks from those who demanded a clear commitment to franchise reform and a redistribution of seats and from those Whigs who felt any commitment to specific measures to be dangerous,[4] the club thrived, and soon had 160 members in the county, 'from the highest down to the upper end of the middle class'.[5] In 1832 the club provided the finance and organization for the Whig campaigns that won two of the four seats and induced a third victor, Lord Grosvenor, to seek their assistance, despite earlier reluctance.[6] By the 1830s all candidates created *ad hoc* organizations at election time. Typical was that of the Grosvenors in South Cheshire in 1832. It is clear that both the Whigs and the Tories had launched similar bodies. By the late 1830s the Cheshire Conservative Association was also advertising free legal advice to 'persons of conservative principles' about registration as electors.[7] At the same time both parties developed regular organizations in the boroughs. In Stockport, for example, the Operatives' Conservative Association was founded in June 1835 and a similar organization opened in Macclesfield, probably at the same time. Both were strongly Anglican, and to judge from the reports of their anniversary dinners in the late 1830s, upholders of the more reactionary Tories. They toasted the Duke of Wellington and denounced the moderate Old Whig, W. C. Brocklehurst, as 'a joint in O'Connell's tail'.[8] Probably, however, neither party developed elaborate party machinery until after 1867. Thus in Macclesfield, the local Liberal and Conservative Associations, with central committees supervising the activities of three or more agents in each 'ward', gradually developed between 1868 and 1880; similar associations are thought to have emerged at Chester at the same time.[9]

The 'independents' who disappeared as central party organizations gained authority after 1885[10] were replaced by a new kind of member who stood for an agreed package of policies, rather than as a man committed only to approaching all issues with an open mind, concerned primarily with the welfare of his own constituents. From the first years after the changes in local government in the 1880s, it became increasingly difficult for men not sponsored by the party associations to be elected either to the county council or to Parliament.[11] Very few non-party candidates achieved more than a tiny parliamentary vote after 1885, although their candidature sometimes affected the result. An independent' Tory Protectionist won 14 per cent of the vote at Birkenhead in 1906, enough to cause the defeat of Sir Elliot Lees, Conservative member since 1886 and a Free Trader, thus giving Labour its first Cheshire seat.[12] In 1942–3,

[2] Gash, *Politics in Age of Peel*, 393–427.
[3] Jn. Rylands Libr., Bromley-Davenport MSS., correspondence 5/iv, unfol., Davenport to Ld. John Russell, 30 April 1822.
[4] Ibid. unfol., letters 2 Oct. 1824, 6 Dec. 1821.
[5] Ibid. 30 Apr. 1822.
[6] Ibid. 25 Oct. 1825.
[7] *Stockport Advertizer*, 14 June 1837.

[8] Ibid. 2 June 1837. See also ibid. 30 June, 14 July 1837.
[9] C. O'Leary, *Elimination of Corrupt Practices in Brit. Elections, 1867–1918*, 136–40.
[10] Hanham, *Party Management, passim.*
[11] Lee, *Soc. Leaders*, 92–105.
[12] *Dod's Parl. Companion* (1906); Craig, *Parl. Election Results, 1885–1918.*

indeed, by-elections for Wallasey and Eddisbury produced freak results; two independents defeated candidates put forward by the coalition government and unopposed by the main parties, but in 1945 both independents lost.[13]

Deference and Control

In 1832 most landlords believed that they had the right to influence the votes of their tenants and neighbours. Yet the extent to which that right was used, and the element of compulsion, should not be exaggerated. In June 1846 Henry Coppock, the veteran Whig agent, told Davies Davenport that the beer barrel and drapers' 'declarations' were much less used than formerly, and both the candidates and their supporters put to far less expense by shorter polls. Of all the forms of political control previously available to the aristocracy, only the family compact remained powerful at elections.[14] Family agreements were indeed still very important. The candidates were chosen by caucuses of gentle families, with whom rested decisions on whether a seat should be contested, and who might often negotiate about it. Thus in 1835 the Whig and Tory caucuses in South Cheshire agreed to divide the representation between them. To the obvious embarrassment of the Whigs John Tollemache decided to run as a second 'independent' Whig, and the 'official' Whig caucus felt constrained both to dissociate itself publicly from his cause, and to subject him privately to such heavy pressure that he withdrew.[15] Similarly the success of the Grosvenors there in 1832 had owed less to their direct appeal to the electorate than to the secret negotiations which their friends carried out with the Whig and Tory caucuses, to gain the second preference votes of both.[16] In the county seats, at any rate, no one outside the gentry could undertake a campaign or present the electors with a choice wider than that sanctioned by the gentry itself. Sometimes, as in 1847, the caucuses agreed to divide the representation and to offer the electors no choice at all.[17] Only if they set up rival slates, did the many tenant-farmers and smallholders have a certain freedom of action, whose extent could only be determined by minutely analysing the poll-books. Letters sent to Lord Grosvenor at the 1832 election suggest that the opinion of landlords about the propriety of their dictating to their tenants varied greatly. A few were blunt and to the point. Sir Thomas Mostyn-Champny wrote: 'I have only time to say with pleasure that your Lordship can now command the second votes of the Mostyn tenancy at Beeston.'[18] George Cornwall Legh said that he had 'told' his tenants to vote for Egerton and Grosvenor.[19] Far more wrote to say that they would not direct their tenants, but only advise them of their own preferences: thus Lord Vernon had told his agent that his tenants might vote as they pleased, but that, if they chose to consult Vernon, he would recommend Grosvenor and Wilbraham.[20] In Vernon's main manors, three-quarters of the tenants appear to have followed his preference.[21] Such conduct was not simply a specious or cynical exercise. John Tollemache, himself a Whig candidate in later elections, similarly expressed a preference for Wilbraham and Grosvenor, while asserting that 'landlords ought not to press their dependents in a way that might prevent their giving a concientious vote', and allowed the Tory candidate, Sir Philip Egerton, to canvass the

[13] They represented the Common Wealth party, set up by Sir Ric. Acland, former Liberal M.P., to contest by-elections where a 'reactionary' candidate was not being opposed.

[14] Jn. Rylands Libr., Bromley-Davenport MSS., correspondence 5/iv, unfol., 14 June 1846.

[15] Based on reports in local newspapers, notably the *Chest. Courant* and the *Chest. Chron.* for Dec. 1834 and Jan. 1835.

[16] Eaton Hall, Grosvenor MSS., papers of 2nd marquess, unfol.

[17] Jn. Rylands Libr., Bromley-Davenport MSS., correspondence 5/iv.

[18] Eaton Hall, Grosvenor MSS., papers of 2nd marquess, unfol., letter 12 Dec. 1832.

[19] Ibid. 14 Nov. 1832.

[20] Ibid. 10 Oct. 1832.

[21] Ibid. poll book 1832.

tenants personally.[22] Moreover, for every landlord who attempted to direct his tenants, there were two who refused even to make a recommendation: thus Edward Lloyd refused to advise his tenants, for he judged that the true intent of the Reform Bill had been 'to prevent the improper intervention of landlords'.[23] That was not simply a polite way of saying that he supported Grosvenor's opponents. A majority of his tenants did vote for Grosvenor in the event. Many landlords clearly felt it proper for them to commit one of the votes of every tenant, but to leave them free to express a personal preference with their second vote.[24]

In the event the electors in most townships voted together. In a sample of 460 voters from 16 townships in the Congleton voting district, 79 per cent voted in the same way as the majority from their own village. Yet the minority who stood out against their friends and neighbours was substantial.[25] Although the Whigs swiftly accused the Tory landlords of considering 'that their tenants were mere slaves, without any rights whatsoever of exercising their judgement in the election',[26] the bulk of the evidence suggests that the authority of the landlord was more moral and psychological: they reasonably expected their tenants to look to them for leadership, advice, and guidance. Rewards rather than punishments were the devices employed. Thus Joseph White of Sutton Hall proposed to give a good dinner to those of his tenants who voted for Egerton and Grosvenor, and others followed suit.[27] The evidence from Davenport's canvass in 1846–7 suggests a similar situation.[28]

The county seats thus remained subject to the influence rather than the control of the gentry, while the more aggressive forms of manipulation were developing in the new towns. No landowner was so coarse-grained as the Chief Mechanical Engineer of the L.N.W.R., F. W. Webb, who wrote in 1878: 'If the people of Crewe do not study the company's interest, I shall not be responsible for what the directors will do in reference to putting on the rates', meaning an increased poor-rate to support those dismissed.[29] Charges, however, of threatening employees, made against the Brocklehursts at Macclesfield and the Marslands at Stockport, may well be partisan and unreliable. Yet the level of probity in borough politics was manifestly lower than in the county seats. E. D. Davenport, the veteran Whig reformer and a man committed to the secret ballot, complained bitterly in the wake of his defeat at Stockport in 1835, less at the behaviour of the tenants and workmen who followed 'good landlords' than at the independent electors who had sold themselves 'for the highest price offered, and promised their votes in a state of intoxication'.[30]

The statement in 1847, that the 'beer barrel' and 'decarations' were less used,[31] may have been true of the county seats, but not of the boroughs, where treating and undisguised bribery remained rampant, Chester and Macclesfield being amongst those which were extensively corrupt in the 1870s.[32] In 1880 both boroughs were disfranchised, and 15 town governors from Chester and 10 from Macclesfield scheduled for corruption. It was found that £9,000 had been illegally spent by the Conservatives alone at Chester, much of it on treating and on colourable employment. At Macclesfield refreshment tickets worth 6s. or 12s. had been commonly issued by the Brocklehursts in the 1840s as they established their political hegemony in the town, and when their control was challenged in the 1860s they reverted to indiscriminate treating. In 1880

[22] Eaton Hall, Grosvenor MSS., papers of 2nd marquess unfol. undated letter.
[23] Ibid. 1 Dec. 1832.
[24] Ibid. *passim*.
[25] Based on poll book in ibid.
[26] Ibid. unfol. Sir Jn. Stanley to Grosvenor 20 Dec. 1832.
[27] Ibid. 8 Aug. 1832.
[28] Jn. Rylands Libr., Bromley-Davenport MSS., correspondence 5/iv, unfol.
[29] Hanham, *Party Management*, 89–90.
[30] *Stockport Advertizer*, 16 Jan. 1835.
[31] Jn. Rylands Libr., Bromley-Davenport MSS., correspondence, 5/iv, unfol.
[32] Hanham, *Party Management*, 263 n.

more than 80 per cent of the 5,000 voters were thought to have received bribes, 2,782 of them being named.[33] In the county seats it was less easy to identify corrupt practices. Many voters had to travel several miles to the poll, and it was far from clear whether the provision of transport by the candidates was permissible.

The clearest evidence of electoral practices comes from the campaign organization for Earl Grosvenor in 1832. He began by establishing a central committee of prominent supporters who would publicize their support for his candidature, pledge financial assistance, and organize fund-raising ventures. In addition Grosvenor set up divisional committees in each polling district, each presided over by an 'agent' who in turn superintended the 'captains' appointed in every village or hamlet. The captains sent in full canvass returns and reported on the activities of opposing candidates. The canvass returns give the voting intentions of more than 85 per cent of the registered voters. Grosvenor himself wrote to influential gentlemen and clergy, and travelled twice around the constituency attending fund-raising dinners, public meetings, and local government gatherings which large numbers of voters were likely to attend. Late in November the committee organized its plan for the poll itself. The 'captains' were to make all necessary arrangements to get potential supporters to the polls. They were to hire carts or other transport to convey electors; they were to be issued with printed cards telling every voter where and when to assemble; those living furthest from the voting station were to be brought first to the poll; a second canvass throughout the constituency was also ordered. At the next meeting further instructions for the poll were issued. All captains who got supporters to the polls were to have their expenses met and were supplied with one ticket for the refreshments for each such voter. The organization was very successful. In a sample of 32 townships in Nantwich hundred the canvass had estimated that Grosvenor would receive 328 votes. In fact he achieved 346. The only serious error was at Burland where only 9 of the 15 expected supporters appeared. A comparison of the canvass and poll book returns for 6 of those townships shows a 95 per cent accuracy of prediction. There were not major defections in all directions: men voted as they said they would.[34]

To some extent there were counter-pressures from voters upward, upon the candidates and landlords, although the evidence for them is less accessible. Especially in the elections of 1832, 1847, and 1852 the gentry and social leaders were conscious of popular pressures exerted on them. The 1831 and 1832 elections were held against a tense background of 'Captain Swing' riots, which drove some landowners to feel that reform was imperative, and others to fear catastrophe if any concessions were made.[35] More than 500 men took part in a riot when the poll was taken in Stockport in 1835. Sixty special constables sworn during the first day of the poll failed to prevent the smashing of windows and furniture at the home of Major Thomas Marsland, the Tory candidate, and the infantry had to be summoned from Manchester to keep order on the second day.[36] At the 1852 election at Stockport there was an outbreak of religious rioting involving both the Irish Roman Catholic minority, and large Church mobs which burned and demolished Catholic chapels. The *Stockport Advertizer* said that 'from the commencement of the election contest, ... there were no great political principles involved in the struggle, but ... the battleground was Protestantism and Popery', and alleged widespread popular intimidation of electors, although the election day itself was the quietest on record, since the anti-corruption laws had kept all the alehouses and

[33] Ibid. 71-2, 263-70; O'Leary, *Elimination of Corruption*, 136-43; Davies, *Macclesfield*, 288-98.

[34] Eaton Hall, Grosvenor MSS., papers of 2nd marquess, unfol.; J. S. Morrill, 'Grosvenors and Great Reform Bill',

forthcoming.

[35] G. Huxley, *Lady Eliz. and the Grosvenors*, 92-109.

[36] *Stockport Advertizer*, 16 Jan. 1835.

inns shut.[37] After Richard Cobden's defeat at Stockport in 1837, his Radical supporters had less violently organized a boycott of all the tradesmen and publicans who had voted against him. He reported that, to avoid loss of custom, 'butchers and greengrocers in the market place cry out from their stalls, Cobden beef, Cobden potatoes etc.'.[38]

Political Issues

The mid 19th century may have witnessed the politics of deference. Yet it would be foolish to assume that the extensive debate about public issues which preceded every election was mere ritual. In 1832 every candidate had emphasized his attitude to reform. The Whigs and Radicals, although everywhere on the offensive, took the Reform Bill, the *Maxima Carta*, as Sir George Wilbraham called it, not as an end in itself, but as providing the opportunity for wider reforms. Lord Grosvenor was quite clear about the need for them; he aimed 'to renovate and repair, not to pull down and demolish; and to prevent both the decay of age and the dry rot of corruption from undermining the fabric of the constitution and causing it to crumble into a heap of ruins'. Nine of the ten successful candidates emphasized both the pressing need for overhaul, and the conservative nature of the necessary reforms. E. J. Stanley was typical in his proposals, demanding the gradual elimination of slavery in the Empire, the commutation of tithes, and further reform of the church, and also in his thinking the Reform Bill itself 'final as a means but not as an end . . .'. Wilbraham looked for tithe commutation, the reform of monopolies, and rapid moves to emancipate the slaves;[39] John Jervis at Chester demanded reform of the corporations and a new Police Bill;[40] Henry Marsland at Stockport opposed tithes, slavery, economic monopolies, and the corn laws, and demanded triennial parliaments and a programme of economy and retrenchment.[41] But most would not commit themselves to detailed proposals, only undertaking to view sympathetically any bills brought forward on their chosen points. Significantly Admiral Tollemache, who alone committed himself whole-heartedly to detailed proposals, and talked about change not restoration, was heavily defeated when his fellow Whig, Stanley, would not endorse his programme.[42]

Throughout the 1830s candidates made their general view of the alternative administrations clear, and thereby endorsed general programmes of action, yet always within a general context of 'independence', emphasizing that their support was conditional upon the intentions of the party leaders being honoured in the detail of their legislation. Most candidates, particularly in the borough seats, proclaimed an overriding opposition both to the expense of the government and the centralization of power. Specific issues attracting attention in their printed addresses and speeches included the tithe problem (1832, 1835, 1837) and the rights of protestant dissenters (1835). The problem of free trade and the corn laws,[43] in 1837 the dominant point only at Stockport, where Cobden was defeated after a bitter contest, was everywhere the principal issue in 1841. In the county seats it then led to the defeat of two men who had been returned in 1832, 1835, and 1837, the Whigs E. J. Stanley and George Wilbraham, who campaigned for a radical reform of the Corn Laws, but at Stockport, to the triumph of Cobden and the Anti-Corn Law League.[44]

[37] *Stockport Advertizer*, 2 July 1852.
[38] J. Morley, *Life of Ric. Cobden*, i. 116–17.
[39] *Chest. Chron.* 24 Dec. 1832.
[40] *Chest. Courant*, 27 Nov. 1832.
[41] Ibid. 18 Dec. 1832.
[42] *Chest. Chron.* 7 Dec. 1832.

[43] Based on reading the *Chest. Chron.*, *Chest. Courant*, *Macclesfield Courier*, and *Stockport Advertizer* for the 8 weeks before and 3 weeks after each poll.
[44] Based on the same newspapers and, for 1841, the *Stockport Chron.*

In the ensuing elections economic reform declined to secondary significance. The 1847 elections were quietly contested, despite the Chartist success at Macclesfield,[45] and propaganda was more concerned with the personalities of the party leaders than hitherto. In the elections between 1852 and 1868 the county seats were not contested, so that the Tory members felt it unnecessary and unwise to do more than issue desultory and bland promises to judge all proposals on their merits. The borough campaigns were livelier. At Stockport in 1852 all three candidates, the sitting members James Heald (Peelite) and James Kershaw (Whig), and J. B. Smith (President of the Manchester Chamber of Commerce), advocated similar programmes; all accepted the need to remove remaining restrictions on trade, all called for a general extension of education, all accepted the need to enlarge the suffrage. The only political difference was that Heald opposed the secret ballot. The election turned on religious issues, what Heald called 'the late aggression of Rome', and it was his campaign against the extension of Roman Catholic rights which caused the sectarian rioting described earlier.[46]

Elsewhere, too, religious issues were dominant in the 1850s and early 1860s. The Conservative *Birkenhead Advertizer*, for example, disparaged John Laird's victory at Birkenhead in 1861 for his 'holy alliance with the Roman Catholic body'.[47] Church rates were also prominent.[48] The question of further parlimentary reform came to dominate electioneering. In 1865, for example, H. C. Raikes, standing at Chester as a Conservative, expressed a willingness to 'give the working classes a share, but not an undue share, in the election of Members of Parliament' while opposing the ballot,[49] and the Liberal Lord Grosvenor cautiously claimed that 'while opposed to the lowering of the franchise' he was 'in favour of its extension . . . where this can be done without giving undue preponderance to any one class of the population'.[50] Similarly both candidates at Birkenhead would only advocate 'support for a well-considered measure'.[51] Foreign policy was mentioned in election addresses for the first time in 1857, when the merits of Cobden's motion over Canton were referred to by candidates at both Stockport and Macclesfield.[52]

Yet the prevailing electoral mood at elections between 1852 and 1865 was torpid. Even the newspapers failed to find major divisions between the candidates. The county seats were uncontested: Macclesfield returned John Brocklehurst, the Liberal silk magnate, and E. C. Egerton, a Tory lawyer from the great landowning family, without serious challenge; Stockport chose two staunch Liberal manufacturers; only Chester saw a change of M.P.s. Earl Grosvenor held first place throughout, joined by either another Liberal or a former Peelite.[53] H. C. Raikes, Tory candidate there, recorded that 'the prolonged experience, the recognized moderation and frank common sense of Lord Palmerston, together with the general contentment now existing among all classes, have produced a sort of armistice between contending parties, which must not however be mistaken for a permanent peace . . .'.[54] The Liberal *Birkenhead Advertizer* finally declared for the Conservative John Laird: 'a moderate politician, all his opinions . . . characterized by strong common sense. He is opposed to extreme measures, and his views are reasonably Liberal.'[55]

Issues, then, were debated and stated. Yet the election results themselves remind us

[45] For Chartism in Macclesfield, see Davies, *Macclesfield*, 291–4. John Williams, national treasurer of the Chartists, came second behind Brocklehurst. A Macclesfield Chartist, John West, failed to secure election at Stockport in the same year.
[46] Based on *Stockport Advertizer*, Apr. to July, 1852.
[47] *Birkenhead Advertizer*, 14 Dec. 1861.
[48] Ibid. Nov. and Dec. 1861.

[49] Ibid. 17 June 1865.
[50] Ibid.
[51] Ibid. 24 June 1865.
[52] *Stockport Advertizer*, 27 Mar. 1857.
[53] W. O. Stanley, Enoch Salisbury, P. S. Humberstone.
[54] *Birkenhead Advertizer*, 17 June 1865.
[55] Ibid. 18 Mar. 1865.

that caucus politics even more than deferential voting were the key to electoral success. In 1832, 1835, 1837, and 1847, three or four of the five constituencies returned one Tory and one Whig. That was not because of the closeness of the support for each party. In 1832 the Whig E. J. Stanley dissociated himself from the more radical views of Admiral Tollemache and procured his defeat by the Tory Tatton Egerton. At Stockport the radical Whig J. H. Lloyd joined forces with a local Tory mill-owner to keep out two other Whigs with whom he was on bad terms.[56] At Macclesfield two silk manufacturers, one Whig and one Tory, allied together against a Whig banker, Thomas Grimsditch.[57] At Chester no Tory appeared at all, and three Whigs fought for the seats; Robert Grosvenor was accepted as first choice, and the effective battle lay between the other sitting member, J. F. Maddocks, a townsman and 'a zealous reformer without being a visionary', and John Jervis, a barrister and 'foreigner' who carefully praised the Grosvenors while attacking the 'infamous abuses which exist within the Corporate establishments of the Country'. Despite a virulent campaign against him for his Tory ancestors by the *Chester Chronicle*,[58] Jervis trounced Maddocks by a margin of 2 to 1.

In South Cheshire the main battle lay between the Whig reformer George Wilbraham, and the moderate Tory, Sir Philip Egerton, who denounced Lord Grey's Bill, proclaimed the church to be in danger, and attempted to portray the ministry as corrupt and hypocritical. Lord Grosvenor, standing as an independent in 1832, had very few first preference votes and depended upon the second preference votes of both parties. Many Whig gentlemen promised to commit their support to him, once Wilbraham's election was secured; similarly with Tory squires. If the two parties ran neck and neck, he could expect to be squeezed out. In the event, Wilbraham's lead over Egerton at the end of the first day was just sufficient (2,171 to 1,929) for him to commit the second votes of his supporters to Grosvenor on the final day, so that he established a lead of 110 over Egerton.[59]

In 1835 every seat except Chester[60] was split between Whigs and Tories.[61] In North Cheshire both parties agreed not to put up a second candidate. In the southern seat Grosvenor withdrew rather than fight another exhausting campaign and although a second Whig, John Tollemache, canvassed the county, the coolness of Wilbraham's friends towards his campaign forced him to withdraw. At Macclesfield the silkmen again combined to exclude the professedly independent Thomas Grimsditch, even though Brocklehurst campaigned on the reforming record of the Whigs, while Ryle 'approved of the declared intentions and policy of the new [Tory] ministry'.[62] Even more remarkably at Stockport Henry Marsland, a Whig mill-owner, committed his second preference votes to an old local rival, the Tory Thomas Marsland, to keep out E. D. Davenport, the Radical landowner, who alleged that Henry had betrayed him because ancient attacks by Davenport on the combination of manufacturers to defend low wages and the corn laws still rankled with him.[63] There were similar alliances of candidates reflecting opposing political principles at several later elections, notably in 1847 when the Whigs were happy to secure one uncontested seat in North Cheshire, and the Tories wished to avoid bitter divisions within their own ranks following the repeal of the Corn Laws.[64] Such decisions of caucuses about how best to win seats

---

[56] *Chest. Courant*, 18 Dec. 1832.
[57] *Macclesfield Courier*, Nov. and Dec. 1832.
[58] *Chest. Chron.* Nov. and Dec. 1832. e.g., 'we believe it is with Mr. Jervis' relations as with an Irishman's potatoes —that the best part of them is underground.'
[59] Eaton Hall, Grosvenor MSS., papers of 2nd marquess, unfol.; Huxley, *Lady Eliz.* 82–109.
[60] Where the two M.P.s of 1832 were returned un-

opposed.
[61] There were no changes in 1837 either, although every seat except South Ches. was contested.
[62] *Macclesfield Courier*, 3, 10, and 17 Jan. 1835.
[63] *Stockport Advertizer*, 16 Jan. 1835.
[64] Jn. Rylands Libr., Bromley-Davenport MSS., correspondence, 5/iv, unfol.

at minimum expense remained the most potent single factor until after 1867 in county and borough elections.

By 1885 the growth of party machinery in most constituencies, the influence which the party headquarters in London could increasingly bring to bear on the choice of candidates, the availability of outside funds, the larger electorate, the secret ballot, and even the end of double constituencies, which precluded deals resulting in split representation, were combining to make party conflict the essence of political action; the great 'national' issues became the essential feature of election addresses and debates. Henceforth, Cheshire politics lost most of their distinctiveness. Election results rarely diverged from the national trend, and, the increasing intrusion of 'outsiders' symbolized the new relationship between Cheshire politics and those elsewhere.[65] Tables X and XI clearly show the dominance of the Conservative party in the county. Only in 1906 and the first election of 1910 did the Conservatives fail to hold at least half the seats, although they only achieved a 'clean sweep' in 1924. They polled more votes than any other party in 22 of the 23 general elections after 1865 and received more than half the total vote in over half the general elections since the rise of the Labour party in the years before 1914. Their lead in 1923 over the Liberals was only 2.3 per cent, and in 1945 that over Labour only 2.4 per cent, but otherwise was very considerable. The Labour party, succeeding the Liberals as the second party in 1918, has retained that position in Cheshire without interruption since 1924, but not until 1935 did it gain more than 30 per cent of the vote, and only in 1951, when Liberals stood in only 2 of the 18 seats, did it achieve 40 per cent. The figures in Table XI, however, can be misleading, for not every seat was contested by all parties on every occasion. In 1892 and 1895, although the Conservative:Liberal proportions of the vote remained almost identical with those of 1886, there was a considerable 'swing' to the Conservatives, since four seats held by them in 1886 were not contested in the later elections. Similarly the Liberals' lead in votes over the Conservatives in 1906 would have been larger had they contested Birkenhead.

After 1885 the Conservatives contested almost every seat. In January 1910 they put up no candidate at Birkenhead, and only one candidate for the double seat at Stockport. In 1918 they did not contest Stockport or Crewe; in 1922 they did not oppose a 'Lloyd-George' National Liberal at Crewe and put up only one candidate at Stockport; in 1931 they put up no one at Birkenhead East, and in 1931, 1935, and 1945 did not oppose the National Liberal candidate at Eddisbury. Labour, by contrast, did not field a candidate in every constituency until 1945, and between 1918 and 1935, averaged only 9 candidates for the 15 seats as did the Liberals. After 1945 Labour fought every seat, while the Liberals fought only 2, 4, and 6 of the 18 seats in 1951, 1955, and 1959, but most of the seats in 1964, 1966, and 1970. To offset that imbalance and provide a fairer method of comparison, Table XII gives the average percentage of the total vote won by the candidates at each party at each election, and also, from 1950, the average for all candidates of that party in the United Kingdom. Those figures too demonstrate that the Conservative predominance is not illusory. Indeed the Cheshire Tories polled better than their rivals even in those years when they lagged behind nationally (1945, 1950, 1951, 1964, 1966).

[65] Based on Craig, *Brit. Parl. Election Results 1885–1910, 1918–45, 1950–70*. The tables include all the constituencies listed by the Boundary Commission Reports as Ches. county or borough seats, whereas the following exclude Birkenhead, Stretford, and Wythenshawe from their calculations. Other material is drawn from: R. B. McCallum and A. Readman, *Brit. General Election of 1945*; H. G. Nicholas, *Brit. Gen. Election of 1950*; D. E. Butler, *Brit. Gen. Election of 1951*, *Brit. Gen. Election of 1955*; D. E. Butler and R. Rose, *Brit. Gen. Election of 1959*; D. E. Butler and A. King, *Brit. Gen. Election of 1964*, *Brit. Gen. Election of 1966*; D. E. Butler and M. Pinto-Duschinsky, *Brit. Gen. Election of 1970*.

The 23 general elections between 1885 and 1970 fall into three groups with contrasted electoral patterns. In the 5 elections between 1885 and 1900 there was extraordinary electoral stability, the Conservatives always polling between 52·7 and 51·2 per cent of the popular vote. In 1886 they gained three seats from the Liberals,[66] but in 1892, 1895, and 1900 only one or two seats changed hands.[67] Similarly there was very little difference between the results from different seats. In each of the seven seats contested both in 1885 and 1886 there was a swing from the Liberals to the Conservatives. In only one case, Northwich, did it exceed 5 per cent. Similarly in 1892, 6 of the 7 constituencies recorded a swing of less than 5 per cent, that time to the Liberals, except at Northwich once again, where there was one of over 9 per cent.[68] During the whole period only once, at Crewe in 1895, was there a swing of more than 10 per cent.

The 1906 Liberal landslide inaugurated a new phase of far greater electoral flux. There were larger swings between the Liberals and the Tories; that at Altrincham in 1906 being 17·2 per cent. Indeed by contrast with the five preceding elections, all but one constituency in 1906 recorded a swing of more than 5 per cent to the Liberals compared with 1900. In most constituencies there was one of more than 5 per cent back to the Conservatives in January 1910. Far more important, that swing coincided with the emergence of the Labour party as an electoral force. Only one candidate from outside the Conservative and Liberal organizations had stood between 1885 and 1900: G. S. Christie as an Independent Labour Party candidate at Hyde in 1895, where he won under 5 per cent of the vote. In 1906 the Labour party candidate at Stockport topped the poll, 750 votes ahead of the single Liberal, and 2,700 votes of the first of the two Conservatives. Labour also contested Birkenhead, which the Tories had won in 1900 without a contest, winning easily in a three-cornered contest against the sitting Conservative, and a Tory Protectionist. Labour held both seats in the elections of 1910.

Henceforth there was a prolonged struggle between Liberal and Labour, over which was to become the second party in the county. In the early 20th century the two parties were certainly appealing to the same electors; not until 1929 did Labour win seats in three-cornered contests with both Liberals and Conservatives, and between 1918 and 1945 only two Liberals ever won seats where they were faced by Labour as well as Tory opponents. Some remarkable results ensued. Between 1918 and 1922 there was a general revival of Liberal fortunes. The average vote of Cheshire Tory candidates dropped from 59·0 to 50·4 per cent: the average vote of Liberal candidates rose from 25·7 to 36·6 per cent. At Birkenhead East, where the Liberals had come a poor third in 1918, their candidate won the seat in the absence of a Labour candidate.

The elections of 1923, 1924, 1929, and 1931 saw the most spectacular changes of all. In 1923, there was a swing from the Conservatives to the Liberals of at least 7½ per cent in all seats except one, and in 1924, an equally large swing back. Nevertheless, except for a few results like that at Birkenhead East in 1922, all the seats moved in much the same way at the same time. There was a swing from the Tories to the Liberals in 1922 and 1929, and an opposite one to the Conservatives in 1924 and 1931, in every seat. There was a swing from Conservative to Labour in every seat in 1923, 1929, 1935, and 1945, and from Labour to Conservative in 1924 and 1931. Only the distribution of votes between Liberals and Labour looks more confused, their comparative shares changing in different directions in different seats in 1922, 1923, 1929, and 1931.

Between the World Wars the Conservatives contested almost every seat, while the other parties sometimes fought most, sometimes only a few seats. Thus Labour con-

---

[66] Chester, Hyde, Northwich.

[67] 1892: Northwich; 1895: Crewe and one seat at Stockport; 1900: as 1895.

[68] A seat already regained by the Liberals at a by-election in 1887.

tested 10 seats in 1922, but only 6 in 1923, then 9 in 1924, 11 in 1929, and 9 in 1931. The Liberals contested between 10 and 13 at every election in the 1920s, but only 4 and 5 in 1931 and 1935. One result was that virtually no candidates did so poorly as to forfeit their deposits. Two Liberals lost deposits in 1918, but no candidates, other than independents, did so again until the Liberal rout of 1950, when 10 of their 16 candidates received less than the required eighth. Both Liberals in 1951 lost their deposits, as did 2 of their 4 candidates in 1958, and 2 of 6 in 1959, 9 of the 15 in 1964, 3 of the 13 in 1966, and 7 of the 14 in 1970. Remarkably no official Labour or Conservative candidate ever lost his deposit in Cheshire until Labour lost one at Cheadle in 1970.

By 1945 the Labour party were firmly established as the second party in Cheshire. They contested every seat after 1945, but never dislodged the Tories from control of a majority of the seats or gained the higher proportion of the popular vote. The period after 1945 was also one of remarkable electoral stability. No seat changed hands in 1951, 1955, or 1959, and 12 seats out of 18, 9 Conservative, 3 Labour, have remained with the same party throughout the period, a contrast with 1885–1900, when only 4 out of 12 seats, and 1918–45, when only 5 out of 14 remained in the uninterrupted possession of one party. In 1950–1 every seat recorded a swing from Labour to Conservative, but none of over 5 per cent, 15 of the 17 swinging by less than 3 per cent; in 1955 there was a swing to the Conservatives, in all but 3 remodelled seats, ranging between 0·2 and 4·0 per cent. In 1959, however, despite the national swing to the Conservatives of 1·5 per cent, in 14 Cheshire seats there was a swing to Labour of between 0·2 and 3·9 per cent.

In 1964, 1966, and October 1974[69] there was a swing to Labour in all 18 seats and in 1970 a swing in all 18 to the Conservatives. The Liberals meantime had had an unhappy record in Cheshire. Between 1950 and 1970 their 70 candidates attained more than a fifth of the vote on only 4 occasions, each time in Cheadle, a new suburban seat created in 1948. It afforded the Liberals their only electoral triumph in Cheshire after the Second World War. In 1950 their candidates came third with 16·6 per cent of the vote, their second highest in the county. In 1951, it fell to 12·4, but in 1955 rose to 15·6 per cent, again their highest share. The breakthrough came in 1959 when their candidate pushed Labour into third place, but with a quarter of the vote was still a long way behind the Tories. In 1964 their share rose to 34·8 per cent mainly at the expense of the Conservatives, whose share fell to 46·7 per cent. That was, however, the only contest fought by all three parties in both 1959 and 1964 where the Labour share did drop. The Liberals had a basis for a major assault on the seat itself; in 1966 Dr. Michael Winstanley, who had previously doubled their vote in Stretford, captured Cheadle with a majority of 675, and held it until 1970.

In various ways, this section has chronicled the growing uniformity of Cheshire with national politics. The results from the various Cheshire constituencies have become more and more similar both to one another and to the national trend. Furthermore, the M.P.s elected in the 1970s were no longer men born within the county or linked with it by family, property, or employment. The politics of Cheshire had, finally, lost that distinctiveness and inwardness which had for centuries been amongst their essential features. By the 1960s, unlike the 1860s, 1760s, 1660s, or 1560s, it was possible to comprehend Cheshire's parliamentary politics without any special grasp of its economic, social, and institutional character. In June 1970 a voter asked one of the poll

69 No 'swing' can be calculated between the elections of 1970 and Feb. 1974 because of the major changes made in the constituency boundaries in the meantime.

clerks at a polling station in the Altrincham and Sale constituency why the names of Edward Heath and Harold Wilson did not appear on the ballot paper.[70] He was attesting the final triumph of party politics, and of mass communication. The representative of the people had become the delegate of the party.

[70] Private communication.

TABLES

THE following tables relate to the parliamentary constituencies lying within the ancient county of Chester, including the county of the city of Chester and the areas separated in 1888 as county boroughs. They also include constituencies separated from the county before the Second World War and excluded from the calculations of the Oxford psephologists, i.e. Birkenhead, Stretford, and Wythenshawe. The tables take no account of the changes made under the Local Government Act, 1972.

TABLE I: REPRESENTATION OF CHESHIRE 1832–1974

Dates	County Constituencies		Borough Constituencies		Total of M.P.s
	Double	Single	Double	Single	
To 1832	1	0	1[a]	0	4
1832–59	2	0	3[b]	0	10
1859–67	2	0	3[b]	1[c]	11
1867–85	3	0	3[b]	1[c]	13
1885–1918	0	8	1[d]	2[e]	12
1918–45	0	9	1[d]	3[f]	14
1945–50	0	9	1[d]	4[g]	15
1950–74	0	10	0	8[h]	18
1974–	0	11	0	8[h]	19

[a] Chester.
[b] Chester, Macclesfield, Stockport.
[c] Birkenhead.
[d] Stockport.
[e] Birkenhead, Chester.
[f] Birkenhead East, Birkenhead West, Wallasey.

[g] Altrincham and Sale, Birkenhead East, Birkenhead West, Wallasey.
[h] Altrincham and Sale, Bebington, Birkenhead, Stockport North, Stockport South, Stretford, Wallasey, Wythenshawe.

TABLE II: GROWTH OF THE ELECTORATE 1832–1901

Column A: Number of registered electors (approximate).
Column B: Ratio of electors to inhabitants.

Constituency	1832		1854		1871		1901	
	A	B	A	B	A	B	A	B
Chester	2,000	1:11	2,500	1:11	7,000	1:7	8,000	1:5·5
Stockport	1,000	1:40	1,500	1:35	7,500	1:8	13,000	1:6
Macclesfield	700	1:30	1,100	1:27	5,500	1:9	—	—
Birkenhead	—	—	—	—	4,500	1:12	18,000	1:6
County	10,000	1:33	12,000	1:37	21,000	1:25	120,000	1:6

TABLE III: CONTESTED ELECTIONS 1660–1974 (EXCLUDING BY-ELECTIONS)

County contests	1660–1734	1741–1831	1832–80	1885–1911	1918–74
Possible	21	19	27	56	160
Actual	11	0	9	47	155
Proportion	52%	—	33%	84%	97%
Borough contests					
Possible	21	19	41	24	99
Actual	11	6	36	23	98
Proportion	52%	32%	88%	96%	99%

TABLE IV: LENGTH OF SERVICE OF M.P.s 1543–1945

	Number of members	Average number of parliaments served in	Average number of years of parliamentary service
1545–1659			
County seats	49	1·4	—
Borough seats	32	2·1	—
1660–1740			
County seats	16	2·9	—
Borough seats	17	2·7	—
1741–1831			
County seats	10	3·8	18·0
Borough seats	14	2·9	16·3
1832–85			
County seats	17	3·7	18·4
Borough seats	31	2·5	11·0
1885–1918			
County seats	28	2·4	10·2
Borough seats	16	2·2	9·5
1918–45			
All seats	49	2·4	9·4

(Those who served in two periods are included under both. Figures are for service in Cheshire seats only.)

TABLE V: COUNTY OF BIRTH OF CHESHIRE M.P.s 1832–1974

	Cheshire	Lancashire	Elsewhere
1832–85			
All seats	29	7	11
County seats	15	1	0
Borough seats	14	6	11
1885–1918			
All seats	14	14	16
County seats	12	9	7
Borough seats	2	5	9
1918–45			
All seats	8	15	26
1945–74			
All seats	8	10	26

TABLE VI: PRIMARY OCCUPATIONS OF CHESHIRE M.P.s 1832–1974

A Landowners
B Manufacturers
C Merchants, shipowners, bankers
D Lawyers
E Trade union officials
F Teachers and lecturers
G Journalists
H Officers in armed services
I Other

	A	*B*	*C*	*D*	*E*	*F*	*G*	*H*	*I*
1832–85									
All seats	21	9	8	8	0	0	0	0	1
County seats	15	0	1	0	0	0	0	0	0
Borough seats	6	9	7	8	0	0	0	0	1
1885–1918									
All seats	6	15	4	8	1	0	4	1	5
County seats	5	10	0	6	0	0	1	0	2
Borough seats	1	5	4	2	1	0	3	1	3
1918–45									
All seats	1	8	11	8	3	0	3	7	8
1945–74									
All seats	1	1	15	9	2	7	1	0	8

TABLE VII: COUNTY OF BIRTH OF CHESHIRE M.P.s BY PARTY 1885–1974

	Cheshire	Lancashire	Elsewhere
1885–1918			
Conservative	6	8	12
Liberal	8	6	2
Labour	0	0	2
1918–45			
Conservative	4	10	20
Liberal	3	3	2
Labour	1	2	4
1945–74			
Conservative	5	6	17
Liberal	1	1	0
Labour	2	3	9

TABLE VIII: PRIMARY OCCUPATIONS OF CHESHIRE M.P.s BY PARTY 1885–1974

A Landowners
B Manufacturers
C Merchants, shipowners, bankers
D Lawyers
E Trade union officials
F Teachers and lecturers
G Journalists
H Officers in armed services
I Other

	A	B	C	D	E	F	G	H	I
1885–1918									
Conservative	6	4	4	6	0	0	2	1	3
Liberal	0	11	0	2	0	0	0	0	2
Labour	0	0	0	0	1	0	1	0	0
1918–45									
Conservative	1	6	10	6	0	0	1	6	4
Liberal	0	2	1	1	0	0	1	0	3
Labour	0	0	0	1	3	0	1	1	1
1945–74									
Conservative	1	0	12	7	0	1	1	0	6
Liberal	0	0	1	0	0	0	0	0	1
Labour	0	1	2	2	2	6	0	0	1

TABLE IX: EDUCATIONAL BACKGROUND OF CHESHIRE M.P.s 1885–1974

(Figures in brackets give the total number of each group)

	Conservative	Liberal	Labour
1885–1918	(26)	(16)	(2)
Public school/private tutor	22	13	0
Oxford and Cambridge	14	8	0
Other universities	0	0	0
1918–45	(34)	(8)	(7)
Public school/private tutor	27	3	1
Oxford and Cambridge	12	2	1
Other universities	5	1	0
1945–74	(28)	(2)	(14)
Public school/private tutor	24	0	1
Oxford and Cambridge	15	0	6
Other universities	5	1	5

Table X: Number of M.P.s Elected for Each Party 1885–1974

(Figures in brackets give the number returned unopposed)

General election	Conservative	Liberal	Labour
1885	7	5	0
1886	10 (2)	2	0
1892	9	3	0
1895	11 (4)	1	0
1900	9 (4)	3	0
1906	0	10	2
1910, Jan.	4	6	2
1910, Dec.	6	4	2
1918	11 (3)	2 (1)	1 (1)
1922	11 (1)	2[a]	1
1923	7	5	2
1924	14	0	0
1929	8 (1)	2	4
1931	13 (4)[b]	1	0
1935	12 (1)[b]	2	0
1945	11[b]	0	4
1950	14	0	3
1951	14	0	3
1955	15	0	3
1959	15	0	3
1964	12	0	6
1966	9	1	8
1970	13	0	5
1974, Feb.	11	1	7
1974, Oct.	12	0	7

[a] Including one supporter of Lloyd George's National Liberals.
[b] Including one National Liberal voting with, and unopposed by, the Conservatives.

Table XI: Number and Proportion of Votes Cast for Each Party at General Elections 1885–1974

A Number of candidates (opposed)   B Votes   C Percentage polled

	Conservative			Liberal			Labour			Other		
	A	B	C	A	B	C	A	B	C	A	B	C
1885	12	51,140	51·2	12	48,777	49·8						
1886	10	41,938	52·7	10	37,584	47·3						
1892	12	56,124	52·6	12	50,657	47·4						
1895	8	41,311	52·7	8	37,142	47·3						
1900	8	40,948	52·4	8	37,188	47·6						
1906	12	57,070	42·2	11	61,812	45·7	2	14,373	10·7	1	2,118	1·6
1910, Jan.	11	72,251	47·8	12	62,273	39·8	2	18,583	12·4			
1910, Dec.	12	73,068	50·8	11	58,817	39·9	2	13,343	9·3			
1918	8	112,123	53·3	7	41,976	20·0	8	52,670	25·1	1	3,407	1·6
1922	11	159,498	41·3	10	127,145	32·9	10	99,729	25·8			
1923	14	181,817	43·4	13	172,131	41·1	6	65,110	15·5			
1924	14	251,761	58·1	10	76,650	17·7	9	105,331	24·2			
1929	13	240,602	42·0	12	162,109	28·0	11	166,457	28·8	1	8,355	1·3
1931	10	337,854	63·5	5	77,157	14·5	9	116,986	22·0			
1935	12	377,636	59·0	4	51,135	8·0	12	211,419	33·0			
1945	15	344,693	43·7	10	103,358	13·1	15	325,589	41·2	2	15,266	2·0
1950	17	439,056	50·5	16	103,013	11·8	17	326,200	37·5	3	1,948	0·2
1951	17	498,218	55·4	2	10,865	1·2	17	390,022	43·4			
1955	18	470,582	58·3	4	23,643	2·9	18	313,454	38·8			
1959	18	487,108	56·2	6	50,243	5·8	18	329,695	38·0			
1964	18	403,972	45·5	15	157,585	17·7	18	326,942	36·8			
1966	18	410,160	46·6	13	123,849	14·1	18	346,527	39·3	1	608	0
1970	18	445,110	49·6	14	121,283	13·5	18	326,817	36·5	2	3,297	0·4
1974, Feb.	19	429,802	42·1	19	249,262	24·6	19	342,790	33·5			
1974, Oct.	19	404,902	42·0	19	203,446	21·1	19	356,265	36·9	2	1,105	0·1

TABLE XII: AVERAGE PERCENTAGE OF VOTES PER CANDIDATE FOR EACH PARTY AT GENERAL ELECTIONS 1918–74

	Conservative	Liberal	Labour
1918	59·0	25·7	28·5
1922	50·4	36·6	30·3
1923	47·4	45·2	30·7
1924	54·5	28·0	34·0
1929	41·9	30·3	32·0
1931	65·5	35·7	28·7
1935	56·9	32·2	35·1
1945	45·8	18·5	39·8
1950	49·8 (43·7)	12·6 (11·8)	38·0 (46·7)
1951	51·7 (48·6)	10·0 (14·7)	41·7 (49·2)
1955	57·2 (50·2)	12·9 (15·1)	39·6 (47·3)
1959	55·2 (49·6)	17·0 (16·9)	38·3 (44·5)
1964	45·6 (43·4)	20·5 (18·5)	37·8 (44·1)
1966	44·4 (41·8)	19·5 (16·1)	42·7 (48·7)
1970	48·6 (46·5)	15·3 (13·5)	39·2 (43·5)
1974, Feb.	42·1	24·6	33·5
1974, Oct.	42·0	21·1	36·9

(Figures in brackets are U.K. averages for 1950–70 derived from the works of the psephologists of Nuffield College, Oxford.)

FORESTS

Delamere and Mondrem, p. 172. Macclesfield, p. 178. Wirral, p. 184.

THERE were four forests in Cheshire: Wirral forest lay in the Wirral peninsula, Delamere and Mondrem in central Cheshire, and Macclesfield in the east.[1] They were always regarded as forests and not as chases, although they were held by a subject during their earlier history. No evidence has been found of forests in Cheshire before the Norman Conquest, and none of the forests is referred to by name in Domesday Book, but by 1086 the earl had put land which was later in Delamere into his forest, and it already included land not held by him in demesne.[2] The Domesday account of Cheshire also contains the description of a forest belonging to Earl Hugh in 'Atiscros' hundred in north Wales.[3] The forest of Wirral came into being in the early 12th century according to later tradition, and the earliest references by name to the forests of Delamere and Macclesfield occur in charters of Earl Hugh II (d. 1181).[4] Express references to Mondrem do not occur until the 13th century though the chief forestership of Delamere and Mondrem was claimed to date from the early 12th century.[5]

The forest of Wirral was created in a region where there was little recorded woodland in 1086 and a relatively high density of population.[6] Delamere and Mondrem included uplands of Triassic sandstone overlaid in the valleys of the Gowy and Weaver by clay, sand, or gravel. References to woodland and settlements in the upland area were infrequent in Domesday Book. The forest of Macclesfield included the exposed moorlands of the Pennines and the adjacent slopes which were probably wooded. In both districts recorded settlements were few in Domesday Book.

Forest administration in Cheshire was in many respects similar to that of other forests. There were hereditary chief foresterships of Wirral and of Delamere with Mondrem, eight hereditary foresterships in Macclesfield, and two hereditary foresterships in Delamere and Mondrem. There were foresters on foot subordinate to the chief foresters of Wirral, Delamere, and Mondrem, and riding foresters in Wirral, Delamere, and Macclesfield. In 1353 the Black Prince, then earl of Chester, created for Sir John Chandos the office of keeper and surveyor of all the Cheshire forests with an annual fee of £53 13s. 4d.[7] Further appointments to the surveyorship are recorded in 1370 and 1386, and in 1400 Thomas Wensley was appointed surveyor, master forester, and rider of Macclesfield, Delamere, and Mondrem.[8] He was succeeded in 1403 by John Stanley, and the offices remained in the Stanley family until the later 15th century.[9] No references to agisters and verderers have been found before 1347. Woodwards are not mentioned by name until later, though reference was made in 1351 to men who were fulfilling their function.[10]

Forest jurisdiction does not appear to have excluded that of the serjeants of the

[1] The help of Dr. I. M. Green with these articles is gratefully acknowledged.

[2] *Dom. Bk.* (Rec. Com.) i, ff. 263b, 267b.

[3] Ibid. f. 268b.

[4] *Blk. Prince's Reg.* iii. 430; T. P. Highet, *Early Hist. of Davenports of Davenport* (Chetham Soc. 3rd ser. ix), 21, 81; Ormerod, *Hist. Ches.* ii. 211.

[5] Chester 33/1 rott. 1, 7; see below, p. 172.

[6] The following paragraph is based on *Domesday Geog. of Northern Eng.*, ed. H. C. Darby and I. S. Maxwell, cap. 6.

[7] *Blk. Prince's Reg.* iii. 122.

[8] *36 D.K.R.* 297, 111; *Cal. Pat. 1399–1401*, 31.

[9] *36 D.K.R.* 446; *37 D.K.R.* 666, 484, 511.

[10] *Blk. Prince's Reg.* iii. 16.

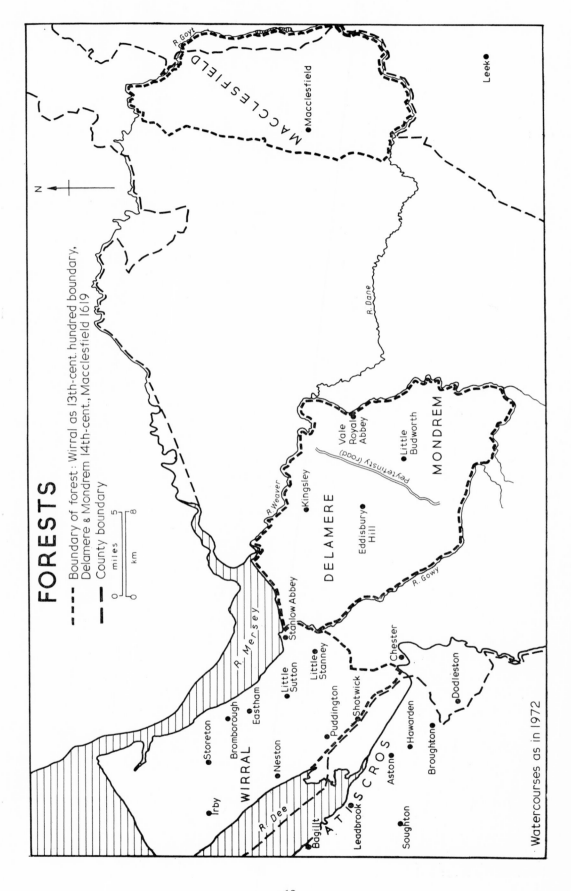

FORESTS

- - - - - Boundary of forest: Wirral as 13th-cent. hundred boundary,
Delamere & Mondrem 14th-cent., Macclesfield 1619

— — — County boundary

miles 0 5
km 0 8

MACCLESFIELD

Leek●

●Macclesfield

R. Goyt

R. Dane

MONDREM

Vale
Royal●
Abbey

●Little
Budworth

Peytefinsty (road)

R. Weaver

●Kingsley

DELAMERE

Eddisbury●
Hill

R. Gowy

Stanlow Abbey●

R. Mersey

Little●
Sutton

Little●
Stanney

Chester●

●Dodleston

●Shotwick

Puddington●

Eastham●

●Hawarden

Bromborough●

●Storeton

●Neston

WIRRAL

Aston●

●Broughton

R. Dee

ATI S CROS

●Irby

Leadbrook●

Bagillt●

Soughton●

Watercourses as in 1972

N

peace in Delamere, Mondrem, and Macclesfield, but Earl Ranulph III (d. 1232) acquitted the freemen of Wirral from puture or hospitality for all serjeants except six foresters on foot, provided that twelve serjeants should be found and kept if required.[11] The rights of hospitality enjoyed by the foresters of Wirral, Delamere, and Mondrem are noteworthy, though their other privileges are comparable with those of foresters elsewhere.[12] The annexation of the earldom by the Crown in 1237 seems to have brought no immediate change in forest administration, and in 1241 Henry III ordered that the woods were to be kept as they had been in the time of Earl Ranulph, and not otherwise wasted or assarted.[13] In 1249, however, it was decided to farm the county to the justice of Chester, and forests, with certain other items, were excluded from the farm and committed to an escheator. A protest by the community of Cheshire was unavailing.[14] In 1259 a similar protest was made when the Lord Edward's letter appointing Thomas Orby keeper of the forests and escheats was read out in the county court. It was said that attention should be given only to the justice or his deputy in forest matters, and that no attachments should be allowed or judgements made except by him.[15] The escheatorship remained, and although the county was sometimes held at farm by the justice there is no evidence that the forests were excepted from that farm. From 1301 forest revenue appears in the chamberlain's accounts. The grant of the manor, hundred, and forest of Macclesfield in 1270 to Eleanor, wife of the Lord Edward, was the first of a succession of such grants to royal ladies.[16] Forest offences there were dealt with by the justice in his annual eyre at Macclesfield.[17] The forest revenues were accounted for by a collector, who was also keeper of the gaol at Macclesfield.[18] From 1403 the chief forester was also steward of Macclesfield manor, both offices being hereditary in the Stanley family.[19]

Forest law in Cheshire was in the main that of other forests, but there were some different customs in Cheshire. They arose partly from the concessions made by Ranulph III in his 'Magna Carta' for Cheshire.[20] In clause 8 the earl conceded to his barons freedom to assart their own lands within the bounds of their husbandry (*agricultura*) in the forest; to grow crops on lawn or land formerly cultivated, without payment for settlement (*herbergacio*);[21] to take housebote and haybote in their own woods without view of the foresters; and to give or sell their own wood at will. Their men were not to be impleaded for the aforesaid unless they were taken with the mainour. These concessions were extended to the knights and free tenants of Cheshire. It appears from clause 17 that even greater liberties within the forests had been sought but rejected.

The custom relating to payment for assarts in Cheshire was different from that elsewhere, where payment was made on the crops grown on assarted land.[22] In Macclesfield an annual rent was paid for each acre assarted.[23] In Delamere and Mondrem a charge, of 6s. 8d. an acre in Delamere and 5s. an acre in Mondrem, was levied at the time of assarting.[24] It is not clear whether or not a charge was made in Wirral.[25]

---

11 R. Stewart-Brown, *Serjeants of Peace in Med. Eng.* 118.
12 Ibid. 1–14.   13 *Cal. Close*, 1237–42, 330.
14 Ibid. 1247–51, 185.
15 *Cal. Chest. Co. Ct. R.* 2.
16 *Cal. Pat.* 1266–72, 459.
17 *Cal. Chest. Co. Ct. R.* pp. xxix–xxxii.
18 Ormerod, *Hist. Ches.* iii. 540.   19 See p. 182.
20 *Cart. St. Werburgh's Abbey, Chest.* i (Chetham Soc. N.S. lxxix), 104–6.
21 Tait suggested that the word means a payment for cutting wood for building or repairing houses: *Cart. Chest. Abbey*, i, 104 n. 5. Cf. *Revised Med. Latin Word-List*, ed. R. E. Latham, where occupation or settlement of land is suggested. Tait was probably right to infer some kind of payment. A survey of 33 Edw. I found that land

in the forest which had been cultivated and was not wooded could be approved at will without view or licence and without fine, subject always to the charge of 6s. 8d. for each acre approved: H. J. Hewitt, *Med. Ches.* (Chetham Soc. N.S. lxxxviii), 15.
22 *Sel. Pleas of the Forest* (Selden Soc. xiii), pp. lxxviii–lxxx.   23 e.g. *Cal. Chest. Co. Ct. R.* 223–5.
24 *Cal. Inq. Misc.* i, pp. 297–8.
25 Ibid. where it was found that although the men of Wirral had the right to assart according to the terms of Earl Ranulph's charter, two justiciars had attached them for land thus brought into cultivation. Cf. the claim of Richard Starky of Tranmere to assart his own soil by giving the earl 5s. an acre of heath and 6s. 8d. an acre of wood: 3 *Sheaf*, iv, p. 64.

Secondly, the right to take housebote and haybote without view seems to have afforded the owners of woods greater liberty than elsewhere, where housebote and haybote were taken under supervision.[26] The question of the rights of those holding land in the forest recurred in 1351 when the Black Prince placed restrictions on pannage, estovers, and the taking of heath, turves, and gorse on demesne land.[27]

Other differences in Cheshire custom became apparent at that time. In 1347 justices were appointed to hold eyres in the Cheshire forests because of the destruction of vert and venison, and because the assize of the forest had not been well kept.[28] The justices imposed amercements for matters not previously regarded as offences, and in 1351 the Prince issued instructions concerning the forests which provoked petitions from the inhabitants of Wirral, Delamere, and Mondrem about the violation of their customary rights.[29] The most important differences related to the lawing of dogs, the carrying of bows, and the holding of swanimote courts. The free tenants of Delamere and Mondrem claimed that there had never been lawing there, and although there had been lawing in Wirral, the lords and parceners of vills claimed exemption from the liability.[30] The Black Prince ordered that no bows or arrows were to be carried off the highway or in the covert, and only on the highway if the cord was removed.[31] The men of Wirral, Delamere, and Mondrem objected that they were accustomed to carry bows throughout the forest without removing the cord. They also claimed that the swanimote courts, which the prince had ordered to be held every three weeks by the foresters to make presentments of all offences to the justiciar before each county court, were an innovation. No reference has been found to swanimote courts before 1351, but they were held in Delamere and Macclesfield in the 15th century, and it seems that in that respect Cheshire had been brought into line with other forests.

The procedure for dealing with forest offenders does not become clear until Edward I's reign. Forest pleas were dealt with by the justice of Chester, in the case of Macclesfield at his annual eyre held there. Special inquiries were also sometimes ordered. In 1304 justices were commissioned whose terms of reference included an inquiry into purprestures, and in 1326 justices were commissioned to investigate and settle various matters in Macclesfield and its forest.[32] The most important of such periodic commissions were the eyres ordered by the Black Prince in 1347 and 1357.

In August 1347 the justice's lieutenant was ordered not to proceed with perambulations of the Cheshire forests without the presence of the justiciar or of the prince's steward.[33] In November the justice was notified of the appointment of justices to hold eyres in the Cheshire forests, and shortly afterwards an inquisition was ordered into damage and trespasses in the prince's forests, parks, and manors in Macclesfield hundred.[34] Claims to forest privileges as well as offences were heard by the justices and heavy amercements were imposed, extending to matters not previously regarded as offences. As a result of the protests which followed some fines were mitigated.[35]

The prince decided to visit his earldom for the first time in 1353 to deal personally with complaints which had reached him, and an eyre for Cheshire and Flintshire was ordered at which one panel of justices, headed by Sir Richard Willoughby, was to deal with forest pleas, and another, headed by Sir William Shareshull, pleas of land, fran-

[26] The assize of the forest laid down that owners of woods could take wood freely to satisfy their needs, but only under supervision and without wasting the forest: *Sel. Chart.* ed. W. Stubbs (9th edn.), 187. A statute of 1327 enacted that although owners of woods could take housebote and haybote without being attached, they were to do so only by view: 1 Edw. III, Stat. II, c. 2.
[27] *Blk. Prince's Reg.* iii. 15–16.
[28] Ibid. i. 139–40.

[29] Ibid. 24–6, 139–40. Less is known about customary rights in Macclesfield.
[30] See pp. 186–7.
[31] Carrying bows in the forest had been prohibited by the assize of the forest: *Sel. Chart.* (ed. Stubbs), 186.
[32] *Cal. Pat.* 1301–7, 238; 1324–7, 296.
[33] *Blk. Prince's Reg.* i. 113.
[34] Ibid. 139–40, 157.
[35] Ibid. iii. 27.

chises, trespasses, and the Crown.[36] The community of Cheshire, however, objected that the holding of a general eyre was contrary to custom.[37] A fine of 5,000 marks was accepted and the eyre was respited for thirty years.[38] A court of trailbaston was held instead at which charges were brought against officials of the prince, including several against the foresters of Wirral. The chamberlain and former justice's lieutenant and escheator were accused of various practices including poaching and destroying game in the forests, but the charges were dismissed because of lack of circumstantial detail.[39] The forest eyre which was to have been held was respited 'until the legal period had elapsed', but regards were nevertheless held in Macclesfield, Delamere, and Mondrem.[40] A second eyre was held in 1357 despite fears of a conspiracy to defeat its findings.[41] The inquiry into offences and privileges was far-reaching, and on this occasion the communities of Wirral and Delamere and Mondrem negotiated communal fines of £1,000 and £2,000 respectively. No communal fine was paid by Macclesfield, but fines imposed on individuals and groups within the community were heavy.[42] The eyres of 1347 and 1357 should be seen as expedients to raise money from the earldom.[43]

Wirral was disafforested in 1376, and in the remaining forests clearance continued. By the 17th century Mondrem was virtually excluded from the forest area, and in 1627 the boundaries of Delamere were not significantly different from those at disafforestation in 1812.[44] In 1503 an inquiry into purprestures and other trespasses was held in Delamere and Macclesfield.[45] Attempts were still being made to enforce the forest laws in Delamere a century later.[46] There were deer in both forests until the Civil War of the 17th century, but the deer in Delamere were destroyed at that time and not replaced.[47]

---

[36] Ibid. iii. 111.
[37] For a valuable reconstruction of the events of 1353, see P. H. W. Booth, 'Financ. Admin. of Lordship and Co. Chest. 1272–1377' (Liverpool Univ. M.A. thesis, 1974), cap. 4.
[38] *Blk. Prince's Reg.* iii. 112, 115.
[39] Chester 29/65 rott. 4–4d, 11d.
[40] *Blk. Prince's Reg.* iii. 115; *Ches. Chamberlains' Accts.* (R.S.L.C. lix), 207.

[41] *Blk. Prince's Reg.* iii. 278.
[42] *Ches. Chamb. Accts.* 248–9.
[43] Booth, 'Financ. Admin.' cap. 4.
[44] Map, Chester R.O., CR 63/2/692 (196).
[45] *37 D.K.R.* 512; Chester 33/9.
[46] *39 D.K.R.* 94; Ches. R.O., DAR/G/50/3.
[47] *Cal. Treas. Bks.* 1660–7, 160; Ches. R.O., DAR/A/32; E 178/5184 ff. 2v–3.

NEITHER forest was mentioned by name in Domesday Book, but there were references to five places which had been put wholly or partly into the earl's forest, and three can be positively identified as lying within the later bounds of Delamere forest. Three vills which had been wholly afforested, 'Aldredelie', Conersley, and 'Done', were waste in 1086 and were held by the earl in demesne.[1] The two partly afforested estates at Weaverham and Kingsley were held by under-tenants. At both there were hays for taking roe deer, and at Kingsley there was also a hawk's eyrie.[2] Although it was claimed in 1353 that the chief forestership of Delamere and Mondrem dated from the time of Earl Ranulph I (d. c. 1129), the earliest contemporary evidence for Delamere seems to be the charter by which Earl Hugh II (d. 1181) granted land at Little Budworth and half the vert and venison of Delamere to Robert le Grosvenor.[3] Clear indications of the existence of Mondrem do not occur until the later 13th century.[4] From that time the charge for assarts in Mondrem was different from that in Delamere, and by the 14th century there was a forestership of Mondrem, but the forest was so closely associated with Delamere that it is impracticable to deal separately with its history.

The bounds of the forests may be reconstructed from various sources, principally the 14th-century lists of vills paying a customary render called frithmote and of vills liable to provide hospitality for the chief forester and his subordinates.[5] Those vills lay between the rivers Gowy in the west, Weaver in the east, Mersey in the north, and an unnamed tributary of the Weaver in the south. It appears, therefore, that the area within those limits was the approximate extent of forest, within which Delamere lay north and west, and Mondrem south and east, of an old road called Peytefinsty, which has been identified as that from Tarporley to Weaverham.[6] The forest region contracted during the later Middle Ages, a process of which the details are lost. From c. 1600

the remainder, which almost entirely excluded the old forest of Mondrem, was usually referred to as Delamere.

Bounded by river valleys west and east and by marshland adjoining the river Mersey to the north, the interior is mostly sandstone uplands, dotted with meres or pools from which Delamere takes its name. There were few recorded settlements on the uplands in 1086.[7] The process of clearing and settling the interior was continuous, and can be illustrated from the many assarts recorded on the forest rolls of the 13th and 14th centuries.[8] Nevertheless there were still wolves in the forest in the early 14th century, and wild swine caused enough damage for the Black Prince to order in 1359 that they be caught and sold.[9]

In 1353 Richard Done claimed that the office of chief forester of Delamere and Mondrem, which he then held, had been granted by Earl Ranulph I to Ranulph Kingsley, with a horn as his title to office; that it remained in the family of Ranulph Kingsley until the death of his grandson, Richard Kingsley, who left several daughters; whereupon it was allotted to one of the daughters, Joan, and thus passed to Richard Done.[10] That account does not accord fully with an order of 1247 that Ranulph le Ruter and Avice his wife be put in seisin of the forestership of Delamere held by Avice's father, Richard Kingsley, so that each of Richard's four daughters was to hold the office for one year in turn and to share the profits with her sisters.[11] Avice later quitclaimed her share in favour of Richard Done.[12] Although the chief forestership descended in the Done family until the 17th century, it appears that the Dones' right to sole tenure was not uncontested.[13] After the deaths of Sir John Done in 1629 and of his son John in 1630, the office passed to John Crewe, husband of Mary, one of the daughters and coheirs of Sir John Done, and in 1709 to Richard Arderne, grandson of Eleanor, another daughter of Sir John Done.[14] John

---

[1] *Dom. Bk.* i, f. 263b. For 'Aldredelie' and 'Done' see *P.N. Ches.* (E.P.N.S.), iii. 161, 239–40.

[2] *Dom. Bk.* i, ff. 267b, 263b.

[3] Ches. R.O., DAR/G/61; Ormerod, *Hist. Ches.* ii. 211.

[4] Chester 33/1 rott. 1, 7. If Mondrem was created later than Delamere it would explain why Little Budworth and part of the land belonging to the forestership of Delamere apparently lay within Mondrem.

[5] *Ches. Chamb. Accts.* 35; Ches. R.O., DAR/G/61; and see map p. 173. The bounds have been discussed by Hewitt, *Med. Ches.* 169–70, and B. M. C. Husain, *Ches. under Norman Earls*, 55–9, who used as evidence the list of vills which paid a rent of custom pigs, although the chamberlains' accounts do not say that those vills were within the forest, e.g. *Ches. Chamb. Accts.* 35. There is also an undated list of vills in B.L. Harl. MS. 2115, f. 80, printed by Ormerod, *Hist. Ches.* ii. 107. They lie within those boundaries already described, with the exception of Stoke, south of the tributary of the Weaver, 'Bedalehethe', and 'Ayton' (unidentified).

[6] In 1275 the charge for assarts made by the men of Delamere was 5s. an acre between 'Peytevinnisti' and Weaver towards Nantwich and 6s. 8d. on the other side of 'Peytevinnisti' towards Frodsham: *Cal. Inq. Misc.* i, pp. 297–8. In 1351 it was claimed that 6s. 8d. an acre was the customary charge for assarts in Delamere and 5s. in Mondrem: *Blk. Prince's Reg.* iii. 23; 3 *Sheaf*, xix, p. 34; xxxiv, p. 38; and see map.

[7] *Dom. Geog. of Northern Eng.*, ed. Darby and Maxwell, 381–2.

[8] Chester 33/1 rott. 1–9; Chester 33/3; Chester 33/4 rott. 5–6d., 8–12, 15–33; Chester 33/6 rott. 22–36, 47–54d.; Chester 33/7.

[9] *Ches. Chamb. Accts.* 41; *Blk. Prince's Reg.* iii. 375.

[10] Ches. R.O., DAR/G/61. The principal difficulty of this pedigree is that only three generations, Ranulph (I) of Kingsley, Ranulph (II), and Richard (I), are given for 120 years: Ormerod, *Hist. Ches.* ii. 87 n. Ranulph (II) of Kingsley was granted land at Millington by John, constable of Chester, between 1178 and 1189: G. Barraclough, *Facsimiles of Early Ches. Charts.* 15–16. Richard of Kingsley evidently died c. 1247: *Cal. Close*, 1242–7, 336. For a woodcut of the Delamere horn, see Ormerod, *Hist. Ches.* ii. 112.

[11] *Cal. Close*, 1242–7, 336.

[12] B.L. Add. Ch. 50531, printed 3 *Sheaf*, xliii, p. 39.

[13] For illustrations of the Dones' tenure of the chief forestership, see e.g. *36 D.K.R.* 141, 80, 241, 154, 324; *37 D.K.R.* 210, 212, 213; *39 D.K.R.* 100. According to Ormerod, the Dones' right to sole tenure was contested by Richard Grosvenor, but the record which he attributes to 31 Edw. I is shown by the names of the justices to date from 31 Edw. III: *Hist. Ches.* ii. 108. Sir William Troutbeck, who succeeded the Grosvenors at Little Budworth, claimed a moiety of the chief forestership in the reign of Hen. VIII: *26 D.K.R.* 20.

[14] *Ches. Inq. p.m. 1603–60*, i (R.S.L.C. lxxxiv), 184–6; Ches. R.O., DAR/A/3/17, 18; DAR/D/63.

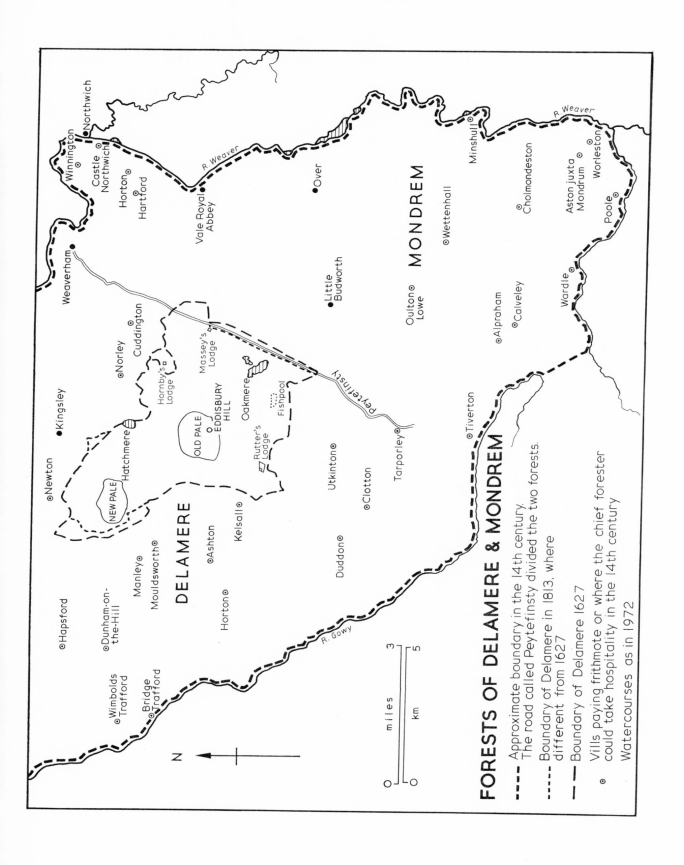

FORESTS OF DELAMERE & MONDREM

- - - - Approximate boundary in the 14th century.
The road called Peytefinsty divided the two forests.

· · · · · Boundary of Delamere in 1813, where
different from 1627

— — — Boundary of Delamere 1627

◎ Vills paying frithmote or where the chief forester
could take hospitality in the 14th century

Watercourses as in 1972

Arderne was chief forester when Delamere was disafforested in 1812.[15]

A detailed statement of the chief forester's perquisites was made by Richard Done in 1353.[16] A jury found that he was entitled to food for himself and his under-foresters and oats for his horse in certain vills; to fern, retropannage, wind-fallen wood, crops of oaks felled by hatchets, and half the bark of fallen oaks; to ½d. for each ox, cow, bull, bullock, or goat taken in the forest between Michaelmas and Martinmas; to all sparrowhawks, merlins, hobbys, swarms of bees, waifs, pelf, the right shoulder of all beasts found there, and the right to keep hounds and greyhounds to hunt vermin. The foresters were also entitled to the residue of any wild beast found wounded or dead, the haunches and sides having been sent to Chester. The chief forester's right to hospitality or puture was comparable to that of the serjeants of the peace. The earl or the chief forester could grant exemption from owing puture.[17]

In 1626 Sir John Done wrote to the Commissioners of the Forests with particulars of his profits of office, which he estimated as worth £88 16s. 8d. annually.[18] They were almost identical with those claimed in 1353, with the omission of retropannage and the addition of the right to appoint ten keepers and two woodwards, with allowance in the forest for their cattle and horses. The chief forester's fishing rights in the forest were the subject of contention in the 17th century. The chief forester had not apparently enjoyed a prescriptive right to the fishing in the Middle Ages. Oakmere had belonged to Vale Royal abbey, and the fishing elsewhere in the forest was sometimes leased, as in 1446.[19] In 1661 John Crewe secured a grant of the rabbits and the fishing,[20] but the fishing was disputed by the Egerton family, Sir Philip Egerton having been granted a lease of the pools in 1674. In 1708 Crewe claimed that the fishpools had been enjoyed by his ancestors, but John Egerton argued that his family had long enjoyed a lease of the pools and that they were not included in the grant of 1661. Egerton secured a renewal of his lease, but Crewe was promised compensation.[21] In 1812 the chief forester claimed compensation for profits of office lost through disafforestation amounting yearly, value in land and rabbits in the various walks, to £504 in addition to the customary rents.[22]

There were other hereditary forestership, one attached to Delamere and the other to Mondrem. The former was held to have originated in the grant made by Earl Hugh II between 1153 and 1160 of half the vert and venison of Delamere and land at Little Budworth to Robert Grosvenor.[23] Warin Grosvenor at his death in the early 14th century held a forestership in Delamere to which his son Warin was heir.[24] In 1347–8 the office was granted to John Hoofield because of trespassers in the forest committed by Richard Grosvenor.[25] In 1352 John Wettenhall was appointed for two years, being succeeded for one year by Thomas Done of Crowton.[26] Further appointments were made in 1357 and 1359.[27] Sir William Troutbeck, who in 1431 bought Little Budworth manor from Margaret, daughter of Richard Grosvenor's daughter Cecily,[28] claimed in right of the manor to be sole forester in the area bounded by the road from Stamford Bridge to Northwich and by a line from Northwich via Darley brook to Tarporley and thence to Stamford Bridge.[29] Troutbeck's niece—Margaret—and her husband Sir John Talbot in 1533–4 conveyed the moiety of the vert and venison of Delamere to John Done of Utkinton.[30]

A forestership in Mondrem was found in 1310 to have been held by Henry Weaver by service of keeping the forest by one armed footman; the office was not dependent on any land but was worth 40s. yearly, to be taken in food in the accustomed places in that part of Mondrem.[31] Henry was presumably related to Henry Weaver, a forester in 1270–1, and to Thomas Weaver, described as a forester of Delamere, whose release from prison was ordered in 1280.[32] In 1315–16 Robert Kelsall accounted for the farm of 26s. 8d. for the forest of Mondrem which had been Henry Weaver's.[33] At the forest eyre of 1347 Thomas Weaver, then forester of Mondrem, was charged with destruction of the vert through assarting.[34] His office and lands were taken into the hand of the Black Prince, and he had not recovered possession at the time of his death.[35] No further references to the forestership have been found.

There is a little evidence about another forestership. Earl Ranulph III granted land to his 'faithful forester', Ranulph of Marton.[36] Stephen Marton was mentioned with the other foresters as being fined in 1270–1.[37] The land was surrendered to Vale Royal abbey, and Ranulph Marton received in compensation another serjeanty and land at Gayton in Wirral.[38] Ranulph son of Ranulph Marton was one of the four foresters-in-fee at the regard of 1287–8, but no later references to that forestership have been found.[39]

The office of rider of Delamere was held by Gilbert de Wyleye in 1301–2.[40] William Wastneys gave £4 to hold the office at farm in 1309, and in 1320 it was granted to Oliver Ingham.[41] In 1334 a release of

[15] Ches. R.O., DAR/D/63.
[16] Ibid. DAR/G/61; Ormerod, *Hist. Ches.* ii. 108–9, prints an English version of the claim from B.L. Harl. MS. 2115, f. 232.
[17] Stewart-Brown, *Serjeants of Peace*, 115–16.
[18] Ormerod, *Hist. Ches.* ii. 111. 'Searn' or 'sengern', there and in Ormerod's source B.L. Harl. MS. 2038, f. 119, is probably a mis-reading for *feugera* (fern), included in Richard Done's claim in 1353.
[19] *Cal. Pat.* 1272–81, 247; 37 *D.K.R.* 511.
[20] Ches. R.O., DAR/E/74, and for material concerning the chief forester's right to rabbits, DAR/A/67, DAR/A/71.
[21] *Cal. Treas. Bks.* 1705–6, 196–7, 603, 604; 1708, 7, 8, 27; 1709, 128, 291, 302; 1710, 332.
[22] Ches. R.O., DAR/D/63.
[23] Ormerod, *Hist. Ches.* ii. 211.
[24] 26 *D.K.R.* 54.
[25] 36 *D.K.R.* 243.

[26] Ibid. 518, 152.
[27] Ibid. 112, 473.
[28] Ormerod, *Hist. Ches.* ii, 211–12.
[29] Ibid. 39.
[30] Ibid. 108.
[31] *Cal. Inq. p.m.* v, pp. 170–1. The 'accustomed places' may have been those where the under-forester could take puture, mentioned in Ormerod, *Hist. Ches.* ii. 108.
[32] Ormerod, *Hist. Ches.* ii. 108; *Cal. Close,* 1279–88, 21.
[33] *Ches. Chamb. Accts.* 85.
[34] Chester 33/3 rot. 4d.
[35] *Blk. Prince's Reg.* iii. 134.
[36] Ormerod, *Hist. Ches.* ii. 176.
[37] Ibid. 108.
[38] *Cal. Close,* 1279–88, 102; *Cal. Chart. R.* 1300–26, 204.
[39] Chester 33/1 rot. 1.
[40] *Ches. Chamb. Accts.* 5.
[41] 36 *D.K.R.* 510; *Ches. Chamb. Accts.* 91.

the ridership was granted by John Whitchurch to John Ward, who was mentioned as still in office in 1347–8.[42] In 1349–50 the ridership was said to have been leased to Thomas Clive, and in 1353 to have been granted for life to Sir John Chandos, who in that year was appointed chief forester, rider, and surveyor of all the Cheshire forests.[43] Nevertheless, further appointments to the ridership at a daily wage of 3d. were made in 1360 and 1362.[44] The office was restored for life in 1378 to John Betchton, who had been ousted by Sir John Delves.[45] In 1502 Ralph Birkenhead was appointed, and in 1514 his office, described as that of ranger, was granted for life to Ralph Egerton.[46] Further appointments to the rangership for life were made in 1527, 1547, 1559, and 1562, the last three with an annuity of £4 11s. 3d.[47] In 1631 the office was held by Viscount Savage, who was ordered to ensure that the subordinate forest officials carried out their duties, because the succession to the chief forestership was being contested at that time.[48] The ranger's right to take one buck and one doe each year from every walk of the forest caused a disagreement with the chief forester, John Crewe, who claimed that Savage was taking his fee deer notwithstanding a restraint of game which had been placed on the forest.[49] In 1639 the ranger was ordered to take his fee deer thenceforth according to the seasons and as prescribed by the foresters.[50]

By 1353 it appears that the chief forester had a staff of eight under-foresters and two grooms (garçons), and in 1443 he was granted an annuity of £10 for his expenses of office and the maintenance of eight foresters.[51] In 1626 there were ten keepers and two woodwards.[52]

There is evidence of regards in Delamere and Mondrem by Edward I's reign when at least four occurred.[53] Judging by the infrequency of references in the 14th century, regards were not held very regularly then.[54] No references to verderers or agisters have been found.

Revenue from the pleas of Delamere was accounted for in 1237–8, but details about the administration of forest law survive only from Edward I's reign.[55] Pleas of vert and venison for Delamere and Mondrem were dealt with by the justice of Chester, but how frequently is not known. Periodically special investigations were made, such as that by a panel of justices into purprestures in Delamere and Wirral in 1304 which provoked a protest from the people of Cheshire.[56] The forest eyres of 1347 and 1357 were the most important of such investigations. In 1347 many trespasses of vert and venison were brought before the justices, and charters of forest privileges were inspected.[57] Heavy penalties were imposed which extended to matters not previously regarded as offences, e.g. digging turves and keeping unlawed dogs.[58]

As a result of the eyre, the Black Prince issued instructions concerning the Cheshire forests.[59] Objections to those and other instructions were made by the inhabitants of Delamere and Mondrem, who set out their grievances in three petitions, two of which were presented also in the name of the men of Wirral. In the first they objected to the writs sent by the chamberlain of Chester to the foresters ordering them to levy 4s. extra above the rents of 6s. 8d. in Delamere and 5s. in Mondrem for approved wastes.[60] In 1347 fines had been imposed on the crops sown on assarted land, which was the custom in other counties. In the petitions made jointly with the men of Wirral, the inhabitants of Delamere and Mondrem protested against the prohibition of unlawed dogs for hunting vermin, and claimed that dogs had never been lawed in Delamere and Mondrem. To the prince's order that turves, heath, or gorse could be dug only in the fields alongside each town by view of the foresters and not in a hunting station or covert, they objected that they had always taken them anywhere in the forest without view. They claimed the right to take estovers on their demesne soil and common pasture without view and at any time of the year, contrary to the prince's order that estovers should be taken only between Easter and Whitsun, and that only one herdsman for each town was to be allowed into the covert. They also protested against swanimote courts, and against the restrictions on their right to housebote and haybote in their demesne wood, which had been granted by Ranulph III. The men of Delamere and Mondrem added that although a payment for pasture called frithyeld was being exacted, they were being prevented from pasturing their cattle in the earl's forest.[61] Following the petitions the prince lifted the fines imposed for unlawed dogs in Delamere and Mondrem, and mitigated those for taking turves and furze on demesne land.[62]

In 1353 a regard was held in Delamere and Mondrem and its findings were reserved until the next eyre,[63] which took place in 1357, when the inquiry into trespasses and liberties paralleled that of 1347. In 1357, however, the men of Delamere and Mondrem compounded for a communal fine of £2,000 to be paid over five years. It is not known how the fine was apportioned, but the duke of Lancaster and the earl of Arundel were exempted.[64] In 1503 justices were commissioned to inquire into purprestures and other trespasses in Delamere, Mondrem, and Macclesfield.[65] Most cases had occurred relatively recently, but the outcome is unknown.[66]

In 1351 the Black Prince had instructed that swanimote courts were to be held in the forests every three weeks, and there was a reference to such a court in 1357 when Thomas Weaverham, who had been indicted there, was pardoned for his good

[42] Cal. Pat. 1330–4, 544; Ches. Chamb. Accts. 121.
[43] Ches. Chamb. Accts. 148, 207; 36 D.K.R. 112.
[44] 36 D.K.R. 545; Blk. Prince's Reg. iii. 382, 443.
[45] Cal. Pat. 1377–81, 249.
[46] 26 D.K.R. App. 2, 20; 39 D.K.R. 94.
[47] 39 D.K.R. App. 1, 94; 26 D.K.R. 19; Cal. Pat. 1558–60, 59; ibid. 1560–3, 246.
[48] Ches. R.O., DAR/A/16.
[49] Cal. S.P. Dom. 1633–4, 370.
[50] Ches. R.O., DAR/A/3/16.
[51] Ormerod, Hist. Ches. ii. 108; 37 D.K.R. 213.
[52] Ormerod, Hist. Ches. ii. 111.
[53] Chester 33/1 rott. 1–3.
[54] Ches. Chamb. Accts. 91, 121, 161, 207.
[55] Ches. in Pipe R. 44.
[56] Cal. Pat. 1301–7, 238; B.L. Harl. MS. 2149, ff. 121v.–122.
[57] Chester 33/4 rott. 5d.–6d., 8–11d., 30–33.
[58] Ches. Chamb. Accts. 130.
[59] Blk. Prince's Reg. iii. 15–16.
[60] Ibid. 23.
[61] Ibid. 24–6.
[62] Ibid. 27.
[63] Ches. Chamb. Accts. 207.
[64] Ibid. 247–8, 261.
[65] 37 D.K.R. 512.
[66] Chester 33/9; no fines appear on the chamberlain's account for 1503–4: S.C. 6/Hen. VII/1519.

service in Gascony.[67] Some 15th-century commissions survive for holding the court of lesser swanimote in Delamere and Mondrem,[68] of which the earliest, dating from 1428, commissioned John Done and William Bulkeley. From 1466 the commissions were at pleasure, the shortest interval between them being eighteen months, and the last was issued in 1494.

It is not known how frequently the medieval earls of Chester hunted in Delamere and Mondrem. James I hunted in Delamere in 1617, when he knighted the chief forester.[69] The king's house of Delamere was mentioned in 1245 as having been committed to Wrennok son of Kenewrek to dwell in.[70] In 1337 the Black Prince, having heard of the great damage that resulted from the distance of the foresters' dwellings, ordered a chamber to be built in the forest.[71] Another order for building a lodge was issued in 1351, and three years later the prince instructed that an unroofed chamber on Peckforton manor be removed to Eddisbury Hill for the forester of Delamere.[72] By 1536 there were two lodges, which had been built, according to the then chief forester, by his grandfather, John Done, and where keepers had lived ever since.[73] In 1626 there were four lodges, in one of which the chief forester lived.[74] At the time of disafforestation the chief forester reported that he lived in the chamber and his deputy in New Pale Lodge; he added that there were three other lodges, Hornsby's, Massey's, and Merrick's, and a small inclosure for the keeper of Newton's walk, but no lodges or inclosure for the other four walks.[75] The chamber stood in an inclosure called the Old Pale. When the Old and New Pales had been inclosed is not known, but according to Sir John Done (d. 1629) it was 'very long since', and both appear on the plan of 1627. It appears from Sir John Done's statement that their purpose was to aid the feeding of the deer, and for the keeper's own beasts.[76]

It is not clear whether there were deer in Mondrem in the Middle Ages, but there are references to both red and fallow deer in Delamere from the 13th century.[77] Leland remarked on the lack of corn in the forests because of the deer.[78] There was concern about the state of the game in the forest in the Black Prince's time; in 1351 he asked the abbot of St. Werburgh's to spare the forest for a while by taking only three bucks and does each year instead of the six to which he was entitled.[79] Deer were sometimes taken from the forest for the earl's use, as in 1252 when Henry III sent agents to take 100 bucks from Delamere for his use in Darnhall and Macclesfield parks.[80] References to gifts of deer occur most often in the 13th and 14th centuries. In 1282, for

example, six bucks were granted to the countess of Lincoln.[81] By the 17th century restraints were again being placed on the taking of game.[82] In 1626 Sir John Done reported that between 60 and 80 deer were killed yearly, and in 1627 two of his keepers testified that there were 320 deer in their two walks.[83] The deer were destroyed in the Civil War, and although restocking was considered in 1661, it was said that it would be expensive because the soil was barren and there was no shelter for the deer, since there were scarcely any trees left except for fuel.[84] Accordingly nothing was done.

The state of the woodland, like that of the game, had become a matter of concern by the Black Prince's time. He tried to ensure that Vale Royal abbey, which lay within the forest bounds, did not abuse its privilege of taking housebote, and he strictly regulated the taking of timber by others.[85] From the 13th century to the 16th timber was sent for the repair of the Dee mills at Chester.[86] In 1303–4 it was used for repairing Beeston castle, and in 1312–13 for chambers in Chester castle.[87] Delamere in particular was a source of oaks, gifts of which were made by the Black Prince to several of his clerks and men who fought for him in Gascony.[88]

By the 17th century the supply of timber trees had diminished: Sir John Done claimed that there were none, and he had to buy some to repair the lodge. Very few were felled for fuel.[89] Done's keepers reported in 1627 that the only timber felled was for the use of the chamberlain and the judges at Chester.[90] In 1651, however, it was estimated that there had been about 2,200 oaks in Delamere before the Civil War.[91] In 1788 the forest apparently contained no significant quantity of timber.[92]

Payments for privileges were another source of profit from the forest. By the 14th century payments for pasturing pigs at the time of pannage between Michaelmas and Martinmas were made on a sliding scale.[93] Certain vills gave 17 pigs each year to the earl as a payment for pasturing their pigs, whether there were acorns in the forest or not. The render had been commuted to cash by 1328.[94] Payments for pannage were being farmed out by 1348, together with payments for agistment, fishing, and escapes.[95] From the 13th century those who allowed their animals to escape into the forest had been fined.[96]

In 1357 an experiment to increase the revenue from pannage was tried.[97] Instead of collecting payments for permission to pasture pigs, a prohibition was placed on the forest, and the foresters impounded all beasts found there, and made their owners redeem them. The scheme failed because the revenue from fines did not match the amounts previously

67 *Blk. Prince's Reg.* iii. 285.
68 *37 D.K.R.* 210, 510–12.
69 Ormerod, *Hist. Ches.* ii. 210.
70 *Cal. Lib.* 1245–61, 15.
71 *36 D.K.R.* 141; *3 Sheaf,* xxxi, p. 69; xxxiii, p. 80.
72 *Blk. Prince's Reg.* iii. 9, 166.
73 *L. & P. Hen. VIII,* xii (1), p. 317.
74 *3 Sheaf,* xxxiii, p. 80.
75 Ches. R.O., DAR/D/63.
76 Ibid. DAR/A/16.
77 *Cal. Close,* 1251–3, 301; 1272–9, 210.
78 Leland, *Itin.* ed. Toulmin Smith, iv. 4, 25.
79 *Blk. Prince's Reg.* iii. 13.
80 *Cal. Close,* 1251–3, 128.
81 Ibid. 1279–88, 161.
82 Ches. R.O., DAR/A/3/11; DAR/A/3/13; DAR/A/3/15; DAR/A/21.
83 Ormerod, *Hist. Ches.* ii. 111; Ches. R.O., DAR/A/27.
84 *Cal. Treas. Bks.* 1660–7, 160; Ches. R.O., DAR/A/32.
85 *Blk. Prince's Reg.* iii. 8–9.
86 e.g. *Cal. Pat.* 1272–81, 105; 1281–92, 135; *Ches. Chamb. Accts.* 215; *37 D.K.R.* 358; *39 D.K.R.* 93.
87 *Ches. Chamb. Accts.* 42, 80.
88 *Blk. Prince's Reg.* iii. 57, 127, 314, 453, 456.
89 Ches. R.O., DAR/A/16.
90 Ibid. DAR/A/27.
91 Ibid. DAR/H/16.
92 *C.J.* xliii. 585.
93 *Ches. Chamb. Accts.* 3.
94 Ibid. 2, 104.
95 Ibid. 120.
96 e.g. ibid. 46.
97 Booth, 'Financ. Admin.' 213–14.

received in payments for pannage. From 1359 pannage was again farmed, usually in conjunction with other payments, such as those for cutting turf.[98] The latter were sometimes farmed separately, as in 1396.[99] The agistment, pannage, turbary, osiers, twigs, and bark were leased to the chief foresters in 1562, 1573, and 1602.[1] At disafforestation the lease was held by Earl Cholmondeley.[2]

Frithmote was another customary payment. When it first appears in the 14th century it was a payment made each year after Christmas by certain forest vills.[3] Its origin and purpose are obscure. In 1351 the Black Prince allowed those who paid at the frithmotes to be excused from attending the newly instituted swanimotes, which seems to suggest that frithmote was a payment for non-attendance at a court.[4] In 1354, however, the duke of Lancaster claimed that his tenants at Kelsall paid 20s. yearly to be quit of frithmote, and for foggage for their animals, which was being denied them.[5] Kelsall's contribution to frithmote is known to have been 20s.[6] An inquisition was ordered, but the Black Prince and his council had been told that the payment was for frithmote and not for foggage. The problem is further complicated by the fact that there was a customary payment for foggage called frithyeld paid each year on St. Andrew's day (30 November), which the inhabitants of Delamere and Mondrem were paying in 1351; they were then being denied the right to pasture their cattle.[7] It seems that frithmote and frithyeld were being confused, and the confusion evidently persisted, since in 1503–4 frithmote was levied on St. Andrew's day.[8] Frithmote continued to be levied, and by the 17th century was being collected by the under-keepers from the constables of each township. Frithmote and the payment for custom pigs were sold to the chief forester in 1674, and continued to be collected until disafforestation, when the chief forester claimed compensation for their loss.[9] There were evidently difficulties in securing payment of frithmote in the late 17th and 18th centuries, as letters of reminder from the chief foresters to the constables show.[10]

From the 14th century it is possible to form an impression of the revenue derived from the forests. There were only minor fluctuations in the annual receipts, which were chiefly composed of the customary payments for frithmote and custom pigs and the yield of agistment and pannage. During the Black Prince's time an attempt was made to increase the revenue. Sales of timber and licences to sell wood increased the revenue markedly between 1361 and 1371 compared with the preceding decade.[11] Possibilities of further increases by selling the turbary outside the covert and increasing the yield from pannage were explored.[12] The most lucrative of such experiments were the forest eyres of 1347 and 1357. In the *Valor* made of the Black Prince's lands following his death, that of Delamere was £51 7s., no separate mention being made of Mondrem.[13] In 1400–1 the chief forester accounted for £42 19s. 1d.[14] In 1559–60 he accounted for £34 0s. 9d., and that amount was the same in a rental of 1711–12.[15] In 1812 the agistment and pannage yielded £43 10s.[16]

In addition to gifts of deer and oaks grants of privilege were made. An indication of the customary rights of forest dwellers has been given in the account of the Black Prince's attempt to curtail them, but individuals and communities enjoyed special privileges. Stanlow abbey's land at Willington was exempted from forest pleas by Earl John (d. 1237).[17] Two religious houses with special privileges were the abbeys of St. Werburgh and Vale Royal. The former was granted a general right of hunting in the Cheshire forests by Earl Ranulph II (d. 1153), but surrendered it in 1285 for the right to take six bucks and six does yearly in Delamere. In the same year the abbot's right to a tithe of all venison taken in the Cheshire forests by the king or his men, to keep greyhounds and coursing dogs for hunting hares and foxes, and to receive one stag yearly on St. Werburgh's day were confirmed.[18] In 1272 it was found that the abbot was further entitled to break up and clear land, to make mills and millpools, to put sheepfolds in his manors in the forest, to take venison in his passage through the forest, and to have two cartloads of dead wood for the abbey kitchen daily from Delamere except during the close month.[19] A petition of 1357 mentioned other privileges: freedom to take estovers, furze, heath, and fern without view of the foresters, and the right to mast and common for swine.[20] The endorsements to the petition show that some of the abbey's claims were disallowed, and the convent fined with the prince for £100 at the eyre for all their trespasses.[21]

Vale Royal abbey, which lay within the forest boundaries, also possessed special privileges. Its manors of Darnhall, Over, Weaverham, and

---

[98] *37 D.K.R.* 432, 642, 674, 511–12.
[99] *36 D.K.R.* 273.
[1] *3 Sheaf*, xxiii, p. 39; *Cal. Pat.* 1560–3, p. 332; 1572–5, p. 208; Ches. R.O., DAR/A/3/12.
[2] Ches. R.O., DAR/D/63.
[3] *Ches. Chamb. Accts.* 2, 16, 104, 119, 148–9, 201, 206, 222, 232, 246, 259.
[4] *Blk. Prince's Reg.* iii. 16. It has been suggested that frithmote is to be identified with 'fridmanesmote' which occurs in the 13th century pipe rolls: *Ches. in Pipe R.* 91 n. It is possible, however, that the latter payment was 'freeman's silver' paid for exemption from summonses issued by the serjeants of the peace or their bedells: Stewart-Brown, *Serjeants of Peace*, 9–10.
[5] *Blk. Prince's Reg.* iii. 172.
[6] *Ches. Chamb. Accts.* 35.
[7] Chester 33/4 rott. 19, 20; *Blk. Prince's Reg.* iii. 26.
[8] S.C. 6/Hen. VII/1519 m. 2d. The fact that frithmote was then paid on St. Andrew's day makes an identification with frithyeld more likely, but in 1302–3 frithmote was paid after Christmas: *Ches. Chamb. Accts.* 16.
[9] Ches. R.O., DAR/C/70, an unnumbered collection of documents about frithmote, including several items about the sale of the rents in 1674, when frithmote was described as a payment by customary tenants who gave 17 pigs to feed on the waste. The rents sold totalled £21 0s. 4d., being £17 12s. 4d. frithmote and £3 8s. for custom pigs. For the chief forester's claim in 1812, see ibid. DAR/D/63.
[10] Ibid. DAR/C/70.
[11] Booth, 'Financ. Admin.' 213–14, 282–283a.
[12] *Blk. Prince's Reg.* iii. 273.
[13] Booth, op. cit. 304.
[14] S.C.6 774/13 m.1.
[15] *3 Sheaf*, xxiii, p. 38; Ches. R.O., DAR/A/6.
[16] Ches. R.O., DAR/D/63.
[17] *Coucher Bk. of Whalley*, ii (Chetham Soc. [1st. ser.] xi), 471–2.
[18] *Cart. Chest. Abbey*, i. 88.
[19] Ibid. 90.
[20] *Blk. Prince's Reg.* iii. 286–7; inspeximus of charter of Earl Ranulph granting mast and common, *Cal. Chart. R.* 1257–1300, 310.
[21] *Blk. Prince's Reg.* iii. 287.

Conersley were disafforested, and the convent had the right to assart in its woods, to take estovers, housebote, and haybote, and to have a beekeeper in the forest. It had a quarry in the forest, and was allowed to take what was needed for glass-making.[22] Like St. Werburgh's Vale Royal sometimes found its liberties challenged. In 1328 the abbot petitioned the king in parliament in person, because the Delamere foresters were denying the abbey's rights, and obtained charters which were read aloud in the county court.[23] The abbey's liberties were also challenged in the Black Prince's time. In 1351 restrictions were placed on its right to take housebote, and in 1357 its claims to estovers and pasturage were disputed. The prince's attorney argued that the abbey was entitled to pasture only in its own vills, not in the forest generally as was claimed. Thereupon the bounds of the commons belonging to the vills were surveyed, and the abbey's pasturage limited.[24] Others who enjoyed forest privileges included the bishop of Coventry and Lichfield who had quittance of pleas of assarting and free pannage for his pigs.[25] In 1299 the bishop was licensed to impark his wood at Tarvin, and in the following year was given deer to stock his park.[26]

The survey of Delamere in 1627 showed that there were 8,346 a. uninclosed and belonging to the king out of a total of 12,672.[27] The forest boundaries had contracted virtually to exclude Mondrem, and there were only minor alterations subsequently before disafforestation. There was evidently an unsuccessful move at that time to disafforest Delamere, and Lord Strange was seeking to buy the lands thus disafforested.[28] The forest survived the Civil War, but in 1661 Andrew Newport and Richard Dutton petitioned to inclose 3,000 a. where there had been many inclosures made and cottages built.[29] Opinions were taken about the possibility of replacing the deer which had been destroyed during the war and a survey of encroachments was ordered.[30] In 1664 Lord Gerard and Andrew Newport obtained a grant of the demesnes of Delamere at a yearly rent of 6d. an acre for every acre recovered for 30 years, with a fourth part of the improved value for 60 years.[31] In 1673 the Lord Chief Justice ordered the continuation of the forest, but in 1677 and 1678 the question of inclosing and disafforesting much of it was revived, first by Lord Gerard and subsequently by John Taylor.[32] Taylor's petition was taken over by the marquess of Powis, and a survey of encroachments was proposed in 1688, whereby compositions were to be taken for encroachments and the commons to be inclosed if possible.[33] It was thought that the yearly value of the forest would rise thereby to between five and six thousand pounds.

Delamere was not disafforested, however, until the 19th century. An Act for inclosing it was passed in 1812 with amending Acts in 1814 and 1818. It was intended by the first that the award should be made within three years, but because the claims to common rights were so complicated amending Acts were necessary to allow partial awards to be made and the Crown lands to be allotted and inclosed.[34] Those lands, assessed at half of the forest's value, consisted of 3,847 a., which were mostly planted with timber and were administered by the Surveyor General of Woods and Forests.[35]

MACCLESFIELD

No direct reference was made to the forest of Macclesfield in Domesday Book, and the earliest is apparently that in the charter, issued between 1153 and 1160, by which Earl Hugh II granted 'Anhus' to Richard Davenport by the service of forestry in fee and appointed Richard supreme forester (*supremus forestarius*) of the earl's forest of Leek and Macclesfield.[1] Lack of evidence makes it difficult to establish the extent of the forest during the Middle Ages. The linking of Leek with Macclesfield in the Davenport charter suggests the possibility that the earl's forest extended beyond Cheshire to his manor of Leek (Staffs.) in the 12th century. The earl's forest of Leek was mentioned in Ranulph III's charter for the burgesses of Leek.[2] It was apparently detached from Macclesfield forest in the 13th century following the grant of Leek manor to Dieulacres abbey.[3] By 1288 it appears that the southern boundary of Macclesfield forest was near Bosley. An inquisition held then found that inclosures at Bosley had not injured the forest, because they prevented the game escaping out of the forest into Staffordshire.[4] The other boundaries are also uncertain. The lands attached to the foresterships in the inquest of service of 1288 were all within the later bounds of the forest. The eastern boundary may be indicated by a charter of the Lord Edward in 1259 removing the restrictions on the woods belonging to the men of the parts of Lyme which had arisen from Earl Ranulph's putting the woods in defence.[5] The

[22] *Ledger Bk. Vale Royal Abbey* (R.S.L.C. lxviii), 24.
[23] Ibid. 45–54.
[24] Ibid. 138–42.
[25] Chester 33/4 rot. 19d.; *Blk. Prince's Reg.* iii. 19.
[26] *Cal. Pat. 1292–1301*, 439; *Cal. Close, 1296–1302*, 145.
[27] Map, Chester R.O., CR 63/2/692 (196); cf. Ches. R.O., DAR/A/6.
[28] *Cal. S.P. Dom. 1627–8*, 53.
[29] *Cal. Treas. Bks. 1660–7*, 160.
[30] Ibid. 307.
[31] *Cal. S.P. Dom. 1663–4*, 538.
[32] Ches. R.O., DAR/A/6; *Cal. S.P. Dom. 1677–8*, 203; *Cal. Treas. Bks. 1685–9*, 325, 1002, 1159.
[33] *Cal. Treas. Bks. 1685–9*, 1777, 1912.
[34] Delamere Forest Incl. Acts, 52 Geo. III, c. 136 (Local and Personal); 54 Geo. III, c. 99 (Local and Personal); 58 Geo. III, c. 47 (Local and Personal).
[35] *4th Rep. Commissioners of Woods, Forests and Land*

Revenue, H.C. 110, p. 29 (1823), xi.
[1] Highet, *Davenports of Davenport*, 21, 81, and p. 3 for a possible identification of 'Anhus'. Ormerod thought that 'Aldredelie', an afforested vill in Domesday Book, was Nether Alderley, from which he inferred the existence of Macclesfield forest in 1086: *Dom. Bk.* i, f. 263b; Ormerod, *Hist. Ches.* iii. 538. 'Aldredelie' seems, however, to have been a lost vill in Delamere forest: *P.N. Ches.* (E.P.N.S.) iii. 239–40. No evidence has been found to support Ormerod's suggestion that the reference to Newbold Astbury meant that the vill was afforested in 1086: *Dom. Bk.* i, f. 267; Ormerod, *Hist. Ches.* iii. 21.
[2] J. Sleigh, *Hist. Leek*, 11–12.
[3] The history of the abbot's chase at Leek is reserved for treatment in *V.C.H. Staffs.*
[4] *Cal. Chest. Co. Ct. R.* 233.
[5] G. Barraclough, *Earldom and Co. Palatine of Chest.* 35; cf. *Annales Cestrienses* (R.S.L.C. xiv), 77.

charter apparently aimed at confirming the concessions made in 1249 by Henry III in response to a complaint by the barons and community of Cheshire.[6] It is not known which Earl Ranulph had placed the restrictions, or whether they referred to land inside or outside the boundaries of the forest; nor is the meaning of 'Lyme' clear in the context.[7] Lyme could be used to describe the eastern boundary of Cheshire, as in clause 14 of the 'Magna Carta' issued by Earl Ranulph III.[8] On the other hand Henry III's concession of 1249 referred to those who held lands and woods within the wood of Lyme outside the demesne woods and forest of the king, and in later references the wood of Lyme meant that in Lyme Handley.[9] The first description of the boundaries which can be definitely dated is that of 1619, which shows the forest occupying an area bounded on the north, east, and south by the rivers Mersey, Goyt, and Dane, and on the west by a line from Otterspool Bridge through Offerton Green, Norbury, Poynton, Prestbury, Gawsworth, and North Rode.[10]

Much of the forest region consisted of the Pennine moorlands and the adjacent uplands where recorded settlements were few in 1086.[11] Extensive woodland was recorded as appurtenant to the earl's manors of Macclesfield, measuring 6 leagues by 4, and at Adlington where the woodland was 11 leagues by two. At Macclesfield there were 7 hays, and at Adlington 7 hays and 2 hawks' eyries.[12] There were still wolves near Macclesfield at the beginning of the 14th century, for it was reported in 1303 that a machine had been made to catch them.[13]

By the later 13th century the custom in Macclesfield forest was to pay an annual rent for assarts according to acreage assarted.[14] The location and extent of such assarts can be seen from the surviving rolls of the eyre at Macclesfield between 1284 and 1290.[15] In 1286, for example, encroachments were reported at Hurdsfield, Stanley, Disley, Lyme Handley, and Gawsworth.[16] In the following year a jury inquired into an approvement of 207½ a. in Bosley made since King John's reign.[17] Land clearance continued from the 14th century to the 16th, as assarts recorded on the forest rolls show.[18] Licences to impark were also granted. In 1462

Robert Legh of Adlington received licence to inclose Adlington Wood, Whiteley Green, and Heys, and in 1516 John Sutton received licence to impark an area stretching from Gawsworth to Macclesfield mills in Sutton Downes and from Langley to Wythenshawe.[19] A survey, attributed to the later years of Henry VIII, shows the extent of inclosures at that date.[20] It has been suggested that inclosure was encouraged in the 16th century, as the resulting fines and rents increased the revenue from the forest.[21] By 1559–60 such rents were by far the largest item in the forest bailiff's account.[22]

Although Richard Davenport was appointed supreme forester of Leek and Macclesfield between 1153 and 1160, the Davenports, who from the 13th century were hereditary serjeants of Macclesfield hundred, did not describe themselves as foresters until the original charter was enrolled in the county court in 1596.[23] By the later 13th century there were eight hereditary foresterships. According to the inquest of service of 1288, Richard Vernon held Marple and Wybersley in free forestry and was to answer the king's summons with the arms of his bailiwick; while in the army he was not to be burdened with the custody of the forest. The other seven foresters held their land by the same service. Robert Downes held Taxal and Downes, John Sutton land in Sutton and Disley, Thomas Worth 'Ratonfeld' (Whitfield in Upton), Robert Champagne High Lee in Sutton Downes, and Jordan Disley land in Disley. No land was attached to the office of Thomas Orby, and the lands of Roger Stanley were not specified.[24] A list of a similar date shows that Stanley's lands were at Stanley in Disley, and names a ninth forester, Adam son of Alan Sutton, who, like John Sutton, held land at Sutton. The names of three other foresters were different: Henry Worth replaced Roger Worth, Richard High Lee Robert Champagne, and Grim Stanley Roger Stanley. Three of the nine were described as holding by charter of Earl Ranulph and one, Adam son of Alan Sutton, by charter of Earl Hugh.[25] In 1287 an inquisition found that Earl Hugh II had enfeoffed Adam, great-grandfather of Richard Sutton, of 2 bovates of land to be held by serjeanty of forestry.[26] The office descended in the Sutton family and a deputy for

[6] Cal. Close, 1247–51, 185.
[7] Barraclough suggested Ranulph III and discussed several possible identifications for Lyme, suggesting tentatively that the south-eastern boundary from Dieulacres and Leek towards Newcastle may have been meant: op. cit. 38. For the term 'to put woods in defence' see Sel. Pleas of the Forest (Selden Soc. xiii), pp. xciii–xciv.
[8] Cart. Chest. Abbey, i. 105.
[9] P.N. Ches. i. 198.
[10] Ormerod, Hist. Ches. iii. 539 n. For the location of the places mentioned see P.N. Ches. i. 9–10. The locations of 'the hill called Norbury Low' and 'the straight road near the house of Robert Hanford' are uncertain, and the boundary of the forest can be only tentatively sketched thereabouts. A slightly different version of the bounds from B.L. Harl. MS. 2038, f. 8 was printed by Ormerod, Hist. Ches. iii. 539 n. There is also an undated list of vills in the forest in Harl. MS. 2115, f. 79. See also Ormerod, Hist. Ches. iii. 541 n. for vills owing suit to the court of the manor and forest. The vills in the lists conform with the boundaries of 1619.
[11] Dom. Geog. Northern Eng., ed. Darby and Maxwell, 383.
[12] Dom. Bk. i, ff. 263b, 264.
[13] Ches. Chamb. Accts. 25.
[14] Between 1355 and 1357 an attempt was made to claim that lands in the forest rented at 8d. an acre were held in

ancient demesne, and in 1359 a similar claim was made about lands in Bollington: Blk. Prince's Reg. iii. 199, 204, 259, 335. For a discussion of the claim see Margaret Sharp, 'Contributions to Hist. of Earldom and Co. Chest. 1237–1399' (Manchester Univ. Ph.D. thesis, 1925), i. 316–19.
[15] Cal. Chest. Co. Ct. R. 207–48.
[16] Ibid. 223–5.
[17] Ibid. 233.
[18] Chester 33/5, 33/6, 33/9 rott. 5–13.
[19] Cal. Chart. R. 1427–1516, 188; 26 D.K.R. App. 2, 115.
[20] Chetham Coll. Libr., Adlington MS. Mun. E. 8. 22, ff. 152v.–153, printed in F. Renaud, Contributions to Hist. of Ancient Parish of Prestbury (Chetham Soc. [1st ser.], xcvii), 222–8.
[21] C. Stella Davies, Hist. of Macclesfield, 40–1.
[22] 3 Sheaf, xxiii, pp. 58, 60, 65–7, 70, 82; xxiv, pp. 12, 14, 16–17, 25.
[23] Highet, Davenports of Davenport, 3–5.
[24] Cal. Chest. Co. Ct. R. 115.
[25] B.L. Cotton MS. Cleop. D. vi, f. 4, printed in Ormerod, Hist. Ches. iii. 538–9 n. The list shows that the second place where Robert de Downes held land, indecipherable in the inquest of service, was Downes. The date of the list has not been established.
[26] Cal. Chest. Co. Ct. R. 233.

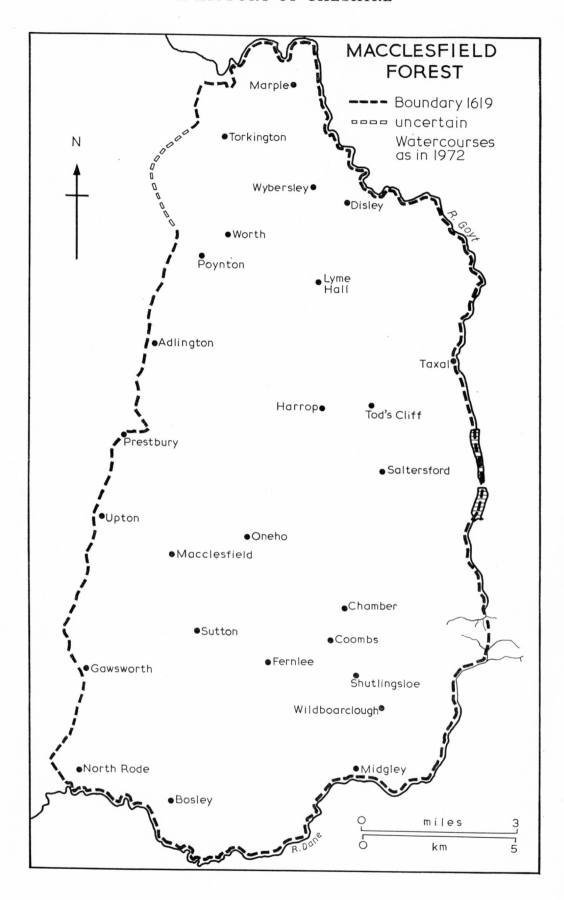

MACCLESFIELD
FOREST

- - - Boundary 1619
□□□□ uncertain
Watercourses
as in 1972

Marple

Torkington

Wybersley

Disley

R. Goyt

Worth

Poynton

Lyme
Hall

Adlington

Taxal

Harrop

Tod's Cliff

Prestbury

Saltersford

Upton

Oneho

Macclesfield

Chamber

Sutton

Coombs

Fernlee

Gawsworth

Shutlingsloe

Wildboarclough

North Rode

Midgley

Bosley

R. Dane

miles 3

km 5

Richard Sutton was present at the swanimote court of 1581.[27] The forestership of Marple and Wybersley already existed in Earl Ranulph III's time, when it was mentioned in a charter of the earl for William Vernon, ancestor of Richard Vernon, who produced the charter at the Macclesfield eyre in 1287.[28] The office remained in the Vernon family until the death of Sir George Vernon in Henry VIII's reign. It was inherited by his daughter Margaret who, with her second husband William Mather, appointed a deputy to attend the swanimote court in 1581.[29] The forestership of Taxal and Downes descended in the Downes family until the death of John Downes in 1621.[30] That attached to land at 'Ratonfeld' was apparently still in the Worth family in 1351, when Thomas Worth was one of the foresters of Macclesfield,[31] but then it passed to the Downes family: an inquest of 1460 found that Robert Downes had died seised of the office, worth 23s. 4d. yearly.[32] A deputy of Roger Downes attended the swanimote court in 1581.

The forestership of High Lee held by Robert Champagne in 1288 had passed to Robert Foxtwist by 1351.[33] Four years after Foxtwist's forfeiture for homicide in 1354[34] his lands and office were granted for life to John Cresswell.[35] In 1411 they were granted to Peter Legh, on the surrender by John Savage of a grant made to him.[36] A further grant was made to Peter Legh in 1438, and the office descended in his family.[37] An inquest of 1528 found that Peter Legh had been seised of land and a forestership in Sutton, and the office was mentioned in 1542.[38] Sir Peter Legh attended the swanimote court in 1581. The forestership held by Jordan Disley in 1288 had apparently passed by 1333 to Richard Pecton, John Makkesone, and John's wife Agnes.[39] John Pecton was a forester in 1351.[40] The later descent is not clear. It may have passed to the Sherd family, represented in 1581 by William Sherd,[41] but the Sherds' forestership may alternatively have been that attached to land at Stanley in Disley held by Roger Stanley in 1288. Richard Stanley was a forester in 1351, and in 1357 he secured licence to enfeoff his daughter Joyce with his serjeanty on her marriage to Roger Simondessone of Mottram.[42] In 1389 John Sherd and Joyce his wife were pardoned for acquiring land in Disley and the office of bailiff of a ninth part of the forestry in fee of Macclesfield, with ultimate reversion to Joyce's heirs,[43] suggesting that John Sherd was Joyce Stanley's second husband.

The forestership held by Thomas Orby in 1288 had been held earlier in Edward I's reign by Richard Orby.[44] By Edward III's reign the office had passed to the Fitton family and in 1351 Thomas Fitton of Gawsworth was a forester. In 1459 Laurence Fitton was said to have died seised of the office, and a deputy for Sir Edward Fitton attended the swanimote court in 1581.[45]

The foresters' privileges[46] included the right to hunt hares, foxes, squirrels, and certain other animals.[47] They were entitled to the fishing, hawks, and eagles in the forest, the right shoulder of every animal taken there and the residue of all beasts found dead, the four quarters having been sent to Macclesfield. They could have holly for their beasts in their own bounds, and outside their bounds when the lord sold the holly. They could also have foggage when the lord sold the foggage. Within their bounds they could take what they needed from the woods for inclosure, building, and fuel without livery from anyone. They had the right to all millstones found in the forest and the bark of trees brought down, were quit of pannage for their own and their men's pigs, and were entitled to have in common the best pig of the lord's pannage and 1d. each every day during the time of pannage.[48]

In 1270 the manor, hundred, and forest of Macclesfield were granted to Eleanor, wife of Edward I, beginning a long period when the lordship of Macclesfield was granted to successive royal ladies. In 1347 the chief forester of Macclesfield was Peter Arderne and the riding forester Robert Legh.[49] In 1353 Sir John Chandos was appointed chief forester, keeper, and surveyor of Macclesfield forest, steward of the manor, and bailiff of the hundred. The post of keeper and surveyor of all the Cheshire forests was created for him in the same year.[50] Chandos was succeeded as surveyor in 1370 by Niel Loring, whose deputy in Macclesfield forest was Peter Legh.[51] In 1385 the earl of Stafford was appointed forester, steward, and bailiff of Macclesfield hundred.[52] Three years earlier Peter Legh and his brother had been appointed bailiffs of Macclesfield and stewards of the hundred and forest courts.[53] In 1391 Peter was appointed to the stewardship of the manor, and in 1395 to the ridership of the forest for life.[54] From 1385 he was named in commissions to hold the three hundreds after the eyre at Macclesfield, and in 1397 was retained in the king's service for life.[55] In 1399, however, he was

[27] Ormerod, *Hist. Ches.* iii. 757–9, 539 n. Sutton was listed as a forester-in-fee in 1581: *26 D.K.R.* App. 2, 115.
[28] *Cal. Chest. Co. Ct. R.* 229–30.
[29] Ormerod, *Hist. Ches.* iii. 839–41, 539 n.
[30] Ibid. 777–9.
[31] *Blk. Prince's Reg.* iii. 15; cf. Ormerod, *Hist. Ches.* iii. 539 n. suggesting that Robert Downes of Shrigley already possessed the forestership in 1342.
[32] *37 D.K.R.* 220; Ormerod, *Hist. Ches.* iii. 703.
[33] *36 D.K.R.* 421 (appointment of John Savage to the forestership formerly of Robert Foxtwist and land in High Lee); *Blk. Prince's Reg.* iii, 15, 43.
[34] *Blk. Prince's Reg.* iii. 172–3.
[35] Ibid. 316–17.
[36] *36 D.K.R.* 297.
[37] *Cal. Pat. 1436–41,* 138.
[38] *39 D.K.R.* 171–2, 172–3.
[39] *28 D.K.R.* 28.
[40] *Blk. Prince's Reg.* iii. 15.
[41] Ormerod, *Hist. Ches.* iii. 830–1.
[42] *Blk. Prince's Reg.* iii. 15, 253; *36 D.K.R.* 443.

[43] *36 D.K.R.* 311.
[44] *29 D.K.R.* 65.
[45] *37 D.K.R.* 278; *39 D.K.R.* 121, 123, 124.
[46] B.L. Cotton MS. Cleop. D. vi, f. 4, printed with a few inaccuracies in Ormerod, *Hist. Ches.* iii. 538 n. appears to be the earliest version; B.L. Harl. MS. 2074, f. 240; J. P. Earwaker, *East Ches.* ii. 7; Chetham Coll. Libr., Adlington MS. Mun. E. 8. 22, f. 155v. printed, with missing words supplied from another version, Renaud, *Ancient Parish of Prestbury,* 197.
[47] *Murilegos, taxos, lodos* (Ormerod); *locaros* (Cotton MS. Cleop. D. vi, f. 4); weasels, otters, pikes (Earwaker).
[48] Earwaker adds 'crokes and baxstones', 'merciaments of all trespassers' in the forest, and pelf.
[49] *Blk. Prince's Reg.* i. 158; Chester 33/6 rot. 36.
[50] *Blk. Prince's Reg.* iii. 53, 95, 122.
[51] *36 D.K.R.* 297, 289.
[52] Ibid. 310.
[53] Ibid. 288.
[54] Ibid. 290–1.
[55] Ibid. 289–91, 310, 311, 181, 296.

executed by Henry Bolingbroke as one of Richard II's principal supporters in Cheshire.[56] In 1400 Thomas Wensley was appointed steward of Macclesfield and surveyor, chief forester, and rider of Macclesfield, Delamere and Mondrem, and was succeeded in these offices in 1403 by John Stanley, steward of Prince Henry's household.[57] In 1414 Stanley was appointed to those offices for life, and in 1439 Ralph, Lord Cromwell, and Thomas Stanley were appointed jointly on surrender by Lord Cromwell of his appointment.[58] In 1459 it was recorded that after the deaths of Cromwell and Stanley the offices passed to Stanley's son Thomas.[59] The chief forestership apparently descended in the Stanley family with the stewardship of the manor.[60] Both offices, together with lands in the forest, were restored to the earl of Derby in 1661.[61] A separate grant of the surveyorship and office of rider was made in 1516 to John Sutton and his heirs, with the controllership of all the king's officers in Macclesfield forest.[62] The earl of Derby, however, held the ridership in 1581.[63]

At the beginning of the 16th century the office occurs of governor of the king's servants in the lordship and forest of Macclesfield; Christopher Savage was appointed to it in 1503, and confirmed in it for life in 1511.[64] Edmund and Richard Savage were appointed to the office in 1531 and John Savage in 1552.[65] The office, described in similar terms to the controllership granted to John Sutton in 1516, may have been identical with the office of bailiff or collector of the forest held by the Savage family since the 15th century. That office can be traced from 1326, when Hugh Meignill was appointed.[66] In Edward III's reign tenure was disputed between Adam Mottram and John Somerford, each of whom claimed it *jure uxoris*.[67] For some years Mottram and Somerford held office in alternate years.[68] In 1381 Henry le Marshall was appointed collector by the princess of Wales, to whom the lordship had been granted, but by 1400 the office was held by John Mottram.[69] In 1409 Mottram surrendered his lands and offices because of his indebtedness, and by 1414 had been replaced by John Savage, previously his deputy.[70] The office descended in the Savage family, ultimately passing to the Cholmondeleys.[71]

Other officers are mentioned. In 1347 there were seven under-foresters, and in Charles I's reign three

keepers and a deputy bow-bearer.[72] The earliest known reference to the regard dates from 1285, when two of the regarders named were described as knights.[73] The regard was mentioned the following year, and regards are known to have been held in 1348 and 1353.[74] Writs for electing regarders were issued in 1404, 1406, and 1412.[75] References to the office were made in 1581 and 1638.[76] There were three verderers and four agisters in 1347.[77] In 1581 the earl of Derby was both verderer and agister, and by the latter date there were also woodwards for some vills. Verderers and woodwards were mentioned as forest officers in 1638.[78]

There are indications of maladministration in the 14th century. In 1325 and 1326 when the lordship was in the king's hands justices were commissioned to investigate various matters there, the commission of 1326 referring to unlicensed assarts, and to the usurpation of fees by the foresters, and of common pasture by the king's tenants.[79] In 1335 the men of Macclesfield forest petitioned for a remedy against Queen Isabel's bailiff, who had taken large quantities of venison and timber, and was refusing to allow anyone to be summoned to the eyre for forest offences.[80] Damage to the forest was one of the subjects of an inquiry ordered by the Black Prince in 1347.[81] The foresters' conduct was evidently unsatisfactory, as in 1347 they were forbidden to take the windfalls which they were claiming, and were to draw their fee only once yearly.[82] In 1358 the justices of the forest were ordered to do right to the foresters after hearing their petitions and claims, but three years later the foresters were threatened with loss of office and forfeiture of their lands if they were not diligent and painstaking.[83]

Though there is a reference to the pleas and perquisites of the manor, borough, hundred, and forest of Macclesfield in 1238–9, there are no details about the administration of forest law until 1285.[84] By that date the justice of Chester was holding an annual eyre at Macclesfield for the pleas of the hundred, the borough, and the forest.[85] In 1285, for example, the forest proceedings included purprestures, the imposition of amercements for trespasses, claims to forest privileges, and fines imposed for animals which had escaped into the forest.[86] In 1288 the steward of Queen Eleanor's forests sat with the justice, and he was also present at the eyre in 1290.[87] The operation of local courts at Macclesfield may be

56 M. V. Clarke and V. H. Galbraith, 'Deposition of Richard II', *Bull. John Rylands Libr.* xiv. 172 (a MS. probably originating from Dieulacres). No evidence has been found to support Adam of Usk's statement that Legh was chief warden of Delamere 'and by authority of that office, had oppressed and ground down the country people': *Chronicon* (ed. Thompson), 26–7, 176–7. The chief forestership of Delamere and Mondrem was, as far as is known, in the possession of the Done family, though Legh may have succeeded Thomas Clifford as surveyor of Macclesfield, Delamere, and Wirral: *36 D.K.R.* 111.
57 *Cal. Pat.* 1399–1401, 31; *36 D.K.R.* 446.
58 *37 D.K.R.* 484.
59 Ibid. 676.
60 Ormerod, *Hist. Ches.* iii. 538; 3 *Sheaf*, xxx, p. 31; *39 D.K.R.*, 95.
61 *Cal. S.P. Dom.* 1660–1, 66.
62 *26 D.K.R.* 29.
63 Ormerod, *Hist. Ches.* iii. 539 n.
64 *37 D.K.R.* 646; *39 D.K.R.* 182.
65 *39 D.K.R.* 182; *Cal. Pat.* 1550–3, 294.
66 *Cal. Pat.* 1324–7, 259.
67 Ormerod, *Hist. Ches.* iii. 540 refers to an inquisition which gives the name of Adam Mottram's wife as Ellen, daughter and co-heir of John *le gaolar*: *Blk. Prince's Reg.* iii. 199.
68 Booth, 'Financ. Admin.' 132–4.
69 *36 D.K.R.* 326; S.C. 6 774/13 m. 1.
70 *36 D.K.R.* 355; Renaud, *Ancient Parish of Prestbury*, 206–7.
71 Ormerod, *Hist. Ches.* iii. 540; Renaud, op. cit. 207–21.
72 Chester 33/6 rot. 36; E 178/5184, f. 2v.
73 *Cal. Chest. Co. Ct. R.* 211.
74 Chester 33/5; Chester 33/6 rot. 40.
75 *36 D.K.R.* 313–14.
76 Ormerod, *Hist. Ches.* iii. 539 n.; E 178/5184 f. 2v.
77 Chester 33/6 rot. 36.
78 Ormerod, *Hist. Ches.* iii. 539 n.; E 178/5184 f. 2v.
79 *Cal. Pat.* 1324–7, 225, 293.
80 *Rot. Parl.* ii. 94.
81 *Blk. Prince's Reg.* i. 157.
82 Ibid. 156–7.
83 Ibid. iii. 291, 428.
84 *Ches. in Pipe R.* 44; *Cal. Chest. Co. Ct. R.* 207–15.
85 *Cal. Chest. Co. Ct. R.* pp. xxix–xxxii.
86 Ibid. 211–14.
87 Ibid. 233, 240.

seen more clearly from the court rolls, surviving from the 14th century. In addition to the justice's eyre and the three hundreds after the eyre, there were courts for the hundred and the borough, and a halmote for the manor and forest. The halmote appears to have fulfilled the functions of a manorial court.[88]

Occasionally justices were specially commissioned to inquire into forest offences. In 1281 two were commissioned to try those who had entered the forest and driven away deer. Men from neighbouring counties were apparently involved, since the jury was to be provided by the justice of Chester and the sheriffs of Staffordshire and Derbyshire.[89] A similar problem arose in 1361 concerning the duke of Lancaster's tenants in Derbyshire and Staffordshire. The Black Prince ordered the justiciar's lieutenant and the duke's steward to hold a court on the boundary of Macclesfield forest.[90] In 1399 Thomas Wensley and others were commissioned to hear complaints that men from Derbyshire and Staffordshire had driven off 700 head of stock into their counties.[91] In 1347 and 1357 Macclesfield was visited by the justices appointed by the Black Prince. The fines imposed on individuals or groups within the community are known to have been heavy at the second eyre. In 1359 the poor tenants of Macclesfield petitioned for a reduction of their fine of £60 to 40 marks.[92] A fine of £162 12s. 8d. was imposed on the earl of Salisbury, £100 on Thomas Fitton of Gawsworth, and £57 1s. 6d. on John Stafford. The burgesses of Macclesfield were fined £40, and the men of the forest £87 for various trespasses and for not lawing their dogs.[93] The fines imposed on Robert Legh and Sir John Hyde were mitigated; Hyde was a bachelor of the Black Prince retained in his service at the time.[94] In 1351 the prince ordered that swanimote courts be held every three weeks by the foresters, and there is evidence for the holding of such courts in Macclesfield from the 15th century.[95]

It is not known how frequently the earls of Chester hunted in Macclesfield. Edward I did so in 1290.[96] By 1347 there was a hunting lodge at the Coombs which the chamberlain was ordered to repair.[97] In 1361 the Black Prince ordered two lodges to be made in Macclesfield hundred to safeguard the game.[98] The chamber was mentioned in the survey of Whelley waste in 1638.[99] It was near the Coombs, which were inclosures for preserving the deer and were mentioned in 1291.[1] In 1301–2 expenditure was recorded for making an inclosure round the chase of Coombs, and in 1303–4 for the wages of eight men who had repaired the lord's share of the fence of the Coombs.[2] The duty of

repairing the hedges rested partly on landholders. In 1345 tenants of Macclesfield hundred claimed that they could not obtain enough wood to make the hedges in the Coombs, and asked to be discharged from their service for a reasonable sum, and for the hedges to be surveyed to see whether it would be more profitable to maintain them or leave them unfinished.[3] In 1355, however, the Black Prince's officials were ordered to have the Coombs inclosed, as the prince had been informed that it could be done cheaply.[4] In 1388 Hamon Bollin was responsible for 72½ roods of the hedge, and for finding 33 men to beset the Coombs (*pro stabilitate facienda*) when the lord hunted there.[5] The duty of providing four pairs of hounds yearly and a huntsman to follow the earl's hounds when he hunted the Coombs was attached to Fernlee and Foe Leigh in Sutton Downes.[6]

Deer from the forest were sometimes taken for the earl's use. In 1353, for example, the Black Prince ordered that six roes be taken from the forest and sent to Chester, evidently in preparation for his visit there.[7] Gifts of deer were also made. In 1247 Roger of Mold received four bucks and two does to stock his park, and in 1363 a hind and a roe deer were given to Thomas Stafford.[8] In 1638 it was stated that the deer chiefly took their summer feed in the Coombs, and their winter feed in Wildboarclough, whither the deer had passage despite the inclosures which had been made.[9]

The forest contained oaks, of which gifts were also made, especially by the Black Prince. In 1365, for instance, five men were given a total of 23 oaks to repair their houses which had fallen down while they were with the prince in Aquitaine.[10] Some gifts of oaks were made from Lyme wood in Lyme Handley. John Davenport received three such gifts from the Black Prince, totalling ten oaks.[11]

The pastures in the forest, which were chiefly in the upland areas, were important for Macclesfield manor. Vaccaries belonging to Queen Eleanor were mentioned in 1285 and 1286.[12] In 1285 it was presented that the queen's bailiffs had made an ox-house at Swyneshurst, where men were living to the great hurt of the forest. By the 14th century horses as well as cattle were bred at Macclesfield.[13] In 1442 the pastures of Saltersford, Harrop, Tod's Cliff, Wildboarclough, Midgeley, and Shutlingsloe were leased to Sir Thomas Stanley for six years at £16 yearly, and grants of the pastures in tail male were made in 1452 and 1462, with escapes of cattle and fines belonging to the same, at an annual rent of £5.[14] The pastures remained in the Stanley family until they were obtained during the Interregnum by Sir William Brereton.[15] They were recovered by the

[88] For courts at Macclesfield 1350–1400 see Booth, 'Financ. Admin.' 300–1.
[89] *Cal. Pat. 1272–81*, 475.
[90] *Blk. Prince's Reg.* iii. 407.
[91] *Cal. Pat. 1399–1401*, 83.
[92] *Blk. Prince's Reg.* iii. 335.
[93] *Ches. Chamb. Accts.* 262.
[94] *Blk. Prince's Reg.* iii. 356–7, 368–9.
[95] Records of the meetings of the swanimote court appear in the rolls of the court of the manor and forest, e.g. S.C. 2/256/7, S.C. 2/285/7.
[96] *Cal. Chest. Co. Ct. R.* 246.
[97] *Blk. Prince's Reg.* i. 158.   [98] Ibid. iii. 407.
[99] E 178/5184 f. 2v.   [1] *Cal. Close 1288–96*, 177.
[2] *Ches. Chamb. Accts.* 9, 44.
[3] *Cal. Pat. 1343–5*, 514.

[4] *Blk. Prince's Reg.* iii. 194–5.
[5] 36 *D.K.R.* 180.
[6] *Blk. Prince's Reg.* iii. 455; 39 *D.K.R.* 121.
[7] *Cal. Lib. 1226–40*, 404; *1245–51*, 137; *Blk. Prince's Reg.* iii. 112.
[8] *Cal. Close, 1242–7*, 157; *Blk. Prince's Reg.* iii. 461.
[9] E 178/5184 ff. 2v.–3.
[10] *Blk. Prince's Reg.* iii. 484.
[11] Ibid. 406, 460, 480.
[12] *Cal. Chest. Co. Ct. R.* 212, 225.
[13] Hewitt, *Med. Ches.* 52–8.
[14] 37 *D.K.R.* 673, 655, 486.
[15] The pastures were confirmed to the earl of Derby in 1640: Lancs. R.O., DDK 11/24; the earl's estates in the forest were sold to Sir William Brereton in 1652: DDK 1462/1.

earl of Derby in 1661, but no rent seems to have been paid after the Restoration, and in 1684 the earl was discharged from payment of his arrears and from any future rent.[16]

Payment for pannage seems to have yielded little, In 1467 pannage was leased with the tolls of markets and fairs in Macclesfield at 13s. 4d. yearly, and in 1482 it was leased with waifs and strays for two years at 13s. 4d.[17] In 1559–60 it was recorded that the sum of 14s. 4d. for the toll of markets with pannage and strays in the forest had been leased to Robert Delahaye in the reign of Henry VIII.[18] Another source of revenue in the 14th century was the iron forges. Two forges, charged to yield over £17 during the financial year 1348–9, would have yielded more but were in the lord's hands because of the pestilence.[19] Coal-mines in the forest were mentioned in 1575.[20] In addition to those sources of profit there were the fines imposed for forest offences, especially at the eyres of 1347 and 1357. From c. 1350 it is possible to work out details of the annual revenue from the forest bailiwick. Between 1350 and 1376 the annual current revenue was usually more than £100, though the value set on the bailiwick at the Black Prince's death was only £88.[21] The current revenue for 1559–60 was made up largely of rents (£69 2s 2½d.), the farm of the park and mill (£15), and the rent from the pastures (£5), which with two other items totalled £89 12s. 10½d.[22]

The forest dwellers enjoyed customary rights. At the eyre of 1285 the townships of Bosley, Bollington, Adlington, Poynton, Norbury, Heppales, Torkington, Rode, and Gawsworth successfully defended their right to cut oaks in their demesne woods without view of the foresters. A claim was made that all forest dwellers could take wood for building, hedging, and fuel without view, but it was decided to speak to the king, and meanwhile the practice was to be prevented by the foresters.[23] The rights evi-

dently derived from the concessions made by Ranulph III in the 'Magna Carta' to barons, knights, and free tenants of the right to take housebote and haybote at will, and to dispose freely of their woods.[24] The town of Macclesfield in 1285 claimed the right to cut oaks in the king's demesne woods without view, and reiterated the claim in 1359 together with a claim to common of pasture and estovers.[25] Details of the commons adjoining townships are given in the survey attributed to the later years of Henry VIII.[26]

Grants of privilege were also made. Those of St. Werburgh's abbey in the Cheshire forests have been discussed above.[27] Dieulacres abbey was granted quittance from payment of pannage in all the Cheshire forests, a liberty exercised in Macclesfield until an attempt was made to prevent it by Queen Eleanor's officials. The abbey's claim was upheld in 1288.[28] Ranulph III granted Marple and Wybersley to William de Vernon with free agistment, pannage, and assarting there, and free agistment and pannage at the pasture of 'Bluntebroc'.[29]

In 1590 the earl of Derby petitioned unsuccessfully for the disafforestation of Macclesfield.[30] A detailed survey of the lordship, including the forest, was made in 1610.[31] At a survey of Whelley waste in 1638 detailed evidence about the forests, including inclosures, commons, courts, and officers, was given, and the chief keeper, Edward Bostock, described the route taken on his walk. There were then still deer in the forest, but, according to one deponent, unless action was taken about the numerous inclosures the king's game would decay and be of little worth.[32] Macclesfield forest effectively came to an end when the earl of Derby acquired outright the pastures which had been leased to his family by the earls of Chester since the 15th century. The pastures were discharged from rent in 1684. Thereafter the forest survived only as an administrative area in connexion with the court of the manor and forest.[33]

WIRRAL

ACCORDING to later tradition the forest came into being when Earl Ranulph I (d. c. 1129) granted the manors of Storeton and Puddington to Alan Sylvester, with a horn as his title to office.[1] The original charter records only the grant of land at Storeton and Puddington to be held as ½ knight's fee, making no reference to the forest, the forestership, or the horn.[2] It has been suggested that the charter was issued by Ranulph II rather than Ranulph I,

between 1129 and 1139.[3] The earliest indication of the forest's existence seems to be in a charter of Ranulph III issued between 1194 and 1208 for the freemen of Wirral, releasing them from maintaining serjeants of the peace other than six foresters on foot, unless circumstances required otherwise.[4]

The forest apparently included the whole of the Wirral peninsula. The most detailed statement about its extent comes from the list of vills contributing to

[16] Ibid. DDK 12/22; DDK 459/10; DDK 1462/1.
[17] 37 D.K.R. 172, 487.
[18] 3 Sheaf, xxiii, p. 52.
[19] Booth, 'Financ. Admin.' 116.
[20] Cal. Pat. 1572–5, p. 412.
[21] Booth, 'Financ. Admin.' 132–4, 305. See also the tables in Sharp, 'Contributions', ii, App. 12, no. 5.
[22] 3 Sheaf, xxiii, pp. 58, 60, 65–7, 70, 82; xxiv, pp. 12, 14, 16–17, 25.
[23] Cal. Chest. Co. Ct. R. 213.
[24] Cart. Chest. Abbey, i. 104.
[25] Cal. Chest. Co. Ct. R. 213; Blk. Prince's Reg. iii. 336, stating that the claim had been allowed at the forest pleas of 13 Edw. III. The names mentioned show that the date should be 13 Edw. I.
[26] Renaud, Ancient Parish of Prestbury, 222–8.

[27] See p. 177.
[28] Cal. Chest. Co. Ct. R. 239.
[29] Ibid. 229.
[30] Cal. S.P. Dom. 1580–91, 655.
[31] E 178/3639. A survey of the lordship of Macclesfield was made 9 Jas. I, L.R. 2/200 ff. 147–358, with details of tenants' holdings.
[32] E 178/5184.
[33] Ormerod, Hist. Ches. iii. 541.
[1] Ormerod, Hist. Ches. ii. 355.
[2] John Rylands Libr. Chart., no. 1807.
[3] R. Stewart-Brown, 'The Charter and Horn of the Master Forester of Wirral', T.H.S.L.C. lxxxvii. 97–112. A photograph of the horn faces p. 107.
[4] Stewart-Brown, Serjeants of Peace, 118.

the fine for disafforestation in 1384–5.[5] They were all within the boundaries of the hundred as fixed after 1086, and the creation of the forest may explain why the eastern boundary of the hundred was altered at some date later than Domesday Book.[6] The forest was apparently co-extensive with the later hundred.

The peninsula was relatively densely populated in 1086, and references to woodland there were infrequent in Domesday Book.[7] Land clearance seems later to have made considerable progress. St. Werburgh's abbey was an important landholder in the peninsula, and abbots are often found assarting land, cutting down timber, and digging marl-pits.[8] Nevertheless, the 'wilderness of Wirral', mentioned in *Sir Gawain and the Green Knight*, was a resort for bands of armed men in the later 14th century.[9]

In 1361 William Stanley, citing earlier evidence, claimed that the forestership which had been conferred on Alan Sylvester descended in his family to his great-granddaughters, Joan and Agnes. Joan died without heirs, so the office passed to Agnes and her husband, Thomas de Baumvill, and thence to their son Philip de Baumvill, whose forest office was mentioned in the inquest of service of 1288.[10] Philip died leaving three daughters of whom one, Joan, the wife of William Stanley, inherited the forestership.[11] The office descended in the Stanley family, William Stanley being chief forester at disafforestation in 1376.[12]

The chief forester was assisted by six foresters on foot who, according to Ranulph III's charter, could take hospitality or puture throughout Wirral except in the four manors of Eastham, Bromborough, Irby, and Sutton belonging to St. Werburgh's abbey.[13] In Edward III's reign the obligation to provide puture was disputed. In 1351 John Domville, who held two vills in the forest, refused to feed the foresters, and forbade his tenants to do so.[14] At the trailbaston court two years later jurors of various hundreds presented that the foresters had often gone to men's houses with horses and grooms to exact their puture, though by right liability was limited to foresters on foot.[15] Puture was among the rights claimed by William Stanley at the forest eyres of 1347 and 1357. On the earlier occasion he claimed the right to take money in lieu of puture from certain vills, a practice which had grown up in Edward I's reign. In 1361 when his son, also William, sought possession of the forestership, it was found that the chief forester was entitled to take money from some vills and puture in kind from the remainder.[16]

As chief forester William Stanley in 1347 claimed other privileges also, including money for animals that escaped into the forest, the right shoulder of any beast found, the hide and offal of any beasts found wounded, and pelf. William also claimed his office and profits in 1357, but he died before a settlement was reached. His son William secured possession of the office in 1361, but escape money and pelf were exempted from his profits of office.[17]

The patent issued by Edward III in November 1376 confirming the disafforestation of Wirral stated that the inheritance of William Stanley was not to be prejudiced thereby, and all those who used to contribute to his puture and profits were to continue doing so.[18] That he continued to claim his office and profits is clear from the releases he afterwards granted from the payment of puture, and from the inspeximus made in 1387 of his earlier claims.[19] In 1397 he was granted an annuity of 20 marks for the loss of his profits of office, and when the annuity was confirmed to his son in 1398 reference was made to the office of which he had been disseised without right.[20] The Stanley forestership was mentioned as late as 1512.[21]

By the beginning of the 14th century the office of rider had emerged. In 1302 the office was held by Walter de Mundham with a daily wage of 6d.[22] William Stafford, yeoman of the Black Prince's chamber, was appointed in 1341 and was still in office in 1354–5.[23] The office of under-rider appears in 1353.[24]

Regards were being held in the forest by the later 13th century. According to William Stanley's account for 1349–50 they were held every third year, but references to them occur only irregularly.[25] Several are known to have been held in Edward I's reign.[26] The names of the twelve regarders for 1286 survive; two are described as knights. They inspected purprestures and other articles of the regard by view of Richard Massey, the deputy justice of Chester, and Richard Hemington, the chamberlain's clerk. Regards are also known to have been held in 1347 and in 1350 or 1351.[27] The latter should have been held in the preceding year, but was postponed until the arrival of the Black Prince's council. That which should have been held in 1353 was postponed until the next eyre, which took place in 1357.[28] A verderer was mentioned in the petition of the men of Wirral in 1351.[29] No reference has been found to the holding of the swanimote courts which were instituted by the Black Prince in the same year.[30]

A petition of 1351 claimed that men had been indicted by the verderer, the forester, and twelve others for hunting vermin, and were denied mainprise or deliverance unless they paid a ransom to

[5] Chester 33/8, printed by Stewart-Brown, 'The Disafforestation of Wirral', *T.H.S.L.C.* lix. 174–80; cf. Ormerod, *Hist. Ches.* ii. 356.
[6] In 1086 the hundred of 'Wilaveston' included several townships later in Broxton hundred: *P.N. Ches.* (E.P.N.S.) iv. 167. For later boundaries of hundred and probably of forest, see map.
[7] *Dom. Geog. Northern Eng.*, ed. Darby and Maxwell, 357.
[8] Hewitt, *Med. Ches.* 10–14.
[9] *Sir Gawain and the Green Knight*, ed. J. R. R. Tolkien and E. V. Gordon (1967), 20; *36 D.K.R.* 189.
[10] *Cal. Chest. Co. Ct. R.* 116.
[11] *Cal. Fine R. 1272–1307*, 200.
[12] *Cal. Pat. 1374–7*, 378.
[13] Stewart-Brown, *Serjeants of Peace*, 118.
[14] *Blk. Prince's Reg.* iii. 34.
[15] Chester 29/65 rot. 4d.

[16] *Blk. Prince's Reg.* iii. 429–36.
[17] Ibid.
[18] *Cal. Pat. 1374–7*, 378.
[19] *T.H.S.L.C.* lix. 167–8; Ormerod, *Hist. Ches.* ii. 355–6.
[20] *36 D.K.R.* 445.
[21] *39 D.K.R.* 244.
[22] *Ches. Chamb. Accts.* 6, 24.
[23] Ibid. 229.
[24] Chester 33/2, doc. attached in front of rot. 1; Chester 29/65 m. 4; cf. *Blk. Prince's Reg.* iii. 38.
[25] *Ches. Chamb. Accts.* 147.
[26] Chester 33/1 rott. 9–12; Chester 33/2.
[27] Chester 33/4 rot. 12; *Ches. Chamb. Accts.* 147, 200.
[28] *Ches. Chamb. Accts.* 207.
[29] *Blk. Prince's Reg.* iii. 25–6.
[30] Ibid. 16.

the lord; also that accusations had been made by the same men for venison and other trespasses without the verdict of an inquisition.[31] Oppressive practices by the foresters were brought forward at the trailbaston court of 1353. William Stanley was found guilty of taking money from certain townships for allowing tenants to pasture their flocks in the woods in the time of fawning. He also admitted taking hens and forced labour from the townships in harvest time. The under-rider had taken a boat against the owners' will, had damaged it, and refused to make amends. He was also found guilty of two charges of assault. The foresters were acquitted of a more general charge of intimidating the common people.[32]

Details of the proceedings against forest offenders survive from the later 13th century. Breaches of forest law were dealt with by the justice, and special investigations were also sometimes ordered.[33] In 1304 the inquiry into assarts and purprestures by justices of oyer and terminer extended to Wirral, and in 1333 an inquisition was ordered to discover whether the abbot of St. Werburgh's had assarted any waste; he was said to have assarted 400 a. without licence.[34]

Wirral was subjected to a forest eyre in 1347, as were the other forests, and many offences were reported. Assarts, destruction of timber, and the digging of marl-pits were recorded. Claims to forest privileges were also dealt with.[35] Petitions were sent to the Black Prince about privileges from the abbeys of St. Werburgh's and Basingwerk and the earl of Salisbury. St. Werburgh's claimed the right to make new ploughings and marl-pits on its demesne soil, and to take estovers without view of the foresters. Basingwerk complained that, although its privileges had been proved, a fine had been exacted. The earl of Salisbury protested against the foresters' actions at his exempt manor of Neston. Another petition to the Black Prince was made by Henry Hooton who objected to the building of two hunting stations and the seizure into the prince's hand of a plot of land, most of which he had lawfully assarted.[36]

In 1351 the prince issued instructions for the Cheshire forests which had the effect of curtailing customary privileges, and the men of Wirral jointly with the men of Delamere and Mondrem listed their grievances in two petitions.[37] Two of the issues were the taking of estovers and the lawing of dogs. The prince's instructions had laid down strict conditions for the taking of estovers, but the men of Delamere, Mondrem, and Wirral claimed the right to take them without view. Following their petitions the prince ordered that in Wirral estovers should be surveyed and allotted each year.[38] It had also been claimed in one of the petitions that the free tenants of Delamere and Mondrem and the lords and parceners of towns in Wirral were always accustomed to keep greyhounds and dogs unlawed for hunting the hare, the fox, and

other vermin. The fine on the men of Wirral was reduced to £20,[39] but apparently William Stanley and John Lassels argued that they had not consented to pay, and in 1353 it was suggested that the whole hundred had agreed to the fine and that every lord and parcener should therefore be charged.[40]

The fines imposed on individuals at the eyre were heavy, and in 1351 it was decided to make proportionate reductions according to means. When sounded about their willingness to pay, those involved offered a joint fine of 100 marks for a general pardon. They further stipulated that they should be allowed to hunt the hare and fox, and that point seems to have been conceded. The prince's reply was to imprison those who refused to pay, though they were released shortly afterwards on giving security for their fines. The fine of 100 marks was apparently accepted.[41] The prince was lenient to Hamon Massey, whose fine was reduced to £3 6s. 8d.; he was pardoned 5s. 4d. for an unlawed dog.[42]

In 1357 Wirral was again subjected to a forest eyre. On that occasion the community negotiated a fine of £1,000, for new ploughings and sowing land with corn, waste and destruction of woods, building houses and windmills, making bricks, and trespasses of vert and venison.[43] In 1363 the Black Prince ordered the chamberlain to send the indenture which he had made with the men of Wirral to London, as they had asked him for a charter of pardon when the payments were complete. A transcript of what seems to be such a charter of pardon survives.[44]

References were made in the 14th century to 'tristres' or hunting stations, but none has been found to a hunting lodge or to hunting by the earls.[45] The forest was stocked with red and fallow deer which were sometimes taken for the earl's use. In 1363, for example, the Black Prince ordered 100 harts and 100 bucks to be taken, salted, and packed in barrels, and sent to him at Bordeaux.[46] In the following year it was reported that William Stanley had taken 18 harts, 49 bucks, 1 soar, 3 sorels, and 1 pricket in the last season of grease, and 5 prickets, 4 hinds, 13 does, 2 stags, 3 calves, and 11 fawns in the last season of fermeson.[47] Gifts of deer are also recorded. In 1244, for instance, the justice of Chester was allowed to take 10 does in the forest as a present for his wife.[48]

In 1244 the justice was ordered to have built four wooden towers in the forest, but the state of the woodland already seems to have been causing concern by 1251, when the knights and free tenants were ordered to deal with their woods only as they had in Earl Ranulph's time.[49] The forest rolls bear witness to the destruction of timber from Edward I's reign. Many cases of felling trees were reported at the eyre of 1347, and in 1351 the Black Prince ordered that the woods which had been taken in hand because of the destruction of vert were not to be delivered

---

[31] *Blk. Prince's Reg.* iii. 25–6.
[32] Chester 29/65 rott. 4–4d.
[33] The earliest reference to forest proceedings in Wirral seems to be that in *Cal. Inq. Misc.* i, pp. 297–8, referring to action taken by Thos. Bolton, justice 1267–70.
[34] *Cal. Pat. 1301–7*, 238; *Cal. Fine R. 1327–37*, 351.
[35] Chester 33/4 rott. 1–5d., 12–15d., 20–33.
[36] *Blk. Prince's Reg.* iii. 21–4.
[37] Ibid. 24–6.
[38] Ibid. 34.
[39] Ibid. 27.
[40] Ibid. 102.

[41] Ibid. 12, 30–1, 33, 36; *Ches. Chamb. Accts.* 168–9.
[42] *Blk. Prince's Reg.* iii. 94, 98.
[43] *Ches. Chamb. Accts.* 247.
[44] *Blk. Prince's Reg.* iii. 458; B.L. Harl. MS. 2022, f. 9c.
[45] *Blk. Prince's Reg.* iii. 24.
[46] Ibid. 458.
[47] Ibid. 466. For seasons of grease (3 May to 14 Sept.) and fermeson (11 Nov. to 2 Feb.), *Sel. Pleas of the Forest* (Selden Soc. xiii), 146, 142.
[48] *Cal. Close, 1242–7*, 275.
[49] *Cal. Lib. 1240–5*, 247; *Cal. Pat. 1247–58*, 106.

without a special order.[50] In 1358 William Stanley was allowed to take four oaks from Greves in Puddington because the prince had heard that William had no wood for fuel in the forest.[51] Six years later William was licensed to receive brushwood at Somerton from those who were willing to give it to him for his household use and fuel.[52]

Apart from the deer Wirral by the 14th century was chiefly important as a source of revenue, most of which came from fines imposed for breaches of the forest laws. In 1349–50 the chief forester reported that there was no revenue from agistment or pannage because the lord had no soil in the forest, and, because no regard was held in that year, no income was received.[53]

Customary rights in the forest were mostly similar to those in Delamere and Mondrem, as the joint petitions of 1351 make clear. In Wirral, however, unlike Delamere and Mondrem, lawing of dogs did take place. In 1275 an inquisition found that abbots, priors, knights, and freeholders who were lords of towns or moieties of towns were used to keeping dogs unlawed.[54] A court for lawing dogs was held in 1311 before the justice.[55] Fines were imposed on those whose dogs were unlawed. The last court of survey was said to have been held before Robert Holland, justice from 1307 to 1309. In 1348 the chief forester and the rider were ordered to hold an inquisition into unlawed dogs and to impose fines of 5s. 4d. or one ox for each dog found unlawed.[56] Following the claim, made in 1351, that lords or parceners of vills could keep unlawed dogs, the fines which had been imposed were reduced.[57]

Assarting practice may have been different in Wirral. Ranulph III had conceded liberty to his barons, knights, and free tenants to assart within the limits of their husbandry within the forests; in Delamere, Mondrem, and Macclesfield a charge was made for assarts. The inquisition of 1275 found that the men of Wirral had the right to assart according to the terms of Earl Ranulph's charter, but that they had been attached for such ploughings in the time of two justices of Chester.[58] It may be inferred that the men of Wirral were being charged contrary to custom,[59] but according to another source a payment of 5s. for each acre of heath and 6s. 8d. for each acre of wood assarted was made to the earl.[60]

Privileges in the forest were granted to St. Werburgh's abbey, which was exempt from puture for foresters in its four manors in Wirral,[61] and to John of Gaunt, who received a licence to hunt hares and foxes in 1359.[62] Stanlow abbey, with its grange at Stanney in the forest, was disafforested by Ranulph III.[63]

Wirral was disafforested in 1376 by a charter of Edward III in accordance with the Black Prince's wish expressed shortly before his death in that year. It is possible that the prince issued some sort of document to disafforest Wirral but did not live to execute it. Letters patent later in 1376 confirmed the charter. Because there had been no inquisition *ad quod damnum* the commonalty of Wirral petitioned for a statute to confirm the charter and letters patent, alleging as reasons for the disafforestation the damage caused by the beasts of the forest, the destruction of parish churches and the withdrawal of services there, and the impoverishment of the inhabitants by the forest regulations. Although no other evidence has been found of the destruction of churches, there can be no doubt about the inconvenience to the inhabitants. There is no indication that a statute was enacted. In 1384–5, however, a fine of 600 marks was made with Richard II for disafforestation. The inhabitants of Wirral were evidently prepared to pay to ensure that the disafforestation would be allowed.[64]

---

[50] Chester 33/4 rott. 1–5d.; *Blk. Prince's Reg.* iii. 10.
[51] 36 *D.K.R.* 443.
[52] *Blk. Prince's Reg.* iii. 466.
[53] *Ches. Chamb. Accts.* 147.
[54] *Cal. Inq. Misc.* i, pp. 297–8.
[55] Chester 29/24 rott. 5–5d. (reference supplied by Mr. P. H. W. Booth).
[56] Chester 33/2 doc. attached before rot. 1.
[57] *Blk. Prince's Reg.* iii. 27.

[58] *Cal. Inq. Misc.* i, pp. 297–8.
[59] Hewitt, *Med. Ches.* 11–12.
[60] 3 *Sheaf*, iv, p. 64.
[61] Stewart-Brown, *Serjeants of Peace*, 118.
[62] *Blk. Prince's Reg.* iii. 334.
[63] *Coucher Bk. Whalley Abbey*, i (Chetham Soc. [1st ser.] x), 11–12.
[64] *Cal. Pat.* 1374–7, 378; *T.H.S.L.C.* lix. 170–80. Mr. Booth is thanked for his opinion on the disafforestation.

POPULATION TABLE 1801–1971

THE population table printed below follows the pattern of those published for Leicestershire, Wiltshire, and Shropshire.[1] It shows the population of every area mentioned as a parish or as a distinct part of a parish for civil administrative purposes in any *Census Report* between 1801 and 1971, and that of the more important of the other local government areas for which totals have been struck.[2] The administrative areas chosen for inclusion are ancient counties (1801–1901) and administrative counties (1891–1971), hundreds (1801–81), urban and rural districts (1881–1971), boroughs (1801–41), municipal boroughs (1851–1971), and county boroughs (1891–1971), ancient parishes (1801–71), townships, chapelries (1801–71),[3] and civil parishes (1881–1971). The population is always expressed for the areas contituted at the date of the census concerned. The choice of areas, and the dates at which each is given, have depended on a series of alterations made in the 19th century both in the conduct and in the areas of local government.[4]

Counties. Under the Divided Parishes Acts, 1876–82, changes were made in parish boundaries, as a result of which part of Warrington C.P.[5] which lay in Lancashire was transferred to Latchford C.P. in Cheshire. The Local Government Act, 1888, created administrative counties, which were in many cases, though not in Cheshire, identical with ancient counties. Where an urban sanitary district extended into two counties, it was taken to be in that administrative county which contained most of its population. In 1888 Cheshire was thus enlarged by the addition of parts of Stockport C.B. and Stalybridge M.B. which were formerly in Lancashire, and diminished by the deduction of parts of Mossley U.S.D. and Warrington C.B. which were transferred to Lancashire and part of New Mills U.S.D. which was transferred to Derbyshire. Differences between ancient and administrative counties were increased by the Local Government Act, 1894, which made possible adjustments of county boundaries to conform with those of civil parishes and rural districts, similar to those made for urban districts under the former Act. In 1895 Tittenley C.P. was transferred to Shropshire; in 1896 part of Latchford C.P. (extended to include parts of Appleton, Walton Inferior, and Latchford Without C.P.s) was transferred to Lancashire, and in 1898 part of Dukinfield C.P. was similarly transferred to Lancashire.[6] In 1896 the boundaries of Cheshire were extended to include part of Threapwood, transferred from Flint, and in 1898 part of Ashton-under-Lyne C.P., transferred from Lancashire.[7] In 1901 Reddish U.D. and part of Heaton Norris C.P. were transferred from Lancashire to Cheshire, and a further part of Heaton Norris was added in 1913.[8] In 1931 Baguley, Northenden, and Northen Etchells C.P.s were transferred to Manchester C.B.[9] Cheshire was also affected by changes made under the Local Government Act, 1929. In 1936 parts of Yeardsley cum Whaley U.D., of Disley C.P., of Kettleshulme C.P., and of Taxal C.P. were transferred to Derbyshire, and parts of Grappenhall C.P., Walton Inferior C.P., Lymm U.D., Acton Grange C.P., Moore C.P., Norton C.P., and Thelwall C.P. to Lancashire. At the same date Ludworth and Mellor C.P.s were transferred from Derbyshire to Cheshire. In 1933, 1935, and 1936 an exchange of territory also took place between the administrative county and the county boroughs. Further exchanges were made in 1952 and 1954.[10]

Hundreds were included in all the *Census Reports* until 1881. The constituent parishes of hundreds in 1831 are shown on pp. 190–2 with notes to show differences 1801–21 and 1841. From 1851 to 1881 the *Census Reports* give the total population of each hundred exclusive of municipal boroughs within it, but do not show their constituent parishes.

Urban and rural districts first appeared as urban and rural sanitary districts under the Public Health Act, 1872. Rural sanitary districts were based upon the poor-law unions, comprising the remainder of the unions

---

[1] For an explanation of the difference between the Leics. and Wilts. tables and previous population tables published in the *V.C.H.* and of the reason for the new pattern, see *V.C.H. Leics.* iii. 176. Cf. *V.C.H. Wilts.* iv. 315–17.

[2] e.g. no figures are given for ecclesiastical, parliamentary, petty sessional, or registration areas, for poor-law unions, or for wards of boroughs and urban districts.

[3] To reduce the length of the table, the population of townships for which totals were struck on not more than two occasions, 1801–71, is given not in the table itself but in the notes at the foot of each page.

[4] For a full explanation of the changes in the areas treated in the *Census Reports* see Inter-Departmental Cttee. on Soc. and Econ. Research, *Guides to Official Sources, No. 2: Census Reports, 1801–1931*, 95–104.

[5] For abbreviations used see note at beginning of population table.

[6] 58 & 59 Vic. c. 86 (Local); Loc. Govt. Bd. Order, P. 1, 167 (9 Nov. 1896); Loc. Govt. Bd. Order, P. 1,416 (9 Nov. 1898).

[7] 59 & 60 Vic. c. 236 (Local); Loc. Govt. Bd. Order, P. 1,416 (9 Nov. 1898).

[8] Loc. Govt. Bd.'s Prov. Orders Conf. (No. 11) Act, 1 Edw. VII, c. 169; Loc. Govt. Bd.'s Prov. Orders Conf. (No. 13) Act, 3 & 4 Geo. V, c. 137.

[9] Manchester Extension Act, 20 & 21 Geo. V, c. 173.

[10] Stockport (Extension) Order, Statutory Instrument, 1952, no. 588; Chester (Extension) Order, Statutory Instrument, 1954, no. 317.

after the urban sanitary districts had been taken out. The urban sanitary districts were co-extensive with the city of Chester and the municipal boroughs then existing, namely Birkenhead, Congleton, Crewe, Hyde, Macclesfield, and the parts of Stalybridge, Stockport and Warrington in Cheshire, together with those areas controlled by improvement act commissioners or by local boards of health.[11] The functions of a sanitary authority became an integral part of every borough council's responsibilities. The Local Government Act, 1894, changed the rural sanitary districts and those urban sanitary districts which were not in municipal or county boroughs into rural and urban districts respectively. That Act and the Local Government Act, 1929, authorized changes in the number and area of the districts.

The constituent civil parishes of urban districts are grouped in the population table under the urban districts, since the districts form compact and administratively unified areas: in most cases a civil parish co-extensive with the urban district was created. Civil parishes in urban districts ceased to exist as units of local government under the Local Government Act, 1933. Nevertheless the population of urban civil parishes was included in the *Census Report* of 1951. Where changes in the boundaries of urban districts are mentioned in the *Census Reports* they have been shown in the notes to the population table. Where the date of the district's formation is not mentioned it may be assumed to have been formed in 1872.

The constituent civil parishes of rural districts are shown on pp. 193–200 where a brief history of each district is also given. Changes in the boundaries of rural districts have been so frequent and complex that it has not been possible to describe them in the notes to the population table, and apparently large changes in the population of rural districts must thus be considered with caution. Since changes which involved the transfer or amalgamation of whole parishes are shown in the list on pp. 193–200, reference to that list makes possible a rough comparison of population at different dates, but for exact comparison the figures and notes for each constituent parish should also be consulted.

Boroughs and municipal boroughs. The subdivision of boroughs into municipal and parliamentary was necessitated by the Parliamentary Reform Act, 1832, which took away parliamentary representation from some boroughs, created new ones with parliamentary status, and altered the parliamentary limits of others. The Municipal Corporations Act, 1835, confirmed the position of all the Cheshire municipal boroughs except Altrincham, which became a municipal borough only in 1937, and Over. Of the Cheshire municipal boroughs Congleton included the same area as the ancient borough, but Chester, Macclesfield, and Stockport were larger, as was Warrington, which was chiefly situated in Lancashire but extended into Cheshire. Ten municipal boroughs were created subsequently, Stalybridge in 1857,[12] Birkenhead and Crewe in 1877, Hyde in 1881, Dukinfield in 1899, Wallasey in 1910, Sale in 1936, Altrincham and Bebington in 1937, and Ellesmere Port in 1955. Birkenhead, Chester, and Stockport were constituted county boroughs under the provisions of the Local Government Act, 1888, and Wallasey became a county borough in 1913.

Parishes. Most figures in the population table relate to parishes or parts of parishes, and the alterations in the boundaries and status of parishes are the most important factors influencing the form of the table.[13]

An ancient parish divided between two or more hundreds is entered only once in the table, with the total population of all its parts together. The distribution of those parts, however, is shown in the table of hundreds.

In 1871 areas which levied their own poor-rates were renamed civil parishes, but the grouping under ancient parishes was retained in the *Census Reports* until 1881, although ancient parishes as such had no civil significance by then. For the purpose of the table it has been found best to make the change between 1871 and 1881. Urban and rural districts first appeared in the 1881 *Census Report*, and the new grouping under urban districts can, where necessary, follow upon the grouping under ancient parishes. The component parts of the latter are therefore grouped in the table under the appropriate ancient parishes until 1871, while from 1881 each civil parish has a separate entry unless it was part of an urban district. Cross-references and notes make it possible to trace the changes.

The boundaries of parishes have undergone many changes. By an Act of 1857[14] extra-parochial places were made into parishes for poor-relief purposes, unless they were very small, in which case, if the owners and occupiers of two-thirds of the land consented, they were annexed to an adjoining parish. By another Act of 1868[15] any extra-parochial place which had evaded the provisions of the earlier Act was joined to the civil parish with which it had the longest common boundary. The Divided Parishes Acts of 1876, 1879, and 1882 provided for the annexation of detached parts of civil parishes to one or more of the surrounding civil parishes. The Local Government Act, 1888, permitted the alteration of civil parish boundaries and

[11] See pp. 77–9.
[12] Part of Stalybridge M.B. was in Lancs. The entire M.B. was included in the admin. co. of Ches. created in 1888.
[13] *Census*, 1801, is particularly unreliable in its general description of nearly every place as a 'parish'. The un-

reliability was admitted in the intro. to *Census*, 1811, and the status of places given in 1801 has therefore been ignored.
[14] Act for Relief of Poor in E.P.P.s, 20 Vic. c. 19.
[15] Poor Law Amendment Act, 31 & 32 Vic. c. 122.

the amalgamation of civil parishes by Local Government Board orders. Under the Local Government Act, 1894, a civil parish divided between two urban districts or between a rural and an urban district became two separate civil parishes.

Place-names. The spelling of place-names follows in general that of the Ordnance Survey.

Census Reports. The figures of population are based solely upon the information given in the *Census Reports.* From 1801 to 1831 the returns were usually made by the parish overseers. More than one day was allowed for enumeration, and the army (including the militia), navy, seamen in registered shipping, and convicts in the hulks were omitted from parish totals. The militia was included in the county total in 1811. From 1841 the conduct of the census passed to the General Register Office, the enumeration was more strictly completed on the fixed day, and members of the classes formerly excluded from the returns were included in the parishes in which they happened to pass the night of the census. The dates of the censuses were:[16]

10 Mar. 1801	5 Apr. 1891
27 May 1811	31 Mar. 1901
28 May 1821	2 Apr. 1911
30 May 1831	19 June 1921
6 June 1841	26 Apr. 1931
30 Mar. 1851	8 Apr. 1951
7 Apr. 1861	23 Apr. 1961
2 Apr. 1871	25 Apr. 1971
3 Apr. 1881	

The notes and commentary. Changes in boundaries and comments on extraordinary changes in administrative status are shown in the notes on each page of the table. The notes do not purport to supply a complete list of such changes: all those recorded in the *Census Reports* are included in the notes, except those involving very small areas without population, but the *Census Reports* are not, apparently, comprehensive. It is improbable, however, that important changes have been omitted.

The explanations in the *Census Reports* of the reasons for particular changes in population, apart from boundary changes, have been formed into a separate commentary (below, pp. 241–9), where their chronological arrangement makes it easier to trace social and economic changes in the county as a whole. An asterisk (*) placed by the relevant figure in the table indicates the existence of such a note.

Acreages of parishes, though included in population tables in some earlier volumes of the *Victoria County History,* have been excluded from the Cheshire table. Acreages were first expressed in the *Census Report* in 1831, when they were calculated on a system devised by John Rickman. Some were corrected in 1851 from information derived from Tithe Commission records and Ordnance Survey maps.[17] Later, at varying dates, the figures were again amended from information received from the Ordnance Survey department. After 1881 boundary changes which significantly affected areas were described in the *Census Reports* and the descriptions have been copied in the notes to the table. Small changes were apparently not always notified and the assessment of acreages seems sometimes to have varied slightly. It would therefore be difficult to choose a date for which areas could be given with equal certainty for all parishes. To have supplied all the different assessments given in the *Census Reports* would have added greatly to the complexity of the table.

THE HUNDREDS AND THEIR CONSTITUENT PARISHES

THIS list of the hundreds, their divisions, and their constituent parishes is chiefly based on the *Census Report* of 1831. Extra-parochial places are included. The footnotes show differences in the constituent parishes, 1801–21 and 1841. After 1851 the *Census Reports* grouped parishes under registration districts and gave only the total population of the hundreds. Where a parish is divided the location of the other part of the parish is shown in the footnotes.

[16] *Guides to Official Sources No. 2,* p. 2; *Census,* 1971.   [17] *Guides to Official Sources No. 2,* pp. 14, 20.

HUNDREDS AND THEIR PARISHES

BROXTON

Higher Division

Aldford (part of)[1]
Bunbury (part of)[2]
Coddington
Farndon
Handley (part of)[3]
Harthill
Kingsmarsh
Malpas (part of)[4]
Shocklach
Threapwood[5]
Tilston

Lower Division

Aldford (part of)[6]
Backford (part of)[7]
Christleton
Dodleston (part of)[8]
Eccleston
Handley (part of)[9]
Plemstall (part of)[10]
Pulford
St. Mary (part of)[11]
St. Oswald (part of)[12]
Sutton, Guilden
Tarvin (part of)[13]
Tattenhall
Waverton

BUCKLOW

Ashton upon Mersey
Bowdon[14]
Budworth, Great (part of)[15]
Grappenhall
Knutsford

Lymm
Mobberley
Rostherne (part of)[16]
Runcorn

EDDISBURY

First Division

Budworth, Little
Bunbury (part of)[17]
Delamere[18]
Middlewich (part of)[19]
Over
St. Oswald's (part of)[20]

Second Division

Barrow
Budworth, Great (part of)[21]
Frodsham
Plemstall (part of)[22]
Tarvin (part of)[23]
Thornton le Moors

[1] i.e. Aldford, Churton by Aldford. The remainder of Aldford A.P. is in Broxton hundred, lower division.

[2] i.e. Burwardsley. The remainder of Bunbury A.P. is in Eddisbury hundred, first division.

[3] i.e. Handley. The remainder of Handley A.P. is in Broxton hundred, lower division.

[4] Extends into Maylor hundred (Flints.).

[5] In 1841 Threapwood, an E.P.P., was returned as partly situated in the higher division of Broxton hundred, and partly in Maylor hundred, Flints., where it was returned 1801-31.

[6] i.e. Buerton and Edgerley. The remainder of Aldford A.P. is in Broxton hundred, higher division. The tns. of Great Boughton and the chap. of Churton Heath in St. Oswald's A.P. were wrongly returned as part of Aldford A.P. in Broxton hundred, lower division, 1811-31. No return was made for Edgerley tns. in 1811.

[7] i.e. Caughall. The remainder of Backford A.P. is in Wirral hundred, higher division.

[8] i.e. Dodleston, Lower Kinnerton. Dodleston A.P. extends into Maylor hundred (Flints.).

[9] i.e. Golborne David. The remainder of Handley A.P. is in Broxton hundred (higher division).

[10] i.e. Hoole, Picton, Mickle Trafford. The remainder of Plemstall A.P. is in Eddisbury hundred, second division. The tns. of Caughall was returned in Plemstall A.P. in 1811.

[11] i.e. Marlston cum Lache, Moston, Upton-by-Chester. Gloverstone was returned in St. Mary's A.P. in 1811. St. Mary's A.P. extends into Wirral hundred (higher division) and into the city of Chester.

[12] i.e. Bache, Huntington, Lea Newbold, Newton by Chester, Saighton, Wervin. St. Oswald's A.P. extends into Eddisbury hundred (first division), Wirral hundred (higher division), and the city of Chester.

[13] i.e. Foulk Stapleford. Tarvin A.P. is mainly in Eddis-

bury hundred (second division).

[14] Agden and Bollington tns. are partly in Bowdon and partly in Rostherne A.P.s.

[15] i.e. Anderton, Antrobus, Appleton, Aston by Budworth, Barnton, Bartington, Great Budworth, Cogshall, Comberbach, Crowley, Dutton, Little Leigh, Marbury, Marston, Peover Inferior, Pickmere, Plumley, Seven Oaks, Stretton, Tabley Inferior, Lower Whitley, Over Whitley, Wincham. Great Budworth A.P. extends into Eddisbury hundred (second division) and Northwich hundred.

[16] i.e. Agden (part of), Bollington (part of), High Legh, Marthall cum Warford, Mere, Millington, Peover Superior, Rostherne, Tabley Superior, Tatton. Agden was returned under Bowdon A.P., 1811-41. In 1811 Bollington was entirely returned under Bowdon A.P.

[17] i.e. Alpraham, Beeston, Bunbury, Calveley, Haughton, Peckforton, Ridley, Spurstow, Tilstone Fearnall, Tiverton, Wardle. Part of Bunbury A.P. is in Broxton hundred (higher division).

[18] Delamere A.P. was created in 1812 by the inclosure of Delamere forest.

[19] i.e. Weaver. Middlewich A.P. is mainly in Northwich hundred.

[20] i.e. Iddinshall. St. Oswald's A.P. extends into Broxton hundred (lower division), Wirral hundred (higher division), and the city of Chester.

[21] i.e. Castle Northwich, Hartford, Winnington. Great Budworth A.P. extends into Bucklow and Northwich hundreds.

[22] i.e. Bridge Trafford. Plemstall A.P. extends into Broxton hundred (lower division).

[23] i.e. Ashton, Burton, Clotton Hoofield, Duddon, Hockenhull, Horton cum Peel, Kelsall, Mouldsworth, Bruen Stapleford, Tarvin. Part of Tarvin A.P. is in Broxton hundred (lower division).

First Division	*Second Division*
Tarporley	Weaverham
Whitegate	Willington E.P.P.

MACCLESFIELD

Alderley	Prestbury[25]
Astbury (part of)[24]	Rostherne (part of)[26]
Cheadle	Stockport
Gawsworth	Taxal
Mottram in Longdendale	Wilmslow
Northenden	

NANTWICH

Acton	Nantwich[29]
Audlem[27]	Sandbach (part of)[30]
Baddiley	Whitchurch (part of)[31]
Barthomley[28]	Wistaston
Coppenhall	Wrenbury[32]
Marbury	Wybunbury[33]

NORTHWICH

Astbury (part of)[34]	Sandbach (part of)[38]
Brereton cum Smethwick	Swettenham
Budworth, Great (part of)[35]	Warmingham
Davenham[36]	
Lawton, Church	
Middlewich (part of)[37]	

WIRRAL

Higher Division	*Lower Division*
Backford (part of)[39]	Bebington
Bromborough (part of)[40]	Bidston
Burton	Bromborough (part of)[46]
Eastham[41]	Heswall
Holy Trinity (part of)[42]	Hilbre Island[47]
Neston	Thurstaston
St. Mary's (part of)[43]	Upton
St. Oswald's (part of)[44]	Wallasey
Shotwick	West Kirby
Shotwick Park	Woodchurch
Stanlow	
Stoke[45]	

[24] i.e. Somerford Booths. Most of Astbury A.P. is in Northwich hundred.

[25] Macclesfield town is in Prestbury A.P.

[26] i.e. Snelson. Most of Rostherne A.P. is in Bucklow hundred.

[27] Dodcott cum Wilkesley chap. is partly in Audlem A.P. and partly in Wrenbury A.P. [28] Partly in Staffs.

[29] Willaston tns. is partly in Nantwich A.P. and partly in Wybunbury A.P.

[30] i.e. Betchton and Hassall. Most of Sandbach A.P. is in Northwich hundred. [31] Mainly in Salop.

[32] Dodcott cum Wilkesley tns. is partly in Audlem A.P.

[33] See note 29.

[34] i.e. Buglawton, Congleton, Davenport, Hulme Walfield, Moreton cum Alcumlow, Newbold Astbury, Odd Rode, Radnor, Smallwood, Somerford. Astbury A.P. extends into Macclesfield hundred.

[35] i.e. Allostock, Birches, Hulse, Lach Dennis, Lostock Gralam, Northwich, Nether Peover, Witton cum Twambrooks.

[36] Part of Rudheath tns. is in Davenham and part in Sandbach A.P.

[37] i.e. Byley cum Yatehouse, Clive, Croxton, Kinderton with Hulme, Middlewich, Minshull Vernon, Mooresbarrow cum Parme, Newton, Occlestone, Ravenscroft, Sproston, Stublach, Sutton, Wimboldsley. Middlewich A.P. extends into Eddisbury hundred (first division).

[38] i.e. Arclid, Blackden, Bradwall, Church Hulme, Cotton, Cranage, Goostrey, Leese, Rudheath, Sandbach, Twemlow, Wheelock. Sandbach A.P. extends into Nantwich hundred.

[39] i.e. Backford, Chorlton, Lea, Great Mollington. Backford A.P. extends into Broxton hundred (lower division).

[40] Part of Bromborough A.P. is in Wirral hundred (lower division).

[41] Part of Whitby tns. is in Eastham, part in Stoke A.P.

[42] i.e. Blacon cum Crabwall. Most of Holy Trinity A.P. is in the city of Chester.

[43] i.e. Little Mollington. St. Mary's A.P. extends into the city of Chester and Broxton hundred (lower division).

[44] i.e. Croughton. St. Oswald's A.P. extends into the city of Chester, Broxton hundred (lower division), and Eddisbury hundred (first division). [45] See note 41.

[46] i.e. Brimstage. Most of Bromborough A.P. is in Wirral hundred (higher division).

[47] In 1841 Hilbre Island was returned as an E.P.P.

CITY OF CHESTER

Boughton, Spital
Cathedral Church and Little St. John
Chester Castle[48]
Holy Trinity[49]
St. Bridget
St. John the Baptist

St. Martin
St. Mary (part of)[50]
St. Michael
St. Olave
St. Oswald (part of)[51]
St. Peter

RURAL DISTRICTS AND THEIR CONSTITUENT CIVIL PARISHES

No attempt has been made in this list to trace changes in the composition of civil parishes or to show what happened to any parish when it ceased to form part of a rural district unless it became part of another rural district or an urban district. For such information the population table and its notes should be consulted.

The poor-law unions comprised the constituent parishes of the rural districts as shown in this list, together with the urban districts and municipal boroughs geographically situated within the rural districts.

ALTRINCHAM R. D.

Formed under the Public Health Act, 1872. Dissolved in 1894, when all its parishes were transferred to Bucklow R.D.

Agden
Ashley
Ashton upon Mersey
Aston by Budworth
Baguley
Bexton
Bollington
Carrington
Dunham Massey
Etchells, Northen
Hale
Knutsford, Nether
Knutsford, Over
Legh, High
Marthall cum Warford
Mere
Millington

Mobberley
Northenden
Ollerton
Partington
Peover Inferior
Peover Superior
Pickmere
Plumley
Pownall Fee (part of)
Rostherne
Tabley Inferior
Tabley Superior
Tatton
Timperley
Toft
Warburton

ASHTON-UNDER-LYNE R.D.

Formed under the Public Health Act, 1872. Most of Ashton-under-Lyne R.D. lay in Lancs. In 1894 the Ches. parishes were transferred to Tintwistle R.D.

Hattersley
Matley

Tintwistle

BIRKENHEAD R.D.

Formed under the Public Health Act, 1872. Dissolved in 1894, when its constituent parishes were transferred to Wirral R.D.

Bidston cum Ford

Noctorum

---

[48] In 1811 and 1821 there was no return for Chester Castle, and in 1841 and 1851 there were separate returns for Chester Castle gaol and Chester Castle barracks.

[49] Part of Holy Trinity A.P. is in Wirral hundred (higher division).

[50] Part of St. Mary's A.P. is in Wirral hundred (lower division) and Broxton hundred (lower division).

[51] Part of St. Oswald's A.P. is in Broxton hundred (lower division), Wirral hundred (lower division), and Eddisbury hundred (first division).

BUCKLOW R.D.

Formed under the Local Government Act, 1894.

Agden
Ashley
Ashton upon Mersey—constituted an U.D. 1895
Aston by Budworth
Baguley—transferred to Manchester C.B. 1931
Bexton
Bollington
Carrington
Dunham Massey
Etchells, Northen—transferred to Manchester C.B. 1931
Hale—constituted an U.D. 1900
Knutsford, Nether—constituted an U.D. 1895
Knutsford, Over—constituted an U.D. 1895
Legh, High
Marthall—created 1951
Marthall cum Warford—dissolved 1951
Mere
Millington

Mobberley
Northenden—transferred to Manchester C.B. 1931
Ollerton
Partington
Peover Inferior
Peover Superior
Pickmere
Plumley
Ringway—created 1900
Rostherne
Styal—dissolved 1936
Tabley Inferior
Tabley Superior
Tatton
Timperley—dissolved 1936
Toft
Warburton
Warford, Little—created 1951

An area which was formerly a detached part of Bollington C.P., being wholly surrounded by Bowdon C.P., became part of the latter under the provisions of the Divided Parishes Act, 1882. It was not added to Bowdon U.D. and therefore became a separate C.P. under the provisions of the Local Government Act, 1894. It was dissolved in 1936 and its area subsequently included in Bowdon U.D.

CHESTER R.D.

Formed under the Public Health Act, 1872.

Aldford—transferred from Tarvin R.D. 1936
Bache
Backford
Barrow—transferred from Tarvin R.D. 1936
Blacon cum Crabwall—dissolved 1936
Broughton, Great
Buerton—transferred from Tarvin R.D. 1936
Capenhurst
Caughall
Chester Castle—said to have been outside U.D. and R.D. in 1881. Put into Chester R.D. 1889
Chorlton by Backford
Christleton
Churton Heath—transferred from Tarvin R.D. 1936
Claverton
Croughton
Dodleston
Dunham on the Hill
Eaton
Eccleston
Elton
Hapsford
Hoole (part of)—re-named 1894
Hoole Village—created 1894
Huntington—transferred from Tarvin R.D. 1936
Ince—transferred to Ellesmere Port U.D. 1933
Kinnerton, Lower

Lea by Backford
Lea Newbold—transferred from Tarvin R.D. 1936
Ledsham—transferred from Wirral R.D. 1933
Littleton
Marlston cum Lache
Mollington—created 1901
Mollington, Great—dissolved 1901
Mollington, Little—dissolved 1901
Moston
Newton by Chester—dissolved 1936
Picton
Poulton
Puddington—transferred from Wirral R.D. 1933
Pulford
Rowton—transferred from Tarvin R.D. 1936
Saighton—transferred from Tarvin R.D. 1936
Saughall—created 1948
Saughall, Great—dissolved 1948
Saughall, Little—dissolved 1948
Shotwick
Shotwick Park
Stanlow—transferred to Ellesmere Port and Whitby U.D. 1910
Stanney, Great—transferred to Ellesmere Port and Whitby U.D. 1910
Stanney, Little
Stoke

Sutton, Guilden—transferred from Tarvin R.D.
    1936
Thornton le Moors
Trafford, Bridge
Trafford, Mickle
Trafford, Wimbolds
Upton-by-Chester
Wervin
Woodbank

CONGLETON R.D.

Formed under the Public Health Act, 1872.

Arclid
Betchton
Blackden—dissolved 1936
Bradwall
Brereton—created 1936
Brereton cum Smethwick—dissolved 1936
Cotton—dissolved 1936
Cranage
Davenport—dissolved 1936
Elton
Goostrey—created 1936
Goostrey cum Barnshaw—dissolved 1936
Hassall
Hulme, Church
Hulme Walfield

Kermincham—dissolved 1936
Leese—dissolved 1936
Moreton cum Alcumlow
Moston—dissolved 1936
Newbold Astbury
Newton—dissolved 1894
Radnor—united with Somerford 1936
Rode, Odd
Smallwood
Somerford
Somerford Booths
Swettenham
Tetton
Twemlow
Wheelock—dissolved 1936

DISLEY R.D.

Formed under the Local Government Act, 1894, from the part of Disley C.P. formerly in Hayfield R.D.

Disley (part of)

MARKET DRAYTON R.D.

Formed under the Public Health Act, 1872. Market Drayton R.D. lay mainly in Salop. The Ches. parish of Tittenley was transferred to Salop. in 1895.

HAYFIELD R.D.

Formed under the Public Health Act, 1872. Hayfield R.D. was mainly in Derb. but part of Disley C.P. was in Ches. and was constituted Disley R.D. in 1894.

MACCLESFIELD R.D.

Formed under the Public Health Act, 1872.

Adlington
Alderley, Nether
Alderley, Over
Birtles—dissolved 1936
Bosley
Butley—dissolved 1936
Capesthorne—dissolved 1936
Chelford
Chorley (part of)
Eaton
Fallibroome—dissolved 1936
Gawsworth
Henbury—created 1936
Henbury cum Pexall—dissolved 1936
Hurdsfield
Kettleshulme
Lyme Handley
Macclesfield Forest

Marton
Mottram St. Andrew
Newton—dissolved 1936
Pott Shrigley
Poynton—united with Worth 1880
Poynton with Worth—created 1880
Prestbury
Rainow
Rode, North
Siddington
Snelson
Sutton
Taxal—dissolved 1936
Tytherington—dissolved 1936
Upton—dissolved 1936
Warford, Great
Wildboarclough
Wincle

Withington—created 1936
Withington, Lower—dissolved 1936
Withington, Old—dissolved 1936

Woodford—dissolved 1939
Worth—united with Poynton 1880

MALPAS R.D.

Formed under the Local Government Act, 1894. It was dissolved in 1936, when Marbury cum Quoisley, Norbury, and Wirswall parishes were transferred to Nantwich R.D. and the remainder to Tarvin R.D.

Agden
Bickley
Bradley
Chidlow
Chorlton
Cuddington
Duckington
Edge
Hampton
Larkton
Macefen
Malpas

Marbury cum Quoisley
Newton by Malpas
Norbury
Oldcastle
Overton
Stockton
Threapwood—transferred from Wrexham R.D. 1895
Tushingham cum Grindley
Wigland
Wirswall
Wychough

NANTWICH R.D.

Formed under the Public Health Act, 1872.

Acton
Alpraham
Alvaston—united with Worleston 1899
Aston juxta Mondrum
Audlem
Austerson
Baddiley
Baddington
Barthomley
Basford
Batherton
Beeston—transferred to Tarvin R.D. 1892
Bickerton
Blakenhall
Bridgemere
Brindley
Broomhall
Buerton
Bulkeley
Bunbury
Burland
Burwardsley—transferred to Tarvin R.D. 1892
Calveley
Checkley cum Wrinehill
Cholmondeley
Cholmondeston
Chorley
Chorlton
Coole Pilate
Coppenhall, Church—dissolved 1936
Crewe
Dodcott cum Wilkesley
Doddington
Edleston
Egerton

Faddiley
Hankelow
Haslington
Hatherton
Haughton
Henhull
Hough
Hunsterson
Hurleston
Lea
Leighton
Marbury cum Quoisley—transferred from Malpas R.D. 1936
Minshull, Church
Minshull Vernon
Newhall
Norbury—transferred from Malpas R.D. 1936
Peckforton
Poole
Ridley
Rope
Shavington cum Gresty
Sound
Spurstow
Stapeley
Stoke
Tilstone Fearnall—transferred to Tarvin R.D. 1892
Tiverton—transferred to Tarvin R.D. 1892
Walgherton
Wardle
Warmingham
Weston
Wettenhall
Willaston

Wirswall—transferred from Malpas R.D. 1936
Wistaston
Woodcott
Woolstanwood

Worleston
Wrenbury cum Frith
Wybunbury

Northwich R.D.

Formed under the Public Health Act, 1872.

Acton—renamed Acton Bridge 1967
Allostock
Anderton
Barnton
Birches—united with Lach Dennis 1892
Bostock
Budworth, Little
Byley
Clive—dissolved 1936
Cogshall—dissolved 1936
Comberbach
Crowton
Croxton—united with Byley, 1892
Cuddington
Darnhall
Davenham
Delamere
Eaton—dissolved 1936
Eddisbury—dissolved 1936
Hartford
Hulse—united with Lach Dennis 1892
Kinderton—created 1894, dissolved 1936
Kinderton cum Hulme—dissolved 1894
Lach Dennis
Leftwich—dissolved 1936
Leigh, Little
Lostock Gralam
Marbury
Marston
Marton

Mooresbarrow cum Parme—united with Sproston 1892
Moulton
Newhall—united with Lach Dennis 1892
Newton—dissolved 1894
Oakmere
Occlestone—united with Wimboldsley 1892
Onston—united with Crowton 1892
Oulton Lowe—united with Little Budworth 1892
Peover, Nether
Ravenscroft—united with Byley 1892
Rudheath
Rushton—transferred from Tarporley U.D. 1936
Shipbrook—united with Whatcroft 1892
Shurlach—united with Rudheath 1892
Sproston
Stanthorne
Stublach—united with Lach Dennis 1892
Sutton—united with Newton 1892
Tarporley—transferred from Tarporley U.D. 1936
Utkinton—transferred from Tarporley U.D. 1936
Wallerscote—united with Winnington 1892
Weaver—united with Darnhall 1892
Weaverham
Whatcroft
Wimboldsley
Wincham
Winnington—dissolved 1936

An area which was formerly a detached part of Marton C.P., being wholly surrounded by Over C.P., became part of the latter parish under the provisions of the Divided Parishes Act, 1882; it was not added to Winsford U.D. and therefore became a separate parish under the provisions of the Local Government Act, 1894.

Runcorn R.D.

Formed under the Public Health Act, 1872.

Acton Grange—dissolved 1936
Alvanley
Antrobus
Appleton
Aston—created 1936
Aston by Sutton—dissolved 1936
Aston Grange—dissolved 1936
Bartington—dissolved 1936
Budworth, Great
Clifton—dissolved 1936
Crowley—dissolved 1936

Daresbury
Dutton
Frodsham
Frodsham Lordship—dissolved 1936
Grappenhall—transferred from Warrington R.D. 1894
Halton
Hatton
Helsby
Keckwick—dissolved 1936
Kingsley

Kingswood—dissolved 1936

Latchford—transferred from Warrington R.D. 1894, and to Warrington C.B. (Lancs.) 1896

Latchford Without—created 1894, dissolved 1936

Manley

Moore

Newton by Daresbury—dissolved 1936

Newton by Frodsham—dissolved 1936

Norley

Norton

Preston Brook—created 1936

Preston on the Hill—dissolved 1936

Seven Oaks—dissolved 1936

Stockham—dissolved 1936

Stockton Heath—created 1897

Stretton

Sutton

Thelwall—transferred from Warrington R.D. 1894, dissolved 1936

Walton—created 1936

Walton Inferior—dissolved 1936

Walton Superior—dissolved 1936

Weston—dissolved 1936

Whitley—created 1936

Whitley, Higher—dissolved 1936

Whitley, Lower—dissolved 1936

STOCKPORT R.D.

Formed under the Public Health Act, 1872. Part of Stockport R.D. lay in Lancs. By 1904 its constituent parishes were all included in urban districts.

Bosden—transferred to Hazel Grove and Bramhall U.D. 1900

Bramhall—transferred to Hazel Grove and Bramhall U.D. 1900

Brinnington (part of)—part transferred to Stockport C.B. 1901, part to Bredbury and Romiley U.D. 1902

Cheadle Bulkeley (part of)—transferred to Cheadle and Gatley U.D. 1886

Cheadle Moseley (part of)—transferred to Cheadle and Gatley U.D. 1886

Compstall—created 1897, constituted Compstall U.D. 1902

Etchells, Stockport—transferred to Cheadle and Gatley U.D. 1886

Handforth—constituted Handforth U.D. 1904

Norbury—transferred to Hazel Grove and Bramhall U.D. 1900

Offerton—transferred to Hazel Grove and Bramhall U.D. 1900

Torkington—transferred to Hazel Grove and Bramhall U.D. 1900

Werneth (part of)—renamed Compstall 1897

TARVIN R.D.

Formed under the Public Health Act, 1872.

Agden—transferred from Malpas R.D. 1936

Aldersey

Aldford—transferred to Chester R.D. 1936

Ashton

Barrow—transferred to Chester R.D. 1936

Barton

Beeston—transferred from Nantwich R.D. 1892

Bickley—transferred from Malpas R.D. 1936

Bradley—transferred from Malpas R.D. 1936

Broxton

Buerton—transferred to Chester R.D. 1936

Burton

Burwardsley—transferred from Nantwich R.D. 1892

Caldecott

Carden

Chidlow—transferred from Malpas R.D. 1936

Chorlton—transferred from Malpas R.D. 1936

Chowley

Churton by Aldford

Churton by Farndon

Churton Heath—transferred to Chester R.D. 1936

Clotton Hoofield

Clutton

Coddington

Cotton Abbotts

Cotton Edmunds

Crewe

Cuddington—transferred from Malpas R.D. 1936

Duckington—transferred from Malpas R.D. 1936

Duddon

Edge—transferred from Malpas R.D. 1936

Edgerley

Farndon

Golborne Bellow

Golborne David

Grafton

Hampton—transferred from Malpas R.D. 1936

Handley

Harthill

Hatton

Hockenhull

Horton

Horton cum Peel

Huntington—transferred to Chester R.D. 1936

Huxley

Iddinshall

Kelsall

Kings Marsh

Larkton—transferred from Malpas R.D. 1936

Lea Newbold—transferred to Chester R.D. 1936

Macefen—transferred from Malpas R.D. 1936

Malpas—transferred from Malpas R.D. 1936

Mouldsworth

Newton by Malpas—transferred from Malpas R.D. 1936

Newton by Tattenhall

Oldcastle—transferred from Malpas R.D. 1936

Overton—transferred from Malpas R.D. 1936

Prior's Heys

Rowton—transferred to Chester R.D. 1936

Saighton—transferred to Chester R.D. 1936

Shocklach, Church—transferred from Wrexham R.D. 1894

Shocklach Oviatt—transferred from Wrexham R.D. 1894

Stapleford, Bruen

Stapleford, Foulk

Stockton—transferred from Malpas R.D. 1936

Stretton

Sutton, Guilden—transferred to Chester R.D. 1936

Tarvin

Tattenhall

Threapwood—transferred from Malpas R.D. 1936

Tilston

Tilstone Fearnall—transferred from Nantwich R.D. 1892

Tiverton—transferred from Nantwich R.D. 1892

Tushingham cum Grindley—transferred from Malpas R.D. 1936

Waverton

Wigland—transferred from Malpas R.D. 1936

Willington

Wychough—transferred from Malpas R.D. 1936

TINTWISTLE R.D.

Formed under the Local Government Act, 1894, from the Ches. parishes formerly in Ashton-under-Lyne R.D.

Hattersley—dissolved 1936

Matley—dissolved 1936

Tintwistle

WARRINGTON R.D.

Formed under the Public Health Act, 1872. The greater part of Warrington R.D. lay in Lancs. In 1894 its three Ches. parishes were transferred to Runcorn R.D.

Grappenhall

Latchford

Thelwall

WHITCHURCH R.D.

Formed under the Public Health Act, 1872. Part of Whitchurch R.D. lay in Salop. In 1894 the Ches. parishes were transferred to Malpas R.D.

Agden

Bickley

Bradley

Chidlow

Chorlton

Cuddington

Duckington

Edge

Hampton

Larkton

Macefen

Malpas

Marbury cum Quoisley

Newton by Malpas

Norbury

Oldcastle

Overton

Stockton

Tushingham cum Grindley

Wigland

Wirswall

Wychough

WIRRAL R.D.

Formed under the Public Health Act, 1872. It was dissolved in 1933, when its constituent parishes were transferred to Birkenhead C.B., Bebington U.D., Ellesmere Port U.D., Hoylake U.D., Wirral U.D. and Chester R.D.

Arrowe

Barnston

Bidston cum Ford—transferred from Birkenhead R.D. 1894

Brimstage

Burton

Caldy

Eastham

Frankby

Gayton

Grange

Greasby

Heswall cum Oldfield

Hoose—transferred to West Kirby and Hoylake U.S.D. 1891

Hooton

Irby

Kirby, West—transferred to West Kirby and Hoylake U.S.D. 1891

Landican—transferred to Birkenhead C.B. 1928

Ledsham

Meols, Great—transferred to West Kirby and Hoylake U.S.D. 1891

Meols, Little—transferred to West Kirby and Hoylake U.S.D. 1891

Moreton—transferred to Wallasey C.B. 1928

Ness

Netherpool—transferred to Ellesmere Port U.D. 1910

Newton cum Larton—united with Grange 1889

Noctorum—transferred from Birkenhead R.D. 1894 and to Birkenhead C.B. 1933

Overpool—transferred to Ellesmere Port U.D. 1910

Pensby

Poulton cum Spital

Prenton—transferred to Birkenhead C.B. 1928

Puddington

Raby

Saughall Massie

Storeton

Sutton, Great

Sutton, Little

Thingwall—transferred to Birkenhead C.B. 1928

Thornton, Childer

Thornton Hough

Thurstaston

Upton by Birkenhead

Whitby—constituted Ellesmere Port and Whitby U.D. 1902

Willaston

Woodchurch

WREXHAM R.D.

Formed under the Public Health Act, 1872. Most of Wrexham R.D. lay in Denb. but it extended into Flints. and Ches. In 1894 Church Shocklach and Shocklach Oviatt were transferred to Tarvin R.D., and Threapwood to Malpas R.D.

Shocklach, Church

Shocklach Oviatt

Threapwood (part of)

POPULATION TABLE 1801–1971

NOTE: The pop. of tns. for which totals were struck on not more than two occasions, 1801–71, is given, not in the table, but in the footnotes under their respective A.P.s. For those tns. see Index.

	1801	1811	1821	1831	1841	1851	1861	1871	1881	1891	1901	1911	1921	1931	1951	1961	1971
CHESHIRE:																	
Ancient County	191,751[a]	227,031*[b]	270,098	334,391	395,660*	455,725	505,428	561,201	644,037	730,058[c]	815,099						
Administrative County with associated C.B.s										743,869	827,191[d]	954,779[e]	1,025,724[f]	1,087,655	1,258,507[g]	1,368,979	1,546,387[h]
ACTON A.P.[i]	2,362	2,589	2,923	2,917	3,198	3,165	3,125	3,193[j]									
ACTON tns.	262	286	273	309	321	351	297	278	See Acton C.P.								
ASTON JUXTA MONDRUM tns.	111	146	159	152	164	171	146	188	See Aston juxta Mondrum C.P.								
AUSTERSON tns.	59	57	65	69	55	55	57	55	See Austerson C.P.								
BADDINGTON tns.	121	113	140	132	137	155	135	123	See Baddington C.P.								
BRINDLEY tns.	148	153	167	153	184	186	227*	187	See Brindley C.P.								
BURLAND tns.	371	434	505	515	639	627	672	656	See Burland C.P.								
CHOLMONDESTON tns.	168	189	208	180	206	186	176	203	See Cholmondeston C.P.								
COOLE PILATE tns.	39	43	48	48	59	43	44	52	See Coole Pilate C.P.								
EDLESTON tns.	88	84	95	104	96	99	89	94	See Edleston C.P.								
FADDILEY tns.	224	241	291	316	320	314	285	297	See Faddiley C.P.								
HENHULL tns.	45	57	90	62	114	110	90	155	See Henhull C.P.								
HURLESTON tns.	162	176	191	198	192	221	181	141	See Hurleston C.P.								
POOLE tns.	168	176	185	188	201	167	187	162	See Poole C.P.								
STOKE tns.	127	140	137	124	119	143	171	201	See Stoke C.P.								
WORLESTON tns.	269	294	369	367	391	337	368	365	See Worleston C.P.								
ACTON C.P.	Part of Acton A.P., q.v.								227	247	258	226	239	206	293	293	276
ACTON C.P.[l]	Part of Weaverham A.P., q.v.								597	534	516	533	555	516	550[k]	551	See Acton Bridge C.P.
ACTON BRIDGE C.P.[l]																	635
ACTON GRANGE C.P.	Part of Runcorn A.P., q.v.								173	453	145	142	145	112[m]	See Walton C.P.		
ADLINGTON C.P.	Part of Prestbury A.P., q.v.								858	819	765	683	630	689[n]	823	1,022	973
AGDEN C.P.	Part of Malpas A.P., q.v.								93	73	60	73	80	75	60	71	82
AGDEN C.P.	Part of Bowdon A.P. and Rostherne A.P., q.v.								104	106	115	102	89	85[o]	79	185	178
ALDERLEY A.P.	1,178	1,293	1,477	1,338	1,538	1,404	1,418	1,364									
ALDERLEY, NETHER tns.	483	541	668	587	679*	606*	617	560	See Alderley, Nether C.P.								
ALDERLEY, OVER tns.	408	424	473	402	455*	450	421	414	See Alderley, Over C.P.								
WARFORD, GREAT tns.	287	328	336	349	404*	348*	380	390	See Warford, Great C.P.								
ALDERLEY, NETHER C.P.	Part of Alderley A.P., q.v.								573	517	522	614[p]	704	757	529	608	659
ALDERLEY, OVER C.P.	Part of Alderley A.P., q.v.								399	385	358	366	291	333	282	314	293
ALDERLEY EDGE U.D. and, from 1936, C.P.[q]											2,856	3,143	3,088	3,145	3,689	3,621[r]	4,470
ALDERLEY EDGE C.P.	Part of Wilmslow A.P.										2,223	2,484	2,450	2,399	See Alderley Edge U.D. and C.P.		
BOLLIN FEE C.P.	Part of Wilmslow A.P.										633	659	638	746[s]	See Alderley Edge U.D. and C.P. and Wilmslow U.D. and C.P.		
ALDERSEY C.P.	Part of Coddington A.P., q.v.								109	114	113	109	106	92	96	75	98
ALDFORD A.P.[t]	516	642	765	796	835	835	731	815									
ALDFORD tns.	331	391	491	488	488	521	438*	497*	See Aldford C.P.								
BUERTON tns.	39	56	60	59	81	63	68	38*	See Buerton C.P.								
CHURTON BY ALDFORD tns.	140	195[u]	210	238	254	251	217	274*	See Churton by Aldford C.P.								
EDGERLEY tns.	6	—[u]	4	11	12	0	8	6	See Edgerley C.P.								
ALDFORD C.P.	Part of Aldford A.P., q.v.								501	457	409	431	374	347	322	280	274
ALLOSTOCK C.P.	Part of Budworth, Great A.P., q.v.								501	501	494	484	454	436	564	617	694
ALPRAHAM C.P.	Part of Bunbury A.P., q.v.								438	404	481	407	465	436	381	389	380

Parish, &c.	Derivation / notes	Population figures (census years)								
ALSAGER C.P. and, from 1894, U.D.	Part of Barthomley A.P., q.v.	1,601	...	2,597	2,693	2,852	5,575	7,806	10,329	
ALTRINCHAM U.S.D. and C.P. (from 1937 M.B.)	Part of Bowdon A.P., q.v.	11,250	12,440	16,831	17,813	20,450[v]	21,356	39,789[w]	41,122	40,787
ALTRINCHAM R.D.	See Bucklow R.D.									
ALVANLEY C.P.	Part of Frodsham A.P., q.v.	321	328	319	306	278	306	287[x]	332	443
ALVASTON C.P.	Part of Nantwich A.P., q.v.	57	30	See Worleston C.P.						
ANDERTON C.P.	Part of Budworth, Great A.P., q.v.	343	369	360	353	368	327	424	459	410
ANTROBUS C.P.	Part of Budworth, Great A.P., q.v.	430	425[y]	373	387	366	380	726[z]	694	716
APPLETON C.P.	Part of Budworth, Great A.P., q.v.	2,067	2,759	744[a]	794	800	1,196*	2,974	4,636	6,826
ARCLID C.P.	Part of Sandbach A.P., q.v.	325	316	321	397	309	306	462	433	376
ARROWE C.P.	Part of Woodchurch A.P., q.v.	127	128	121	111	106	91[b]	See Birkenhead C.B. and C.P. and Wirral U.D.		
ASHLEY C.P.	Part of Bowdon A.P., q.v.	385	412	424	418	391	359	338	421	345
ASHTON C.P.	Part of Tarvin A.P., q.v.	388	367	408	421	448	430	394	474	1,013
ASHTON UPON MERSEY A.P.	1,597	1,819	1,924	2,078	2,414	2,894	4,507	6,628		
ASHTON UPON MERSEY tns. (part of in 1871)[c]	778	819	918	901	974	1,105	1,174	...	1,476*	1,055*
SALE tns.	819	901	1,049	1,104	1,309	1,720	...	3,031*	5,573*	

1,055* See Ashton upon Mersey C.P.
5,573* See Sale U.D. and M.B.

(a) This figure was corrected to 192,305 in 1851.

(b) This figure includes the local militia which numbered 3,466.

(c) In 1884 part of Warrington C.P. (Lancs.) (pop. 2 in 1891) was transferred to Latchford C.P. in Ches. The bounds, of the ancient co. and of the administrative co. in 1891 is reached by adding part of Stockport C.B. (pop. 16,368 in 1891), part of Stalybridge U.S.D. (pop. 7,278 in 1891), both in the ancient co. of Lanc., and by deducting part of Mossley U.S.D. (pop. 2,887 in 1891), part of Warrington U.S.D. (pop. 5,785 in 1891), both in the ancient co. of Lanc., and part of New Mills U.S.D. (pop. 1,163 in 1891) in the ancient co. of Derb.

(d) In 1895 part of Ches., viz. Tittenley C.P. (pop. 34 in 1891) was transferred to Salop., and in 1896 and 1898 further parts, viz. parts of Appleton C.P. and of Latchford Without C.P. (pop. respectively 467 and 183 in 1901) and of Dukinfield C.P. (pop. 39 in 1901) were transferred to Lancs. In 1896 the bounds. of Ches. were extended to include part of Threapwood, transferred from Flints., and part of Ashton-under-Lyne (pop. 45 in 1901) from Lancs.

(e) In 1901 Ches. was extended to include Reddish U.D. and part of Heaton Norris C.P. (pop. 82 in 1901), transferred from Lancs.

(f) In 1913 a further part of Heaton Norris U.D. and C.P. (pop. 11,188 in 1911) was transferred to Ches. from Lancs.

(g) Comprised the administrative co. as constituted in 1931 together with part of Derb. administrative co. viz. Ludworth and Mellor C.P.s (pop. respectively 1,926 and 1,712 in 1931), but without part of Lymm U.D. (pop. 4 in 1931) and parts of the following C.P.s: Grappenhall, Walton Inferior, Acton Grange, Moore, Norton, and Thelwall (pop. respectively 213, 434, 12, 23, 28, and 3 in 1931), which were transferred to Lancs., and part of Yeardsley cum Whaley U.D. (pop. 1,745 in 1931), parts of Disley R.D. and C.P. (pop. 75 and 523 in 1931), part of Kettleshulme C.P. (pop. 3 in 1931), and parts of Taxal C.P. (pop. 646 and 26 in 1931) which were transferred to Derb.

(h) In 1965 parts of Congleton R.D. and Nantwich R.D. were transferred from Ches. to Staffs., and parts of Whitchurch U.D. (pop. 5 in 1961), formerly in Salop., and of Kidsgrove U.D. and Newcastle under Lyme R.D., formerly in Staffs., were transferred to Ches.

(i) Newhall tns. was returned under Acton A.P. 1811-41, but lies in Audlem A.P. and Wrenbury A.P., q.v.

(j) This fig. includes 36 inhabitants of Sound tns., which lay partly in Acton A.P.

(k) In 1936 part of Acton C.P. (pop. 28 in 1931) was transferred to Dutton C.P. Part of Weaverham cum Milton C.P. (pop. 63 in 1931) was transferred to Acton C.P.

(l) In 1967 Acton C.P. was renamed Acton Bridge C.P.: Ches. C.C. Minute No. 6, 23 Feb. 9167.

(m) Dissolved 1936. Part (pop. 100 in 1931) was transferred to Walton C.P. and the remainder to Warrington R.D. (Lancs.).

(n) In 1936 part of Adlington C.P. (pop. 2 in 1931) was transferred to Bollington U.D. and C.P.

(o) In 1936 part of Lymm C.P. (pop. 2 in 1931) was transferred to Agden C.P.

(p) In 1910 part of Nether Alderley C.P. (pop. 35 in 1901) was transferred to Alderley Edge C.P.

(q) In 1894 Chorley C.P. was renamed Alderley Edge U.D. and was extended to include a further part of Chorley C.P. (pop. 9 in 1901). At the same date Alderley Edge C.P. was created out of that part of Chorley C.P. in Alderley Edge U.D. In 1936 Alderley Edge U.D. was extended to include parts of Wilmslow U.D. and Chorley C.P. (pop. 109 and 25 respectively in 1931). By extending the C.P. to include part of Bollin Fee C.P. (pop. 746 in 1931) the former became co-extensive with the U.D.

(r) In 1954 part of Wilmslow U.D. (pop. 20 in 1951) was transferred to Alderley Edge C.P. and C.P.

(s) Dissolved 1936, part (pop. 746 in 1931) being transferred to Alderley Edge U.D. and C.P., and part without population to Wilmslow C.P.

(t) Great Boughton tns. and Churton Heath chap. in St. Oswald parish were wrongly returned with Aldford A.P. 1811-41, and their pop. was included in the total for the parish.

(u) In 1811 the pop. of Edgerley tns. was included in the total for Aldford tns.

(v) In 1920 parts of Carrington C.P. and of Dunham Massey C.P. (pop. 1,279 in 1911) were transferred to Altrincham U.D. and C.P.

(w) In 1936 part of Altrincham U.D. and C.P. (pop. 68 in 1931) was transferred to Hale U.D. and C.P.

(x) In 1936 part of Alvanley C.P. (pop. 22 in 1931) was transferred to Helsby C.P.

(y) In 1881 a detached part of Antrobus C.P. (pop. 3 in 1881) was transferred to Seven Oaks C.P.

(z) In 1936 Crowley C.P. (pop. 139 in 1931) and Seven Oaks C.P. (pop. 163 in 1931) were added to Antrobus C.P.

(a) In 1896 part of Appleton C.P. (pop. 467 in 1891) was transferred to Latchford C.P. and Lancs. admin. co., and in 1897 part of Appleton C.P. (pop. 2,543 in 1901) became Stockton Heath C.P.

(b) Dissolved 1933. Part (pop. 71 in 1931) was transferred to Birkenhead C.B. and C.P. and part (pop. 20 in 1931) to Irby C.P. in Wirral U.D.

(c) Ashton on Mersey tns. extends into Bowdon A.P. but is returned entirely in Ashton on Mersey A.P.

	1801	1811	1821	1831	1841	1851	1861	1871	1881	1891	1901	1911	1921	1931	1951	1961	1971
ASHTON UPON MERSEY C.P. and, from 1895, U.D.	Part of Ashton upon Mersey A.P., q.v.					3,326	4,234	5,563	7,234	7,773	See Sale U.D.						
ASTBURY A.P.	7,095	8,035	10,388[d]	14,673	14,619[d]	16,501	19,351	18,443									
BUGLAWTON chap.	517	584	948	2,087*	1,864*	2,052	2,014*	1,629*	See Buglawton C.P.								
CONGLETON chap.	3,861	4,616	6,405	9,352	9,222*	10,520	12,344	11,344	See Congleton M.B.								
DAVENPORT tns.	89	89	96	103	125	111	117	86	See Davenport C.P.								
HULME WALFIELD tns.	122	118	108	109	121	131	111	107	See Hulme Walfield C.P.								
MORETON CUM ALCUMLOW tns.	116	140	129	141	148	133	119	114	See Moreton cum Alcumlow C.P.								
NEWBOLD ASTBURY tns.	575	596	569	598	641	705	741	783	See Newbold Astbury C.P.								
ODD RODE tns.	917	1,003	1,143	1,300	1,518	1,853	2,503*	2,964*	See Odd Rode C.P.								
RADNOR tns.	14	12	14	20	11	24	25	34	See Radnor C.P.								
SMALLWOOD tns.	492	496	584	554	606	619	590	602	See Smallwood C.P.								
SOMERFORD tns.	142	114	107	112	99	79	82	91	See Somerford C.P.								
SOMERFORD BOOTHS tns.	250	267	285	297	264	274	220	241	See Somerford Booths C.P.								
ASTON C.P.[e]	Part of Budworth, Great A.P., q.v.								449	384	423	406	385	364	244	220	125[f]
ASTON BY BUDWORTH C.P.	Part of Runcorn A.P., q.v.								285	280	249	276	255	220	300	295	261
ASTON BY SUTTON C.P.	Part of Runcorn A.P., q.v.								33	35	40	48	37	36	See Aston C.P.	See Aston C.P.	
ASTON GRANGE C.P.															See Aston C.P.	See Aston C.P.	
ASTON JUXTA MONDRUM C.P.	Part of Acton A.P., q.v.								183	195	194	200	168	139	141	140	146
AUDLEM A.P.[g]	2,375	2,350	2,795[h]	2,978	2,827	2,870	2,287	2,666									
AUDLEM tns.	965	1,040	1,307	1,558	1,621*	1,591	1,510	1,521	See Audlem C.P.								
BUERTON tns. (part of)	405	429	524	464	512	444	464	504	See Buerton C.P.								
DODCOTT CUM WILKESLEY tns.[g]	755	622	670	637	392	560	197	266*	See Dodcott cum Wilkesley C.P.								
HANKELOW tns.	207	216	258	289	279	253	89	95	See Hankelow C.P.								
NEWHALL tns. (part of)	See Wrenbury A.P.								See Newhall C.P.								
TITTENLEY tns.	43	43	36	30	23	22	27	36	See Tittenley C.P.								
AUDLEM C.P.	Part of Audlem A.P., q.v.									1,371	1,455	1,480	1,394	1,346	1,315	1,172	1,293
AUSTERSON C.P.	Part of Acton A.P., q.v.								61	54	53	54	42	50	31	214	114
BACHE C.P.	Part of St. Oswald's A.P., q.v.								27	23	36	402*	19	62	68	o	86
BACKFORD A.P.																	
BACKFORD tns.	404	420	450	487	556	447	525	550	See Backford C.P.								
CAUGHALL tns.	138	146	140	165	200	155	150	130	See Caughall C.P.								
CHORLTON BY BACKFORD tns.	17	18[j]	23	26	16	11	19	19	See Chorlton by Backford C.P.								
LEA BY BACKFORD tns.	68	53	78	86	85	68	85	81	See Lea by Backford C.P.								
MOLLINGTON, GREAT tns.	111	113	122	118	140	122	186	189	See Mollington, Great C.P.								
BACKFORD C.P.	Part of Backford A.P., q.v.								125	137	141	155	135	124	119	174	145
BADDILEY A.P. and C.P.	276	288	270	267	275	281	272	323*	285	246[k]	211	237	233	219	219	196	235
BADDINGTON C.P.	Part of Acton A.P., q.v.								147	141	123	142	116	112	132[l]	112	130
BAGULEY C.P.	Part of Bowdon A.P., q.v.								736	814	834	970	1,375*	1,453*[m]	Part of Manchester C.B. (Lancs.)		
BARNSTON C.P.	Part of Woodchurch A.P., q.v.								280	404	522	641	693	See Wirral U.D.			
BARNTON C.P.	Part of Budworth, Great A.P., q.v.								1,538	2,297	2,792	3,051	3,359	3,198	3,918	4,485	4,245
BARROW A.P. and C.P.[n] (part of)[p]	501	585	642	678	668	659	623	634	724	734	727	699	677	910	1,065	1,050	990[o]
BARTHOMLEY A.P. (part of)[p]	1,425	2,016	2,091	2,218	2,409	2,441	2,721	3,463									
ALSAGER chap.	275	349	359	446*	445	473	703*	1,148*	See Alsager C.P.								
BARTHOMLEY tns.	184	465	450	449	422	450	416	405	See Barthomley C.P.								
CREWE tns.	289	280	297	295	396	365	387	371	See Crewe C.P.								
HASLINGTON chap.	677	922	985	1,028	1,146	1,153	1,215	1,539*	See Haslington C.P.								

The figures below are given in census-year order (earliest to latest). Dotted leaders in the source indicate years for which no separate return was made. An asterisk (*) marks a boundary change; superscript letters refer to the footnotes.

Township / Civil parish	Population figures
BARTHOMLEY C.P. — Part of Barthomley A.P., q.v.	372, 315, 292, 295, 277, 257, 263, 285, 248
BARTINGTON C.P. — Part of Budworth, Great A.P., q.v.	96, 83, 75, 71, 74, 64; See Dutton C.P.
BARTON C.P. — Part of Farndon A.P., q.v.	121, 88, 92, 105, 94, 103, 85, 72, 83
BASFORD C.P. — Part of Wybunbury A.P., q.v.	77, 54, 69, 70, 53, 177*, 229, 172, 160
BATHERTON C.P. — Part of Wybunbury A.P., q.v.	25, 29, 29, 28, 70, 53, 58, 64, 44
BEBINGTON A.P.	1,026, 1,206, 1,678, 2,193, 5,008, 10,016, 15,105, 23,725*
BEBINGTON, HIGHER tns.	143, 191, 216, 273, 844, 1,478*, 2,086, 3,172*; See Bebington, Higher C.P.
BEBINGTON, LOWER tns.	263, 279, 316, 440, 1,187*, 1,492*, 2,485, 3,768*; See Bebington, Lower C.P. and U.D.
POULTON CUM SPITAL tns.	87, 83, 101, 120, 209*, 294*, 360, 374; See Poulton cum Spital C.P.
STORETON tns.	180, 179, 220, 192, 214, 233, 256, 263; See Storeton C.P.
TRANMERE chap.	353, 474, 825, 1,168, 2,554, 6,519*, 9,918, 16,143*; See Tranmere C.P.
BEBINGTON M.B.[q]	47,844, 52,814, 61,582
BEBINGTON CUM BROMBOROUGH C.P.	39,715
BRIMSTAGE C.P.	135
EASTHAM C.P.	5,598
POULTON CUM SPITAL C.P.	1,257
RABY C.P.	308
STORETON C.P.	325
THORNTON HOUGH C.P.	506
BEBINGTON, HIGHER C.P. (part in Bebington, Higher U.D.) (part in Birkenhead C.B., q.v.) — Part of Bebington A.P., q.v.	4,122, 4,372; See Bebington, Higher U.S.D.
BEBINGTON, HIGHER U.S.D. and, from 1894, C.P.	1,959, 2,163, 2,951[r], 1,540, 1,689, 1,765
BEBINGTON, LOWER U.S.D. and C.P. — Part of Bebington A.P., q.v.	4,050, 5,216, 8,398, 11,401*, 14,687
BEBINGTON AND BROMBOROUGH U.D. and C.P.s	26,740; See Bebington M.B.
BEESTON C.P. — Part of Bunbury A.P., q.v.	328, 302, 285, 308, 296, 268, 284, 259, 221
BETCHTON C.P. — Part of Sandbach A.P., q.v.	823, 813, 692, 714, 708, 614, 719, 887, 950
BEXTON C.P. — Part of Knutsford A.P., q.v.	94, 115, 124, 101, 98, 132, 11[t], 7, 9

(d) The total for Astbury A.P. in 1821 was wrongly given as 14,383, and in 1841 as 14,355.

(e) In 1936 Aston by Sutton C.P. (pop. 220 in 1931) and Aston Grange C.P. (pop. 36 in 1931) were amalgamated to form Aston C.P.

(f) In 1967 part of Aston C.P. was transferred to Runcorn U.D.

(g) In 1851 the figs. for Audlem A.P. 1801–41 were corrected as follows: 1801, 2,439; 1811, 2,587; 1821, 2,979; 1831, 3,352; 1841, 3,371. The totals are reached by omitting the whole of Dodcott cum Wilkesley tns. and by including the whole of Newhall tns.

(h) In 1821 the pop. of Audlem A.P. was returned as 3,085.

(i) Before 1841 the entire pop. of Dodcott cum Wilkesley tns. was returned in Audlem A.P. In 1851 and 1861 Dodcott cum Wilkesley was wholly returned in Wrenbury A.P., q.v.

(j) In 1811 Caughall was wrongly returned in Plemstall A.P.

(k) In 1882 part of Baddiley C.P. (pop. 20 in 1891) was transferred to Burland C.P., and in 1888 part of Baddiley C.P. (pop. 2 in 1891) was transferred to Brindley C.P.

(l) In 1936 Baddington C.P. (pop. 8 in 1931) was transferred to Nantwich U.D.

(m) In 1933 Barnston C.P. was transferred from Wirral R.D. to Wirral U.D. and part of Brimstage C.P. (pop. 5 in 1931) was added.

(n) In 1821 and 1831 the constituent tns. of Great and Little Barrow were separately returned, their pops. being: Great Barrow 1821, 393; 1831, 436; Little Barrow 1821, 249; 1831, 242.

(o) In 1963 parts of Christleton, Guilden Sutton, and Mickle Trafford C.P.s were transferred to Barrow C.P., and parts of Barrow C.P. were transferred to Christleton, Guilden Sutton, and Mickle Trafford C.P.s.

(p) Barthomley A.P. extends into Pirehill hundred (Staffs.).

(q) Created 1937 from Bebington U.D. The latter had been created in 1933 from Bebington and Bromborough U.D. (pop. 26,740 in 1931), Poulton cum Spital C.P., Storeton C.P., and parts of Brimstage C.P., Childer Thornton C.P., Eastham C.P., Hooton C.P., Raby C.P., Thornton Hough C.P., and Willaston C.P. (pop. 5,137 in 1931).

(r) In 1894 the part of Higher Bebington C.P. in Birkenhead C.B. was constituted Rock Ferry C.P., but it was transferred in 1898 to Birkenhead C.B. Higher Bebington U.D. thus became co-extensive with the civil parish.

(s) Created 1922 by uniting Bromborough U.D. and C.P. (pop. 2,652 in 1921) with Higher and Lower Bebington U.D.s (pop. respectively 1,765 and 14,687 in 1921).

(t) In 1936 part of Bexton C.P. (pop. 118 in 1931) was transferred to Knutsford U.D. and C.P.

	1801	1811	1821	1831	1841	1851	1861	1871	1881	1891	1901	1911	1921	1931	1951	1961	1971
BICKERTON C.P.	Part of Malpas A.P., q.v.								325	335	323	326	300	259	256	205	206
BICKLEY C.P.	Part of Malpas A.P., q.v.								400	391	383	394	352	302	325	311	328
BIDSTON A.P.[u]	* 684	735	1,014	3,434	9,236	25,818	38,366[v]	45,901[w]									
BIDSTON CUM FORD tns.	199	198	257	251	291	293	282	286	See Bidston cum Ford C.P.								
BIRKENHEAD chap.	110	105	200	2,569	8,223*	24,285*	36,212	42,891	See Birkenhead M.B.								
CLAUGHTON WITH GRANGE tns. (part of in 1861 and 1871)	67	88	119	224	240	714*	1,309[x]	2,073*	See Claughton with Grange C.P.								
MORETON tns.	210	230	273	247	330	350	361	455*	See Moreton C.P.								
SAUGHALL MASSIE tns.	98	117	165	143	152	176	202	196	See Saughall Massie C.P.								
BIDSTON CUM FORD C.P.	Part of Bidston A.P., q.v.								270	254	465	969*	899	506[y]	{See Birkenhead C.B. and Wallasey C.B.		
BIRCHES C.P.	Part of Budworth, Great A.P., q.v.								8	See Lach Dennis C.P.							
BIRKENHEAD C.B. and, from 1898–1928 and from 1933, C.P.[z]										99,857	110,915	130,794	145,577	147,803	142,501	141,813	137,852
BEBINGTON, HIGHER C.P. (part of)[a]										1,465							
BIRKENHEAD C.P.										58,287				145,053			
CLAUGHTON WITH GRANGE C.P.										3,510	See Birkenhead C.B. and C.P.						
LANDICAN C.P.											See Birkenhead C.B. and C.P.			66			
OXTON C.P.										4,429	See Birkenhead C.B. and C.P.						
PRENTON C.P.														2,032			
THINGWALL C.P.														652			
TRANMERE C.P.										30,680	See Birkenhead C.B. and C.P.						
BIRKENHEAD M.B. and U.S.D.[b]									84,006	See Birkenhead C.B.							
BEBINGTON, HIGHER C.P. (part of)									2,163								
BIRKENHEAD C.P.									51,610								
CLAUGHTON WITH GRANGE C.P.									2,934								
OXTON C.P.									3,312								
TRANMERE C.P.									23,987								
BIRKENHEAD R.D.									391	456	See Wirral R.D.						
BIRTLES C.P.	Part of Prestbury A.P., q.v.								58	60	51	55	44	50	See Henbury C.P.		
BLACKDEN C.P.	Part of Sandbach A.P., q.v.								142	148	110	119	124	121	See Goostrey C.P.		
BLACON CUM CRABWALL C.P.	Part of Holy and Undivided Trinity A.P., q.v.								235	261	258	267	487	788[c]	{See Chester C.B. and Mollington C.P.		
BLAKENHALL C.P.	Part of Wybunbury A.P., q.v.								193	186	196	227	218	178	169	141	148[d]
BOLLIN FEE C.P.	Part of Wilmslow A.P., q.v.								2,856	3,137[e]							
part in Chorley U.D.									244	277	See Alderley Edge U.D.						
part in Wilmslow U.D.									2,612	2,860	See Wilmslow U.D. and C.P.						
BOLLINGTON C.P.	Part of Bowdon A.P. and Rostherne A.P., q.v.								272	223	215	193	170	174	175	231	205
BOLLINGTON C.P.	Part of Prestbury A.P., q.v.								5,464	5,335	See Bollington U.D.						
part in Bollington U.S.D.									3,963	3,913							
rural part									1,501	1,422[f]							
BOLLINGTON U.D.											5,245	5,224	5,094	5,027	5,313[g]	5,644	6,602

Parish	Ancient parish / notes	1801	1811	1821	1831	1841	1851	1861	1871	1881	1891	1901	1911	1921	1931
BOSDEN C.P.	Part of Cheadle A.P., q.v. .... See Hazel Grove U.D.														
BOSLEY C.P.	Part of Prestbury A.P., q.v.						400	364	353	388	361	359	421	413	379
BOSTOCK C.P.	Part of Davenham A.P., q.v.						198	213	197	196	156	139	146[h]	200	200
BOUGHTON, GREAT C.P.	Part of St. Oswald's A.P., q.v.				1,962	2,342	2,212	739	1,034	1,336	1,625	2,690*	3,165[i]	4,673	7,832
BOWDON A.P.[j]		6,066	6,953	7,442[k]	7,932[k]	9,373[k]	11,033[l]	14,822*	19,744[m]						
AGDEN tns. (part of)[n]	See Agden C.P.	85	90	77	99	45	48	38	34						
ALTRINCHAM chap.	See Altrincham C.P. and U.D.	1,692	2,032	2,302	2,708	3,399	4,488	6,628*	8,478*						
ASHLEY tns.	See Ashley C.P.	288	350	392	379	377	375*	380*							
BAGULEY tns. (part of, in 1871)	See Baguley C.P.	423	464	458	468	505	570	611*	600*						
BOLLINGTON tns. (part of)[o]	See Bollington C.P.	202	233	84	See Rostherne A.P.	304	105	111	93						
BOWDON tns.	See Bowdon U.D.	340	403	433	458	549	1,164	1,827	2,262*						
CARRINGTON chap.	See Carrington C.P.	435	480	531	552	559	536	521	469						
DUNHAM MASSEY tns.	See Dunham Massey C.P.	872	936	1,090	1,105	1,257	1,255	1,535*	1,790*						
HALE tns.	See Hale C.P.	783	929	958	945	974	995	1,160*	1,711*						
PARTINGTON tns.	See Partington C.P.	358	412	434	466	457	485	445	511						
TIMPERLEY tns.	See Timperley C.P.	588	624	683	752	947	1,008	1,571*	2,112*						
BOWDON U.S.D. and C.P.	Part of Bowdon A.P., q.v.						2,559	2,792	2,788	3,044	2,965	3,285	3,529[p]	4,477	4,891
BRADWALL C.P.	Part of Malpas A.P., q.v.						145	133	124	117	142	136	105	95	78
BRAMHALL C.P.	Part of Stockport A.P., q.v. — See Hazel Grove and Bramhall U.D.	662	758	924	1,245*	1,358	1,307	2,682	3,365				223[q]	195	202

(u) The pop. of Bidston A.P. returned in the censuses 1821–51 was exclusive of Birkenhead.

(v) In 1861 and 1871 separate returns were made for the part of Claughton with Grange tns. in Woodchurch A.P., q.v.

(w) In 1928 parts of Bidston cum Ford C.P. (pop. respectively 10 and 423 in 1921) were transferred to Wallasey C.B. and C.P. and Birkenhead C.B. and C.P. The parish was dissolved in 1933, and its pop. transferred to Birkenhead C.B. and C.P., part without pop. being transferred to Wallasey C.B.

(x) Birkenhead M.B. was constituted a C.B. under the Local Govt. Act, 1888. In 1891 the boundary of the C.B. was extended to the middle of the bed of the River Mersey. In 1898 Birkenhead C.B. and C.P. were further extended to include part of Lower Bebington C.P. and Birkenhead C.P. (pop. nil in 1901) and Birkenhead C.P. was extended to include Tranmere, Claughton with Grange, Oxton, and Rock Ferry C.P.s, and thus became co-extensive with the C.B. until 1928, when Landican C.P., Prenton C.P., and Thingwall C.P. were transferred from Wirral R.D. to Birkenhead C.B.

In 1928 Birkenhead C.B. and C.P. was extended to include part of Bidston cum Ford C.P. (pop. 423 in 1921).

In 1933 Birkenhead C.B. and C.P. was further extended to include Noctorum C.P. (pop. 473 in 1931), Woodchurch C.P. (pop. 113 in 1931), part of Arrowe C.P. (pop. 71 in 1931), part of Bidston cum Ford C.P. (pop. 506 in 1931), and part of Upton by Birkenhead C.P. (pop. 2,547 in 1931). Birkenhead C.P. was extended to include Landican, Prenton, and Thingwall C.P.s and thus became co-extensive with the C.B. once more.

(y) See above, note (w).

(z) See above, note (x).

(a) In 1894 that part of Higher Bebington C.P. in Birkenhead C.B. was constituted Rock Ferry C.P. In 1898 it was included in Birkenhead C.P.

(b) Birkenhead M.B. was incorporated in 1877.

(c) In 1936 Blacon cum Crabwall C.P. was dissolved, part (pop. 774 in 1931) being transferred to Chester C.B., and part (pop. 14 in 1931) to Mollington C.P.

(d) In 1965 part of Blakenhall C.P. was transferred to Newcastle under Lyme R.D. (Staffs.).

(e) In 1888 Bollin Fee C.P. was extended to include part of Pownall Fee (pop. 28 in 1891). Bollin Fee C.P. was also said to have been affected by the Divided Parishes Act, 1882. In 1894 part of Bollin Fee C.P. (pop. 3,208 in 1901) was transferred to Wilmslow C.P., and part of Fulshaw C.P. (pop. 251 in 1901) was transferred to Bollin Fee C.P. The altered C.P. was wholly included in Alderley Edge U.D., q.v.

(f) In 1894 Kerridge C.P. was created out of the rural part of Bollington C.P. In 1900 Bollington U.D. and C.P. was extended to include Kerridge C.P.

(g) In 1936 Bollington U.D. was extended to include parts of Adlington C.P., Butley C.P., and Tytherington C.P. (pops. respectively 2, 18, and 15 in 1931).

(h) In 1936 part of Bostock C.P. (pop. 3 in 1931) was transferred to Moulton C.P. Bostock C.P. was extended to include part of Wharton C.P. (pop. 20 in 1931).

(i) In 1936 part of Great Boughton C.P. (pop. 954 in 1931) was transferred to Chester C.B. Part of Hoole C.P. (pop. 126 in 1931) was added to Great Boughton C.P.

(j) From 1801 to 1831 the population of Agden tns., and in 1801 and 1811 that of Bollington tns., were returned in Bowdon A.P.

(k) In 1821 the total for Bowdon A.P. was stated to have been 7,442; in 1831, 8,213; in 1841, the whole of Agden and Bollington tns. were included, and in 1841 the whole of Agden tns. In 1851 the figure for 1841 was corrected to 9,385.

(l) In 1851 the total for Bowdon A.P. was given as 11,228, but that figure was corrected to 11,033 in 1861.

(m) In 1871 the total included 1,304 inhabitants of Ashton upon Mersey tns. which lay mainly in Ashton upon Mersey A.P. Part of Baguley tns. was in that year included in the total for Northenden A.P., q.v.

(n) See above, note (j).

(o) See above, note (j).

(p) In 1894 part of Bowdon U.D. and C.P. (pop. 29 in 1931) was transferred to Altrincham U.D., and part of Dunham Massey C.P. (pop. 85 in 1931) was transferred to Bowdon U.D.

(q) In 1936 part of Bradwall C.P. (pop. 1,075 in 1931) was transferred to Sandbach U.D. and C.P. Bradwall C.P. was extended to include part of Kinderton C.P. (pop. 10 in 1931).

	1801	1811	1821	1831	1841	1851	1861	1871	1881	1891	1901	1911	1921	1931	1951	1961	1971
BREDBURY AND ROMILEY U.D., and, from 1936, C.P.									5,553	5,821	7,107	8,683[r]	9,168	10,876	17,818[s]	21,621[t]	28,529
BREDBURY C.P.	Part of Stockport A.P., q.v.								3,734	3,901	4,691	5,785[r]	6,023	7,154			
ROMILEY C.P.[u]	Part of Stockport A.P., q.v.								1,819	1,920	2,416	2,898	3,145	3,722			
BRERETON C.P.[u]															613	817	960
BRERETON CUM SMETHWICK A.P. and C.P.	556	587	624	661	667	649	592	620	613	568	552	529	506	469	See Brereton C.P.		
BRIDGEMERE C.P.	Part of Wybunbury A.P., q.v.								134	157	149	163	162	149	141	133	99
BRIMSTAGE C.P.	Part of Bromborough A.P., q.v.								186	199[w]	181	189	183	161[v]	See Bebington M.B.		
BRINDLEY C.P.	Part of Acton A.P., q.v.								185	154[w]	127	154	177	187	123	153	186
BRINNINGTON C.P.	Part of Stockport A.P., q.v.								5,994	7,061	502[x]	See Bredbury C.P.					
part in Stockport M.B. and C.B.									5,542	6,576							
rural part									452	485							
BROMBOROUGH A.P.	404	342	446	449	573	538	1,279	1,511									
BRIMSTAGE tns.	127	123	141	136	161	126	185	197	See Brimstage C.P.								
BROMBOROUGH tns.	277	219	305	313	412	412	1,094*	1,314*	See Bromborough U.S.D. and C.P.								
BROMBOROUGH U.S.D. and C.P.									1,335	1,662	1,891[y]	1,974	2,652	See Bebington and Bromborough U.D.			
BROOMHALL C.P.	Part of Wrenbury A.P., q.v.								127	127	114	131	139	184	243	211	219
BROXTON HUNDRED	13,064	13,651	15,723	16,415	17,483	17,034	18,499	20,194	20,522*								
BROXTON C.P.	Part of Malpas A.P., q.v.								521*	558	543	541	493	507	471	444	392
BUCKLOW HUNDRED	28,768	32,403	37,192	42,942	48,625	54,875	60,039	71,854	83,234								
BUCKLOW R.D.									See Altrincham R.D.								
BUDWORTH, GREAT A.P.[z]	11,314	12,628[a]	14,264	15,963	17,103	17,990	18,852	20,747									
ALLOSTOCK tns.	419	462	461	448	427	474	536	540	See Allostock C.P.								
ANDERTON tns.	191	220	210	327	331	251	334*	281*	See Anderton C.P.								
ANTROBUS tns.	351	385	453	476	489	489	514	495	See Antrobus C.P.								
APPLETON tns.	1,206	1,173	1,435	1,699	1,753	1,828	1,828	1,947	See Appleton C.P.								
ASTON BY BUDWORTH chap.	396	402	380	409	405	430	459	444	See Aston by Budworth C.P.								
BARNTON tns.	402	480	612	730	859	1,117	1,219	1,363*	See Barnton C.P.								
BARTINGTON tns.	77	81	81	76	89	87	63	118*	See Bartington C.P.								
BIRCHES tns.	13	12	8	9	8	8	9	7	See Birches C.P.								
BUDWORTH, GREAT tns.	463	504	501	586	677	643	613	614	See Budworth, Great C.P.								
COGSHALL tns.	57	90	110	77	108	101	103	114	See Cogshall C.P.								
COMBERBACH tns.	142	163	226	295	303	295	266	281	See Comberbach C.P.								
CROWLEY tns.	147	139	149	146	175	169	183	204	See Crowley C.P.								
DUTTON tns.	301	313	325	329	361	337	442*	461	See Dutton C.P.								
HARTFORD tns. (part of)[b]	472	667	772	863	994	933	909	1,123*	See Hartford C.P.								
HULSE tns.	37	42	54	55	53	51	65	74	See Hulse C.P.								
LACH DENNIS tns.	43	50	44	32	33	28	28	34	See Lach Dennis C.P.								
LEIGH, LITTLE chap.	380	340	359	381	387	407	409	407	See Leigh, Little C.P.								
LOSTOCK GRALAM tns.	361	453	525	537	574	519	467*	568	See Lostock Gralam C.P.								
MARBURY tns.	20	41	35	26	37	23	17	37	See Marbury C.P.								
MARSTON tns.	284	349	404	465	479	559	745*	772	See Marston C.P.								
NORTHWICH tns.	1,338	1,382	1,490	1,481	1,368	1,377	1,190	1,244	See Northwich U.D.								
NORTHWICH, CASTLE tns.	385	422	575	692	746	1,135	1,395*	1,650*	See Northwich, Castle C.P.								

									Reference
PEOVER INFERIOR tns.	131	99	88	108	104	121	109	122	See Peover Inferior C.P.
PEOVER, NETHER chap.	256	238	250	226	248	232	258	258	See Peover, Nether C.P.
PICKMERE tns.	148	168	217	228	241	242	247	256	See Pickmere C.P.
PLUMLEY tns.	303	367	366	378	385	376	365	365	See Plumley C.P.
SEVEN OAKS tns.	103	147	141	149	149	148	159	158	See Seven Oaks C.P.
STRETTON tns.	220	233	277	324	362	367	373	364	See Stretton C.P.
TABLEY INFERIOR tns.	127	129	110	134	100	123	130	139	See Tabley Inferior C.P.
WHITLEY, HIGHER tns.	283	266	244	283	330	322	367*	340	See Whitley, Higher C.P.
WHITLEY, LOWER tns.	137	233	236	237	219	216	211	210	See Whitley, Lower C.P.
WINCHAM tns.	367	420	491	589	650	684	642	911*	See Wincham C.P.
WINNINGTON tns.	196	192	230	256	321	405	460	529	See Winnington C.P.
WITTON CUM TWAMBROOKS chap.	1,531	1,966	2,405c	2,912	3,338	3,493	3,677*	4,229*	See Witton cum Twambrooks C.P.
Witton cum Twambrooks C.P.	601	532	510	476	486	486	412	403	
BUDWORTH, GREAT C.P.				Part of Budworth, Great A.P., q.v.					
BUDWORTH, LITTLE A.P. and C.P.	434	470	524	621	599	578	582	601	
	541	554	552	585d	600	568e	508	531	
BUERTON C.P.				Part of Aldford A.P., q.v.					
	64	62	72	61	73	55	54	29	
BUERTON C.P.				Part of Audlem A.P., q.v.					
	471	459	395	421	405	426	408	428	
BUGLAWTON U.S.D. and C.P.				Part of Astbury A.P., q.v.					
	1,550	1,572	1,438	1,452	1,382	1,651f	(See Congleton M.B., Eaton C.P., and Rode, North C.P.)	229	
BULKELEY C.P.				Part of Malpas A.P., q.v.					
	172	180	168	152	137	120	146	214	
BUNBURY A.P.	3,073	3,453	4,021	4,373	4,678	4,753	4,727	4,631	
ALPRAHAM tns.	335	333	409	418	520	518	530	576	See Alpraham C.P.
BEESTON tns.	377	410	441	434	426	397	355	317	See Beeston C.P.
BUNBURY tns.	519	574	667	834	926*	931	990	965	See Bunbury C.P.
BURWARDSLEY chap.	204	250	272	394	458	479	500	522	See Burwardsley C.P.
CALVELEY tns.	144	201	221	170	190	212	285	263	See Calveley C.P.
HAUGHTON tns.	151	138	175	172	161	155	172	144	See Haughton C.P.
PECKFORTON tns.	260	281	294	331	309	286	221	205	See Peckforton C.P.
RIDLEY tns.	122	123	123	100	123	133	129	111	See Ridley C.P.
SPURSTOW tns.	339	373	533	588	508*	562	514	499	See Spurstow C.P.
TILSTONE FEARNALL chap.	130	145	166	170	189	155	173	215	See Tilstone Fearnall C.P.
TIVERTON tns.	377	493	591	618	687	747	704	652	See Tiverton C.P.
WARDLE tns.	115	132	129	144	181	178	154	162	See Wardle C.P.
BUNBURY C.P.	884	857	820	943	1,006	882	915g	833	917	Part of Bunbury A.P., q.v.

(t) In 1901 part of Bredbury C.P. (pop. 20 in 1901) was transferred to Stockport C.B. and C.P., and in 1902 part of Brinnington C.P. (pop. 98 in 1901) was included in Bredbury C.P.

(s) In 1936 Bredbury and Romiley C.P.s were united to form Bredbury and Romiley C.P., which thus became co-extensive with the U.D. The U.D. and C.P. was extended to include part of Compstall U.D. and C.P. (pop. 804 in 1931), and part of Hyde M.B. (pop. 20 in 1931).

(t) In 1952 part of Bredbury and Romiley U.D. and C.P. (pop. 151 in 1951) was transferred to Stockport C.B.

(u) Created 1936 by the union of Brereton cum Smethwick C.P. and Davenport C.P.

(v) In 1933 part of Brimstage C.P. (pop. 5 in 1931) was transferred to Barnston C.P. in Wirral U.D., and Brimstage as thus altered was transferred to Bebington M.B.

(w) In 1888 Brindley C.P. was extended to include part of Baddiley C.P. (pop. 2 in 1891).

(x) In 1804 that part of Brinnington C.P. in Stockport C.B. (pop. 6,528 in 1901) was transferred to Stockport C.B.

(y) In 1895 Bromborough U.D. and C.P. was extended to include part of Poulton cum Spital C.P. (pop. 67 in 1901).

(z) Rudheath tns. is situated mainly in Davenham A.P. but extends into Great Budworth and Sandbach A.P.s. In 1821 the pop. of that part of Rudheath tns. in Great Budworth A.P. was 80 and in 1871, 88.

(a) In 1851 the total for 1811 was corrected to 14,264. In 1821 and 1831 the figures given in the census were respectively 14,346 and 15,955.

(b) From 1811 to 1851 Hartford was wholly returned under Great Budworth A.P., but it was partly situated in Weaverham A.P., where part of its pop. was returned in 1861 and 1871. In 1851 the total for Weaverham A.P. included 17 inhabitants of Hartford.

(c) Included 80 inhabs. of Rudheath tns. which was mainly situated in Davenham A.P., q.v

(d) In 1882 Little Budworth C.P. was amalgamated with Oulton Lowe C.P. (pop. 47 in 1881).

(e) In 1936 parts of Little Budworth C.P. (pop. respectively 18 and 20 in 1931) were transferred to Delamere and Okamere C.P.s.

(f) In 1936 Buglawton U.D. was dissolved, part (pop. 1,617 in 1931) being transferred to Congleton M.B., and part (pop. 34 in 1931) to Eaton C.P.

(g) In 1936 part of Tilstone Fearnall C.P. (pop. 28 in 1931) was transferred to Bunbury C.P.

	1801	1811	1821	1831	1841	1851	1861	1871	1881	1891	1901	1911	1921	1931	1951	1961	1971
BURLAND C.P.	Part of Acton A.P., q.v.								657	622[h]	581	636	634	595	546	522	565
BURTON A.P.	427	447	481	458	428	467	425	437									
BURTON tns.	288	300	326	313	282	291	265	272	See Burton C.P.								
PUDDINGTON tns.	139	147	155	145	146	176	160	165	See Puddington C.P.								
BURTON C.P.	Part of Burton A.P., q.v.								257	266	222	264	282	438*	See Neston U.D.		
BURTON C.P.	Part of Tarvin A.P., q.v.								70	65	53	41	49	41	42	41	38
BURWARDSLEY C.P.	Part of Bunbury A.P., q.v.								440	383	329	318	354	298	310	268	181
BUTLEY C.P.	Part of Prestbury A.P., q.v.								552	523	471	461	470	554[l]	See Bollington C.P. and Prestbury C.P.		
BYLEY C.P.	Part of Middlewich A.P., q.v.								137	203	199[j]	178	176	146	217[k]	177	132
CALDECOTT C.P.	Part of Shocklach A.P., q.v.								55	49	44	56	47	42	33	26	20
CALDY C.P.	Part of Kirby, West A.P., q.v.								187	170	202	183	266	426*	See Hoylake U.D.		
CALVELEY C.P.	Part of Bunbury A.P., q.v.								279	321	312	316	271	270	202	217	191
CAPENHURST C.P.	Part of Shotwick A.P., q.v.								159	158	159	146	139	157	253	338	300
CAPESTHORNE C.P.	Part of Prestbury A.P., q.v.								111	114	76	83	102	97	See Siddington C.P.		
CARDEN C.P.	Part of Tilston A.P., q.v.								169	156	163	158	133	151	98	96	87
CARRINGTON C.P.	Part of Bowdon A.P., q.v.								438	568	514	522	531	504	627	642	488
CATHEDRAL CHURCH PRECINCT	E.P.P. and C.P. in Chester City and M.B., q.v.								245	See Chester C.B. and C.P.							
CAUGHALL C.P.	Part of Backford A.P., q.v.								19	19	21	23	15	13	9	18	46
CHEADLE A.P.	3,582	5,120	6,508	8,154	10,145	10,479	10,852	11,996	See Cheadle C.P.								
CHEADLE BULKELEY tns.	1,577	2,509	3,229	4,228*	5,463	5,489	6,115	6,927*	See Cheadle C.P.								
CHEADLE MOSELEY tns.	971	1,296	1,534	1,946	2,288	2,319	2,329	2,612*	See Cheadle C.P.								
HANDFORTH CUM BOSDEN tns.	1,034	1,315	1,745	1,980[l]	2,394*	2,671	2,408*	2,457	See Handforth cum Bosden U.D. and C.P.								
CHEADLE C.P.[m]	Part of Cheadle A.P., q.v.								12,263	16,830	See Cheadle and Gatley U.D. and C.P.						
part of, in Stockport C.B., q.v.									6,294	10,022	See Stockport C.P.						
rural part, after 1886 in Cheadle and Gatley U.D., q.v.									5,969	See Cheadle C.P. in Cheadle and Gatley U.D.							
CHEADLE AND GATLEY U.S.D. and, from 1930, C.P.[n]									8,252		10,820	9,913	11,036	18,473*	31,511[o]	45,621	60,799
CHEADLE C.P. (part of, to 1901)	Part of Cheadle A.P., q.v.								6,808		9,044	7,867[p]	8,845	See Cheadle and Gatley U.D. and C.P.			
STOCKPORT ETCHELLS C.P.	Part of Stockport A.P., q.v.								1,444		1,776	2,046	2,191	See Cheadle and Gatley U.D. and C.P.			
CHECKLEY CUM WRINEHILL C.P.	Part of Wybunbury A.P., q.v.								170	182	206	240	242	235	220	221	98[q]
CHELFORD C.P.	Part of Prestbury A.P., q.v.								313	342	374	384	355	341	392	437	431
CHESTER C.B. and C.P.[r]										37,105	38,309	39,028	40,802	41,440	48,237[s]	59,268[t]	62,911
CHESTER CITY: from 1835 M.B. and from 1872 U.S.D.	15,052	16,140	19,949	21,344	23,115	27,766	31,110	35,257*	36,794								
CATHEDRAL CHURCH PRECINCT E.P.P. and C.P.	—	233	270	389	329	377	376	413	245								
CHESTER CASTLE E.P.P. and C.P.	193	—	—	32*	436	591[u]	128*	434[v]									

HOLY AND UNDIVIDED TRINITY A.P. and C.P. (part of)	2,264	2,224	3,036	3,226	3,340*	3,375*	3,606	3,793	3,020
ST. BRIDGET A.P. and C.P.	636	733	805	747	675	861	1,040*	1,077	1,104
ST. JOHN, LITTLE E.P.P.w					51		61		
ST. JOHN THE BAPTIST A.P. and C.P.	3,831	4,244	5,098	6,035	6,752*	8,493	9,835	11,943x	13,247
ST. MARTIN A.P. and C.P.	574	682	565	528	532*	536*	694*	752	779
ST. MARY ON THE HILL A.P. and C.P. (part of)	2,129y	2,469	3,376	3,085	2,975	3,415	4,499*	5,149	5,276
ST. MICHAEL A.P. and C.P.	725	655	712	643	649*	775	922	888	758
ST. OLAVE A.P. and C.P.	438	381	587	456	430	518	480	689	579
ST. OSWALD A.P. and C.P. (part of)	3,377	3,416	4,334	5,209	5,959	6,702	7,534	9,902	11,724
ST. PETER A.P. and C.P.	810	933	1,016	863	847	948	798*	686*	622
SPITAL BOUGHTON E.P.P. and C.P.	75	170	150	131	191	158	163	169	139
CHESTER R.D.	8,309	10,824	10,989	12,447	13,365	16,165	25,197	28,324	34,671z
CHESTER CASTLE C.P.a	414	249	230	224	163	228*	123	38	8
CHIDLOW C.P.	Part of Malpas A.P., q.v.				17	14	19	16	11	13	11	10	10
CHOLMONDELEY C.P.	Part of Malpas A.P., q.v.				285	318	298	287	278	278	266	238	185
CHOLMONDESTON C.P.	Part of Acton A.P., q.v.				187	214	162	170	195	158	172	168	175
CHORLEY C.P.	Part of Wilmslow A.P., q.v.										1,961	2,141
part in Chorley U.D.											1,675	1,838	See Alderley Edge C.P.
rural part											286	303	See Chorley C.P.

(h) In 1882 part of Baddiley C.P. (pop. 2 in 1891) was transferred to Burland C.P. as a result of the Divided Parishes Act.

(i) Dissolved 1936, part (pop. 536 in 1931) being transferred to Prestbury C.P., and part (pop. 18 in 1931) to Bollington U.D. and C.P.

(j) In 1892 Croxton and Ravenscroft C.P.s (pops. respectively 49 and 20 in 1881) were amalgamated with Byley C.P.

(k) In 1936 parts of Leese C.P. (pop. 38 in 1931) and of Rudheath (pop. 7 in 1931) were transferred to Byley C.P.

(l) Between 1831 and 1871 the pops. of Handforth and of Bosden were separately returned, viz. 1831: Handforth 591, Bosden 1,389; 1841: Handforth 681, Bosden 1,713; 1851: Handforth 650, Bosden 2,021; 1861: Handforth 629, Bosden 1,779; 1871: Handforth 662, Bosden 1,795. In 1886 the part of Cheadle C.P. not in Stockport C.B. was included in Cheadle and Gatley U.D., q.v. In 1804 the part of Cheadle C.P. (pop. 15,099 in 1901) in Stockport C.B. was transferred to Stockport C.P.

(m) In 1879 Cheadle Bulkeley and Cheadle Moseley C.P.s were united to form Cheadle C.P.

(n) Created 1886 from that part of Cheadle C.P. not in Stockport C.B., and from Stockport Etchells C.P. In 1901 part of Cheadle C.P. (pop. 7,950 in 1911) was transferred to Stockport C.B. and C.P. In 1930 Cheadle C.P. and Stockport Etchells C.P. were united to form Cheadle and Gatley C.P. which was co-extensive with the U.D.

(o) In 1936 part of Handforth U.D. (pop. 93 in 1931) was transferred to Cheadle and Gatley U.D., and part of Cheadle and Gatley U.D. and C.P. (pop. 31 in 1931) was transferred to Wilmslow U.D. and C.P.

(p) See above, note (n).

(q) In 1965 part of Checkley cum Wrinehill C.P. was transferred to Newcastle under Lyme R.D. (Staffs.).

(r) In 1884 the C.P.s in Chester City were amalgamated to form Chester C.P. Cheshire was designated a C.B. under the Local Government Act, 1888.

(s) In 1936 Chester C.B. and C.P. was extended to include parts of Blacon cum Crabwall, Great Boughton, Hoole, Marlston cum Lache, and Newton by Chester C.P.s (pop. respectively 774, 954, 404, 41, and 2,134 in 1931).

(t) In 1954 Chester C.B. and C.P. was extended to include parts of Hoole and Upton-by-Chester C.P.s (pop. respectively 8,705 and 10 in 1951).

(u) In 1841 and 1851 the pop. of Chester Castle barracks and gaol were separately returned, viz. 1841: 258 (barracks), 178 (gaol); 1851: 376 (barracks), 215 (gaol).

(v) In 1881 Chester Castle C.P. was stated to lie outside Chester M.B. and U.S.D. It was put into Chester R.S.D. in 1889.

(w) In 1851 Little St. John, previously returned with St. Oswald A.P., was stated to comprise the Blue Coat Hospital and six alms-houses for decayed widows. Though locally situated in St. Oswald parish, the poor were maintained by the corporation of Chester who claimed to be the owners of the hospital and alms-houses.

(x) In 1871 and 1881 St. John the Baptist parish was stated to include part of Hoole tns. (pop. 1,328 in 1871 and 2,342 in 1881).   (y) This figure was corrected to 2,251 in 1851.

(z) In 1963 part of Little Stanney C.P. was transferred from Chester R.D. to Ellesmere Port M.B., part of Christleton C.P. to Tarvin R.D., and part of Cotton Edmunds and Tarvin C.P.s from Tarvin R.D. to Chester R.D. In 1967 another part of Little Stanney was transferred from Chester R.D. to Ellesmere Port M.B.

(a) Chester Castle was part of Chester R.D., not of Chester C.B. and C.P.

(b) In 1936 part of Chorley C.P. (pop. 25 in 1931) was transferred to Alderley Edge U.D. and C.P.

	1801	1811	1821	1831	1841	1851	1861	1871	1881	1891	1901	1911	1921	1931	1951	1961	1971
CHORLEY C.P.	Part of Wrenbury A.P., q.v.								166	145	132	140	134	162	167	143	111
CHORLEY U.S.D.[c]									2,067	2,270							
BOLLIN FEE C.P. (part of)									244	277							
CHORLEY C.P. (part of)									1,675	1,838							
FULSHAW C.P. (part of)									104	155							
POWNALL FEE C.P. (part of)									44[d]	See Fulshaw C.P.							
CHORLTON C.P.	Part of Malpas A.P., q.v.								102	102	104	90	93	90	82	71	57
CHORLTON C.P.	Part of Wybunbury A.P., q.v.								78	85	79	92	86	76	78	92	83[e]
CHORLTON-BY-BACKFORD C.P.	Part of Backford A.P., q.v.								66	71	86	70	86	82	113	77	74
CHOWLEY C.P.	Part of Coddington A.P., q.v.								39	37	35	52	57	61	65	51	21
CHRISTLETON A.P.	857	770	954	893[f]	875	971	1,006	987	See Christleton C.P.								
CHRISTLETON tns.	651	560	701	633	625	719	698	704	See Christleton C.P.								
COTTON ABBOTTS tns.	21	22	17	11	15	17	20	23	See Cotton Abbotts C.P.								
COTTON EDMUNDS tns.	73	75	85	79	77	68	59	50	See Cotton Edmunds C.P.								
LITTLETON tns.	24	44	43	48	48	45	66	58	See Littleton C.P.								
ROWTON tns.	88	69	108	122	110	122	163	152	See Rowton C.P.								
CHRISTLETON C.P.	Part of Christleton A.P., q.v.								835	902[g]	859	937	896	997	1,311	2,047	2,240[h]
CHURTON BY ALDFORD C.P.	Part of Aldford A.P., q.v.								256	196	223	220	194	191	175	168	130
CHURTON BY FARNDON C.P.	Part of Farndon A.P., q.v.								113	121	126	136	360	145*	109	116	122
CHURTON HEATH C.P.	Part of St. Oswald's A.P., q.v.								8	7	7	16	7	15	15	18	16
CLAUGHTON WITH GRANGE C.P.	Part of Bidston A.P., q.v.																12
CLAVERTON E.P.P. and C.P.[i]						0	0	0	0	0	0	0	0	0	4	6	
CLIFTON C.P.	Part of Runcorn A.P., q.v.								203	215	213	204	198	178	See Sutton C.P.		
CLIVE C.P.	Part of Middlewich A.P., q.v.								165	173	147	145	145	178	See Winsford U.D.		
CLOTTON HOOFIELD C.P.	Part of Tarvin A.P., q.v.								342	373	369	360	359	382	350	307	300
CLUTTON C.P.	Part of Farndon A.P., q.v.								71		78	60	66	56	67	119	125
CODDINGTON A.P.	Part of Farndon A.P., q.v.	320	358	346	345	324	256	325	297	See Coddington C.P.							
ALDERSEY tns.	154	157	138	153	138	103	119	133	See Aldersey C.P.								
CHOWLEY tns.	56	68	78	70	77	58	67	54	See Chowley C.P.								
CODDINGTON tns.	110	133	130	122	109	95	139	110	See Coddington C.P.								
CODDINGTON C.P.	Part of Coddington A.P., q.v.								115	106	103	108	96	95	115	105	95
COGSHALL C.P.	Part of Budworth, Great A.P., q.v.								90	86	86	84	92	93	See Comberbach C.P.		
COMBERBACH C.P.	Part of Budworth, Great A.P., q.v.								310	392	411	380	395	388	624	546	620
COMPSTALL C.P. and, from 1902, U.D.	Part of Stockport A.P. and Werneth C.P.										875	908	944	865[j]	(See Bredbury and Romiley C.P. and U.D., and Hyde M.B. and C.P.		
CONGLETON M.B. and C.P.	Part of Astbury A.P., q.v.					10,520*	12,344*	11,344*	11,116	10,744	10,707	11,309	11,762	12,885	15,502[k]	16,823	20,341
CONGLETON R.D.									19,851	14,417	12,220	12,821	13,219	13,124	13,261	14,096	19,175[l]
COOLE PILATE C.P.	Part of Acton A.P., q.v.								62	49	53	62	49	52	70	60	58
COPPENHALL A.P.	362	380	512	498	747	5,066	8,981	19,904*	See Coppenhall, Church C.P. / See Crewe M.B.								
COPPENHALL, CHURCH tns.	241	266	366	350	544	495	822	2,094*	See Coppenhall, Church C.P.								
COPPENHALL, MONKS tns.	121	114	146	148	203	4,571*	8,159*	17,810*	See Crewe M.B.								
COPPENHALL, CHURCH C.P.	Part of Coppenhall A.P., q.v.								2,879	4,165	—[m]	731	783	996	See Crewe M.B.		
COTTON C.P.	Part of Sandbach A.P., q.v.								43	27	21	24	25	33	See Cranage C.P.		
COTTON ABBOTTS C.P.	Part of Christleton A.P., q.v.								13	12[n]	12	11	10	11	8	5	3
COTTON EDMUNDS C.P.	Part of Christleton A.P., q.v.								48	59[n]	62	66	61	65	28	37	28[o]

Place	Notes	Population figures (as printed, most recent → earliest)
CRANAGE C.P.	Part of Sandbach A.P., q.v.	1,448 1,276 1,217[p] 399 423 410 361 382 442
CREWE M.B. and U.S.D. and COPPENHALL, MONKS C.P.[q]		51,421 53,195 52,423[s] 46,069 46,497 44,960 42,074 28,761[r] 24,385
CREWE C.P.	Part of Coppenhall A.P., q.v.	146 147 182[t] 363 404 365 406 448 423
CREWE C.P.	Part of Barthomley A.P., q.v.	30 43 61 47 84 54 56 40 53
CROUGHTON C.P.	Part of Farndon A.P.	19 21 38 21 23 36 29 41 29
CROWLEY C.P.	Part of St. Oswald's A.P., q.v.	See Antrobus C.P. … 139 146 172 182 190 196
CROWTON C.P.	Part of Budworth, Great A.P., q.v.	362 371 420 474 488 487 479 531[u] 463
CROXTON C.P.	Part of Middlewich A.P., q.v.	See Byley C.P. … 49
CUDDINGTON C.P.	Part of Malpas A.P., q.v.	146 159 219 236 226 271 255 272 271
CUDDINGTON C.P.	Part of Weaverham A.P., q.v.	4,447 3,765 2,898[v] 608 520 503 465 505 408
DARESBURY C.P.	Part of Runcorn A.P., q.v.	330[x] 283 235[w] 86 104 135 153 152 139
DARNHALL C.P.	Part of Whitegate A.P., q.v.	193 205 212[z] 210 241 285 300[y] 333 167
DAVENHAM A.P.		2,891 3,250 3,567[a] 4,521 5,335 6,294 6,855 7,543[b]
BOSTOCK tns.	See Bostock C.P.	169 154 154 190 218 174 207 173
DAVENHAM tns.	See Davenham C.P.	554* 518 552 488 413 379 317 327
EATON tns.	See Eaton C.P.	21 11 16 11 13 18 13 15
LEFTWICH tns.	See Leftwich C.P.	2,749 2,627 2,528* 2,001* 1,799 1,192 979 899
MOULTON tns.	See Moulton C.P.	511* 395* 328 318 243 196 187 103
NEWHALL tns.	See Newhall C.P.	17 28 27 26 22 17 10 13
RUDHEATH tns.[c]	See Rudheath C.P.	429* 411 435 435 367 363 303 264
SHIPBROOK tns.	See Shipbrook C.P.	77 94 81 89 83 92 84 90
SHURLACH tns.	See Shurlach C.P.	170 150 174 159 98 64 57 49
STANTHORNE tns.	See Stanthorne C.P.	177* 161 156 169 149 148 134 120
WHARTON tns.	See Wharton C.P.	2,597* 2,234* 1,775 1,400* 1,060 853 888 753
WHATCROFT tns.	See Whatcroft C.P.	72 72 68 49 56 71 71 85

(c) Chorley U.S.D. consisted of parts of Bollin Fee, Chorley, Fulshaw, and Pownall Fee. Pownall Fee C.P. was dissolved in 1894, part (pop. 2,750 in 1901) being transferred to Wilmslow U.D. and C.P., and part (pop. 1,153 in 1901) being constituted Styal C.P. Fulshaw C.P. was dissolved at the same time, part (pop. 1,403 in 1901) being transferred to Wilmslow U.D. and C.P., and part (pop. 251 in 1901) to Bollin Fee C.P. Thus altered, Chorley U.D. was renamed Alderley Edge U.D., and Alderley Edge A.P. was created, q.v.

(d) In 1882 part of Pownall Fee (pop. 37 in 1901) was transferred to Fulshaw C.P. under the Divided Parishes Act, and in 1888 a further part (pop. 28 in 1891) to Bollin Fee C.P.

(e) In 1965 part of Balterley C.P. (pop. 2 in 1961) was transferred from Newcastle under Lyme R.D. to Chorlton C.P.

(f) In 1831 the total for Christleton A.P. was wrongly returned as 1,409.

(g) In 1888 part of Christleton C.P. (pop. 7 in 1801) was transferred to Waverton C.P.

(h) In 1963 the boundaries of Christleton, Barrow, Cotton Edmunds, and Tarvin C.P.s were readjusted but no change in pop. was involved.

(i) No return was made for Claverton between 1801 and 1841.

(j) Dissolved 1936, part (pop. 804 in 1931) being transferred to Bredbury and Romiley U.D. and C.P., and part (pop. 61 in 1931) to Hyde M.B. and C.P.

(k) In 1936 parts of Buglawton C.P. (pop. 1,617 in 1931), Eaton C.P. (pop. 120 in 1931), Hulme Walfield C.P. (pop. 19 in 1931), and Newbold Astbury C.P. (pop. 25 in 1931) were transferred to Congleton M.B.

(l) In 1965 parts of Church Lawton and Odd Rode C.P.s formerly in Congleton R.D. were transferred to Kidsgrove U.D. (Staffs.), and part of Kidsgrove C.P. (pop. 58 in 1961) was transferred to Congleton R.D.

(m) In 1894 part of Church Coppenhall C.P. (pop. 4,892 in 1901) was included in Monks Coppenhall C.P.

(n) In 1888 part of Cotton Abbotts C.P. (pop. 5 in 1891) was transferred to Cotton Edmunds C.P.

(o) In 1963 parts of Foulk Stapleford, Hockenhull, and Tarvin C.P.s were transferred to Cotton Edmunds C.P., and parts of Cotton Edmunds C.P. were transferred to Foulk Stapleford, Hockenhull, and Tarvin C.P.s.

(p) In 1936 part of Cranage C.P. (pop. 13 in 1931) was transferred to Lach Dennis, and Cotton C.P. (pop. 33 in 1931) and part of Leese C.P. (pop. 56 in 1931) were transferred to Cranage C.P.

(q) Crewe M.B. was incorporated in 1877.

(r) In 1892 Crewe M.B. was extended to include parts of Church Coppenhall C.P., Shavington cum Gresty C.P., and Wistaston C.P. (pops. respectively 4,892, 924, and 328 in 1901), and in 1894 Monks Coppenhall C.P. was extended to include those areas.

(s) In 1936 Crewe M.B. was extended to include Church Coppenhall C.P., and parts of Crewe, Haslington, Leighton, Shavington cum Gresty, Warmingham, Wistaston, and Woolstanwood C.P.s (total pop. 2,252 in 1931).

(t) In 1936 part of Crewe C.P. (pop. 186 in 1931) was transferred to Crewe M.B. and Monks Coppenhall C.P.

(u) In 1892 Onston C.P. (pop. 93 in 1881) was united with Crowton C.P.

(v) In 1936 part of Weaverham C.P. (pop. 402 in 1931) was transferred to Cuddington C.P.

(w) In 1936 Keckwick and Newton by Daresbury C.P.s (pop. respectively 54 and 179 in 1931) were united with Daresbury C.P.

(x) In 1967 part of Daresbury C.P. was transferred to Runcorn U.D. and part of Norton C.P. was transferred to Daresbury C.P.

(y) In 1892 Weaver C.P. (pop. 139 in 1881) was united with Darnhall C.P.

(z) In 1931 part of Darnhall C.P. (pop. 6 in 1931) was transferred to Winsford U.D. and C.P. In 1936 part of Over (pop. 24 in 1931) in Winsford U.D. was transferred to Darnhall C.P.

(a) In 1821 and 1831 the totals for Davenham A.P. were wrongly returned as 3,470 and 4,515.

(b) See below, note (c).

(c) Rudheath tns. was situated chiefly in Davenham A.P. but extended into Great Budworth and Sandbach A.P.s. In 1821 97 of its inhabitants were stated to be attributable to Great Budworth and Sandbach A.P.s and in 1871 88 and 4 inhabitants were returned in Great Budworth and Sandbach respectively.

Place	1801	1811	1821	1831	1841	1851	1861	1871	1881	1891	1901	1911	1921	1931	1951	1961	1971
DAVENHAM C.P.	Part of Davenham A.P., q.v.								585	670	706	616	616	644	2,305[d]	2,149[e]	2,504
DAVENPORT C.P.	Part of Astbury A.P., q.v.								82	89	80	87	68	81	See Brereton C.P.		
DELAMERE A.P.[f]	—	—	424	742[g]	914	1,050	1,146	1,329									
Delamere tns.	—	—	262	424	412	498	474	524*	See Delamere C.P.								
Eddisbury tns.	—	—	—	178	204	191	228	232	See Eddisbury C.P.								
Kingswood tns.	—	—	72	—[h]	103	109	160	187	See Kingswood C.P.								
Oakmere tns.	—	—	90	140	195	252	284	386*	See Oakmere C.P.								
DELAMERE C.P.	Part of Delamere A.P., q.v.								578		612	666	671	713	1,170[i]	1,193	1,304
DISLEY C.P. (part of, in 1891)	Part of Stockport A.P., q.v.									512							
DISLEY R.D. and C.P.	Part of Stockport A.P., q.v.								3,312	2,260[j]	2,827	2,958	3,022	3,212	2,865	3,188	3,986
DODCOTT DUM WILKESLEY C.P.	Part of Audlem A.P. and Wrenbury A.P., q.v.								654	569[k]	626	626	542	547	451	451	422
DODDINGTON C.P.	Part of Wybunbury A.P., q.v.								47	60	70	61	57	66	1,094	51	127
DODLESTON A.P. (part of)[l]	282	324	351	356	371	352	403	388									
Dodleston tns.	185	229	266	252	298	258	304	288	See Dodleston C.P.								
KINNERTON, LOWER tns.	97	95	85	104	73	94	99	100	See Kinnerton, Lower C.P.								
DODLESTON C.P.	Part of Dodleston A.P., q.v.								283	273	307	303	302	247	267	405	363
DUCKINGTON C.P.	Part of Malpas A.P., q.v.								62	47	51	62	56	65	59	65	52
DUDDON C.P.	Part of Tarvin A.P., q.v.								176	160	186	203	194	194	202	234	301
DUKINFIELD U.D., C.P. after 1894, and, from 1899, M.B.[m]	Part of Stockport A.P., q.v.								16,942	17,408	18,929[n]	19,442	19,509	19,311	18,451[o]	17,316	17,315
DUKINFIELD C.P.									29,675	29,239							
part in Stalybridge M.B.									12,733	11,831[p]							
part in Dukinfield U.S.D.									16,942	17,408							
DUNHAM MASSEY C.P.	Part of Bowdon A.P., q.v.								1,977	2,079	2,644	2,928	1,668	1,694[q]	523[r]	525	535
DUNHAM ON THE HILL C.P.	Part of Thornton A.P., q.v.								276	287	282	284	275	316	446	589	562
DUTTON C.P.	Part of Budworth, Great A.P., q.v.								452	416	426	484	402	454[s]	516	481	314[t]
EASTHAM A.P.[u]	1,142	1,090	1,430	1,580	2,377	2,411	2,641	3,426									
Eastham tns.	348	325	368	350	372	419	522	621*	See Eastham C.P.								
Hooton tns.	91	109	112	103	120	110	141	140	See Hooton C.P.								
Netherpool tns.	13	29	24	19	32	23	25	30	See Netherpool C.P.								
Overpool tns.	89	71	74	93	96	72	88	81	See Overpool C.P.								
SUTTON, GREAT tns.	153	166	182	162	203	203	224	286	See Sutton, Great C.P.								
SUTTON, LITTLE tns.	166	219	329	387	426	432	474	711	See Sutton, Little C.P.								
THORNTON, CHILDER tns.	112	96	177	296	361	319	435	637	See Thornton, Childer C.P.								
WHITBY tns. (part of)	170[v]	75	164	170	767*	833*	732*	920*	See Whitby C.P.								
EASTHAM C.P.	Part of Eastham A.P., q.v.								639	1,729*	913	1,084	1,098	2,990[w]	See Bebington M.B.		
EATON C.P.	Part of Davenham A.P., q.v.								17	24	26	20	20	75*	See Davenham C.P.		
EATON C.P.	Part of Eccleston A.P., q.v.								132	239	182	204	111	143	706	73	84
EATON C.P.	Part of Prestbury A.P., q.v.								401	357	346	333	347	325	242[x]	257	349
ECCLESTON A.P.	280	320	358	361	321	376	349	405	See Tarporley U.D.								
Eaton tns.	81	54	66	73	64	87	82	110	See Eaton C.P.								
Eccleston tns.	199	266	292	288	257	289	267	295	See Eccleston C.P.								
ECCLESTON C.P.	Part of Eccleston A.P., q.v.								323	343	320	321	293	291	272	261	203
EDDISBURY HUNDRED	17,851	20,761	24,593	26,891	28,510	30,258	30,339	33,013	36,073								
EDGE C.P.	Part of Malpas A.P., q.v.								248	244	212	251	250	238	267	243	218
EDGERLEY C.P.	Part of Aldford A.P., q.v.								7	5	6	12	4	11	6	6	10

Place	Figures
EDLESTON C.P.	Part of Acton A.P., q.v. ......
EGERTON C.P.	Part of Malpas A.P., q.v. ......
ELLESMERE PORT U.D., from 1950 C.P., and from 1955 M.B.[y]	
ELLESMERE PORT AND WHITBY U.D.[a]	10,366 · 10,366[a] · 13,063 · 18,911 · 32,653 · 44,681 · 61,637[z] (also 10,253* · 12,891 · 18,267*)
ELLESMERE PORT C.P.	See Ellesmere Port U.D.
STANNEY, GREAT C.P.	644 · 448 · 252 · 172 · 174 · 201[c] See Moston C.P.
ELTON C.P.	Part of Thornton A.P., q.v. 197 · 203* · 208 · 275 · 485 · 410 · 478 · 53 · 190
ELTON C.P.	Part of Warmingham A.P., q.v. 549 · 482 · 374 · 485 · 1,142
ETCHELLS, NORTHEN C.P.	Part of Northenden A.P., q.v. Part of Manchester C.B. (Lancs.).
ETCHELLS, STOCKPORT C.P.	Part of Stockport A.P., q.v. 756 · 758 · 823 · 906 · 1,369
FADDILEY C.P.	Part of Acton A.P., q.v. 234 · 217 · 232 · 223 · 211 · 193 · 159 · 147
FALLIBROOME C.P.	Part of Prestbury A.P., q.v. 35 · 42 · 39 · 43 · 49 · 72 See Cheadle and Gatley U.S.D. / See Prestbury C.P.
BARTON A.P.	See Barton C.P.
BARTON tns.	718 · 764 · 857 · 864 · 999 · 1,013 · 992 · 995 ; 143 · 177 · 168 · 169 · 146 · 131 · 120 · 123
CHURTON BY FARNDON	
CHURTON BY FARNDON tns.	See Churton by Farndon C.P.
CLUTTON tns.	See Clutton C.P. 117 · 128 · 122 · 117 · 132 · 147 ; 100 · 110 · 89 · 74
CREWE tns.	See Crewe C.P. 72 · 84 · 100 · 96 · 110 · 67 · 51 · 53 · 102 · 73
FARNDON tns.	See Farndon C.P. 29 · 38 · 51 · 47 · 67 · 102
FARNDON C.P.	Part of Farndon A.P., q.v. 357 · 337 · 423 · 429 · 521 · 558 · 557 · 598
FRANKBY C.P.	Part of Kirby, West A.P., q.v. 556 · 560 · 564 · 546 · 573 · 560 · 564 · 688 · 818 · 1,162 ; 185 · 221 · 248 · 270 · 255 · 286 See Hoylake U.D.

(d) In 1936 parts of Eaton C.P. (pop. 75 in 1931) and Leftwich C.P. (pop. 1,021 in 1931) were transferred to Davenham C.P.

(e) In 1955 part of Davenham C.P. (pop. 34 in 1951) was transferred to Northwich U.D.

(f) Delamere A.P. was created in 1812 as a result of the inclosure of the royal forest of Delamere.

(g) In 1851 this figure was corrected to 828.

(h) In 1851 the pop. of Kingswood was stated to have been 86 in 1831.

(i) In 1936 part of Delamere C.P. (pop. 402 in 1931) was transferred to Utkinton C.P., and part of Eddisbury C.P. (pop. 19 in 1931) and part of Little Budworth C.P. (pop. 18 in 1931) were transferred to Delamere C.P.

(j) In 1891 Disley was stated to be partly in Derb. In 1894 the part of Disley C.P. in Derb. (pop. 1,520 in 1901) was constituted Newton C.P., and the part in Ches. Disley R.D. and C.P.

(k) In 1889 part of Dodcott cum Wilkesley C.P. (pop. 23 in 1891) was transferred to Acton C.P.

(l) Dodleston A.P. extended into the county of Flint.

(m) Dukinfield U.D. comprised part of Dukinfield C.P. only until 1894 when the part of Dukinfield C.P. in Stalybridge M.B. (pop. 11,701 in 1901) was transferred to Stalybridge C.P.

(n) In 1908 part of Dukinfield U.D. (pop. 39 in 1901) was transferred to Ashton-under-Lyne U.D. and C.P. and from Ches. admin. co. to Lancs. admin. co., and part of Ashton-under-Lyne U.D. and C.P. (pop. 45 in 1901) was transferred to Dukinfield U.D. and C.P.

(o) In 1936 part of Dukinfield M.B. (pop. 17 in 1931) was transferred to Hyde M.B., and parts of Hyde M.B. (pop. 16 in 1931) and Matley C.P. (pop. 75 in 1931) were transferred to Dukinfield M.B.

(p) See above, note (m).

(q) In 1920 part of Dunham Massey C.P. (pop. 1,386 in 1921) was transferred to Altrincham U.D. and C.P.

(r) In 1936 part of Dunham Massey C.P. (pop. 893 in 1931) was transferred to Altrincham U.D. and C.P. and part (pop. 85 in 1931) to Bowdon C.P. and U.D.

(s) In 1936 Bartington C.P. (pop. 64 in 1931) and part of Acton C.P. (pop. 28 in 1931) were transferred to Dutton C.P.

(t) In 1967 part of Dutton C.P. was transferred to Runcorn U.D.

(u) Whitby tns. was situated partly in Eastham A.P. and partly in Stoke A.P. In 1801 and 1811 no separate returns for each part were made, and the total for Eastham A.P. in those years included the whole of Whitby.

(v) See above, note (u).

(w) In 1933 parts of Childer Thornton and Hooton C.P.s (pop. respectively 2 and 104 in 1931) were transferred to Eastham C.P. Part of Eastham C.P. (pop. 17 in 1931) was transferred to Childer Thornton C.P. in Ellesmere Port U.D. and part (pop. 12 in 1931) was transferred to Willaston C.P. in Neston U.D. Thus altered, Eastham C.P. was transferred to Bebington U.D., q.v.

(x) In 1936 Eaton C.P. was extended to include part of Buglawton C.P. (pop. 34 in 1931) and part of Eaton (pop. 120 in 1921) was transferred to Congleton M.B.

(y) Created 1933 from Ellesmere Port and Whitby U.D. with its constituent parishes of Ellesmere Port and Great Stanney and the altered parishes of Childer Thornton, Hooton, Ince, and Little Sutton. In 1950 Ellesmere Port C.P. was extended to include the other parishes in the U.D., with which it thus became co-extensive. In 1955 Ellesmere Port was constituted a M.B. In 1963 and 1967 parts of Little Stanney C.P. were transferred from Chester R.D. to Ellesmere Port M.B.

(z) Created 1902 from Whitby C.P. In 1910 Ellesmere Port and Whitby U.D. was extended to include Great Stanney, Stanlow, Netherpool, and Overpool C.P.s. In 1911 Ellesmere Port C.P. (pop. 10,145 in 1911) was formed by the union of Netherpool (pop. 15 in 1911), Overpool (pop. 93 in 1911), and Whitby (pop. 10,145 in 1911) C.P.s. Stanlow C.P. (pop. 31 in 1911) was added to Great Stanney C.P.

(a) See above, note (m).

(b) See above, note (a).

(c) In 1936 Sandbach U.D. and C.P. was extended to include part of Elton C.P. (pop. 287 in 1931).

	1801	1811	1821	1831	1841	1851	1861	1871	1881	1891	1901	1911	1921	1931	1951	1961	1971
FRODSHAM A.P.	3,542	4,098	4,991[d]	5,547	5,821	6,382	5,890	6,429									
ALVANLEY tns.	314	287	284	346	314	312	330	325	See Alvanley C.P.								
FRODSHAM lordship	301	756	973	1,024	1,022	1,010	968	1,014	See Frodsham Lordship C.P.								
FRODSHAM tns.	1,250	1,349	1,556	1,746	1,806	2,179	1,869*	2,095	See Frodsham C.P.								
HELSBY tns.	268	297	378	534	572	602	570	716*	See Helsby C.P.								
KINGSLEY tns.	661	656	924	934	1,007	1,067	995	1,121*	See Kingsley C.P.								
MANLEY tns.	264	262	333	331	385	395	294*	339	See Manley C.P.								
NEWTON tns.	108	100	109	130	100	119	136	124	See Newton C.P.								
NORLEY tns.	376	391	434	502	615	698	728	695	See Norley C.P.								
FRODSHAM C.P.	Part of Frodsham A.P., q.v.								2,489	3,333[e]	2,728	3,049	3,025	3,140	5,245[f]	5,661	8,581
FRODSHAM LORDSHIP C.P.	Part of Frodsham A.P., q.v.								1,087	1,513[e]	1,403	1,637	1,604	1,563	See Frodsham C.P.		
FULSHAW A.P.	Part of Wilmslow A.P., q.v.								1,187[g]	1,385[h]	See Wilmslow U.D. and C.P. and Bollin Fee C.P.						
part in Chorley U.D.									104[g]	155							
part in Wilmslow U.D.									1,083	1,230							
GAWSWORTH A.P. and C.P.	697	757	804	847	806	788	713	607*	588	633	573	567	573	709[j]	1,093	1,375[j]	1,804
GAYTON C.P.	Part of Heswall A.P., q.v.								199	199	180	238	219	527[k]	See Wirral U.D.		
GODLEY C.P.	In Hyde M.B., q.v.								82*	81	68	85	75	103	102	100	85
GOLBORNE BELLOW C.P.	Part of Tattenhall A.P., q.v.								90*	74	67	62	67	84	59	63	53
GOLBORNE DAVID C.P.	Part of Handley A.P., q.v.																
GOOSTREY C.P.[1]															794	940	1,962
GOOSTREY CUM BARNSHAW C.P.	Part of Sandbach A.P., q.v.								365	336	352	405	442	508	See Goostrey C.P.		
GRAFTON C.P.	Part of Tilston A.P., q.v.								0	2	2	7	4	13	4	12	6
GRANGE C.P.	Part of Kirby, West A.P., q.v.								108	184[m]	299	445	665	1,624[n]	See Hoylake U.D.		
part in West Kirby and Hoylake U.S.D.										28							
rural part										156							
GRAPPENHALL A.P.	1,092	1,305	1,652	2,607	2,948	3,250	3,586	3,878									
GRAPPENHALL tns.	338	361	400	441	587	708	701	734*	See Grappenhall C.P.								
LATCHFORD chap.	754	944	1,252*	2,166*	2,361	2,542	2,885	3,144*	See Latchford C.P.								
GRAPPENHALL C.P.	Part of Grappenhall A.P., q.v.								788	984	987	1,803*	1,945	2,449	5,655	7,746[o]	8,505
GREASBY C.P.	Part of Thurstaston A.P. and Kirby, West A.P., q.v.								236	237	290	476	585	747	See Hoylake U.D.		
Hale C.P. and, from 1900, U.D.	Part of Bowdon A.P., q.v.								2,222	3,114	4,562[p]	8,351	9,300	10,667	12,152[q]	14,800	17,063
HALTON C.P.	Part of Runcorn A.P., q.v.								1,439	1,555[r]	1,238	1,294	1,508	1,694	1,490[s]	1,467	See Runcorn U.D.
part in Runcorn U.S.D.									314								
rural part									1,125								
HAMPTON C.P.	Part of Malpas A.P., q.v.								348	362	326	346	384	366	290	258	307
HANDFORTH C.P. and, from 1904, U.D.	Part of Cheadle A.P., q.v.								736	794	911	934	904	1,031[t]	See Cheadle and Gatley U.D. and Wilmslow U.D.		
HANDLEY A.P.	265	273	332	389	386	381	364	437									
GOLBORNE DAVID tns.	62	58	76	80	84	74	70	105*	See Golborne David C.P.								
HANDLEY tns.	203	215	256	309	302	307	294	332*	See Handley C.P.								
HANDLEY C.P.	Part of Handley A.P., q.v.								274*	281	259	246	261	250	277	206	150
HANKELOW C.P.	Part of Audlem A.P., q.v.								219	226[u]	210	224	217	175	193	206	212
HAPSFORD C.P.	Part of Thornton A.P., q.v.								75	86	86	107	110	112	132	99	89
HARTFORD C.P.	Part of Budworth, Great A.P., q.v.								1,451	1,570	850[v]	883	896	1,420*	2,919	2,272[w]	3,587
part in Northwich U.S.D.									565	726							
rural part									886	844							

Place	Ancient parish / note	Population figures
HARTHILL, A.P. and C.P.		107, 220, 147, 166, 158, 130, 122, 120, 100, 95, 81, 101, 105, 95, 89, 66, 44
HASLINGTON C.P.	Part of Barthomley A.P., q.v.	1,814, 1,827, 1,791, 2,359, 2,451, 2,633, 3,223[x], 2,879, 4,351
HASSALL C.P.	Part of Sandbach A.P., q.v.	309, 337, 301, 295, 318, 340, 288, 218, 217
HATHERTON C.P.	Part of Wybunbury A.P., q.v.	322, 314, 280, 290, 274, 287, 321, 313, 278
HATTERSLEY C.P.	Part of Mottram A.P., q.v.	263, 286, 287, 256, 268, 280[y]; See Hyde M.B. and C.P. and Longdendale U.D. and C.P.
HATTON C.P.	Part of Runcorn A.P., q.v.	365, 327, 319, 303, 327, 297, 362, 340, 352
HATTON C.P.	Part of Waverton A.P., q.v.	143, 143, 134, 131, 129, 132, 126, 147, 133
HAUGHTON C.P.	Part of Bunbury A.P., q.v.	131, 142, 163, 218, 147, 150, 188, 147, 147
HAZEL GROVE AND BRAMHALL U.D. and C.P.[z]		9,791, 9,631, 10,127, 13,300, 19,674[a], 29,917, 39,619
HELSBY C.P.	Part of Frodsham A.P., q.v.	812, 1,154, 1,572, 1,891, 1,890, 1,960, 2,739[b], 3,634, 4,517
HENBURY cum PEXALL C.P.[c]	Part of Prestbury A.P., q.v.	431, 375, 368, 360, 394, 352, 400, 424, 686
HENHULL C.P.	Part of Acton A.P., q.v.	149, 128, 102, 120, 118, 123, 59[d], 56, 73
HESWALL A.P.		268, 438, 386, 406, 546, 657, 749, 910
GAYTON tns.		100, 115, 153, 110, 149, 144, 193, 188; See Gayton C.P.
HESWALL CUM OLDFIELD tns.		168, 323, 233, 296, 397, 513, 556, 722; See Heswall cum Oldfield C.P.
HESWALL CUM OLDFIELD C.P.		876, 1,210, 2,167, 3,616*, 4,349*, 5,532*; See Wirral U.D.
HILBRE ISLAND E.P.P.[e]	Part of Heswall A.P., q.v.	—, 10, 19, 7; See Meols, Little C.P.
HOCKENHULL C.P.	Part of Tarvin A.P., q.v.	26, 27, 20, 28, 21, 20, 31, 31, 23[f]

(d) In 1821 the total for Frodsham A.P. was wrongly returned as 5,451.

(e) In 1882 as a result of the Divided Parishes Act part of Frodsham C.P. (pop. 150 in 1891) was transferred to Frodsham Lordship C.P.

(f) In 1936 Frodsham Lordship C.P. (pop. 1,563 in 1931) and those lands (pop. 0 in 1931) common to both Frodsham C.P. and Frodsham Lordship C.P. were transferred to Frodsham C.P.

(g) In 1882 as a result of the Divided Parishes Act part of Pownall Fee C.P. (pop. 37 in 1891) was transferred to Fulshaw C.P.

(h) Dissolved 1894, part (pop. 1,403 in 1901) being transferred to Wilmslow U.D. and C.P. and part (pop. 257 in 1901) to Bollin Fee C.P.

(i) In 1936 part of Gawsworth C.P. (pop. 41 in 1931) was transferred to Macclesfield M.B. and C.P.

(j) In 1955 part of Gawsworth C.P. (pop. 53 in 1957) was transferred to Macclesfield M.B.

(k) In 1933 Gayton C.P. was extended to include part of Thornton Hough (pop. 6 in 1931) and thus altered, Gayton was transferred to Wirral U.D.

(l) Created 1936 from Goostrey cum Barnshaw and Blackden C.P.s (pop. respectively 508 and 121 in 1931).

(m) In 1889 Newton cum Larton C.P. (pop. 66 in 1891) was united with Grange C.P. In 1894 the part of Grange C.P. in West Kirby and Hoylake U.D. (pop. 17 in 1901) was transferred to Hoylake and West Kirby C.P.

(n) In 1933 Grange C.P. was extended to include part of Saughall Massie C.P. (pop. 31 in 1931), and thus altered was transferred to Hoylake U.D.

(o) In 1955 part of Stockton Heath C.P. (pop. 70 in 1951) was transferred to Stockton Heath C.P. and part of Grappenhall C.P. (pop. 5 in 1951) was transferred to Grappenhall C.P.

(p) In 1900 Ringway C.P. was created from the rural part of Hale C.P.

(q) In 1936 part of Hale U.D. and C.P. (pop. 71 in 1931) was transferred to Altrincham U.D. and C.P. and part of Altrincham U.D. (pop. 68 in 1931) and part of Bucklow R.D. (viz. parts of Ringway and Timperley C.P.s, pop. respectively 339 and 8 in 1931) were transferred to Hale U.D.

(r) In 1884 part of Halton A.P. (pop. 400 in 1891) was transferred to Runcorn C.P.

(s) In 1936 part of Halton C.P. (pop. 674 in 1931) was transferred to Runcorn U.D. and C.P.

(t) Dissolved 1936, part (pop. 938 in 1931) being transferred to Wilmslow U.D. and C.P., and part (pop. 93 in 1931) to Cheadle and Gatley U.D. and C.P.

(u) In 1888 part of Audlem C.P. (pop. 14 in 1891) was transferred to Hankelow C.P.

(v) In 1894 the part of Hartford C.P. in Northwich U.S.D. (pop. 1,699 in 1901) was transferred to Northwich C.P.

(w) In 1955 part of Hartford C.P. (pop. 955 in 1951) was transferred to Northwich U.D.

(x) In 1936 part of Haslington C.P. (pop. 13 in 1931) was transferred to Crewe M.B. and part of Wheelock (pop. 262 in 1931) was transferred to Haslington C.P.

(y) Dissolved 1936, part (pop. 181 in 1931) being transferred to Longdendale U.D. and C.P. and part (pop. 99 in 1931) to Hyde M.B. and C.P.

(z) Created 1900 from Offerton, Bosden, Bramhall, Norbury, and Torkington C.P.s (pop. respectively 558, 2,570, 4,645, 1,679, and 339 in 1901). In 1901 part of Hazel Grove and Bramhall U.D. and C.P. (pop. 1,857 in 1901) was transferred to Stockport C.B. and C.P.

(a) In 1935 and 1936 part of Hazel Grove and Bramhall U.D. and C.P. (pop. 872 in 1931) was transferred to Stockport C.B. and C.P. and part (pop. 57 in 1931) to Marple U.D. and C.P. In 1939 Woodford C.P. (pop. 801 in 1931) was transferred to Hazel Grove and Bramhall U.D. and C.P.

(b) In 1936 part of Alvanley C.P. (pop. 22 in 1931) was transferred to Helsby C.P.

(c) Created 1936 from Henbury cum Pexall C.P. (pop. 352 in 1931), part of Birtles C.P. (pop. 50 in 1931), and part of Macclesfield C.P. (pop. 2 in 1931).

(d) In 1936 part of Henhull C.P. (pop. 26 in 1931) was transferred to Nantwich U.D. and C.P.

(e) No return was made for Hilbre Island 1801–31. From 1881 it was included in the return for Little Meols. In 1851 it was said to have been connected with St. Oswald parish.

(f) In 1963 part of Cotton Edmunds C.P. was transferred to Hockenhull C.P. and parts of Hockenhull C.P. to Cotton Edmunds and Tarvin C.P.s.

	1801	1811	1821	1831	1841	1851	1861	1871	1881	1891	1901	1911	1921	1931	1951	1961	1971
HOLLINGWORTH U.D. and C.P.	Part of Mottram A.P., q.v.								2,658	2,895	2,447	2,580	2,466	2,299	See Longdendale U.D. and C.P.		
HOLY AND UNDIVIDED TRINITY A.P.	2,300	2,278	3,111	3,298	3,401*	3,490*	3,675	4,007									
part in Chester City	2,264	2,224	3,036	3,226	3,340*	3,375*	3,606	3,793									
BLACON CUM CRABWALL tns.	36	54	75	72	61	115	69	214	See Blacon cum Crabwall C.P.								
HOOLE C.P.	Part of Plemstall A.P., q.v.								3,062	4,066[g]	See Hoole U.D. and Hoole Village C.P.						
part in Hoole U.D.									2,899								
rural part									163								
Hoole U.D. and, from 1894, C.P.									2,899	3,892	5,341	5,929	5,994	5,889	9,058[h]	See Chester C.B., Sutton, Guilden C.P., and Hoole Village C.P.	
HOOLE VILLAGE C.P.[1]											218	251	275	226	188[j]	283[k]	282
HOOSE C.P.	Part of Kirby, West A.P., q.v.								1,208	1,658	See Hoylake and West Kirby C.P.						
HOOTON C.P.	Part of Eastham A.P., q.v.								161	537*	200	226	204	246[l]	See Bebington M.B.		
HORTON C.P.	Part of Tilston A.P., q.v.								94	96	119	129	112	120	104	77	63
HORTON CUM PEEL C.P.	Part of Tarvin A.P., q.v.								40	36	32	42	34	37	26	21	23
HOUGH C.P.	Part of Wybunbury A.P., q.v.								275	320	324	327	344	299	330	390	531
HOYLAKE U.D.[m]															30,936	32,273	32,277
CALDY C.P.															607		
FRANKBY C.P.															413		
GRANGE C.P.															7,657		
GREASBY C.P.															4,367		
HOYLAKE AND WEST KIRBY C.P.															17,892		
HOYLAKE AND WEST KIRBY U.D. and C.P.	See Kirby, West and Hoylake U.S.D.										10,911*	14,029*	17,068	16,631	See Hoylake U.D.		
HULME, CHURCH C.P.	Part of Sandbach A.P., q.v.								658	860	866	926	1,112	1,143	1,460	1,816	3,782
HULME WALFIELD C.P.	Part of Astbury A.P., q.v.								113	115	108	84	93	80	143[n]	124	122
HULSE C.P.	Part of Budworth, Great A.P., q.v.								41	See Lach Dennis C.P.							
HUNSTERSON C.P.	Part of Wybunbury A.P., q.v.								193	172	165	180	200	175	159	168	176
HUNTINGTON C.P.	Part of St. Oswald's A.P., q.v.								120	110	121	117	126	144	2,614	1,603	1,273
HURDSFIELD C.P. part in Macclesfield M.B.	Part of Prestbury A.P., q.v.								3,967	3,725							
rural part									3,530	3,282[o]	458[o]	447	464	441[p]	418	465	680
HURLESTON C.P.	Part of Acton A.P., q.v.								124	117	123	123	127	110	69	85	80
HUXLEY C.P.	Part of Waverton A.P., q.v.								236	229	259	283	295	253	255	239	242[q]
HYDE M.B. and, from 1923, C.P.[r]	Part of Mottram in Longdendale A.P., q.v.								28,630	30,670	32,766	33,437	33,424	32,075[s]	31,494[t]	31,741	37,095
GODLEY C.P.	Part of Stockport A.P., q.v.								1,392	1,408	1,691	1,660	1,735				
HYDE C.P.	Part of Mottram in Longdendale A.P., q.v.								17,876	20,354	23,668[u]	24,054	23,974				
NEWTON C.P.	Part of Stockport A.P., q.v.								7,340	7,333	7,407	7,723	7,715				
WERNETH C.P. (part of)	Part of Mottram in Longdendale A.P., q.v.								2,022	1,575[v]							
IDDINSHALL C.P.	Part of St. Oswald's A.P., q.v.								18	17	21	12	15	14	6	11	8
INCE A.P. and C.P.	443	426	460	487	475	422	371	388	334	1,080*	290	271	328	277	See Ellesmere Port U.D.		
IRBY C.P.	Part of Thurstaston A.P. and Woodchurch A.P., q.v.								154	174	146	161	233	1,062[w]	4,032	See Wirral U.D.	
KECKWICK C.P.	Part of Runcorn A.P., q.v.								83	82	65	64	63	54	See Daresbury C.P.		
KELSALL C.P.	Part of Tarvin A.P., q.v.								638	692	670	709	781	874	1,030	1,119	1,516

Parish / Township	Population figures and notes
KERMINCHAM C.P.	Part of Swettenham A.P., q.v. … See Swettenham C.P.
KETTLESHULME C.P.	Part of Prestbury A.P., q.v. … 129, 133, 152, 156, 163, 183, … 316
KINDERTON C.P.y	329, 347, 321, 358, 380, 349, 338x, 329
KINDERTON CUM HULME C.P. part in Middlewich U.S.D.	432z, 529, 457, 286 … See Middlewich U.D., Bradwall, Sproston C.P., etc.
rural part	393, 439
and C.P.	148, 150 ; 541, 589 … See Kinderton C.P. and Middlewich C.P.
KINGSLEY C.P.	1,207, 1,111a, 1,066, 1,014, 1,051, 1,011, 1,503b, 1,346, 1,698
KING'S MARSH E.P.P. and C.P.c	54, 72, 65, 65, 63, 63, 56, 46, 35
KINGSWOOD C.P.	235, 233, 248, 463*, 490, 557d … 40, 46, — , — , 58*, 70, 72, 91, 62 … See Kingsley, Manley, and Norley C.P.s
KINNERTON, LOWER C.P.	112, 114, 113, 120, 127, 111, 120, 142, 128, 115
KIRBY, WEST A.P.	Part of Dodleston A.P., q.v. … 906e, 921, 1,140, 1,289, 1,641, 1,951, 2,059, 2,724
CALDY tns.	92, 98, 66, 102, 104, 142, 147, 168 … See Caldy C.P.
FRANKBY tns.	70f, 90, 125, 114, 125, 138, 137, 170* … See Frankby C.P.
GRANGE tns.	101, 93, 235, 124, 132, 105, 93, 77 … See Grange C.P.
GREASBY tns. (part of)	123g, 113, 114, 141, 147, 158, 190, 172 … See Greasby C.P.
HOOSE chap.	60, 100, 172, 196, 444, 589, 664, 809* … See Hoose C.P.
KIRBY, WEST tns.	148, 141, 159, 232, 330, 435, 413, 492* … See Kirby, West C.P.
MEOLS, GREAT tns.	140, 148, 131, 198, 172, 170, 184, 337* … See Meols, Great C.P.
MEOLS, LITTLE tns.	123, 85, 126, 134, 170, 169, 430* … See Meols, Little C.P.
NEWTON CUM LARTON tns.	49, 50, 48, 56, 53, 44, 62, 69 … See Newton cum Larton C.P.

(g) Part of Hoole C.P. was included in Hoole U.D. in 1881 and in 1894 the remainder was constituted Hoole Village C.P.

(h) In 1936 Guilden Sutton C.P. (pop. 41 in 1931), Hoole Village C.P. (pop. 45 in 1931), and Newton by Chester C.P. (pop. 447 in 1931) were transferred to Hoole U.D. Part of Hoole U.D. (pop. 404 in 1931) was transferred to Chester C.B. and part (pop. 126 in 1931) to Great Boughton C.B. Hoole U.D. was dissolved in 1954, part (pop. 8,705 in 1951) being transferred to Chester C.B., part (pop. 209 in 1951) to Guilden Sutton C.P., and part (pop. 144 in 1951) to Hoole Village C.P.

(i) See above, note (g).

(j) In 1936 part of Hoole Village C.P. (pop. 45 in 1931) was transferred to Hoole U.D., part (pop. 126 in 1931) to Great Boughton C.P., and part (pop. 19 in 1931) to Guilden Sutton C.P.

(k) In 1954 part of Hoole U.D. (pop. 144 in 1951) was transferred to Hoole Village C.P.

(l) In 1933 part of Hooton C.P. (pop. 104 in 1931) was transferred to Bebington U.D. and part (pop. 142 in 1931) to Childer Thornton C.P. In 1950 Hooton C.P. was united with Ellesmere Port C.P.

(m) Created 1933.

(n) In 1936 part of Hulme Walfield C.P. (pop. 19 in 1931) was transferred to Congleton M.B. and C.P.

(o) In 1894 the part of Hurdsfield C.P. (pop. 3,114 in 1901) in Macclesfield M.B. was transferred to Macclesfield C.P.

(p) In 1936 part of Hurdsfield C.P. (pop. 13 in 1931) was transferred to Macclesfield M.B. and C.P.

(q) In 1963 part of Huxley C.P. was transferred to Foulk Stapleford C.P. and part of Foulk Stapleford C.P. was transferred to Huxley C.P.

(r) Incorporated in 1881.

(s) In 1923 Hyde C.P. was extended to include Godley and Newton C.P.s and thus became co-extensive with the M.B.

(t) In 1936 Hyde M.B. and C.P. was extended to include part of Compstall U.D. and C.P.

(pop. 61 in 1931), part of Dukinfield M.B. and C.P. (pop. 17 in 1931), part of Hattersley C.P (pop. 99 in 1931), and part of Matley C.P. (pop. 97 in 1931). At the same date part of Hyde M.B. and C.P. (pop. 16 in 1931) was transferred to Dukinfield M.B. and C.P. and another part (pop. 20 in 1931) to Bredbury and Romiley U.D. and C.P.

(u) In 1894 Hyde C.P. was extended to include the part of Werneth C.P. in Hyde M.B. (pop. 1,773 in 1901).

(v) See above, note (u).

(w) In 1933 Irby C.P. was extended to include part of Arrowe C.P. (pop. 20 in 1931) and was transferred from Wirral R.D. to Wirral U.D.

(x) In 1936 part of Kettleshulme C.P. (pop. 3 in 1931) was transferred to Whaley Bridge U.D. (Derb.).

(y) Created 1894 from part of Kinderton cum Hulme C.P. (pop. 91 in 1901) and part of Newton C.P. (pop. 195 in 1901). The remainder of Kinderton cum Hulme C.P. (pop. 562 in 1901) was transferred to Middlewich C.P.

(z) Dissolved 1936, part (pop. 379 in 1931) being transferred to Middlewich U.D., part (pop. 43 in 1931) to Sproston C.P., and part (pop. 10 in 1931) to Bradwall C.P.

(a) In 1881 part of Norley C.P. (pop. 8 in 1891) was transferred to Kingsley C.P.

(b) In 1936 part of Kingsley C.P. (pop. 23 in 1931) was transferred to Norley C.P. and Newton by Frodsham C.P. (pop. 421 in 1931) and part of Kingswood C.P. (pop. 47 in 1931) were transferred to Kingsley C.P.

(c) King's Marsh became a parish for the purpose of the Act 20 Vict. c. 19.

(d) Dissolved 1936, part (pop. 482 in 1931) being transferred to Manley C.P., part (pop. 47 in 1931) to Kingsley C.P., and part (pop. 28 in 1931) to Norley C.P.

(e) Greasby tns., which extended into Thurstaston A.P., was wholly returned in West Kirby A.P., 1801-31.

(f) In 1851 this figure was corrected to 90.

(g) See above, note (e).

	1801	1811	1821	1831	1841	1851	1861	1871	1881	1891	1901	1911	1921	1931	1951	1961	1971
KIRBY, WEST C.P.	Part of Kirby, West A.P., q.v.																1,118
KIRBY, WEST AND HOYLAKE U.S.D.[h]										6,545	See Hoylake and West Kirby U.D. and C.P.						
GRANGE C.P. (part of)										28							
HOOSE C.P.										1,658							
KIRBY, WEST C.P.										2,441							
MEOLS, GREAT C.P.										456							
MEOLS, LITTLE C.P.										1,962							
KNUTSFORD A.P.	2,870	2,855	3,535	3,599	4,006	4,375	4,194	4,306									
BEXTON tns.	49	58	69	76	77	87	66	71	See Bexton C.P.								
KNUTSFORD, NETHER tns.	2,052	2,114	2,753*	2,823	3,185*[l]	3,539*	3,485	3,597	See Knutsford, Nether C.P.								
KNUTSFORD, OVER tns.	320	243	231	217	225	208	204	206	See Knutsford, Over C.P.								
OLLERTON tns.	244	229	246	283	283	300	272	260	See Ollerton C.P.								
TOFT tns.	205	211	236	200	236	241	167*	172	See Toft C.P.								
KNUTSFORD U.D. and C.P.[j]	Part of Knutsford A.P., q.v.								3,895	4,240	5,172	5,760	5,415	5,879	6,617[k]	9,389	13,776
KNUTSFORD, NETHER C.P.	Part of Knutsford A.P., q.v.								410	403	See Knutsford U.D.						
KNUTSFORD, OVER C.P.	Part of Budworth, Great A.P., q.v.								See Knutsford U.D.								
LACH DENNIS C.P.	Part of Woodchurch A.P., q.v.								62	194[l]	184	164	158	155	687[m]	171	281
LANDICAN C.P.	Part of Woodchurch A.P., q.v.								75	76	71	80	75	See Birkenhead C.B. and C.P.			
LARKTON C.P.	Part of Malpas A.P., q.v.								48	33	34	46	37	37	53	47	46
LATCHFORD C.P.	Part of Grappenhall A.P., q.v.								4,282								
part in Warrington C.B. (Lancs.)									3,959								
rural part									323	440[n]							
LATCHFORD WITHOUT C.P.[o]											295	755*	797	1,266*	See Stockton Heath C.P.		
LAWTON, CHURCH A.P. and C.P.	445	488	512	516	622	693	724	753	823	803	850	849	852	874	971	1,051	2,157[p]
LEA C.P.	Part of Wybunbury A.P., q.v.								70	64	70	51	50	37	47	58	41
LEA-BY-BACKFORD C.P.	Part of Backford A.P., q.v.								68	72	73	104	145	165	233	194	193
LEA NEWBOLD C.P.	Part of St. Oswald's A.P., q.v.								46	45	49	47	44	39	29	31	18
LEDSHAM C.P.	Part of Neston A.P., q.v.								82	83	82	152*	152	139	116[q]	144	126
LEESE C.P.	Part of Sandbach A.P., q.v.								107	117	90	113	113	119[r]			
LEFTWICH C.P.	Part of Davenham A.P., q.v.								2,864	3,398[s]	848[t]	846	886	1,021	See Northwich U.D.		
part in Northwich U.S.D.									2,360	2,710							
rural part									504	688							
LEGH, HIGH C.P.	Part of Rostherne A.P., q.v.								850	844	794	778	729	688	1,184	866	1,038
LEGH, LITTLE C.P.	Part of Budworth, Great A.P., q.v.								455	410	366	352	351	422	528	449	512
LEIGHTON C.P.	Part of Nantwich A.P., q.v.								172	164	126	136	156	141	138[u]	147	104
LEIGHTON C.P.	In Neston and Parkgate U.S.D. and C.P., q.v.																
LISCARD C.P.	See Wallasey U.D.																
LITTLETON C.P.	Part of Christleton A.P., q.v.								106	103	151	276	301	336	482	522	528
LONGDENDALE U.D. and C.P.[v]										11,640		2,106*	2,115	1,928	4,591	4,626	10,359
LOSTOCK GRALAM C.P.	Part of Budworth, Great A.P., q.v.								777	896					1,522[w]	2,008	2,002
LYME HANDLEY C.P.	Part of Prestbury A.P., q.v.								296	251	242	241	264	211	174	175	156
LYMM A.P. and, from 1881, U.D. and C.P.	1,622	1,908	2,090	2,305	2,658	3,156	3,769	4,541*	4,665	4,995	4,707	4,989	5,283	5,643	6,412[x]	7,338	10,497
MACCLESFIELD HUNDRED	56,437	70,623	87,749	123,349	153,621	114,523	104,352	105,992	93,401								
MACCLESFIELD M.B.; from 1881 U.S.D., and from 1894, C.P.						39,048*	36,101*	35,450	37,514	36,009	34,624[y]	34,797	33,846	34,905	35,999[z]	37,644[a]	44,401

HURDSFIELD C.P. (part of)									3,530	3,282
MACCLESFIELD C.P. (part of)									28,619	27,667
SUTTON C.P. (part of)									5,365	5,060
MACCLESFIELD R.D.									17,589	17,329
MACCLESFIELD FOREST C.P.	207	187	172	181	166	125	122	98	79	
MALPAS A.P. (part of)b	62	47	45	73	52	65	62	76	95	

Far right (later-year columns, MACCLESFIELD R.D.): 15,775 16,628 17,045 19,161 19,931 23,351 28,210

Parish								Reference
Part of Prestbury A.P., q.v.								
Part of Malpas A.P., q.v.	4,470	4,326	4,917	5,127	5,211	5,269	5,163	5,112
AGDEN tns.	90	100	122	104	97	98	110	102 — See Agden C.P.
BICKERTON tns.	270	308	370	373	401	398	379	377 — See Bickerton C.P.
BICKLEY tns.	435	419	431	451	489	467	397	394 — See Bickley C.P.
BRADLEY tns.	77	63	78	95	99	125	110	133* — See Bradley C.P.
BROXTON tns.	275	331	352	454	464	513	546	622* — See Broxton C.P.
BULKELEY tns.	184	165	178	185	190	197	196	190 — See Bulkeley C.P.
CHIDLOW tns.	17	12	15	15	12	12	18	20 — See Chidlow C.P.
CHOLMONDELEY tns.	292	251	297	272	260	269	306	292 — See Cholmondeley C.P.
CHORLTON tns.	94	94	124	155	150	132	113	105 — See Chorlton C.P.
CUDDINGTON tns.	424	225	247	260	240	282	268	290 — See Cuddington C.P.
DUCKINGTON tns.	61	72	81	86	85	81	86	59 — See Duckington C.P.
EDGE tns.	266	276	298	310	313	263	270	262 — See Edge C.P.
EGERTON tns.	103	111	115	114	143	127	115	119 — See Egerton C.P.
HAMPTON tns.	159	190	207	273	290	309	332	370 — See Hampton C.P.
LARKTON tns.	50	64	60	44	53	54	35	35 — See Larkton C.P.
MACEFEN tns.	46	54	48	48	58	59	47	56 — See Macefen C.P.
MALPAS tns.	906	938	1,127	1,004	1,022	1,054	1,037	962* — See Malpas C.P.
NEWTON BY MALPAS tns.	23	16	18	17	19	31	23	22 — See Newton by Malpas C.P.
OLDCASTLE tns.	205	94	93	98	95	108	100	115 — See Oldcastle C.P.
OVERTON tns.	97	101	101	111	110	122	107	106 — See Overton C.P.
STOCKTON tns.	23	28	32	30	31	31	27	23 — See Stockton C.P.
TUSHINGHAM CUM GRINDLEY tns.	194	168	283	328	320	315	324	270* — See Tushingham cum Grindley C.P.
WIGLAND tns.	160	204	265	240	203	193		171* — See Wigland C.P.
WYCHOUGH tns.	19	30	36	35	30	19	24	17* — See Wychough C.P.

(h) Created 1891; renamed Hoylake and West Kirby U.D. and C.P. in 1897. In 1894 Hoylake and West Kirby C.P. was created from the following C.P.s in Hoylake and West Kirby U.D.: part of Grange, Hoose, Little Meols, Great Meols, and West Kirby (pop. respectively 17, 2,701, 2,830, 821, and 4,542 in 1901).

(i) In 1841 the pop. of Nether Knutsford was wrongly returned as that of Over Knutsford.

(j) Created 1895 from the union of Over and Nether Knutsford (pop. respectively 480 and 4,692 in 1901).

(k) In 1936 Knutsford U.D. and C.P. was extended to include part of Bexton C.P. (pop. 118 in 1931), part of Tabley Superior C.P. (pop. 118 in 1931), and part of Toft C.P. (pop. 58 in 1931).

(l) In 1892 Lach Dennis C.P. was extended to include Hulse, Birches, Stublach, and Newhall C.P.s (pop. respectively 41, 8, 37, and 19 in 1881).

(m) In 1936 Lach Dennis C.P. was extended to include part of Cranage C.P. (pop. 13 in 1931) and part of Leese C.P. (pop. 25 in 1931).

(n) In 1884 part of Warrington C.P. (pop. 2 in 1891) was transferred to Latchford C.P. Most of Latchford C.P. lay in the admin. co. of Lancs. in 1888. In 1894 Latchford Without C.P. was created from the rural part of Latchford C.P. and in 1896 Latchford Without C.P., extended to include parts of Latchford Without and Appleton C.P.s (pop. respectively 183 and 467 in 1901), was transferred to Lancs.

(o) See above, note (n).

(p) In 1965 the boundaries between Church Lawton C.P. and Kidsgrove U.D. (Staffs.) were altered.

(q) In 1933 Ledsham C.P. was extended to include part of Willaston C.P. (pop. 34 in 1931).

(r) Dissolved 1936, part (pop. 56 in 1931) being transferred to Cranage C.P., part (pop. 38 in 1931) to Byley C.P., and part (pop. 25 in 1931) to Lach Dennis C.P.

(s) In 1882 part of Leftwich C.P. (pop. 419 in 1891) was transferred to Witton cum Twambrooks C.P. under the Divided Parishes Act.

(t) In 1894 part of Leftwich C.P. (pop. 2,699 in 1901) was transferred to Northwich U.D. and C.P.

(u) In 1936 part of Leighton C.P. (pop. 4 in 1931) was transferred to Crewe M.B. and Monks Coppenhall C.P.

(v) Created 1936 from Hollingworth U.D. (pop. 2,299 in 1931), Mottram in Longdendale U.D. (pop. 2,636 in 1931), and parts of Hattersley (pop. 181 in 1931) and Matley (pop. 29 in 1931) C.P.s.

(w) In 1936 part of Lostock Gralam C.P. (pop. 831 in 1931) was transferred to Northwich U.D. and part (pop. 2 in 1931) to Rudheath C.P.

(x) In 1933 and 1936 part of Lymm U.D. (pop. 2 in 1931) was transferred to Agden C.P. and part (pop. 4 in 1931) to Woolston C.P., Lancs.

(y) In 1894 Macclesfield C.P. was extended to include the parts in Macclesfield M.B. of Hurdsfield C.P. (pop. 3,114 in 1901) and Sutton C.P. (pop. 4,887 in 1901).

(z) In 1936 parts of Fallibroome C.P. (pop. o in 1931), Gawsworth C.P. (pop. 41 in 1931), Hurdsfield C.P. (pop. 13 in 1931), Sutton C.P. (pop. 22 in 1931), Tytherington C.P. (pop. 303 in 1931), and Upton C.P. (pop. 270 in 1931) were transferred to Macclesfield M.B., and part of Macclesfield (pop. 2 in 1931) was transferred to Henbury C.P.

(a) In 1955 part of Gawsworth C.P. (pop. 53 in 1951) was transferred to Henbury C.P.

(b) Iscoyd tns. lay in Maylor hundred, Flints, and Branfield hundred, Denb.

	1801	1811	1821	1831	1841	1851	1861	1871	1881	1891	1901	1911	1921	1931	1951	1961	1971
MALPAS C.P.	Part of Malpas A.P., q.v.								939	1,164	1,139	1,166	1,098	1,101	1,219	1,310	1,493
MALPAS R.D.											4,488	4,643	4,465	4,283			
MANLEY C.P.	Part of Frodsham A.P., q.v.	778	833	811	784	758	779	758	306	296	305	327	328	358	793[c]	706	806
MARBURY A.P.	702																
MARBURY CUM QUOISLEY tns.	372	391	395	403	383	355	387	381	See Marbury cum Quoisley C.P.								
NORBURY tns.	330	387	438	408	401	403	392	377*	See Norbury C.P.								
MARBURY C.P.	Part of Budworth, Great A.P., q.v.								26	56	61	51	44	37			12
MARBURY CUM QUOISLEY C.P.	Part of Marbury A.P., q.v.								346	340	317	317	299	282	291	276	236[d]
MARLSTON CUM LACHE C.P.	Part of St. Mary's A.P., q.v.								126	105	103	113	115	101	102[e]	98	115
MARPLE U.D. and C.P.	Part of Stockport A.P., q.v.								4,421	4,844	5,595	6,483	6,608	7,389	13,073[f]	16,300	23,665
MARSTON C.P.	Part of Budworth, Great A.P., q.v.								969	961[g]	878	807	777	530	729	693	578
MARTHALL C.P.	Part of Rostherne A.P. and Marthall cum Warford C.P., q.v.														167	171	160
MARTHALL CUM WARFORD C.P.	Part of Rostherne A.P., q.v.								268	233	244	524*	633	626[h]	{See Marthall and Warford, Little C.P.s.		
MARTON C.P.	Part of Prestbury A.P., q.v.								308	290	289	282	283	249	227	236	235
MARTON C.P.	Part of Whitegate A.P., q.v.								695	606	549	598	606	597	548[i]	785	589
MATLEY C.P.	Part of Mottram in Longdendale A.P., q.v.								205	174	196	289	273	348[j]	{See Dukinfield M.B., Hyde M.B., Longdendale U.D., and Stalybridge M.B.		
MEOLS, GREAT C.P.	Part of Kirby, West A.P., q.v.								402	456	See Hoylake and West Kirby U.D.						
MEOLS, LITTLE C.P.	Part of Kirby, West A.P., q.v.								926	1,902	See Hoylake and West Kirby U.D.						
MERE C.P.	Part of Rostherne A.P., q.v.								512	401	437	467	409	379	653	661	650
MIDDLEWICH A.P.	3,779	4,048	4,350	4,787[k]	4,755	4,498	4,752	4,920[l]									
BYLEY tns.	130	135	132	123	149	110	124	145	See Byley C.P.								
CLIVE tns.	102	118	123	123	117	155	193	165	See Clive C.P.								
CROXTON tns.	45	55	52	43	48	49	46	45	See Croxton C.P.								
KINDERTON CUM HULME tns.	404	449	469	495	555	450	477	485	See Kinderton cum Hulme (from 1894 Kinderton) C.P.								
MIDDLEWICH tns.	1,190	1,232	1,212	1,325	1,242	1,235	1,203	1,283	See Middlewich C.P.								
MINSHULL VERNON tns.	357	255	349	385	403	375	402	390	See Minshull Vernon C.P.								
MOORESBARROW CUM PARME tns.	27	27	25	25	36	25	25	21	See Mooresbarrow cum Parme C.P.								
NEWTON tns.	943	1,201	1,520	1,649	1,512	1,500	1,657	1,730*	See Newton C.P.								
OCCLESTONE tns.	85	86	94	93	94	117	110	94	See Occlestone C.P.								
RAVENSCROFT tns.	13	4	26	16	23	10	32	35	See Ravenscroft C.P.								
SPROSTON tns.	150	144	148	128	171	156	163	158	See Sproston C.P.								
STUBLACH tns.	68	54	64	66	71	67	47	38	See Stublach C.P.								
SUTTON tns.	30	28	32	18	38	23	26	38	See Sutton C.P.								
WEAVER tns.	129	131	177	196	191	140	148	154	See Weaver C.P.								
WIMBOLDSLEY tns.	106	129	121	102	106	86	99	74	See Wimboldsley C.P.								
MIDDLEWICH U.S.D. and, from 1893, C.P.[m]									3,379	3,706	4,669	4,909	5,115	5,458	6,736[n]	6,863	7,848
KINDERTON CUM HULME C.P. (part of)									393	439							
MIDDLEWICH C.P.									1,325	1,283							
NEWTON C.P. (part of)									1,661	1,984							
MILLINGTON C.P.	Part of Rostherne A.P., q.v.								266	273	225	233	262	258	324	301	248

MINSHULL, CHURCH A.P. and C.P.

Place																
MINSHULL, CHURCH A.P. and C.P.	417	258	528	468	467	380	392	391	377	321	318	314	282	265	247	340 / 285
MINSHULL VERNON C.P.	Part of Middlewich A.P., q.v.															
MOBBERLEY A.P. and C.P.	993	1,152	1,198	1,245	1,275	1,272	1,271	1,462	1,292	1,353	1,406	1,550	1,735	1,913°	2,295	2,528
MOLLINGTON C.P.[p]										232	246	252	336	335^q	481	577
MOLLINGTON BANASTRE C.P.	Part of St. Mary's A.P., q.v.													See Mollington C.P.		
MOLLINGTON, GREAT C.P.	Part of Backford A.P., q.v.	51	53											See Mollington C.P.		
MOORE C.P.	Part of Runcorn A.P., q.v.	237	224	237	398	526	408	440	433	481	494^r	624	603^s			
MOORESBARROW CUM PARME C.P.	Part of Middlewich A.P., q.v.					27					See Sproston C.P.					
MORETON C.P.	Part of Bidston A.P., q.v.	424	464	597	970	4,029*	See Wallasey C.B. and C.P.									
MORETON CUM ALCUMLOW C.P.	Part of Astbury A.P., q.v.	117	106	132	134	130	196	203	284							
MOSTON C.P.	Part of St. Mary's A.P., q.v.	19	49	53	37	81*	850	553	495							
MOSTON C.P.	Part of Warmingham A.P., q.v.	180	183	145	148	134	See Tetton C.P.		427^u							
MOTTRAM IN LONGDENDALE A.P.	5,949	7,665	10,086	15,536	21,215	23,354	22,495	21,373								
GODLEY tns.	270	451	514	636	1,185*	1,353	1,222	See Godley C.P.								
HATTERSLEY tns.	455	473	563	477*	610*	497	400*	276	See Hattersley C.P.							
HOLLINGWORTH tns.	910	1,089	1,393	1,760*	2,012*	2,347	2,155	2,280	See Hollingworth C.P. and U.D.							
MATLEY tns.	285	311	324	262	251	252	231	207	See Matley C.P.							
MOTTRAM IN LONGDENDALE tns.	1,021	1,346	1,580	1,820	2,290^v	3,027	2,491	2,715	See Mottram in Longdendale C.P. and U.D.							
NEWTON tns.	948	1,446	1,944	2,144*	3,247*	3,199	3,406	2,590*	See Newton C.P.							
STAYLEY tns.	1,005	1,445	2,159*	5,997*	7,501*	7,481	6,440*	6,295	See Stayley C.P.							
TINTWISTLE tns.	1,055	1,104	1,609	2,440*	3,905	4,579	6,187	5,588*	See Tintwistle C.P.							
MOTTRAM IN LONGDENDALE C.P. and U.D.	Part of Mottram in Longdendale A.P., q.v.					2,913	2,636	2,883	3,049	3,128	3,270	2,883	2,636	See Longdendale U.D. and C.P.		
MOTTRAM ST. ANDREW C.P.	Part of Prestbury A.P., q.v.	365	183	365	381	388	386	397	444	597^w	628	665				
MOULDSWORTH C.P.	Part of Tarvin A.P., q.v.	183	172	167	186	172	194	260	277	266						
MOULTON C.P.	Part of Davenham A.P., q.v.	1,113	1,293	1,210	1,004	1,143	1,220	1,218^x	1,512	2,085						

(c) In 1936 part of Kingswood C.P. (pop. 482 in 1931) was transferred to Manley C.P.

(d) In 1965 part of Whitchurch U.D. (Salop.) (pop. 5 in 1961) was transferred to Marbury cum Quoisley C.P.

(e) In 1936 part of Marlston cum Lache C.P. (pop. 41 in 1931) was transferred to Chester C.B. and C.P.

(f) In 1936 part of Bredbury C.P. (pop. 10 in 1931), part of Hazel Grove and Bramhall U.D. and part of Kinderton C.P. (pop. 51 in 1931), and the whole of Ludworth C.P. (Derb.) (pop. 1,926 in 1931) and of Mellor C.P. (Derb.) (pop. 1,712 in 1931) were transferred to Marple U.D. and C.P.

(g) In 1889 part of Marston C.P. (pop. 18 in 1891) was transferred to Wincham C.P.

(h) In 1951 Marthall cum Warford C.P. was divided into Marthall C.P. and Little Warford C.P.

(i) In 1936 parts of Marton C.P. (pop. respectively 91 and 10 in 1931) were transferred to Winsford U.D. and C.P. and Oakmere C.P., and Marton C.P. was extended to include part of Over C.P. (pop. 4 in 1931).

(j) Dissolved 1936, part (pop. 75 in 1931) being transferred to Dukinfield M.B., part (pop. 97 in 1931) to Hyde M.B., part (pop. 29 in 1931) to Longdendale U.D., and part (pop. 147 in 1931) to Stalybridge M.B.

(k) In 1831 the total for Middlewich A.P. was wrongly given as 4,785.

(l) This total included 65 inhabitants of Leese tns. which was chiefly in Sandbach A.P. but extended into Middlewich.

(m) Middlewich U.D. consisted of Middlewich C.P. and parts of Newton and Kinderton cum Hulme C.P.s. In 1893, Middlewich U.D. was extended to include parts of Newton C.P. (pop. 2,872 in 1901) and Kinderton cum Hulme C.P. (pop. 562 in 1901). In 1894 these were added to Middlewich C.P. which thus became co-extensive with the U.D.

(n) In 1936 Middlewich U.D. and C.P. was extended to include part of Tetton C.P. (pop. 20 in 1931) and part of Kinderton C.P. (pop. 379 in 1931).

(o) In 1936 Mobberley C.P. was extended to include part of Great Warford C.P. (pop. 18 in 1931).

(p) Created 1901 from the union of Great and Little Mollington C.P.s. (pop. respectively 188 and 44 in 1901).

(q) In 1936 Mollington C.P. was extended to include part of Blacon cum Crabwall C.P. (pop. 14 in 1931).

(r) In 1933 part of Moore C.P. (pop. 23 in 1931) was transferred to Penketh C.P. (Lancs.).

(s) In 1967 part of Moore C.P. was transferred to Runcorn U.D.

(t) In 1915 parts of Hoylake and West Kirby C.P. (pop. 132 in 1921) were transferred to Moreton C.P., and Moreton C.P. was extended to include part of Saughall Massie C.P. (pop. 8 in 1921). In 1928 Moreton C.P. was included in Wallasey C.B. and C.P.

(u) In 1970 Elton C.P. (pop. 174 in 1961) and Tetton C.P. (pop. 309 in 1961) were joined to form a new C.P. named Moston.

(v) This figure was corrected to 1,744 in 1851.

(w) In 1936 Mottram St. Andrew was extended to include Newton C.P. (pop. 82 in 1931).

(x) In 1936 part of Bostock C.P. (pop. 3 in 1931) was transferred to Moulton C.P.

	1801	1811	1821	1831	1841	1851	1861	1871	1881	1891	1901	1911	1921	1931	1951	1961	1971
NANTWICH A.P.	3,714	4,236	5,033[y]	5,357	5,921	5,871	6,763	7,234									
ALVASTON tns.	11	33	37	41	40	37	28	23	See Alvaston C.P.								
LEIGHTON tns.	200	156	270	261	237	190	217	241	See Leighton C.P.								
NANTWICH tns.	3,463	3,999	4,661	4,886	5,489*	5,579*	6,225*	6,673*	See Nantwich C.P. and U.D.								
WILLASTON tns. (part of)	See Wybunbury A.P.[z]					147	228*	222*	See Willaston C.P.								
WOOLSTANWOOD tns.	40	48	65	70	64	65	65	75	See Woolstanwood C.P.								
NANTWICH HUNDRED	17,637	19,568	22,331	23,072	24,853	28,850	34,292	47,659	32,212								
NANTWICH R.D.									27,017	26,925	23,197	24,995	25,015	26,626	27,633	27,796	34,093[a]
NANTWICH U.S.D. and C.P.	Part of Nantwich A.P., q.v.								7,495	7,412	7,722	7,815	7,296	7,133	8,843[b]	10,438	11,683
NESS C.P.	Part of Neston A.P., q.v.								376	354	355	451	527	523	See Neston U.D.		
NESTON A.P.	2,901	2,909	3,216	3,518	3,809	3,578	4,049	4,334									
LEDSHAM tns.	56	75	74	70	81	94	93	89	See Ledsham C.P.								
LEIGHTON tns.	266	287	404	333	374	319	363	334	See Neston and Parkgate U.S.D.								
NESS tns.	347	462	394	480	485	454	346*	344	See Ness C.P.								
NESTON, GREAT tns.	1,486	1,332	1,418	1,638	1,701	1,524	1,764	1,856	See Neston, Great C.P.								
NESTON, LITTLE tns.	254	243	316	412	438	511	580	662	See Neston, Little C.P.								
RABY tns.	131	150	145	165	190	195	214	223	See Raby C.P.								
THORNTON HOUGH tns.	165	179	204	144	208	164	349	429*	See Thornton Hough C.P.								
WILLASTON tns.	196	181	261	276	332	317	340	397*	See Willaston C.P.								
NESTON U.D.[c]															9,726	11,865	16,879
BURTON C.P.															667		
NESS C.P.															596		
NESTON CUM PARKGATE C.P.															7,005		
WILLASTON C.P.															1,458		
NESTON AND PARKGATE U.S.D. and, from 1894, C.P.[d]									3,405	3,577	4,154	4,596	5,195	5,676	See Neston U.D.		
LEIGHTON C.P.									259	325	In Neston and Parkgate U.S.D. and C.P., q.v.						
NESTON, GREAT C.P.									2,119	2,240	In Neston and Parkgate U.S.D. and C.P., q.v.						
NESTON, LITTLE C.P.									1,027	1,012[e]	In Neston and Parkgate U.S.D. and C.P., q.v.						
NETHERPOOL C.P.	Part of Eastham A.P., q.v.								31	329*	21	See Ellesmere Port C.P.					
NEWBOLD ASTBURY C.P.	Part of Astbury A.P., q.v.								768	608	593	527	554	571	564[f]	595	550
NEWHALL C.P.	Part of Audlem and Wrenbury A.P.s, q.v.								712	734	718	764	703	645	720	672	647
NEWHALL C.P.	Part of Davenham A.P., q.v.								19	See Lach Dennis C.P.							
NEWTON C.P.	Part of Middlewich A.P., q.v.								1,962	2,369[g]	See Kinderton and Middlewich C.P.s						
part in Middlewich U.S.D., q.v.									1,661	1,984							
rural part									301	385							
NEWTON C.P.	In Hyde M.B., q.v.																
NEWTON C.P.	Part of Prestbury A.P., q.v.								78	55	88	44	62	82	See Mottram St. Andrew C.P.		
NEWTON BY CHESTER C.P.	Part of St. Oswald's A.P., q.v.								268	507	1,268	1,852*	1,871	2,581[h]	See Chester C.B. and Hoole U.D.		
NEWTON BY DARESBURY C.P.	Part of Runcorn A.P., q.v.								189	185	169	160	122	179	See Daresbury C.P.		
NEWTON BY FRODSHAM C.P.	Part of Frodsham A.P., q.v.								119	106	130	311*	381	421	See Kingsley C.P.		
NEWTON BY MALPAS C.P.	Part of Malpas A.P., q.v.								16	17	19	15	17	13	9	15	12

Parish	Reference / notes	Population figures (census years, approx. 1801 → 1961)
NEWTON BY TATTENHALL C.P.	Part of Tattenhall A.P., q.v.	116, 117, 159, 219, 217, 198, 160, 148, 128
NEWTON CUM LARTON C.P.	Part of Kirby, West A.P., q.v.	68, *See Grange C.P.*, 202, 203, 322, 314, 271, 241, 218, 207
NOCTORUM C.P.	Part of Woodchurch A.P., q.v.	121, 212, 203, 192, 473*, *See Birkenhead C.B. and C.P.*
NO MANS LAND E.P.P.[1]		34, 25
NORBURY C.P.	Part of Marbury A.P., q.v.	330, 346, 322, 314, 271, 241, 218
NORBURY C.P.	Part of Stockport A.P., q.v	1,499, 1,495, *See Hazel Grove and Bramhall C.P.*
NORLEY C.P.	Part of Frodsham A.P., q.v.	721[j], 689, 656, 740, 790, 820, 852[k], 841, 930
NORTHENDEN A.P.		1,406, 1,386, 1,420, 1,560, 2,127, 3,097, 3,236, *Part of Manchester C.B. (Lancs.)*
Etchells, Northen tns.[m]	See Stockport A.P. … *See Etchells, Northen C.P.*	538, 608, 776, 742, 727, 1,687[i], 1,359, 1,430
Northenden tns.	*See Northenden C.P.*	538, 608[n], 630, 659, 678, 679, 680, 738, 709, 721, 915*
NORTHENDEN C.P.	Part of Northenden A.P., q.v.	1,172, 1,560, 2,127
NORTHWICH HUNDRED		23,455, 26,541, 31,204, 33,046, 38,149, 41,638, 41,296, 47,208, 37,350
NORTHWICH R.D.		18,380, 21,218, 22,073, 23,270, 24,436, 26,498, 37,709, 39,498, 43,169
NORTHWICH U.S.D.[o] and, from 1894, C.P.		12,246, 14,914, 17,611, 18,151, 18,381, 18,732[p], 17,489[q], 19,542, 18,136
Hartford C.P. (part of)		565, 726
Leftwich C.P. (part of)		2,360, 2,710[r]
Northwich, Castle C.P. (part of)		1,022, 2,386
Winnington C.P.		2,126, 2,386
Witton cum Twambrooks C.P.		469, 563
NORTHWICH, CASTLE C.P.	In Northwich U.S.D., q.v.	5,704, 7,591[s]
NORTON C.P.	Part of Runcorn A.P., q.v.	345, 430, 294, 277, 238, 210, 142[t], 126 {See Runcorn U.D. and Daresbury C.P.}

(y) In 1821 the total for Nantwich A.P. was wrongly given as 5,633.

(z) In 1851 this figure was corrected to 122.

(a) In 1965 parts of Blakenhall, Checkley cum Wrinehill, and Weston C.P.s in Nantwich R.D. were transferred to Newcastle under Lyme R.D. (Staffs.), and parts of Whitchurch U.D. (Salop.) (pop. 5 in 1961) and part of Balterley C.P. in Newcastle under Lyme R.D. (Staffs.) (pop. 5 in 1961) were transferred to Nantwich R.D.

(b) In 1936 parts of Baddington C.P. (pop. 8 in 1931), of Henhull C.P. (pop. 26 in 1931), of Stapeley C.P. (pop. 124 in 1931), of Willaston C.P. (pop. 1,170 in 1931), and of Worleston C.P. (pop. 178 in 1931) were transferred from Nantwich R.D. to Nantwich U.D. and C.P.

(c) Created 1933 from part of Neston and Parkgate U.D. and C.P. (pop. 5,676 in 1931), Ness C.P. (pop. 523 in 1931), and parts of Burton (pop. 438 in 1931), Eastham (pop. 12 in 1931), Thornton Hough (pop. 14 in 1931), and Willaston (pop. 1,248 in 1931) C.P.s.

(d) Neston and Parkgate U.D. included Great Neston, Leighton, and Little Neston C.P.s. In 1894 these C.P.s were united to form Neston cum Parkgate C.P.

(e) In 1882 two parts of Little Neston (pop. 13 in 1891) were transferred to Raby C.P. under the provisions of the Divided Parishes Act. In 1889 part of Little Neston C.P. (pop. 67 in 1891) was transferred to Raby C.P.

(f) In 1936 part of Newbold Astbury C.P. (pop. 25 in 1931) was transferred to Congleton M.B. and C.P.

(g) In 1892 Newton C.P. was extended to include Sutton C.P. In 1894 part of Newton C.P. (pop. 195 in 1901) was transferred to Kinderton C.P. and the remainder (pop. 2,872 in 1901) was put into Middlewich C.P.

(h) Dissolved 1936, part (pop. 2,134 in 1931) being transferred to Chester C.B. and part (pop. 447 in 1931) to Hoole U.D.

(i) No return was made for No Mans Land before 1851 or after 1861. In 1871 the tns. of Beard, Thornsett, Oversett, and Whittle (Derb.) was said to include a former E.P.P. known as No Mans Land.

(j) In 1881 part of Norley (pop. 8 in 1891) was transferred to Kingsley C.P.

(k) In 1936 parts of Kingsley C.P. (pop. 23 in 1931) and Kingswood C.P. (pop. 28 in 1931) were transferred to Norley C.P.

(l) This total includes 34 inhabitants of Baguley, which was chiefly situated in Bowdon A.P.

(m) In 1801 and 1811 Northern Etchells and Stockport Etchells were returned together, and they have been entered under Stockport A.P. The pop. of Northern Etchells in those years was estimated in the 1851 census to have been 646 and 649 respectively.

(n) In 1811 Northenden tns. was returned under Stockport A.P.

(o) Northwich U.S.D. comprised Castle Northwich C.P., Hartford C.P., Leftwich C.P. (part), Northwich C.P., Winnington C.P. (part), and Witton cum Twambrooks C.P. In 1894 Northwich C.P. was extended to include the other C.P.s and parts of C.P.s in the U.S.D., with which it thus became co-extensive.

(p) In 1936 Northwich U.D. and C.P. was extended to include parts of Lostock Gralam and Winnington C.P.s (pop. respectively 831 and 1,264 in 1931).

(q) In 1955 Northwich U.D. and C.P. was extended to include parts of Davenham, Hartford, Rudheath, and Whatcroft C.P.s (pop. 2,671 in 1951).

(r) See below, note (s).

(s) In 1882 under the Divided Parishes Act Witton cum Twambrooks C.P. was extended to include part of Leftwich C.P. (pop. 419 in 1891).

(t) In 1936 parts of Norton C.P. (pop. respectively 3 and 42 in 1931) were transferred to Runcorn U.D. and C.P. and to Preston Brook C.P. Norton C.P. was extended to include Stockham C.P. (pop. 21 in 1931).

Table of township and civil parish populations, 1801–1971 (Cheshire). Census years 1801–1971 (1941 omitted); asterisks and bracketed letters are reference markers.

Area	1801	1811	1821	1831	1841	1851	1861	1871	1881	1891	1901	1911	1921	1931	1951	1961	1971
OAKMERE C.P.	Part of Delamere A.P., q.v.								408	387	370	421	357	425	467[u]	583	527
OCCLESTONE C.P.	Part of Middlewich A.P., q.v.								101	See Wimboldsley C.P.							
ODD RODE C.P.	Part of Astbury A.P., q.v.								3,194	3,121	3,187	3,326	3,237	3,307	3,331	3,574	4,239[v]
OFFERTON C.P.	Part of Stockport A.P., q.v.								358	372	See Hazel Grove and Bramhall C.P.						
OLDCASTLE C.P.	Part of Malpas A.P., q.v.								123	87	96	88	97	84	71	74	66
OLLERTON C.P.	Part of Knutsford A.P., q.v.								287	269	270	259	221	274	228	314	363
ONSTON C.P.	Part of Weaverham A.P., q.v.								93	See Crowton C.P.							
OULTON LOWE C.P.	Part of Over A.P., q.v.								47	See Budworth, Little C.P.							
OVER A.P.	1,161	2,126	2,514	2,928	3,137[w]	2,926	3,454	4,542									
OULTON LOWE tns.	52	62	60	55	47	57	53	52	See Oulton Lowe C.P.								
OVER tns. (part of)[x]	881	1,796	2,157	2,601	2,816	2,575	3,138	4,259*	See Over C.P.								
WETTENHALL tns.	228	268	297	272	274	294	263	231	See Wettenhall C.P.								
OVER C.P.	In Winsford U.D., q.v.																
OVERPOOL C.P.	Part of Eastham A.P., q.v.								86	112	91	See Ellesmere Port C.P.					
OVERTON C.P.	Part of Malpas A.P., q.v.								125	101	122	112	107	98	101	109	91
OXTON C.P.	In Birkenhead M.B. and C.P., q.v.																
PARTINGTON C.P.	Part of Bowdon A.P., q.v.								438	576	587	758*	605	816	957	6,574	9,269
PECKFORTON C.P.	Part of Bunbury A.P., q.v.								208	193	176	183	140	161	140	114	107
PENSBY C.P.	Part of Woodchurch A.P., q.v.								30	51	48	74	92	784*	See Wirral U.D.		
PEOVER INFERIOR C.P.	Part of Budworth, Great A.P., q.v.								112	132	144	148	130	100	111	137	123
PEOVER, NETHER C.P.	Part of Budworth, Great A.P., q.v.								211	220	222	220	247	200	295	376	461
PEOVER SUPERIOR C.P.	Part of Rostherne A.P., q.v.								609	541	549	573	629	617	696	629	738
PICKMERE C.P.	Part of Budworth, Great A.P., q.v.								241	224	203	235	281	341	411[y]	371	438
PICTON C.P.	Part of Plemstall A.P., q.v.								112	104	95	90	106	97	83	86	68[z]
PLEMSTALL A.P.[a]	581	628	710	737	804	877	2,019	1,115									
HOOLE tns.	177	213	237	249	294	427	1,596*	704[a]	See Hoole C.P.								
PICTON tns.	96	100	93	97	113	81	108	104	See Picton C.P.								
TRAFFORD, BRIDGE tns.	61	67	61	58	63	66	50	55	See Trafford, Bridge C.P.								
TRAFFORD, MICKLE tns.	247	248	319	333	334	303	265	252	See Trafford, Mickle C.P.								
PLUMLEY C.P.	Part of Budworth, Great A.P., q.v.								366	381	333	359	471	459	483	840	828
POOLE C.P.	Part of Acton A.P., q.v.								146	150	155	131	137	114	99	112	100
POTT SHRIGLEY C.P.	Part of Prestbury A.P., q.v.								385	354	313	326	407	441	415	376	226
POULTON C.P.	Part of Pulford A.P., q.v.								161	170	150	155	151	119	187	117	81
POULTON CUM SEACOMBE C.P.	In Wallasey M.B., q.v.																
POULTON CUM SPITAL C.P.	Part of Bebington A.P., q.v.								399	489	487[b]	551	548	768*	See Bebington U.D.		
POWNALL FEE C.P.	Part of Wilmslow A.P., q.v.								2,882[c]	3,081							
part in Chorley U.S.D.									869	827							
part in Wilmslow U.S.D.									44								
rural part									1,969	2,254							
POYNTON WITH WORTH C.P.	Part of Prestbury A.P., q.v.								2,166	2,274	2,544	2,793	2,770	3,944*	5,483	7,750	10,784
PRENTON C.P.	Part of Woodchurch A.P., q.v.								111	267	412	1,303*	See Birkenhead C.B.				
PRESTBURY A.P.	21,438	27,504	34,976[d]	42,257	52,078	59,265	55,680	53,403									
ADLINGTON tns.	847	940	1,057	1,066	1,159	1,104	987*	893*	See Adlington C.P.								
BIRTLES tns.	35	32	47	54	60	65	73	54	See Birtles C.P.								
BOLLINGTON tns.	1,231	1,518	1,723	2,685	4,350	4,655	5,439*	5,040*	See Bollington C.P.								
BOSLEY chap.	417	482	546	597	552	568	461*	425*	See Bosley C.P.								
BUTLEY tns.	516	635	579*	808	602	709	674*	591*	See Butley C.P.								
CAPESTHORNE chap.	88	70	65	72	95	138	114	106	See Capesthorne C.P.								
CHELFORD chap.	163	188	203	191	201*	263	256	273	See Chelford C.P.								
EATON tns.	184	228	327	525	535	584	485*	448*	See Eaton C.P.								

Population table (Cheshire parishes, townships and chapelries). Census figures read left-to-right by year.

Place									Reference
FALLIBROOME tns.	31	25	31	36	25	28	35	44*	See Fallibroome C.P.
HENBURY tns.	333	385	428	453	421	464	445	422*	See Henbury C.P.
HURDSFIELD tns.	582	734	1,082	3,551	3,083*	4,016*	3,836	3,947	See Hurdsfield C.P.
KETTLESHULME tns.	291	404	354	336	232	352	357	321*	See Kettleshulme C.P.
LYME HANDLEY tns.	222	247	253	268	222	264	237	269	See Lyme Handley C.P.
MACCLESFIELD tns.	8,743	12,299	17,746	24,137*	23,129	29,648*	26,837	27,475*	See Macclesfield M.B.
MACCLESFIELD FOREST chap.	215	285	260	256	279	269	208	242	See Macclesfield Forest C.P.
MARTON chap.	310	320	341	307	354	313	296	312*	See Marton C.P.
MOTTRAM ST. ANDREW tns.	319	349	382	380	387	408	460	428*	See Mottram St. Andrew C.P.
NEWTON tns.	—[e]	108	95	103	90	122	85*	77*	See Newton C.P.
POTT SHRIGLEY chap.	369	330	331	391	334	467	450	425	See Pott Shrigley C.P.
POYNTON chap.	432	497	540	854	747	1,247	1,284	1,230*	See Poynton with Worth C.P.
PRESTBURY tns.	466	415	440	390	470	373	358	318*	See Prestbury C.P.
RAINOW chap.	1,390	1,595	1,530	1,759*	1,807	1,605*	1,550	1,316*	See Rainow C.P.
RODE, NORTH tns.	256	240	262	287	256	277	285	274*	See Rode, North C.P.
SIDDINGTON chap.	423	448	481	513	479	459	433	394*	See Siddington C.P.
SUTTON chap.	1,739	2,096	2,991	7,035*	5,856	7,525*	6,756*	6,338*	See Sutton C.P.
TYTHERINGTON tns.	226	355	382	389	427	374	395	335	See Tytherington C.P.
UPTON tns.	56	67	52	85	64	111	171	196*	See Upton C.P.
WILDBOARCLOUGH tns.	338	392	414	347*	476	447*	293	253*	See Wildboarclough C.P.
WINCLE chap.	351	428	466	455	453	336	343	306*	See Wincle C.P.
WITHINGTON, LOWER tns.	540	584	615	782*	584	570*	578	543	See Withington, Lower C.P.
WITHINGTON, OLD tns.	137[f]	178	164	191	191	189	161	161	See Withington, Old C.P.
WOODFORD tns.	188	254	383	564	403	430*	392*	351*	See Woodford C.P.
WORTH tns.	254	376	406	490	655	885	751*	716*	See Worth C.P.
PRESTBURY C.P.[h]	Part of Prestbury A.P., q.v.	292	311	314	291	344	487	1,693[g] / 2,159 / 2,891	
PRESTON BROOK C.P.	560	493	454	440	449	355	401	417	
PRESTON ON THE HILL C.P.[i]	Part of Runcorn A.P., q.v.								See Preston Brook C.P. 157
PRIOR'S HEYS E.P.P. and C.P.									
PUDDINGTON C.P.	Part of Burton A.P., q.v.	—	20	21	22	25	22	9 / 11 / 12 / 14 / 15 / 17	
PULFORD A.P.	275	303	318	335	289	338	354	440	
POULTON tns.	170	171	186	206	161	204	222	267	See Poulton C.P.
PULFORD tns.	105	132	132	129	128	134	132	173	See Pulford C.P.
PULFORD C.P.	264	298	305	254	267	261	285	313	
RABY C.P.	239	298	350	339[k]	394	365	351	347	See Bebington M.B.

(u) In 1936 parts of Little Budworth C.P. (pop. 20 in 1931) and Marton C.P. (pop. 10 in 1931) were transferred to Oakmere C.P.

(v) In 1965 part of Kidsgrove U.D. (Staffs.) (pop. 58 in 1961) was transferred to Odd Rode C.P., and part of Odd Rode C.P. to Kidsgrove U.D.

(w) In 1841 the total for Over A.P. was wrongly given as 2,863.

(x) Part of Over tns. was in Whitegate A.P., but was wholly returned in Over A.P. until 1851.

(y) In 1936 part of Pickmere C.P. (pop. 21 in 1931) was transferred to Wincham C.P.

(z) In 1963 Picton C.P. was involved in small boundary changes with Bridge Trafford and Wimbolds Trafford C.P.s.

(a) In 1811 Caughall tns. in Backford A.P. was wrongly returned under Plemstall A.P. Part of Hoole tns., which was chiefly situated in Plemstall A.P., lay in St. John the Baptist A.P. where 1,328 of its inhabitants were returned in 1871.

(b) In 1895 part of Poulton cum Spital C.P. (pop. 67 in 1901) was transferred to Bromborough C.P.

(c) In 1882 and 1888 parts of Pownall Fee C.P.s (pop. respectively 37 and 28 in 1891) were transferred to Fulshaw and Bollin Fee C.P.s. Pownall Fee was dissolved in 1894, part (pop. 2,750 in 1901) being transferred to Wilmslow C.P., and the remainder (pop. 1,153 in 1901) being constituted Styal C.P., q.v.

(d) In 1821 the pop. of Prestbury A.P., including Macclesfield, was wrongly returned as 17,230.

(e) No return. The pop. was included in that of Butley.

(f) No return.

(g) In 1936 Prestbury C.P. was extended to include parts of Butley, Fallibroome, and Upton C.P.s (pop. respectively 536, 72, and 8 in 1931).

(h) Created 1936 from Preston on the Hill C.P. (pop. 355 in 1931) and part of Norton C.P. (pop. 42 in 1931). In 1967 part of Preston Brook C.P. was transferred to Runcorn U.D.

(i) No separate return was made for Prior's Heys 1801–41. Its pop. was probably returned with Tarvin tns. It became a C.P. for the purpose of 20 Vic. c. 19.

(j) In 1933 Puddington C.P. was extended to include part of Willaston C.P. (pop. 14 in 1931).

(k) In 1882 Raby C.P. was extended to include two parts of Little Neston C.P. (pop. 13 in 1891) under the Divided Parishes Act. In 1889 another part of Little Neston C.P. (pop. 67 in 1891) was transferred to Raby C.P.

	1801	1811	1821	1831	1841	1851	1861	1871	1881	1891	1901	1911	1921	1931	1951	1961	1971
RADNOR C.P.	Part of Astbury A.P., q.v.								29	30	See Somerford C.P.						
RAINOW C.P.	Part of Prestbury A.P., q.v.								1,281	1,255	1,205	1,175	1,087	1,109	1,088	1,005	1,141
RAVENSCROFT C.P.	Part of Middlewich A.P., q.v.								20	See Byley C.P.							
REDDISH C.P. (part of)	In Stockport C.B., q.v.																
RIDLEY C.P.[1]	Part of Bunbury A.P., q.v.								98	109	109	137	225*	160	138	123	108
RINGWAY C.P.[1]	Part of Prestbury A.P., q.v.										491	452	459	602	203[m]	239	218
RODE, NORTH C.P.	Part of Prestbury A.P., q.v.								263	247	276	274	247	268	230	195	176
ROMILEY C.P.	See Bredbury and Romiley U.D.																
ROPE C.P.	Part of Wybunbury A.P., q.v.								84	75	62	74	83	92	177	148	863
ROSTHERNE A.P.	3,065	3,370	3,791[n]	3,730	3,953	4,190	4,058	4,073									
AGDEN tns. (part of)	See Bowdon A.P.																
BOLLINGTON tns. (part of)	See Bowdon A.P.																
LEGH, HIGH chap.	787	860	854	983	982	1,024	1,004	939	See Legh, High C.P.								
MARTHALL CUM WARFORD tns.	260	270	267	281	254	225	253	274	See Marthall cum Warford C.P.								
MERE tns.	498	568	566	552	588	583	556	540	See Mere C.P.								
MILLINGTON tns.	196	285	334	330	312	370	338	343	See Millington C.P.								
PEOVER SUPERIOR tns.	451	480	543	561	580*	543	531	599	See Peover Superior C.P.								
ROSTHERNE tns.	235	250	373	376	386	388	393	391	See Rostherne C.P.								
SNELSON tns.	126	118	137	136	199*	169	158	159	See Snelson C.P.								
TABLEY SUPERIOR tns.	392	409	450	442	510	537	490	485	See Tabley Superior C.P.								
TATTON tns.	120	130	87	69	80	128	109	108	See Tatton C.P.								
ROSTHERNE C.P.	Part of Rostherne A.P., q.v.								382	407	413	382	319	284	245	195	189
ROWTON C.P.	Part of Christleton A.P., q.v.								187	181	205	165	183	168	228	297	350
RUDHEATH C.P.	Part of Davenham A.P., q.v.								504	644	954[o]	950	1,356	2,733*	4,883[p]	3,264[q]	3,163
RUNCORN A.P.	4,860	5,947	7,738	10,326[r]	12,698	15,047	16,457	19,460									
ACTON GRANGE tns.	139	135	148	149	175	172	180	200	See Acton Grange C.P.								
ASTON BY SUTTON chap.	186	167	197	166	206	218	207	220	See Aston by Sutton C.P.								
ASTON GRANGE tns.	47	29	36	36	27	16	42	28	See Aston Grange C.P.								
CLIFTON tns.	28	36	26	36	34	30	30	113*	See Clifton C.P.								
DARESBURY chap.	134	114	146	143	184	157	136	169*	See Daresbury C.P.								
HALTON chap.	628	894	1,066	1,322	1,397	1,570	1,505	1,620*	See Halton C.P.								
HATTON tns.	241	271	397	391	382	377	357	397*	See Hatton C.P.								
KECKWICK tns.	69	61	56	74	75	89	115	77*	See Keckwick C.P.								
MOORE tns.	156	186	243	298	317	336	269*	344	See Moore C.P.								
NEWTON BY DARESBURY tns.	96	114	124	165	193	185	191	230*	See Newton by Daresbury C.P.								
NORTON tns.	220	221	294	306	294*	344	380	394*	See Norton C.P.								
PRESTON ON THE HILL tns.	333	381	391*	461	607*	594*	596	609*	See Preston on the Hill C.P.								
RUNCORN tns.	1,379	2,060	3,103*	5,035*	6,951	8,688*	10,063*	12,066*	See Runcorn C.P.								
STOCKHAM tns.	46	38	52	52	43	34	42	43	See Stockham C.P.								
SUTTON tns.	223	265	266	237	275	362	356	363	See Sutton C.P.								
THELWALL chap.	309	326	327	332	334	347	468	453	See Thelwall C.P.								
WALTON INFERIOR tns.	271	285	353	340	349	375	395	459*	See Walton Inferior C.P.								
WALTON SUPERIOR tns.	193	175	219	238	229	220	160*	215	See Walton Superior C.P.								
WESTON tns.	162	189	294	532	626*	933*	965	1,460[o]	See Weston C.P.								
RUNCORN C.P.	In Runcorn U.S.D. q.v.																
RUNCORN R.D.									18,897	22,467	23,244	28,216	28,934	32,725	35,573	39,961	44,930[s]

Table of ancient parishes, townships and civil parishes with census population figures (figures listed earliest → latest as printed; an asterisk (*) reproduces the asterisk shown against certain figures).

Area	Population figures (by census, as printed)
RUNCORN U.S.D. and, from 1884, C.P.[t]	15,126 (corrected 14,812), 20,050, 16,491, 17,353, 18,476, 18,127, 23,931[u], 26,035, 35,999[s]
RUNCORN C.P.	
HALTON C.P. (part of)	314
RUSHTON C.P.	Part of Tarporley A.P. and Tarporley U.D, q.v.
SAIGHTON C.P.	Part of St. Oswald's A.P, q.v.
ST. BRIDGET A.P. and C.P.	344, 362, 308, 327, 362, 347, 415[v], 390, 375
ST. JOHN, LITTLE A.P. and C.P.	245, 308, 312
ST. JOHN THE BAPTIST A.P. and C.P.	See Chester M.B.
ST. MARTIN A.P. and C.P.	See Chester M.B.
ST. MARY ON THE HILL A.P.[w]	
part in Chester City and M.B.	2,426[x], 2,793, 3,736, 3,545, 3,596, 4,157, 5,464, 6,494
	2,129[x], 2,469, 3,376, 3,085, 2,975, 3,415, 4,499*, 5,149, 5,276 — See Chester C.P.
rural parts, viz.	
MARLSTON CUM LACHE tns.	87, 110, 108, 130, 148, 157, 163, 136 — See Marlston cum Lache C.P.
MOLLINGTON BANASTRE tns.	23, 26, 28, 24, 25, 16, 29, 44 — See Mollington Banastre C.P.
MOSTON tns.	14, 6, 18, 17, 11, 14, 15, 18 — See Moston C.P.
UPTON BY CHESTER tns.	173, 182, 206, 289*, 437*, 555*, 758*, 1,147 — See Upton C.P.
ST. MICHAEL A.P. and C.P.	See Chester M.B.
ST. OLAVE A.P. and C.P.	See Chester M.B.
ST. OSWALD'S A.P.[y]	
part in Chester City constituted St. Oswald's C.P.	3,377, 3,416, 4,334, 5,209, 5,959, 6,702, 7,534, 9,908
rural parts, viz.	4,580, 4,776, 6,070, 6,955, 7,775, 8,759, 9,845, 12,524, 11,724
BACHE tns.	8, 21, 21, 34, 18, 25, 34, 26 — See Bache C.P.
BOUGHTON, GREAT tns.[z]	544, 660, 911, 900, 949, 1,164, 1,387*, 1,733 — See Boughton, Great C.P.
CHURTON HEATH chap.[a]	8, 7, 8, 14, 3, 22, 44, 11* — See Churton Heath C.P.
CROUGHTON tns.	33, 30, 27, 39, 27, 22, 28, 29 — See Croughton C.P.
HUNTINGTON tns.	111, 124, 133, 112, 143, 129, 113, 119 — See Huntington C.P.
IDDINSHALL tns.	18, 18, 25, 24, 30, 22, 22, 18 — See Iddinshall C.P.
LEA NEWBOLD tns.	42, 58, 61, 43, 42, 39, 35, 33 — See Lea Newbold C.P.
NEWTON BY CHESTER tns.	141, 128, 192, 213, 226, 245, 298, 252 — See Newton by Chester C.P.
SAIGHTON tns.	242, 247, 291, 303, 313, 329, 272, 309 — See Saighton C.P.
WERVIN tns.	56, 67, 67, 65, 60, 78, 92 — See Wervin C.P.

(l) Created in 1900 from part of Hale C.P.

(m) In 1936 part of Ringway C.P. (pop. 339 in 1931) was transferred to Hale U.D. and C.P.

(n) In 1851 the total for 1821 was stated to have been 3,611.

(o) In 1892 Rudheath C.P. was extended to include Shurlach C.P. (pop. 157 in 1901).

(p) In 1936 part of Rudheath C.P. (pop. 7 in 1931) was transferred to Byley C.P. and Rudheath C.P. was extended to include part of Lostock Gralam C.P. (pop. 2 in 1931).

(q) In 1955 part of Rudheath C.P. was transferred to Northwich U.D.

(r) This figure was corrected to 10,313 in 1851.

(s) In 1967 Halton C.P. and parts of Aston, Daresbury, Dutton, Moore, Norton, Preston Brook, and Sutton C.P.s (pop. 2,401 in 1961) were transferred from Runcorn R.D. to Runcorn U.D.

(t) Runcorn U.D. included Runcorn C.P. and part (pop. 314 in 1881) of Halton C.P.; in 1884 part of Halton C.P. (pop. 400 in 1891) was transferred to Runcorn C.P., which thus became co-extensive with Runcorn U.S.D.

(u) In 1936 Runcorn U.D. and C.P. was extended to include Weston C.P. (pop. 3,783 in 1931) and part of Halton C.P. (pop. 674 in 1931).

(v) In 1936 Rushton C.P. was extended to include part of Eaton C.P. (pop. 277 in 1931), and part of Rushton C.P. (pop. 84 in 1931) was transferred to Utkinton C.P.

(w) Gloverstone was returned as a tns. in St. Mary's A.P. in 1811. In 1801 its pop. was 122, but in 1811 no pop. was recorded. Gloverstone was said to have been converted into barracks by the latter date.

(x) In 1851 the pop. of that part of St. Mary's parish in Chester City in 1801 was corrected to 2,251 and the total pop. of the parish to 2,548.

(y) In 1821 the pop. of St. Oswald's A.P. was wrongly returned as 5,126 and in 1831 as 6,041.

(z) Wrongly returned with Aldford A.P. 1811–31.

(a) Wrongly returned with Aldford A.P. 1811–31.

	1801	*1811*	*1821*	*1831*	*1841*	*1851*	*1861*	*1871*	*1881*	*1891*	*1901*	*1911*	*1921*	*1931*	*1951*	*1961*	*1971*
ST. PETER A.P. and C.P.	See Chester M.B.																
SALE U.S.D. and (except in 1931) C.P., and, from 1936, M.B.[b]	Part of Ashton upon Mersey A.P., q.v.								7,915	9,644	12,088	15,044	16,329	28,071	43,168	51,336	55,769
ASHTON UPON MERSEY U.D. and C.P.													9,704	18,367			
SALE C.P.																	
SANDBACH A.P.[c]	4,496	5,391	6,352[d]	7,214	9,299	8,552	9,046	9,651[c]									
ARCLID tns.	92	82	65	79	121	282*	265	255	See Arclid C.P.								
BETCHTON tns.	578	701	759	818	809	822	798	838*	See Betchton C.P.								
BLACKDEN tns.	136	152	191	170	266*	164*	157	149	See Blackden C.P.								
BRADWALL tns.	252	258	282	297	344	291	437*	587*	See Bradwall C.P.								
COTTON tns.	77	81	81	86	101	92*	62	71	See Cotton C.P.								
CRANAGE tns.	385	387	433	438	512	410*	391	462	See Cranage C.P.								
GOOSTREY tns.	231	261	298	292	325	268	268	321	See Goostrey C.P.								
HASSALL tns.	181	205	218	200	260	219	246	283*	See Hassall C.P.								
HULME, CHURCH chap.	314	346	397	406	1,008*	555*	573	568	See Hulme, Church C.P.								
LEESE tns. (part of, in 1871)[e]	86	126	135	126	151	119*	121	58	See Leese C.P.								
SANDBACH tns.	1,844	2,311	2,905	3,710	4,587	4,659	4,989	5,259	See Sandbach C.P.								
TWEMLOW tns.	131	152	130	152	241	123*	151	153	See Twemlow C.P.								
WHEELOCK tns.	189	329	458	440	574	548	588	643*	See Wheelock C.P.								
SANDBACH U.S.D. and C.P.[g]	Part of Sandbach A.P., q.v.								5,493	5,824	5,558	5,723	5,864	6,411	9,253[f]	9,862	13,306
SAUGHALL, GREAT C.P.	Part of Shotwick A.P., q.v.								619	699	703	819	809	865	See Saughall C.P.		
SAUGHALL, LITTLE C.P.	Part of Shotwick A.P., q.v.								92	101	137	148	219	304	See Saughall C.P.		
SAUGHALL, MASSIE C.P.	Part of Bidston A.P., q.v.								191	189	186	210	315[h]	749[i]	1,518	2,178	2,426
SEVEN OAKS C.P.	Part of Budworth, Great A.P., q.v.								183	177[j]	162	149	134	163	See Antrobus C.P.		
SHAVINGTON CUM GRESTY C.P.	Part of Wybunbury A.P., q.v.								1,067	1,509	1,149[k]	1,270	1,373	2,303*	1,830[l]	2,027	3,518
SHIPBROOK C.P.	Part of Davenham A.P., q.v.							67	See Whatcroft C.P.								
SHOCKLACH A.P.	350	367	422	431	427	405	414	376									
CALDECOTT tns.	59	56	84	75	69	62	66	68	See Caldecott C.P.								
SHOCKLACH, CHURCH tns.	146	156	158	140	178	175	180	149	See Shocklach, Church C.P.								
SHOCKLACH OVIATT tns.	145	155	180	216	180	168	168	159	See Shocklach, Oviatt C.P.								
SHOCKLACH, CHURCH C.P.	Part of Shocklach A.P., q.v.								135	158	147	159	146	162	127	89	81
SHOCKLACH OVIATT C.P.	Part of Shocklach A.P., q.v.								135	158	167	193	191	149	125	117	99
SHOTWICK A.P.[m]	485	657	719[n]	713	868	874	931	1,003									
CAPENHURST tns.	147	165	161	159	154	148	131	171	See Capenhurst C.P.								
SAUGHALL, GREAT tns.	147	304	343	367	480	493	545	571	See Saughall, Great C.P.								
SAUGHALL, LITTLE tns.	48	64	38	40	47	69	94	101	See Saughall, Little C.P.								
SHOTWICK tns.	95	81	94	96	112	100	98	92	See Shotwick C.P.								
WOODBANK tns.	48	43	39	51	75	64	63	68	See Woodbank C.P.								
SHOTWICK C.P.	Part of Shotwick A.P., q.v.								77	77	82	77	76	73	70	72	55
SHOTWICK PARK E.P.P. and C.P.[o]	25	24	23	18	16	13	4	11	14	8	8	29	19	26	78	64	69
SHURLACH C.P.	Part of Davenham A.P., q.v.								179	See Rudheath C.P.							
SIDDINGTON C.P.	Part of Prestbury A.P., q.v.								406	406	392	383	366	344	394[p]	504	489
SMALLWOOD C.P.	Part of Astbury A.P., q.v.								578	577	530	548	591	615	585	502	489
SNELSON C.P.	Part of Rostherne A.P., q.v.								180	185	170	201	187	200	160	184	154
SOMERFORD C.P.	Part of Astbury A.P., q.v.								78	71	98[q]	119	116	102	531	309	295

Parish	Reference / Population figures
SOMERFORD BOOTHS C.P.	Part of Astbury A.P., q.v.
SOUND C.P.	Part of Acton and Wrenbury A.P.s, q.v.
SPITAL BOUGHTON E.P.P. and C.P.	186 · 204 · 160 · 162 · 187 · 172 · 195 · 201 · 216 / 223 · 218 · 237 · 243 · 276 · 246 · 234 · 249 · 274
SPROSTON C.P.	See Chester M.B.
SPURSTOW C.P.	Part of Middlewich A.P., q.v.
STALYBRIDGE M.B. and U.S.D. (part of, until 1891), from 1801 M.B. and from 1894 C.P.[t]	Part of Bunbury A.P., q.v.
	224 · 230 · 216[s] · 167 · 176 · 172 · 167 · 196[r] · 141 / 343 · 352 · 323 · 333 · 381 · 373 · 434 · 412 · 451
	14,286 · 18,130 · 15,323 · 16,384 · 26,783 · 27,673 · 26,513 · 25,216 · 24,831 · 22,541[u] · 21,947 · 22,805
ASHTON-UNDER-LYNE C.P. (part of)[v]	Part of Ashton-under-Lyne (Lancs.) C.P.
DUKINFIELD C.P. (part of)	7,278
STALEY C.P. (part of)[y]	Part of Stockport A.P., q.v.
	11,831 · 7,674 · 422* · 89*
STANLOW E.P.P. and C.P.[w]	Part of Mottram in Longdendale A.P., q.v.
	10 · 12 · 16 · 13 · 14 · 26 · 18 · 30 · 18
STANNEY, GREAT C.P.	See Stanney, Great C.P.
STANNEY, LITTLE C.P.	See Ellesmere Port and Whitby U.D.
	23 · 58
STANTHORNE C.P.	Part of Stoke A.P., q.v.
	157 · 145 · 187 · 163 · 192 · 170 · 268 · 220 · 194[x] · 161
STAPELEY C.P.	Part of Stoke A.P., q.v.
	193 · 206 · 204 · 191 · 214 · 290 · 136[y] · 160
STAPLEFORD, BRUEN C.P.	Part of Davenham A.P., q.v.
	602 · 686 · 607 · 652 · 622 · 634 · 513[z] · 484 · 448[a]
STAPLEFORD, FOULK C.P.	Part of Wybunbury A.P., q.v.
	151 · 130 · 145 · 118 · 128 · 114 · 119 · 106 · 83[a]
STALEY C.P. (part of)[b]	Part of Tarvin A.P., q.v.
part in Stayley U.S.D.	234 · 204 · 233 · 238 · 205 · 205 · 153 · 137 · 183[a]
part in Stalybridge U.S.D.	See Stalybridge M.B.
rural part	7,363 · 2,674
	3,651 · 38

(b) In 1930 Sale U.D. was extended to include Ashton upon Mersey U.D. (pop. 7,773 in 1921) and in 1936 Sale U.D. was extended to include Ashton upon Mersey C.P.

(c) In 1821 and 1871 the totals for Sandbach A.P. include respectively 17 and 4 inhabitants of Rudheath. Leese tns. extended into Middlewich A.P., where part of its pop. was returned in 1871.

(d) In 1821 the pop. of Sandbach A.P. was wrongly returned as 6,369.

(e) See above, note (c).

(f) In 1936 Sandbach U.D. and C.P. was extended to include parts of Bradwall, Elton, and Wheelock C.P.s (pop. respectively 1,075, 287, and 494 in 1931).

(g) Created 1948 from the union of Great and Little Saughall C.P.s.

(h) In 1915 part of Hoylake and West Kirby C.P. (pop. 95 in 1921) was transferred to Saughall Massie C.P., and parts of Saughall Massie C.P. (pop. 25 and 8 in 1921) were transferred to Hoylake and West Kirby C.P. and Moreton C.P.

(i) Dissolved 1933, part (pop. 31 in 1931) being transferred to Grange C.P. in Hoylake U.D. and part (pop. 718 in 1931) to Wallasey C.B.

(j) In 1881 Seven Oaks C.P. was extended to include part of Antrobus C.P. (pop. 3 in 1891).

(k) In 1892 part of Shavington cum Gresty (pop. 924 in 1901) was transferred to Crewe M.B., and in 1894 it was included in Monks Coppenhall C.P.

(l) In 1936 part of Shavington cum Gresty C.P. (pop. 740 in 1931) was transferred to Crewe M.B. and Monks Coppenhall C.P.

(m) In 1821 and 1831 separate returns were made for Kingswood tns. (pop. 44 and 86 respectively). In 1821 and 1831 the total for Shotwick A.P. was wrongly returned as 799.

(n) This figure was corrected to 387 in 1851.

(o) Shotwick Park became a parish for the purposes of 20 Vic. c. 19.

(p) In 1936 Siddington C.P. was extended to include Capesthorne C.P. (pop. 97 in 1931).

(q) In 1895 Somerford C.P. was extended to include Radnor C.P. (pop. 26 in 1901).

(r) In 1892 Sproston C.P. was extended to include Mooresbarrow cum Parme C.P. (pop. 26 in 1901).

(s) In 1936 Sproston C.P. was extended to include part of Kinderton C.P. (pop. 43 in 1931).

(t) Stalybridge M.B., incorporated in 1857, comprised part of Dukinfield tns., part of Stayley tns., and part of Hartshead tns. in Ashton-under-Lyne A.P. (Lancs.). In 1881 the borough was extended to include Stayley U.S.D. and a further part of Ashton-under-Lyne (pop. 518). In 1888 it was wholly included in Ches. admin. co. In 1894 Stalybridge C.P. was created from the parts in Stalybridge M.B. of Stayley C.P. (pop. 8,750 in 1901) and Ashton-under-Lyne C.P. (pop. 7,402 in 1901).

(u) In 1936 Stalybridge M.B. and C.P. was extended to include part of Matley C.P. (pop. 147 in 1931).

(v) In 1888 the part of Ashton-under-Lyne (Lancs.) C.P. in Stalybridge M.B. which had been in Lancs. ancient co. was included in Ches. admin. co.

(w) Stanlow, formerly an E.P.P., was deemed a C.P. for the purposes of the Act 20 Vic. c. 19.

(x) In 1963 and 1967 parts of Little Stanney were transferred to Ellesmere Port M.B. and in 1963 parts of Ellesmere Port M.B. and Thornton le Moors C.P. were transferred to Little Stanney.

(y) In 1936 Winsford U.D. and C.P. was extended to include part of Stanthorne C.P. (pop. 121 in 1931).

(z) In 1936 Nantwich U.D. and C.P. was extended to include part of Stapeley C.P. (pop. 124 in 1931) and in 1938 Stapeley C.P. was extended to include part of Willaston C.P. (pop. 37 in 1931).

(a) In 1963 part of Bruen Stapleford C.P. was transferred to Foulk Stapleford C.P., as were parts of Cotton Edmunds and Huxley C.P.s. Parts of Foulk Stapleford C.P. were transferred to Bruen Stapleford, Cotton Edmunds, and Huxley C.P.s.

(b) Stayley C.P. was partly in Mossley U.S.D. in Lancs. ancient and admin. cos. In 1881 Stayley U.S.D. was added to Stalybridge M.B. The part of Stayley C.P. in Stayley U.S.D. therefore added to the part in Stalybridge M.B., q.v.

	1801	1811	1821	1831	1841	1851	1861	1871	1881	1891	1901	1911	1921	1931	1951	1961	1971
STOCKHAM C.P.[c]	Part of Runcorn A.P., q.v.								25	47	38	32	27	21	See Norton C.P.		
STOCKPORT A.P.[c]	28,344	35,411	44,957	66,610	84,301[d]	91,423	98,005	96,049									
BRAMHALL tns.	1,033	1,134	1,359	1,401	1,396	1,508	1,615	1,960*	See Bramhall C.P.								
BREDBURY tns.	1,358	1,706	2,010	2,374	3,301	2,991	3,408*	3,596*	See Bredbury C.P. in Bredbury and Romiley U.D.								
BRINNINGTON tns.	890	1,705	2,124	3,987	5,331	5,203	5,346	5,042*	See Brinnington C.P.								
DISLEY chap.	995	1,415	1,533	2,037*	2,191	2,225	2,265	2,817*	See Disley C.P.								
DUKINFIELD tns.	1,737	3,053	5,096	14,681*	22,394	26,418	29,953*	26,329*	See Dukinfield C.P.								
ETCHELLS, STOCKPORT tns.[e]	1,269	1,276	749	701	749	805	860	977	See Etchells, Stockport C.P.								
HYDE tns.	1,063	1,806	3,355	7,144*	10,170	11,569	13,722*	14,223*	See Hyde M.B.								
MARPLE chap.	2,031	2,254	2,646	2,678	3,462	3,558	3,338	4,100*	See Marple C.P.								
NORBURY tns.	592	451	680	671	808	848	1,305	1,291	See Norbury C.P.								
OFFERTON tns.	351	493	401	431	354	352	297	316	See Offerton C.P.								
ROMILEY tns.	825	1,015	1,181	1,290	1,465	1,364	1,468	1,804*	See Romiley C.P.								
STOCKPORT tns.	14,830	17,545	21,726*	25,469*	28,431*	30,589*	30,746	29,931*	See Stockport C.P.								
TORKINGTON tns.	218	254	293	284	345	358	218*	261	See Torkington C.P.								
WERNETH tns.	1,152	1,304	1,804	3,462*	3,904	3,635	3,464*	3,402	See Werneth C.P.								
STOCKPORT C.B. and, from 1936, C.P.[f]						40,175[o]	40,843	39,827	45,003	70,263	78,897	108,682[g]	123,309[h]	125,490	141,650[i]	142,543[j]	139,644
BRINNINGTON C.P. (part of)									5,542	6,576							
CHEADLE C.P. (part of)									6,294	10,022							
HEATON NORRIS C.P. (part of)									33,167								
REDDISH C.P.										16,368		14,252	15,386	15,463			
STOCKPORT C.P.										37,297	78,897[l]	94,430[m]	97,077	96,617			
STOCKPORT M.B. and U.S.D. (part of)[m]																	
BRINNINGTON C.P. (part of)													10,846[k]	13,410			
CHEADLE C.P. (part of)																	
STOCKPORT R.D.	Part of Stockport A.P., q.v.								21,935	10,159	2,288[p]						
STOCKTON C.P.	Part of Malpas A.P., q.v.								35	21	28	24	28	20	12	12	15
STOCKTON HEATH C.P.[q]	Part of Budworth, Great A.P. and Appleton C.P., q.v.										2,543*	4,370*	4,684	4,844	6,674[r]	6,684[s]	6,506
STOKE A.P.[t]	335	361	461	398	399	402	431	514									
STANNEY, GREAT tns.	12	16	18	32	53	56	65	65	See Stanney, Great C.P.								
STANNEY, LITTLE tns.	203	229	228	201	163	177	204	201	See Stanney, Little C.P.								
STOKE tns.	120	116	129	101	111	93	102	84*	See Stoke C.P.								
WHITBY tns. (part of)	See Eastham A.P., part of Whitby tns. in		86	64	72	76*	60	164*	See Whitby C.P.								
STOKE C.P.	Part of Acton A.P., q.v.								197	206	191	211	225	213	229	184	156
STOKE C.P.	Part of Stoke A.P., q.v.								70	78	67	74	88	101	74	165	167[u]
STORETON C.P.	Part of Bebington A.P., q.v.								244	256	263	280	279	215	See Bebington U.D.		
STRETTON C.P.	Part of Budworth, Great A.P., q.v.								396	396	310	346	352	371	1,083	579	419
STRETTON C.P.	Part of Tilston A.P., q.v.								97	92	92	80	80	79	58	43	49
STUBLACH C.P.	Part of Middlewich A.P., q.v.								37[v]	See Lach Dennis C.P.							
STYAL C.P.[w]	Part of Wilmslow A.P. and Pownall Fee C.P., q.v.										1,153	1,309	1,245	1,336	See Wilmslow U.D. and C.P. and Mobberley C.P.		
SUTTON C.P.	Part of Middlewich A.P., q.v.								32	See Newton C.P.							

Area	Annotation / population figures
SUTTON C.P.	Part of Prestbury A.P., q.v. … 6,684 · 6,366x · 1,294 · 1,257 · 1,295 · 1,426 · 1,948y · 2,016 · 2,521
part in Macclesfield M.B.	5,365 · 5,060 · 1,306
rural part	1,319 · 1,306
SUTTON, GREAT C.P.	Part of Runcorn A.P., q.v. … 377 · 405 · 409 · 397 · 453 · 622* · 667z · 733 · 535a — See Ellesmere Port U.D. and C.P.
SUTTON, GUILDEN A.P. and C.P.	Part of Eastham A.P., q.v. … 158 · 120 · 131 · 132 · 180 · 221 · 223 · 234 · 269 · 347 · 397 · 368 · 404 · 442b · 718c · 669d
SUTTON, LITTLE C.P.	Part of Eastham A.P., q.v. … 866 · 1,094 · 1,109 · 1,327 · 1,635 · 2,258 — See Ellesmere Port U.D. and C.P.
SWETTENHAM A.P.	Part of Swettenham A.P., q.v. … 416 · 400 · 435 · 421 · 420
KERMINCHAM tns.	179 · 173 · 176 · 174 · 191 — See Kermincham C.P.
SWETTENHAM tns.	237 · 227 · 259 · 247 · 229 · 200 · 187 · 197 — See Swettenham C.P.
SWETTENHAM C.P.	321e · 314 · 286
TABLEY INFERIOR C.P.	Part of Budworth, Great A.P., q.v. … 176 · 171 · 186 · 181 · 169 · 150 · 186 · 171 · 181 · 148 · 109f · 98 · 119
TABLEY SUPERIOR C.P.	Part of Rostherne A.P., q.v. … 119 · 150 · 129 · 120 · 493 · 478 · 461 · 452 · 368g · 382 · 370
TARPORLEY A.P.	1,866 · 1,852 · 2,123 · 2,391 · 2,546 · 2,632 · 2,577 · 2,652
EATON tns.	460 · 369 · 477 · 502 · 525 · 522 · 465 · 465 — See Eaton C.P.
RUSHTON tns.	274 · 285 · 315 · 330 · 301 · 349 · 342 · 366 — See Rushton C.P.
TARPORLEY tns.	674 · 701 · 800 · 995 · 1,114 · 1,171 · 1,212 · 1,243 — See Tarporley C.P.
UTKINTON tns.	458 · 497 · 531 · 564 · 606 · 590 · 558 · 578 — See Utkinton C.P.

(c) See below, note (e).

(d) In 1841 the pop. of Stockport A.P. was incorrectly returned as 84,282.

(e) In 1801 and 1811 the pop. of Northen Etchells and Stockport Etchells was returned together. In 1851 the pop. of Stockport Etchells at those dates was estimated as 623 and 627 respectively.

(f) Stockport M.B. was constituted Stockport C.B. by the Local Government Act, 1888. It included part of Heaton Norris C.P., formerly in Lancs. ancient co.

(g) In 1901 Stockport C.B. was extended to include Reddish U.D. and C.P., formerly in Lancs. admin. co., and Stockport C.B. and C.P. was extended to include parts of Bredbury, Heaton Norris, Brinnington, Cheadle, and Hazel Grove and Bramhall C.P.s (pop. 30, 51, 1,197, 7,950, and 4,169 in 1911).

(h) In 1913 Stockport C.B. was extended to include a further part of Heaton Norris U.D. and C.P. (pop. 10,846 in 1921). The remainder of Heaton Norris was included in Manchester C.B., Lancs.

(i) In 1935 Stockport C.B. and C.P. was extended to include part of Hazel Grove and Bramhall U.D. and C.P. (pop. 872 in 1931) under the Stockport Extension Act, 1934. In 1936 Stockport C.B. and C.P. was extended to include the C.P.s of Heaton Norris and Reddish, and the C.B. and C.P. thus became co-extensive.

(j) In 1952 Stockport C.B. and C.P. was extended to include part of Bredbury and Romiley U.D. (pop. 151 in 1951).

(k) See above, note (h).

(l) In 1894 Stockport C.B. and C.P. was extended to include the parts in Stockport C.B. of the following C.P.s: Heaton Norris (pop. 17,066 in 1901), Cheadle (pop. 15,099 in 1901), and Brinnington (pop. 6,528 in 1901).

(m) See above, note (g).

(n) Stockport M.B. included part of Heaton Norris tns. in Manchester A.P. (Lancs. ancient co.). The figures for 1851–81 refer to the pop. of the part of Stockport in Ches. viz. Stockport tns. and part of Brinnington, Cheadle Bulkeley, and Cheadle Moseley tns.

(o) This figure includes 134 in Stockport barracks.

(p) In 1901 part of Brinnington C.P. (pop. 1,197 in 1911) was transferred to Stockport C.B. and in 1902 the remainder (pop. 821 in 1911) was transferred to Bredbury and Romiley U.D. In 1902 Compstall C.P. was constituted Compstall U.D., and two years later Handforth C.P. was constituted Handforth U.D.

(q) Created 1897 from part of Appleton C.P. (pop. 2,543 in 1901).

(r) In 1933 part of Latchford Without C.P. (pop. 1,266 in 1931) was transferred from Warrington C.B. (Lancs.) to Stockton Heath C.P.

(s) In 1955 Stockton Heath C.P. was extended to include part of Grappenhall C.P. (pop. 70 in 1951) and Grappenhall C.P. was extended to include part of Stockton Heath C.P. (pop. 5 in 1951).

(t) The totals for Stoke A.P. in 1801 and 1811 exclude the pop. of Whitby tns., which was wholly returned in Eastham A.P., q.v. In 1841 the total given for Stoke A.P. (346) excludes Great Stanney, returned as an E.P.P.

(u) In 1963 the boundary between Stoke C.P. and Thornton le Moors C.P. was altered.

(v) In 1889 Stublach C.P. was extended to include part of Rudheath (pop. 22 in 1891). In 1892 Stublach C.P. was united with Lach Dennis C.P., q.v.

(w) Created 1894 from the rural part of Pownall Fee C.P. (pop. 1,153 in 1901).

(x) In 1894 the part of Sutton C.P. (pop. 4,887 in 1901) in Macclesfield M.B. was included in Macclesfield M.B.

(y) In 1936 Macclesfield M.B. and C.P. was extended to include part of Sutton C.P. (pop. 22 in 1931).

(z) In 1936 Sutton C.P. was extended to include part of Clifton C.P. (pop. 178 in 1931).

(a) In 1967 part of Sutton C.P. was transferred to Runcorn U.D.

(b) In 1936 part of Guilden Sutton C.P. (pop. 41 in 1931) was transferred to Hoole U.D. and C.P. and part of Hoole Village C.P. (pop. 19 in 1931) was transferred to Guilden Sutton C.P.

(c) In 1954 part of Hoole U.D. (pop. 209 in 1951) was transferred to Guilden Sutton C.P.

(d) In 1963 Guilden Sutton C.P. exchanged a small portion of land with Barrow C.P.

(e) In 1936 Swettenham C.P. was extended to include Kermincham C.P. (pop. 129 in 1931).

(f) In 1936 Tabley Inferior C.P. was extended to include part of Wincham C.P. (pop. 7 in 1931).

(g) In 1936 part of Tabley Superior C.P. (pop. 118 in 1931) was transferred to Knutsford U.D. and C.P.

	1801	1811	1821	1831	1841	1851	1861	1871	1881	1891	1901	1911	1921	1931	1951	1961	1971
TARPORLEY U.S.D.[h]															(See Rushton, Tarporley, and Utkinton C.P.s		
EATON C.P.	Part of Tarporley A.P. and U.S.D., q.v.								465	461	394	409	377	353[i]			
RUSHTON C.P.	Part of Tarporley A.P. and U.S.D., q.v.								334	324	333	305	310	310[j]			
TARPORLEY C.P.	Part of Tarporley A.P. and U.S.D., q.v.								1,350	1,419	1,454	1,414	1,391	1,355[k]	1,538[l]	1,552	1,722
UTKINTON C.P.	Part of Tarporley A.P. and U.S.D., q.v.								520	498	463	476	440	434[k]			
TARVIN A.P.	2,683	3,120	3,486[m]	3,415	3,585	3,511	3,319	3,299	2,669	2,702	2,644	2,604	2,518	2,452			
ASHTON tns.	342	365	414	405	401	430	411	398	See Ashton C.P.								
BURTON tns.	71	77	78	84	79	99	77	60	See Burton C.P.								
CLOTTON HOOFIELD tns.	278	312	388	401	417	390	398	324	See Clotton Hoofield C.P.								
DUDDON tns.	163	243	243	203	200	191	168	172	See Duddon C.P.								
HOCKENHULL tns.	41	40	38	35	35	22	36	28	See Hockenhull C.P.								
HORTON CUM PEEL tns.	36	39	36	36	45	33	40	41	See Horton cum Peel C.P.								
KELSALL tns.	469	557	598	648	686	626	542	618	See Kelsall C.P.								
MOULDSWORTH tns.	142	125	138	180	165	158	175	153	See Mouldsworth C.P.								
STAPLEFORD, BRUEN tns.	161	198	268	159	165	145	153	147	See Stapleford, Bruen C.P.								
STAPLEFORD, FOULK tns.	212	243	263	244	285	236	245	236	See Stapleford, Foulk C.P.								
TARVIN tns.[n]	768	921	1,022	1,020	1,087	1,181	1,074	1,122	See Tarvin C.P.								
TARVIN C.P.	Part of Tarvin A.P., q.v.								1,274	1,193	1,093	1,137	1,122	1,251	1,505	1,400	2,705[o]
TARVIN R.D.									11,186	12,387	12,614	13,187	13,390	13,279	14,606	14,497	18,123[p]
TATTENHALL A.P.	746	809	1,016	1,141[q]	1,119	1,204	1,262	1,433	See Golborne Bellow C.P.								
GOLBORNE BELLOW tns.	81	75	86	96	129	105	108	142*	See Golborne Bellow C.P.								
NEWTON BY TATTENHALL tns.	59	66	75	67	86	117	121	129	See Newton by Tattenhall C.P.								
TATTENHALL tns.	606	668	855	978	904	982	1,033	1,162*	See Tattenhall C.P.								
TATTENHALL C.P.	Part of Tattenhall A.P., q.v.								1,089*	975	975	1,043	1,055	1,008	1,049	1,167	1,600
TATTON C.P.	Part of Rostherne A.P., q.v.								145	149	120	119	63	61	42	17	40
TAXAL A.P.	385	469	662	587	853	898	1,329*	1,421	See Taxal C.P.								
TAXAL tns.	160	182	241	184	190	205	277*	262	See Taxal C.P.								
YEARDSLEY CUM WHALEY tns.	225	287	421	403	663	693	1,052	1,159	See Yeardsley cum Whaley U.D. and C.P.								
TAXAL C.P.	Part of Taxal A.P., q.v.								313	308	342	568*	670	679[r]			
TETTON C.P.	Part of Warmingham A.P., q.v.								161	158	142	150	155	141	306[s]	309	See Moston C.P.
THELWALL C.P.	Part of Runcorn A.P., q.v.								496	770[t]	481	517	462	509[u]	See Grappenhall C.P.		
THINGWALL C.P.	Part of Woodchurch A.P., q.v.								162	173	156	200	416	See Birkenhead C.B.			
THORNTON, CHILDER C.P.	Part of Eastham A.P., q.v.								621	743	685	688	851	792[v]	See Ellesmere Port U.D. and C.P.		
THORNTON HOUGH C.P.	Part of Neston A.P., q.v.								456	487	547	602	598	586[w]	See Bebington M.B.		
THORNTON LE MOORS A.P.	772	807	853	913	914	942	913	877									
DUNHAM ON THE HILL tns.	260	289	306	322	306	332	320	323	See Dunham on the Hill C.P.								
ELTON tns.	167	165	179	210	225	216	190	206	See Elton C.P.								
HAPSFORD tns.	78	92	89	83	102	102	84	82	See Hapsford C.P.								
THORNTON LE MOORS tns.	156	158	162	180	165	186	206	172	See Thornton le Moors C.P.								
TRAFFORD, WIMBOLDS tns.	111	103	117	118	116	106	113	94	See Trafford, Wimbolds C.P.								
THORNTON LE MOORS C.P.	Part of Thornton le Moors A.P., q.v.								157	145	130	178	191	166	223	225	216[x]
THREAPWOOD E.P.P. and C.P. (part of, until 1896)[y]	—	—	—	—	316	256	224	233	192	206	305	275	294	279	290	239	219

THURSTASTON A.P.[z]	112	63	127	92	168	142	162	151									
GREASBY tns. (part of)	—	—	—	—	28	19	14	21	See Greasby C.P.								
IRBY tns. (part of)	—	—	—	—	26	25	25	9									
THURSTASTON tns.	112	63	127	92	114	98	123	121	See Thurstaston C.P.								
THURSTASTON C.P.	Part of Thurstaston A.P., q.v.								113	145	141	138	207	210	See Wirral U.D.		
TILSTON A.P.	599	711	833	873	923	837	817	721									
CARDEN tns.	124	183	195	207	233	190	208	166	See Carden C.P.								
GRAFTON tns.	23	17	21	18	14	12	11	13	See Grafton C.P.								
HORTON tns.	111	116	141	148	142	139	122	123	See Horton C.P.								
STRETTON tns.	84	101	106	105	84	71	94	75	See Stretton C.P.								
TILSTON tns.	257	294	370	395	450	425	382*	344	See Tilston C.P.								
TILSTON C.P.	Part of Tilston A.P., q.v.								360	305	320	382	368	347	377	426	489
TILSTONE FEARNALL C.P.	Part of Bunbury A.P., q.v.								149	202	184	175	168	146	146[a]	99	112
TIMPERLEY C.P.	Part of Bowdon A.P., q.v.								2,241	2,461	3,215	4,090	4,263	7,080[b]	See Altrincham U.D. and C.P., Hale U.D. and C.P., and Sale M.B. and C.P.		
TINTWISTLE C.P. (part of, in 1891)[c]	Part of Mottram A.P., q.v.								3,442	2,116	1,622[d]	1,648	1,530	1,392	See Tintwistle R.D. and C.P.		
TINTWISTLE R.D. (and, from 1936, C.P.)											2,105	2,193	2,071	2,020	1,364[e]	1,436	1,480
TITTENLEY C.P.	Part of Audlem A.P., q.v.								25	34	In Shropshire after 1895.						
TIVERTON C.P.	Part of Bunbury A.P., q.v.								520	514	525	544	565	525	489	477	456
TOFT C.P.	Part of Knutsford A.P., q.v.								173	208	176	187	162	214	118[f]	118	75
TORKINGTON C.P.	Part of Stockport A.P., q.v.								244	294	See Hazel Grove and Bramhall U.D. and C.P.						
TRAFFORD, BRIDGE C.P.	Part of Plemstall A.P., q.v.								60	66	60	53	58	50	38	38	39[g]
TRAFFORD, MICKLE C.P.	Part of Plemstall A.P., q.v.								244	284	268	274	251	263	348	459	393[g]
TRAFFORD, WIMBOLDS C.P.	Part of Thornton le Moors A.P., q.v.								97	93	90	86	86	73	122	105	108[g]

(h) Dissolved 1936.

(i) Dissolved 1936, part (pop. 277 in 1931) being transferred to Rushton C.P., part (pop. 18 in 1931) to Tarporley C.P., and part (pop. 58 in 1931) to Utkinton C.P.

(j) In 1936 part of Rushton C.P. (pop. 84 in 1931) was transferred to Utkinton C.P.

(k) In 1936 Utkinton C.P. was extended to include parts of Delamere, Eaton, and Rushton C.P.s (pop. respectively 19, 58, and 84 in 1931), and part of Utkinton C.P. (pop. 9 in 1931) was transferred to Tarporley C.P.

(l) In 1936 Tarporley C.P. was extended to include parts of Eaton and Utkinton C.P.s (pop. respectively 18 and 9 in 1931).

(m) The pop. of Tarvin A.P. was wrongly returned as 3,485 in 1821.

(n) The pop. of Prior's Heys E.P.P. was returned with that of Tarvin tns. 1801–41.

(o) In 1963 part of Tarvin C.P. was transferred to Chester R.D., and parts of Christleton, Cotton Edmunds, and Hockenhull C.P.s were transferred to Tarvin C.P.

(p) In 1963 parts of Cotton Edmunds and Tarvin C.P.s were transferred from Tarvin R.D. to Chester R.D., and part of Christleton C.P. was transferred from Chester R.D. to Tarvin R.D.

(q) The pop. of Tattenhall A.P. was wrongly returned as 1,080 in 1831.

(r) Dissolved 1936, part (pop. 7 in 1931) being transferred to Wildboarclough C.P., part (pop. 646 in 1931), to Whaley Bridge U.D. and C.P., and part (pop. 26 in 1931) to Hartington Upper Quarter C.P. (Derb.).

(s) In 1936 Middlewich U.D. and C.P. was extended to include part of Tetton C.P. (pop. 20 in 1931) and Tetton C.P. was extended to include Moston C.P. (pop. 134 in 1931).

(t) In 1884 part of Thelwall C.P. (pop. 12 in 1891) was transferred to Latchford C.P.

(u) In 1933 part of Thelwall C.P. (pop. 3 in 1931) was transferred to Woolston C.P. in Warrington R.D. (Lancs.). Thus altered, Thelwall was united with Grappenhall C.P. in 1936.

(v) In 1933 part of Childer Thornton C.P. (pop. 2 in 1931) was included in Eastham C.P. in Bebington U.D., and the former C.P. was extended to include parts of Eastham and Hooton C.P.s (pop. respectively 17 and 142 in 1931). Thus altered, the C.P. was transferred to Ellesmere Port U.D.

(w) In 1933 Neston cum Parkgate C.P. was extended to include part of Thornton Hough C.P. (pop. 14 in 1931) and Gayton C.P. in Wirral U.D. was extended to include another part (pop. 6 in 1931). Thus altered, Thornton Hough C.P. was transferred to Bebington M.B.

(x) In 1963 parts of Little Stanney, Stoke, and Wervin C.P.s were transferred to Thornton le Moors C.P., and parts of Thornton le Moors C.P. were transferred to Little Stanney, Stoke, and Wervin C.P.s.

(y) Threapwood was an E.P.P. which extended into Maylor hundred (Flints.). It was deemed a C.P. for the purposes of 20 Vic. c. 19 and was wholly included in Ches. admin. co. from 1896. Until 1841 Threapwood was returned as being in Flints. only.

(z) Until 1841 Irby and Greasby were wholly returned under Woodchurch and West Kirby A.P.s respectively, in each of which they were partly situated.

(a) In 1936 Bunbury C.P. was extended to include part of Tilstone Fearnall C.P. (pop. 28 in 1931).

(b) Dissolved 1936, part (pop. 7,072 in 1931) being transferred to Altrincham U.D. and C.P., and part (pop. 8 in 1931) to Hale U.D. and C.P.

(c) In 1891 part of Tintwistle C.P. was situated in Lancs. admin. co.

(d) In 1894 part of Tintwistle C.P. (pop. 1,643 in 1901) was transferred to Mossley C.P. (Lancs.).

(e) In 1936 Hattersley and Matley C.P.s were dissolved and Tintwistle R.D. and C.P. thus became co-extensive.

(f) In 1936 Knutsford U.D. and C.P. was extended to include part of Toft C.P. (pop. 58 in 1931).

(g) In 1963 there were small mutual changes in the boundaries of Bridge Trafford, Mickle Trafford, and Wimbolds Trafford C.P.s.

	1801	1811	1821	1831	1841	1851	1861	1871	1881	1891	1901	1911	1921	1931	1951	1961	1971
TRANMERE C.P. in Birkenhead M.B. and C.B., q.v.	Part of Bebington A.P., q.v.																
TUSHINGHAM WITH GRINDLEY C.P.	Part of Malpas A.P., q.v.								221	256	264	252	250	234	217	183	173
TWEMLOW C.P.	Part of Sandbach A.P., q.v.								163	139	143	120	106	107	176	155	243
TYTHERINGTON C.P.	Part of Prestbury A.P., q.v.								312	376	304	338	376	318[h]	See Bollington U.D. and C.P. and Macclesfield M.B. and C.P.		
UPTON C.P.	Part of Prestbury A.P., q.v.								185	225	224	217	250	278[i]	See Macclesfield M.B. and C.P. and Prestbury C.P.		
UPTON BY BIRKENHEAD A.P. and C.P.	141	163	183	191	237	227	293	540*	622	687	788	1,006	1,132	2,564[j]	See Birkenhead C.P. and Wallasey C.P.		
UPTON-BY-CHESTER C.P.	Part of St. Mary's A.P., q.v.								1,112	1,313	1,769	1,559*	2,292	2,667	6,343	7,708[k]	10,441
UTKINTON C.P.	Part of Tarporley A.P., q.v.								See Tarporley U.S.D.						507	535	587
WALGHERTON C.P.	Part of Wybunbury A.P., q.v.								166	143	178	151	151	159	199	153	134
WALLASEY A.P.[l]	663	943	1,169	2,737	6,261*	8,339	10,723	14,944	See Wallasey U.S.D.								
LISCARD tns.	211	289	345	967	2,873	4,100*	5,625	8,070*	See Wallasey U.S.D.								
POULTON CUM SEACOMBE tns.	178	214	380	1,212	2,446	3,044*	3,683	4,923*	See Wallasey U.S.D.								
WALLASEY tns.	274	440	444	558*	942*	1,195*	1,415	1,951*	See Wallasey U.S.D.								
WALLASEY C.B. and C.P.[m]													90,809	97,626[n]	101,369[o]	103,209	97,215
WALLASEY U.S.D.; from 1910 M.B. and from 1913 C.B.									21,192	33,229	53,579	78,504	See Wallasey C.B.				
LISCARD C.P.									11,612	16,323	28,661	38,659*					
POULTON CUM SEACOMBE C.P.									7,640	14,839	20,749	30,566*					
WALLASEY C.P.									1,940	2,067	4,169	9,279*					
WALLERSCOTE C.P.									11	See Winnington C.P.							
WALTON C.P.[p]	Part of Weaverham A.P., q.v.														1,549	1,514	1,658
WALTON INFERIOR C.P.	Part of Runcorn A.P., q.v.								498	425	719	1,068*	1,193	1,460[q]	See Walton C.P.		
WALTON SUPERIOR C.P.	Part of Runcorn A.P., q.v.								246	225	215	200	202	175	See Walton C.P.		
WARBURTON A.P. and C.P.	466	470	509	510	509	489	484	452	426	416	403	403	379	354	376	328	287
WARDLE C.P.	Part of Bunbury A.P., q.v.								152	164	193	154	151	140	285	239	207
WARFORD, GREAT C.P.	Part of Alderley A.P., q.v.								351	378	394	622	831	900	1,035[r]	1,023	906
WARFORD, LITTLE C.P.[s]	Part of Alderley A.P., q.v.														544	517	489
WARMINGHAM A.P.	917	1,041	1,078[t]	1,167	1,396	1,271	1,205	1,289									
ELTON tns.	331	377	379	430	570*	444	507	504	See Elton C.P.								
MOSTON tns.	120	162	143	184	224	207	170	217*	See Moston C.P.								
TETTON tns.	120	157	170	181	182	197	170	166	See Tetton C.P.								
WARMINGHAM C.P.	346	345	386	372	420	423	358	402	320	264	218	247	221	215	199[u]	215	222
WARRINGTON M.B. (part of)[v]						2,419	2,723	2,897	3,973	5,785							
WAVERTON A.P.	594	622	707	720	776	788	736	788									
HATTON tns.	152	147	157	150	156	164	146	162	See Hatton C.P.								
HUXLEY tns.	196	212	247	246	279	267	253	260	See Huxley C.P.								
WAVERTON tns.	246	263	303	324	341	357	337	366	See Waverton C.P.								
WAVERTON C.P.	Part of Waverton A.P., q.v.								330	371[w]	384	538	545	479	476	523	1,297

236

	1801	1811	1821	1831	1841	1851	1861	1871	1881	1891	1901	1911	1921	1931	1951	1961
WEAVER C.P.	Part of Middlewich A.P., q.v.															
WEAVERHAM A.P.	1,819	2,020	2,360	2,321	2,596	2,745	2,782	……	3,013					5,264[y]	7,764	7,936
ACTON tns.	210	263	301	335	382	424	484	496	See Acton C.P.							
CROWTON tns.	297	355	455	361	454	466	413	440	See Crowton C.P.							
CUDDINGTON tns.	212	217	282	277	253	316	317	370*	See Cuddington C.P.							
HARTFORD tns. (part of)	See Budworth, Great A.P.			……		17	18	17	See Hartford C.P.							
ONSTON tns.	53	60	71	92	85	96	98	98	See Onston C.P.							
WALLERSCOTE tns.	7	5	10	8	7	6	11		See Wallerscote C.P.							
WEAVERHAM tns. (part of, after 1851)[x]	1,040	1,120	749	818	834	979	1,530	1,581	See Weaverham C.P.							
WEAVERHAM LORDSHIP (part of, after 1851)								139	See Darnhall C.P.							
WEAVERHAM C.P.	See Weaverham tns.															
WERNETH C.P.	Part of Stockport A.P., q.v.								1,699	1,761	1,882	1,989	2,111	3,179*	See Hyde C.P. and Compstall C.P.	
WERNETH C.P. part in Hyde M.B.														3,129	2,587*	See Hyde C.P. and Compstall C.P.
rural part														2,022	1,107	
WERVIN C.P.	Part of St. Oswald's A.P., q.v.								92	94	97	89	103	……	117	145[a]
WESTON C.P.	Part of Runcorn A.P., q.v.								1,684	2,339	2,145	2,246	……	3,783*	See Runcorn U.D. and C.P.	
WESTON C.P.	Part of Wybunbury A.P., q.v.								519	485	474	530	531	544	570	730[b]
WETTENHALL C.P.	Part of Over A.P., q.v.								214	182	214	210	219	186	154	139
WHARTON C.P.	Part of Davenham A.P., q.v.								See Winsford U.D.							
WHATCROFT C.P.	Part of Davenham A.P., q.v.								57	135[c]	141	136	141	119	82	65[d] / 40
WHEELOCK C.P.	Part of Sandbach A.P., q.v.								794	826	685	672	731	756[e]	{See Sandbach U.D. and C.P. and Haslington C.P.}	
WHITBY C.P.	Part of Eastham and Stoke A.P.s, q.v.								1,488				4,082	5,107*	See Ellesmere Port and Whitby U.D.	
WHITCHURCH A.P. (part of), viz. Wirswall tns.[f]	See Wirswall C.P.															
WHITEGATE A.P.																
DARNHALL tns.	103	112	113	83	91	107	113		See Darnhall C.P.							
MARTON tns.	197	175	207	198	197	176	177	661	See Marton C.P.							
OVER tns. (part of)	628	691	789	909	872	1,529	1,535	1,721	See Over C.P.							
WEAVERHAM tns. (part of)	431	516	582	711	675	639	636	779	110[g]	84	104	See Weaverham C.P.				

(h) Dissolved 1936, part (pop. 15 in 1931) being transferred to Bollington U.D. and C.P. and the remainder (pop. 303 in 1931) to Macclesfield M.B. and C.P.

(i) Dissolved 1936, part (pop. 270 in 1931) being transferred to Macclesfield M.B. and C.P. and the remainder (pop. 8 in 1931) to Prestbury C.P.

(j) Dissolved 1933, part (pop. 2,547 in 1931) being transferred to Birkenhead C.B. and C.P., and part (pop. 17 in 1931) to Wallasey C.B. and C.P.

(k) In 1954 Chester C.B. and C.P. was extended to include part of Upton by Chester C.P. (pop. 10 in 1951).

(l) In 1821 and 1831 the totals for Wallasey A.P. were wrongly returned as 1,160 and 3,247 respectively.

(m) In 1912 Wallasey C.P. was extended to include Liscard and Poulton cum Seacombe C.P.s. Wallasey M.B. was constituted a C.B. in 1913.

(n) In 1928 Wallasey C.B. was extended to include part of Bidston cum Ford and Moreton C.P.s (pop. respectively 10 and 4,029 in 1921).

(o) In 1933 Wallasey C.B. and C.P. was extended to include parts of Saughall Massie and Upton by Birkenhead C.P.s (pop. respectively 718 and 17 in 1931).

(p) Created 1936 from Walton Superior C.P. (pop. 175 in 1931) and parts of Acton Grange and Walton Inferior C.P.s (pop. respectively 100 and 1,026 in 1931).

(q) Dissolved 1936, part (pop. 1,026 in 1931) being transferred to Walton C.P. and part (pop. 434 in 1931) to Warrington C.B. (Lancs.).

(r) In 1936 Mobberley C.P. was extended to include part of Great Warford C.P. (pop. 18 in 1931).

(s) Created 1951 from part of Marthall cum Warford C.P.

(t) In 1821 the total for Warmingham A.P. was wrongly returned as 1,069.

(u) In 1936 Crewe M.B. and Monks Coppenhall C.P. was extended to include part of Warmingham C.P. (pop. 13 in 1931).

(v) Warrington M.B. was incorporated in 1847. Most of it lay in Lancs. ancient co. except parts of the tns. of Latchford and Thelwall. On the creation of admin. cos. in 1888 Thelwall C.P. was wholly included in Ches. and in 1896 Latchford C.P. was transferred to Lancs.

(w) In 1888 Waverton C.P. was extended to include part of Christleton C.P. (pop. 7 in 1891).

(x) In 1801, 1811, 1861, and 1871 Weaverham lordship was returned with Weaverham tns. After 1841 parts of Weaverham tns. and Weaverham lordship were stated to be in Whitegate A.P., and are returned in the total for that parish after 1851.

(y) In 1936 parts of Weaverham C.P. (pop. respectively 63 and 402 in 1931) were transferred to Acton and Cuddington C.P.s.

(z) In 1894 Hyde C.P. was extended to include part of Werneth C.P. (pop. 1,773 in 1901), the remainder of which was renamed Compstall C.P. in 1897.

(a) In 1963 the boundaries between Wervin C.P. and Thornton le Moors C.P. and between Wervin C.P. and Wimbolds Trafford C.P. were altered.

(b) In 1965 part of Weston C.P. was transferred to Newcastle under Lyme R.D. (Staffs.), and part of Balterley C.P. (pop. 3 in 1961) was transferred from Newcastle under Lyme R.D. to Weston C.P.

(c) In 1892 Whatcroft C.P. was extended to include Shipbrook C.P. (pop. 73 in 1901).

(d) In 1955 Northwich U.D. was extended to include part of Whatcroft C.P. (pop. 82 in 1951).

(e) Dissolved 1936, part (pop. 494 in 1931) being transferred to Sandbach U.D. and C.P. and part (pop. 262 in 1931) to Haslington C.P.

(f) Most of Whitchurch A.P. lay in Salop.

(g) This figure includes 14 inhabitants of Weaverham lordship.

	1801	1811	1821	1831	1841	1851	1861	1871	1881	1891	1901	1911	1921	1931	1951	1961	1971
WHITLEY C.P.[h]	Part of Budworth, Great A.P., q.v.								306	303	323	336	343	339	530	530	506
WHITLEY, HIGHER C.P.	Part of Budworth, Great A.P., q.v.								214	205	201	171	162	171	See Whitley C.P.	See Whitley C.P.	
WHITLEY, LOWER C.P.	Part of Budworth, Great A.P., q.v.								150	152	142	154	117	104	109	93	85
WIGLAND C.P.	Part of Malpas A.P., q.v.								227	220[l]	200	182	189	162	168[l]	142	148
WILDBOARCLOUGH C.P.	Part of Prestbury A.P., q.v.								462	502	597	806*	997	1,296[k]	See Neston U.D.		
WILLASTON C.P.	Part of Neston A.P., q.v.								1,986	2,070	2,400	2,715	2,764	2,834	1,882[l]	1,818	2,229
WILLINGTON E.P.P. and C.P.[m] (Part of Nantwich and Wybunbury A.P.s, q.v.)	84	109	101	115	103	123	106	121	145	153	146	139	142	167	132	116	132
WILMSLOW A.P.	3,233	3,710	3,927	4,296	4,973	4,952	6,616	7,816									
BOLLIN FEE tns.	1,506	1,755	1,761	1,784	2,212*	1,884	2,143	2,536*	See Bollin Fee C.P.								
CHORLEY tns.	391	426	478	474	561*	803*	1,760*	1,937*	See Chorley C.P.								
FULSHAW tns.	214	232	256	291	305*	358	532	887*	See Fulshaw C.P.								
POWNALL FEE tns.	1,122	1,297	1,432	1,747	1,895*	1,907	2,181	2,501*	See Pownall Fee C.P.								
WILMSLOW U.S.D. and, from 1894, C.P.[n]									5,664	6,344	7,361	8,153	8,282	9,760	19,536[o]	21,389	29,040
BOLLIN FEE C.P. (part of)									2,612	2,860[p]							
FULSHAW C.P. (part of)									1,083	1,230							
POWNALL FEE C.P. (part of)									1,969	2,254[q]							
WIMBOLDSLEY C.P.	Part of Middlewich A.P., q.v.								93	219[r]	183	194	179	145	189	168	186
WINCHAM C.P.	Part of Budworth, Great A.P., q.v.								1,172	1,229[s]	1,054	1,091	1,175	1,003	800[t]	751	864
WINCLE C.P.	Part of Prestbury A.P., q.v.								284	254[u]	261	248	229	208	202	183	164
WINNINGTON C.P.	Part of Budworth, Great A.P., q.v.								681	2,246[v]	1,604[w]	1,503	1,662	1,268[x]	See Northwich U.D. and C.P., Hartford C.P., and Weaverham C.P.		
part in Northwich U.S.D., q.v.									469	563							
rural part									212	1,683							
WINSFORD U.D. and, from 1936, C.P.[y]									10,041	10,440	10,382	10,770	10,956	10,998	12,738	12,760	24,932
OVER C.P.									6,534	6,835	7,063	7,300	7,354	7,306[z]			
WHARTON C.P.									3,507	3,605	3,319	3,470	3,602	3,092[a]			
WIRRAL HUNDRED	10,744	11,579	13,881	19,100	33,678	59,630	69,448	105,041									
WIRRAL R.D.									49,494	18,251	18,099	19,022	24,753	28,904			
WIRRAL U.D.[b]									15,016						17,362	21,894	26,885
BARNSTON C.P.															2,578		
GAYTON C.P.															832		
HESWALL CUM OLDFIELD C.P.															6,773		
IRBY C.P.															4,032		
PENSBY C.P.															2,996		
THURSTASTON C.P.															151		
WIRSWALL C.P.	Part of Whitchurch A.P., q.v.								116	106	138	162	147	158	169	154	135
WISTASTON A.P. and C.P.	258	295	332	350	355	298	331	378	407	610	494[c]	697	718	1,504[d]	2,818	4,519	6,573
WITHINGTON C.P.[e]	In Northwich U.S.D., q.v.														661	590	507
WITHINGTON, LOWER C.P.	Part of Prestbury A.P., q.v.								582	550	578	533	495	531	See Withington C.P.	See Withington C.P.	
WITHINGTON, OLD C.P.[b]	Part of Prestbury A.P., q.v.								155	131	121	148	136	125	See Withington C.P.	See Withington C.P.	
WITTON CUM TWAMBROOKS C.P.	Part of Budworth, Great A.P., q.v. ... In Northwich U.S.D., q.v.																

WOODBANK C.P.	Part of Shotwick A.P., q.v.								59	84	72	85	74	88	77	73	74
WOODCHURCH A.P.[f]	736	753	835	929	1,409	2,927	3,922[g]	4,026[g]									
ARROWE tns.	96	82	72	91	122	105	109	120	See Arrowe C.P.								
BARNSTON tns.	129	110	93	112	206	239	252	292	See Barnston C.P.								
IRBY tns. (part of, after 1831)[h]	105	110	145	123	107	155	152	142	See Irby C.P.								
LANDICAN tns.	45	47	53	61	67	57	64	64	See Landican C.P.								
NOCTORUM tns.	17	14	30	28	30	32	31	63*	See Noctorum C.P.								
OXTON tns.	137	128	169	234	546	2,007*	2,670	2,610	See Oxton C.P.								
PENSBY tns.	22	27	22	21	31	41	38	30	See Pensby C.P.								
PRENTON tns.	81	84	99	104	110	99	123	106	See Prenton C.P.								
THINGWALL tns.	52	75	78	77	76	96	114	125	See Thingwall C.P.								
WOODCHURCH tns.	52	76	74	78	114	96	94	110	See Woodchurch C.P.								
WOODCHURCH C.P.	Part of Woodchurch A.P., q.v.								127	129	140	138	129	113	See Birkenhead C.P.		
WOODCOTT C.P.	Part of Wrenbury A.P., q.v.								33	30	23	26	26	18	18	22	23
WOODFORD C.P.	Part of Prestbury A.P., q.v.								362	332	304	338	413	801*	See Hazel Grove and Bramhall U.D. and C.P.		
WOOLSTANWOOD C.P.	Part of Nantwich A.P., q.v.								117	107	133	131	132	137	87[i]	95	144
WORLESTON C.P.	Part of Acton A.P., q.v.								338	339[j]	485	540	463	548	383[k]	336	364

(h) Created 1936 by the amalgamation of Higher Whitley (pop. 339 in 1931) and Lower Whitley (pop. 171 in 1931) C.P.s.

(i) In 1888 Wildboarclough C.P. was extended to include part of Wincle C.P. (pop. 6 in 1891).

(j) In 1936 Wildboarclough C.P. was extended to include part of Taxal C.P. (pop. 7 in 1931).

(k) In 1933 Willaston C.P. was extended to include part of Eastham C.P. (pop. 12 in 1931) and part of Willaston (pop. 14 in 1931) was transferred to Puddington C.P. Thus altered Willaston was transferred to Neston U.D.

(l) In 1938 Stapeley C.P. was extended to include part of Willaston C.P. (pop. 37 in 1931).

(m) Willington E.P.P. was described until 1841 as a tns. in Whalley A.P. (Lancs.).

(n) In 1894 Wilmslow C.P. was created from the parts in Wilmslow U.D. of Bollin Fee, Fulshaw, and Pownall Fee C.P.s.

(o) In 1936 Wilmslow U.D. and C.P. was extended to include part of Cheadle and Gatley U.D. and C.P. (pop. 31 in 1931), part of Handforth U.D. and C.P. (pop. 938 in 1931), and part of Styal C.P. (pop. 1,336 in 1931). Part of Wilmslow U.D. and C.P. (pop. 109 in 1931) was transferred to Alderley Edge U.D. and C.P.

(p) In 1888 Bollin Fee C.P. was extended to include part of Pownall Fee C.P. (pop. 28 in 1891).

(q) See above, note (p).

(r) In 1892 Wimboldsley C.P. was extended to include Occlestone C.P. (pop. 68 in 1901).

(s) In 1889 Wincham C.P. was extended to include part of Marston C.P. (pop. 18 in 1891).

(t) In 1936 Wincham C.P. was extended to include part of Pickmere C.P. (pop. 21 in 1931) and part of Wincham (pop. 7 in 1931) was transferred to Tabley Inferior C.P.

(u) In 1888 Wildboarclough C.P. was extended to include part of Wincle C.P. (pop. 6 in 1891).

(v) In 1892 Winnington C.P. was extended to include Wallerscote C.P. (pop. 17 in 1901).

(w) In 1894 part of Winnington C.P. (pop. 1,390 in 1901) was transferred to Northwich U.D. and C.P.

(x) Dissolved 1936, part (pop. 1,264 in 1931) being transferred to Northwich U.D. and C.P., and part (pop. 4 in 1931) to Hartford C.P.

(y) From 1894 Winsford U.D. included an unnamed C.P. formerly a detached part of Over which, being part of Marton C.P. under the provisions of the Divided Parishes Act, 1882, but not separated from Winsford U.D., became a separate C.P. under the provisions of the Local Government Act, 1894. Winsford C.P. was created in 1936 from parts of Clive, Darnhall, Marton, Over, Stanthorne, and Wharton C.P.s (pop. respectively 178, 6, 91, 7,278, 121, and 3,672 in 1931) and the unnamed C.P.s without pop. in Winsford U.D. and Northwich R.D.

(z) Dissolved 1936, parts (pop. respectively 7,278, 24, and 4 in 1931) being transferred to Winsford U.D. and C.P., Darnhall C.P., and Marton C.P.

(a) Dissolved 1936, part (pop. 3,672 in 1931) being transferred to Winsford U.D. and C.P. and part (pop. 20 in 1931) to Bostock C.P.

(b) Created 1933 from Barnston C.P. (pop. 1,453 in 1931), Gayton C.P. (pop. 527 in 1931), Irby C.P. (pop. 1,062 in 1931), Pensby C.P. (pop. 784 in 1931), and Thurstaston C.P. (pop. 210 in 1931).

(c) In 1894 Crewe M.B. and Monks Coppenhall C.P. was extended to include part of Wistaston C.P. (pop. 328 in 1901).

(d) In 1936 Crewe M.B. and Monks Coppenhall C.P. was extended to include a further part of Wistaston C.P. (pop. 244 in 1931).

(e) Created 1936 from the amalgamation of Lower Withington (pop. 531 in 1931) and Old Withington (pop. 125 in 1931) C.P.s.

(f) See below, note (h).

(g) In 1861 and 1871 275 and 364 inhabitants of Claughton with Grange C.P. were returned in Woodchurch A.P.

(h) Irby tns. extended into Thurstaston A.P., for which part a separate return was made after 1831. The totals for Woodchurch A.P. before 1841 include the whole of Irby tns.

(i) In 1936 part of Woolstanwood C.P. (pop. 56 in 1931) was transferred to Crewe M.B. and Monks Coppenhall C.P.

(j) In 1899 Worleston C.P. was extended to include Alvaston C.P. (pop. 61 in 1901).

(k) In 1936 Nantwich U.D. and C.P. was extended to include part of Worleston C.P. (pop. 178 in 1931).

	1801	1811	1821	1831	1841	1851	1861	1871	1881	1891	1901	1911	1921	1931	1951	1961	1971
WRENBURY A.P.[1]	891	1,040	1,181	1,158	1,355	2,060	2,505	2,210									
BROOMHALL tns.	140	166	196	181	157	142	166	119	See Broomhall C.P.								
CHORLEY tns.	126	186	183	168	183	173	166	172	See Chorley C.P.								
DODCOTT CUM WILKESLEY tns. (part of, in 1841 and 1871)[m]	See Audlem A.P.				197	631	672	354	See Dodcott cum Wilkesley C.P.								
NEWHALL tns. (part of, after 1841)[n]	819	859	854	1,011	936	331	737	778	See Newhall C.P.								
SOUND tns.[o]	192	207	247	255	255	261	246	217	See Sound C.P.								
WOODCOTT tns.	29	26	29	30	36	32	33	33	See Woodcott C.P.								
WRENBURY CUM FRITH tns.	404	455	526	524	527	490	531	537	See Wrenbury cum Frith C.P.								
WRENBURY CUM FRITH C.P.	Part of Wrenbury A.P., q.v.								509	475	491	494	501	589	708	815	1,000
WYBUNBURY A.P.[p]	3,174	3,461	3,889	3,938	4,419	4,389	4,985	5,905									
BASFORD tns.	55	64	86	85	85	69	60	62	See Basford C.P.								
BATHERTON tns.	25	29	29	34	32	28	24	25	See Batherton C.P.								
BLAKENHALL tns.	199	219	225	245	257	226	236	188	See Blakenhall C.P.								
BRIDGEMERE tns.	230	208	233	236	219	220	187	187	See Bridgemere C.P.								
CHECKLEY CUM WRINEHILL tns.	240	152	211	235	213	203	202	170	See Checkley cum Wrinehill C.P.								
CHORLTON tns.	106	90	91	109	141	114	113	114	See Chorlton C.P.								
DODDINGTON tns.	51	62	39	37	41	86	71	56	See Doddington C.P.								
HATHERTON tns.	191	379	418	447	396	394	377	367	See Hatherton C.P.								
HOUGH tns.	206	238	202	252	275	309	346	352	See Hough C.P.								
HUNSTERSON tns.	235	200	239	226	245	212	212	217	See Hunsterson C.P.								
LEA tns.	73	73	71	56	68	58	62	63	See Lea C.P.								
ROPE tns.	79	90	95	119	123	96	88	87	See Rope C.P.								
SHAVINGTON CUM GRESTY tns.	189	199	274	320	441	453	629*	931*	See Shavington cum Gresty C.P.								
STAPELEY tns.	249	261	329	356	448	462	578*	623	See Stapeley C.P.								
WALGHERTON tns.	211	206	246	213	229	213	194	155	See Walgherton C.P.								
WESTON tns.	348	426	463	401	496	514	500	520	See Weston C.P.								
WILLASTON tns. (part of, after 1831)	209	214	209	122[q]	181	202	539*	1,172*	See Willaston C.P.								
WYBUNBURY tns.	278	351	429	445	529	530	567	616	See Wybunbury C.P.								
WYBUNBURY C.P.	Part of Wybunbury A.P., q.v.								595	544	516	599	671	644	752	747	794
WYCHOUGH C.P.	Part of Malpas A.P., q.v.								15	10	16	17	14	16	13	15	12
YEARDSLEY CUM WHALEY U.S.D. and C.P.	Part of Taxal A.P., q.v.								1,272	1,235	1,487	1,659	1,699	1,745	Part of Whaley Bridge U.D. (Derb.).		

(l) In 1851 the totals for Wrenbury A.P. were corrected as follows: 1801, 1,646; 1811, 1,662; 1821, 1,851; 1831, 1,795; 1841, 1,747. See also note following. From 1821 to 1841 inclusive the totals for Wrenbury A.P. recorded in the censuses (934, 903, and 1,100 respectively) did not include the pop. of Sound tns., which was returned in Wybunbury A.P. in those years.

(m) Dodcott cum Wilkesley tns. was situated partly in Audlem A.P., where it was wholly returned before 1841. In 1841 and 1871 separate returns were made for that part of Dodcott in Wrenbury A.P. and in 1851 and 1861 the tns. was wholly returned in Wrenbury. Those variations are reflected in the A.P. totals for the years concerned.

(n) Newhall tns. was wrongly returned under Acton A.P. 1811–41 but its pop. has been listed under Wrenbury A.P., in which most of the tns. was situated. Newhall, however, extended also into Audlem A.P., and a separate return for that part was made after 1841, q.v.

(o) Most of Sound tns. lay in Wrenbury A.P., but it extended into Acton A.P. In 1811 Sound was wrongly returned as situated in Audlem A.P. and from 1821 to 1841 in Wybunbury A.P. In 1871 36 inhabitants of Sound tns. were included in the total for Acton A.P., q.v.

(p) Until 1831 the totals for Wybunbury A.P. include the whole pop. of Willaston tns. After 1831 part of its pop. was returned in Nantwich A.P., q.v. The totals for Wybunbury A.P. from 1821 to 1841 included the pop. of Sound tns. which was wrongly returned as part of Wybunbury A.P. at those dates. The figure for 1821 (4,146) is an error for 4,136.

(q) In 1851 this figure was corrected to 199.

COMMENTARY

NOTES in the *Census Reports* explaining some of the changes in population not caused by boundary alterations are listed below, under ancient parishes until 1881. The notes occur with varying frequency and seem to follow no particular plan. The presence of a note of this nature relating to any return is indicated in the population table by an asterisk.

1801

No comments were given for this year.

1811

CHESHIRE. The population of the county included the Chester Local Militia, numbering 1,332 including officers assembled for 14 days' exercise on 15 May 1811, the Stockport Regiment, numbering 1,111, assembled on 20 May, and the Macclesfield Regiment, numbering 1,023, assembled on 27 May.

1821

GRAPPENHALL (Latchford). Increase attributed to establishment of cotton factory.

KNUTSFORD (Nether Knutsford). Building of house of correction has increased population.

MOTTRAM IN LONGDENDALE (Newton). Increase of steam-weaving stated to have increased population.

PRESTBURY (Butley). Included one man over 100 years old.

RUNCORN (Runcorn). Quarries which provide stone for the docks and other public works at Liverpool have caused an increase in population.

STOCKPORT (Stockport). Included a woman over 100 years old.

1831

ASTBURY (Buglawton). Increase attributed to continued development of silk manufacture.

BARTHOMLEY (Alsager). Increase attributed to inclosure of Alsager common.

CHEADLE (Cheadle Bulkeley). Increase attributed to cotton manufacture.

CHESTER (Chester Castle). Return did not include 87 male and 8 female prisoners.

GRAPPENHALL (Latchford). Increase attributed to extension of cotton manufactory.

MOTTRAM IN LONGDENDALE (Hollingworth, Mottram, Newton, and Stayley). Increase attributed to extension of cotton factories.

PRESTBURY (Hurdsfield). Increase attributed to flourishing state of silk trade in 1825.

RUNCORN (Runcorn). Quarries, which provide stone for docks and other public works at Liverpool, have caused a great increase in population.

ST. MARY ON THE HILL (Upton by Chester). Increase attributed to building of lunatic asylum.

STOCKPORT (Disley, Dukinfield, Stockport, and Werneth). Increase attributed to cotton trade.

WALLASEY (Wallasey). Increase attributed to growth of building, owing to its proximity to Liverpool.

1841

CHESHIRE. 187 males and 141 females stated to have emigrated to the colonies and foreign countries since 31 Dec. 1840. The Regiment of King's Cheshire Yeomanry Cavalry consisting of 491 men was temporarily absent, being quartered at Liverpool and therefore included in the returns for Lancashire.

ALDERLEY (Nether Alderley, Great Warford). Temporary increase of 67 and 53 labourers and their families respectively, working on the railway.

ASTBURY (Buglawton). Decrease ascribed partly to depression of silk manufacture.

ASTBURY (Congleton). Included 118 persons in the Congleton workhouse.

AUDLEM (Audlem). Included 43 labourers temporarily employed on the canal.

BEBINGTON (Lower Bebington). Included 37 persons in quarantine hospital.

BEBINGTON (Poulton cum Spital). Included 51 persons in Wirral union workhouse.

BIDSTON (Birkenhead). Increase attributed to proximity to Liverpool. Included 10 persons in the lock-up house.

BUNBURY (Bunbury). Temporary increase of 64 excavators and railway plate-layers employed on the Chester and Crewe railway.

BUNBURY (Spurstow). 60 labourers temporarily absent at Birmingham, employed in cutting a canal.

CHEADLE (Handforth). Temporary increase of 43 labourers employed on the railway.

DAVENHAM (Leftwich). Included 122 persons in Northwich union workhouse.

DAVENHAM (Wharton). Temporary decrease of 74 persons being flat-men with their families employed at Liverpool in consequence of the River Weaver being run off for repairs.

EASTHAM (Whitby). Temporary increase of 203 persons, being labourers excavating canal basin and boatmen with their families, in consequence of the stoppage of the canal.

HOLY TRINITY. Included 298 persons in Chester workhouse and 59 in Chester city gaol.

KNUTSFORD (Nether Knutsford). Included 130 persons in Knutsford union workhouse and 320 in the house of correction.

MOTTRAM IN LONGDENDALE (Godley). Temporary increase of 58 labourers and their families employed on the Manchester and Sheffield railway.

MOTTRAM IN LONGDENDALE (Hattersley). Temporary increase of 100 miners, labourers, and their families employed on the Manchester and Sheffield railway.

MOTTRAM IN LONGDENDALE (Hollingworth). Included 11 persons in the poorhouse.

MOTTRAM IN LONGDENDALE (Mottram in Longdendale). Included 4 persons in the workhouse. Temporary increase of 45 labourers with their families employed on the Manchester and Sheffield railway.

MOTTRAM IN LONGDENDALE (Newton). Temporary increase of 250 labourers with their families employed on the Manchester and Sheffield railway.

MOTTRAM IN LONGDENDALE (Tintwistle). Included 15 persons in the workhouse. Temporary increase of 120 labourers with their families employed on the Manchester and Sheffield railway.

NANTWICH (Nantwich). Included 132 persons in the union workhouse and 3 in the lock-up house.

PRESTBURY (Chelford). Temporary increase of 16 labourers employed on the railway.

PRESTBURY (Macclesfield). Included 106 persons in the Macclesfield union workhouse and 7 in the debtors' prison.

PRESTBURY (Rainow). Included 47 persons in the Rainow union workhouse.

PRESTBURY (Sutton). Included 76 persons in the Sutton union workhouse.

PRESTBURY (Wildboarclough). Decrease of 120 persons arising from the stoppage of a calico printing establishment.

PRESTBURY (Withington, Lower). Temporary increase of 156 being excavators, etc., with their families, employed on the railway.

ROSTHERNE (Peover Superior, Snelson). Temporary increase of 46 and 43 labourers and their families respectively, employed on the railway.

RUNCORN (Norton, Preston on the Hill, Runcorn, Weston). Included respectively 32, 101, 508, and 62 persons in boats and barges.

ST. JOHN Included 14 persons in the female penitentiary.

ST. MARTIN. Included 73 persons in the Chester infirmary.

ST. MARY ON THE HILL (Upton-by-Chester). Included 163 persons in the county lunatic asylum.

ST. MICHAEL. Included 25 persons in the training college.

SANDBACH (Blackden, Church Hulme). Temporary increase of 65 and 130 labourers with their families respectively, employed on the railway.

STOCKPORT (Stockport). Included 265 persons in the workhouse, 95 males and 20 females in the barracks, and 21 persons in the infirmary. 99 persons had emigrated since 30 Dec. 1840.

WALLASEY (Wallasey). Great increase attributed to proximity to the town of Liverpool, and the facility afforded by steamers crossing the Mersey. Numerous boarding schools have been established.

WARMINGHAM (Elton). Temporary increase of 114 labourers with their families employed on the railway.

WILMSLOW (Bollin Fee, Chorley, Fulshaw, Pownall Fee). Temporary increase of 326, 92, 22, and 103 persons respectively employed on the railway.

1851

ALDERLEY (Nether Alderley, Great Warford). Decrease accounted for by removal of labourers temporarily resident in 1841.

BEBINGTON (Higher, Lower Bebington). Increase attributed to situation on Cheshire side of the Mersey opposite Liverpool. Population had nearly quadrupled since 1841.

BEBINGTON (Poulton cum Spital). Included 120 persons in Wirral union workhouse.

BEBINGTON (Tranmere). The causes which have contributed to the increase of population in Birkenhead have led to similar results in Tranmere.

BIDSTON (Birkenhead). Population has increased threefold since 1841, arising from extensive improvements and building speculations which, combined with the facilities of steam communication on the Mersey, have caused it to become the residence of a portion of the mercantile community of Liverpool.

BIDSTON (Claughton with Grange). Great increase attributed to its position on the Cheshire side of the Mersey opposite Liverpool.

CONGLETON. Workhouse has been discontinued and inmates moved to Arclid, q.v.

COPPENHALL (Monks Coppenhall). Great increase attributable to rapid growth of Crewe, which has become of considerable importance from being the point of junction of several lines of railway.

DAVENHAM (Leftwich). Included 154 persons in Northwich union workhouse.

EASTHAM (Whitby). Rapidly increasing in population from its position on the Cheshire side of the river Mersey.

HOLY TRINITY. Included 228 persons in the Chester workhouse and 56 persons in Chester city gaol.

KNUTSFORD (Nether Knutsford). Included 126 persons in Altrincham union workhouse and 362 in the house of correction.

MACCLESFIELD. Included 228 persons in the union workhouse.

NANTWICH (Nantwich). Included 153 persons in Nantwich union workhouse.

PRESTBURY (Rainow). Workhouse discontinued in 1842 and inmates moved to Macclesfield union workhouse. Decrease of population arises from the removal of labourers and artisans to the neighbouring towns in search of employment.

PRESTBURY (Sutton). Workhouse now merged with Macclesfield union workhouse.

PRESTBURY (Wincle). Decrease arises from stoppage of a cotton mill.

PRESTBURY (Withington, Lower). Same comment as for Alderley.

PRESTBURY (Woodford). Decrease attributed to discontinuance of some printing works.

RUNCORN (Preston on the Hill, Runcorn, Weston). Included respectively 50, 220, and 234 persons in barges

ST. MARTIN. Included 88 persons in Chester Infirmary.

ST. MARY ON THE HILL (Upton-by-Chester). Increase caused by a greater number of inmates, i.e. 238, in a lunatic asylum.

SANDBACH (Arclid). Increase accounted for by establishment of Congleton union workhouse since 1841, containing 164 persons.

SANDBACH (Blackden, Cotton, Cranage, Leese, Twemlow). Same comment as for Alderley.

SANDBACH (Church Hulme). Same comment as for Alderley; many temporary dwellings returned in 1841 have also been removed.

STOCKPORT. Included 368 persons in the workhouse.

STOKE (Whitby). See note for part of Whitby in Eastham parish.

WALLASEY (Liscard, Poulton cum Seacombe, Wallasey). Increase attributed to proximity to Liverpool, the facility afforded by steamers for crossing the Mersey, and the numerous boarding schools which have been established there.

WILMSLOW (Chorley). Further increase arises from establishment of a railway station.

WOODCHURCH (Oxton). Population has nearly quadrupled since 1841 owing to position on the Cheshire side of the Mersey.

1861

N.B. From 1861 the notes to the main population table seldom contain information about persons in workhouses and other public institutions. Separate tables supply those figures in the *Census Reports*, and no attempt has been made to include the information in these notes.

ACTON (Brindley). Increase attributed to removal of labourers from adjacent township of Acton, where several cottages have been pulled down.

ALDFORD (Aldford). Decrease attributed to emigration and migration.

ALDFORD (Great Boughton). Increase attributed to proximity to Chester.

ASHTON UPON MERSEY (Ashton upon Mersey, Sale). Since the opening of railway communication with Manchester many villa residences have been built.

ASTBURY (Odd Rode). Increase attributed to mining operations.

BARTHOMLEY (Alsager). Increase attributed to facilities of railway communication and proximity to the Potteries.

BOWDON (Altrincham, Ashley, Baguley, Bowdon, Dunham Massey, Hale, Timperley). Same comment as for Ashton upon Mersey.

BROMBOROUGH (Bromborough). Increase attributed to establishment of an extensive candle manufactory.

BUDWORTH, GREAT (Anderton). Included 80 persons in boats.

BUDWORTH, GREAT (Dutton). Increase attributed to erection of workhouse.

BUDWORTH, GREAT (Lostock Gralam). Decrease attributed to migration to Anderton for employment in saltworks.

BUDWORTH, GREAT (Marston, Northwich, Castle, Witton cum Twambrooks). Increase attributed to removal of persons from Northwich, consequent on the undermining of their houses by salt springs, etc.

BUDWORTH, GREAT (Whitley, Higher). Increase attributed to residence of labourers employed elsewhere.

CHEADLE (Bosden). Decrease attributed to migration of miners.

CONGLETON. Increase attributed to extension of the silk trade.

COPPENHALL (Monks Coppenhall). Increase attributed to employment of persons connected with the railways.

DAVENHAM (Moulton, Wharton). Increase attributed to extension of the salt trade.

EASTHAM (Whitby). Decrease attributed to the facilities of railway conveyance having caused a partial cessation of canal traffic.

FRODSHAM (Frodsham). Decrease attributed to absence of labourers employed in 1851 on railway works.

FRODSHAM (Manley). Decrease attributed to discontinuance of employment in stone quarries.

KINGSMARSH. Decrease attributed to migration.

KNUTSFORD (Toft). Decrease mainly attributed to reduction in number of members of a large establishment, owing to the death of the proprietors.

MACCLESFIELD. Decrease attributed to continued depression in the silk trade.

MOTTRAM IN LONGDENDALE (Godley, Newton). Decrease attributed to discontinuance of employment in cotton mills.

MOTTRAM IN LONGDENDALE (Hattersley, Hollingworth, Tintwistle). Decrease attributed to removal of workmen employed in 1851 on the railway and Manchester waterworks.

NANTWICH (Willaston). Increase attributed to proximity to Nantwich.

NESTON (Ness). Several houses have been pulled down.

PLEMSTALL (Hoole). Increase attributed to proximity to Chester railway station.

PRESTBURY (Adlington). Decrease mainly attributed to cessation of work at a colliery.

PRESTBURY (Bollington). Increase attributed to employment afforded in the cotton factories.

PRESTBURY (Bosley). Decrease attributed to conversion of silk and cotton mills into corn mills and to the pulling down of houses.

PRESTBURY (Butley). Decrease attributed to reduction in number of hands employed in silk factory.

PRESTBURY (Eaton). Decrease attributed to decline in the silk trade.

PRESTBURY (Newton, Woodford). Decrease attributed to migration of young persons in search of employment.

PRESTBURY (Sutton). Same comment as for Macclesfield.

PRESTBURY (Wildboarclough). Decrease attributed to discontinuance of employment in an extensive cotton-printing establishment.

PRESTBURY (Worth). Decrease attributed to migration owing to want of employment in the collieries.

RUNCORN (Moore, Walton Superior). Decrease attributed to removal of families to towns etc.

RUNCORN (Runcorn). Increase attributed to the demand for labour in manufactories and adjacent copper works, to the extension of the docks, and the prosperity of the shipbuilding trade.

ST. BRIDGET. Increase chiefly confined to detached portion which formerly consisted of fields but is now known as the Queen's Park.

ST. MARTIN. Increase attributed to the erection of barracks and cottages.

ST. MARY ON THE HILL. Increase mainly attributable to the establishment of neighbouring chain, cable, and anchor works, etc., and of carriage works belonging to the northern division of the Great Western Railway.

ST. MARY ON THE HILL (Upton-by-Chester). Increase attributed to enlargement of the lunatic asylum and to the erection of houses and cottages.

ST. OSWALD (Great Boughton). Increase attributed to proximity to Chester.

ST. PETER. Decrease attributed to removal of families to adjoining parishes consequent on the pulling down of houses.

SANDBACH (Bradwall). Increase attributed to establishment of reformatory for male prisoners and the erection of houses for railway officials.

STOCKPORT (Bredbury). Increase mainly attributed to extended colliery operations, the manufacture of hats, and the railway works in progress.

STOCKPORT (Dukinfield). Increase mainly attributed to extension of employment in cotton mills.

STOCKPORT (Hyde). Increase attributed to establishment of cotton mills and construction of a railway.

STOCKPORT (Torkington). Decrease attributed to removal of families from dilapidated houses and to the discontinuance of a boarding school.

STOCKPORT (Werneth). Decrease attributed to reduction in number of hands employed in the cotton mills owing to improvements in machinery.

TAXAL. Increase attributed to railway advantages and proximity to cotton mills and collieries.

TILSTON (Tilston). Decrease attributed to pulling down of cottages.

WILMSLOW (Chorley). Increase attributed to proximity to Manchester and to facilities of railway communication.

WYBUNBURY (Shavington cum Gresty). Increase attributed to erection of houses for the accommodation of persons employed in the Crewe railway works.

WYBUNBURY (Stapeley). Increase attributed to building of houses near Nantwich railway station.

WYBUNBURY (Willaston). See note under Nantwich.

1871

ALDFORD (Aldford, Churton by Aldford). Increase mainly attributed to presence of large number of operatives employed in restoration of Eaton Hall.

ALDFORD (Buerton). Decrease attributed to pulling down of houses on Marquess of Westminster's estate.

ASHTON UPON MERSEY (Ashton upon Mersey, Sale). Increase attributed to building of residences for Manchester merchants, warehousemen, and others.

ASTBURY (Buglawton). Decrease attributed to depressed condition of the silk trade.

ASTBURY (Odd Rode). Increase attributed to the prosperous state of the coal and iron trades.

AUDLEM (Hankelow). Increase attributed to influx of labourers and their families.

BADDILEY. Same comment as for Audlem.

BARTHOMLEY (Alsager). Increase attributed to erection of villa residences by master potters from the Staffordshire districts.

BARTHOMLEY (Haslington). Increase attributed to enlargement of the London and North-Western Railway Company's works since 1861.

BEBINGTON (Higher, Lower Bebington). Increase attributed to the fact that many merchants, clerks, and others, live there because of proximity to Liverpool.

BIDSTON (Claughton with Grange). Increase attributed to building of private residences by Liverpool merchants.

BIDSTON (Moreton). Increase attributed to the fact that several farms have fallen into the hands of one purchaser, who is said to have effected great improvements by pulling down old houses and building others, erecting a church, widening the public roads, constructing sewers, etc.

BIDSTON (Tranmere). Increase attributed to the operations of land and building societies which have been established within the last 10 years, mainly as a result of its proximity to and facility of communication with Liverpool and Birkenhead.

BOWDON (Altrincham, Ashley, Baguley, Bowdon, Dunham Massey, Hale, Timperley). Same comment as for Ashton upon Mersey.

BROMBOROUGH (Bromborough). Increase attributed to establishment of a large candle factory.

BUDWORTH, GREAT (Anderton). Included 98 persons in boats and barges.

BUDWORTH, GREAT (Barnton). Increase attributed to extension of trade on River Weaver and on the canal.

BUDWORTH, GREAT (Bartington). Included 36 persons living in boats.

BUDWORTH, GREAT (Hartford). Increase attributed to extension of salt trade and building of new houses for labouring classes.

BUDWORTH, GREAT (Castle Northwich, Wincham, Witton cum Twambrooks). Increase attributed to extension of the salt trade and to improved railway communications.

CHEADLE (Cheadle Bulkeley, Cheadle Moseley). Increase attributed to their being resorted to as a place of residence by persons engaged in business at Manchester. Since 1861 a large school known as 'The Manchester Warehousemen and Clerks' Orphan School' has been erected in Cheadle Moseley.

CHESTER. Increase attributed to great augmentation of railway employment on the northern side of the city, the Birmingham Wagon Company employing about one hundred men; iron and brass foundries employ more men than formerly; the Canal Company's boatbuilding yard has lately been established; and the shoe trade now forms a prominent branch of industry. In addition, many merchants and others engaged in business at Liverpool and Birkenhead now reside in this neighbourhood.

CONGLETON. Decrease attributed to depressed condition of the silk trade.

COPPENHALL (Church and Monks Coppenhall). Increase attributed to enlargement of the London and North-Western Railway Company's works since 1861.

DAVENHAM (Davenham, Rudheath, Stanthorne). Increase attributed to building of houses.

DAVENHAM (Moulton, Wharton). Increase attributed to extension of the salt trade.

DELAMERE (Delamere, Oakmere). Increase attributed to the opening of the West Cheshire railway and to the building of houses and cottages.

EASTHAM (Childer Thornton, Eastham, Great Sutton). Increase attributed to building of houses since 1861.

EASTHAM (Whitby). Increase attributed to briskness of business at Ellesmere Port in transferring cargoes from boats on the canal to vessels in the Mersey. Return included 163 persons on board vessels.

FRODSHAM (Frodsham, Helsby, Kingsley, Manley). Increase attributed to building of houses, chiefly for accommodation of farm labourers, and persons employed at quarries and railway works.

GAWSWORTH. Decrease attributed to migration of young persons to towns.

GRAPPENHALL (Latchford). Increase attributed to building of houses by persons engaged in business at Warrington.

HANDLEY (Golborne David, Handley). Increase mainly attributed to influx of labourers building a railway.

HESWALL (Heswall cum Oldfield). Increase attributed to building of villa residences by Liverpool merchants and others.

KIRBY, WEST (Frankby). Increase attributed to building of a hall with farmstead and cottages attached.

KIRBY, WEST (Hoose, West Kirby, Little Meols). Increase attributed to building of houses since the opening of the railway from Birkenhead to Hoylake.

KIRBY, WEST (Great Meols). Same comment as for Bidston (Tranmere).

LYMM. Increase attributed to extension of the fustian-cutting trade.

MALPAS (Bradley, Broxton, Hampton). Increase attributed to influx of workers building a railway.

MALPAS (Duckington, Malpas, Tushingham with Grindley, Wigland, Wychough). Decrease attributed to diminished demand for agricultural labour and consequent migration.

MARBURY (Norbury). Decrease attributed to migration in search of higher wages.

MIDDLEWICH (Newton). Included 75 persons in boats.

MOBBERLEY. Increase mainly attributed to extension of the silk and crepe trades.

MOTTRAM IN LONGDENDALE (Hattersley, Mottram). Decrease attributed to closing of a large cotton factory.

MOTTRAM IN LONGDENDALE (Stayley). Decrease attributed to closing of two large cotton manufactories in consequence of the death of the proprietor.

MOTTRAM IN LONGDENDALE (Tintwistle). Increase in Micklehurst attributed to the erection of cotton manufacturing and spinning mills and to the flourishing state of the flannel trade.

NANTWICH (Nantwich). Increase attributed to prosperous condition of the shoe trade.

NANTWICH (Willaston). Same comment as for Coppenhall.

NESTON (Little Neston). Same comment as for Heswall.

NESTON (Thornton Hough). Increase attributed to erection of a church and several cottages by a resident.

NESTON (Willaston). Increase attributed to facilities afforded for railway communication.

NORTHENDEN (Northenden). Increase attributed to proximity to Manchester and to the building of villa residences.

OVER (Over). Increase mainly attributed to establishment of a cotton factory.

PRESTBURY (Adlington, Butley, Fallibroome, Mottram St. Andrew, Newton, Poynton, Prestbury, Upton, Woodford, Worth). Decrease mainly attributed to demolition of old houses.

PRESTBURY (Bollington). Decrease mainly attributed to closing of two cotton mills.

PRESTBURY (Bosley, Eaton, Henbury, Marton, North Rode, Siddington). Same comment as for Gawsworth.

PRESTBURY (Kettleshulme, Rainow). Decrease attributed to migration in search of employment.

PRESTBURY (Sutton, Wildboarclough, Wincle). Decrease attributed to depression in silk trade.

PRESTBURY (Tytherington). Decrease attributed to the demolition of several houses, the occupiers of which were removed to adjoining townships.

RUNCORN (Aston Grange). Decrease attributed to migration of 3 families in consequence of the dilapidated condition of their houses.

RUNCORN (Clifton). Increase attributed to temporary presence of men and their families employed in construction of a railway line through the district.

RUNCORN (Daresbury, Hatton). Increase attributed to presence of workmen rebuilding Stretton and Daresbury churches.

RUNCORN (Halton). Increase mainly attributed to building and extension of tanneries.

RUNCORN (Keckwick). Decrease mainly attributed to closing of a brickyard.

RUNCORN (Newton by Daresbury, Walton Superior). Increase mainly attributed to building of a large mansion.

RUNCORN (Norton, Preston on the Hill). Included 101 and 45 persons respectively in boats; Norton also included 22 in a barn.

RUNCORN (Runcorn). Increase attirbuted to establishment of soap and alkali works.

RUNCORN (Walton Inferior). Increase attributed to building of several houses since 1861.

RUNCORN (Weston). Increase attributed to additional dwelling accommodation having been provided for the labourers employed at the stone quarries, alkali works, docks, etc.

ST. OSWALD (Churton Heath). Same comment as for Aldford (Buerton).

ST. PETER. Decrease attributed to the conversion of dwelling houses into business premises.

SANDBACH (Betchton, Hassall). Increase attributed to prosperous condition of salt trade.

SANDBACH (Bradwall). Increase attributed to prosperous condition of the iron and wire-working trades.

SANDBACH (Wheelock). Increase attributed to prosperity of trade in iron and salt.

STOCKPORT (Bramhall). Same comment as for Davenham (Davenham, Rudheath, Stanthorne).

STOCKPORT (Bredbury). Increase attributed to flourishing state of the hat trade.

STOCKPORT (Brinnington). Decrease attributed to migration of factory operatives in consequence of the depression in trade caused by the American war. A number of houses have been pulled down, their sites being required for a railway.

STOCKPORT (Disley). Increase attributed to building of houses for workpeople.

STOCKPORT (Dukinfield). Decrease attributed to effect of the American war on the cotton trade.

STOCKPORT (Stockport Etchells). Increase considered to be natural growth of population of a prosperous agricultural district.

STOCKPORT (Hyde). Increase attributed to extension of cotton mills.

STOCKPORT (Marple). Increase attributed to extension of cotton manufactories.

STOCKPORT (Romiley). Increase attributed to the extension of cotton and hat manufactories.

STOCKPORT (Stockport). Decrease attributed to migration of factory operatives in consequence of the depression in trade caused by the American war.

STOKE (Stoke). Included 39 persons in boats.

STOKE (Whitby). See note under Eastham parish.

TATTENHALL (Golborne Bellow, Tattenhall). Same comment as for Handley.

TAXAL (Yeardsley cum Whaley). Increase attributed to extension of the cotton trade.

UPTON BY BIRKENHEAD. Same comment as for Bidston (Tranmere).

WALLASEY (Liscard, Poulton cum Seacombe, Wallasey). Increase attributed to the introduction of gas and water works, and improved service of ferry steamers, the establishment (at Seacombe) of an iron shipbuilding yard and patent guano works, and the increase of commerce at the Birkenhead docks.

WARMINGHAM (Moston). Same comment as for Sandbach (Bradwall).

WEAVERHAM (Cuddington). Same comment as for Delamere.

WILMSLOW (Bollin Fee, Chorley, Fulshaw, Pownall Fee). Increase mainly attributed to building of villa residences for accommodation of persons engaged in business at Manchester.

WOODCHURCH (Noctorum). Same comment as for Bidston (Claughton with Grange).

WYBUNBURY (Shavington cum Gresty). Same comment as for Coppenhall.

WYBUNBURY (Willaston). See note under Nantwich parish.

1881

A note states that the apparent decrease of population in the sub-district of Tattenhall is chiefly attributed to the fact that the population in 1871 included a number of labourers who were temporarily engaged in building a railway line. It should be noted, however, that only Broxton, Golborne Bellow, Golborne David, Handley, and Tattenhall townships in Tattenhall sub-district were stated in 1871 to include such labourers.

1891

EASTHAM. Included 848 persons engaged on the Manchester Ship Canal.

ELTON (in Thornton A.P.). Included 30 persons engaged on the Manchester Ship Canal.

HOOTON. Included 256 persons engaged on the Manchester Ship Canal.

INCE. Included 772 persons engaged on the Manchester Ship Canal.

NETHERPOOL. Included 304 persons in 26 temporary wooden huts engaged on the Manchester Ship Canal.

STANLOW. Included 320 persons engaged on the Manchester Ship Canal.

STANNEY, GREAT. Included 15 persons engaged on the Manchester Ship Canal.

WERNETH. Decrease attributed to fact that five hat manufactories and one large cotton mill which were working in 1881 were closed in 1891.

WHITBY. Included 1,024 persons engaged on the Manchester Ship Canal.

1901

HOYLAKE CUM WEST KIRBY. Increase mainly attributed to its development as a popular holiday resort.

STOCKTON HEATH. Increase mainly attributed to its proximity to Warrington.

1911

BACHE. Large increase due to inclusion in 1911 of part of the Chester county lunatic asylum; in 1901 all the inmates of this asylum were included in the population of Upton by Chester C.P.

BEBINGTON, LOWER. Large increase mainly attributed to development of the soap-making industry.

BIDSTON CUM FORD. Large increase attributed mainly to its development as a residential suburb, consequent on improved travelling facilities.

BRADWALL. Large increase attributed mainly to development of motor-wagon works.

ELLESMERE PORT. Large increase attributed mainly to industrial development.

GRAPPENHALL. Large increase attributed mainly to proximity to the town of Warrington.

HESWALL-CUM-OLDFIELD. Large increase mainly attributed to development as residential suburb of Liverpool.

HOYLAKE CUM WEST KIRBY. Large increase attributed mainly to its development as a health resort and to its proximity to Liverpool and Birkenhead.

KINGSWOOD. Large increase attributed mainly to the establishment of consumption sanatoria.

LATCHFORD WITHOUT. Same comment as for Grappenhall.

LEDSHAM. Large increase attributed mainly to the establishment of smallholdings.

LISCARD. Large increase attributed mainly to proximity to city of Liverpool.

LOSTOCK GRALAM. Large increase attributed mainly to the development of alkali manufacture.

MARTHALL CUM WARFORD. Large increase attributed mainly to the establishment of the David Lewis Epileptic Colony.

NEWTON BY CHESTER. Large increase attributed mainly to its proximity to the city of Chester.

NEWTON BY FRODSHAM. Large increase attributed mainly to the establishment of a branch of the National Children's Home and Orphanage.

PARTINGTON. Large increase attributed mainly to number of persons on board vessels in the docks situated in the parish.

POULTON CUM SEACOMBE. Same comment as for Liscard.

PRENTON. Large increase attributed mainly to its proximity to the town of Birkenhead.

STOCKTON HEATH. Same comment as for Grappenhall.

TAXAL. Large increase attributed mainly to its development as a residential suburb.

UPTON BY CHESTER. See note for Bache.

WALLASEY. Same comment as for Liscard.

WALTON INFERIOR. Same comment as for Grappenhall.

WILLASTON (in Neston A.P.). Same comment as for Heswall-cum-Oldfield.

1921

BAGULEY. Large increase attributed mainly to the greater number of patients in the sanatorium.

HESWALL-CUM-OLDFIELD. Increase attributed mainly to residential development due to proximity of parish to city of Liverpool.

MORETON. Increase attributed mainly to the erection of bungalows, caravans, tents, etc., by persons unable to obtain house accommodation in the neighbouring towns.

RIDLEY. Increase attributed mainly to the conversion of four large farms into smallholdings.

1931

APPLETON. Large increase attributed mainly to residential development.

BARNSTON. Same comment as for Appleton.

BASFORD. Same comment as for Appleton.

BOUGHTON, GREAT. Same comment as for Appleton.

BLACON CUM CRABWALL. Same comment as for Appleton.

BURTON. Same comment as for Appleton.

CALDY. Same comment as for Appleton.

CHEADLE AND GATLEY. Same comment as for Appleton.

CHESTER CASTLE. Increase attributed to increase in personnel of the military barracks.

CHURTON BY FARNDON. Included 209 persons in a holiday camp.

EASTHAM. Same comment as for Appleton.

EATON. Same comment as for Appleton.

ELLESMERE PORT. Same comment as for Appleton.

GAYTON. Same comment as for Appleton.

GRANGE. Same comment as for Appleton.

HARTFORD. Same comment as for Appleton.

HESWALL-CUM-OLDFIELD. Same comment as for Appleton.

IRBY. Same comment as for Appleton.

LATCHFORD WITHOUT. Same comment as for Appleton.

MOSTON (St. Mary's A.P.). Same comment as for Appleton.

NOCTORUM. Same comment as for Appleton.

PENSBY. Same comment as for Appleton.

POULTON CUM SPITAL. Large increase attributed mainly to an increase in the number of poor-law institution inmates.

POYNTON-WITH-WORTH. Same comment as for Appleton.

RUDHEATH. Same comment as for Appleton.

SAUGHALL MASSIE. Same comment as for Appleton.

SHAVINGTON CUM GRESTY. Same comment as for Appleton.

SUTTON, GREAT. Same comment as for Appleton.

TIMPERLEY. Same comment as for Appleton.

UPTON BY BIRKENHEAD. Same comment as for Appleton.

WEAVERHAM. Same comment as for Appleton.

WESTON (Runcorn A.P.). Large increase attributed mainly to the building of houses for the purpose of accommodating factory employees.

WILLASTON (Neston A.P.). Same comment as for Appleton.

WISTASTON. Same comment as for Appleton.

WOODFORD. Same comment as for Appleton.

1951, 1961, 1971

No comments were given for these years.

INDEX